STORIES OF THE CIVIL RIGHTS MOVEMENT

NONVIOLENT RESISTANCE
IN THE CIVIL RIGHTS MOVEMENT

by Gail Terp

Content Consultant
William P. Jones
Professor of History
University of Wisconsin–Madison

Core Library

An Imprint of Abdo Publishing
abdopublishing.com

abdopublishing.com

Published by Abdo Publishing, a division of ABDO, PO Box 398166,
Minneapolis, Minnesota 55439. Copyright © 2016 by Abdo Consulting
Group, Inc. International copyrights reserved in all countries. No part of
this book may be reproduced in any form without written permission from
the publisher. Core Library™ is a trademark and logo of Abdo Publishing.

Printed in the United States of America, North Mankato, Minnesota

032015
092015

Cover Photo: Bettmann/Corbis/AP Images
Interior Photos: Bettmann/Corbis/AP Images, 1; John G. Moebes/Corbis,
4; Chuck Burton/Corbis, 6; Bettmann/Corbis, 8, 18, 26, 40; North Wind
Picture Archives, 12, 14; Everett Collection/Newscom, 21; AP Images, 22,
24, 30, 34, 37, 43, 45; Harold Valentine/AP Images, 28; Horace Cort/AP
Images, 32

Editor: Jon Westmark
Series Designer: Becky Daum

Library of Congress Control Number: 2015931580

Cataloging-in-Publication Data
Terp, Gail.
 Nonviolent resistance in the civil rights movement / Gail Terp.
    p. cm. -- (Stories of the civil rights movement)
Includes bibliographical references and index.
ISBN 978-1-62403-882-2
1. African Americans--Civil rights--History--20th century--Juvenile literature.
2. Civil rights movements--United States--History--20th century--Juvenile
literature. 3. United States--Race relations--Juvenile literature.   I. Title.
973--dc23
                                                                2015931580

CONTENTS

CHAPTER ONE

SITTING FOR CHANGE

It was around three o'clock in the afternoon on February 1, 1960. Four young men entered a Woolworth's department store in Greensboro, North Carolina. They bought school supplies. After paying they sat down at the store's lunch counter and tried to order coffee. The waitress refused to serve them.

David Richmond, Franklin McCain, Ezell Blair Jr., and Joseph McNeil became known as the "Greensboro Four."

The waitress was following store rules. The lunch counter was segregated. Segregation rules said African Americans had to do things separately from whites. The Woolworth's lunch counter was marked "Whites Only."

The young men were college freshmen. They had been talking about segregation for months. They had each experienced it and knew it was wrong. They wanted to resist segregation by refusing to obey the unjust rules.

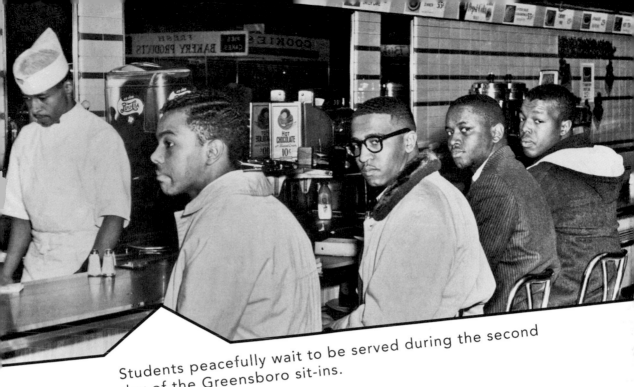

Students peacefully wait to be served during the second day of the Greensboro sit-ins.

They decided to hold a sit-in. They chose Woolworth's because it had both a store and a lunch counter. They wanted to show that Woolworth's was being unfair. Woolworth's was willing to take their money in the store. But it would not let them sit at the lunch counter.

The store's manager asked the students to leave. They refused. As they sat, some white people gathered to watch them. Many called the young men insulting names. The students sat and waited. When the store closed for the day, they got up and left.

By February 6, approximately 400 African-American men and women had joined the Greensboro sit-ins.

As the young men returned to their dorms, they were elated. They felt they had done something important. They had stood up to unfairness. They were not the first to fight unjust laws in a peaceful way. They were not the first to hold a sit-in. But they did start something big that day. Over the next several days, hundreds of Greensboro students held sit-ins throughout the city. And over the next few months, sit-ins spread throughout the South.

Nonviolent Resistance in the United States

The students who sat in at Woolworth's were practicing nonviolent resistance. They resisted by choosing to disobey the rules of segregation. They were nonviolent, meaning they did not fight back even though others insulted them. By sitting where they were not supposed to, they quietly showed they thought the law was wrong.

African Americans faced segregation laws in many areas of their lives. There were laws that said where they could and could not live, laws that said where they could and could not sit, and laws that kept them from getting jobs.

African Americans wanted a way to effectively show that they were not being treated fairly. Many civil rights activists looked to Mohandas Gandhi's example on how to effectively protest. Gandhi fought injustice in India from the 1920s to the 1940s. The British government ruled India for much of that time.

Under British rule, the Indian people suffered many injustices. Some rebelled with violence. But it was Gandhi's nonviolent resistance that helped India gain independence from Britain.

In 1942 the Congress on Racial Equality (CORE) formed. The group wanted to use Gandhi's method of nonviolent resistance to change racist attitudes in the United States. CORE organized sit-ins and other nonviolent actions. In the 1950s, civil rights leader Dr. Martin Luther King Jr. began working with CORE. King helped lead

Gandhi's Salt March

When India was under British control, the people could not collect their own salt. They had to buy it and pay a tax to the British government. In 1930 Gandhi and others marched 240 miles (386 km) to the coast. They walked for three weeks. They talked to people along the way about what they were doing. More than 12,000 people gathered at the coast. Here Gandhi picked up a small lump of natural salt. Soon he was arrested. The salt tax continued. But the march showed the Indian people a new way to bring attention to injustice.

Gandhi

- Fought British rule in India
- Lawyer
- Inspired by many religions
- Focused on patient nonviolent action
- Protested by refusing to eat
- Fought against India's class structure
- Helped bring India's independence

Both

- Used nonviolence
- Led marches
- Inspired others
- Helped people gain civil rights
- Were assassinated

King

- Fought for civil rights in the United States
- Minister
- Inspired by Christianity
- Did not want to be a public leader at first
- Focused on nonviolence's ability to create tension
- Helped African Americans gain equal rights to whites
- Used Gandhi as a role model

Gandhi and King

This diagram compares the lives of Mohandas Gandhi and Martin Luther King Jr. Both used nonviolent resistance to bring about big changes. How are these two figures similar? What are some differences that you find interesting or surprising?

some of the largest peaceful rallies of the 1950s and 1960s. Through organizations like CORE and activists like King, nonviolent resistance became an effective tool that helped end many unfair laws and bring lasting change to the United States.

CHAPTER TWO

A LONG WAY FROM FREEDOM

The United States has a long history of racial oppression. Starting in the 1600s, white colonists brought people from Africa to work as slaves. By 1804 all of the northern states had outlawed slavery. But slavery remained in the South. Slaves were the property of their owners. Slaves could not travel without a written pass. They were not allowed to learn to read or write. They needed permission to marry.

Slaves were often sold at auctions. Members of the same family could be sold to different owners.

A network of whites and free African Americans helped runaway slaves make their way to freedom.

Slaves who did not obey their owner's rules were punished. Sometimes they were killed.

Escape

African Americans knew that slavery was unfair. They found ways to resist it. Sometimes slaves did poor work, wasted time, or damaged tools. Others ran away. This was difficult and dangerous. They faced terrible consequences if they were caught running away.

Segregation and Jim Crow

Slavery ended officially in 1865 with the Thirteenth Amendment to the US Constitution. In 1868 the

Fourteenth Amendment gave every person born or naturalized in the United States full citizenship. It promised citizens equal protection under the law. The Fifteenth Amendment gave African-American men the right to vote in 1870.

Many whites in the South resisted these changes. They did not want African Americans to be considered equal citizens, so they developed state and local laws that segregated society. These were called Jim Crow laws. They kept African Americans separate from whites. There were laws that controlled where African Americans could eat,

The Emancipation Proclamation

Abraham Lincoln became president in 1861. Shortly after he was sworn in, the Civil War (1861–1865) began. The fighting was over whether slavery should be legal. After the war had gone on for almost two years, Lincoln decided to use a new strategy to defeat the South. On January 1, 1863, he issued the Emancipation Proclamation. This document freed the slaves in the states that were fighting to keep slavery. It also allowed escaped slaves to join the army and navy.

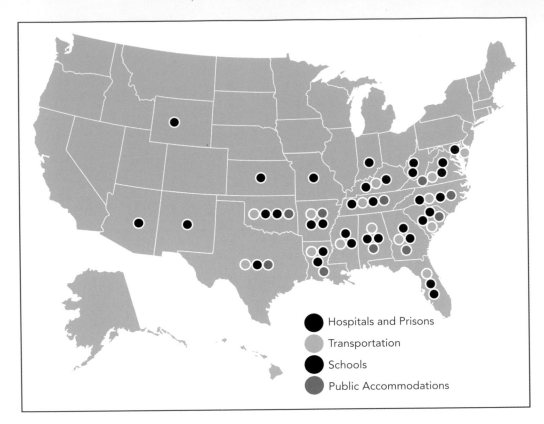

Legend:
- Hospitals and Prisons
- Transportation
- Schools
- Public Accommodations

Segregation under Jim Crow

Jim Crow laws affected things ranging from what schools African Americans could attend to where they could sit at public accommodations, such as movie theaters and restaurants. This map shows the Jim Crow laws in each state. How does the map help you understand segregation?

shop, sit, work, and go to school. Often the facilities for whites were far better than those available to African Americans. The laws existed throughout the United States but were especially numerous in the South.

Jim Crow laws often said that African-American children could not go to white schools. African-American schools, if they existed at all, were much poorer than white schools. African-American students often had to walk to school. One woman described what school was like for her:

> I tell you, I had to walk to school every day and back no matter if it was storming. . . . Nothing rode the bus but whites. And they would ride and throw trash, throw rocks and everything at us on the road. . . . We weren't allowed to say one word to them or throw back or nothing, because if you threw back at them you was going to jail. . . . We didn't have nothing at our school. They give the teachers some chalk and a couple of erasers for the board, but no kind of supplies. Not even heat.

> Source: William H. Chafe. Remembering Jim Crow: African Americans Tell about Life in the Segregated South. New York: New Press, 2001. Print. 155.

Changing Minds

This passage tells about how Jim Crow laws affected one girl. Write a letter to the white children on the bus from this girl's point of view. How can she convince them their behavior was wrong? What could she say that would help them see that the Jim Crow laws were unfair?

CHAPTER THREE

THE SIT-INS OF 1960

The Greensboro sit-in sparked more resistance across the country. Civil rights organizations became involved. Within weeks sit-ins started in nine states. Two of the most important sit-in sites were Nashville, Tennessee, and Atlanta, Georgia.

Nashville

College students in Nashville had begun planning their sit-ins in the fall of 1959. For months they had

Members of CORE and a labor union in New York City show their support for the North Carolina sit-ins on February 13, 1960.

been meeting with James Lawson. Lawson was a Nashville minister. He was training the students how to use nonviolent resistance. They practiced sitting quietly while others yelled and pushed them. They learned how to control their feelings. They learned how to not fight back.

Almost two weeks after the Greensboro sit-in, on February 13, 1960, the students in Nashville were ready. There were 124 of them. They broke into groups. The groups went to stores that had lunch counters. As they sat, they heard insults but ignored them.

CIVIL RIGHTS VOICES
James Lawson

This movement should not be considered one for Negroes but one for people who consider this a movement against injustice. This would include members of all races.

James Lawson was a strong believer in nonviolence. His workshops taught how to use nonviolence to fight injustice. He was not as well known as some other civil rights leaders, but he had great influence. King described him as the greatest teacher of nonviolence in America.

them that he was against segregation. On May 10, 1960, city officials and local businesses agreed to desegregate Nashville's public facilities. Almost three months after the first sit-ins, the lunch counters in Nashville opened to all.

Atlanta

The college students in Atlanta began their sit-ins in March 1960, a few weeks after those in Greensboro. In their first sit-in, 200 students split up and went to ten eating establishments. Nearly 80 were arrested. After spending a day in jail, they were released.

The sit-ins continued. But they did not lead to change. So the students asked King to protest with

An Early Sit-in

Sit-ins were not new in the United States. One of the earliest sit-ins was held in 1943 in Washington, DC. Three African-American women sat at a lunch counter. They ordered hot chocolates. The waitress charged them more than white customers. The women refused to pay. They were arrested and taken to jail. There were many sit-ins after this incident. But it took ten years for the DC lunch counters to desegregate.

King walks past a protester after being arrested for taking part in the Atlanta sit-ins on October 19, 1960.

them. This was a hard decision for King, who already had an arrest on his record. If he was arrested again, he could go to jail for several months. On October 19, King joined approximately 80 others at a downtown store. He was arrested and sentenced to four months of hard labor. Many people were outraged by the harsh sentence. Some important people, including the US Attorney General, Robert Kennedy, protested.

President John F. Kennedy called King's wife to show his sympathy. King was released after two days.

The students continued the sit-ins. The stores in downtown Atlanta were losing business. On March 7, 1961, city leaders agreed to desegregate the lunch counters the following fall, when the local schools were scheduled to integrate. The students complained about the delay. But they accepted the agreement in the end.

FURTHER EVIDENCE

This chapter is about the sit-ins of the 1960s. What was one of the chapter's main points about nonviolent resistance? What are some pieces of evidence in the chapter that support this main point? Check out the website at the link below about a museum with a sit-in exhibit. Write a few sentences about how this exhibit supports this chapter's main point.

Sit-ins

mycorelibrary.com/nonviolent-resistance

CHAPTER FOUR

THE FREEDOM RIDES OF 1961

Many students who took part in sit-ins in the South wanted to continue working for civil rights beyond the lunch counter. Some participants helped form the Student Nonviolent Coordinating Committee (SNCC). The SNCC decided to work with CORE for equality in public transportation. Members of the civil rights movement had been working to desegregate buses for many

On segregated buses, African Americans were forced to ride in the back and give up their seats for whites.

King rides a bus beside a white minister on December 21, 1956, the day the Supreme Court ordered the buses in Montgomery, Alabama, to be integrated.

years. In 1955 and 1956, African Americans in Montgomery, Alabama, staged a 381-day nonviolent boycott of public buses. The US Supreme Court ordered the city and state to desegregate the buses in response to the boycott.

The court had also made rulings about buses that traveled from state to state. In 1946 the US Supreme Court ruled that interstate buses must be integrated. And in 1958, it expanded the ruling to include bus stations that served interstate buses.

Even though the US Supreme Court made these rulings, many people felt the laws were not being enforced in the South. CORE created a plan in 1961 to test the laws. Members of the SNCC also joined. African Americans and whites would take buses through the South. The African Americans would sit in the front, and the white passengers would sit in the back. The plan was called the Freedom Rides.

The Freedom Rides

The Freedom Rides started with three days of nonviolence training.

A white man blocks the bus carrying Freedom Riders in Anniston, Alabama. Others slashed the tires while the bus was stopped.

Then on May 4, two buses left Washington, DC, with 13 riders. There were seven African Americans and six whites. The first few days were uneventful. But on May 9, 1961, several white men attacked some of the African-American riders in a bus station waiting room. Two of the riders were hurt, but they continued to ride.

The buses arrived in Anniston, Alabama, on May 14. When the first bus pulled into the station, it was met by a screaming mob. The mob surrounded the bus. Using metal pipes, clubs, and chains, they smashed windows and slashed tires. The police came and escorted the bus to the Anniston city limits.

Shortly after the police left, the bus had to stop. Its tires were too damaged to go on. A mob surrounded the bus again. The police returned but did not stop the mob. Someone threw a firebomb through one of the broken windows. The bomb exploded, filling the bus with smoke. The riders fled the bus. After a while, the police drove the mob away. Ambulances took the riders to the hospital.

The second bus pulled into Anniston about an hour after the first. Eight white men entered the bus and attacked some of the Freedom Riders. The men rode the bus to Birmingham, Alabama. At the station, they took two of the Freedom Riders into an alley and beat them with pipes. One was left paralyzed.

When this happened, CORE leader James Farmer called off the ride. He felt it had become too dangerous. But in Nashville, members of the

Federal troops patrol First Baptist Church in Montgomery, Alabama. The troops broke up a mob of protesters outside the church, which allowed the people inside to escape.

SNCC felt differently. They decided to continue the Freedom Rides.

On May 20, one bus with a new set of Freedom Riders left Birmingham for Montgomery, Alabama. At the Montgomery bus station, a large mob met them. Most of the riders escaped. But three were badly beaten.

The next night, the riders gathered at a local African-American church. They were joined by almost 1,200 supporters. An angry mob of approximately 3,000 stood outside. The people in the church sang.

The mob outside threw rocks and bricks. US Attorney General Robert Kennedy sent federal soldiers to protect the church. They forced the mob to leave. It was not until early morning that the people trapped in the church were able to escape.

More students joined the rides. Police arrested many. Finally on September 22, 1961, the Interstate Commerce Commission ordered that desegregation on interstate buses be enforced. This was an important win for the Freedom Riders, though it would take many months for some states to enforce the ruling.

EXPLORE ONLINE

The focus of Chapter Four is on the Freedom Rides. The website at the link below shows the route that the buses followed. How does seeing the route on the map give you a better idea of the trip? What new information do the map captions give you to think about?

Freedom Rides

mycorelibrary.com/nonviolent-resistance

CHAPTER FIVE

CONTINUING NONVIOLENT RESISTANCE

The violence against the Freedom Riders helped bring more national attention to the civil rights movement, which continued to grow. On August 28, 1963, approximately 250,000 people gathered peacefully in Washington, DC. The massive demonstration helped bring about the Civil Rights Act of 1964. The act promised equal rights to all people no matter what their race, color, religion, gender, or

King marches with thousands of others on August 28, 1963, in Washington, DC. King delivered one of his most famous speeches at the rally.

national origin. While this was a major victory for the civil rights movement, there was still more work to be done.

Selma to Montgomery March of 1965

One area of continued injustice involved voting. Before 1965 whites in many southern states prevented African Americans from voting. They gave them unfair literacy tests. They taxed them. They even arrested them. The SNCC and King wanted to raise awareness of these unfair practices. They planned a 54-mile (87-km) march in Alabama. It would start in Selma and end in Montgomery, the state capital.

On March 7, 1965, approximately 600 people gathered near a church in Selma and started to march. State troopers were waiting for them at a local bridge. The troopers told the marchers to turn around. But the marchers did not move. They bowed their heads and waited. The troopers charged. Many were on horses. The troopers attacked the marchers

State troopers break up the first march from Selma to Montgomery on March 7, 1965. The day became known as "Bloody Sunday" because of the violence.

with clubs, whips, and tear gas. Seventy people were hospitalized. Many more were injured.

Two days later, a second march occurred. A crowd of 1,500 gathered at the church. They marched across the bridge. King led them in a prayer. Then they returned to the church.

The third march began on March 21. There was a group of more than 3,000. They walked in a line that stretched a mile (1.6 km) long. Police walked with them to keep them safe. The march lasted four days. Many slept in tents at night. Some rode back to Selma to sleep. The marchers arrived in Montgomery on March 24. The next morning, they walked to the Alabama state capitol building. A crowd of 25,000 listened as King and many others spoke. The march from Selma to Montgomery helped bring about the Voting Rights Act of 1965.

The Voting Rights Act of 1965

On August 6, President Lyndon B. Johnson signed the Voting Rights Act into law. It outlawed unfair voting rules in all the states. It stopped the use of literacy tests. It outlawed taxing voters. Many have called it the most effective civil rights law ever passed. By the end of the 1960s, many more African Americans registered to vote.

Nonviolent Work Goes On

Following the success of the Selma to Montgomery marches, King continued to use nonviolence to bring about change. In 1966 he helped organize the Chicago Freedom Movement. In Chicago and across the country, many realtors in white neighborhoods would not sell homes to African Americans. King organized marches in white neighborhoods to protest. The movement helped lead to the Fair Housing Act of 1968.

But King was not able to see the Fair Housing Act signed into law. On April 3, 1968, he spoke at a rally in Memphis. The next day, he was shot and killed. People all over the world mourned.

Internal Divisions

By the end of the 1960s, many nonviolent resisters were worn out from the constant threat of danger. They saw that nonviolent action could not protect them against violent whites. Some began to arm themselves

The Fair Housing Act of 1968

On April 11, just one week after King's death, President Johnson signed the Civil Rights Act of 1968. It was also called the Fair Housing Act. It said the sale and rental of housing must be fair. States could not allow housing discrimination based on race, color, or gender.

President Johnson signs the Civil Rights Act of 1968 seven days after King's death.

for self-defense. Others felt it was time to build African-American leadership that did not depend on whites to achieve change. One of these people was SNCC leader Stokely Carmichael. He called the movement Black Power.

Lasting Legacy

Although some civil rights leaders went away from nonviolent resistance in the late 1960s, the strategy left a distinguishing mark on the civil rights movement. It effectively focused national attention on important issues, which allowed the movement to bring lasting change to the United States.

President Johnson gave a speech before he signed the Voting Rights Act of 1965:

> *But even if we pass this bill, the battle will not be over. What happened in Selma is part of a far larger movement which reaches into every section and State of America. . . . Their cause must be our cause too. Because it is not just Negroes, but really it is all of us, who must overcome the crippling legacy of bigotry and injustice. . . . For Negroes are not the only victims. How many white children have gone uneducated, how many white families have lived in stark poverty, how many white lives have been scarred by fear, because we have wasted our energy and our substance to maintain the barriers of hatred and terror?*
>
> Source: Lyndon B. Johnson. "Remarks on the Signing of the Voting Rights Act." Capitol Rotunda, Washington, DC. August 6, 1965. Address.

What's the Big Idea?

Take a close look at the excerpt from President Johnson's speech. Which group of people is he addressing in this part of the speech? What is he trying to tell them? How does he support his claim?

SNAPSHOT OF NONVIOLENT RESISTANCE

A bus burns after being attacked by an angry mob. The Freedom Riders escaped the blaze, but many were beaten before the police took action.

Date

May 1, 1961

Key Players

Freedom Riders, white protesters, Anniston police

What Happened

Police escorted the bus to the edge of Anniston, Alabama, after an initial attack at the bus station. Soon after the police left, the bus broke down due to damage caused by the first attack. A mob of white protesters gathered. They set the bus on fire and beat the riders. Eventually the police broke up the mob and took the injured riders to the hospital.

Impact

Despite the attack, more people joined the Freedom Rides. The federal government took action to protect the riders. After months of rides and continued attacks, desegregation on interstate buses was finally enforced.

Tell the Tale

Chapter One discusses the first Greensboro sit-in. When the four students got back to their dorm, they must have told the other students about the sit-in. Write the story as one of the students might have told it. Use details from the chapter. Make sure you set the scene, develop a sequence of events, and include a conclusion.

Take a Stand

Chapter Three discusses the sit-ins that occurred across the South. The sit-in participants were breaking the law. Do you think they were right to break the law? What facts and details support your opinion?

You Are There

Chapter Five discusses the Selma to Montgomery
March of 1965. Imagine you are one of the protesters
on the third march. Describe what you see and hear.
Are people singing? Who is marching along with you?
Describe camping at night. What is your tent like?
What do you eat? Use your imagination!

Say What?

Studying the civil rights movement can mean learning
new vocabulary. Find five words in this book that
you did not know before. Look up the words in a
dictionary. Then write the meanings in your own
words, and use each word in a new sentence.

GLOSSARY

amendment
a change or addition to a document, such as the US Constitution

boycott
to protest by refusing to buy or use goods and services

desegregate
to end a policy of racial separation

injustice
the lack of justice or fairness

integrate
to make open to all cultures and races

literacy
the ability to read and write

naturalized
to become a citizen of a country

nonviolent resistance
to peacefully disobey an unjust rule or law

racist
a person who believes that a certain human race is better than another

realtor
a person who sells land or buildings

LEARN MORE

Books

Pinkney, Andrea Davis. *Sit-in: How Four Friends Stood Up by Sitting Down*. New York: Little, Brown and Company, 2010.

Rappaport, Doreen. *Nobody Gonna Turn Me Around*. Cambridge, MA: Candlewick, 2006.

Rice, Dona. *Martin Luther King Jr*. New York: TIME for Kids, 2011.

Websites

To learn more about Stories of the Civil Rights Movement, visit **booklinks.abdopublishing.com**. These links are routinely monitored and updated to provide the most current information available.

Visit **mycorelibrary.com** for free additional tools for teachers and students.

INDEX

ABOUT THE AUTHOR

Gail Terp is a retired elementary teacher who now writes for kids and beginning adult readers. Her blog, *Best Blog for Kids Who Hate to Read*, is a family blog for reluctant readers and their families. Terp lives in Troy, New York.

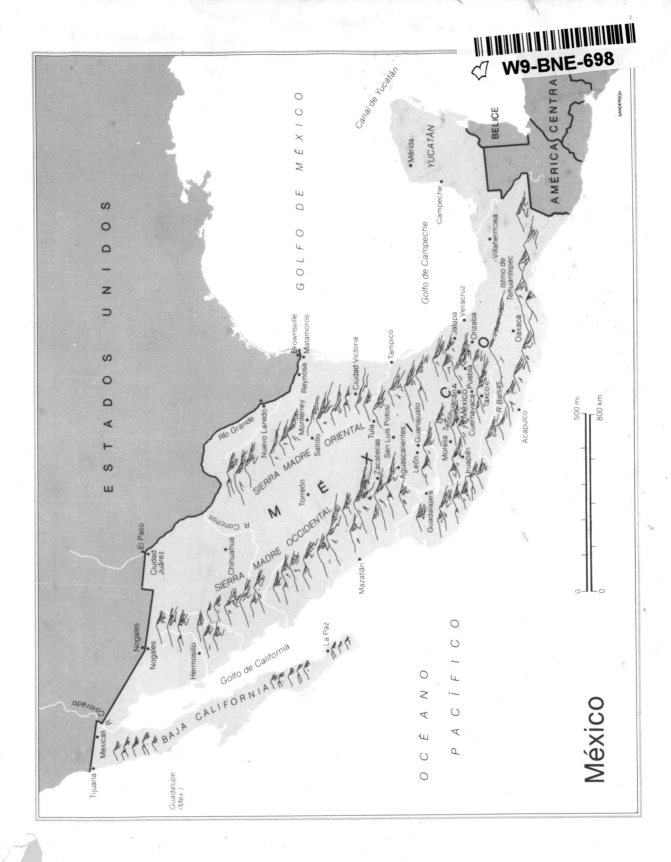

México

¿Cómo se dice...?

Fourth Edition

¿Cómo se dice...?

Ana C. Jarvis
Chandler-Gilbert Community College

Raquel Lebredo
California Baptist College

Francisco Mena
Crafton Hills College

D. C. Heath and Company
Lexington, Massachusetts   Toronto

Acquisitions Editor: Denise St. Jean
Developmental Editors: José Blanco, Gina Russo
Production Editor: Janice Molloy
Cover and Text Designer: Alwyn Velásquez
Production Coordinator: Michael O'Dea
Photo Coordinator: Martha Shethar
Photo Researcher: Carole Frohlich
Text Permissions Editor: Margaret Roll
Illustrations: Penny Carter
Marble used on cover and in text: Westlight/Backgrounds

Published simultaneously in Canada.

Printed in the United States of America.

International Standard Book Number: 0–669–19614–2

Library of Congress Catalog Card Number: 89–84202

10 9

Ana C. Jarvis, a native of Paraguay, was born in Asunción and attended school in Buenos Aires, Argentina. She received her Ph.D. in Spanish from the University of California, Riverside, in 1973. Presently an Instructor of Spanish at Chandler-Gilbert Community College in Chandler, Arizona, Dr. Jarvis previously taught at Mesa Community College, the University of California, Riverside, San Bernardino Valley College, Brigham Young University, and Riverside City College. In addition to authoring numerous Spanish textbooks, she has published several short stories in Spanish, and is presently at work on a novel. In 1988 she was chosen "Faculty Member of the Year" at Chandler-Gilbert Community College.

Raquel Lebredo was born in Camagüey, Cuba. She attended school in Havana and later enrolled in the University of Havana, where she received a Ph.D. in Education in 1950. She was subsequently employed as an elementary school principal, and taught literature and language at a preparatory school in Havana. After living in Spain for a period of time, she moved in 1968 to the United States. Dr. Lebredo was awarded a Ph.D. in Spanish from the University of California, Riverside, in 1973. Since then she has taught Spanish at Claremont Graduate School, Crafton Hills College, the University of Redlands, and California Baptist College. She has authored several Spanish textbooks, and in 1985 she was chosen "Faculty Member of the Year" by the student body at California Baptist College.

Francisco Mena, a native of Madrid, Spain, received his Ph.D. in Spanish from the University of California, Riverside, in 1973. He has taught Spanish language and literature courses at Oberlin College, California State University, Chico, the University of Redlands, and Crafton Hills College. In addition to authoring numerous Spanish textbooks in the United States, he has published a book about Federico García Lorca and several collections of poems in Spain. His work has been included in several anthologies of contemporary Spanish poets, and he is listed in *Quién es quién en las letras españolas, 1978* (Who's Who in Spanish Letters), as an important contributor to contemporary Spanish literature.

¿Cómo se dice... ?, Fourth Edition, is a complete, flexible program designed to present the fundamentals of Spanish to two- and four-year college and university students. This edition continues to feature the balanced, eclectic approach to language instruction that has made it one of the most widely used programs of its kind. To achieve its goal of helping learners attain linguistic proficiency, **¿Cómo se dice... ?**, Fourth Edition, systematically involves them in activities requiring the communicative use of all four language skills: listening, speaking, reading, and writing. Because cultural awareness is as important to successful communication as linguistic competence, special care has been devoted in the Fourth Edition to providing up-to-date, practical insights into the cultural diversity of the Spanish-speaking world. Since it is essential to understand the underlying philosophy and organization of the program to use it to greatest advantage, the Student's Text and other components are described in detail below.

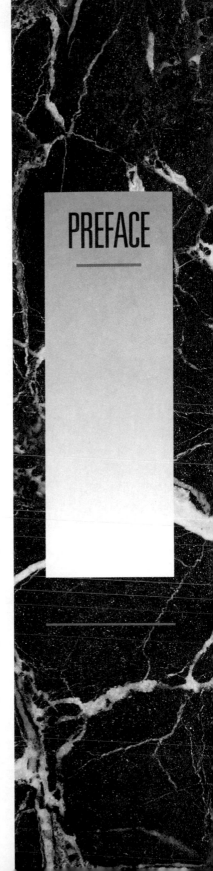

The Student's Text

The organization of this central component of the **¿Cómo se dice... ?**, Fourth Edition, program reflects its emphasis on the active use of Spanish for practical communication in context. Major divisions of the Student's Text are:

- Three introductory *Pasos* that enable learners to communicate in Spanish using high-frequency, basic language from the outset of the course
- Eighteen regular lessons, each focusing on a high-frequency, communicative situation and featuring the following elements:

Objectives: A list of grammatical and communicative goals begins each lesson.

Dialogues: New vocabulary and structures are first presented in the context of a conversation in idiomatic Spanish dealing with the high-frequency situation that is the lesson's central theme. An English translation is provided on the following page.

Vocabulario: All new words and expressions introduced in the dialogue are listed by parts of speech or under the general heading *Otras palabras y expresiones.* The *Vocabulario adicional* section offers other words and phrases related to the lesson theme.

¿Lo sabía Ud.... ?: These notes convey information on cultural themes or points arising in the dialogues in simple, easy-to-read Spanish.

Pronunciación: Lessons 1–9 present and practice the sounds of the Spanish language, with special attention to features of pronunciation that pose problems for speakers of English.

Estructuras gramaticales: Each new grammatical structure featured in the dialogue is explained clearly and concisely in English, so that the explanation may be used independently as an out-of-class reference. The explanations are followed by numerous examples of the structure's use for communicative purposes. Exceptions to the grammar rules cited in the explanations or instances where knowledge of the English structure may interfere with learning the equivalent Spanish structure are signaled by the *¡Atención!* head.

Práctica: One or more activities following each grammar explanation reinforce the new concept and provide further insight into the structure's use for communication.

¡A ver cuánto aprendió!: This series of increasingly less structured activities allows learners to synthesize the lesson's new vocabulary and structures. *¡Conversemos!* checks comprehension of the dialogue and promotes class discussion of its content. *Repase el vocabulario* uses a variety of proven activity formats to review new vocabulary presented in the lesson. *Situaciones* involves pairs or small groups of students in using new structures and vocabulary orally, in brief conversational exchanges, or in writing to resolve realistic situations. *Para escribir* guides students to express themselves in writing in a variety of formats: notes, postcards, letters, compositions, and journal entries.

En la vida real: This new section at the end of each lesson involves learners in more complex, extended communicative tasks, such as interviews, problem-solving, and role-playing. Some involve reading and using the information gained from an authentic text, for example, a newspaper ad or a travel brochure. Most are designed for work in pairs or small groups. All involve spontaneous use of language in practical, meaningful, communicative tasks intended to motivate learners and to underscore the usefulness of language study.

In addition, the following features appear at regular intervals throughout the Student's Text:

Y ahora, ¡vamos a leer!: Beginning with Lesson 2, all even-numbered lessons end with readings designed to reinforce the structures and vocabulary presented in the preceding lessons and to develop students' reading skills. Comprehension questions follow each reading.

Self-Tests: After *Paso 3* and Lessons 3, 6, 9, 12, 15, and 18, these sections enable learners to review the structures and vocabulary of the three preceding lessons. Their organization by lesson and by grammatical structure allows students to monitor their progress quickly and to target specific concepts for further study when necessary.

Panorama hispánico: At the end of *Paso 3* and after every two lessons through Lesson 16, *Panorama hispánico* presents interesting facts and a colorful photo essay on the lifestyle, culture, geography, economy, and history of one of the diverse key areas of the Spanish-speaking world.

Appendixes: Five appendixes provide learners with useful reference tools throughout the course. *Appendix A* summarizes the sounds and key pronunciation features of the Spanish language, with abundant examples. Conjugations of high-frequency regular, stem-changing, and irregular Spanish verbs constitute *Appendix B*. In *Appendix C* a glossary of all grammatical terms used in the text, with examples, is provided. Questions to be used in the "College Bowl" game following Lesson 18 summarize the textbook's cultural content in *Appendix D*. *Appendix E* is the answer key to the *Self-Test* sections.

Supplementary Materials for the Student

Student Cassette: A free cassette, containing recordings of the dialogues from all textbook lessons, is packaged with each copy of the Student's Text. Available for the first time with **¿Cómo se dice... ?**, Fourth Edition, this cassette is designed to maximize learners' exposure to the sounds of natural spoken Spanish.

Workbook/Laboratory Manual: Each lesson of this component is correlated to the corresponding Student's Text lesson and contains a *Workbook Activities* section and a *Laboratory Activities* section. The array of writing exercises in the *Workbook Activities* section reinforces the structures and vocabulary presented in the textbook. In the *Laboratory Activities* section supporting printed materials are provided for all of the pronunciation, listening comprehension, and listening and writing activities featured in the **Audio Program** described below.

Audio Program: The **Audio Program** accompanying **¿Cómo se dice... ?**, Fourth Edition, has been significantly expanded to emphasize further development of listening comprehension skills. Each lesson features taped readings of the dialogues at natural speed and with pauses for student repetition. *Pronunciation* activities parallel those found in Lessons 1–9 of the textbook. *Let's Practice* offers a variety of oral activities that reinforce the structures and vocabulary presented in each textbook lesson. *Listening Comprehension* features lively, contextualized conversations followed by comprehension questions designed to help students focus on listening for information in context. The *Listening and Writing Activities* require learners to carry the process one step further, filling in information presented in taped passages that simulate realistic listening experiences such as advertisements, announcements, and newscasts. A dictation concludes this section.

Student Software Program: Additional, computer-aided practice in using structures and vocabulary from the textbook is provided by this program. In-depth error analysis which guides learners toward self-correction of errors is a key feature of this component.

Supplementary Materials for the Instructor

Instructor's Annotated Edition: The *Instructor's Guide* that begins this component provides a detailed description of the entire **¿Cómo se dice... ?**, Fourth Edition, program with suggestions for its implementation. In the annotated version of the Student's Text that follows, specific suggestions for implementing and supplementing the features of each lesson are provided right on the appropriate Student's Text pages.

Testing Program: Eighteen tests, one for each of the eighteen lessons, monitor students' progress on a regular basis. Two mid-term and two final examinations test cumulative achievement and round out the printed version of the **Testing Program.** Both listening comprehension and writing skills are evaluated by all of the tests.

HeathTest Plus: This new computerized testing program enables the instructor to modify and customize the existing test item bank by selecting specific or random items, and by adding, deleting, or modifying items. It is available in IBM® and Macintosh® versions to adopters of **¿Cómo se dice... ?**, Fourth Edition.

Instructor's Resource Kit: This conveniently boxed, expanded supplement package component assists the instructor in presenting, reviewing, expanding, and reinforcing the materials in the textbook. New to the **Instructor's Resource Kit** for **¿Cómo se dice... ?**, Fourth Edition are:

- The **Heath Spanish Overhead Transparencies Kit,** 32 full-color visuals designed to present key introductory level vocabulary and structures in context. In the accompanying **Instructor's Resource Manual** a variety of teaching strategies and suggested activities are offered for each transparency. In addition these transparencies have been correlated to **¿Cómo se dice... ?**, Fourth Edition, by means of an overhead projector symbol in the **Instructor's Annotated Edition.**
- The **Heath Spanish Situation Cards Kit,** a set of 120 cards with its own **Instructor's Guide,** enables the instructor to monitor students' development of oral proficiency.

Other materials included in the **Instructor's Resource Kit** are the printed version of the **Testing Program;** the **Tapescript** of the **Audio Program;** the **Heath Spanish History Booklet,** with supplementary information on the history, politics, and cultures of Spain and Latin America; and the **Instructor's Manual and Videoscripts** for the *Entre amigos* **Video Program,** described below.

Entre amigos **Video Program:** Two 90-minute videocassettes present ten episodes in the lives of a group of university-age friends from a variety of Spanish-speaking countries. Each lively, engaging episode is correlated to the Student's Text by means of a videocassette symbol. The complete video program and

Instructor's Manual and Videoscripts were created by authors Ana C. Jarvis and Raquel Lebredo specifically for **¿Cómo se dice... ?**. The accompanying **Student Activity Manual** may be purchased with the video program or ordered separately.

We would like to hear your comments on and reactions to **¿Cómo se dice... ?**, Fourth Edition. Reports on your experiences using this program would also be of great interest and value to us. Please write us care of D. C. Heath and Company, College Division, 125 Spring Street, Lexington, MA 02173 or call our toll–free number: 1–800–235–3565.

Acknowledgments

We wish to express our appreciation to the following colleagues for the many valuable suggestions they offered in their reviews of the Third Edition and of the revised manuscript of the Fourth Edition.

Robert L. Adler
  *University of Alabama
  at Birmingham*
Iris Allocati
  Citrus Community College
Ann Bachman
  Seminole Community College
Malcolm Compitello
  Michigan State University
Octavio de la Suarée
  William Paterson College
Diana M. Diehl
  University of Delaware
Kenneth G. Eller
  *University of Nebraska
  at Omaha*
Robert Fedorchek
  Fairfield University
Rosa M. Fernández
  University of New Mexico
Walter Fuentes
  College of Charleston
George Pesacreta
  Palomar College

Alvin L. Prince
  Furman University
Montserrat Solá-Solé
  *University of the
  District of Columbia*
William N. Stivers
  Pepperdine University
Charles P. Thomas
  University of Wisconsin
Janet J. Hampton
  *University of the
  District of Columbia*
Paul Jacques
  Grossmont College
Christopher Maurer
  Harvard University
Virginia M. McCready
  Pasadena City College
Oliver T. Myers
  *University of Wisconsin,
  Milwaukee*

Special thanks are also due the following individuals whose time and expertise greatly contributed to the finalization of the manuscript: Lisa Sadulsky, whose careful typing of the manuscript relieved us of a heavy burden, Ruth Eisele, who created the answer key for the Student's Text exercises and the end vocabularies, and Janice Macián, who wrote the annotations for the **Instructor's Annotated Edition.** We also extend our sincere appreciation to the Modern Languages editorial staff of D. C. Heath and Company, College Division. Janice Molloy, José Blanco, Gina Russo, and Denise St. Jean provided us with invaluable assistance, constructive criticism, and sound suggestions at every stage in the preparation and production of the manuscript.

A.C.J.
R.L.
F.M.

CONTENTS

LECCIÓN <u>4</u> *¡Vamos a Madrid!* 102

PANORAMA HISPÁNICO 3 | *España (II)* 124

LECCIÓN <u>5</u> *Un viaje al Perú* 128

LECCIÓN <u>6</u> *En un restaurante cubano* 146

SELF-TEST *Lecciones 4–6* 170

PANORAMA HISPÁNICO 4 | *México*   178

LECCIÓN 7   *Las vacaciones de Teresa*   182

Pronunciación: The Spanish *ll* and *ñ*   186
Estructuras gramaticales   186
  1. Constructions with **gustar**   186
  2. Possessive pronouns   188
  3. Time expressions with **hacer**   190
  4. Preterit of regular verbs   191
  5. Direct and indirect object pronouns used together   193

LECCIÓN 8   *Un día muy ocupado*   200

Pronunciación: The Spanish *l, r, rr,* and *z*   204
Estructuras gramaticales   205
  1. Reflexive constructions   205
  2. Some uses of the definite article   210
  3. Preterit of **ser, ir,** and **dar**   212
  4. Preterit of **e:i** and **o:u** stem-changing verbs   213

PANORAMA HISPÁNICO 5 | *América Central*   220

LECCIÓN 9   *Planes de vacaciones*   224

Pronunciación: La entonación   227
Estructuras gramaticales   229
  1. Irregular preterits   229
  2. Uses of **por**   231
  3. Uses of **para**   232
  4. The imperfect   234

SELF-TEST   *Lecciones 7–9*   240

Photograph Credits
Color photographs

25 George Holton/Photo Researchers. 29 (l) Thomas Bowman/PhotoEdit; (tr) Bob Daemmrich; (br) Robert Frerck/Odyssey Productions. 30 (t) D. Donne Bryant; (b) Ron Grishaber/PhotoEdit. 31 (l) Beryl Goldberg; (tr) Bob Daemmrich. 32 Owen Franken. 35 Mark Antman/The Image Works, Inc. 52 Owen Franken. 71 Victor Englebert. 72 Peter Menzel. 73 (t) Robert Frerck/Odyssey Productions; (bl) Mark Antman/The Image Works, Inc.; (br) Carl Purcell. 74 (tl) (tr) Mark Antman/The Image Works, Inc.; (b) Robert Frerck/Odyssey Productions. 75 (bl) (tr) Mark Antman/The Image Works, Inc. 76 Peter Menzel. 80 Ulrike Welsch. 102 Peter Menzel. 106 Larry Mangino/The Image Works, Inc. 122 Peter Menzel. 124 Robert Frerck/Odyssey Productions. 125 (bl) Marvin Koner/COMSTOCK; (tr) G. Rancinan/Sygma. 126 (tl) Peter Borsari/Gamma-Liaison; (tr) Mark Antman/The Image Works, Inc.; (br) Peter Menzel. 127 (bl) (tr) Mark Antman/The Image Works, Inc. 128, 132 Carl Purcell. 146 Stuart Cohen/COMSTOCK. 151 Paul Conklin. 178 Stuart Cohen/COMSTOCK. 179 (bl) (tr) José Blanco; (mr) Robert Frerck/Odyssey Productions. 180 (tl) Peter Menzel/Stock, Boston; (br) Peter Menzel. 181 (tl) (mr) (br) Robert Frerck/Odyssey Productions. 182 Robert Frerck/Odyssey Productions. 185 Peter Menzel. 200, 218 Robert Frerck/Odyssey Productions. 220 David Kupferschmid. 221 (bl) Bob Daemmrich; (tr) Owen Franken. 222 (tl) Robert Frerck/Odyssey Productions; (tr) (br) Chip and Rosa María de la Cueva Peterson. 223 (bl) Robert Frerck/Odyssey Productions; (tr) Bill Gentile/Picture Group. 224 Stuart Cohen/COMSTOCK. 227 Georg Gerster/COMSTOCK. 246 Robert Frerck/Odyssey Productions. 250 Katherine McGlynn/The Image Works, Inc. 263 Robert Frerck/Odyssey Productions. 264 Owen Franken. 265 (bl) COMSTOCK; (tr) Paul Conklin. 266 (bl) Chip and Rosa María de la Cueva Peterson; (tr) Peter Menzel; (br) Stuart Cohen/COMSTOCK. 267 (mb) Robert Frerck/Odyssey Productions; (tr) Paul Conklin/PhotoEdit. 268 Chip and Rosa María de la Cueva Peterson. 272 Suzanne Brookens/The Stock Market. 288 Owen Franken. 292 Mark Antman/The Image Works, Inc. 305, 312 Robert Frerck/Odyssey Productions. 313 (tr) (br) Victor Englebert. 314 (l) Beryl Goldberg; (r) Stuart Cohen/COMSTOCK. 315 (tl) (tr) Victor Englebert; (b) Ulrike Welsch. 316, 320 Robert Frerck/Odyssey Productions. 332 Mark Antman/The Image Works, Inc. 336 Peter Menzel. 350 Robert Frerck/Odyssey Productions. 351 (ml) Robert Frerck/Odyssey Productions; (tr) Peter Menzel; (br) Victor Englebert. 352 (bl) Owen Franken; (tr) Peter Menzel. 353 (l) Victor Englebert; (tr) G. Rancinan/Sygma; (br) Stuart Cohen/COMSTOCK. 354 Victor Englebert. 357 Mark Antman/The Image Works, Inc. 378 Peter Menzel. 382 Mark Antman/The Image Works, Inc. 395 (tl) (tr) Stuart Cohen/COMSTOCK; (b) Beryl Goldberg. 396 (t) Bob Daemmrich; (bl) D. Fineman/Sygma; (br) George Rose/Gamma-Liaison. 397 (bl) Susan Greenwood/Gamma-Liaison; (tr) Bob Daemmrich. 398 Stuart Cohen/COMSTOCK. 402 Joe Viesti/Viesti Associates, Inc. 414 Stuart Cohen/COMSTOCK. 418, 433 Mark Antman/The Image Works, Inc.

Black and white photographs

49 (l) Peter Menzel. 50 (tl) Peter Menzel; (tr) Andrew Brilliant & Carol Palmer; (bl) Mark Antman/The Image Works; (br) Andrew Brilliant & Carol Palmer.

¿Cómo se dice...?

INTRODUCCIÓN

En la universidad

—Buenos días, profesor.
—Buenos días, señorita.
   ¿Cómo se llama usted?
—Me llamo Ana María Vargas.

—Buenas tardes, doctor Gómez.
—Buenas tardes, señor Campos.
   ¿Cómo está usted?
—Muy bien, gracias. ¿Y usted?
—Bien, gracias.

—Buenas noches, señora.[1]
—Buenas noches, Amanda.
   ¿Qué hay de nuevo?
—No mucho...

---

[1] In Spanish-speaking countries, young people
frequently address their elders as **señor** or **señora.**

—¡Hola, José Luis!
—Hola, Teresa. ¿Qué tal?
—Bien, ¿y tú?
—No muy bien...
—¡Caramba! ¡Lo siento...!

—Hasta luego, profesora.
—Adiós.

—Hasta mañana, Paco.
—Hasta mañana, Isabel.

AT THE UNIVERSITY
Good morning, professor.
Good morning, Miss. What
is your name?
My name is Ana María Var-
gas.

Good afternoon, Doctor
Gómez.
Good afternoon, Mr. Cam-
pos. How are you?
Very well, thank you. And
you?
Fine, thank you.

Good evening, ma'am.
Good evening, Amanda.
What's new?
Not much . . .

Hello, José Luis!
Hi, Teresa. How's it going?
Fine, and with you?
Not very well . . .
Gee! I'm sorry . . . !

See you later, Professor.
Good-bye.

See you tomorrow, Paco.
See you tomorrow, Isabel.

Vocabulary

TITLES

doctor (Dr.) doctor[1] *(m.)*
doctora (Dra.) doctor[1] *(f.)*
profesor professor, teacher *(m.)*
profesora professor, teacher *(f.)*
señor (Sr.) Mr., sir, gentleman
señora (Sra.) Mrs., madam, lady
señorita (Srta.) Miss, young lady

GREETINGS AND FAREWELLS

adiós good-bye
buenas noches good evening, good night
buenas tardes good afternoon
buenos días good morning
hasta luego see you later
hasta mañana see you tomorrow
hola hello, hi

GENERAL VOCABULARY

caramba gee
en la universidad at the university

gracias thank you, thanks
lo siento I'm sorry
muy very
¿qué? what?
tú you (when addressing a child, a friend, or a relative)
usted (Ud.) you (when addressing someone older or in authority)

USEFUL QUESTIONS AND ANSWERS

¿Cómo se llama usted? What's your name?
Me llamo... My name is . . .
¿Cómo está usted? How are you?
¿Qué tal? How's it going? (informal)
bien fine
muy bien very well
no muy bien not very well
¿Qué hay de nuevo? What's new?
No mucho... Not much . . .

---

[1] In most Spanish-speaking countries, lawyers and most professionals who hold a college degree are addressed as **doctor, doctora.**

▶ Cardinal numbers 0–10   *(Números cardinales 0–10)*

♦ If you learn to count from zero to ten, you will be able to give your phone number in Spanish.

0	cero	4	cuatro	8	ocho
1	uno	5	cinco	9	nueve
2	dos	6	seis	10	diez
3	tres	7	siete		

♦ Now learn how to ask someone what his or her phone number is.

¿Cuál es tu[1] número de teléfono?   *What is your phone number?*

¡A ver cuánto aprendió!

A. With a classmate, practice giving appropriate responses to the following statements and questions.

1. Buenos días.
2. ¿Cómo está usted?
3. Buenas tardes.
4. ¿Qué hay de nuevo?
5. Buenas noches.
6. ¿Qué tal?
7. ¿Cómo se llama usted?
8. Hasta mañana, señor (señora, señorita).
9. Hasta luego.
10. ¡Hola!

---

[1] **tu** = *your* (when addressing a friend or a very young person).

B. Situaciones *(Situations)*

What would you say in the following situations? What might the other person say?

1. You greet your teacher in the morning and ask how he or she is.
2. You greet Mr. Vega in the afternoon.
3. You say "hi" to your best friend and ask him or her what's new.
4. You greet Miss Olmedo in the evening.
5. You greet a young person and ask him or her how it's going.
6. You say "see you tomorrow" to Dr. María Méndez.
7. You say good-bye to a friend.
8. You ask an older person what his or her name is.
9. Someone tells you he's not feeling too well.
10. Someone asks what's new with you.

C. This is a page from someone's address book. Tell us the phone number of each of the following people.

NOMBRES	TELÉFONOS
María Luisa Pagán	325-4270
José María Pereyra	476-0389
Teresita Peña	721-4693
Amanda Pidal	396-7548
Angel Pardo	482-3957
Prof. Benito Paredes	396-1598
Dra. Raquel Parra	476-8539
Tito Paz	721-0653
David Pizarro	482-7986
María Inés Pinto	396-8510

1. La doctora Parra
2. José María
3. El señor Pardo
4. Tito
5. La señora Pagán
6. El profesor Paredes
7. La señorita Peña
8. Amanda

En la vida real

ENCUENTROS (*ENCOUNTERS*)

Imagine that you and a classmate meet outside of class. How would you greet each other in Spanish? How would you find out each other's complete name and phone number? How would you say good-bye? Act out this situation with a partner. You may want to include these additional phrases:

¿Cómo te va? *How is it going (for you)?*
Hasta la vista. *Until I see you again.*
Chau. *Bye.*

¡AL TELÉFONO!

You and a classmate are in a Spanish-speaking country. Take turns reading the telephone numbers you must call according to the following needs.

1. You are having car trouble.
2. You need to cash a check.
3. You need some medicine.
4. You want to send roses to a friend.
5. You want to see a play.
6. You have to travel by plane.
7. You need your picture taken.
8. Somebody stole your wallet.
9. Someone needs to go to the emergency room.
10. You need a place to live.
11. You want to buy a plane ticket to Mexico.
12. You want to see Picasso's paintings.
13. One of your friends has been hospitalized.
14. You want to travel to a nearby city.
15. You have a toothache.

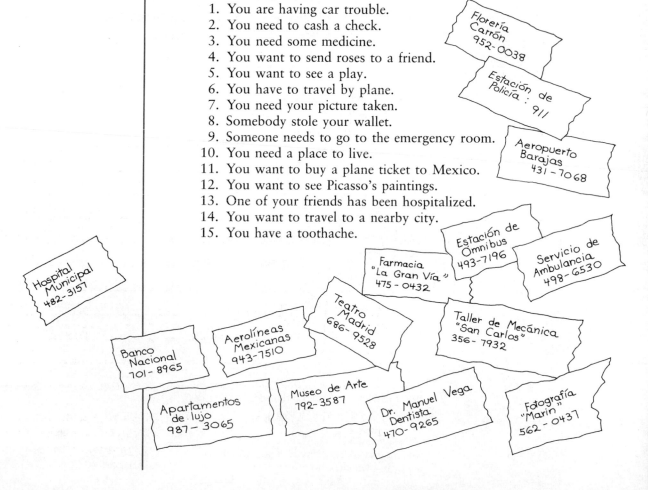

Florería Carrón 952-0038

Estación de Policía: 911

Aeropuerto Barajas 431-7068

Hospital Municipal 482-3157

Estación de Omnibus 493-7196

Servicio de Ambulancia 498-6530

Farmacia "La Gran Vía" 475-0432

Taller de Mecánica "San Carlos" 356-7932

Teatro Madrid 686-9528

Banco Nacional 701-8965

Aerolíneas Mexicanas 943-7510

Apartamentos de lujo 987-3065

Museo de Arte 792-3587

Dr. Manuel Vega Dentista 470-9265

Fotografía "Marín" 562-0437

Conversaciones breves

SRTA. PEÑA	—*(En la puerta)* Buenos días, profesor. Con permiso.
PROFESOR	—Buenos días. Pase y tome asiento.
SRTA. PEÑA	—Muchas gracias.
PROFESOR	—Señorita Peña, el[1] doctor Mena.
SRTA. PEÑA	—Mucho gusto, doctor Mena.
DR. MENA	—El gusto es mío, señorita Peña.

JULIA	—¡Hola! ¿Cómo te llamas?
ROSA	—Me llamo Rosa Díaz. ¿Y tú?
JULIA	—Julia Sandoval.

CARLOS	—Profesor, ¿cómo se dice «de nada» en inglés?
PROFESOR	—Se dice *«you're welcome»*.
CARLOS	—¿Qué quiere decir *«I'm sorry»*?
PROFESOR	—Quiere decir «lo siento».

---

[1] When you are speaking about a third person (indirect address) and use a title with the name, the definite article is required.

MARÍA	—Oye, Juan, ¿cuál es tu dirección?
JUAN	—Calle Lima, número treinta.
MARÍA	—Gracias. Hasta la vista, Juan.
JUAN	—Chau. Saludos a Marité.[1]

| OSCAR | —¿Qué día es hoy, Pedro? |
| PEDRO | —Hoy es miércoles. |

| SRTA. PAZ | —¡Perdón! Por favor, ¿qué hora es? |
| SR. VEGA | —Son las dos y media. |

_____

[1]Nickname for María Teresa.

BRIEF CONVERSATIONS

MISS P. *(At the door)* Good morning, Professor. Excuse me.

PROF. Good morning. Come in and have a seat.

MISS P. Thank you very much.

PROF. Miss Peña, (this is) Dr. Mena.

MISS P. It's a pleasure, Dr. Mena.

DR. M. The pleasure is mine, Miss Peña.

J. Hello! What's your name?

R. My name is Rosa Díaz. And yours?

J. Julia Sandoval.

C. Professor, how do you say **"de nada"** in English?

PROF. You say "you're welcome."

C. What does "I'm sorry" mean?

PROF. It means **"lo siento."**

M. Listen, Juan, what's your address?

J. Thirty Lima Street.

M. Thanks. I'll see you later, Juan.

J. Bye. Say hi to Marité.

O. What day is today, Pedro?

P. Today is Wednesday.

MISS P. Excuse me! What time is it, please?

MR. V. It's two-thirty.

Vocabulary

POLITE EXPRESSIONS

con permiso   excuse me
de nada   you're welcome
el gusto es mío   the pleasure is mine
muchas gracias   thank you very much
mucho gusto   pleased to meet you
pase, adelante   come in
perdón   excuse me
por favor   please
tome asiento   have a seat
saludos a...   say hello to . . .

SOME USEFUL QUESTIONS

¿Cómo se dice... ?   How do you say . . . ?
¿Cómo te llamas?[1]   What's your name?
¿Cuál es tu dirección?[2]   What's your address?
¿Qué día es hoy?   What day is today?

¿Qué hora es?   What time is it?
Son las...   It's . . . (when referring to time of day)
¿Qué quiere decir... ?   What does . . . mean?

GENERAL VOCABULARY

calle   street
¿cómo?   how
conversaciones breves   brief conversations
¿cuál?   what?, which?
chau[3]   bye
dirección, domicilio   address
en   in, at
en español   in Spanish
en la puerta   at the door
hasta la vista   until I see you again
hoy   today
hoy es...   today is . . .
miércoles   Wednesday
quiere decir...   it means . . .
se dice...   you say, one says

Restaurante DUROC
Reservaciones: 2617959 - 2600629
Av. de las Américas No. 60-66

---

[1] When addressing a child or a very young person.   [2] When addressing an older person or someone in authority, say **¿Cuál es su dirección?**   [3] From the Italian **"ciao."**

► Days of the week   *(Los días de la semana)*

lunes	martes	miércoles	jueves	viernes	sábado	domingo
	1	*2*	*3*	*4*	*5*	*6*
7	*8*	*9*	*10*			

lunes   *Monday*   viernes   *Friday*
martes   *Tuesday*   sábado   *Saturday*
miércoles   *Wednesday* domingo   *Sunday*
jueves   *Thursday*

—¿Qué día es hoy? ¿**Lunes**?   *What day is today? Monday?*
—No, hoy es **martes.**   *No, today is Tuesday.*

♦ In Spanish-speaking countries, the week starts on Monday.

♦ Note that the days of the week are not capitalized in Spanish.

♦ The days of the week are masculine in Spanish, and they are frequently used with the masculine definite article **el**—*i.e.*, **el lunes, el jueves, el domingo.**

Programación de Telecaribe

VIERNES

6:00 Telecaribe
6:50 Noticiero Cartagena T.V.
7:00 Champagne
7:30 Esta sí es la Costa
8:00 Coralito

9:00 Noticiero Televista
9:30 Las Amazonas
10:00 Amor Gitano
11:00 Noticiero Cartagena T.V.
11:10 Cierre

► Cardinal numbers 11–30   *(Números cardinales 11–30)*

11	once	18	dieciocho	25	veinticinco
12	doce	19	diecinueve	26	veintiséis
13	trece	20	veinte	27	veintisiete
14	catorce	21	veintiuno[1]	28	veintiocho
15	quince	22	veintidós	29	veintinueve
16	dieciséis[1]	23	veintitrés	30	treinta
17	diecisiete	24	veinticuatro		

► Telling time   *(La hora)*

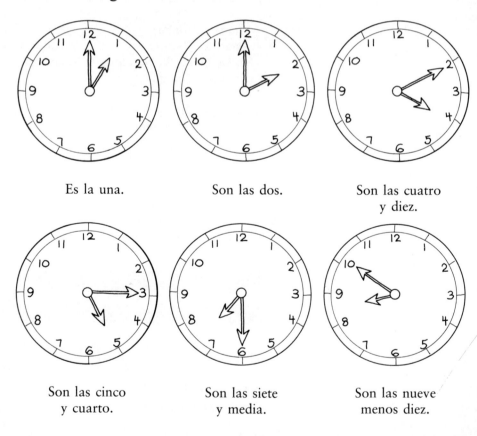

Es la una.   Son las dos.   Son las cuatro
y diez.

Son las cinco   Son las siete   Son las nueve
y cuarto.   y media.   menos diez.

---

[1]The numbers 16 to 29 may also be spelled thus: **diez y seis...** , **veinte y uno...** , and so on. The most common spelling, however, is the single word form used in this text.

To ask what time it is, use **¿qué hora es?** The following points should be remembered when telling time in Spanish.

♦ **Es** is used with **una.**

Es la una y cuarto.					*It is a quarter after one.*

Son is used with all the other hours.

Son las dos y cuarto.					*It is a quarter after two.*
Son las cinco y diez.					*It is ten after five.*

♦ The feminine definite article is always used before the hour.

Es **la** una y veinte.					*It is twenty after one.*
Son **las** cuatro y media.					*It is four-thirty.*

♦ The hour is given first, then the minutes.

Son las **cuatro** y **diez.**					*It is ten after four (literally, "four and ten").*

♦ The equivalent of *past* or *after* is **y.**

Son las doce **y** cinco.					*It is five after twelve.*

♦ The equivalent of *to* or *till* is **menos.** It is used with fractions of time up to a half hour.

Son las ocho **menos** veinte.					*It is twenty to eight.*

♦ Use the following word order when telling time in Spanish.

Es la or **Son las**	+	*hour*	+	**y** or **menos**	+	*minutes*

ATENCIÓN

The equivalent of *at + time* is **a + la(s) + time.**

—¿Qué hora es?					*What time is it?*
—Son las cinco menos diez.					*It's ten to five.*
—¿A qué hora es la clase?					*At what time is the class?*
—La clase es a las cinco.					*The class is at five o'clock.*

¡A ver cuánto aprendió!

A. ¡Conversemos! *(Let's talk)*

Team up with a classmate and respond appropriately to the following questions or statements.

1. Mucho gusto, señor (señora, señorita).
2. ¿Cómo te llamas?
3. ¿Cuál es tu dirección? *(Say street numbers one by one.)*
4. ¿Cuál es tu número de teléfono?
5. ¿Qué hora es, por favor?
6. ¿Qué día es hoy?
7. ¿Cómo se dice «*Thank you very much*» en español?
8. ¿Qué quiere decir «**Lo siento**»?
9. Muchas gracias.
10. ¿A qué hora es la clase?

B. The person asking these questions is always a day ahead. Respond, following the model.

MODELO: ¿Hoy es lunes?
    No, hoy es domingo.

1. ¿Hoy es miércoles?
2. ¿Hoy es domingo?
3. ¿Hoy es viernes?
4. ¿Hoy es martes?
5. ¿Hoy es sábado?
6. ¿Hoy es jueves?

C. Read the following numbers aloud in Spanish.

15	22	12
26	13	21
30	18	14
11	29	16

D. ¿Qué hora es?

Give the time indicated on the clocks that follow. Start with clock number one.

E. Complete the following dialogues.

1. *Julia talks with a classmate.*

JULIA   — _____

ELENA   —Me llamo Elena Martínez.

JULIA   — _____

ELENA   —486–3497.

JULIA   — _____

ELENA   —Calle Roma número veintiocho.

2. *Professor Mena and Mr. Roberto Soto are in the classroom. Today is Friday.*

PROF. MENA   —¿Cómo se llama usted, señor?

ROBERTO   — _____

PROF. MENA   —Mucho gusto, señor Soto.

ROBERTO   — _____

PROF. MENA   —¿Qué día es hoy?

ROBERTO   — _____

PROF. MENA   —¿Cómo se dice «*twenty-five*» en español?

ROBERTO   — _____

PROF. MENA   —¿Qué quiere decir «*Until I see you again*»?

ROBERTO   — _____

PROF. MENA   —Muy bien. Hasta luego, señor Soto.

ROBERTO   — _____

3. *A student thanks her teacher.*

MARISA   — _____

PROFESORA   —De nada, señorita García. Hasta luego.

MARISA   — _____

F. **Situaciones**

What would you say in each of the following situations? What might the other person(s) say?

1. You ask your teacher how to say "you're welcome" in Spanish.
2. You ask a little girl what her name is.
3. You ask a classmate what her address is.
4. You ask your teacher what **"permiso"** means.
5. You introduce Dr. Cortés to your teacher.
6. Someone knocks on your door and you ask him or her to come in and have a seat.
7. You ask someone what time it is.
8. You want someone to say hello to your best friend.
9. You ask someone what day it is.
10. You ask a classmate what time class is.

En la vida real

PRESENTACIONES *(INTRODUCTIONS)*

For this activity, work in groups of three. In each group, one person introduces the other two. Find out everybody's address, and talk about what day it is and what time it is. Finally, test each other on the meaning of certain words (Spanish–English; English–Spanish). You might want to include the following words or phrases:

Encantado. (If you are male) ⎫
Encantada. (If you are female) ⎬ *Charmed (A pleasure).*
A sus órdenes. *At your service.*

HORARIO DE CLASES *(CLASS SCHEDULE)*

This is María Elena's schedule. With a classmate, try to figure out when her classes are.

MODELO: —¿Cuándo es la clase de tenis?
 —*La clase de tenis es los sábados.*
 —¿A qué hora?
 —*A las nueve.*

HORA	LUNES	MARTES	MIÉRCOLES	JUEVES	VIERNES	SÁBADO
8:00	Sicología		Sicología		Sicología	
9:00	Biología		Biología		Biología	Tenis
10:00 11:30		Historia		Historia		
12:15 1:00	A	L	M U	E R	Z	O[1]
1:00	Literatura		Literatura		Literatura	Laboratorio de Biología
5:00		Educación Física		Educación Física		
7:00	Danza Aeróbica		Danza Aeróbica			

UNA ACTIVIDAD ESPECIAL

With the help of a dictionary and/or your instructor, work with a classmate to make up each other's schedules.

---
[1] Lunch.

En la clase

You will see the people and objects in the illustration below in a typical classroom. Learn these words, which will be used frequently both in class and in this book.

► Useful expressions for the class   *(Expresiones útiles para la clase)*

You will hear your professor use the following directions and general terms in class. You should familiarize yourself with them.

♦ When the professor is speaking to the whole class:

Abran sus libros, por favor.	*Open your books, please.*
Cierren sus libros, por favor.	*Close your books, please.*
Escriban, por favor.	*Write, please.*
Escuchen, por favor.	*Listen, please.*
Estudien la lección...	*Study lesson . . .*
Hagan el ejercicio número...	*Do exercise number . . .*
Pronuncien, por favor.	*Pronounce, please.*
Repitan, por favor.	*Repeat, please.*
Siéntense, por favor.	*Sit down, please.*
Vayan a la página...	*Go to page . . .*
Levanten la mano.	*Raise your hands.*
Repasen el vocabulario.	*Review the vocabulary.*

♦ When the professor is speaking to one student:

Continúe, por favor.	*Go on, please.*
Lea, por favor.	*Read, please.*
Vaya a la pizarra, por favor.	*Go to the chalkboard, please.*

♦ Some other words used in the classroom:

dictado	*dictation*
examen	*exam*
presente	*present, here*

► Colors   *(Colores)*

♦ You will see different colors in the classroom. Learn how to say them in Spanish.

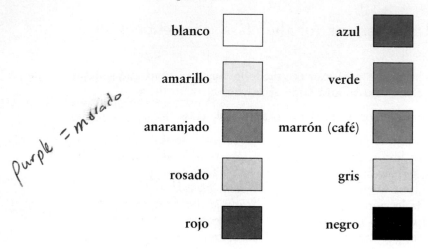

blanco		azul	
amarillo		verde	
anaranjado		marrón (café)	
rosado		gris	
rojo		negro	

Purple = morado

PRÁCTICA

Point out the following objects in the classroom and indicate their colors.

libro de español	escritorio	puerta
pizarra	tiza	pluma
pared	silla	cuaderno

Estructuras gramaticales

► *1.* Gender, Part 1   *(Género, Parte I)*

♦ In Spanish, all nouns—including those denoting non-living things— are either masculine or feminine.

Masculine	*Feminine*
el hombre	la mujer
el profesor	la profesora
el cuaderno	la tiza
el lápiz	la ventana
el estudiante	la estudiante
el secretario	la secretaria

♦ Nouns ending in **-o** or denoting male beings are masculine: **cuaderno** *(notebook);* **hombre** *(man).*

◆ Nouns ending in **-a** or denoting female beings are feminine: **profesor***a* *(female professor);* **mujer** *(woman).*

ATENCIÓN

Some common exceptions include the words **el día** *(day)* and **el mapa** *(map),* which end in **-a** but are masculine, and the word **la mano** *(hand),* which ends in **-o** but is feminine.

◆ Some helpful rules to remember about gender are:

◇ Some masculine nouns ending in **-o** have a corresponding feminine form ending in **-a**: **secretario/secretari***a*.

◇ Some nouns ending in a consonant add **-a** for the corresponding feminine: **profesor/profesor***a*.

◇ Many nouns which refer to people have the same form for both genders: **el estudiante/la estudiante.** In such cases, gender is indicated by the article **el** (masculine) or **la** (feminine).

PRÁCTICA

Indicate whether the following nouns are feminine or masculine.

1. mapa	6. profesora	11. ventana	16. mano
2. tiza	7. pizarra	12. pluma	17. cuaderno
3. escritorio	8. libro	13. hombre	18. doctor
4. secretaria	9. mujer	14. día	
5. silla	10. puerta	15. secretario	

▶ *2.* Plural forms   *(Formas del plural)*

◆ The plural of nouns is formed by adding **-s** to words ending in a vowel and **-es** to words ending in a consonant.

señora → señoras   reloj → relojes
  silla → sillas   borrador → borradores
  libro → libros   conversación → conversaciones[1]

◆ Nouns ending in **-z** change the **z** to **c** and add **-es.**

lápiz → lápices   luz *(light)* → luces

◆ When referring to two or more nouns of different genders, the masculine form is used in the plural.

dos chicas y un chico → tres chicos

---

[1]Note that the plural form does not have a written accent.

PRÁCTICA

Give the plural of the following nouns.

1. mapa
2. reloj
3. tiza
4. lápiz
5. ventana

6. puerta
7. lección
8. escritorio
9. borrador
10. día

▶ **3. Definite and indefinite articles** *(Artículos determinados e indeterminados)*

A. The definite article

◆ Spanish has four forms equivalent to the English definite article *the*.

	Masculine	*Feminine*	*English*
Singular	el	la	*the*
Plural	los	las	

el profesor   **los** profesores
la profesora   **las** profesoras
el lápiz   **los** lápices

ATENCIÓN

It is always a good idea to learn new nouns with their corresponding definite articles—this will help you identify their gender.

B. The indefinite article

◆ The Spanish equivalents of *a (an)* and *some* are as follows.

	Masculine	*Feminine*	*English*
Singular	un	una	*a (an)*
Plural	unos	unas	*some*

un libro   **unos** libros
una silla   **unas** sillas
un profesor   **unos** profesores

PRÁCTICA

Give the corresponding definite and indefinite article for each of the following nouns.

	Definite	Indefinite	
1.	_____	_____	profesores
2.	_____	_____	mujer
3.	_____	_____	sillas
4.	_____	_____	libro
5.	_____	_____	día
6.	_____	_____	hombre
7.	_____	_____	ventana
8.	_____	_____	mapas
9.	_____	_____	mano
10.	_____	_____	plumas

▶ *4.* Uses of **hay**   (Los usos de **hay**)

   ◆ The form **hay** means *there is* and *there are*. It has no subject and is invariable.

   —¿Cuántos mapas **hay** en la   *How many maps are there in*
     clase?   *the classroom?*
   —Hay **dos** mapas.   *There are two maps.*

PRÁCTICA

Go to the illustration on page 18 and answer the following questions.

1. ¿Cuántos (*How many*) estudiantes hay en la clase?
2. ¿Hay un profesor o dos?
3. ¿Cuántos libros hay?
4. ¿Hay un reloj en la clase?
5. ¿Cuántos hombres hay? ¿Cuántas mujeres hay?
6. ¿Hay un mapa en la clase?

¡A ver cuánto aprendió!

A. Review the colors; then think about the following objects and give their color(s) in Spanish.

1. an orange
2. the flag of the United States
3. a tree
4. coffee
5. coal
6. snow
7. a canary
8. a cloudy sky
9. rosy cheeks
10. your clothes
11. your shoes
12. the cover of **¿Cómo se dice... ?**

B. Using **hay,** say how many objects or people there are in each of the drawings.

MODELO: *Hay dos sillas.*

1.

2.

3.

4.

5.

6.

7.

C. Match each item in column A with its English equivalent in column B.

A	**B**
1. Estudien la lección dos.	a. Open the window, please.
2. Hagan los ejercicios, por favor.	b. Close the door.
	c. Repeat, please.
3. Siéntese, por favor.	d. Write the dictation.
4. Vayan a la página diez.	e. Go to page ten.
5. Abra la ventana, por favor.	f. Sit down, please.
	g. Study lesson two.
6. Repitan, por favor.	h. Read the book, please.
7. Vaya a la pizarra.	i. Go to the chalkboard.
8. Cierre la puerta.	j. Do the exercises, please.
9. Escriban el dictado.	
10. Lea el libro, por favor.	

En la vida real

En la clase

With a classmate, do an inventory of everything in your classroom, using the word **hay.**

Una actividad especial

A splash of color! This is an open-air market in Guatemala. How many colors that you see here can you name in Spanish? You need to include:

morado *purple*
claro *light*
oscuro *dark*
(i.e., **azul oscuro** = *dark blue*)

Mercado al aire libre en Guatemala.

Check your progress! An answer key is provided in Appendix E.

A. Cardinal numbers 0–30

Write the following numbers in Spanish.

9	5	13	2	0	10	27
11	14	18	30	12	15	

B. Gender of nouns: the definite and indefinite articles

Give the correct form of the definite (**el** or **la**) and indefinite (**un** or **una**) articles for each of the following nouns.

1. puerta
2. libro
3. mapa
4. mujer
5. borrador

6. secretario
7. mano
8. hombre
9. día
10. silla

C. Plural forms

Make the following words plural.

1. el señor y la señorita
2. un reloj
3. la doctora y el profesor
4. un lápiz

5. la conversación
6. una mujer
7. la ventana
8. la pluma y el cuaderno

D. Colors

Think about the following items, then give their color(s) in Spanish.

1. a banana
2. cherries
3. the sky
4. the flag of the United States

5. the grass
6. tar
7. chocolate
8. a pumpkin

E. Telling time

Write the following times in Spanish.

1. It's one-thirty.
2. It's a quarter to three.
3. It's ten after four.
4. It's twelve o'clock.
5. It's two-fifteen.

F. Just words . . .

Match the items in column A with those in column B.

	A		B
1.	¿Cómo está Ud., señora?	a.	*Desk.*
2.	¿Qué día es hoy?	b.	792–3950.
3.	¿Cómo se dice «*chalk*» en español?	c.	Veinticinco.
4.	¿Qué quiere decir «escritorio»?	d.	José Luis Peña.
5.	¿Cómo se llama Ud.?	e.	No mucho.
6.	¿Hoy es miércoles?	f.	No, jueves.
7.	Muchas gracias.	g.	Bien, gracias.
8.	¿Cuál es su número de teléfono?	h.	Tiza.
9.	¿Cómo se dice «*blackboard*» en español?	i.	De nada.
10.	Hasta luego.	j.	Lunes.
11.	¿Cuál es tu dirección?	k.	Gracias.
12.	¿Qué hora es?	l.	Pizarra.
13.	¿Qué hay de nuevo?	m.	Las cuatro y cuarto.
14.	Tome asiento.	n.	Calle Palma, número quince.
15.	¿Cuántos estudiantes hay en la clase?	o.	Adiós.

Estados Unidos

El español en los Estados Unidos

PANORAMA HISPÁNICO

1

- Hoy día hay más de 20 millones de hispanos en los Estados Unidos. Es el grupo minoritario de mayor crecimiento *(growth)* en el país.

- Tejas, California, Nueva York y Florida son los estados que tienen la mayor concentración de hispanos. En otras áreas como Nueva Inglaterra, Illinois y Washington D.C., el número de hispanos aumenta todos los años.

- Los nombres de muchas ciudades, estados y zonas geográficas de los Estados Unidos vienen del español. Arizona, California, Los Ángeles, El Paso, La Sierra Nevada y Río Grande tienen un significado especial en español. ¿Puede Ud. decir cuáles son?

- En las regiones donde viven muchos hispanos existen programas de educación bilingüe. Estos programas ayudan a los jóvenes hispanos a integrarse a la sociedad y a la cultura norteamericana.

- El español es actualmente el idioma más popular en las escuelas y universidades de los Estados Unidos. Más de 200.000 estudiantes universitarios toman español cada año.

▶ En Tejas, como en muchos otros estados, existe un sistema de educación bilingüe para ayudar a los niños hispanos en sus estudios en la escuela primaria. ¿Qué ventajas, en su opinión, ofrece la educación bilingüe?

▲ En California, Tejas, Arizona, Florida y Nueva York, existen servicios bilingües para ayudar al gran número de personas de habla hispana que residen en estos estados. Estos servicios son de tipo social, educativo y legal. ¿Hay muchas personas de habla hispana en la ciudad donde Ud. vive?

▼ Como parte del proceso colonizador, las órdenes religiosas españolas establecieron numerosas misiones en el suroeste de los Estados Unidos. Un ejemplo es la Misión de San Francisco de Asís en Taos, probablemente la más conocida en Nuevo México. ¿Puede mencionar Ud. algunas otras misiones en el suroeste?

San Diego, a unas pocas millas de Tijuana, México, es la puerta de entrada de miles de mexicanos a los Estados Unidos. Muchos prefieren quedarse cerca de la frontera y, en San Diego, se radican principalmente en el Barrio *(neighborhood)* Logan, bajo el Puente Coronado. ¿Conoce Ud. la ciudad de San Diego?

Aunque la radio y la televisión en español se han desarrollado más que la prensa escrita en los Estados Unidos, hay periódicos y revistas en español en todas las grandes ciudades del país, y aun en muchas de las ciudades pequeñas. En la foto, dos jóvenes mexicoamericanos leen las noticias; uno, en *Noticias del mundo*, un diario hispano de Los Ángeles; el otro, en el *Register* de Orange County, California. ¿Hay periódicos en español en la ciudad donde Ud. vive? ¿Cuáles?

La Pequeña Habana, en la ciudad de Miami, se extiende a lo largo de la calle Ocho y las zonas adyacentes. Creada por los cubanos, casi todas las tiendas, cafés, restaurantes y mercados del barrio tienen nombres en español, que es el idioma que se oye hablar por las calles. El español no es una lengua extranjera en esa zona. ¿Hay algunos estudiantes cubanos en su universidad?

En 1910 unos mil quinientos puertorriqueños vivían en los Estados Unidos. Hoy día hay más de un millón de puertorriqueños sólo en la ciudad de Nueva York, más que en San Juan, la capital de Puerto Rico. En Nueva York los puertorriqueños han establecido sus propias revistas de información cultural y política, sus propios restaurantes y lugares de diversión. En la foto, un conjunto musical puertorriqueño anima la carroza de una de las estaciones de televisión hispanas de Nueva York. ¿Conoce Ud. algunos puertorriqueños en la universidad donde Ud. estudia?

Puente Internacional en el Lago Amistad, localizado en la frontera entre los Estados Unidos y México. Observe que el símbolo de ambos países es el águila, pero el águila mexicana está encima de un cáctus y tiene una serpiente en el pico. ¿Qué otros estados norteamericanos limitan con México?

Una estudiante habla por teléfono en Barcelona, España.

OBJECTIVES

Pronunciation	The Spanish **a** and **e**
Structure	Subject pronouns • Present indicative of regular **-ar** verbs • Gender, Part II • Negative and interrogative sentences • Present indicative of **ser** • Cardinal numbers 31–1,000
Communication	You will learn vocabulary used in both making and receiving phone calls.

Al teléfono

Raquel desea hablar con Marta.

RAQUEL —Hola. ¿Está Marta?
MARISA —No, no está. Lo siento.
RAQUEL —¿A qué hora regresa?
MARISA —A las nueve de la noche.
RAQUEL —Entonces llamo[1] más tarde.
MARISA —Muy bien. Adiós.

Carmen habla con María.

MARÍA —Bueno.
CARMEN —Hola. ¿Está María?
MARÍA —Sí, con ella habla... ¿Carmen?
CARMEN —Sí. ¿Qué tal, María?
MARÍA —Muy bien, gracias. ¿Qué hay de nuevo?
CARMEN —Nada. ¡Oye! ¿Estudiamos[1] inglés[2] hoy?
MARÍA —Sí, y mañana estudiamos[1] francés.
CARMEN —Muy bien. Hasta luego, entonces.

Pedro desea hablar con Ana.

ROSA —Dígame.
PEDRO —Hola. ¿Está Ana?
ROSA —Sí. ¿Quién habla?
PEDRO —Pedro Morales.
ROSA —Un momento, por favor.
ANA —(A Rosa) ¿Quién es?
ROSA —Es Pedro Morales.
ANA —Hola, Pedro. ¿Qué tal?
PEDRO —Bien, ¿y tú?
ANA —Más o menos.
PEDRO —¿Por qué? ¿Problemas sentimentales?
ANA —No, económicos. ¡Yo necesito dinero!
PEDRO —¡Yo también! ¡Oye! ¿Tú trabajas en el hospital esta noche?
ANA —No, hoy no trabajo por la noche.

---

[1]The present indicative is often used in Spanish to express a near future.   [2]Names of languages and nationalities are not capitalized in Spanish.

ON THE PHONE

Raquel wishes to speak with Marta.

R. Hello. Is Marta there?
M. No, she's not. I'm sorry.
R. At what time is she coming back?
M. At nine o'clock at night.
R. Then I'll call later.
M. Very well. Good-bye.

Carmen speaks with María.

M. Hello.
C. Hello. Is María there?
M. Yes, speaking . . . Carmen?
C. Yes. How's it going, María?
M. Very well, thank you. What's new?
C. Nothing. Listen! Are we studying English today?
M. Yes, and tomorrow we are studying French.
C. Very well. See you later, then.

Pedro wishes to speak with Ana.

R. Hello.
P. Hello. Is Ana there?
R. Yes. Who is speaking?
P. Pedro Morales.
R. One moment, please.
A. *(To Rosa)* Who is it?
R. It's Pedro Morales.
A. Hi, Pedro. How's it going?
P. Fine, and with you?
A. So-so.
P. Why? Love problems?
A. No, financial ones! I need money!
P. So do I! Listen! Are you working at the hospital tonight?
A. No, I'm not working tonight. (Today, I'm not working at night).

Vocabulario

NOMBRES

el **dinero**   money
el **francés**   French (language)
el **inglés**   English (language)
la **noche**   evening, night

VERBOS

desear   to wish, want
estudiar   to study
hablar   to speak
llamar   to call
necesitar   to need
regresar   to return
ser   to be
trabajar   to work

OTRAS PALABRAS Y EXPRESIONES

a   at, to
al teléfono   on the telephone
a la(s) + *time*   at + *time*
¿a qué hora?   (At) what time?
con   with
con ella habla   this is she (speaking)
de   of, from
de la noche   in the evening (definite time)

dígame   hello (answering the phone)
en   on
entonces   then, in that case
¿está... + *name*?   is . . . *(name)* there?
esta noche   tonight
hola, bueno   hello
mañana   tomorrow
más o menos   so-so, more or less
más tarde   later
nada   nothing
no está   he or she is not (here)
o   or
¡oye!   listen!
por la noche   in the evening, at night (no definite time)
¿por qué?   why?
problemas económicos   financial problems
problemas sentimentales   love problems
¿quién?   who?
¿quién es?   who is it?
sí   yes
también   also, too
un momento   one moment

Vocabulario adicional   *(Additional vocabulary)*

el **alemán**   German (language)
En Berlín hablan **alemán.**

el **chino**   Chinese (language)
Nosotros no hablamos **chino.**

el **español**   Spanish (language)
En Madrid hablan **español.**

el **italiano**   Italian (language)
Sofía Loren habla **italiano.**

el **japonés**   Japanese (language)
Hablan **japonés** en Tokio.

el **portugués**   Portuguese (language)
En Brasil no hablan español; hablan **portugués**.

el **ruso**   Russian (language)
Nosotros estudiamos **ruso** en la universidad.

de la **mañana**   in the morning
Estudiamos a las ocho **de la mañana**.[1]

de la **tarde**   in the afternoon
Regresa a las cinco **de la tarde**.

por la **mañana**[1]   in the morning
Estudiamos **por la mañana**.

por la **tarde**   in the afternoon
Regresa **por la tarde**.

---

[1] Notice the use of **de la** (**mañana, tarde, noche**) when a specific time is mentioned. **Por la** (**mañana, tarde, noche**) is used when no specific time is mentioned.

¿Lo sabía Ud.... ?[2]

- Contestando el teléfono *(Answering the phone)*:
  En España *(Spain):* «Diga», «Dígame», «¿Sí?»
  En Cuba y en otras regiones del Caribe: «Oigo»
  En México: «Bueno»
  En Argentina: «¿Sí?», «Hable», «Hola».
- En Latinoamérica y en España los estudiantes generalmente estudian juntos *(together)*.
- «Español» y «castellano» son *(are)* equivalentes.
- En Brasil no hablan español; hablan portugués.
- Unos *(about)* 341.000.000[3] de personas hablan español como *(as)* idioma *(language)* nativo.
- Para los horarios *(schedules)* de aviones, trenes y autobuses, y para muchas invitaciones, se usa el sistema de 24 horas. Por ejemplo, las cuatro de la tarde son las dieciséis horas.

Dos estudiantes en una clase de ciencias en la Universidad de Ibaeta en San Sebastián, España.

---

[2] *Did you know . . . ?*   [3] Note that in Spanish numbers, a period is used instead of a comma to indicate thousands.

Pronunciación

▶ *A.* The Spanish **a**

The Spanish **a** is pronounced like the *a* in the English word *father*. Listen to your teacher and repeat the following words.

Ana	tal	está
nada	habla	trabaja
gracias	hasta	mañana

▶ *B.* The Spanish **e**

The Spanish **e** is pronounced like the *e* in the English word *met*. Listen to your teacher and repeat the following words.

qué	desea	teléfono
usted	noche	regresa
entonces	problemas	sentimentales

Estructuras gramaticales

▶ *1.* Subject pronouns   *(Pronombres personales usados como sujetos)*

Singular	*Plural*	
yo *I*	**nosotros**	*we* (m.)
	nosotras	*we* (f.)
tú *you* (familiar)	**vosotros**	*you* (m., familiar)
	vosotras	*you* (f., familiar)
usted *you* (formal)	**ustedes**	*you* (formal)
él *he*	**ellos**	*they* (m.)
ella *she*	**ellas**	*they* (f.)

♦ The **tú** form is used as the equivalent of *you* generally when addressing a friend, a coworker, a relative, or a child. The **Ud.** form is used when speaking to people in higher positions, or generally when expressing deference or respect. In most Spanish-speaking countries today, young people tend to call each other **tú** even if they have just met.

♦ The plural form of **tú** is **vosotros,** which is only used in Spain. In Latin America, the plural form **ustedes** (abbreviated **Uds.**) is used as the plural form of both **usted** (abbreviated **Ud.**) and **tú.**

♦ The masculine plural forms can refer to the masculine gender alone or to both genders together.

Ellos (Luis y Carlos) hablan español.

They (Luis and Carlos) speak Spanish.

Ellos (María, Marta y Raúl) hablan inglés.

They (María, Marta, and Raúl) speak English.

Nosotros (Ana María, Carlos y yo) trabajamos en el hospital.

We (Ana María, Carlos, and I) work at the hospital.

PRÁCTICA

A. Say the following in Spanish.

1. we *(f.)*
2. I
3. you *(form., pl.)*
4. he
5. they *(m.)*
6. you *(fam., sing.)*
7. they *(f.)*
8. we *(m.)*
9. you *(form., sing.)*
10. she

B. Give the plural of the following subject pronouns.

1. yo
2. ella
3. él
4. tú
5. Ud.

▶ *2.* Present indicative of regular **-ar** verbs   *(Presente de indicativo de los verbos regulares terminados en **-ar**)*

♦ Spanish verbs are classified in three main patterns of conjugation, according to the infinitive ending. The three infinitive endings are **-ar, -er,** and **-ir.**

hablar   *to speak*

		Singular	
yo	hablo	Yo **hablo** español.	*I speak Spanish.*
tú	hablas	Tú **hablas** francés.	*You (fam.) speak French.*
Ud.	habla	Ud. **habla** alemán.	*You (form.) speak German.*
él	habla	Él **habla** italiano.	*He speaks Italian.*
ella	habla	Ella **habla** portugués.	*She speaks Portuguese.*
		Plural	
nosotros	hablamos	Nosotros **hablamos** español.	*We speak Spanish.*
vosotros	habláis	Vosotros **habláis** francés.	*You (fam.) speak French.*
Uds.	hablan	Uds. **hablan** alemán.	*You (form.) speak German.*
ellos	hablan	Ellos **hablan** italiano.	*They speak Italian.*
ellas	hablan	Ellas **hablan** portugués.	*They speak Portuguese.*

—¿Qué idioma **hablas?**	*What language do you speak?*
—Yo **hablo** español.	*I speak Spanish.*
—¿Y Pierre?	*And Pierre?*
—Él **habla** francés.	*He speaks French.*

♦ Regular verbs ending in **-ar** are all conjugated as **hablar** in the chart above. Some other common **-ar** verbs are:

desear	*to want, desire*	**necesitar**	*to need*
estudiar	*to study*	**regresar**	*to return*
llamar	*to call*	**trabajar**	*to work*

ATENCIÓN

Notice that the verb forms for **Ud., él,** and **ella** are the same. In addition, **Uds., ellos,** and **ellas** share common verb forms. This is true for all verbs in all tenses.

♦ The infinitive of Spanish verbs consists of a stem (such as **habl-**) and an ending (such as **-ar**).

♦ The stem **habl-** does not change. The endings change with the subject.

♦ The Spanish present tense is equivalent to three English forms:

Yo **hablo** inglés. $\begin{cases} \textit{I speak English.} \\ \textit{I do speak English.} \\ \textit{I am speaking English.} \end{cases}$

♦ Because the verb endings indicate who is performing the action, the subject pronouns are frequently omitted.

Necesito dinero.	*I need money.*
Estudiamos inglés.	*We study English.*
Deseo hablar con Roberto.	*I want to speak with Roberto.*

♦ Subject pronouns can, however, be used for emphasis or clarification.

Tú hablas francés.	*You speak French.*
Ella habla inglés y **yo** hablo alemán.	*She speaks English, and I speak German.*

ATENCIÓN

In Spanish, as in English, when two verbs are used together, the second verb remains in the infinitive.

Deseo **hablar** con Roberto.   *I want to speak with Roberto.*

PRÁCTICA

A. Give the corresponding forms of the following regular verbs.

1. *yo:* trabajar, hablar, necesitar, regresar
2. *tú:* necesitar, estudiar, llamar, desear
3. *Luis:* trabajar, hablar, llamar, regresar
4. *Ud.:* trabajar, hablar, necesitar, estudiar
5. *nosotros:* necesitar, estudiar, llamar, desear
6. *ellos:* trabajar, hablar, llamar, desear

B. Complete the following sentences with the present indicative of the verbs in parentheses.

1. Ana y Eva _____ (trabajar) en el hospital.
2. Carlos y yo _____ (necesitar) cuadernos.
3. Teresa también _____ (estudiar) ruso.
4. Tú _____ (desear) hablar con Pedro.
5. Yo _____ (llamar) más tarde.
6. ¿A qué hora _____ (regresar) nosotros?

C. Using the verbs **trabajar, hablar, necesitar, regresar, llamar, estudiar,** and **desear,** talk about what is going on in these illustrations.

▶ *3.* Gender, Part II   *(Género, Parte II)*

In **Paso** 3 you learned that words which end in **-o** in Spanish are generally masculine, and those which end in **-a** are generally feminine. There are other useful rules to help you determine the gender of nouns that do not end in **-o** or **-a.**

◆ Nouns ending in **-sión, -ción, -tad, -dad,** and **-umbre** are feminine.

la televi**sión**	*television*
la conversa**ción**	*conversation*
la liber**tad**	*liberty, freedom*
la ciu**dad**	*city*
la certid**umbre**	*certainty*

◆ Many words ending in **-ma** are masculine.[1]

el poe**ma**	*poem*
el telegra**ma**	*telegram*
el progra**ma**	*program*
el siste**ma**	*system*
el cli**ma**	*climate*
el idio**ma**	*language*
el proble**ma**	*problem*
el te**ma**	*subject, theme*

◆ You must learn the gender of nouns that have other endings and that do not refer to male or female beings. Remember that it is helpful to memorize each noun with its corresponding article.

la pared *wall*　　　　　　　　　**el** borrador *eraser*

PRÁCTICA

Read the following words, adding the corresponding definite article (**el, la, los,** or **las**).

1. pared	9. mano
2. mesa	10. lumbre
3. turismo	11. libertad
4. hospital	12. idiomas
5. problemas	13. organización
6. ciudad	14. día
7. sociedad	15. solución
8. silla	16. conversación

---

[1]Some feminine words ending in **-ma** are: **la cama** *(bed)* and **la rama** *(branch)*.

▶ *4.* Negative and interrogative sentences *(Oraciones negativas e interrogativas)*

A. Negative sentences

♦ To make a sentence negative, simply place the word **no** in front of the verb.

Yo trabajo en el hospital.	*I work at the hospital.*
Yo **no** trabajo en el hospital.	*I don't work at the hospital.*

Ella habla inglés.	*She speaks English.*
Ella **no** habla inglés.	*She doesn't speak English.*

♦ If the answer to a question is negative, the word **no** will appear twice: at the beginning of the sentence, as in English, and in front of the verb.

—¿Habla Ud. español?	*Do you speak Spanish?*
—**No,** yo **no** hablo español.	*No, I don't speak Spanish.*

Or, omitting the subject pronoun:

—**No, no** hablo español.	*No, I don't speak Spanish.*

B. Interrogative sentences

♦ In Spanish, there are several ways of asking a question to elicit a *yes* or *no* answer.

¿**Elena** habla español?

¿Habla **Elena** español?   } **Sí,** Elena habla español.

¿Habla español **Elena**?

♦ These three questions ask for the same information and have the same meaning. The subject may be placed at the beginning of the sentence, after the verb, or at the end of the sentence.

♦ Note that Spanish uses two question marks: an inverted one at the beginning of the sentence and an upright one at the end.

♦ Another common way of asking a question in Spanish is by adding tag questions such as ¿**no**? and ¿**verdad**? at the end of a statement.

Elena habla español, ¿**verdad**?	*Elena speaks Spanish, doesn't she?*

ATENCIÓN

Spanish does not use an auxiliary verb, such as *do* or *does,* in negative or interrogative sentences.

PRÁCTICA

A. The following statements contain the wrong information. Correct them, basing your answers on the dialogue.

MODELO: Eva estudia esta noche.
Eva no estudia esta noche.

1. Ana trabaja esta noche.
2. Raquel desea hablar con Pedro.
3. Carmen y María estudian japonés hoy.
4. Ana necesita libros.
5. Pedro desea hablar con Rosa.
6. Marta regresa a las nueve de la mañana.
7. Carmen habla con Raquel.
8. Carmen y María estudian italiano mañana.

B. One of your classmates doesn't speak English. How would you ask her these questions in Spanish?

1. Do you work?
2. Do you need money?
3. Do you study in the morning?
4. Do you speak Russian?
5. Do you want to speak with the professor?
6. The professor isn't home. Do you want to call later?
7. Are you returning to the university tomorrow?
8. Is the professor working tonight?

▶ *5.* Present indicative of **ser**   *(Presente de indicativo del verbo **ser**)*

ser *to be*		
Singular		
yo	soy	*I am*
tú	eres	*you are* (fam.)
Ud.		*you are* (form.)
él	es	*he is*
ella		*she is*
Plural		
nosotros	somos	*we are*
vosotros	sois	*you are* (fam.)
Uds.		*you are* (form.)
ellos	son	*they are* (m.)
ellas		*they are* (f.)

♦ Some important Spanish verbs are irregular. This means they do not follow the regular conjugation pattern of the **-ar, -er,** and **-ir** verbs.

♦ The verb **ser,** *to be,* is irregular. Its forms, like the forms of other irregular verbs, must be memorized.

♦ The verb **ser** is commonly used to express identity, place of origin, occupation, and nationality. It is also used in telling time, as seen in **Paso 2.**

KODAK ES COLOR

PRÁCTICA

Where are these people from? Tell us, using the information found in the illustrations. Also, tell us the capital of each country.

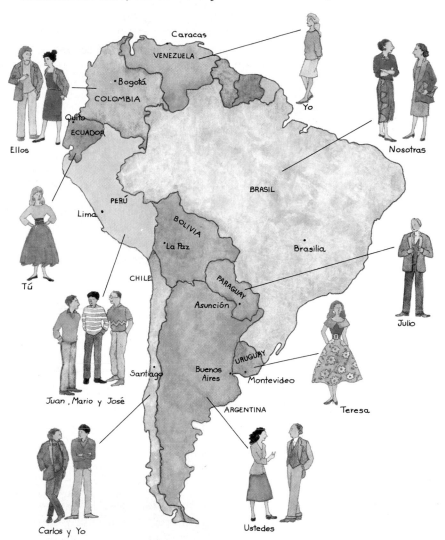

MODELO: Ud.
   Ud. es de Bolivia. La capital de Bolivia es La Paz.

1. Teresa
2. yo
3. Carlos y yo
4. Juan, Mario y José
5. tú

6. ellos
7. nosotras
8. Uds.
9. Julio

▶ *6.* Cardinal numbers 31–1,000   *(Números cardinales 31–1.000)*

31	**treinta y uno**	101	**ciento uno** (and so on)
32	**treinta y dos** (and so on)	200	**doscientos**
40	**cuarenta**	300	**trescientos**
41	**cuarenta y uno** (and so on)	400	**cuatrocientos**
50	**cincuenta**	500	**quinientos**
60	**sesenta**	600	**seiscientos**
70	**setenta**	700	**setecientos**
80	**ochenta**	800	**ochocientos**
90	**noventa**	900	**novecientos**
100	**cien**	1.000	**mil**

—¿Cuánto cuesta el lápiz?	*How much does the pencil cost?*
—Cuesta **cincuenta y cinco** centavos.	*It costs fifty-five cents.*
—¿Cuánto cuestan los libros?	*How much do the books cost?*
—Cuestan **treinta y ocho** dólares.	*They cost thirty-eight dollars.*

◆ When counting beyond 100, **ciento** is used.

◆ Note that **y** appears only in numbers between 16 and 99.

◆ In Spanish, one does not count in hundreds beyond 1,000; thus, 1,100 is expressed as **mil cien**. After 1,000, the numbers are represented thus: **dos mil, tres mil, catorce mil,** and so on. Note that in Spanish numbers, a period is used instead of a comma to indicate thousands.

PRÁCTICA

A. Complete the following group of numbers.

    1. cuarenta y dos, cuarenta y cuatro,... cincuenta
    2. cincuenta, cincuenta y cinco, sesenta,... cien
    3. cien, doscientos, trescientos,... mil
    4. diez mil, veinte mil, treinta mil,... cien mil
    5. ciento diez, doscientos veinte, trescientos treinta,... mil cien

Radio Total Bogotá	1160 AM
Radio Total Cali	1470 AM
Radio Total Medellin	1530 AM

GRC **Grupo Radial Colombiano**

B. Look at the following illustration and tell us how much everything costs.

MODELO: —¿Cuánto cuesta la silla?
—*La silla cuesta ochenta dólares.*

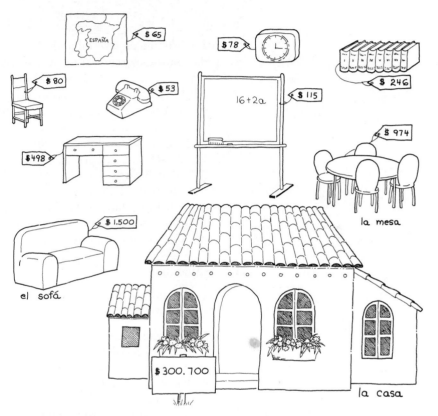

¡A ver cuánto aprendió!

A. ¡Conversemos!

Reread the dialogues in this lesson and be ready to discuss the following.

1. ¿Con quién desea hablar Raquel?
2. ¿A qué hora regresa Marta?
3. ¿Con quién habla María?
4. ¿Qué estudian Carmen y María hoy?
5. ¿Estudian francés o italiano mañana?
6. ¿Qué necesita Ana?
7. ¿Pedro también necesita dinero?
8. ¿Trabaja Ana esta noche?

B. ¡Repase el vocabulario! *(Review the vocabulary!)*

Complete the following sentences with the appropriate words; then read them aloud.

1. ¡Oye! ¿ _____ (nosotros) inglés hoy?
2. —¿Qué hay de nuevo?
   — _____
3. ¿Problemas sentimentales o _____ ?
4. ¿Nosotros regresamos a las ocho _____
   _____ mañana?
5. ¿No está? Entonces llamo más _____ .
6. Nosotros _____ hablar español con el profesor.
7. ¿ _____ es? ¿Pedro Morales?
8. Jorge necesita dinero y yo _____ .
9. Sí, está. Un _____ , por favor.
10. —¿Qué tal?
    —Más o _____ .
11. En Río de Janeiro hablan _____ y en París hablan
    _____ .
12. ¿Qué idioma _____ en Roma? ¿Italiano?

C. Situaciones

You are talking on the telephone. What would you say in the following situations? What might the other person say?

1. You want to ask whether Carlos is home.
2. You tell a caller to wait a moment.
3. You ask who is speaking.
4. Someone asks to speak to you. You say, "This is he (she)."
5. You tell someone you'll call later.
6. Someone has asked to talk to you and you want to know who it is.

Para escribir 🖊   *(To write)*

Complete the following sentences in your own words using appropriate verb forms and vocabulary items.

1. El doctor Campos trabaja en el hospital y el profesor...
2. John Wilson estudia español y José García...
3. Yo necesito un lápiz y Teresa...
4. Nosotros trabajamos por la noche y ellos...
5. En México hablan español y en Chicago...
6. Yo deseo hablar con Jorge y tú...
7. Ella regresa a las cuatro de la tarde y yo...
8. En Roma hablan italiano y en Pekín...

En la vida real

ENTREVISTA

Choose a partner and ask each other the following questions, using the **tú** form.

Pregúntele a su compañero (-a)...

1. ...qué idiomas habla.
2. ...dónde trabaja.
3. ...si *(if)* estudia por la mañana o por la noche.
4. ...si habla español con el profesor (la profesora).
5. ...si necesita dinero.
6. ...con quién desea hablar.
7. ...si estudia portugués.
8. ...si regresa a la universidad mañana.

¡POR TELÉFONO!

With a classmate, act out the following phone conversations.

1. Greet each other, and make plans for studying together. Find out about each other's work schedule.
2. Call your classmate's roommate or a member of his or her family (who will not be home) and find out when he or she will be back.

¡MUCHO GUSTO!

Here are some people you should try to get acquainted with:

Mucho gusto. Me llamo Alina Rojas y soy de Cuba. Soy profesora de español. Hablo inglés y español.

¿Qué tal? Me llamo Ana María y soy de Buenos Aires, Argentina. Y yo me llamo Carlos y soy de Chile. Somos estudiantes.

¡Buenas tardes! Me llamo Francisco Acosta y soy de México. Soy piloto. Trabajo para *(for)* Aero-México.

¡Mucho gusto! Me llamo Cristina Vargas Peña y soy de Costa Rica. Soy dentista y trabajo en Los Ángeles, California.

¿Cómo están ustedes? Yo soy Julio Santacruz y soy de Madrid. Soy actor de televisión y deseo trabajar en Hollywood.

¡Buenos días! Me llamo Carmen Sandoval y soy de Caracas, Venezuela. Soy secretaria y trabajo para la compañía de teléfonos. Estudio idiomas en la universidad.

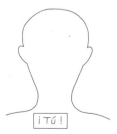

¡ TÚ !

¡Mucho gusto!

Now . . . what can you tell us about your new friends?

1. Julio Santacruz
2. Ana María y Carlos
3. La Sra. Rojas
4. La doctora Vargas Peña
5. El Sr. Acosta
6. La Srta. Sandoval

Un mensaje telefónico

Based on the information provided in the phone message, complete the statements which follow.

```
┌─────────────────────────────────────────────────┐
│            Hospital El Samaritano                │
│  MENSAJE PERSONAL                                │
│  Para    Carlos Vega                             │
│  De parte de   Jorge Ibarra                      │
│  De la compañía   Hotel Plaza                    │
│  Teléfono        386 - 4127                       │
│  Llamó por teléfono a la(s)  10:30               │
│  ☑ de la mañana   ☐ de la tarde   ☐ de la noche  │
│                                                  │
│  MENSAJE                                         │
│  1. Desea hablar con usted.  ☐                   │
│  2. Llama más tarde.         ☑                   │
│  3. Llama mañana.            ☐                    │
│  ──────────────────────────────────────          │
│  ASUNTO  Problemas con las reservaciones         │
│  del hotel para la convención                    │
│  Día  Miércoles                                  │
└─────────────────────────────────────────────────┘
```

1. El mensaje es para _____ .
2. El señor Vega trabaja en el _____ .
3. El mensaje es de parte de _____ .
4. El señor Ibarra trabaja para el _____ .
5. El número de teléfono del hotel es _____ .
6. El mensaje es _____ .
7. El señor Ibarra llamó a las _____ de la _____ del día _____ .
8. En el hotel hay problemas con _____ .

Una actividad especial

Each member of the class will complete a card, like the one below, providing personal data. The cards will then be exchanged, and each student will read the information provided by his or her classmate to the rest of the class, making all necessary changes.

```
┌─────────────────────────────────────────────┐
│  Yo soy Carlos Bustamante.                   │
│  Soy de Bogotá, Colombia.                    │
│  Trabajo en (ciudad) Medellín.               │
│  Estudio biología.                           │
│  Necesito dinero y libros.                   │
└─────────────────────────────────────────────┘
```

Modelo: *Carlos Bustamante es de Bogotá...* and so on.

Buscando trabajo. Dos estudiantes leen los anuncios en el periódico en Sevilla, España.

OBJECTIVES

Pronunciation	The Spanish **i** and **o**
Structure	Possession with **de** • Adjectives: Forms, position, and agreement with articles and nouns • Possessive adjectives • Present indicative of regular **-er** and **-ir** verbs • Present indicative of the irregular verbs **tener** and **venir** • Use of **tener que** + *infinitive*
Communication	You will learn vocabulary related to personal data.

Susana desea solicitar trabajo

Susana y su amigo Quique conversan en la cafetería de la universidad mientras beben café y comen sándwiches de jamón y queso. La muchacha es rubia, bonita y muy inteligente. Quique es alto, moreno, guapo y simpático. Susana lee un anuncio en el periódico y decide solicitar el empleo. Quique cree que ella no debe trabajar.

La compañía IBM necesita recepcionista. Debe hablar inglés y tener conocimiento de computadoras. Enviar su solicitud a Avenida Simón Bolívar #342, Caracas.

QUIQUE —¡Susana, tú tienes cuatro clases! No tienes tiempo para trabajar.

SUSANA —Todas mis clases son por la mañana. Tengo la tarde libre.

QUIQUE —Pero tienes que estudiar...

SUSANA —Bueno, mis clases no son muy difíciles.

QUIQUE —¡La clase de la Dra. Peña no es fácil!

SUSANA —No es difícil. *(Mira el anuncio.)* Avenida Simón Bolívar... Yo vivo cerca de allí...

QUIQUE —¿Cerca? Tú vives en la calle Seis.

SUSANA —No es lejos. Bueno, me voy.

QUIQUE —¿A qué hora vienes mañana?

SUSANA —A las ocho. Nos vemos.

QUIQUE —Hasta luego, Susana. ¡Buena suerte!

(En la compañía IBM, Susana llena la solicitud.)

Vocabulario

COGNADOS

la **cafetería** cafeteria
la **clase** class
la **compañía** company
la **computadora** computer

inteligente intelligent
el (la) **recepcionista**[1] receptionist
el **sándwich**[2] sandwich

NOMBRES

el (la) **amigo(-a)** friend
el **anuncio** ad
la **avenida** avenue
el **café** coffee
el **conocimiento** knowledge
el **jamón** ham
la **muchacha, chica** girl, young
    woman
el **muchacho, chico** boy, young
    man
el **periódico, diario** newspaper
el **queso** cheese
la **solicitud** application
la **tarde** afternoon
el **tiempo** time
el **trabajo, empleo** job

VERBOS

beber, tomar to drink
comer to eat
conversar, charlar, platicar
    (Méx.) to talk, to chat
creer to think, to believe
deber must, to have to, should
decidir to decide
enviar, mandar to send
leer to read
llenar to fill, to fill out
mirar to look at, to watch (T.V.)
solicitar to apply for

tener *(irreg.)* to have
venir *(irreg.)* to come
vivir to live

ADJETIVOS

alto(-a) tall
bonito(-a), lindo(-a) pretty
difícil difficult
fácil easy
guapo(-a) handsome
libre free
moreno(-a) dark, brunette
rubio(-a), güero(-a) *(Méx.)*
    blond(e)
simpático(-a) nice, charming
todos(-as) all

OTRAS PALABRAS Y
EXPRESIONES

a to
allí there
buena suerte good luck
bueno... well . . .
cerca (de) close (to), near
lejos (de) far (from)
me voy I'm leaving
mientras while
nos vemos I'll see you
para to, in order to
pero but

---

[1] Nouns ending in **-ista** change only the article to indicate gender: el **recepcionista** *(m.)*; la **recepcionista** *(f.)*.   [2] In addition to **sándwich**, **emparedado** or **bocadillo** is used in Spain.

Vocabulario adicional

antipático(-a) unpleasant
Antonio no es **antipático;** es muy
simpático.

delgado(-a) thin, slender
Roberto es alto y **delgado.**

gordo(-a) fat
¿María es delgada o **gorda?**

norteamericano(-a) North American
Los muchachos son **norteamericanos.**

pelirrojo(-a) red-headed
Teresa no es rubia; es **pelirroja.**

Ésta *(This)* es la solicitud de trabajo que llena Susana cuando solicita el puesto en la compañía IBM.

SOLICITUD DE TRABAJO (Job Application)

Apellidos y nombres *García López, Susana*
(Last name & names)

Dirección *Calle 6 # 258*

Zona Postal *70-824*   Teléfono *862-4221*
(Zip Code)

Fecha de nacimiento
(Date of birth)

DÍA (day)	MES (mo)	AÑO (yr)
7	12	70

Estado civil *(Marital status)*   Sexo *(Sex)*   Edad *(Age)*

1. X soltero(-a) *(single)*   Masculino ___   *20 años*

2. __ casado(-a) *(married)*   Femenino X

3. __ divorciado(-a) *(divorced)*

4. __ viudo(-a) *(widower, widow)*

Esposo/esposa ___
(Husband/wife)

Nombre y edad de los hijos[1] ___
(Children's names and ages)

Nacionalidad *Venezolana*

Lugar de nacimiento *Caracas*
(Place of birth)

Ocupación *Estudiante*

Lugar donde trabaja ___
(Place of work)

Número de seguro social ___
(Social security number)

Número de la licencia para conducir ___
(Driver's license number)

---

[1] **Hijos** = *children (sons and daughters).*

¿Lo sabía Ud....?

■ En España y en Latinoamérica, muchas personas tienen sobrenombres *(nicknames)*. Por ejemplo *(For example)*: Enrique: **Quique;** Roberto o Alberto: **Beto;** Francisco: **Paco;** María Teresa: **Marité;** Antonia: **Toña;** Mercedes: **Mecha;** Dolores: **Lola;** José: **Pepe;** Luis: **Lucho;** Manuel: **Manolo.**

■ En los países hispánicos las personas generalmente usan dos apellidos: el apellido del padre y el apellido de la madre. Por ejemplo, los hijos(-as) de María **Rivas** y Juan **Pérez** usan los apellidos **Pérez Rivas.**

■ En una guía telefónica *(phone book)* en español, alfabetizan *(they alphabetize)* los nombres según *(according to)* los dos apellidos. Por ejemplo:

Peña Aguilar, Rosa
Peña Aguilar, Sara Luisa
Peña Gómez, Raúl
Quesada Álvarez, Javier
Quesada Álvarez, Octavio
Quesada Benítez, Ana María

Pronunciación

▶ *A.* The Spanish **i**

The Spanish **i** is pronounced like the double *e* in the English word *see.* Listen to your teacher and repeat the following words.

decidir	días	niño
civil	cinco	hijo
fácil	difícil	solicitud

▶ *B.* The Spanish **o**

The Spanish **o** is a short, pure vowel. It corresponds to the *o* in the English word *no*, but without the glide. Listen to your teacher and repeat the following words.

hospital	México	vengo
como	vivo	ocho
otro	número	esposo

Estructuras gramaticales

▶ *1.* Possession with **de**   *(El caso posesivo)*

◆ The **de** + *noun* construction is used to express possession or relationship. Spanish does *not* use the apostrophe.

Raúl 's children
los hijos **de** Raúl
(the children of Raúl)

la clase **de la Dra. Peña**   *Dr. Peñas's class*
el nombre **de la muchacha**   *the girl's name*

ATENCIÓN

Note the use of the definite article before the words **hijos, clase,** and **muchacha.**

—¿Quién es Francisco Acosta?   *Who is Francisco Acosta?*
—Es **el esposo de** Carmen.   *He is Carmen's husband.*

—¿Cúal es **el número de telé-   *What is Irene's phone number?*
fono** de Irene?
—243–8567.   *243–8567.*

PANORAMA DEL MERCADO FINANCIERO

PRÁCTICA

A. Show the relationship in each set of figures below, expressing possession or relationship (e.g., the Spanish equivalent of *Maria's husband*).

B. Be an interpreter. Write the following in Spanish.

1. Miss Vera's students
2. the young lady's age
3. the doctor's husband
4. the professors' problems
5. Amanda's marital status
6. Carmen's nationality
7. Javier's last name
8. Marta's social security number

▶ *2.* Adjectives: Forms, position, and agreement with articles and nouns *(Adjetivos: Formas, posición y concordancia con artículos y nombres)*

A. Forms of adjectives

◆ In Spanish, adjectives agree in gender and number with the nouns they modify. Adjectives ending in **-o** form the feminine by changing the **-o** to **-a.**

el chico rubio	la chica rubia
el lápiz rojo	la pluma roja

◆ Adjectives ending in **-e** or in a consonant have the same form for the masculine and the feminine.

el chico inteligente	la chica inteligente
el esposo feliz *(happy)*	la esposa feliz
el libro fácil	la clase fácil

◆ The only exceptions are:

◇ Adjectives of nationality that end in a consonant add an **-a** in the feminine.

el muchacho español	la muchacha española
el señor inglés *(English)*	la señora inglesa

◇ Adjectives ending in **-or, -án, -ón,** or **-ín** add an **-a** in the feminine.

el alumno trabajador
la alumna trabajadora ⎬ *the hardworking student*

ATENCIÓN

Adjectives that have an accent in the masculine form drop it in the feminine:[1] **inglés → inglesa.**

◆ To form the plural, adjectives follow the same rules as nouns. Adjectives ending in a vowel add **-s;** adjectives ending in a consonant add **-es;** those ending in **-z** change the **-z** to **-c** and add **-es.**

las profesoras norteamericanas
los profesores españoles
los esposos felices

---

[1] For rules on accent marks, see Appendix A.

♦ When an adjective modifies two or more nouns of different genders, the masculine plural form is used.

la chica mexicana
el chico mexicano } la chica y el chico mexicanos

B. Position of adjectives

♦ Descriptive adjectives—such as adjectives denoting color, size, and so forth—generally follow the noun.

Miguel es un chico **inteligente.**
Necesito dos plumas **rojas.**

♦ Adjectives denoting nationality always follow the noun.

El profesor **mexicano** trabaja en la universidad.

C. Agreement of articles, nouns, and adjectives

♦ In Spanish, the article, the noun, and the adjective agree in gender and number.

un muchacho alto   **una** muchacha alta
los muchachos altos   **las** muchachas altas

PRÁCTICA

A. Change the articles and adjectives in each sentence according to the new nouns.

   1. Todos los muchachos son altos.
      _____ muchachas _____ .
   2. ¿Teresa es rubia o morena?
      ¿Carlos _____ ?
   3. El estudiante es muy inteligente y simpático.
      Los estudiantes son _____ .
   4. Necesito la pluma roja.
      _____ lápices _____ .
   5. El español no es difícil.
      _____ idiomas no son _____ .
   6. El chico es feliz.
      _____ chicas son _____ .

B. Using as many descriptive adjectives as possible, describe the following people, places, or things.

1. Julio Iglesias
2. Madonna
3. Magic Johnson
4. el español
5. el libro de español
6. su *(your)* ciudad favorita
7. los estudiantes de la clase
8. el profesor (la profesora) de español
9. las chicas de la clase
10. los muchachos de la clase
11. Margaret Thatcher
12. Fernando Valenzuela

▶ *3.* Possessive adjectives   *(Los adjetivos posesivos)*

FORMS OF THE POSSESSIVE ADJECTIVES

Singular	*Plural*	
mi	mis	*my*
tu	tus	*your* (fam.)
su	sus	{ *your* (form.) *his* *her* *its* *their*
nuestro(-a)	nuestros(-as)	*our*
vuestro(-a)	vuestros(-as)	*your* (fam.)

—¿**Tu** esposo es de Buenos Aires?

—No, **mi** esposo es de Asunción.

Is your husband from Buenos Aires?

No, my husband is from Asuncion.

♦ Possessive adjectives always precede the nouns they introduce and are never given vocal emphasis as in English. They agree in number with the nouns they modify.

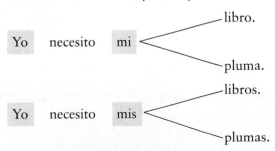

♦ **Nuestro** and **vuestro** are the only possessive adjectives that have the feminine endings **-a** and **-as.** The others take the same endings for both genders.

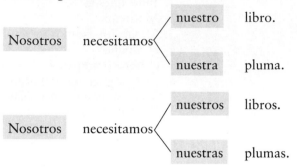

| Nosotros | necesitamos | nuestro | libro. |
| | | nuestra | pluma. |

| Nosotros | necesitamos | nuestros | libros. |
| | | nuestras | plumas. |

♦ Possessive adjectives agree with the thing possessed and *not* with the possessor. For example, two male students referring to their female professor will say *nuestra* **profesora.**

♦ Because **su** and **sus** each have several possible meanings, the form **de él** (or **de ella, de ellos, de ellas, de Ud.,** or **de Uds.**) can be substituted to avoid confusion. The "formula" is: *article + noun + de + pronoun.*

| sus plumas | las plumas **de él** (**ella, Ud.,** etc.) |
| su libro | los libros **de él** (**ella, Ud.,** etc.) |

PRÁCTICA

A. Give the following possessive adjectives in Spanish.

1. *(my)* _____ cuaderno
2. *(our)* _____ clases
3. *(your)* (**Ud.** form) _____ profesora
   (*or* _____ profesora _____
   _____)
4. *(her)* _____ teléfono (*or* _____
   teléfono _____ _____)
5. *(your)* _____ periódico
6. *(his)* _____ hijos (*or* _____ hijos
   _____ _____)
7. *(my)* _____ clases
8. *(her)* _____ estado civil (*or* _____
   estado civil _____ _____)
9. *(their)* _____ apellido (*or* _____
   apellido _____ _____)
10. *(your)* (**tú** form) _____ profesores
11. *(your)* (**Ud.** form) _____ nombre
12. *(our)* _____ trabajo

B. Be an interpreter. What are these people saying?

1. Where does your husband work, ma'am?
   My husband works at the university.
2. Do your friends need money, Mr. Vera?
   Yes, my friends need 2,000 pesos.
3. Do you need your notebook, Lolita?
   Yes, I need my notebook and my pen.
4. Our classes are very difficult.
   Well, my classes are difficult, too.
5. Do you need her address, Anita?
   No, I need his address.

▶ *4.* Present indicative of regular **-er** and **-ir** verbs
*(Presente de indicativo de los verbos regulares
terminados en **-er** y en **-ir**)*

comer	*to eat*	vivir	*to live*
yo	como	yo	vivo
tú	comes	tú	vives
Ud.		Ud.	
él	come	él	vive
ella		ella	
nosotros(-as)	comemos	nostros(-as)	vivimos
vosotros(-as)	coméis	vosotros(-as)	vivís
Uds.		Uds.	
ellos	comen	ellos	viven
ellas		ellas	

◆ Other verbs conjugated like **comer** are:

aprender	*to learn*	beber	*to drink*
creer	*to believe*	vender	*to sell*
leer	*to read*	deber	*to owe*

para vivir mejor

*Conjunto Residencial
Islas*

♦ Other verbs conjugated like **vivir** are:

abrir	*to open*	**escribir**	*to write*
recibir	*to receive*	**decidir**	*to decide*

—¿Qué **comen** Uds.?   *What are you eating?*
—Nosotros **comemos** queso y   *We are eating cheese and*
    Elsa **come** jamón.   *Elsa is eating ham.*

—¿Dónde **viven** ellos?   *Where do they live?*
—**Viven** en la calle Magnolia.   *They live on Magnolia Street.*
—¿Dónde **vives** tú?   *Where do you live?*
—**Vivo** en la calle Juárez.   *I live on Juarez Street.*

PRÁCTICA

A. Give the corresponding forms of the following verbs.

1. *yo:* vivir, deber, creer, escribir
2. *tú:* aprender, abrir, comer, decidir
3. *ella:* leer, vivir, creer, recibir
4. *tú y yo:* vender, decidir, beber, vivir
5. *Luis y Rosa:* vivir, deber, creer, escribir
6. *Ustedes:* recibir, beber, deber, escribir

B. Interview a classmate. Ask him or her the following questions.

1. ¿Dónde vives?
2. ¿Comes en la cafetería?
3. ¿Comen Uds. sándwiches?
4. ¿Bebes café?
5. ¿Escribes en español o en inglés?
6. ¿Leen Uds. en español?
7. ¿Lees bien el español?[1]
8. ¿Qué periódico lees tú?
9. ¿Aprendes mucho en la clase de español?
10. ¿Vendes tus libros?
11. ¿Reciben mucho dinero tus amigos?
12. ¿Debes trabajar mañana?

---

[1] The definite article is used with names of languages except after the prepositions **en** and **de**, or the verbs **hablar** and frequently **estudiar**.

C. Write what these people do, must do, or decide to do.

1. Yo / café
2. Nosotros / español
3. Uds. / periódico
4. Carlos y Rosa / con una pluma roja
5. Tú / la puerta
6. Las chicas / en un apartamento
7. Ud. / jamón y queso
8. Nosotros / estudiar mucho
9. Susana / solicitar el empleo
10. Los profesores / no / mucho dinero

▶ *5.* Present indicative of the irregular verbs **tener** and **venir** *(Presente de indicativo de los verbos irregulares **tener** y **venir**)*

tener *to have*		venir *to come*	
yo	tengo	yo	vengo
tú	tienes	tú	vienes
Ud. ⎫ él ⎬ tiene ella ⎭	tiene	Ud. ⎫ él ⎬ viene ella ⎭	viene
nosotros(-as)	tenemos	nosotros(-as)	venimos
vosotros(-as)	tenéis	vosotros(-as)	venís
Uds. ⎫ ellos ⎬ tienen ellas ⎭	tienen	Uds. ⎫ ellos ⎬ vienen ellas ⎭	vienen

—¿**Tiene** Ud. hijos? *Do you have children?*
—Sí, **tengo** dos. Ellos **vienen** más tarde. *Yes, I have two. They are coming later.*

PRÁCTICA

A. Change the verbs according to the new subjects.

1. *Yo* tengo dinero. (Él, Uds., Ud. y yo, Su esposo, Ellas)
2. *Él* viene con Roberto. (Tú, Juana y él, Juan, Uds., Yo, Ud.)

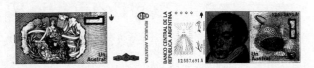

B. Interview a classmate. Ask him or her the following questions.

1. ¿Tienes mi número de teléfono?
2. ¿Tienes mi dirección?
3. ¿Tiene la profesora tu número de seguro social?
4. ¿Tienen Uds. mucho trabajo en la clase de español?
5. ¿Tú tienes la tarde libre mañana?
6. ¿Vienes a clase los sábados?
7. ¿Vienes con tus amigos?
8. ¿Vienen todos los estudiantes a clase?
9. ¿Vienen Uds. a la universidad por la noche o por la mañana?
10. ¿A qué hora vienen Uds. a la clase de español?

▶ *6.* Use of **tener que** + *infinitive* (Uso de **tener que** + infinitivo)

 ♦ **Tener que** is the Spanish equivalent of *to have to.*

Yo **tengo** que leer los libros.	*I have to read the books.*
—¿Tú **tienes** que trabajar hoy?	*Do you have to work today?*
—No, hoy **no tengo que** trabajar.	*No, I do not have to work toda*

PRÁCTICA

A. Change the verbs according to the new subjects.

1. *Yo* tengo que trabajar. (Tú, Nosotros, Él, Ellos, Uds.)
2. *Él* tiene que estudiar. (María, Uds., Tú, Ellos, Nosotros, Yo)

B. You are the instructor. Tell the students what they have to do, using **tener que.**

1. Uds. / venir a clase mañana
2. tú / venir a las ocho
3. Juan / trabajar mucho
4. María y Carmen / estudiar la Lección 2
5. Uds. / hablar español en clase
6. Él / leer los libros en la clase

Clasificados de El Espectador.
Si tiene que vender...

¡A ver cuánto aprendió!

A. ¡Conversemos!

Reread the dialogue in this lesson and be ready to discuss the following.

1. ¿Dónde conversan Susana y Quique?
2. ¿Qué beben mientras conversan?
3. ¿Qué comen?
4. ¿Susana es rubia o morena?
5. ¿Es guapo Quique?
6. ¿Dónde lee Susana el anuncio?
7. ¿Qué decide solicitar Susana?
8. ¿Qué necesita la compañía IBM?
9. ¿Qué conocimientos debe tener la recepcionista?
10. ¿A qué dirección debe enviar Susana su solicitud?
11. ¿Cuándo tiene Susana tiempo libre?
12. ¿Es fácil o difícil la clase de la Dra. Peña?
13. ¿En qué calle vive Susana?
14. ¿A qué hora viene Susana mañana?
15. ¿Qué llena Susana en la compañía IBM?

B.

By combining the words in the three columns (one word for each column starting with A), you can form many different sentences. Write five affirmative and five negative sentences.

A	B	C
Yo	ser	profesor
La chica	estudiar	en el hospital
Uds.	trabajar	bien
Ud.	comer	dos hijos
Ana y Luisa	solicitar	para la compañía Ford
Nosotros	llenar	café
El doctor Jiménez	aprender	la solicitud
Tú	vivir	las preguntas
	beber	inglés
	tener	de Madrid
	leer	mexicano
		jamón y queso
		el periódico
		en la calle Roma
		empleo

C. ¡Repase el vocabulario!

Match the items in column A with those in column B.

	A		**B**
1.	Anita charla	a.	es difícil.
2.	Nosotros vivimos en la	b.	la solicitud.
3.	No tenemos esposos. Somos	c.	Avenida Paz.
		d.	café.
4.	Yo trabajo para	e.	la compañía Sandoval.
5.	Ella es muy	f.	seguro social.
6.	No es fácil;	g.	linda.
7.	Nosotros tenemos la tarde	h.	con Roberto.
8.	Ahora debe llenar	i.	libre.
9.	Ellos beben	j.	solteras.
10.	Yo no tengo tu número de	k.	para estudiar.
11.	Leen el anuncio	l.	en el diario.
12.	Vengo a solicitar	m.	de jamón y queso.
13.	No tengo tiempo	n.	trabajo.
14.	Comemos sándwiches		

D. Situaciones

What would you say in the following situations? What might the other person say?

1. You are helping a Spanish-speaking woman fill out a form. Ask for her name and surname, her address, where she is from, her age, and whether she is married, single, divorced, or widowed. If appropriate, ask her if she has children.
2. Ask someone if he or she wishes to eat a ham and cheese sandwich and drink coffee.
3. You are trying to convince your friend to go on a blind date. Describe the young woman or the young man to him or her.

EMPLEOS
67 — OFRECEN
68 — SOLICITAN
69 — MECANOGRAFIA

PROFESIONALES
73 — MEDICOS
74 — SICOLOGOS
75 — ODONTOLOGOS

En la vida real

ENTREVISTA

Choose a partner, then interview each other using the **tú** form.

Pregúntele a su compañero(-a) de clase...

1. ...si su mejor *(best)* amigo(-a) es rubio(-a), moreno(-a) o pelirrojo(-a).
2. ...que días tiene la clase de español.
3. ...cuántas clases tiene.
4. ...a qué hora viene a la universidad.
5. ...cuándo tiene la tarde libre.
6. ...si vive cerca o lejos de la universidad.
7. ...si vive en una calle o en una avenida.
8. ...si por la noche estudia o mira televisión.

LOS AMIGOS

With a classmate discuss and compare your best friends. Ask each other as many questions as necessary to get as much information as possible about them. What they are like (¿cómo es él/ella?), where they are from, and so on. Some additional words you may want to include:

trabajador(a)	*hardworking*	**tímido(-a)**	*shy*
haragán, perezoso(-a)	*lazy*	**rico(-a)**	*rich*
optimista	*optimist*	**pobre**	*poor*
pesimista	*pessimist*		

C—EMPLEOS

NECESITAMOS TRABAJO...

Some friends of yours are looking for jobs. Help them by answering their questions about the following classified ads. (Continued on the next page.)

IMPORTANTE LABORATORIO FARMACEUTICO NACIONAL
BUSCA
TECNICO
Capacitado para crear y dirigir una línea de productos OTC
- Se requiere persona con experiencia en este campo.
- Condiciones a convenir.
Interesados escribir adjuntando curriculum a GIS-PERT PUBLICIDAD, c. Balmes, 10 08007-Barcelona; indicando en el sobre la Ref.º 21.210.

Multinacional Alemana dedicada a la hidráulica, ubicada en el Vallés Occidental, precisa:
SECRETARIA/O
DPTO. COMPRAS
SE REQUIERE:
- Dominio del idioma alemán a nivel conversación.
- Experiencia Administrativa en área de Compras.
- Facilidad de trato con proveedores.
- Edad 22-37 años.
Condiciones económicas según aptitudes.
Interesadas escribir historial a:
OPTIM
C. Estació, n.º 9, 1.º, 1.ª
08814 PALAU DE PLEGAMANS
Indicar ref. 2.475.

OPTIM

EMPRESA FINANCIERA
PRECISA
DIRECTOR DE SERVICIO EXTRANJERO
SE REQUIERE:
⇨ Capacidad de organización y gestión.
⇨ Edad: entre 35 y 45 años.
⇨ Perfecto dominio del idioma inglés y conocimientos de otros idiomas.
⇨ Experiencia mínima de 3 años en el servicio de extranjero.
⇨ Titulado en Ciencias Económicas o Empresariales.
SE OFRECE:
⇨ Incorporación inmediata.
⇨ Remuneración a convenir, de acuerdo con la experiencia y conocimientos aportados por el candidato.
⇨ Proceso de selección con garantía de absoluta reserva en los datos aportados.
Los candidatos enviarán "curriculum vitae" antes del día 20 de noviembre, acompañado de fotografía, dirección y teléfono al Apartado 1.540 de Vigo.

(Oferta INEM nº 2.971 OR.)

1. ¿Qué empresa necesita secretario(-a)?
2. Si deseo trabajar de secretaria en la compañía Optim, ¿qué idioma necesito hablar?
3. ¿En qué ciudad está el Laboratorio Farmacéutico Nacional?
4. ¿Qué experiencia mínima debo tener si solicito el puesto de director de servicio extranjero?
5. ¿Para solicitar qué puestos necesito tener una foto?
6. ¿Qué edad se requiere para trabajar en la empresa financiera?
7. ¿Cuándo debo enviar el *curriculum vitae* a la empresa financiera?

UNA ACTIVIDAD ESPECIAL

Imagine that you are applying for a job and have to fill out this application.

SOLICITUD DE TRABAJO

Apellidos y nombres _____ Fecha de nacimiento

Dirección _____

DÍA	MES	AÑO

Zona Postal _____ Teléfono _____

Estado civil   Sexo   Edad

1. ___ soltera(-a)   Masculino _____   _____

2. ___ casado(-a)   Femenino _____

3. ___ divorciado(-a)

4. ___ viudo(-a)

Esposo/esposa _____

Nombre y edad de los hijos _____

Nacionalidad _____

Lugar de nacimiento _____

Ocupación _____

Lugar donde trabaja _____

Número de seguro social _____

Número de la licencia para conducir _____

Y ahora, *¡vamos a leer!*

La familia de Hilda López

La señora Hilda López es de Santiago, pero ahora vive en California. Es
enfermera° y trabaja en un hospital de Los Ángeles. Sus padres° son médicos,° y viven en Valparaíso, una ciudad de Chile.

· Julio, el esposo de la señora López, es ingeniero.° Ellos tienen tres
hijos: Eduardo, Irene y Teresa. Los niños° hablan inglés y español. En la
escuela° leen y escriben en inglés.

La familia vive en la ciudad de Los Ángeles, en la calle Figueroa, número ciento treinta. Emilio López, el padre° de Julio, es viudo y vive con
ellos.

nurse / parents
M.D.'s
engineer
children
at school

father

¡A ver cuánto recuerda!   *(Let's see how much you remember!)*

1. ¿De qué país es la señora López?
2. ¿Vive en Chile ahora?
3. ¿Dónde trabaja?
4. ¿Cuál es el estado civil de la señora López?
5. ¿Cuál es la profesión de la señora López? ¿De su esposo?
6. ¿Cuántos hijos tienen?
7. ¿Qué idiomas hablan los niños?
8. ¿En qué calle vive la familia? ¿En qué ciudad?
9. ¿Es divorciado el padre de Julio?
10. ¿Con quién vive el señor López?

Para escribir

Following the style and format of the paragraph you have just read, and using
the questions above as a guide, write a brief composition about yourself, starting with:

Me llamo _____ ; soy de _____ . Ahora vivo _____ ...

Una reunión familiar en Cali, Colombia.

España

España (I)

PANORAMA HISPÁNICO 2

- Los moros, del norte de África, dominaron España por más de 700 años y su influencia se observa todavía en la arquitectura de ciudades como Toledo, Córdoba, Granada y Sevilla.

- Después de Madrid, Barcelona, la capital de Cataluña, es la ciudad más importante de España. Tiene más de cinco millones de habitantes. En 1992 se celebran en esta ciudad los Juegos Olímpicos.

- El turismo tiene una gran importancia para la economía española. Más de 45 millones de personas visitan España durante la primavera y el verano. Entre los atractivos que ofrece el país están el clima, sus hermosas playas *(beaches)* en las costas del Mediterráneo y su rica historia.

- En la mayoría de los pueblos y ciudades españolas, las plazas son el centro de las actividades sociales y económicas. En los cafés de las plazas se reúnen los amigos a charlar, mientras que en los edificios alrededor de la plaza hay bancos, almacenes, hoteles, etc.

◀ La espléndida Plaza Mayor de Salamanca es la más impresionante de España. Salamanca es una de las ciudades más elegantes y sobrias de Europa. Es famosa por su universidad, fundada en 1218. Por las tardes, durante el verano, los estudiantes conversan en los cafés al aire libre que hay en la plaza. La universidad donde Ud. estudia, ¿es antigua o moderna?

◀ Las Ramblas son el centro de actividades de Barcelona, el puerto más importante de España. Muchos teatros, entre ellos el Teatro de la Ópera, están situados en esta hermosa avenida. Hay también numerosos restaurantes, tiendas y hoteles. ¿Existe un lugar así en la ciudad donde Ud. vive?

◀ Vista parcial del puerto de San Sebastián en el País Vasco. Situada sobre el Mar Cantábrico y muy cerca de la frontera francesa, San Sebastián es uno de los centros pesqueros *(fishing)* más importantes de España. La ciudad es también conocida por su hermosa playa, «La Concha». ¿En qué otras regiones españolas encontramos playas de gran atracción turística?

▲ La ciudad de Ávila, situada al noroeste de Madrid, a 1.127 metros de altura, es la única ciudad española que está totalmente rodeada por murallas de la época romana. Aunque las murallas tienen más de dos mil años, están en perfecto estado de conservación. Ávila es la ciudad donde nació Santa Teresa de Jesús, famosa escritora mística del siglo XVI. ¿En qué parte de los Estados Unidos está situada la ciudad donde Ud. vive?

◀ Una de las grandes atracciones turísticas de Madrid es la Plaza de España, donde se encuentra el monumento a Cervantes. Frente a la estatua del escritor vemos a don Quijote y a Sancho Panza, personajes de su inmortal obra *Don Quijote de la Mancha*. ¿Qué otros sitios de interés le gustaría visitar en Madrid?

▲ El Templo de la Sagrada Familia, en Barcelona, es la obra maestra del arquitecto catalán Antonio Gaudí. Gaudí murió *(died)* sin terminar la construcción del templo, que solamente tiene cuatro de las doce torres planeadas por el arquitecto. ¿Puede Ud. mencionar alguna iglesia o templo famoso en el estado donde Ud. vive?

▶ Benidorm, situada en la Costa Blanca sobre el Mediterráneo, recibe más de 250.000 visitantes cada verano. La ciudad tiene unos cinco kilómetros de playa de arena *(sand)* blanca. Hoy día, Benidorm es un centro cosmopolita e internacional. ¿Qué lugares visita Ud. en el verano?

El pueblo de Alcázar de San Juan en la provincia de Ciudad Real. Ciudad Real es el centro de la región española llamada La Mancha. Esta región es una extensa llanura *(plain)* en la que aparece de vez en cuando *(from time to time)* la silueta de un molino de viento *(windmill)*. La Mancha es famosa en todo el mundo porque es el escenario de las aventuras del famoso personaje de Cervantes, Don Quijote de la Mancha. ¿Qué sabe Ud. de este personaje?

El Patio de los Leones de la Alhambra de Granada. La Alhambra es un palacio inmenso, construido por los árabes durante el siglo *(century)* XIV. Entre los aspectos más destacados de la Alhambra están los jardines con fuentes que tiene el palacio y que forman una especie de laberinto. ¿Qué culturas cree Ud. que tienen influencia en los Estados Unidos?

Celebrando el año nuevo en Santiago, Chile.

OBJECTIVES

Pronunciation   The Spanish **u** and linking

Structure   Expressions with **tener** • The personal **a** • Contractions • Present indicative of the irregular verbs **ir, dar,** and **estar** • **Ir a** + *infinitive* • Present indicative of **e:ie** stem-changing verbs

Communication   You will learn vocabulary related to party activities, foods, and beverages.

¿Bailamos... ?

Adela, una chica uruguaya, invita a muchos de sus compañeros de la universidad a una fiesta de fin de año en su casa. En la fiesta, Humberto y Adela conversan mientras bailan.

ADELA	—Humberto, ¿dónde está tu prima?
HUMBERTO	—Va a venir más tarde. Tiene que traer a mi hermana.
ADELA	—También va a traer unos discos. Oye, ¿dónde vamos a celebrar el año nuevo?[1]
HUMBERTO	—Vamos a ir al baile del Club Náutico más tarde.
ADELA	—¡Magnífico! ¿Por qué no invitamos a Julio y a su novia?
HUMBERTO	—Buena idea; ellos son muy simpáticos. Además, hoy es el cumpleaños de Julio.
ADELA	—¿Ah sí? ¿Cuántos años tiene Julio?
HUMBERTO	—Creo que tiene veintidós.
ADELA	—¿Tienes hambre? ¿Quieres pollo, entremeses, ensalada... ?
HUMBERTO	—No, gracias. No tengo mucha hambre, pero tengo sed.
ADELA	—¿Quieres un coctel, sidra[2], champán, cerveza, sangría[3]... ?
HUMBERTO	—Prefiero un refresco.
ADELA	—¿A qué hora empieza el baile en el Club?
HUMBERTO	—A las diez y media. Voy a invitar a Julio y a Teresa.

Más tarde, en el Club Náutico, todos celebran el año nuevo.

ADELA	—La orquesta es magnífica. ¿Bailamos, Humberto?
HUMBERTO	—Sí.
JULIO	—*(A su novia)* ¿Estás cansada, Teresa?
TERESA	—No, tengo calor. ¿Por qué no vamos todos a la terraza ahora?
JULIO	—Buena idea. ¿Llevamos las bebidas?
TERESA	—Sí, tengo mucha sed.
HUMBERTO	—¿No tienen uvas? En Cuba siempre comemos doce uvas a la medianoche.
MARISA	—Aquí en Montevideo brindamos con sidra.
ADELA	—¡Son las doce! ¡Feliz Año Nuevo!
TODOS	—¡Feliz Año Nuevo! ¡Feliz Año Nuevo... !
HUMBERTO	—Y, ¡feliz cumpleaños, Julio!

---

[1] In Hispanic countries, it is common for people to celebrate the New Year by attending a party in a private home early in the evening, then moving to a club before midnight.   [2] A kind of champagne made from apples.   [3] A drink prepared with red wine and fruit.

Vocabulario

COGNADOS

el **club**   club
el **coctel**   cocktail
el **champán**   champagne
la **ensalada**   salad
la **idea**   idea

mucho(-a)   much, a lot of
la **orquesta**   orchestra, group
la **sidra**   cider
la **terraza**   terrace
uruguayo(-a)   Uruguayan

NOMBRES

el **baile**   dance
la **bebida**   drink, beverage
la **casa**   house, home
la **cerveza**   beer
el (la) **compañero(-a)**   classmate
el **cumpleaños**   birthday
el **disco**   record
los **entremeses**   hors d'oeuvres
la **fiesta**   party
la **hermana**   sister
el **hermano**   brother
la **medianoche**   midnight
la **novia**   girlfriend, fiancée
el **novio**   boyfriend, fiancé
el **pollo**   chicken
el (la) **primo(-a)**   cousin
el **refresco**   soft drink, soda pop
las **uvas**   grapes

VERBOS

bailar   to dance
brindar   to toast
celebrar   to celebrate
dar *(irreg.)*   to give
empezar, comenzar (e:ie)   to
begin, to start
estar *(irreg.)*   to be
invitar   to invite

ir *(irreg.)*   to go
llevar   to take (someone or something someplace)
preferir (e:ie)   to prefer
querer (e:ie)   to want, to wish
traer (yo traigo)   to bring

ADJETIVOS

bueno(-a)[1]   good
cansado(-a)   tired
feliz   happy
magnífico(-a)   great
muchos(-as)   many
nuevo(-a)   new

OTRAS PALABRAS Y EXPRESIONES

a la medianoche   at midnight
además   besides
ahora   now
aquí   here
¿Bailamos... ?   Shall we
dance . . . ?
¿cuántos(-as)?   how many?
fiesta de fin de año   New Year's
Eve party
que   that *(relat. pron.)*
siempre   always
todos(-as)   everybody, all

---

[1]**Bueno** drops the -o when placed before a masculine, singular noun: **un** *buen* **profesor.**

T. No, I'm hot. Why don't we all go to the terrace now?

J. Good idea. Shall we take the drinks?

T. Yes, I'm very thirsty.

H. Don't they have grapes? In Cuba we always eat twelve grapes at midnight.

M. Here in Montevideo we toast with cider.

A. It's twelve o'clock! Happy New Year!

E. Happy New Year! Happy New Year . . . !

H. And happy birthday, Julio!

Vocabulario adicional

¿adónde? where (to)?
¿Adónde vamos?

al mediodía at noon
Ana viene **al mediodía.**

antipático(-a) unpleasant
Josefina es muy **antipática.**

la cinta, el casete tape, cassette
Ella trae las **cintas.**

contento(-a) happy
Estoy **contenta** porque hoy vienen mis amigos.

¿cuánto(-a)? how much?
¿Cuánto dinero tienes?

de quién whose
¿De quién es la cinta? ¿De Ana?

la fiesta de Navidad Christmas party
¿A quién llevas a la **fiesta de Navidad?**

hijo, hija son, daughter
Mi **hija** es rubia y mi **hijo** es moreno.

malo(-a)[1] bad
Es una situación muy mala.

ocupado(-a) busy
Hoy estoy muy **ocupado.**

porque because
No viene **porque** no tiene dinero.

el tocadiscos record player
¿Dónde está **el tocadiscos?**

el vino wine
¿Deseas tomar **vino?**

---

[1] **Malo** drops the -o when placed before a masculine, singular noun: un *mal* hombre.

¿Lo sabía Ud.... ?

- En España y en Latinoamérica, no existe tanta *(as much)* separación entre *(among)* generaciones como en los Estados Unidos. Los niños, los padres y los abuelos frecuentemente van juntos a fiestas y a celebraciones.
- En los países *(countries)* de habla hispana, las chicas y los muchachos generalmente salen *(go out)* en grupos. Van juntos a fiestas, al teatro y a conciertos.
- Los hispanos generalmente celebran el cumpleaños y también el día de su «santo». Muchos padres les dan a sus hijos el nombre del santo que corresponde al día de su nacimiento según el calendario católico. Por ejemplo, si un niño nace *(is born)* el 24 de junio, que es el día de San Juan, el niño puede llamarse Juan. Pero si nace el 24 de junio y sus padres lo llaman Miguel, celebra su cumpleaños en junio y celebra el día de su «santo» el 29 de septiembre, que es el día de San Miguel.
- En los países hispanos no existe una edad mínima para comprar o tomar bebidas alcohólicas.
- En español se dice «¡Salud!» *(Cheers!)* al brindar.

Un café al aire libre en la Gran Vía, una de las calles más importantes de Madrid.

Pronunciación

▶ *A.* The Spanish **u**

The Spanish **u** is shorter in length than the English **u**. It corresponds to the *ue* sound in the English word *Sue*. Listen to your teacher and repeat the following words.

muchacho	Susana	azul	universidad
Humberto	Cuba	bueno	uruguayo

► *B.* Linking

♦ In Spanish, a final consonant is always linked with the next initial vowel sound.

el amigo   ¿Vas al baile?   mis hermanos[1]

♦ When two identical consonants are together, they are pronounced as one.

es simpática   Voy con Norma.

♦ When two identical vowels are together, they are pronounced as one long vowel.

Rodolfo Ochoa   ¿Va Ana?

♦ The final vowel of one word is linked with the initial vowel of the following word to form one syllable.

fin de año   la hermana de Olga
hablo español

Estructuras gramaticales

► *1.* Expressions with **tener**   (*Expresiones con* ***tener***)

♦ Many useful idiomatic expressions are formed with **tener** + *noun*.

tener (mucho) frío	*to be (very) cold*
tener (mucha) sed	*to be (very) thirsty*
tener (mucha) hambre	*to be (very) hungry*
tener (mucho) calor	*to be (very) hot*
tener (mucho) sueño	*to be (very) sleepy*
tener prisa	*to be in a hurry*
tener miedo	*to be afraid*
tener razón	*to be right*
no tener razón	*to be wrong*
tener... años de edad	*to be . . . years old*

—¿**Tienes** calor?   *Are you hot?*
—Sí, y también **tengo** mucha   *Yes, and I'm also very thirsty.*
  sed.

—¿Cuántos años **tienes**?   *How old are you?*
—**Tengo** diecinueve años.   *I'm nineteen years old.*

---

[1] In Spanish the letter **h** is silent.

ATENCIÓN

Note that while Spanish uses **mucho(-a)** + *noun* (as in **mucha hambre**), English uses *very* + *adjective* (as in *very hungry*).

PRÁCTICA

A. ¿Qué tienen?

1. Jorge

2. Yo

3. Tú

4. La profesora

5. Ud.

6. Felipe

7. Marisa y Elena   8. Ella

B. Which expression with **tener** would you use in each of the following situations?

   1. You are in the Arizona desert in the middle of summer.
   2. A big dog is chasing you.
   3. You have only a minute to get to your next class.
   4. You are in Alaska in the middle of winter.
   5. You haven't eaten for an entire day.
   6. You got up at four A.M. and it is now midnight.
   7. You just ran for two hours in the sun.
   8. You are blowing out twenty candles on your birthday cake.

▶ *2.* The personal **a**   *(La **a** personal)*

   ◆ The preposition **a** is used in Spanish before a direct object[1] referring to a specific person or persons. It is called the "personal **a**," and has no equivalent in English.

   Yo llevo **a mi hermana.**   Nosotros invitamos **a los estudiantes.**
          D.O.   D.O.

   I   take   my sister.   *We   invite   the students.*
          D.O.   D.O.

   ◆ The personal **a** is *not* used when the direct object is not a person.

   Yo llevo **los discos.**
          D.O.

   I   take   the records.
          D.O.

---

[1]See **Lección 6** for further explanation of the direct object.

♦ The verb **tener** does not generally take the personal **a**, even if the
direct object is a person.

Tengo **hijos.**   Tenemos **dos hermanas.**
    D.O.   D.O.

I have children.   *We have two sisters.*
    D.O.   D.O.

PRÁCTICA

A. Read the following dialogues, adding the personal **a** when
needed.

   1. —¿Cuántos primos tienes?
      —Tengo _____ dos primos y una prima.
   2. —¿Llama Ud. _____ Carmen o _____
      Elena?
      —Llamo _____ Carmen.
   3. —¿Tu amigo lleva _____ Rosa a la fiesta de Navi-
      dad?
      —No, lleva _____ su novia.
   4. —¿Adónde lleva Ud. _____ las bebidas?
      —A la fiesta.
   5. —¿Tienes _____ muchos hermanos?
      —No, no tengo _____ hermanos.
   6. —¿Qué lees?
      —Leo _____ la lección.

B. Interview a classmate. Ask him or her the following
questions.

   1. ¿A quién invitas siempre a tus fiestas?
   2. ¿Llevas a tu novio(-a) a los bailes de la universidad?
   3. ¿Tienes hermanos? ¿Cuántos?
   4. ¿Traes a tus amigos a clase?
   5. ¿Tienes primos? ¿Cuántos?

C. Be an interpreter. What are these people saying?

   1. Whom are you taking to the Christmas party?
      I am taking my daughter and my son.
   2. Do you have children?
      Yes, I have a son.
   3. Do you invite Carmen to your parties?
      No, she is very unpleasant.

► **3.** Contractions   *(Contracciones)*

♦ There are only two contractions in Spanish: **del** and **al**.

♦ The preposition **de** *(of, from)* followed by the article **el** contracts to **del**.

La hija de + el profesor López ⟶ La hija **del** profesor López

♦ The preposition **a** *(to, toward)* or the personal **a** followed by the article **el** contracts to **al**.

¿Vas **a + el** baile?   ⟶ ¿Vas **al** baile?

Llevo **a + el** primo de Roberto. ⟶ Llevo **al** primo de Robert.

—¿Llevas **al** hermano de Ana?   *Are you taking Ana's brother?*
—No, llevo **a las** hijas de Eva.   *No, I'm taking Eva's daughters.*

ATENCIÓN

A + el and **de + el** must always be contracted to **al** and **del**. None of the other combinations (**de la, de las, de los, a la, a las, a los**) is contracted: **Invitan *a los* hijos *de los* profesores.**

PRÁCTICA

A. Complete the following sentences orally with one of the following: **de la, de las, del, de los, a la, a las, al, a los.**

1. Vengo _____ baile _____ universidad.
2. La señora necesita _____ muchachas.
3. Ellos llaman _____ estudiantes _____ mediodía.
4. El libro es _____ compañera de María.
5. Humberto lleva _____ chicas _____ baile de fin de año.
6. El tocadiscos es _____ primos de Juan.
7. La sidra es _____ señor López.
8. ¿Nosotros tenemos la dirección _____ chicas?

B. Answer the following questions using the cues provided.

1. ¿De quién son los discos? (profesor)
2. ¿De quién es el tocadiscos? (señorita Paz)
3. ¿A quién invitan a la fiesta? (señor Peña)
4. ¿A quiénes trae el señor Peña? (chicos)
5. ¿A quién llaman los chicos? (muchachas)
6. ¿Adónde llevan a las muchachas? (baile / club)

▶ *4.* Present indicative of the irregular verbs **ir, dar,** and **estar**   *(Presente de indicativo de los verbos irregulares **ir, dar** y **estar**)*

	ir *to go*	**dar** *to give*	**estar** *to be*
Singular			
yo	voy	doy	estoy
tú	vas	das	estás
Ud. / él / ella	va	da	está
Plural			
nosotros	vamos	damos	estamos
vosotros	vais	dais	estáis
Uds. / ellos / ellas	van	dan	están

—Susana **da** una fiesta hoy. ¿Tú **vas**?

—No, no **voy** porque **estoy** muy cansada.

—Entonces invito a tu hermana. ¿Dónde **está**?

—**Está** en la universidad. Viene a las tres.

Susana is giving a party today. Are you going?

No, I'm not going because I am very tired.

Then I'm inviting your sister. Where is she?

She is at the university. She is coming at three.

◆ The verb **estar,** *to be,* has been used here to indicate current condition (**Estoy muy cansada.**) and location (**Está en la universidad.**). **Ser,** the other equivalent of the English verb *to be,* has been used up to now to refer to origin (**Él es de Chile.**), nationality (**Ellas son mexicanas.**), characteristics (**Jorge es rubio.**), profession (**Elsa es profesora.**), and time (**Son las doce.**).

◆ Other possible uses of **dar** are: **dar un examen** *(test),* **dar una conferencia** *(lecture).*

PRÁCTICA

A. Change the verbs according to the new subjects.

    1. *Yo* voy a la fiesta. (Nosotros, Tú, Mis amigos, Uds., Ellos)
    2. *Ellos* están bien. (Nosotros, Yo, Tú, Mi hijo, Ud., Tú y José)
    3. *Él* da dinero. (Ud., Yo, Tú, Ella y yo, Ellos, Uds.)

B. Provide the following information about you and your friends.

    1. ¿Cómo está Ud.?
    2. ¿Está Ud. cansado(-a) hoy?
    3. ¿Quién no está en clase hoy?
    4. ¿Con quién va Ud. a las fiestas de la universidad?
    5. ¿Adónde va los sábados por la noche con sus amigos?
    6. ¿Adónde van Uds. mañana?
    7. ¿Van Uds. a un club? (¿A cuál?)
    8. ¿Da Ud. muchas fiestas en su casa?
    9. ¿Da Ud. una fiesta de fin de año?
   10. ¿Dónde están sus amigos ahora?
   11. ¿Está muy ocupado el profesor?
   12. ¿Da el profesor exámenes difíciles o fáciles?

C. Complete the following sentences in a logical manner.

    1. Roberto está allí y nosotros...
    2. Yo doy una fiesta esta noche y tú...
    3. Tú vas a la universidad y yo...
    4. Yo estoy muy cansado pero ellos...
    5. Nosotros damos una fiesta de Navidad y él...
    6. Ellos van hoy y nosotros...

▶ *5.* **Ir a** + *infinitive*   (**Ir a** + infinitivo)

♦ **Ir a** + *infinitive* is used to express future action. It is equivalent to the English expression *to be going to* + *infinitive*. The "formula" is as follows:

ir (conjugated) + **a** + *infinitive*

Voy	**a**	**trabajar.**
I am going		*to work.*

—¿En qué universidad **van a estudiar** Uds.?   *At what university are you going to study?*

—**Vamos a estudiar** en la Universidad de Costa Rica.   *We're going to study at the University of Costa Rica.*

PRÁCTICA

A. What do you think these people are going to do? Consider where they are and what time of day it is.

MODELO: José / en el hospital / por la tarde
     José va a trabajar en el hospital por la tarde.

1. Yo / en mi casa / por la noche
2. Los estudiantes / en la clase / por la mañana
3. Nosotros / en el club / por la noche
4. Tú / en la cafetería / a las doce
5. El profesor / en la universidad / por la tarde
6. Julio y Teresa / en la terraza / a las diez de la noche
7. Susana / en la compañía IBM / por la mañana
8. Uds. / en la fiesta / por la noche

B. In the following sentences change the verbs to the future using the **ir a** + *infinitive* construction.

1. Ellos *venden* refrescos en el club.
2. Mi hermana *come* en la cafetería.
3. Yo *converso* con mis amigos.
4. Nosotros *llamamos* a nuestros primos.
5. Tú *invitas* a los muchachos.
6. Uds. *beben* vino.
7. Uds *traen* los discos.
8. Ud. *lleva* a su hijo al mercado.

C. Using the cues provided, tell us what you and your friends are going to do tomorrow.

1. ¿Adónde va a ir Ud. mañana?   (a la universidad)
2. ¿Adónde va a ir su amigo?   (al trabajo)
3. ¿Con quién va a comer en la cafetería?   (con mi compañero de clase)
4. ¿A qué hora van a comer?   (a las doce)
5. ¿Qué van a comer?   (pollo y ensalada)
6. ¿Adónde va a ir Ud. por la tarde?   (al club)
7. ¿Su amigo va a ir también?   (no)
8. ¿Qué van a hacer Ud. y sus amigos por la noche?   (mirar televisión)

▶ *6.* Present indicative of **e:ie** stem-changing verbs
(*Presente de indicativo de los verbos que cambian en la raíz **e:ie***)

♦ In Spanish, some verbs undergo a stem-change in the present indicative. For these verbs, when **e** is the last stem vowel and it is stressed, it changes to **ie** as follows.

preferir			*to prefer*
yo	prefiero	nosotros	preferimos
tú	prefieres	vosotros	preferís
Ud.		Uds.	
él }	prefiere	ellos }	prefieren
ella		ellas	

—¿A qué hora **piensas** ir a la fiesta?	*What time are you planning to go to the party?*
—**Prefiero** ir a las diez. ¿Y tú?	*I prefer to go at ten. And you?*
—Yo **no quiero** ir. Estoy cansado.	*I don't want to go. I'm tired.*

♦ Note that the stem vowel is not stressed in the verb forms used with **nosotros** and **vosotros**; therefore, the e does not change to **ie**.

♦ Stem-changing verbs have regular endings like other **-ar**, **-er**, and **-ir** verbs.

♦ Some other verbs that undergo the same change are:

cerrar   *to close*   **empezar**   *to begin, to start*
entender   *to understand*   **comenzar**   *to begin, to start*
perder   *to lose, to miss*   **pensar**   *to think*
querer   *to want, to wish, to*   **pensar** (+ *infinitive*)   *to plan*
    love

PRÁCTICA

A. Change the verbs according to the new subjects.

1. *Yo quiero ir con ellas.* (Tu sobrina y yo, Tú, Ellos, Él, Nosotras)
2. *Yo empiezo la clase.* (Tú, Ella y yo, Ellos, Nosotros, Mi amigo)
3. *¿Tú cierras la puerta?* (Ud., Yo, Ella, Nosotros, Uds.)

B. Answer the following questions with complete sentences.

1. ¿Prefiere Ud. vivir en Buenos Aires o en Los Ángeles?
2. ¿Prefieren Uds. comer en su casa o en la cafetería?
3. ¿Entiende Ud. una conversación en español?
4. ¿Entienden Uds. el inglés?
5. ¿Quiere Ud. tomar un refresco?
6. ¿Quiere Ud. un café o un refresco?
7. ¿Entiende Ud. la lección?
8. ¿Piensa Ud. ir a un baile el sábado?

C. Complete the following dialogues, using the verbs given.

1. preferir   —¿Dónde _____ comer Uds.? ¿En un café o en su casa?
               — _____ comer en nuestra casa.

2. querer   —¿Qué _____ comer (Uds.)?
               —Rosa _____ comer pollo y Oscar y yo _____ comer entremeses.

3. pensar   —¿Adónde _____ Uds. ir el domingo?
               — _____ ir al club.

4. cerrar   —¿No _____ (ellos) la cafetería los sábados?
               —No, creo que no _____ los sábados.

5. perder   —Cuando Uds. van a Las Vegas, ¿ _____ mucho dinero?
               —Sí, _____ mucho.

6. empezar   —¿A qué hora _____ Uds. a trabajar?
               —Nosotros _____ a las ocho y Luis _____ a las nueve.

¡A ver cuánto aprendió!

A. ¡Conversemos!

Reread the dialogue in this lesson and be ready to discuss the following.

1. ¿Es uruguayo Humberto?
2. ¿A quiénes invita Adela?
3. ¿Qué va a traer la prima de Humberto?
4. ¿Quiénes son muy simpáticos?
5. ¿Cuántos años tiene Julio?
6. ¿Qué quiere beber Humberto?
7. ¿Adónde van todos más tarde?
8. ¿A qué hora empieza el baile en el Club Náutico?
9. ¿Es buena o mala la orquesta?
10. ¿Por qué van Julio y Teresa a la terraza?
11. ¿Qué llevan a la terraza?
12. ¿Con qué brindan en la fiesta?

B. ¡Repase el vocabulario!

Supply the missing words and read aloud.

1. ¿ _____ es el disco? ¿De Teresa?
2. En las fiestas de _____ de año en Cuba, comen doce _____ a la _____ .
3. La orquesta es muy, muy buena. ¡Es _____ !
4. ¿Por qué no comen? _____ no tienen hambre...
5. ¿ _____ vas? ¿Al club?
6. ¡Feliz año _____ !
7. No es antipático. Es muy _____ .
8. ¿Tienes refrescos? Tengo mucha _____ .
9. No tengo cintas pero tengo _____ .
10. No quiero bailar ahora porque estoy muy _____ .
11. ¿ _____ dinero tiene Ud.? ¿Mil pesos?
12. Tiene dos hijos. La _____ vive en Colombia y el hijo vive en Lima.
13. Vamos a _____ con sidra.
14. Hoy vamos a celebrar el _____ de Julio.
15. ¿Estudiamos esta noche o vas a estar _____ ?

club
campestre
del caribe

DICIEMBRE 31

Celebración de fin de año
para padres-hijos-familiares e invitados de socios
Salón Dorado 9:00 PM

C. Situaciones

What would you say in the following situations? What would the
other person say?

1. You ask someone to dance with you.
2. You ask someone whether he or she wants to drink champagne, a cocktail, or a soft drink.
3. Your friend is hungry and thirsty. Offer him or her things to
   eat and drink.
4. Tell a friend that you are going to bring the drinks for a party.
5. Wish someone a happy new year.
6. Wish someone a happy birthday.

Para escribir

Complete the following sentences.

1. Yo traigo el pollo y tú...
2. Nosotros preferimos sangría y ellos...
3. Ellos platican y nosotros...
4. Ellos van a ir al baile con sus primos y yo...
5. Yo invito a mis amigos y Uds....
6. Yo llevo al hijo del profesor y tú...
7. Yo tengo veinte años y tú...
8. Ellos llevan el vino y yo...
9. Ellos van a brindar con sidra y nosotros...
10. Ellos son de California y nosotros...

CENA Y RUMBA
DE AÑO NUEVO

DELICIOSO BUFFET

Ceviche de Camarón
Pavo Bellavista
Lomo al Oporto
Arroz con Coco y Pasas
Alcachofas y Espárragos Vinagreta
Ensalada de Frutas y
Postre de Navidad.

Diciembre 31   Orquesta Maya

$7.000 por persona
Reservaciones: 610 46 64 - 236 53 36

MASSAI CLUB. Restaurante, Discoteca, Bar, Casino.
Km. 4 Vía La Calera.

En la vida real

ENTREVISTA

Choose a partner, then interview each other, using the **tú** form.

Pregúntele a su compañero(-a) de clase...

1. ...cuántos años tiene.
2. ...si es feliz.
3. ...si da muchas fiestas en su casa.
4. ...si va a dar una fiesta el sábado.
5. ...si baila muy bien.
6. ...si prefiere beber vino, cerveza o refresco.
7. ...si es una buena idea tener una fiesta hoy.
8. ...adónde va a ir esta noche.
9. ...si tiene discos o cintas.
10. ...si quiere comer pollo o entremeses.

UNA VISITA

With a classmate, plan activities you would have in your hometown to entertain a visitor from a Spanish-speaking country. Give your visitor a name and decide which country he or she is from. In your plans include a party, visits to places of interest, and outdoor activities. Decide who is going to do what, and include food and drinks you are going to offer your visitor.

Some additional words or phrases you may want to include are:

la **hamburguesa** *hamburger*
el **perro caliente** *hot dog*
el **pollo frito** *fried chicken*
el **museo** *museum*
el **cine** *movie theatre*
la **discoteca** *disco*
el **teatro** *theater*

el **picnic** *picnic*
la **playa** *beach*
la **montaña** *mountain*

el **partido de** *(game)*
- fútbol americano
- béisbol
- básquetbol
- fútbol *(soccer)*

...FELIZ AÑO NUEVO!
1989
salud... amor y paz para todos!
SON NUESTROS SINCEROS DESEOS
almacenes
SEGURISIMO

UN ESPECTÁCULO

You and a classmate are in Spain and come across this ad about a show. You decide to go see it. What information can you get from the ad? After reading the ad, take turns in answering the questions below.

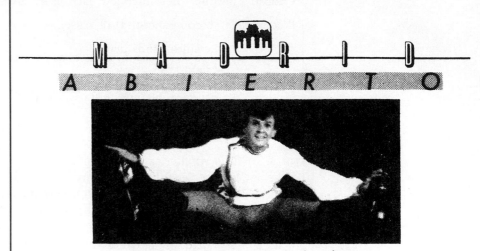

Zdenek Pazdirek, doble campeón checoslovaco.

«Holiday on ice», en el Palacio de Deportes

Música y acrobacias pasadas por hielo

SETENTA artistas del patinaje, de diversas nacionalidades, componen el espectáculo musical y circense **«Holiday on ice»**, de origen holandés, que recorre España en este verano y se presenta en Madrid solamente hasta el 2 de agosto, antes de proseguir su gira hacia Valladolid y Bilbao.

En dos horas aproximadas, el «show» ofrece dos series de números musicales y bailes, acrobacias y malabarismo, dedicadas a México y la URSS, respectivamente. Según sus promotores, destacan, además, la «danza de los platillos», que pone fin a la primera parte, y la actuación de los «clowns» Ribelli, en la segunda. El espectáculo se presenta en función única, a las 21,30 horas. Hay entradas desde 500 a 1.500 pesetas. Los niños menores de doce años disponen de localidades rebajadas. Venta anticipada, de 11 a 14 y de 18 a 21 h., en el **Palacio de Deportes de la Comunidad** (Av. Felipe II, 19. Metro Goya). **J. H.**

1. ¿Cómo se llama el espectáculo?
2. ¿Dónde presentan el espectáculo?
3. ¿Hasta *(until)* cuándo va a estar en Madrid el grupo?
4. De Madrid, ¿adónde va el grupo?
5. ¿Cuántos artistas hay en el grupo?
6. ¿Son todos checoslovacos?
7. ¿Que país *(country)* creen Uds. que es la U.R.S.S.? ¿Holanda? ¿Rumania? ¿Rusia?
8. ¿El espectáculo es a las nueve y media de la mañana o de la noche?
9. En España no usan dólares; usan pesetas. ¿Cuánto dinero necesitan Uds. para comprar las entradas *(buy the tickets)*?
10. ¿En qué calle está el Palacio de Deportes de la Comunidad?

UNA ACTIVIDAD ESPECIAL

Get together with two or three students and plan a party. Discuss the following:

1. How much money you have
2. When you are going to give the party
3. Where you are going to give the party
4. Whom you are going to invite
5. What you are going to eat and who is going to bring the food
6. What you are going to drink and who is going to bring the drinks
7. What you are going to do
8. Who is going to bring the records and tapes
9. What kind of music you want

Take this test. When you finish, check your answers in the answer key provided for this section in Appendix E. Then use a red pen to correct any mistakes you may have made. Ready?

LECCIÓN 1

A. Subject pronouns and present indicative of regular *-ar* verbs

Rewrite each pair of sentences to form one sentence. Use the plural forms of the subject pronouns to include both subjects.

1. Ella habla inglés y español.
   Yo *(f.)* hablo inglés y español.
2. Él trabaja en el hospital.
   Ud. trabaja en el hospital.
3. Ella llama más tarde.
   Ella llama más tarde.
4. Ella estudia ruso y chino.
   Él estudia ruso y chino.
5. Tú *(m.)* necesitas dinero.
   Yo *(f.)* necesito dinero.
6. Él desea hablar con Eva.
   Yo *(m.)* deseo hablar con Eva.

B. Gender, Part II

Use the appropriate form of the definite article (**el, la, los** or **las**) with each of the following nouns.

1. televisión
2. ciudades
3. libertad
4. programas
5. lección
6. problema
7. certidumbre
8. universidades
9. idioma
10. sistema
11. conversaciones
12. telegramas

C. Negative and interrogative sentences

Write the following dialogues in Spanish.

1. Do you speak French?
   No, I don't speak French.
2. Does he need (the) lesson 1?
   No, he doesn't need (the) lesson 1.
3. Are they calling later?
   No, they are not calling later.
4. Do you work at the university?
   No, I don't work at the university.

D. Cardinal numbers 31–1,000

In Spanish, write out the following dates and house numbers.

1. El año *(year)* 1492
2. El año 1776
3. El año 1865
4. El año 1990
5. Calle Paz, número 2552
6. Calle Bolívar, número 5123

E. Present indicative of *ser*

Write the following sentences in Spanish.

1. I am from Mexico, but they are from California.
2. Are you *(fam.)* from Chile? We are from Chile, too.
3. Mr. Vera is (a) professor.
4. Are you *(fam. pl.)* from Venezuela?

F. Just words . . .

Match the questions or statements in column A with the appropriate responses in column B.

A	B
1. Hola. ¿Está Raúl?	a. Yo también.
2. ¿Por qué? ¿Problemas económicos?	b. Habla Pedro Morales.
3. ¡Oye! ¿Qué hay de nuevo?	c. Un momento, por favor.
4. Nosotros estudiamos japonés.	d. No, sentimentales...
5. Deseo hablar con Ana.	e. Dinero.
6. ¿A qué hora regresa?	f. Estudiamos italiano y portugués.
7. ¿Quién habla?	g. María Gomez.
8. ¿Quién es?	h. No, en la universidad.
9. ¿Estudiamos esta noche?	i. Con él habla.
10. ¿Qué idiomas estudian Uds.?	j. No, mañana.
11. ¿Qué necesitan Uds.?	k. A las nueve y media.
12. ¿Trabaja en el hospital?	l. Nada.

LECCIÓN 2

A. Possession with *de*

Unscramble each set of words to form a question.

1. ¿ / de / teléfono / Nora / número / es / cuál / de / el / ?
2. ¿ / difícil / la / doctora / la / es / Peña / clase / de / ?
3. ¿ / dirección / Ernesto / de / los / de / hijos / es / cuál / la / ?

B. Agreement of adjectives, articles, and nouns

Rewrite the following sentences, making all of the nouns feminine. Change the adjectives and articles accordingly.

1. El chico es alto.
2. El doctor es español.
3. Los señores son ingleses.
4. El profesor es mexicano.
5. Los hijos de ella no son felices.

C. Possessive adjectives

Answer the following questions in the affirmative. Use the appropriate possessive adjectives.

1. ¿Ella es la esposa de Roberto?
2. ¿El profesor de Uds. es divorciado?
3. ¿Los hijos de ellos beben café?
4. ¿Los hijos de Uds. solicitan el trabajo?
5. ¿Mis estudiantes deben llenar otra solicitud?

D. Present indicative of regular *-er* and *-ir* verbs

Complete the following sentences, using the appropriate form of the verbs in the list.

vivir	escribir	decidir	leer	comer
creer	beber	aprender	recibir	deber

1. Yo no _____ sándwiches.
2. Adriana _____ en la calle Magnolia.
3. Ellos _____ el inglés, no el español.
4. ¿_____ Uds. café?
5. ¿Tú no _____ en Santa Claus?
6. Ud. _____ el anuncio en el periódico.
7. Juan y yo _____ en alemán.
8. Paco no _____ mucho dinero.
9. Yo _____ en la cafetería.
10. Ud. _____ escribir la lección.

E. Present indicative of the irregular verbs *tener* and *venir*

Complete the following sentences, using the correct forms of **venir** or **tener,** as appropriate.

1. ¿Cuántos hijos _____ Uds.?
2. Ella _____ a la universidad para estudiar.
3. Nosotros no _____ el número de teléfono de Ana.
4. El señor Rojas _____ más tarde.
5. Yo _____ dos hijos. Ellos _____ a la universidad con mi esposa.
6. Yo no _____ a solicitar trabajo.

F. Use of *tener que* + infinitive

Write the following sentences in Spanish.

1. I have to fill out the application.
2. We have to write the ad.
3. They have to work.
4. My husband has to come at eleven.

G. Just words . . . (Part I)

Complete the following sentences using appropriate words or phrases from the vocabulary list in **Lección 2.**

1. Para trabajar en la compañía, debe tener _____ de computadoras.
2. No es moreno; es _____ .
3. Tiene que llenar la _____ para el empleo.
4. La clase de la Dra. Vargas no es fácil; es muy _____ .
5. Ellos beben _____ y _____ sándwiches de _____ y queso.
6. Él _____ el anuncio en el _____ .
7. Trabajo por la mañana, pero tengo la tarde _____ .
8. Ellos no viven _____ ; viven cerca de aquí.

H. Just words . . . (Part II)

Supply the missing categories from a work application according to the information provided.

1. _____ : Marisa Cortés
2. _____ : Calle Lima, 432
3. _____ : Veinticinco años
4. _____ : Caracas, Venezuela
5. _____ : Casada
6. _____ : Profesora
7. _____ : Universidad Nacional

LECCIÓN 3

A. Expressions with *tener*

Write the following sentences in Spanish.

1. My classmates are in a hurry.
2. I'm not hungry, but I'm very thirsty.
3. Are you hot? I'm cold!
4. My friends are sleepy.
5. We are not scared.
6. You are right, Miss Peña. Mary is thirty years old.

B. The personal *a*

Form sentences, using the elements provided. Include the personal **a** when necessary.

1. yo / llevar / mis hermanos / a / la fiesta de Navidad
2. nosotros / llevar / la cerveza / a / la cafetería
3. ellos / invitar / Julio / y / su novia
4. nosotros / tener / cuatro hijos

C. Contractions

Answer the following questions, using the information provided to formulate your answers.

1. ¿De dónde vienen Uds.? (el club)
2. ¿Adónde vas? (el baile de fin de año)
3. ¿A quién llama tu novio? (el hermano de su compañero)
4. ¿A quiénes invitan ellos? (las chicas)
5. ¿De dónde vienes? (la terraza)
6. ¿A quién llevan Uds.? (las muchachas uruguayas)
7. ¿De dónde viene la novia de Roberto? (el hospital)
8. ¿De dónde es la hermana de tu novio? (la ciudad de México)

D. Present indicative of the irregular verbs *ir, dar,* and *estar*

Complete the following sentences, using the present indicative of **ir, dar,** or **estar,** as appropriate.

1. Yo no _____ a la fiesta con mis compañeros.
2. Nosotros _____ un baile aquí esta noche.
3. Mi hermana _____ en su casa.
4. ¿Dónde _____ el champán?
5. Las chicas _____ a la fiesta con sus amigos.
6. Tus primos no _____ mucho dinero.
7. Yo _____ cansado.
8. ¿Adónde _____ tus primos?
9. ¿Dónde _____ tú?
10. Yo no _____ mi número de teléfono.

E. *Ir a* + infinitive

Form sentences that tell what *is* or *is not* going to happen. Use the given elements.

MODELO: mi prima / dar / fiesta / el domingo
      Mi prima va a dar una fiesta el domingo.

1. yo / no hablar / con mi hermana
2. mis hijos / estudiar / en España
3. mi amiga / leer / el anuncio
4. ustedes / bailar / fiesta
5. tú / no vivir / cerca / de la universidad
6. nosotros / brindar / con sidra

F. Present indicative of *e:ie* stem-changing verbs

Complete the following sentences, using the present indicative of the verbs in the list, as necessary.

entender   cerrar   empezar   preferir
pensar   querer   perder   comenzar

1. Mi primo no _____ beber café.
2. Nosotros no _____ la Lección 2.
3. Ella siempre _____ mucho dinero en Las Vegas.
4. ¿ _____ tú la ventana?
5. Las clases _____ esta noche.
6. Nosotros _____ a bailar ahora.
7. Yo no _____ trabajar el domingo.
8. Luis y yo _____ beber refrescos.

G. Just words . . .

Choose the word or phrase in parentheses that best completes each sentence.

1. (Invitamos, Brindamos, Bailamos) a nuestros compañeros a la fiesta.
2. Siempre (comemos, empezamos, estamos) doce uvas a la media-noche el día de fin de año.
3. Aquí no beben (sidra, entremeses, pollo).
4. Esta orquesta es muy buena. ¡Es (magnífica, antipática, feliz)!
5. ¡Feliz año (simpático, nuevo, guapo)!
6. No bebo (coctel, refresco, Coca-Cola) porque yo no tomo be-bidas alcohólicas.
7. Aquí todos (bailamos, brindamos, estamos) con vino.
8. Tengo todos los (tocadiscos, pollos, discos) de Julio Iglesias.

Café al aire libre en la Plaza Mayor en Madrid, España.

OBJECTIVES

Pronunciation   The Spanish **b, v, d,** and **g** (before **a, o,** or **u**)

Structure   Comparison of adjectives and adverbs • Irregular comparison of adjectives and adverbs • Ordinal numbers • Months and seasons of the year • Present indicative of **o:ue** stem-changing verbs • Weather expressions

Communication   You will learn vocabulary related to family relationships and personal characteristics.

¡Vamos a Madrid!

Carol, una muchacha norteamericana, está en España. Asiste a la universidad de Salamanca y vive en una pensión cerca de la Plaza Mayor. Quiere aprender a[1] hablar español perfectamente y por eso nunca pierde la oportunidad de practicar el idioma. Ahora está en un café con dos amigos españoles.

LUIS   —Oye, Carol, ¿puedes ir con nosotros a Madrid este fin de semana?

CAROL   —No puedo; tengo que escribir muchas cartas: a mi abuela, a mi tío, a mi hermano...

LUIS   —Tú extrañas mucho a tu familia, ¿no?

CAROL   —Sí, ...especialmente a mi hermano mayor.

CARMEN   —¿Cómo es tu hermano? ¿Rubio? ¿Moreno?

CAROL   —Es rubio, delgado y de estatura mediana. Estudia medicina.

CARMEN   —¡Muy interesante! ¿Cuándo viene a España? ¿En el verano?

CAROL   —No, va a viajar a México con su esposa y sus dos hijas.

CARMEN   —¡Bah! Es casado... ¡Qué lástima! ¿No tienes otro hermano?

CAROL   —No, lo siento. ¿Quieren ver una fotografía de mis sobrinas?

CARMEN   —Sí. *(Mira la foto.)* ¡Son muy bonitas!

CAROL   —Empiezan a[1] asistir a la escuela el 15 de septiembre.

LUIS   —¡Oye! ¿Por qué no vas a Madrid con nosotros? Es más interesante que escribir cartas...

CAROL   —¿Van en coche?

LUIS   —No, preferimos ir en autobús. Es tan cómodo como el coche, no cuesta mucho y no tenemos que manejar.

CARMEN   —Pensamos ir al Museo del Prado...

CAROL   —Ah... allí están algunos de los cuadros más famosos del mundo.

LUIS   —¡Es muy interesante! ¡Y Madrid tiene unos restaurantes muy buenos! Nosotros siempre almorzamos en la Casa Botín.

CAROL   —Vale. ¡Vamos a Madrid! ¡ ...Si no llueve!

CARMEN   —No, según el pronóstico, va a hacer buen tiempo.

---

[1]The preposition **a** is used after **aprender** and **empezar** when they are followed by a verb in the infinitive.

LET'S GO TO MADRID!

Carol, an American girl, is in Spain. She attends the University of Salamanca and lives in a boarding house near the Plaza Mayor. She wants to learn to speak Spanish perfectly, and that is why she never misses the opportunity to practice the language. Now she is at a café with two Spanish friends.

L. Listen, Carol, can you go with us to Madrid this weekend?

CL. I can't; I have to write a lot of letters: to my grandmother, to my uncle, to my brother . . .

L. You miss your family very much, don't you?

CL. Yes, . . . especially my older brother.

CN. What is your brother like? Blond? Dark-haired?

CL. He's blond, slim, medium height. He is studying medicine.

CN. Very interesting! When is he coming to Spain? In the summer?

CL. No, he's going to travel to Mexico with his wife and two daughters.

CN. Bah! He's married . . . What a pity! Don't you have another brother?

CL. No, I'm sorry. Do you want to see a picture of my nieces?

CN. Yes. (*She looks at the picture.*) They're very pretty!

CL. They start attending school on September fifteenth.

L. Listen! Why don't you come to Madrid with us? It's more interesting than writing letters . . .

CL. Are you going by car?

Vocabulario

COGNADOS

el **café** café
  especialmente especially
la **familia** family
  famoso(-a) famous
la **fotografía**, la
    foto photograph, photo
  interesante interesting

la **medicina** medicine
el **museo** museum
la **oportunidad** opportunity
  perfectamente perfectly
el **restaurante** restaurant
  septiembre September

NOMBRES

la **abuela** grandmother
el **autobús**, el **ómnibus**, el **camión**
  de pasajeros (*Mex.*) bus
la **carta** letter
el **coche**, el **carro**, el **automóvil**,
  el **auto** car, automobile
el **cuadro**, la **pintura** painting,
  picture
la **escuela** school
  España Spain
el **fin de semana** weekend
el **mundo** world
la **pensión** boarding house
la **sobrina** niece
el **tiempo** weather
el **tío** uncle
el **verano** summer

VERBOS

almorzar (o:ue) to have lunch
asistir (a) to attend
costar (o:ue) to cost
extrañar, echar de menos to miss
  (feel homesick)
llover (o:ue) to rain
manejar to drive
poder (o:ue) to be able to, can
practicar to practice

ver (yo veo) to see
viajar to travel

ADJETIVOS

cómodo(-a) comfortable
este this (*m.*)
mayor older
otro(-a) other, another

OTRAS PALABRAS Y EXPRESIONES

algunos(-as) some
¡Ah! Oh!
¿cómo es... ? what is . . . like?
¿cuándo? when
de estatura mediana medium
  height
nunca never
por eso that is why
pronóstico del tiempo weather
  forecast
¡qué lástima! what a pity!
según according to
si if
va a hacer buen tiempo the
  weather is going to be good
vale okay (*Spain*)
vamos let's go

L. No, we prefer to go by bus. It's as comfortable as the car, it doesn't cost much, and we don't have to drive.

CN. We're planning on going to the Museo del Prado . . .

CL. Oh . . . some of the most famous paintings in the world are there.

L. It's very interesting! And Madrid has some very good restaurants! We always have lunch at Casa Botín.

CL. Okay. Let's go to Madrid! . . . If it doesn't rain!

CN. No, according to the forecast, the weather is going to be good.

Vocabulario adicional

bajo(-a)   short *(in height)*
No es alto; es **bajo**.

Estados Unidos   United States
Es uruguayo, pero vive en los Estados Unidos.

grande   big
Tengo un escritorio muy **grande**.

incómodo(-a)   uncomfortable
Tu silla es muy **incómoda**.

pequeño(-a)   small (size)
Es un libro muy **pequeño**.

abuela (grandmother)
suegra (mother-in-law)

abuelo (grandfather)
suegro (father-in-law)

padres (parents)

cuñado (brother-in-law)
yerno (son-in-law)

tía (aunt)
hermana
madre (mother)
mamá (mom)

padre (father)
papá (dad)
hermano

cuñada (sister-in-law)
nuera (daughter-in-law)

sobrina

sobrino (nephew)
nieto (grandson)

prima

primo

nieta (granddaughter)

¿Lo sabía Ud.... ?

- La Universidad de Salamanca es una de las universidades más antiguas y famosas del mundo. Además de los cursos regulares para españoles, ofrece muchas clases para estudiantes extranjeros *(foreign)*.
- El Museo del Prado es uno de los museos más importantes del mundo. Tiene una colección de más de dos mil cuadros y más de trescientas esculturas. Allí están representados los grandes pintores españoles— Goya, Murillo, Velázquez, El Greco y otros. También hay cuadros de otros pintores europeos famosos.

- En la mayoría de los países hispánicos, las universidades no tienen residencias universitarias *(dorms)*. Los estudiantes viven con su familia o en pensiones, donde el precio incluye el cuarto y la comida *(room and board)*.
- En los países hispánicos, hay muchos cafés al aire libre *(sidewalk cafés)*, donde la gente *(people)* conversa mientras come y toma algo *(something)*.
- En los países de habla española, la fecha *(date)* se escribe indicando primero el día y después el mes: 2—5—90 equivale al dos de mayo de 1990.

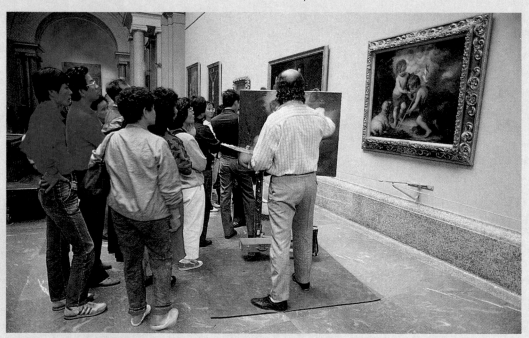

Turistas en el famoso Museo del Prado en Madrid, España.

Pronunciación

▶ *A.* The Spanish **b** and **v**

The Spanish **b** and **v** are pronounced exactly alike. Both sound like a weak English *b,* as in the word *Abe.* In Spanish, they are even weaker when pronounced between vowels. The lips don't quite touch. Never pronounce these consonants like English *v.* Listen to your teacher and repeat the following words.

vale	bien
viajar	abuela
Ana va	rubio
verano	sobrina

▶ *B.* The Spanish **d**

The Spanish **d** is slightly softer than the *d* in the English word *day.* When pronounced between two vowels or at the end of a word, it is similar to the *th* in the English word *they.* Listen to your teacher and repeat the following words.

delgado	oportunidad
de	sábado
debe	medicina
dos	Adela

▶ *C.* The Spanish **g**

1. When followed by **a, o,** or **u,** the Spanish **g** is similar to the *g* in the English word *guy.* Listen to your teacher and repeat the following words.

    delgado　　guapo　　gordo

2. When pronounced between vowels, the Spanish **g** is much softer. Repeat after your teacher.

    amigo　　pregunta　　agosto

3. In the combinations **gue** and **gui,** the **u** is silent. Repeat after your teacher.

    Guevara　　Guillermo　　alguien

Estructuras gramaticales

► *1.* Comparison of adjectives and adverbs
  (Comparación de los adjetivos y adverbios)

A. Comparisons of inequality

♦ In Spanish, the comparative of inequality of most adjectives and adverbs is formed by placing **más** *(more)* or **menos** *(less)* before the adjective or the adverb and **que** *(than)* after it.

más *(more)*		*adjective*		
	+	*or*	+	**que** *(than)*
menos *(less)*		*adverb*		

—¿Tú eres **más alta que** Ana?   *Are you taller than Ana?*
—Sí, ella es mucho **más baja que** yo.   *Yes, she is much shorter than I.*
—¿Cuántos años tiene Ana?   *How old is Ana?*
—Creo que tiene **más de** veinte años.   *I think she's over twenty years old.*

ATENCIÓN

De is used instead of **que** before a numerical expression of quantity or amount.

Tiene **más de** treinta años.   *She's over thirty years old.*
Hay **menos de** veinte estudiantes aquí.   *There are fewer than twenty students here.*

B. Comparisons of equality

♦ To form comparisons of equality with nouns, adjectives, and adverbs in Spanish, use the adjectives **tanto, -a, -os, -as,** or the adverb **tan... como.**

When comparing nouns:	*When comparing adjectives or adverbs:*
tanto (dinero) **tanta** (plata) *(as much)* **tantos** (libros) **tantas** (plumas) *(as many)*	**tan** *(as)* ⟨ bonita ⟨ tarde

—Tengo mucho trabajo.	*I have a lot of work.*
—Yo tengo **tanto** trabajo **como** tú.	*I have as much work as you (do).*
—¿Vas en autobús?	*Are you going by bus?*
—Sí, es **tan** cómodo **como** el coche.	*Yes, it's as comfortable as the car.*

C. The superlative

♦ The superlative construction is similar to the comparative. It is formed by placing the definite article before the person or thing being compared.

definite article + *(noun)* + **más** or **menos** + *adjective*

—¿Quieres ir al Museo del Prado?	*Do you want to go to the Museo del Prado?*
—Sí, allí están **los cuadros más famosos** de España.	*Yes, the most famous paintings in Spain are there.*

ATENCIÓN

Note that the Spanish **de** translates to the English **in** after a superlative.

Son los cuadros más famosos **de** España.	*They are the most famous paintings in Spain.*
Es la chica más bonita **de** la clase.	*She is the prettiest girl in the class.*

PRÁCTICA

A. Complete the following sentences, using the Spanish equivalent of the words in parentheses.

1. Tu primo es _____ tú. *(fatter than)*
   Tú eres _____ que él. *(much thinner)*
2. Mi cuñado es _____ que ella, pero estudia mucho. *(less intelligent)*
3. Mi suegra tiene _____ años, pero mi suegro tiene _____ . *(less than fifty / more than seventy)*
4. Mi abuela tiene _____ mis padres. *(as much money as)*
5. Carlos tiene _____ yo. *(as many records as)*
6. Mi sobrina es _____ su mamá. *(as tall as)*

7. Tu tía habla español _____ mi padre.   *(as well as)*
8. Aquí hay _____ allí.   *(as many girls as)*

B. Compare the people in the picture below with each other.

1. María es _____ Rosa.
2. Rosa es _____ María.
3. Carlos es _____ Rosa y María.
4. Carlos es _____ Juan.
5. Juan es _____ Carlos.
6. Juan es _____ María.
7. Juan es el _____ de todos.
8. Carlos es el _____ de todos.
9. Rosa es la _____ de todos.
10. Juan no es tan _____ Carlos.

C. Establish comparisons between the following people and things using the adjectives provided and adding any necessary words.

1. Magic Johnson / Dudley Moore   (alto)
2. Cuba / Estados Unidos   (pequeño)
3. Michael Jackson / Raymond Burr   (delgado)
4. coche / ómnibus   (cómodo)
5. Maine / Texas   (grande)

D. Be an interpreter. What are these people saying?

1. I do not have as many opportunities as you (do) to practice Spanish.
   You are right. I have more opportunities than you (do).
2. Are you taller than your sister?
   Yes, I am the tallest in the family.
3. You are the most intelligent girl in the world.
   No, you are as intelligent as I (am).

▶ *2.* Irregular comparison of adjectives and adverbs
(Comparativos irregulares de adjetivos y adverbios)

♦ Six adjectives and four adverbs have irregular comparative and superlative forms in Spanish:

Adjectives		*Adverbs*		*Comparative*		*Superlative*	
bueno	*good*	bien	*well*	mejor	*better*	el mejor	*the best*
malo	*bad*	mal	*badly*	peor	*worse*	el peor	*the worst*
mucho	*much*	mucho	*much*	más	*more*	el más	*the most*
poco	*little*	poco	*little*	menos	*less*	el menos	*the least*
grande	*big*			mayor	*older*	el mayor	*the oldest*
pequeño	*small*			menor	*younger*	el menor	*the youngest*

—Yo tengo muy **poco** dinero.   *I have very little money.*
—¡Yo tengo **menos** que tú!   *I have less than you!*

—Eva es una **buena** estu-   *Eva is a good student.*
diante.
—Sí, es **la mejor** de la clase.   *Yes, she's the best in the class.*

♦ When the adjectives **grande** and **pequeño** refer to size, the regular forms are generally used.

Tu casa es **más grande** que la   *Your house is bigger than Car-*
de Carolina.   *olina's.*

♦ When these adjectives refer to age, the irregular forms are used.

Ella es **mucho mayor** que yo.   *She is much older than I.*

♦ **Poco** refers to amount: Tengo **poco** dinero.   *I have little money.*

PRÁCTICA

A. Answer the following questions with complete sentences.

1. Mi nieta tiene veinte años y mi nieto tiene treinta. ¿Quién es mayor? ¿Quién es menor?
2. Mi yerno tiene cuarenta años y mi nuera tiene treinta y ocho. ¿Quién es menor? ¿Quién es mayor?
3. Yo tengo veinte dólares y tú tienes diecisiete. ¿Quién tiene menos dinero? ¿Quién tiene más dinero?
4. ¿Quién habla mejor el español: tú o el profesor (la profesora)?
5. Pedro tiene una «D» en inglés; Antonio tiene una «F». ¿Quién es el peor estudiante?
6. ¿Quién tiene más dinero, tú o tus padres?

B. Be an interpreter. What are these people saying?

1. Do you attend Harvard University?
   Yes, and I think (that) it is the best university in the world.
2. Are you older than your cousin?
   Yes, she is two years younger than I.
3. I have very little money.
   I have less than you (do).

▶ *3.* Ordinal numbers   *(Números ordinales)*

primero(-a)	*first*	**sexto(-a)**	*sixth*
segundo(-a)	*second*	**séptimo(-a)**	*seventh*
tercero(-a)	*third*	**octavo(-a)**	*eighth*
cuarto(-a)	*fourth*	**noveno(-a)**	*ninth*
quinto(-a)	*fifth*	**décimo(-a)**	*tenth*

◆ Ordinal numbers agree in gender and number with the nouns they modify.

el segundo **chico**   la segunda **chica**
los primeros **días**   las primeras **semanas**

◆ Ordinal numbers are seldom used after **décimo** *(tenth)*.

ATENCIÓN

The ordinal numbers **primero** and **tercero** drop the final **-o** before masculine singular nouns.

el **primer** día   el **tercer** día

PRÁCTICA

Supply the ordinal numbers that correspond to the following cardinal numbers.

1. cuatro
2. diez
3. uno
4. siete
5. dos

6. ocho
7. tres
8. nueve
9. cinco
10. seis

► *4.* **Months and seasons of the year** *(Los meses y las estaciones del año)*

El invierno

La primavera

El verano

El otoño

- ◆ To ask for the date, say:

  —¿Qué fecha es hoy?   *What's the date today?*

- ◆ When giving the date, always begin with the expression **Hoy es el...**

  —Hoy es el veinte de mayo.   *Today is May twentieth.*

- ◆ Begin with the number, followed by the preposition **de** *(of)*, then the month.

  quince de agosto   *August 15th*
  diez de septiembre   *September 10th*

—¿Qué fecha es hoy? **¿El pri-**
   mero de mayo?
—No, hoy es **el treinta de**
   abril.

What's the date today? May
first?
No, today is April thirtieth.

> ATENCIÓN

Primero is the only ordinal number used with dates.

PRÁCTICA

A. Give the Spanish equivalent of the following dates.

1. July fourth
2. October thirty-first
3. January first
4. May fifth
5. February twelfth
6. December twenty-fifth
7. March twenty-first
8. April second
9. June twentieth
10. September ninth
11. August thirteenth
12. November eleventh

B. Indicate in which season in the northern hemisphere the following months fall.

1. febrero
2. agosto
3. mayo
4. enero
5. octubre
6. julio
7. abril
8. noviembre

C. With a classmate, give the dates when the following events in your life occur.

1. your birthday
2. your mother's birthday
3. your father's birthday
4. your best friend's birthday
5. the start of classes this semester
6. the end of classes

▶ *5.* Present indicative of **o:ue** stem-changing verbs
(*Presente de indicativo de los verbos que cambian en la raíz **o:ue***)

poder *to be able to*	
puedo	podemos
puedes	podéis
puede	pueden

♦ As you saw in the dialogue for **Lección 4,** some verbs undergo a stem-change in the present indicative. For these verbs, when **o** is the last stem vowel and it is stressed, it changes to **ue.**

—¿A qué hora **vuelven** Uds.?   *At what time are you return-ing?*

—**Volvemos** a las doce.   *We'll return at twelve o'clock.*

—Entonces **almorzamos** a las doce y media.   *Then we'll have lunch at twelve-thirty.*

♦ Note that the stem vowel is not stressed in the verb forms used with **nosotros** and **vosotros;** therefore, the **o** does not change to **ue.**

♦ Other verbs that undergo the same change are:[1]

recordar *to remember*	**costar** *to cost*
encontrar *to find*	**volver** *to return*
volar *to fly*	**llover** (impersonal) *to rain*
almorzar *to have lunch*	**dormir** *to sleep*
contar *to tell, to count*	

PRÁCTICA

A. Change the verbs according to the new subjects.

1. *Yo puedo llevar los discos.* (Uds. Ella, Tú, Nosotros, Jorge)
2. *Ella no encuentra las cartas.* (Nosotros, Uds., Yo, Ellos, Tú)
3. *Mi nieto cuenta de uno a cien.* (Yo, Ellos, Uds., Tú, Nosotros)

B. Marité is talking to her roommate, who is sound asleep. Complete the story, supplying the missing (**o:ue**) verbs. Then read aloud.

MARITÉ   —¡Teresa, me voy! No _____ mis libros. ¿Dónde están? No _____ ir a mi clase sin *(without)* mis libros. ¡Oye! Hoy _____ con Pedro en la cafetería; no tengo dinero y los sándwiches en la cafetería _____ dos dólares. ¡Ay, Teresa!, hoy tengo que llamar a Marta y no _____ su número de teléfono. ¡Teresa!, ¿tú _____ el número de Marta? ¡Oye! ¿Roberto _____ a San Francisco hoy? ¿Vas al aeropuerto con él? *(Mira por la ventana.)* ¡Ay, como _____ ! Necesito tu impermeable *(raincoat).*

---

[1] For a complete list of stem-changing verbs, see Appendix B.

¡Ah!, hoy _____ a casa a las cinco. *(Abre la puerta de Teresa.)* ¡Teresa! ¡Teresa! ¿Por qué no contestas *(answer)*?

TERESA   —*(Mmm...)* Nunca _____ dormir cuando tú estás en casa.

MARITÉ   —Tú _____ mucho. No necesitas dormir más. Me voy. Nos vemos.

C. Arnaldo is very nosy and is always asking questions. We have the answers; give us his questions.

1. ¿_____? Mi tocadiscos cuesta $1.000.
2. ¿_____? Nosotros almorzamos en el restaurante.
3. ¿_____? Volvemos a casa a las cinco.
4. ¿_____? No, yo no duermo mucho.
5. ¿_____? No, no recuerdo el número de teléfono de Ana.
6. ¿_____? Vuelo a San Francisco los domingos.
7. ¿_____? No, no puedo ir a tu casa esta noche.

▶ 6. **Weather expressions**   *(Expresiones usadas para describir el tiempo)*

◆ In the following expressions, Spanish uses the verb **hacer,** *to make,* followed by a noun.

Hace (mucho) frío.	*It is (very) cold.*
Hace (mucho) calor.	*It is (very) hot.*
Hace (mucho) viento.	*It is (very) windy.*
Hace sol.	*It is sunny.*

◆ To ask about the weather say: **¿Qué tiempo hace?** *(What's the weather like?)*

—¿**Qué tiempo hace** hoy?   *What's the weather like today?*
—Hace buen (mal) tiempo.   *The weather is good (bad).*

◆ The following words used to describe the weather do not combine with **hacer;** they are impersonal verbs used only in the infinitive, present participle, past participle, and third-person singular forms of all tenses.

llover (o:ue) *(to rain)*	**Llueve.**	*It is raining.*
nevar (e:ie) *(to snow)*	**Nieva.**	*It is snowing.*
lloviznar *(to drizzle)*	**Llovizna.**	*It is drizzling.*

♦ Other weather-related words are **lluvia** *(rain)* and **niebla** *(fog).*

—¿**Hace** mucho **frío** en Bue-   *Is it very cold in Buenos*
nos Aires?   *Aires?*
—Sí, pero nunca **nieva.**   *Yes, but it never snows.*

—¿Vas a volar hoy a San   *Are you going to fly to San*
Francisco?   *Francisco today?*
—No, porque **hay niebla.**   *No, because it's foggy[1].*

PRÁCTICA

A. Study the words in the following list, then complete the
dialogues.

el **paraguas** *umbrella*   el **abrigo** *coat*
el **impermeable** *raincoat*   el **suéter** *sweater*
la **sombrilla** *parasol*

1. —¿Necesitas un paraguas?
 —Sí, porque en Oregón _____ mucho.
2. —¿No necesitas un abrigo?
 —No, porque _____ .
3. —¿Quieres un impermeable?
 —No, gracias, apenas *(hardly)* _____ .
4. —¿Por qué no quieres llevar el suéter?
 —¡Porque _____ !
5. —¿Vas a llevar la sombrilla?
 —Sí, porque _____ .
6. —¿Necesitas un suéter y un abrigo?
 —Sí, porque _____ .
7. —¿Un impermeable? ¿Por qué? ¿Llueve? ¿Llovizna?
 —No, pero _____ .
8. —¡Qué lluvia! Necesito un _____ y
 un _____ .

B. Tell us what the weather will be like at these different
locations and times.

1. Portland, Oregón–el 2 de enero
2. Anchorage, Alaska–el 25 de diciembre
3. Phoenix, Arizona–el 13 de agosto
4. Londres *(London)*–el 5 de febrero
5. Chicago–el 6 de marzo

---

[1] **hay niebla** = *it's foggy.*

¡A ver cuánto aprendió!

A. ¡Conversemos!

Reread the dialogues in this lesson and be ready to discuss the following.

1. ¿Carol es española?
2. ¿Dónde estudia?
3. ¿Dónde vive?
4. ¿Por qué no puede ir a Madrid este fin de semana?
5. ¿Cómo es el hermano de Carol?
6. ¿Va a venir a España?
7. ¿Con quién va a viajar a México?
8. ¿Tiene Carol otros hermanos?
9. ¿Cuándo empiezan a asistir a la escuela las sobrinas de Carol?
10. Según Luis, ¿por qué es mejor viajar en autobús?
11. ¿Dónde están algunos de los cuadros más famosos del mundo?
12. ¿Dónde almuerzan casi siempre Luis y Carmen?
13. Si llueve, ¿va a ir Carol a Madrid?
14. Según el pronóstico, ¿qué tiempo va a hacer el sábado?

B. ¡Repase el vocabulario!

Match the questions in column A with the answers in column B; then read them aloud.

A	B
1. ¿Dónde está tu familia?	a. No, es muy fea.
2. ¿Qué estudias?	b. Sí, es mi cuñada.
3. ¿Estás incómoda?	c. El 3 de septiembre.
4. ¿Vamos al museo mañana?	d. Medicina.
5. ¿Practicas el español?	e. El 21 de marzo.
6. ¿Es bonita?	f. No, es mi sobrina.
7. ¿No tienen dinero para ir a un hotel?	g. Sí, ¡qué lástima!
8. ¿Es la hermana de tu esposo?	h. ¡Vale!
9. ¿Es tu prima?	i. Sí, es el hijo de mi hija.
10. ¿Van en ómnibus?	j. En los Estados Unidos.
11. ¿Cuándo es tu cumpleaños?	k. No, por eso van a una pensión.
12. ¿Cuándo empieza la primavera?	l. No, vamos en coche.
13. ¿Es tu nieto?	m. Sí, mi silla es muy pequeña.
14. ¿Van a perder la oportunidad de ir a México?	n. Sí, nunca pierdo la oportunidad.
15. ¿Es gorda?	o. No, es delgada.

C. Situaciones

1. Describe the weather to a friend.
2. Tell a Spanish-speaking friend you don't want to miss the opportunity to practice Spanish.
3. Someone asks about your weekend plans. Tell him or her what they are.
4. Tell a Spanish-speaking friend about some important dates in the United States.
5. Ask a friend if he or she wants to see some pictures of your family.

Para escribir

Write a composition describing each member of your family. Include the following information for each person:

- color of hair and complexion
- other personal characteristics (Establish comparisons between the other members of your family and yourself.)
- age
- place of birth and current residence
- place of employment or study
- marital status and number of children

REAL BALLET
NACIONAL DE ESPAÑA

En la vida real

ENTREVISTA

Choose a partner, then interview each other using the **tú** form.

Pregúntele a su compañero(-a) de clase...

1. ...si es más bajo(-a) que su papá.
2. ...si es mayor o menor que el profesor (la profesora).
3. ...si su mamá es alta, baja o de estatura mediana.
4. ...si la clase de español es la más interesante que tiene.
5. ...si habla español perfectamente.
6. ...si este verano va a viajar o piensa estudiar o trabajar.
7. ...qué estación del año prefiere.
8. ...cuál cree que es la ciudad más bonita de los Estados Unidos.
9. ...dónde piensa ir este fin de semana.
10. ...cuándo es su cumpleaños.

OBJETIVOS

You and a classmate have a goal: to someday speak Spanish like a native, and to learn as much as possible about the culture of Spanish-speaking countries. Come up with a list of things you are going to do to reach that goal.

Some additional words and phrases you may want to include:

escuchar   *(to listen to)* ⎱ **canciones** *(songs)*
                            programas de radio
                            las cintas del laboratorio de lenguas

visitar países de habla hispana   *to visit Spanish-speaking countries*
revistas *magazines*
películas españolas y latinoamericanas   *Spanish and Latin American movies*
tener correspondencia *to correspond*
gente *people*

¿QUÉ TIEMPO HACE?

Based on the information provided in the weather forecast, answer the following questions.

Pronóstico general del estado del tiempo

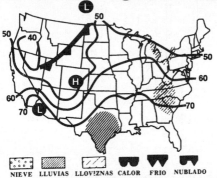

NIEVE LLUVIAS LLOVIZNAS CALOR FRIO NUBLADO

ESTADO GENERAL DEL TIEMPO: Pronóstico para Miami y sus vecindades.

CIELOS: Parcialmente nublados con turbonadas con un 20 por ciento de probabilidades de lluvias. Para el sábado el cielo estará soleado con un 30 por ciento de posibilidades de lluvias.

TEMPERATURAS: Para esta noche las bajas estarán por encima de los 70 grados y las altas para el sábado estarán por encima de los 90 grados.

VIENTOS: Los vientos para ambos días serán del Este a razón de 10 a 15 millas por hora.

AGUAS: Desde Júpiter hasta Cayo Largo incluyendo las Bahamas las aguas estarán ligeramente picadas con vientos del Este a razón de 10 a 15 nudos y olas de 2 a 5 pies de altura. Las aguas estarán moderadamente picadas en la costa.

MAREAS: Las mareas a la entrada de la bahía de Miami, serán:

ALTAS: 12:09 a.m. y 6:45 p.m.
BAJAS: 5:45 a.m. y 6:14 p.m.

Temperaturas mínimas (máximas entre paréntesis) en las siguientes ciudades:

Atlanta 66 (81)	Los Angeles 63 (73)
Boston 52 (70)	Miami 77 (88)
Chicago 64 (79)	Minneapolis 58 (80)
Cleveland 64 (75)	New Orleans 75 (91)
Dallas 75 (91)	New York 57 (72)
Denver 51 (90)	Phoenix 74 (108)
Duluth 53 (71)	St. Louis 68 (85)
Houston 76 (89)	San Francisco 50 (74)
Jacksonville 75 (87)	Seattle 47 (63)
Kansas City 66 (85)	Washington 62 (78).
Little Rock 70 (89)	

Relación de las temperaturas, mínimas (máximas entre paréntesis), en grados centígrados registradas en las siguientes capitales:

Amsterdam 10 (18)	Miami 27 (29)
Asunción 9 (24)	Montevideo 5 (18)
Atenas 19 (28)	Nueva York 12 (21)
Berlín 10 (15)	Panamá 22 (29)
Bonn 8 (15)	París 7 (15)
Bogotá 7 (18)	Quito 8 (17)
Bruselas 7 (18)	Rio de Janeiro 19 (31)
Buenos Aires 4 (17)	Roma 20 (25)
Caracas 17 (23)	San José 17 (23)
Ginebra 7 (14)	San Juan 25 (32)
Guatemala 15 (25)	San Salvador 19 (30)
La Paz 5 (14)	Santo Domingo 22 (31)
Lima 12 (19)	Santiago de Chile 6 (20)
Lisboa 16 (28)	Tegucigalpa 16 (28)
Londres 9 (15)	Tokio 18 (24)
Los Angeles 15 (24)	Viena 10 (15)
Madrid 15 (24)	Washington 13 (24)
México 12 (23)	

1. ¿En qué estado está lloviendo?
2. ¿Qué necesitan usar las personas que viven allí?
3. ¿Está lloviznando en la Florida?
4. ¿Dónde está lloviznando?
5. ¿En qué estado hace frío hoy?
6. ¿En qué ciudad de los Estados Unidos hace más calor hoy?
7. ¿En qué ciudad hace más frío hoy?
8. ¿Hay nieve en Boston hoy?
9. ¿Qué por ciento (*percent*) de probabilidades de lluvia tenemos para hoy en Miami?
10. ¿Va a hacer calor o frío en Miami el sábado?
11. ¿Va a hacer mucho viento hoy?
12. ¿Cuál va a ser la temperatura en la capital de Argentina?

ÁRBOL GENEALÓGICO

Prepare your family tree and call it «**Mi árbol genealógico**». Be sure to include each member's relationship to you.

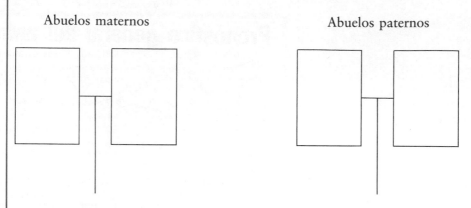

Abuelos maternos   Abuelos paternos

UNA ACTIVIDAD ESPECIAL

Bring pictures of your relatives to class and tell a classmate who they are, giving information about each one. Ask each other any pertinent questions.

Y ahora, *¡vamos a leer!*

¡Vamos a Madrid!

Vista nocturna de la hermosa fuente de La Cibeles, en la plaza del mismo nombre en Madrid, España.

who

with brown eyes

Cindy y Robin son dos chicas norteamericanas que° estudian medicina en la Universidad de Barcelona. Cindy tiene veinte años; es una chica alta, rubia y muy simpática. Robin tiene diecinueve años; es morena, de ojos castaños° y es más alta y más delgada que Cindy. Las dos chicas son muy inteligentes y estudian mucho.

Este fin de semana Robin y Cindy piensan ir a Madrid porque quieren visitar a unos amigos que viven allí. Cindy quiere ir en automóvil pero Robin piensa que es mejor ir en autobús porque es tan cómodo como el coche.

El sábado van a ir al Museo del Prado porque Robin quiere ver los cuadros de Goya y de Velázquez que tienen allí. Por la noche van a ir a un club a bailar. El domingo van a visitar la ciudad de Toledo, y por la noche Cindy quiere comer en un restaurante de la Gran Vía, la famosa calle de Madrid.

to buy
next week

Hoy Robin va a comprar° unos discos de música española para su hermano porque la próxima semana° es su cumpleaños.

¡A ver cuánto recuerda!

1. ¿De dónde son Cindy y Robin?
2. ¿A qué universidad asisten?
3. ¿Cómo es Cindy?
4. ¿Cómo es Robin?
5. ¿Quién es mayor?
6. ¿Adónde piensan ir este fin de semana? ¿Por qué?
7. ¿Por qué piensa Robin que es mejor ir en autobús?
8. ¿Qué pintores (painters) españoles prefiere Robin?
9. ¿Adónde van a ir el domingo?
10. ¿Qué es la Gran Vía?
11. ¿Qué va a comprar Robin?
12. ¿Quién celebra su cumpleaños la semana próxima?

España

PANORAMA HISPÁNICO

España (II)

3

- El gobierno de España es una monarquía constitucional similar a la de Gran Bretaña, pero el rey *(king)* Juan Carlos tiene más poder *(power)* que Isabel II de Inglaterra porque es el jefe supremo de las fuerzas armadas.

- Una de las costumbres más populares de España es la de comer «tapas» en los bares y restaurantes. Las tapas son platos típicos de España, servidos como aperitivos en un café, bar o restaurante.

- Algunos de los pintores más famosos del mundo son españoles: el Greco, Velázquez, Picasso, Miró y Dalí.

- Julio Iglesias es uno de los cantantes españoles de más fama internacional en la actualidad. Es muy popular en los Estados Unidos, donde hay varios de sus discos en inglés.

- El día siete de julio se celebra en Pamplona la fiesta de San Fermín. Ese día sueltan a los toros *(turn the bulls loose)* y los muchachos corren delante de ellos hasta llegar a la plaza de toros para la corrida.

- Entre los deportes *(sports)* más populares de España están el fútbol, el jai-alai y el ciclismo.

Esta joven pareja saborea unas «tapas» en un bar de Málaga. Las tapas son pequeñas porciones de las diferentes comidas típicas de España. Pueden ser un pedazo de tortilla a la española, pollo, camarones, aceitunas, etc. Generalmente las tapas se sirven en los bares por la tarde. ¿Qué platos típicos españoles ha probado Ud.?

Juan Carlos de Borbón, rey de España. España es una monarquía constitucional como Inglaterra. Actualmente, el jefe de gobierno es el líder socialista Felipe González, que aparece en la foto junto al rey. ¿Quién es el jefe de gobierno en Inglaterra?

La fundación Juan Miró está en un edificio diseñado por el arquitecto catalán Josep Lleas Sert, en el Parque de Montjuic. Aquí está el Centro de Estudios de Artes Contemporáneas, establecido por Miró. La fundación contiene muchas de las pinturas y esculturas del gran artista. ¿Quiénes son sus pintores favoritos?

◀ Julio Iglesias vio terminada
su carrera de futbolista al
sufrir un accidente. Entonces
se decidió por la música, y se
convirtió en el cantante español de mayor éxito en el
mundo. Iglesias ha vendido
más de cien millones de discos y, en 1987, recibió el
premio Grammy como el
mejor cantante de música
popular en español. ¿Tiene
Ud. discos de música española? ¿Cuáles?

▶ Esta pareja está comiendo una
riquísima paella en un pueblo cerca
de Barcelona. La paella es un plato
típico de la cocina española. Se
come en todas las regiones de España, pero su preparación varía de
región a región. La más famosa es
la paella valenciana, que es de
mariscos. ¿Puede mencionar Ud.
algunos otros platos típicos de la
comida española?

La celebración del Corpus Christi data de la Edad Media. Esta fiesta religiosa se celebra con gran esplendor durante el mes de mayo con procesiones, corridas de toros y actuaciones de coros. La fiesta comienza el día 15 con la salida de la procesión de la Catedral y termina el día 18. El primer Corpus Christi se celebró en Toledo. ¿Qué fiestas religiosas se celebran en los Estados Unidos?

▲ El Ballet Real aparece aquí en los jardines del Generalife, en Granada. El repertorio del Ballet Real incluye bailes clásicos y folklóricos. Aquí vemos una representación del baile flamenco, típico del Sur de España. ¿Qué tipos de bailes son populares en los Estados Unidos?

◄ La corrida de toros es uno de los espectáculos más populares de España y tiene orígenes antiquísimos. La típica corrida tiene lugar los domingos por la tarde en estadios especiales llamados «plazas de toros», de las cuales hay más de 400 en España. ¿Sabe Ud. en qué país cerca de los Estados Unidos tienen corridas de toros?

Vista panorámica de Lima, la capital del Perú.

OBJECTIVES

Pronunciation   The Spanish **p, t, c,** and **q**

Structure   Present indicative of **e:i** stem-changing verbs •
Pronouns as objects of prepositions • Affirmative
and negative expressions • Present progressive •
Direct object pronouns

Communication   You will learn vocabulary related to travel: going
through customs, obtaining information, and getting a
room at a hotel.

Un viaje al Perú

Teresa, una chica mexicana, va a pasar sus vacaciones en el Perú. Ella acaba de llegar a Lima, donde piensa pasar unos días antes de ir a Machu Picchu para visitar las famosas ruinas de los Incas. Ahora está en el aeropuerto, que es grande y muy moderno. Teresa muestra su pasaporte y luego pasa por la aduana.

En la aduana, Teresa está hablando con el inspector.

INSPECTOR —Debe abrir sus maletas. ¿Tiene Ud. algo que declarar?

TERESA —Tengo una cámara fotográfica y una grabadora. Nada más.

INSPECTOR —Muy bien. Todo está en regla.

TERESA —¿Hay alguna oficina de turismo por aquí?

INSPECTOR —Sí, está allí, a la izquierda.

En el aeropuerto venden objetos de oro y de plata, y Teresa compra algunos para su familia.

En la oficina de turismo, Teresa pide información.

TERESA —Buenos días, señor. ¿Tiene Ud. una lista de hoteles y pensiones?

EMPLEADO —Sí, señorita. También tenemos una lista de restaurantes y lugares de interés. Aquí las tiene.

TERESA —Gracias. ¿Dónde puedo tomar un taxi?

EMPLEADO —La segunda puerta a la derecha. También hay un autobús que la lleva al centro.

Teresa toma el autobús y va a un hotel del centro, donde pide una habitación.

TERESA —Necesito una habitación sencilla con baño privado, por favor. No tengo reservación.

EMPLEADO —Tenemos una con vista a la calle que cuesta dos mil intis[1] por día. También hay otra interior en el tercer piso por mil quinientos intis.

TERESA —Son muy caras para mí. ¿No tiene alguna habitación más barata?

EMPLEADO —No, no hay ninguna. En diciembre hay muy pocos cuartos libres.

TERESA —Prefiero el cuarto interior. ¿Aceptan cheques de viajero?

EMPLEADO —Sí, señorita, los aceptamos, y también aceptamos tarjetas de crédito.

---

[1] Peruvian currency. This exchange rate is subject to change.

A Trip to Peru

Teresa, a Mexican girl, is going to spend her vacation in Peru. She has just arrived in Lima, where she's planning to spend a few days before going to Machu Picchu to visit the famous Incan ruins. She is now at the airport, which is big and very modern. Teresa shows her passport and then goes through customs.

At the customs desk, Teresa is talking with the inspector.

I. You must open your suitcases. Do you have anything to declare?

T. I have a camera and a tape recorder. Nothing else.

I. Very well. Everything is in order.

T. Is there a tourist office near here?

I. Yes, it's over there, to the left.

At the airport they sell gold and silver objects, and Teresa buys some for her family.

At the tourist office, Teresa asks for information.

T. Good morning, sir. Do you have a list of hotels and boarding houses?

E. Yes, Miss. We also have a list of restaurants and places of interest. Here they are.

T. Thanks. Where can I get a taxi?

E. The second door on the right. There is also a bus that takes you downtown.

Teresa takes the bus and goes to a hotel downtown, where she asks for a room.

T. I need a single room with a private bathroom, please. I don't have a reservation.

E. We have one overlooking the street that costs two thousand intis per

TERESA —¿A cómo está el cambio de moneda?
EMPLEADO —Mil novecientos intis por dólar.

Teresa firma el registro.

TERESA —¿Puede alguien llevar mis maletas al cuarto, por favor?
EMPLEADO —Sí, en seguida viene el botones a llevarlas. Aquí tiene la llave.
TERESA —Quiero cenar en mi habitación. ¿Hasta qué hora sirven la cena?
EMPLEADO —La sirven hasta las once.

Vocabulario

COGNADOS

el **aeropuerto** airport
el **dólar** dollar
el **hotel** hotel
la **información** information
el (la) **inspector(a)** inspector
el **interés** interest
interior interior
la **lista** list
moderno(-a) modern
el **objeto** object

la **oficina** office
el **pasaporte** passport
privado(-a) private
el **registro** register
la **reserva,** la **reservación** reservation
las **ruinas** ruins
el **taxi** taxi
las **vacaciones**[1] vacation

NOMBRES

la **aduana** customs
el **baño,** el **cuarto de baño** bathroom
el **botones** bellhop
la **cámara fotográfica** camera
la **cena** dinner, supper
el **centro** downtown (area)
el **cuarto,** la **habitación** room
el **cheque de viajero** traveler's check
el (la) **empleado(-a)** clerk
la **grabadora** tape recorder
el **lugar** place
la **llave** key
la **maleta,** la **valija** suitcase

la **oficina de turismo** tourist office
el **oro** gold
el **piso** floor
la **plata** silver
la **tarjeta de crédito** credit card

VERBOS

aceptar to accept
cenar to have dinner, supper
comprar to buy
declarar to declare
firmar to sign
llegar to arrive
mostrar (o:ue), enseñar to show
pasar to spend (time)

---

[1] **Vacaciones** is always used in the plural form in Spanish.

day. There is also an interior one on the third floor for fifteen hundred intis.

T. They are very expensive for me. Don't you have any cheaper rooms?

E. No, there aren't any. In December there are few vacant rooms.

T. I prefer the interior room. Do you accept traveler's checks?

E. Yes, Miss, we accept them, and we also accept credit cards.

T. What is the exchange rate?

E. One thousand nine hundred intis per dollar.

Teresa signs the register.

T. Can someone take my suitcases to the room, please?

E. Yes, the bellhop will come to take them right away. Here is the key.

T. I want to have dinner in my room. Until what time do they serve dinner?

E. They serve it until eleven o'clock.

pasar (por)   to go through, by
pedir (e:i)   to ask for, request
servir (e:i)   to serve
tomar   to take
visitar   to visit

ADJETIVOS

barato(-a)   inexpensive, cheap
caro(-a)   expensive
libre   vacant, free
pocos(-as)   few
sencillo(-a)   single, simple

OTRAS PALABRAS Y EXPRESIONES

¿A cómo está el cambio de moneda?   What is the exchange rate?
acabar de + *infinitive*   to have just + *past participle*

a la izquierda   to the left
algo   something, anything
antes (de)   before
aquí las tiene...   here you have them, here they are
con vista a   overlooking
en seguida   right away
hasta   until
luego   then, afterwards
mí   me
nada más   nothing else
para   in order to
por   per, for
por aquí   around here
que   which
tener algo que declarar   to have something to declare
todo está en regla   everything is in order
unos días   a few days

Vocabulario adicional

el **almuerzo**   lunch
El **almuerzo**[1] es a las doce.

el **ascensor**, el **elevador**   elevator
¿Hay un **ascensor** aquí?

cancelar   to cancel
Voy a **cancelar** las reservaciones.

confirmar   to confirm
Deseo **confirmar** la reservación.

el **desayuno**   breakfast
Servimos el **desayuno**[1] a las siete.

doble   double
Quiero una habitación **doble**

la **embajada**   embassy
¿Dónde está la **embajada** norteamericana?

el **jabón**   soap
¿Hay **jabón** en el baño?

la **lista de espera**   waiting list
Estoy en **la lista de espera**.

servicio de habitación   room service
El hotel no tiene **servicio de habitación**.

la **tarjeta de turista**   tourist card
Si Ud. es argentino, necesita una **tarjeta de turista**.

la **toalla**   towel
Necesito el **jabón** y la **toalla**.

---

[1] In Spanish, the definite article is used with the words **almuerzo, desayuno,** and **cena.**

¿Lo sabía Ud.... ?

- Lima, la capital del Perú, es una ciudad de contrastes. Junto a *(Next to)* edificios *(buildings)* muy modernos hay otros de arquitectura colonial. El 25% de la población es de origen indio.
- La moneda *(currency)* que utilizan con más frecuencia los latinoamericanos cuando viajan fuera de su país es el dólar norteamericano. Esto se debe a que *(due to the fact that)* es fácil cambiar dólares en la mayoría de los bancos principales de los países hispanoamericanos.

Guardia frente al Palacio Presidencial, en Lima, Perú. El cambio de la guardia es un espectáculo turístico.

Pronunciación

▶ *A.* The Spanish **p**

The Spanish **p** is pronounced like the English *p* as in the word *sparks*, but with no expulsion of air. Listen to your teacher and repeat the following words.

aeropuerto	para	comprar
Perú	poder	pasaje
pagar	puerta	empleado

▶ *B.* The Spanish **t**

The Spanish **t** is pronounced by placing the tongue against the upper teeth, as in the English word *stop*. Listen to your teacher and repeat the following words.

Teresa	aeropuerto	turista
tren	tengo	maleta
restaurante	agente	puerta

▶ *C.* The Spanish **c**

The Spanish sound for the letter c in the combinations **ca, co,** and **cu** is /k/, pronounced as in the English word *scar*, but with no expulsion of air. Listen to your teacher and repeat the following words.

comprar	capital	clase
cuánto	como	comprobante
cuándo	con	documento

▶ *D.* The Spanish **q**

The Spanish **q** is always followed by a **u**; it is pronounced like the *c* in the English word *come,* but without any expulsion of air. Listen to your teacher and repeat the following words.

Quintana	Roque	quien
que	quiere	equipaje
aquí	queso	Quevedo

Estructuras gramaticales

▶ *1.* Present indicative of **e:i** stem-changing verbs
*(Presente de indicativo de los verbos que cambian en la raíz **e:i**)*

servir	*to serve*
sirvo	servimos
sirves	servís
sirve	sirven

◆ Some **-ir** verbs undergo a special stem-change in the present indicative. For these verbs, when **e** is the last stem vowel and it is stressed, it changes to **i**.

—¿Qué **sirven** Uds. en sus fiestas?   *What do you serve at your parties?*

—**Servimos** champán.   *We serve champagne.*

◆ Note that the stem vowel is not stressed in the **nosotros** and **vosotros** verb forms; therefore, the **e** does not change to **i**.

◆ Other verbs[1] that undergo the same change are:

pedir	*to ask for, to request, to order*	**seguir**	*to follow, to continue*
decir	*to say, to tell*	**conseguir**	*to get, to obtain*

◆ The verb **decir** undergoes the same change, but in addition it has an irregular first-person singular form: **yo digo.**

◆ Note that in the present tense **seguir** and **conseguir** drop the **u** before **a** or **o**: **yo sigo, yo consigo.**

PRÁCTICA

A. In the following conversations the verbs are missing. Provide them.

1. decir
—¿Tú _____ que Roberto es feo?
—Sí, yo _____ que es feo, pero Carmen _____ que es guapo.

2. servir
—¿Qué _____ Uds. en sus fiestas?
— _____ entremeses y refrescos. ¿Qué _____ tú?
—Yo _____ sándwiches y cerveza.

3. pedir
—¿Qué _____ Uds. cuando van a un restaurante mexicano?
—Yo _____ tacos y Ernesto _____ enchiladas.

4. conseguir
—Yo no _____ trabajo.
—Tú no _____ trabajo porque no hablas dos idiomas.

B. By combining the words in the three columns (one word for each column starting with A), form complete sentences. Use each verb in column B at least once.

---
[1] For a complete list of stem-changing verbs, see Appendix B.

A	**B**	**C**
yo	decir	el desayuno
el inspector	servir	habitaciones
nosotros	pedir	que necesitamos
Ana y Eva	conseguir	cheques de
mis padres	seguir	viajero
tú		la solicitud
la recepcionista		aduana
		que debo abrir las
		maletas
		jabón y toalla
		al botones
		un cuarto con baño
		privado
		la llave del cuarto
		pollo y refrescos

▶ *2.* **Pronouns as objects of prepositions** *(Pronombres usados como objetos de preposición)*

Singular		**Plural**	
mí	*me*	**nosotros(-as)**	*us*
ti	*you* (fam.)	**vosotros(-as)**	*you* (fam., pl.)
Ud.	*you* (form.)	**Uds.**	*you* (form., pl.)
él	*him*	**ellos**	*them* (m.)
ella	*her*	**ellas**	*them* (f.)

—¿Hablan de **mí**?   *Are you talking about me?*

—No, no hablamos de **ti**.   *No, we are not talking about you.*

—¿Vas **conmigo** o con Carlos?   *Are you going with me or with Carlos?*

—No voy **contigo**; voy **con él**.   *I'm not going with you; I'm going with him.*

- The object of a preposition is the noun or pronoun which immediately follows it: **La fiesta es** *para María/ella.* **Ellos van** *con nosotros.*

- In Spanish, the pronouns that function as objects of prepositions are the same as the subject pronouns, except for the first- and second-person singular forms, **mí** and **ti**. The object pronoun **mí** has a written accent to distinguish it from the possessive pronoun **mi** *(my)*.

◆ When used with the preposition **con,** the first- and second-person singular forms become **conmigo** *(with me)* and **contigo** *(with you),* respectively.

PRÁCTICA

You and your friends are going on a trip and want to buy gifts to bring home. Complete the sentences below, indicating who is traveling with whom or whom the gifts are for.

1. Carlos va _____ *(with me)* y tú vas _____ *(with them).*
2. Yo voy _____ *(with you),* Paquito.
3. Las chicas van _____ *(with you),* señoras.
4. Las toallas no son para _____ *(me),* Anita; son para _____ *(you).*
5. La grabadora es para _____ *(him)* y la cámara fotográfica es para _____ *(us).*
6. Las maletas son para _____ *(her).*

▶ **3. Affirmative and negative expressions** *(Expresiones afirmativas y negativas)*

Affirmative		**Negative**	
algo	*something, anything*	**nada**	*nothing, not anything*
alguien	*someone, somebody, anyone*	**nadie**	*nobody, no one, not anyone*
alguno(-a), algún	*any, some*	**ninguno(-a), ningún**	*no,[1] none, not any*
siempre	*always*	**nunca, jamás**	*never*
también	*also, too*	**tampoco**	*neither, not either*
o... o	*either . . . or*	**ni... ni**	*neither . . . nor*

—¿Tiene **algo** que declarar?	*Do you have anything to declare?*
—No, no tengo **nada.**	*No, I don't have anything.*
—¿Quieren comprar **algunos** objetos?	*Do you want to buy some objects?*
—No, no queremos comprar **ningún** objeto.	*No, we don't want to buy any objects.*

---

[1] In Spanish, **no** is never used as an adjective.

♦ **Alguno** and **ninguno** drop the -o before a masculine singular noun: *algún* niño; *ningún* niño; but *alguna* niña; *ninguna* niña.

ATENCIÓN

Note that **alguno(-a)** may be used in the plural forms, but **ninguno(-a)** is not pluralized.

♦ Spanish sentences frequently use a double negative form to express a degree of negation: the adverb **no** is placed before the verb and the second negative word either follows the verb or appears at the end of the sentence. If, however, the negative word precedes the verb, **no** is never used.

No hablo español **nunca.**
or: **Nunca** hablo español. } *I never speak Spanish.*

No compro **nada nunca.**
or: **Nunca** compro **nada.** } *I never buy anything.*

♦ Note that Spanish often uses several negatives in one sentence.

Yo **no** quiero **nada tampoco.**   *I don't want anything either.*

PRÁCTICA

A. Oscar always contradicts everybody. Play the role of Oscar.

MODELO: Ana necesita *algo*.
*Ana no necesita **nada.***

1. Raquel siempre viaja en el verano.
2. Ana va con Raquel y Jorge va con ella también.
3. Siempre piden habitaciones dobles.
4. Siempre compran algo cuando viajan.
5. Siempre compran algunos objetos de oro.
6. Cenan en la pensión o en la cafetería.
7. Siempre hay alguien en su casa.
8. El esposo de Luisa nunca habla con nadie.

B. Answer these personal questions negatively, using the expressions you have just learned.

1. ¿Quiere Ud. viajar a Bolivia o a Nicaragua?
2. ¿Tiene Ud. algunos amigos rusos?
3. Yo no hablo chino. ¿Y Ud.?
4. ¿Siempre va Ud. a la universidad por la noche?
5. ¿Hay alguien en su casa ahora?
6. ¿Necesita Ud. algo?

C. Be an interpreter. What are these people saying?

1. Do you need anything else?
   No, I do not need anything else.
2. There aren't any vacant rooms in the hotel.
   Yes, there are some, but they are very expensive.
3. Are there any Mexican employees at the American embassy?
   Yes, there are some.
4. I never serve wine.
   I never serve wine, either. I always serve soda or coffee.

► 4. Present progressive   (*Estar* + *gerundio*)

♦ The present progressive describes an action that is in progress. It is formed with the present tense of **estar** and the **gerundio** (equivalent to the English *-ing* form) of the verb.

GERUNDIO

hablar	comer	escribir
habl **-ando**	com **-iendo**	escrib **-iendo**
(speaking)	*(eating)*	*(wriiing)*

Yo **estoy comiendo**
I   am   eating.

| —¿**Estás estudiando?** | *Are you studying?* |
| —No, **estoy escribiendo** una carta. | *No, I am writing a letter.* |

♦ The following forms are irregular:

pedir *(to ask for, request):* **pidiendo**
decir *(to say, tell):* **diciendo**
servir *(to serve):* **sirviendo**
dormir *(to sleep):* **durmiendo**
traer *(to bring):* **trayendo**
leer *(to read):* **leyendo**

♦ Note that as in **traer** and **leer,** the **i** of **-iendo** becomes **y** between vowels.

ATENCIÓN

In Spanish, the present progressive is *never* used to indicate a future action. Some verbs, such as **ser, estar, ir,** and **venir,** are rarely used in the progressive construction.

PRÁCTICA

A. Change the verbs according to the new subjects.

1. *Él* está estudiando. (Tú, Julia y Pedro, Yo, Nosotras)
2. *Yo* estoy leyendo un libro. (Tú y yo, Ella, Tú, Uds.)
3. *Tú* no estás pidiendo los comprobantes. (Ud., Nosotros, Ellas, Yo)

B. Complete the following dialogues, using the present progressive of the verbs given.

1. comer —¿Qué _____ tú?
   —Yo _____ ensalada.
2. leer —¿Qué libro _____ Uds.?
   — _____ *Don Quijote.*
3. servir —¿Qué _____ Uds.?
   —Yo _____ refrescos y Luisa _____ cerveza.
4. decir —¿Qué _____ Juan Carlos?
   —Nada.
5. estudiar —¿Carlos _____ ?
   dormir —No, _____ .

► **5. Direct object pronouns** *(Pronombres usados como complemento directo)*

A. The direct object

♦ In addition to a subject, most sentences have an object which directly receives the action of the verb.

Ellos compran el libro.
  S.   V.   D.O.

In the sentence above, the subject (**Ellos**) performs the action, while **el libro,** the direct object, directly receives the action of the verb. The direct object of a sentence may be either a person or a thing.

♦ The direct object can be easily identified as the answer to the questions *whom?* and *what?* about what the subject is doing.

Ellos compran **el libro.**   *(What are they buying?)*
Pepe llama **a su primo.**   *(Whom is he calling?)*

♦ Direct object pronouns may be used in place of the direct object.

B. Forms of the direct object pronouns

	Singular		*Plural*
me	*me*	nos	*us*
te	*you* (fam.)	os	*you* (fam.)
lo	{ *you* (form., m.) *him, it* (m.)	los	{ *you* (form., m.) *them* (m.)
la	{ *you* (form., f.) *her, it* (f.)	las	{ *you* (form., f.) *them* (f.)

—¿Tiene **la** llave?   *Do you have the key?*
—Sí,   **la**   tengo.   *Yes, I have it.*

—¿Compra Ud. **los** pasajes?   *Are you buying the tickets?*
—Sí   **los**   compro.   *Yes, I'm buying them.*

C. Position of direct object pronouns

♦ In Spanish, object pronouns are normally placed before a conjugated verb.

          D.O.   D.O.
Ellos sirven **la cena.**   *They serve dinner.*
Ellos   **la**   sirven.   *They serve it.*

♦ In negative sentences, the **no** must precede the object pronoun.

          D.O.   D.O.
Ellos sirven **la cena.**   *They serve dinner.*
Ellos   **la**   sirven.   *They serve it.*
Ellos **no**   **la**   sirven.   *They don't serve it.*

♦ When an infinitive is used with a conjugated verb, the direct object pronoun may either be attached to the infinitive or placed before the conjugated verb. The same principle applies with the present participle in progressive constructions.

Puedo firmar**lo.**   } *I can sign it.*
Lo puedo firmar.

Estoy leyéndo**lo.**   } *I am reading it.*
Lo estoy leyendo.

ATENCIÓN

When a direct object pronoun is attached to a present participle (**leyéndolo, firmándola**), an accent mark is added to maintain the correct stress.

PRÁCTICA

A. You and your friends are planning a party. Volunteer to do all of the following tasks.

    MODELO: ¿Quién invita a las chicas?
               Yo *las invito*.

    1. ¿Quién llama a los muchachos?
    2. ¿Quién compra las bebidas?
    3. ¿Quién va a traer los discos?
    4. ¿Quién consigue el tocadiscos?
    5. ¿Quién trae a mi compañera?
    6. ¿Quién está preparando *(preparing)* los entremeses?
    7. ¿Quién va a traer a Luis?
    8. ¿Quién lleva a las chicas a su casa?

B. You and some friends will be traveling in Mexico shortly. Answer another friend's questions about your arrangements. Use direct object pronouns in your answers.

    1. ¿Tus amigos te van a llamar esta noche?
    2. ¿Tienen Uds. reservaciones para el hotel?
    3. ¿Vas a comprar cheques de viajero?
    4. ¿Tienes tu tarjeta de crédito?
    5. ¿Llevas tu cámara fotográfica?
    6. ¿Van a visitar Uds. las ruinas de Teotihuacán?
    7. ¿Quién los va a llevar a Uds.[1] al aeropuerto?
    8. ¿Me llevan con Uds. a México?

C. Be an interpreter. What are these people saying?

    1. Do you love me?
       Yes, I love you.
    2. Are you going to sign the register?
       No, I'm not going to sign it.
    3. Do I have to show my passport?
       Yes, you have to show it, sir.
    4. Do your cousins visit you? *(fam. pl.)*
       Yes, they visit us on Sundays.

familia®

En calidad y economía lo tiene todo.

---

[1] **A Uds.** is needed for clarification because **los** could also be *them*.

¡A ver cuánto aprendió!

A. ¡Conversemos!

Reread the dialogues in this lesson and be ready to discuss the following.

1. ¿Es Teresa norteamericana?
2. ¿Dónde está Lima?
3. ¿Qué ruinas famosas hay en el Perú?
4. ¿Dónde piensa Teresa pasar unos días al comienzo de su viaje?
5. ¿Cómo es el aeropuerto de Lima?
6. ¿Qué compra Teresa en el aeropuerto?
7. ¿Tiene Teresa algo que declarar?
8. ¿Qué pide Teresa en la oficina de turismo?
9. ¿Qué toma para ir al centro?
10. ¿Pide Teresa una habitación sencilla o doble?
11. ¿Qué cuarto prefiere Teresa? ¿Por qué?
12. ¿Cómo puede Teresa pagar el hotel?
13. ¿A cómo está el cambio de moneda?
14. ¿Teresa lleva sus maletas al cuarto o las lleva el botones?
15. ¿Hasta qué hora sirven la cena?

B. ¡Repase el vocabulario!

Select the word or phrase that best completes each sentence.

1. En el aeropuerto debo mostrar...
   a. la llave.   b. el baño.   c. el pasaporte.
2. Quiero una habitación...
   a. en la oficina de turismo.   b. con vista a la calle.
   c. en el autobús.
3. Deseo declarar...
   a. la reservación.   b. esta cámara fotográfica.
   c. la lista de hoteles.
4. Debes pasar por la aduana...
   a. con el restaurante.   b. con el piso.
   c. con las maletas.
5. Voy a comprar algo para...
   a. mis padres.   b. la aduana.   c. la llave.
6. El botones va a llevar...
   a. el interés.   b. la plata.   c. las maletas.
7. ¿Dónde puedo tomar...
   a. el jabón?   b. el ascensor?   c. la tarjeta de turista?
8. Sirven la cena...
   a. a las nueve de la mañana.   b. a las tres de la tarde.
   c. a las nueve de la noche.
9. En el verano hay pocos cuartos...
   a. libres.   b. modernos.   c. casados.

10. En el Hilton una habitación con vista a la calle cuesta ochenta dólares...
    a. por año.   b. por mes.   c. por día.
11. No tengo reservación, pero estoy en...
    a. el centro.   b. la lista de espera.   c. el cuarto.
12. La habitación no es barata; es...
    a. cara.   b. libre.   c. sencilla.

C. Situaciones

What would you say in the following situations? What might the other person say?

1. You are at the hotel. Ask the clerk what time they serve breakfast and whether they have room service.
2. You are at the airport. Tell the inspector that you have nothing else to declare, and ask if everything is in order.
3. You are at the tourist office. Ask the clerk if he or she has a list of hotels and boarding houses and a list of places of interest. Say that you need them right away.
4. You are the clerk at a tourist office. Tell the tourists that there are some buses that can take them downtown and that they can also take a taxi.
5. You are the clerk at a hotel. Tell a tourist that you don't have any single rooms with private bathrooms because there are few vacant rooms in July.

Para escribir

Complete the following dialogues.

1. *Carlos va a Tijuana.*

CARLOS —¿Dónde está tu pasaporte?
ROBERTO — _____
CARLOS —¡Sí, lo necesitas! ¿No vas a ir a México?
ROBERTO — _____
CARLOS —¿Tijuana? ¿Y para eso necesitas todas esas maletas?
ROBERTO — _____
CARLOS —¡No! ¡No puedo llevarlas al coche!

2. *En el hotel.*

TURISTA —¿Tienen habitaciones?
HOTELERO — _____
TURISTA —No, interior.
HOTELERO — _____
TURISTA —¡Cincuenta dólares por día! ¿Aceptan cheques de viajero?
HOTELERO — _____

En la vida real

ENTREVISTA

Choose a partner, then interview each other using the **tú** form.

Pregúntele a su compañero(-a) de clase...

1. ...cuántas maletas lleva cuando viaja.
2. ...si lleva cheques de viajero cuando viaja.
3. ...si siempre lleva su cámara fotográfica cuando viaja.
4. ...qué lugares de interés hay en la ciudad donde vive.
5. ...a qué hora sirven el desayuno en la cafetería de la universidad.
6. ...si quiere llevarlo (la) a almorzar.
7. ...si quiere comprar su grabadora.
8. ...si prefiere objetos de oro o de plata.
9. ...si hay alguien en su cuarto ahora.
10. ...si su cuarto tiene baño privado.

DISCUSIÓN

Four or five students (or more, according to class size) will pretend to own hotels and will make up signs describing accommodations and prices. The rest of the class will discuss the similarities and differences and will decide in pairs or individually where they would like to stay. At the end of this activity each student will explain his or her choice.

A follow-up activity: After staying at the hotel people will have encountered one or more of the following problems:

(no) hay {
agua caliente   *hot water*
sábanas limpias   *clean sheets*
frazadas, cobijas   *blankets*
cucarachas   *roaches*
}

no funciona
(it's not working) {
el aire acondicionado   *air-conditioning*
la calefacción   *heater*
el ascensor, el elevador   *elevator*
}

On a card prepare a list of complaints and drop it in the "suggestion box" (the instructor's desk).

Plaza Las Glorias
Puerto Vallarta
HOTEL & VILLAS

Plaza Las Glorias
Cancún
HOTEL & VILLAS

Plaza Las Glorias
Cozumel
HOTEL & VILLAS

¿DÓNDE HOSPEDARSE? *(Where to stay?)*

Imagine it's the month of August. Say whether these people are going to stay at the **Aloha Puerto Sol** hotel or at the **Atlanterra Sol** hotel. Give reasons for your choice according to the information provided in the following ads. You should also indicate how much each group will have to pay. Start out by saying «**Se van a hospedar en... porque...** »

1. La familia Salcedo: el papá, la mamá y dos niños. Jorgito tiene diez años y Alicia tiene ocho. No tienen mucho dinero.
2. Gustavo y Carolina, que son recién casados *(newlyweds)*. Desean ver un espectáculo y bailar. Tienen mucho dinero.
3. Teresa, Raquel y Rebeca, tres muchachas chilenas que están viajando juntas. Les gusta *(They like)* jugar al tenis y bailar.

ESTANCIAS EN EL HOTEL ALOHA PUERTO SOL****

LE OFRECEMOS:
- Alojamiento en régimen de habitación y desayuno.
- Todas las habitaciones son mini-suites.
- Mini-bar.
- Cesta de fruta en la habitación.
- Botella de vino en la habitación.
- Entrada al Aquapark con 50% de descuento.
- Entrada gratis al Zoo de Fuengirola.
- Programa completo de deportes y animación para adultos y niños (Mini-Club).
- Espectáculos - actuaciones.

ALOHA PUERTO SOL H.D.

Precio por persona y día en habitación doble-habitación y desayuno			SUPL. M.P.	SUPL. P.C SOBRE M.P.	SUPL. INDIV.	DESCUENT 3ª PERSON
01/05 - 15/07 01/10 - 31/10	01 09 - 30/09	16/07 - 31/06				
3.165	4.060	4.455	1.340	610	1.310	15%

Código 048	IVA NO INCLUIDO

ESTANCIAS EN EL HOTEL ATLANTERRA SOL****

LE OFRECEMOS:
- Régimen de habitación y desayuno. Habitación doble.
- Cesta de fruta en la habitación.
- Botella de vino en la habitación.
- 1 hora de tenis gratis.
- 1 copa gratis en la discoteca.
- Programa completo de deportes y animación para niños (Mini-Club) y adultos.
- Espectáculos - actuaciones.
- Salida de la habitación a las 14 horas.
- Condiciones especiales en nuestro restaurante grill «Oasis»
- Oferta novios 10%.

ATLANTERRA SOL H.D.

	Precio por persona y día en habitación doble-habitación y desayuno		SUPL. M.P.	SUPL. PC. SOBRE M/P.	SUPL. INDIV.	DESCUENT 3ª PERSON
	01/10 - 31/10	16/07 al 30/09				
	4.970	6.495	1.490	1.320	2.295	15%
Desc. niños 2 - 15 años	1º 50% 2º 35%	1º 35% 2º 35%	IVA NO INCLUIDO			
Código 054						

UNA ACTIVIDAD ESPECIAL

Get together with a couple of your classmates and plan a trip to a Spanish-speaking country. Get brochures of the country you are going to visit. Find out about hotels, rates of exchange, places of interest, and so on. Discuss how and when you will be leaving, how much spending money you'll bring, what cities and special sites you intend to visit, and what you need to take with you.

Restaurante en la elegante Zona Rosa, centro comercial de la Ciudad de México.

OBJECTIVES

Pronunciation   The Spanish **j**, **g** (before **e** or **i**), and **h**
Structure   Demonstrative adjectives and pronouns • Uses of **ser** and **estar** • Verbs with irregular first-person forms • **Saber** vs. **conocer**; **pedir** vs. **preguntar** • Indirect object pronouns
Communication   You will learn vocabulary related to restaurant menus, ordering meals at a restaurant, and paying the bill.

En un restaurante cubano

Hoy es el 15 de diciembre. Es el aniversario de bodas de Lidia y Jorge Torres. Lidia no sabe que su esposo piensa llevarla a cenar a uno de los mejores restaurantes de Miami para celebrarlo. Cuando ella le pregunta qué van a hacer hoy, él le dice que van a ir al cine o al teatro. Son las nueve de la noche y Lidia está lista para salir.

LIDIA —¿Adónde vamos?

JORGE —Vamos a tomar un taxi.

Llegan al restaurante Miramar.

LIDIA —¡Qué sorpresa! ¡Éste es mi restaurante favorito!

MOZO —Por aquí, por favor. Aquí está el menú.

LIDIA —Gracias. *(Lee el menú.)* Bistec, cordero asado con puré de papas, pavo relleno, camarones...

JORGE —¿Por qué no pides langosta? Es muy sabrosa. ¿O un filete? Aquí preparan unos filetes muy ricos.

LIDIA —¡Ay! ¡No sé qué pedir!

MOZO —Les recomiendo la especialidad de la casa: lechón asado y arroz con frijoles negros. De postre, helado, flan o torta helada.

JORGE —Bueno, yo quiero lechón asado y arroz con frijoles negros. ¿Y tú, Lidia?

LIDIA —Yo quiero sopa, camarones y arroz.

MOZO —¿Y para tomar?

JORGE —Primero un vermut y después media botella de vino tinto.

MOZO —Muy bien, señor. *(Anota el pedido.)*

LIDIA —¿Qué hacemos después de cenar?

JORGE —¿Quieres ir a la fiesta de Eva? Es en el club Los Violines.

LIDIA —No... yo no la conozco muy bien. Prefiero ir al teatro.

JORGE —Buena idea. En el Teatro Martí ponen una obra de teatro muy buena.

LIDIA —Sí, es una comedia española.

El mozo trae la comida.

LIDIA —*(Que está comiendo los camarones)* ¡Estos camarones están muy ricos!

JORGE —Este restaurante es excelente.

LECCIÓN

6

■ ■ ■

AT A CUBAN RESTAURANT

Today is December fifteenth. It's Lidia and Jorge Torre's wedding anniversary. Lidia doesn't know that her husband plans to take her to dinner at one of the best restaurants in Miami to celebrate (it). When she asks him what they are going to do today, he tells her that they're going to go to the movies or to the theater. It is nine o'clock in the evening, and Lidia is ready to go out.

L. Where are we going?

J. We're going to take a taxi.

They arrive at the Miramar Restaurant.

L. What a surprise! This is my favorite restaurant!

W. This way, please. Here is the menu.

L. Thanks. *(She reads the menu.)* Steak, roast lamb with mashed potatoes, stuffed turkey, shrimp . . .

J. Why don't you order lobster? It's very tasty. Or a tenderloin steak? They prepare some delicious steaks here.

L. Oh, I don't know what to order!

W. I recommend to you the specialty of the house: roast pork and rice with black beans. For dessert, ice cream, custard, or ice cream cake.

J. Fine, I want roast pork and rice with black beans. And you, Lidia?

L. I want soup, shrimp, and rice.

W. And to drink?

J. First a vermouth and then a half bottle of red wine.

W. Very well, sir. *(He writes down the order.)*

Después de comer el postre, Lidia y Jorge beben café y conversan. Ya son las diez y media. Jorge pide la cuenta, la paga, le deja una buena propina al mozo y salen.

JORGE   —Feliz aniversario, mi amor. *(Le da un beso.)*

Vocabulario

COGNADOS

el **aniversario** anniversary	**favorito(-a)** favorite
la **comedia** comedy	el **menú** menu
cubano Cuban	la **sorpresa** surprise
la **especialidad** specialty	el **vermut** vermouth
excelente excellent	

NOMBRES

el **amor** love	el **cordero** lamb
el **arroz** rice	la **cuenta** bill
el **beso** kiss	el **filete** tenderloin steak
el **bistec** steak	el **flan** custard
la **botella** bottle	los **frijoles** beans
los **camarones** shrimp	el **helado** ice cream
el **cine** movie theater, movies	la **langosta** lobster
la **comida** food, meal	el **lechón** young pig (pork)

L. What are we doing after dinner?
J. Do you want to go to Eva's party? It's at the Los Violines Club.
L. No . . . I don't know her very well. I prefer to go to the theater.
J. Good idea. At the Martí Theater they are showing a very good play.
L. Yes, it's a Spanish comedy.

The waiter brings the food.

L. *(Who is eating the shrimp)* These shrimp are delicious!
J. This is an excellent restaurant.

After eating dessert, Lidia and Jorge drink coffee and talk. It's now (already) ten-thirty. Jorge asks for the bill, pays it, leaves the waiter a good tip, and they leave.

J. Happy anniversary, my love. *(He gives her a kiss.)*

el **mozo, camarero, mesero** *(Mex.)* waiter[1]
la **obra de teatro** play
el **pavo** turkey
el **pedido,** la **orden** order
el **postre** dessert
la **propina** tip
la **sopa** soup
el **teatro** theater
la **torta helada** ice cream cake

VERBOS

anotar to write down
conocer to know, be acquainted with
dejar to leave (behind)
hacer to do, to make
pagar to pay
pedir to order
preguntar to ask (a question)
preparar to prepare
recomendar (e:ie) to recommend
saber to know
salir to leave, to get (go) out

ADJETIVOS

asado(-a) roasted
helado(-a) iced, ice cold
listo(-a) ready
medio(-a) half
relleno(-a) stuffed
sabroso(-a), rico(-a) tasty, delicious
tinto red (wine)

OTRAS PALABRAS Y EXPRESIONES

aniversario de bodas wedding anniversary
de postre for dessert
después de after
mi amor my love, my darling
poner una obra de teatro to put on a show *or* play
por aquí this way
puré de papas mashed potatoes
ya already

Vocabulario adicional

Para poner la mesa *(To set the table)*

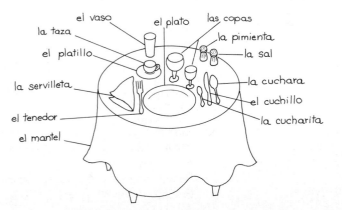

---
[1]*waitress:* camarera, mesera.

RESTAURANTE MIRAMAR

Especialidad en carnes y Mariscos

MENÚ

PARA EL ALMUERZO

Sándwiches[1] de pollo	$ 3.50	Papas fritas (*French fries*)	$ 1.00
Sándwiches de jamón y queso	$ 2.50	Tortilla a la española (*Omelette*)	$ 2.50
Sándwiches de huevo (*egg*)	$ 1.50	Tortilla mexicana	$ .50
Sopa del día	$ 2.00	Frijoles (*Beans*)	$ 1.75
Ensalada	$ 2.00	Arroz	$ 1.80
Hamburguesas[1]	$ 2.50	Arroz con frijoles negros	$ 2.00

PARA LA CENA (*Todos los platos de la lista se sirven[2] con la sopa del día y ensalada.*)

Pescados y mariscos (*Seafood*)

Langosta	$15.00	Trucha	$ 7.50
Salmón[1]	$10.00	Camarones	$ 9.00

Carne (*Meat*)

Albóndigas (*Meatballs*)	$ 6.00	Pavo relleno	$ 7.50
Bistec (*Fillet*)	$12.00	Pollo frito	$ 6.50
Cordero	$ 8.00	Arroz con pollo	
Lechón asado	$ 8.50	(*Chicken and rice*)	$ 6.00

POSTRES

Arroz con leche	$ 2.00	Helado	$ 1.50
Torta de chocolate[1]	$ 2.50	Frutas[1]	$ 1.25
Gelatina[1]	$ 1.50	Queso	$ 1.50
Flan con crema	$ 2.50		

BEBIDAS

Agua mineral (*Mineral water*)	$ 1.00	Café	$ .80
Cerveza	$ 3.00	Té[1]	$ .80
Champán[1]	$ 5.00	Chocolate caliente (*Hot chocolate*)	$ 1.20
Vino blanco	$ 3.50	Jugo de frutas (*Fruit juice*)	$ 1.50
Vino tinto	$ 3.50	Leche fría (*Cold milk*)	$ 1.20
Vermut	$ 3.50		

[1]These words are cognates, so you can guess what they mean.
[2]se sirven = *are served.*

¿Lo sabía Ud.... ?

- La ciudad de Miami en el estado de la Florida se ha convertido en uno de los centros turísticos más importantes del mundo. Cientos de miles de turistas procedentes de América Latina la visitan todos los años. Más de 800.000 hispanos viven en Miami, muchos de ellos cubanos. Por lo tanto, la influencia cubana se ve por todas partes, tanto en el aspecto económico como cultural. El español se usa tanto en Miami que en muchas tiendas hay letreros que dicen: «*English spoken here*».

- En los países de habla hispana, el café se sirve después del postre, nunca durante la comida. Generalmente es café tipo expreso, y se sirve en tazas muy pequeñas.

- Después de comer, los hispanos generalmente se quedan sentados (*remain seated*) alrededor de la mesa y conversan. A esto se le llama «hacer la sobremesa».

- En los países de habla hispana, la propina que generalmente se ofrece en los restaurantes es del 10%, pero hay variación según el país y el tipo de restaurante. Con frecuencia la propina está incluida en la cuenta.

La Pequeña Habana, centro comercial de los cubanos en Miami, Florida.

Pronunciación

▶ *A.* The Spanish **j**

The Spanish **j** sounds somewhat like the *h* in the English word *hit*. It is never pronounced like the English *j* in *John* or *James*. Listen to your teacher and repeat the following words.

Julia	dejar	embajada
pasaje	jabón	equipaje
tarjeta	objeto	jueves

▶ *B.* The Spanish **g** (before **e** or **i**)

When followed by **e** or **i,** the Spanish **g** sounds like the Spanish **j** mentioned above. Listen to your teacher and repeat the following words.

Gerardo	inteligente	agente
agencia	general	Genaro
registro	Argentina	ingeniero

▶ *C.* The Spanish **h**

The Spanish **h** is always silent. Listen to your teacher and repeat the following words.

hay	**Hilda**	**habitación**
Honduras	**hermano**	**hasta**
ahora	**hotel**	**hija**

Estructuras gramaticales

▶ *1.* Demonstrative adjectives and pronouns   *(Los adjetivos y los pronombres demostrativos)*

A. Demonstrative adjectives

♦ Demonstrative adjectives point out persons or things. Like all other adjectives, they agree in gender and number with the nouns they modify. The forms of the demonstrative adjectives are as follows.

Masculine		Feminine		
Singular	*Plural*	*Singular*	*Plural*	
este	estos	esta	estas	*this, these*
ese	esos	esa	esas	*that, those*
aquel	aquellos	aquella	aquellas	*that, those* (at a distance)

—¿Qué necesitas?
—Necesito **esta** pluma, **ese** cuaderno y **aquellos** libros.

What do you need?
I need this pen, that notebook, and those books (over there).

B. Demonstrative pronouns

♦ The demonstrative pronouns are the same as the demonstrative adjectives, except the pronouns have a written accent.

Masculine		Feminine		Neuter	
Singular	*Plural*	*Singular*	*Plural*		
éste	éstos	ésta	éstas	esto	*this* (one), *these*
ése	ésos	ésa	ésas	eso	*that* (one), *those*
aquél	aquéllos	aquélla	aquéllas	aquello	*that* (one), *those* (at a distance)

—¿Quieres este jabón o **ése**?

Do you want this soap or that one?

—No quiero ni **éste** ni **ése**; quiero **aquél**.

I don't want this one or that one; I want that one over there.

◆ Each demonstrative pronoun has a neuter form. They are: **esto,
eso,** and **aquello.** The neuter forms, which do not change in number or gender, are used to refer to situations, ideas, and nonspecific objects or things, equivalent to the English *this, that matter; this,
that business;* and *this, that stuff.*

—¿Entiendes **eso?**　　　　　　*Do you understand that?*
—No, no lo entiendo.　　　　　*No, I don't understand it.*

PRÁCTICA

A. Change the demonstrative adjectives according to the gender
and number of the nouns.

1. *esta* lista de espera, _____ terrazas,
   _____ elevador, _____ cuadros
2. *ese* empleado, _____ orquesta, _____
   tenedores, _____ copas
3. *aquella* señora, _____ cheque, _____
   toallas, _____ cuchillos

B. Using demonstrative pronouns, state your preference.

MODELO: ¿Quiere Ud. esta lista o ésa?
　　　　　Prefiero aquélla.

1. ¿Quiere Ud. estas maletas o ésas?
2. ¿Quiere Ud. estos libros o ésos?
3. ¿Quiere Ud. este refresco o ése?
4. ¿Quiere Ud. esta cámara o ésa?
5. ¿Quiere Ud. esto o eso?

C. Complete the following sentences by translating the words in
parentheses.

1. Firmo este registro y _____ *(that one over there).*
2. Quiero estos lápices y _____ *(those).*
3. Necesito esta llave y _____ *(that one over there).*
4. Voy a comprar esta toalla y _____ *(those).*
5. No quiero esas maletas; quiero _____ *(these).*
6. No voy a comer en ese restaurante. Voy a comer
   en _____ *(this one).*

ÉSTE ES SU NUEVO DINERO

▶ *2.* Uses of **ser** and **estar**   *(Usos de **ser** y **estar**)*

The English verb *to be* has two Spanish equivalents, **ser** and **estar.** As a general rule, **ser** expresses *who* or *what* the subject is *essentially,* and **estar** indicates *state* or *condition.* **Ser** and **estar** are *not* interchangeable.

A. Uses of *ser*

Ser expresses a fundamental quality and identifies the essence of a person or thing.

♦ It describes the basic nature or character of a person or thing. It is also used with expressions of age.

Este restaurante **es** excelente.
Yo **soy** mayor que María Isabel.

♦ It describes the material that things are made of.

Estos objetos **son** de oro y plata.

♦ It is used with adjectives denoting nationality and to indicate origin, profession, trade, and so on.

Sandra **es** norteamericana.
Yo **soy** de Caracas.
Mi mamá **es** profesora.

♦ It is used with expressions of time and with dates.

Hoy **es** miércoles, cuatro de abril.
Son las cuatro y cuarto de la tarde.

✳ ♦ It is used with events as the equivalent of *taking place.*

La fiesta **es** en el club Los Violines.

♦ It is used to indicate possession or relationship.

La grabadora **es** de Julia.
El inspector de aduanas **es** el hermano de Raúl.

PRÁCTICA

Interview a classmate, asking him or her the following questions.

1. ¿Eres norteamericano(-a)?
2. ¿Eres feliz?
3. ¿Tu papá es rubio, moreno o pelirrojo?
4. ¿De dónde eres?
5. ¿Eres mayor o menor que yo?
6. ¿Quién es tu mejor amigo(-a)?

7. Hoy hay una fiesta. ¿Es en tu casa?
8. ¿Qué día es hoy?
9. ¿Qué fecha es hoy?
10. ¿Qué hora es?

B. Uses of *estar*

Estar is used to express more transitory qualities and often implies the possibility of change.

♦ It indicates place or location.

El mozo no **está** aquí. ¿Dónde **está**?

♦ It is used to indicate condition.

Mis padres **están** muy cansados.

♦ With personal reactions, it describes what is perceived through the senses—that is, how a person or thing seems, looks, tastes, or feels.

¡Estos camarones **están** muy ricos!

♦ It is used with the **-ando** and **-iendo** forms of the verb in the present progressive.

Lidia **está comiendo** camarones.

PRÁCTICA

A. Imagine that you and a friend are at a restaurant, and answer the following questions.

1. ¿En qué calle está el restaurante?
2. ¿Ud. está comiendo filete, camarones o pavo?
3. ¿Cómo está la comida? ¿Está sabrosa?
4. ¿Qué está comiendo su amigo(-a)?
5. ¿Ud. está tomando vino tinto o un refresco?
6. ¿Qué está tomando su amigo(-a)?
7. ¿Dónde está el camarero (la camarera)?
8. ¿Qué está haciendo el mozo (la mesera)?
9. ¿Está Ud. leyendo el menú para pedir el postre?
10. ¿Qué está comiendo su amigo de postre?

B. ¿**Ser** or **estar**? Complete the following dialogues, using the correct verb.

1. —¿De dónde _____ tus padres?
   ¿ _____ mexicanos?
   —Sí, pero ahora _____ en California.

—¿Tu papá _____ profesor?

—No, _____ médico.

2. —¿Olga _____ tu prima?

—No, _____ mi sobrina.

—¿Cómo _____ ella?

— _____ alta, morena y
   delgada. _____ muy bonita.

—¿Dónde _____ ella ahora?

— _____ en su casa.

3. —¿Qué hora _____ ?

—Ya _____ las siete.

—¿Dónde _____ la fiesta de Navidad?

— _____ en el Club Náutico. ¿Tú vas a ir?

—No, _____ muy cansada.

4. —¿Qué _____ comiendo (tú)?

— _____ comiendo arroz con pollo.

—¿ _____ rico?

—¡Sí, _____ muy sabroso!

5. —¿Éste _____ tu reloj?

—Sí, _____ mi reloj.

—¿ _____ de oro?

—No. ¡Oye! ¿Qué día _____ hoy?

—Hoy _____ jueves.

C. Be an interpreter. What are these people saying?

1. Are you (an) American, Mr. Cortés?
   No, I am (a) Spaniard. I am from Madrid.
2. How is the food?
   It's very tasty.
3. What's the date today?
   It's September third. Is it your birthday?
   No, it's my wedding anniversary.
4. What are you doing, Anita?
   I'm reading my favorite book.

BIENVENIDO A AIR PANAMA
LO MEJOR LE ESTA ESPERANDO

▶ *3.* Verbs with irregular first-person forms   (*Verbos irregulares en la primera persona*)

♦ The following verbs are irregular in the first-person singular of the present tense.

Verb	*yo form*	*Regular forms*
salir *(to go out)*	**salgo**	sales, sale, salimos, salís, salen
hacer *(to do, make)*	**hago**	haces, hace, hacemos, hacéis, hacen
poner *(to put, place)*	**pongo**	pones, pone, ponemos, ponéis, ponen
traer *(to bring)*	**traigo**	traes, trae, traemos, traéis, traen
conducir *(to drive; to conduct)*	**conduzco**	conduces, conduce, conducimos, conducís, conducen
traducir *(to translate)*	**traduzco**	traduces, traduce, traducimos, traducís, traducen
conocer *(to know)*	**conozco**	conoces, conoce, conocemos, conocéis, conocen
caber *(to fit)*	**quepo**	cabes, cabe, cabemos, cabéis, caben
ver *(to see)*	**veo**	ves, ve, vemos, veis, ven
saber *(to know)*	**sé**	sabes, sabe, sabemos, sabéis, saben

PRÁCTICA

A. Interview a classmate, asking him or her the following questions.

1. ¿Sabes español?
2. ¿Traes tu libro de español a la clase?
3. ¿Ves al profesor (a la profesora) todos los días?
4. ¿Conoces a la familia del profesor (de la profesora)?
5. ¿Traduces la lección al inglés?
6. ¿Haces la tarea *(homework)* los domingos?
7. ¿A qué hora sales de tu casa?
8. ¿Conduces el coche de tus padres?
9. Hay seis chicas en el coche. ¿Cabes tú también?
10. ¿Dónde pones las llaves de tu coche?

B. Complete the following sentences in an original manner.

1. Mi nuera sale por la mañana y yo...
2. Él cabe aquí pero yo...
3. Ella ve a sus suegros los domingos y yo...

4. Él sabe japonés y yo...
5. Yo traduzco al italiano y mi hermano...
6. Marta conduce un Ford y yo...
7. Oscar trae las uvas y yo...
8. Yo pongo los platos en la mesa y mis hermanas...

▶ *4.* **Saber** vs. **conocer; pedir** vs. **preguntar**

A. *Saber* vs. *conocer*

Spanish has two verbs that mean *to know,* **saber** and **conocer.**

♦ When *to know* means *to know something by heart, to know how to do something,* or *to know a fact,* **saber** is used.

No sé los verbos irregulares.	*I don't know the irregular verbs.*
Juan **sabe** hablar ruso.	*John knows how to speak Russian.*
Ellos **saben** dónde está el teatro.	*They know where the theater is.*

♦ When *to know* means *to be familiar with* or *to be acquainted with a person, a thing,* or *a place,* it is translated as **conocer.**

Nosotros **conocemos** a tu tía.	*We know your aunt.*
Elisa **conoce** las novelas de Cervantes.	*She knows (is acquainted with) Cervantes' novels.*
¿**Conoces** Guadalajara?	*Do you know (have you been to) Guadalajara?*

PRÁCTICA

What or whom do these people "know"?

1. —¿ _____ tú al abuelo de Olga?
   —Sí, lo _____ , pero no _____ dónde vive.
2. —Tú _____ Brasil, ¿no?
   —Sí, pero no _____ hablar portugués.
3. —¿Tú _____ el poema «*The Raven*»?
   —¡Lo _____ de memoria!
4. —¿ _____ tú qué hora es?
   —Sí, son las ocho.
5. —Jorge conduce muy mal.
   —Sí, no _____ conducir.

B. *Pedir* vs. *preguntar*

♦ **Pedir** means *to ask for something* in the sense of requesting an object or service.

¿Pido más servilletas?	*Should I ask for more napkins?*
Vamos a pedir la llave.	*We are going to ask for the key.*

♦ **Preguntar** means *to ask a question,* in the sense of requesting information.

Ellos **preguntan** a qué hora sirven la comida.	*They ask at what time dinner is served.*
Voy a preguntar dónde está el mozo.	*I'm going to ask where the waiter is.*

ATENCIÓN

Note that **pedir** means *to ask for;* the preposition *for* has no Spanish equivalent in this case.

PRÁCTICA

What do these people ask? What do they request?

1. —¿Vas a _____ información sobre *(about)* Antonio?
   —No, pero voy a _____ cuál es su número de teléfono.
2. —¿Por qué no _____ (tú) qué obra de teatro ponen hoy?
   —Porque no quiero ir al teatro este fin de semana.
3. —¿Vas a _____ una habitación sencilla o una doble?
   —No sé. Primero voy a _____ cuánto cuesta un cuarto exterior con baño privado.
4. —¿Qué está _____ el botones?
   —La llave del cuarto.

▶ 5. Indirect object pronouns   *(Pronombres usados como complemento indirecto)*

♦ In addition to a subject and a direct object, a sentence may have an indirect object.

Él le da el libro a María.   *He gives the book to María.*
   D.O.   I.O.   D.O.   I.O.

♦ An indirect object describes *to whom* or *for whom* an action is done. An indirect object pronoun can be used in place of an indirect object. In Spanish, the indirect object pronoun includes the meaning *to* or *for:* **Yo *les* mando los libros (a los estudiantes).**

♦ The forms of the indirect object pronouns are as follows.

	Singular		*Plural*
me	*(to) me*	**nos**	*(to) us*
te	*(to) you* (fam. sing.)	**os**	*(to) you* (fam. pl.)
le	*(to) you* (form. sing.) *(to) him* *(to) her*	**les**	*(to) you* (form. pl.) *(to) them* (m., f.)

♦ In Spanish, the indirect object pronouns are the same as the direct object pronouns, except in the third person.

♦ Indirect object pronouns are usually placed in front of the verb.

—¿Qué **te** dice tu papá en la carta?   *What does your Dad say to you in the letter?*

—**Me** dice que viene por unos días.   *He tells me (says to me) that he is coming for a few days.*

♦ In sentences with a conjugated verb followed by an infinitive, the indirect object pronoun may be either placed in front of the conjugated verb or attached to the infinitive.

Le quiero dar un beso.
Quiero dar**le** un beso. } *I want to give him a kiss.*

♦ When used in sentences with the present progressive, an indirect object pronoun may be either placed in front of the conjugated verb or attached to the present participle.

Nos está diciendo que es lunes.
Está diciéndo**nos** que es lunes. } *He's telling us that it's Monday.*

ATENCIÓN

The indirect object pronouns **le** and **les** require clarification when the person to whom they refer is not specified. Spanish provides clarification (or emphasis) by using the preposition **a** + *personal pronoun or noun.*

Le doy la cuenta.	*I am giving the bill . . .* (to whom? to him? to her? to you?)
but: **Le** doy la cuenta **a ella.**	*I am giving the bill to her.*

♦ If the indirect object of a sentence is a noun or a pronoun, the indirect object pronoun must also be used.

Le traigo un libro **a Roberto.**	*I am bringing a book to Roberto.*
¿Les vas a dar el dinero a **ellas?**	*Are you going to give the money to them?*

PRÁCTICA

A. Complete the following sentences with the correct indirect object pronoun.

1. _____ doy el empleo.   (a ella)
2. _____ da los pasajes.   (a mí)
3. _____ damos las botellas.   (a ti)
4. _____ da el telegrama.   (a nosotros)
5. _____ damos el bistec.   (a ellos)
6. _____ vamos a dar las cucharas.   (a ella)
7. _____ doy la propina.   (a Uds.)
8. _____ traemos la sopa.   (a él)
9. _____ compro la maleta.   (a Ud.)
10. _____ escriben las cartas.   (a nosotras)

B. You and your friends are going to set the table for a banquet. Say whether the people in charge are going to give you what you need to complete the task.

MODELO: —¿Van a darle los vasos?
—*Sí, le van a dar los vasos.*

1. ¿Van a darme el mantel?
2. ¿Van a darle los tenedores?
3. ¿Van a darles las cucharitas?
4. ¿Van a darnos las copas?
5. ¿Van a darte las tazas?

6. ¿Van a darles las cucharas?
7. ¿Van a darte los platos?
8. ¿Van a darnos las servilletas?

C. You are going on a trip to Caracas where you will visit your aunt and uncle. Describe to a classmate what you are doing and what you are going to do.

1. ¿Le estás escribiendo a tu tío de Venezuela?
2. ¿Qué le estás diciendo?
3. ¿Qué les vas a llevar a tus tíos?
4. ¿Tu papá te va a dar su cámara fotográfica?
5. ¿Nos vas a escribir de Caracas?
6. ¿Me vas a dejar la llave de tu casa?
7. ¿Qué les vas a traer a tus padres?
8. ¿Le vas a dar un beso a tu mamá antes de irte?

D. Be an interpreter. What are these people saying?

1. What are you going to give me?
   I am going to give you a kiss, my darling.
2. Is the waiter going to bring us the dessert?
   No . . . and we aren't going to leave him a tip.
3. Do you always ask your father for money?
   No, I never ask him for money.
4. Can you bring me a half bottle of wine?
   No, but I can bring you a soda . . .

¡A ver cuánto aprendió!

A. ¡Conversemos!

Reread the dialogue in this lesson and be ready to discuss the following.

1. ¿Cuándo es el aniversario de bodas de Lidia y Jorge?
2. ¿Qué piensa hacer Jorge para celebrarlo?
3. ¿A qué hora está lista Lidia?
4. ¿Qué les da el mozo?
5. ¿Cuál es la especialidad de la casa?
6. ¿Qué pide Lidia?
7. ¿Qué pide Jorge?
8. ¿Qué beben Lidia y Jorge?
9. ¿Por qué no quiere ir Lidia a la fiesta de Eva?
10. ¿Adónde piensan ir después de la cena?
11. ¿Qué le deja Jorge al mozo?
12. ¿Qué le dice Jorge a Lidia al salir del restaurante?

B. ¡Repase el vocabulario!

Match the questions in column A with the answers in column B, then read them aloud.

A

1. ¿Qué celebran hoy?
2. ¿Está rico el pavo relleno?
3. ¿Cuál es la especialidad de la casa?
4. ¿Qué bebidas prefieres?
5. ¿Qué quieres de postre?
6. ¿Vas a pedir agua mineral?
7. ¿Qué está anotando el mozo?
8. ¿Quieres bistec?
9. ¿Adónde vamos esta noche?
10. ¿Es bueno este restaurante?
11. ¿No quieres langosta?
12. ¿Cuánto vas a dejar de propina?
13. ¿Qué venden en McDonald's?
14. ¿Quién paga la cuenta?
15. ¿Quieres café?
16. ¿Es un sándwich de jamón?

B

a. Flan con helado.
b. Sí, quiero pedirla, pero es muy cara.
c. El pedido.
d. Lechón asado con arroz y frijoles negros.
e. Sí, es excelente.
f. Hamburguesas.
g. No, de huevo.
h. Ocho dólares.
i. Sí, está muy sabroso.
j. Ana.
k. Sí, una botella.
l. No, prefiero té.
m. Al teatro.
n. Su aniversario de bodas.
o. Sí, quiero comer carne.
p. Vermut o vino tinto.

C. Situaciones

What would you say in the following situations? What might the other person say?

1. You are at a restaurant. Ask to see the menu; then order salad, meatballs, soup, and mashed potatoes. Tell the waiter or waitress that you want vermouth first. Also tell him or her that you want ice cream cake for dessert.
2. You are a waiter or waitress. Tell your customers that you recommend roast lamb or fried chicken and, for dessert, custard. Ask them if they want coffee or tea.
3. You want to ask your roommate if he or she can set the table. Tell him or her everything that goes on the table: the tablecloth, napkins, spoons, forks, knives, teaspoons, plates, glasses, wine glasses, cups and saucers, salt, and pepper.

4. You are a host or hostess. Ask your guests what they want to drink offering these suggestions: tea, hot chocolate, coffee, cold milk, or fruit juices.

Para escribir ✒

Write a dialogue between a waiter or waitress and a customer. Include the following exchanges.

- asking for a menu
- ordering the food, drink(s), and dessert
- asking for the check

En la vida real

En el restaurante Miramar

You and a classmate are at the Miramar Restaurant. Looking at the menu, ask him or her the following.

Pregúntele a su compañero(-a) de clase...

1. ...qué va a pedir.
2. ...qué le recomienda para comer.
3. ...qué prefiere tomar: vino blanco, champán o refresco.
4. ...qué quiere de postre: arroz con leche, torta o gelatina.
5. ...cuánto es la cuenta.
6. ...cuánto va a dejar de propina.
7. ...qué van a hacer después de cenar.
8. ...si sabe preparar algún plato sabroso.

Un almuerzo especial

You and a classmate are hosting a special weekend for some foreign students. Discuss the breakfast, lunch, and dinner menus you will be preparing, taking into account your guests' different peculiarities.

1. María Inés Soto is a vegetarian.
2. Juan Carlos Reyes loves meat and dairy products.
3. Isabel Peña is on a diet.
4. Francisco Rojas is extremely thin and wants to gain weight.
5. Raquel Arias loves seafood.

Some additional words and phrases that you might include:

el **tocino** *(bacon)*
el **chorizo** *(sausage)* } **con huevos** *(with eggs)*
el **cereal** *cereal*
el **panqueque** *pancake*
el **pan** *bread*
la **mantequilla** *butter*
la **mermelada** *jam*
el **yogur** *yogurt*
las **zanahorias** *carrots*

¡Buen provecho!

You and a friend have decided to go out to dinner tonight. Read the following ads for Hispanic restaurants in Miami, and answer the questions which follow.

SALAS NOCTURNAS

1. Ud. y un amigo quieren comer pescado. ¿A qué restaurante pueden ir?
2. Si quieren hacer reservaciones en ese restaurante, ¿a qué número deben llamar?
3. ¿Cuál es la especialidad del restaurante Las Redes?
4. ¿Por qué es famoso el restaurante Segovia?
5. ¿Cuándo hay música en el restaurante Segovia?
6. ¿Cuánto cuesta el almuerzo allí?
7. ¿Qué comidas típicas cubanas sirven en el restaurante La Carreta?
8. Si quieren dar un banquete, ¿a qué restaurante deben ir?
9. ¿En qué calle está El Bodegón Castilla?
10. ¿Cree Ud. que en El Bodegón Castilla sirven comida italiana o española?

UNA ACTIVIDAD ESPECIAL

You and a classmate have received a $40.00 gift coupon to eat dinner at the Miramar Restaurant. Select what you are going to have, including drinks and dessert. And don't forget to leave a tip!

Y ahora, *¡vamos a leer!*

¡Feliz cumpleaños!

Hoy es el cumpleaños de la abuela de Jorge y Elba Zuluaga. Para celebrarlo, los chicos deciden llevarla al restaurante El Gaucho, que es el favorito de la señora Zuluaga. Hacen reservaciones para las siete porque después de la cena van a llevarla al teatro Las Máscaras a ver una comedia. En el restaurante, el mozo les recomienda la especialidad de la casa: parrillada.[1] Piden parrillada para tres y unas empanadas°. Cuando termin-an° de comer, el camarero trae una torta de cumpleaños con setenta velitas° y todos brindan con champán.

meat pies
they finish
candles

Ya son las nueve y la obra de teatro comienza a las nueve y media. Jorge llama al camarero y pide la cuenta. Cuando salen, la abuela les da un beso a sus dos nietos.

¡A ver cuánto recuerda!

1. ¿Cuántos años tiene la abuela de Jorge y Elba?
2. ¿Celebran el cumpleaños en su casa?
3. ¿Cómo se llama el restaurante favorito de la abuela?
4. ¿Ud. cree que El Gaucho es un restaurante argentino o mexi-cano?
5. ¿A qué hora llegan al restaurante?
6. ¿Van a un baile después de la cena?
7. En el teatro Las Máscaras, ¿ponen hoy un drama?
8. Jorge, Elba y la abuela, ¿son vegetarianos o no? ¿Cómo lo sabe Ud.?
9. ¿Qué sorpresa trae el camarero cuando terminan de comer?
10. ¿Cuántas velitas tiene la torta?
11. ¿A qué hora tienen que estar en el teatro?
12. ¿Qué hace la abuela cuando salen del restaurante?

---

[1] Typical Argentine dish consisting of barbecued beef and sausages.

Take this test. When you finish, check your answers in the answer key provided for this section in Appendix E. Then use a red pen to correct any mistakes you have made. Ready?

LECCIÓN 4

A. Comparison of adjectives and adverbs

Form sentences, using the elements provided. Use the comparative or the superlative, as necessary.

1. Alfredo / estudiante / más / inteligente / clase
2. la lección 12 / menos / interesante / la lección 7
3. mi novia / más / bonita / tu novia
4. Roberto / más / guapo / familia
5. el profesor / tener / menos / veinte estudiantes
6. Ana / tan / alta / Roberto

B. Irregular comparison of adjectives and adverbs

Complete the following sentences, using regular or irregular comparative forms, as necessary.

1. California es _____ que Maine.
2. El profesor de español habla español _____ que los estudiantes.
3. Eva tiene «A» en español, Roberto tiene «B» y Marisa tiene «F». Eva es la _____ alumna. Marisa es la _____ alumna.
4. Yo tengo veinte años y Raquel tiene catorce años. Yo soy _____ que Raquel.
5. Rockefeller tiene _____ dinero que nosotros. Nosotros tenemos _____ dinero que Rockefeller.
6. Rhode Island es _____ que California.

C. Ordinal numbers

Complete the following sentences.

1. Marzo es el _____ mes del año.
2. Mayo es el _____ mes del año.
3. Abril es el _____ mes del año.
4. El _____ mes del año es octubre.
5. Agosto es el _____ mes del año.
6. Enero es el _____ mes del año.

D. Present indicative of *o:ue* stem-changing verbs

Complete the following sentences, using the present indicative of the verbs in the list, as necessary.

recordar   almorzar   costar
contar   volver   poder

1. ¿Cuánto _____ ese libro?
2. Ellos no _____ ir hoy.
3. ¿ _____ Ud. cuál es su número de teléfono?
4. Yo _____ de uno a veinte en español.
5. Tengo hambre. ¿A qué hora _____ (nosotros)?
6. ¿Cuándo _____ tú a España?

E. Weather expressions

Complete the following sentences appropriately.

1. Necesito un paraguas. _____ mucho.
2. ¿No te vas a poner el abrigo? ¡Brrr! ¡ _____
   _____ _____ !
3. ¡No necesito abrigo! ¡Hace _____ !
4. En Alaska _____ mucho en el invierno.
5. Necesitas la sombrilla. Hoy _____ _____
   _____ .
6. No vamos a volar a San Francisco porque hay mucha
   _____ .

F. Just words . . .

Choose the word or phrase in parentheses that best completes each sentence.

1. El hijo de mi hija es mi (yerno, nieto, cuñado).
2. Roberto no es alto; es el más (bajo, guapo, moreno) de la familia.
3. ¡Pedro no es gordo! ¡Es muy (rubio, cómodo, delgado)!
4. Vamos a ver (los cumpleaños, las pinturas, a la abuela) de Picasso en el museo.
5. Tengo que escribir muchas (medicinas, cartas, pensiones) este fin de semana.
6. ¿Quieres (extrañar, asistir, mirar) televisión? ¡Vale!
7. ¿Tú (asistes, extrañas, viajas) mucho a tu familia?
8. ¿No vamos a tener oportunidad de practicar el español? (¡Qué famoso!, ¡Qué lástima!, ¡Qué pequeño!)
9. Ellos nunca quieren viajar en ómnibus; por eso siempre (manejan su auto, comen en este restaurante, hablan francés).

10. ¿Quieres ver algunas (bebidas, fotos, cintas) de mi novia? ¡Es la chica más bonita del mundo!
11. Según el (verano, pronóstico, cumpleaños) del tiempo, va a llover hoy.
12. No es alto. Es de estatura (fea, incómoda, mediana).

LECCIÓN 5

A. Present indicative of *e:i* stem-changing verbs

Give the Spanish equivalent of the following.

1. At the Mexico Restaurant they serve dinner at nine.
2. She requests a room overlooking the street.
3. We follow the bellhop to the room.
4. Do you *(pl.)* get reservations in December?
5. I'm saying (I say) that he must sign the register now.

B. Pronouns as objects of prepositions

Complete the following sentences, using the Spanish equivalent of the words in parentheses.

1. La maleta es para _____ . *(me)*
2. Los empleados están hablando de _____ . *(you, fam.)*
3. Hay sólo dos valijas para _____ . *(them)*
4. La cámara fotográfica es para _____ . *(us)*
5. ¿Quieres visitar la capital _____ ? *(with me)*
6. Bueno. Voy a dejar la grabadora _____ . *(with you,* fam.)

C. Affirmative and negative expressions

Change the following sentences to the affirmative.

1. Ellos no van a querer nada.
2. No hay nadie en el baño.
3. No tengo ningún objeto de oro y plata.
4. Ellos nunca pasan por la aduana.
5. Yo tampoco ceno a las nueve.
6. Jamás tiene las listas de los hoteles.
7. No puedes ir ni a la derecha ni a la izquierda.
8. Ellos nunca quieren nada tampoco.

D. Present progressive

Complete the following sentences, using the present progressive of the verbs in the list, as necessary.

pedir	comer	hablar
leer	decir	dormir

1. Ella _____ que nosotros necesitamos más dinero.
2. Yo _____ con el empleado.
3. Nosotros _____ una novela de Cervantes.
4. ¿Qué _____ tú? ¿Pollo?
5. Luis _____ en su cuarto.
6. ¿Ustedes _____ una habitación con vista a la calle?

E. Direct object pronouns

Complete the following sentences with the Spanish equivalent of the words in parentheses.

1. ¿El libro? No quiero _____ . Es muy caro. *(buy it)*
2. Yo _____ más tarde, Anita. *(call you)*
3. ¿La cena? Ellos _____ a las siete. *(serve it)*
4. Ella tiene una grabadora, pero no va a _____ . *(declare it)*
5. Mamá no _____ al hotel. *(take me)*
6. ¿Las toallas? Yo no _____ . *(need them)*
7. Yo tengo cheques de viajero pero ellos no _____ . *(accept them)*
8. Yo no puedo _____ , señor Vega. *(take you)*
9. Ellos quieren las cámaras fotográficas pero yo no _____ . *(have them)*
10. Nosotros no podemos _____ , señorita Roca. *(call you)*

F. Just words . . .

Choose the correct response to the following questions or statements.

1. ¿Son caras las habitaciones en los hoteles del centro?
   a. No, son de oro y plata.
   b. No, están en el segundo piso.
   c. No, son baratas.

2. ¿Dónde vas a conseguir la lista de hoteles?
   a. En la oficina de turismo.
   b. En el baño.
   c. En un restaurante.
3. ¿Qué documentos debo mostrar?
   a. Veinte dólares.
   b. El pasaporte.
   c. El ascensor.
4. ¿A cómo está el cambio de moneda?
   a. Aquí tiene la llave.
   b. Nada más.
   c. Mil novecientos intis por dólar.
5. ¿Tiene algo que declarar?
   a. Necesito una lista de los lugares de interés.
   b. Esta cámara fotográfica.
   c. Sí, van a declararlo.
6. Necesitamos una habitación doble y dos habitaciones sencillas.
   a. No tenemos ningún cuarto libre, señorita.
   b. Hay pocas habitaciones modernas.
   c. Todo está en regla.
7. ¿Dónde trabaja el inspector?
   a. En el autobús.
   b. En la aduana.
   c. En el hospital.
8. El cuarto con vista a la calle es muy caro.
   a. ¿Quiere una habitación interior?
   b. El ascensor está a la izquierda.
   c. No hay muchas oficinas de turismo por aquí.
9. ¿Qué desea, señorita?
   a. Una habitación sencilla, con baño privado.
   b. El ómnibus está a la derecha.
   c. No tengo nada que declarar.
10. ¿No puedes ir a México?
    a. No, y voy a confirmar los pasajes.
    b. No, voy a cancelar las reservaciones.
    c. No soy de México; soy de Guatemala.
11. ¿Tienen jabón?
    a. Están en la embajada norteamericana.
    b. Sí, tenemos uno con vista a la calle.
    c. Sí, pero no tenemos toallas.
12. ¿Están Uds. en la lista de espera?
    a. Tengo una lista de los lugares de interés de nuestra ciudad.
    b. El botones tiene la lista.
    c. No, nosotros tenemos reservaciones.

LECCIÓN 6

A. Demonstrative adjectives and pronouns

Give the Spanish equivalent of the following.

1. these knives and those *(over there)*
2. that tablecloth and this one *(here)*
3. these offices and those *(over there)*
4. this theater and that one *(over there)*
5. this waiter and that one *(over there)*
6. these napkins and those *(over there)*

B. Summary of the uses of *ser* and *estar*

Form sentences with the elements provided. Use the appropriate forms of **ser** or **estar**, as needed, and add the necessary connectors.

1. ella / mamá / María
2. club nocturno / calle Siete
3. ¡Hmmm! / este lechón asado / muy sabroso
4. Roberto / de España / ahora / en los Estados Unidos
5. sopa / fría
6. reloj / oro
7. hoy / martes / mañana / miércoles
8. mozo / sirviendo / comida
9. fiesta / casa / Julia
10. teatro / muy grande

C. Irregular first person

Complete the following sentences with the present indicative of the verbs in the list, as needed.

traducir	hacer	conocer	saber	salir
poner	caber	ver	traer	conducir

1. Yo _____ un Ford modelo 1989.
2. Yo no _____ dónde están los platos.
3. Yo no _____ en este coche. ¡Hay ocho personas!
4. Yo siempre _____ de casa a las siete y media.
5. Yo _____ las lecciones del inglés al portugués.
6. ¿Dónde está el vermut? Yo no lo _____ .
7. Le aseguro que yo no _____ nada los domingos por la mañana.
8. Yo _____ los tenedores y los cuchillos en la mesa.
9. Yo no _____ al hermano de Francisco.
10. Yo _____ a mis hijos a la universidad.

D. *Saber* vs. *conocer; pedir* vs. *preguntar*

Give the Spanish equivalent of the following sentences.

1. I'm going to ask when their wedding anniversary is.
2. I know that they want to go to that restaurant.
3. I don't know your mother-in-law, Mrs. Peña.
4. He is going to ask for the menu.
5. I don't know (how to) speak Russian.

E. Indirect object pronouns

Rewrite the following sentences, using indirect object pronouns to replace the words in italics.

1. Ella trae la torta helada *para ellos.*
2. Yo voy a preparar un puré de papas *para ti.*
3. Él trae el flan y el helado *para Ud.*
4. Ana va a comprar las tazas *para mí.*
5. El camarero trae una botella de vino tinto *para nosotros.*
6. Traen el filete y la langosta *para ellos.*

F. **Just words . . .**

Match the questions in column A with the appropriate responses in column B.

A	**B**
1. ¿Qué quieres de postre?	a. No, prefiero cordero.
2. ¿Quieres café?	b. Sí, con champán.
3. ¿Quieres albóndigas?	c. No, agua mineral.
4. ¿Cuánto vas a dejar de propina?	d. Los frijoles son muy buenos aquí.
5. ¿Qué vas a pedir?	e. Es una sorpresa...
6. ¿Ya está lista la comida?	f. No, prefiero jugo de frutas. Hace mucho calor.
7. ¿Qué vas a anotar?	g. No, no me gusta el pescado.
8. ¿Qué me recomiendas?	h. No sé. ¿Quieres ver el menú?
9. ¿Quieres salmón?	i. Sí, con crema, por favor.
10. ¿Qué sirven en este restaurante?	j. No, la pimienta.
11. ¿Vas a beber cerveza?	k. Sí, traigan las copas.
12. ¿Quieres chocolate caliente?	l. Sí, ¿dónde están las tazas, los platitos y las cucharitas?
13. ¿Vamos a celebrar nuestro aniversario?	m. Cinco dólares.
14. ¿Van al teatro?	n. Creo que es pescado y mariscos.
15. ¿Qué me vas a traer?	o. El pedido.
16. ¿Vamos a tomar vermut?	p. Sí, porque voy a poner la mesa.
17. ¿Cuál es la especialidad de la casa?	q. La cuenta.
18. ¿Quieres la sal?	r. No, al cine.
19. ¿No vas a servir el té?	s. Arroz con leche o gelatina.
20. ¿Necesitas el mantel y las servilletas?	t. Sí, voy a servirla ahora.

México

México

PANORAMA HISPÁNICO 4

- Con más de veintidós millones de habitantes, la Ciudad de México es el centro urbano más grande del mundo. Es también la capital más antigua del Nuevo Mundo, fundada por los aztecas en el año 1325.

- El turismo es una de las principales fuentes de ingresos para la economía mexicana. Cancún, Acapulco, Puerto Vallarta, Mazatlán y otros centros turísticos reciben millones de visitantes todos los años, principalmente de los Estados Unidos.

- La comida mexicana es muy famosa en los Estados Unidos. Muchos de los alimentos típicos mexicanos, como los frijoles y las tortillas de maíz, son de origen indígena. Los platos más populares son las enchiladas, el mole, el guacamole, los tamales y los tacos.

- Antes de la conquista de México por parte de los españoles, existían allí numerosas culturas indias: los aztecas, los mayas, los toltecas y los miztecas, entre otras. Aún hoy en día existen grandes concentraciones de indígenas en las regiones de Yucatán, Chiapas y Oaxaca.

▶ Pirámide del Mago en Uxmal, en la Península de Yucatán, México. Uxmal es una antigua ciudad del período clásico maya. Al entrar a la zona arqueológica, la primera estructura que se destaca es la Pirámide del Mago. En realidad, no es un solo edificio sino que son cinco templos construidos uno encima *(on top)* del otro. ¿Qué culturas indias existen en los Estados Unidos?

◀ El Paseo de la Reforma en la Ciudad de México. El paseo contiene numerosos monumentos impresionantes, entre ellos: la estatua del Rey Carlos IV de España; el espléndido monumento a Cristóbal Colón; y el del último emperador azteca Cuauhtemoc. ¿Qué monumentos hay en la ciudad de Washington, D.C. que son muy importantes históricamente?

▲ El mercado del pueblo de Tlacolula, en el estado de Oaxaca, es uno de los más famosos de México. Allí se pueden comprar los productos agrícolas y de artesanía que venden los indios de la región, como por ejemplo vasijas de barro y sarapes. Lo más popular de la artesanía de Oaxaca es su cerámica negra. ¿Ha comprado Ud. alguna vez artículos típicos mexicanos?

◀ La península de Yucatán es famosa no sólo por sus ruinas mayas sino también por sus playas llenas de palmeras y por sus aguas cálidas y cristalinas. A 45 minutos de Cancún se encuentra Akumal, que hoy en día es un centro turístico de belleza inigualable. ¿Qué centros turísticos importantes hay en el estado donde Ud. vive?

▲ El primero y el dos de noviembre se celebra en México el Día de los Muertos. En la foto aparece una mujer rezando *(praying)* en el Cementerio de Patzcuaro, en el estado de Michoacán. Los habitantes del pueblo llevan comida a las tumbas de sus familiares y permanecen allí toda la noche. Miles de velas y flores de papel adornan el cementerio, creando un espectáculo impresionante. ¿Cómo se celebra en los Estados Unidos el Día de los Muertos *(Memorial Day)*?

▶ La ciudad de Mérida, capital del estado de Yucatán, México, fue fundada por los españoles en 1542 en el sitio de una antigua ciudad maya. En la ciudad se conservan numerosos edificios de arquitectura colonial, como el Palacio de Gobierno que aparece en la foto. ¿Qué edificios importantes hay en la ciudad donde usted vive?

▲ Mural del famoso artista mexicano Diego Rivera, que presenta la historia y las costumbres de la civilización Totonec. Estos frescos se encuentran alrededor de la impresionante escalera central del Palacio Nacional construido en el sitio donde se encontraba el palacio del emperador Montezuma. Otros famosos frescos de Rivera pueden verse en el Ministerio de Educación, en la Ciudad de México. ¿Puede Ud. describir el mural que aparece en la foto?

▶ Ver una representación del Ballet Folklórico de México es disfrutar de un espectáculo lleno de arte y color. El ballet ofrece representaciones los miércoles y los domingos en el Palacio de Bellas Artes de la Ciudad de México. Sus danzas y trajes típicos son de una gran belleza. ¿Le gustan a Ud. los bailes folklóricos? ¿Cuáles prefiere?

▶ El Parque de Chapultepec, situado al final del Paseo de la Reforma, se encuentra en el corazón de la Ciudad de México. El parque contiene un jardín botánico, un zoológico, un parque de diversiones y un lago donde se puede remar. Hay también numerosos museos, entre los cuales están el famosísimo Museo Antropológico y el Museo de Arte Moderno.

Machu Picchu, la antigua ciudad de los Incas, localizada en las montañas de los Andes.

OBJECTIVES

Pronunciation   The Spanish **ll** and **ñ**

Structure   Constructions with **gustar** • Possessive pronouns • Time expressions with **hacer** • Preterit of regular verbs • Direct and indirect object pronouns used together

Communication   You will learn vocabulary related to traveling.

Las vacaciones de Teresa

Hace media hora que Teresa y su amiga Silvia hablan por teléfono. Teresa le está contando de su viaje al Perú.

TERESA —Me gustó mucho la capital, pero me gustó más Machu Picchu.

SILVIA —¡Y no me mandaste una tarjeta postal!

TERESA —Compré dos, pero no te las mandé; las tengo aquí.

SILVIA —¿Y cuándo piensas dármelas?

TERESA —Mañana. Tengo que devolverte la maleta y el bolso de mano que me prestaste.

SILVIA —¿Llevaste mucho equipaje?

TERESA —Sí, mis dos maletas y la tuya. Pagué exceso de equipaje.

SILVIA —¿Cuánto te costó el pasaje? ¿Viajaste en primera clase?

TERESA —¿Estás loca? Viajé en clase turista. ¡Y me costó setecientos mil pesos![1] Ida y vuelta, claro...

SILVIA —¿Qué tal el vuelo?

TERESA —Un poco largo... Y como el avión salió con dos horas de retraso, llegamos muy tarde.

SILVIA —¿Pasó algo interesante en Lima?

TERESA —Bueno... en la agencia de viajes donde compré el pasaje para Machu Picchu, conocí a un muchacho muy simpático.

SILVIA —¿Viajó contigo? ¡Tienes que contármelo todo!

TERESA —Sí, viajé con él en avión a Cuzco, donde almorzamos juntos. Después, conversamos durante todo el viaje en tren a Machu Picchu.

SILVIA —No sé por qué tus vacaciones siempre son magníficas y las mías son tan aburridas.

TERESA —Pues la próxima vez tenemos que viajar juntas.

SILVIA —Bueno, pero sólo si vamos en tren o en ómnibus. A mí no me gusta viajar en avión.

TERESA —Bueno, viajamos en tren. Oye, es tarde. Nos vemos mañana al mediodía.

SILVIA —Sí, hasta mañana.

---

[1] Mexican currency.

TERESA'S VACATION

Teresa and her friend Sylvia have been talking on the phone for a half hour. Teresa is telling her about her trip to Peru.

T. I liked the capital very much, but I liked Machu Picchu better.

S. And you didn't send me a postcard!

T. I bought two, but I didn't send them to you; I have them here.

S. And when are you planning on giving them to me?

T. Tomorrow. I have to return to you the suitcase and the handbag that you lent me.

S. Did you take a lot of luggage?

T. Yes, my two suitcases and yours. I paid excess luggage fees.

S. How much did the plane ticket cost you? Did you travel first class?

T. Are you crazy? I traveled in tourist class. It cost me seven hundred thousand pesos! Round-trip, of course.

S. How was the flight?

T. A little long . . . And since the plane left two hours behind schedule, we arrived very late.

S. Did anything interesting happen in Lima?

T. Well . . . at the travel agency where I bought the ticket to Machu Picchu, I met a very charming young man.

S. Did he travel with you? You have to tell me everything!

Vocabulario

COGNADOS

la **capital**   capital

el **exceso**   excess

NOMBRES

la **agencia de viajes**   travel agency
el **avión**   plane
el **bolso de mano**   handbag
el **equipaje**   luggage
la **hora**   hour
el **pasaje**, el **billete** *(Spain)*   ticket
    (for plane, train, or bus)
    _____ **de primera clase**   first
    class ticket
el **retraso**   delay
la **tarjeta**   card
    _____ **postal**   postcard
el **tren**   train
la **vez**   time
el **viaje**   trip
el **vuelo**   flight

VERBOS

conocer   to meet
contar (o:ue)   to tell
devolver (o:ue)   to return (some-
    thing)
gustar   to like, to appeal
pasar   to happen
prestar   to lend

ADJETIVOS

aburrido(-a)   boring
juntos(-as)   together

largo(-a)   long
loco(-a)   crazy
próximo(-a)   next

OTRAS PALABRAS Y EXPRESIONES

bueno, bien   okay, fine
la **clase turista**   tourist class
claro   of course
como   since
de   about
de ida   one-way
de ida y vuelta   round-trip
durante   during
exceso de equipaje   excess luggage
hablar por teléfono   to talk on
    the phone
míos, mías   mine
primera clase   first class
pues   then
¿qué tal... ?   how was (is) . . . ?
sólo   only
tarde   late
todo   all
todo el viaje   the whole trip
tuyo(-a)   yours
un poco + *adjective*   a little +
    adjective

Vocabulario adicional

el **asiento**   seat
Necesitamos dos **asientos** en el
    vuelo a Buenos Aires.

el **asiento de pasillo (de ventanilla)**
    aisle seat (window seat)
¿Quiere **asiento de pasillo** o
    asiento de ventanilla?

T. Yes, I traveled with him by plane to Cuzco, where we had lunch together. We then talked during the entire train ride to Machu Picchu.

S. I don't know why your vacations are always great and mine are so boring.

T. Next time we have to travel together.

S. Okay, but only if we go by train or by bus. I don't like to travel by plane.

T. Well, we'll travel by train. Listen, it's late. I'll see you tomorrow at noon.

S. Yes, see you tomorrow.

el **barco**   ship
Quiero viajar en **barco.**

¡Buen viaje!   Have a nice trip!
Adiós, Marisa. **¡Buen viaje!**

corto(-a)   short (length)
El lápiz es muy **corto.**

la **entrada**   entrance
¿Dónde está la **entrada** al aeropuerto?

la **puerta de salida**   gate (i.e., at an airport)
¿Cuál es la **puerta de salida** para el vuelo a Caracas?

la **salida**   exit
No es la entrada; es la **salida.**

la **sección de (no) fumar**   the (non-) smoking section
Quiero un asiento en **la sección de no fumar.**

el (la) **turista**   tourist
Muchos **turistas** visitan México todos los años.

el (la) **viajero(-a)**   traveler
Los **viajeros** llegan esta noche por tren.

tener... de retraso (atraso)   to be . . . behind schedule
El avión **tiene dos horas de retraso.**

¿Lo sabía Ud.... ?

■ **Cuzco,** situado a más de diez mil pies de altura en los Andes peruanos, fue en un tiempo la capital del imperio de los Incas. Hoy día, la ciudad es un gran centro turístico y artístico.

■ **Machu Picchu,** conocida también como la ciudad perdida de los Incas, está situada en la cordillera de los Andes a unos ciento diez kilómetros al noroeste de Cuzco. El imperio de los Incas se extendió desde el sur de Colombia hasta el norte de Chile y Argentina.

La iglesia de San Pedro, en Cuzco, Perú. Note su estilo colonial español.

Pronunciación

▶ *A.* The Spanish **ll**

In most countries, the Spanish **ll** has a sound similar to the *y* in the English word *yes*. Listen to your teacher and repeat the following words.

calle	me llamo	llave	botella
llevar	relleno	pollo	llegar

▶ *B.* The Spanish **ñ**

The Spanish **ñ** is similar to the *ny* in the English word *canyon*. Listen to your teacher and repeat the following words.

español	niño	mañana	España
señor	señorita	otoño	año

Estructuras gramaticales

▶ *1.* Constructions with **gustar**   *(Construcciones con* **gustar***)*

♦ The verb **gustar** means *to like (something or somebody)*. **Gustar** is always used with an indirect object pronoun (**me** in the following example).

Me gusta tu casa.   *I like your house.*
I.O. V   S   S V   D.O.

♦ The two most commonly used forms of **gustar** are: (1) the third-person singular form, **gusta,** used if the subject is singular or if **gustar** is followed by one or more infinitives; and (2) the third-person plural form, **gustan,** used if the subject is plural.

Indirect object pronouns

Me
Te
Le   gusta ⟨ la capital.
Nos   viajar en tren.
Os   comer y beber.
Les

Os
Les   gustan ── las chicas rubias.

♦ Note that the verb **gustar** agrees with the *subject* of the sentence—that is, with the person or thing being liked.

Me gust**a la capital.**	*I like the capital.*
Me gust**an las chicas rubias.**	*I like blonde girls.*

♦ The person who does the liking is the indirect object.

Me gustan las chicas rubias.
I.O.

—¿**Te** gusta la langosta?	*Do you like lobster?*
—Sí, **me** gusta mucho la langosta, pero **me** gustan más los camarones.	*Yes, I like lobster very much, but I like shrimp better.*
—**A Eva le** gusta el pollo.	*Eva likes chicken.*

ATENCIÓN

Note that the words **mucho** and **más** *(better)* immediately follow **gustar**.

♦ The preposition **a** + *noun or pronoun* may be used to emphasize or specify the name of the person referred to by the indirect object pronoun.

A Eva (**A ella**) le gusta el pollo.	*Eva (She) likes chicken.*

PRÁCTICA

A. You and some friends are at a restaurant. Using **gustar**, say what everybody likes to eat and drink.

MODELO: Yo / las papas fritas
(A mí) me gustan las papas fritas.

1. ellas / las albóndigas
2. tú / el jugo
3. nosotros / comer lechón asado
4. Marta y Elena / el agua mineral
5. yo / el pollo frito
6. ellos / el salmón
7. Uds. / las frutas
8. Ud. / tomar vino tinto
9. Eduardo / el pavo relleno
10. los niños / la tortilla española

B. Tell us what you and your relatives like and don't like to do on weekends.

Modelo: A mi mamá...
A mi mamá le gusta ir a bailar.

1. A mí...
2. A mí no...
3. A mis hermanos...
4. A mis hermanos no...
5. A mi papá...
6. A mi papá no...
7. A nosotros...
8. A nosotros no...
9. A mis primos...
10. A mis primos no...

C. Be an interpreter. What are these people saying?

1. Do you like this blue handbag, Lolita?
   No . . . I like the green handbag better.
2. Do your children like to travel by ship, Mr. Vega?
   Yes, they like (to) very much.
3. Do you like this seat, sir?
   No, I don't like window seats.
4. What do you like to do, ladies?
   We like to read and to travel.

▶ *2.* **Possessive pronouns**   *(Pronombres posesivos)*

Singular		Plural		
Masculine	**Feminine**	**Masculine**	**Feminine**	
el mío	la mía	los míos	las mías	*mine*
el tuyo	la tuya	los tuyos	las tuyas	*yours* (fam.)
el suyo	la suya	los suyos	las suyas	{ *yours* (form.) *his* *hers*
el nuestro	la nuestra	los nuestros	las nuestras	*ours*
el vuestro	la vuestra	los vuestros	las vuestras	*yours* (fam.)
el suyo	la suya	los suyos	las suyas	{ *yours* (form.) *theirs*

♦ In Spanish, the possessive pronouns agree in gender and number with the thing possessed. They are generally used with the definite article.

—Aquí están **mis maletas.** ¿Dónde están **las tuyas?**   *Here are my suitcases. Where are yours?*

—**Las mías** están en mi cuarto.   *Mine are in my room.*

—**Nuestro profesor** es de Colombia.   *Our professor is from Colombia.*

—**El nuestro** es de Venezuela.   *Ours is from Venezuela.*

ATENCIÓN

After the verb **ser,** the definite article is frequently omitted when ownership is indicated.

—¿Estos billetes son **suyos,** señor?   *Are these tickets yours, sir?*

—No, no son **míos.**   *No, they're not mine.*

♦ Because the third-person forms of the possessive pronouns (**el suyo, la suya, los suyos, las suyas**) could be ambiguous, they may be replaced for clarification by the following.

el de	⎧ Ud.	el [libro] de él
la de	⎪ él	el **de él**
los de	⎨ ella	el **suyo**
las de	⎪ Uds.	Es **suyo.** *(unclarified)*
	⎪ ellos	Es **el de él.** *(clarified)*
	⎩ ellas	

—Estas maletas son de Eva y de Jorge, ¿no?   *These suitcases are Eva's and Jorge's, aren't they?*

—Bueno, la maleta azul es **de ella** y la maleta marrón es **de él.**   *Well, the blue suitcase is hers, and the brown suitcase is his.*

PRÁCTICA

A. Provide the correct possessive pronouns with each subject.

MODELO: Yo tengo una tarjeta postal. Es...
         Yo tengo una tarjeta postal. Es mía.

1. Mario tiene un billete. Es...
2. Nosotros tenemos dos pasajes. Son...

3. Tú tienes una llave. Es...
4. Inés tiene dos pinturas. Son...
5. Yo tengo dos casas. Son...
6. Ud. tiene una carta. Es...
7. Ellos tienen las toallas. Son...
8. Paco tiene una botella de vino. Es...

B. Make comparisons between the objects and people described and your own acquaintances and possessions. Use appropriate possessive pronouns when answering the questions.

1. Nuestro profesor de español es de Cuba. ¿Y el de ustedes?
2. Mi casa tiene cuatro cuartos. ¿Y la tuya?
3. Mis amigos viven en San Diego. ¿Y los tuyos?
4. Mi cumpleaños es en septiembre. ¿Y el tuyo?
5. Nuestras maletas son verdes. ¿Y las de ustedes?
6. La hermana de ella es muy bonita. ¿Y la de tu amigo?
7. Su idioma es el inglés. ¿Y el tuyo?
8. Mis primas son uruguayas. ¿Y las tuyas?

▶ *3.* Time expressions with **hacer**   *(Expresiones de tiempo con el verbo **hacer**)*

♦ English uses the present perfect progressive or the present perfect tense to express how long something has been going on.

*I **have been living** here for twenty years.*

♦ Spanish uses the following construction.

Hace + *length of time* + **que** + *verb* (in the present tense)
Hace   veinte años   que   vivo aquí.

—**¿Cuánto tiempo hace que** Ud. estudia español?	*How long have you been studying Spanish?*
—**Hace** tres meses **que** estudio español.	*I have been studying Spanish for three months.*
—¿Tienes mucha hambre?	*Are you very hungry?*
—¡Sí! **Hace** ocho horas **que** no como.	*Yes! I haven't eaten for eight hours.*

PRÁCTICA

A. Provide some information about yourself.

1. ¿Cuánto tiempo hace que usted vive en esta ciudad?
2. ¿Cuánto tiempo hace que usted estudia aquí?
3. ¿Cuánto tiempo hace que usted trabaja en esta ciudad?
4. ¿Cuánto tiempo hace que usted habla español?
5. ¿Cuánto tiempo hace que usted no come?
6. ¿Cuánto tiempo hace que usted no ve a sus padres?

B. Be an interpreter. What are these people saying?

1. How long have you been studying Spanish?
   I have been studying it for six months.
2. How long has he been working at the travel agency?
   Five years.
3. How long have you known your professor?
   I have known her for two weeks.
4. Are you still working?
   Yes, I've been working for two hours.

▶ *4.* **Preterit of regular verbs** *(Pretérito de verbos regulares)*

♦ Spanish has two simple past tenses: the preterit and the imperfect. (The imperfect will be studied in **Lección 9.**)

♦ The preterit of regular verbs is formed as follows. Note that the endings for the **-er** and **-ir** verbs are the same.

-**ar** verbs	-**er** verbs	-**ir** verbs
tomar *to take*	**comer** *to eat*	**escribir** *to write*
tom**é**	com**í**	escrib**í**
tom**aste**	com**iste**	escrib**iste**
tom**ó**	com**ió**	escrib**ió**
tom**amos**	com**imos**	escrib**imos**
tom**asteis**	com**isteis**	escrib**isteis**
tom**aron**	com**ieron**	escrib**ieron**

♦ Note that the first-person plural of **-ar** and **-ir** verbs is identical to the present tense forms.

—**Salimos** de casa a las seis.   *We left home at six.*
—¿A qué hora **llegaste** al hospital?   *What time did you arrive at the hospital?*
—**Llegué** a las siete y **empecé** a trabajar.   *I arrived at seven and I started to work.*

♦ Verbs ending in **-gar**, **-car**, and **-zar** change g to **gu**, c to **qu**, and z to **c** before é in the first person of the preterit: **pagar** → **pagué**; **buscar** *(to look for)* → **busqué**; **empezar** → **empecé**.

♦ Verbs of the **-ar** and **-er** groups that are stem-changing in the present indicative are regular in the preterit.

Rosa **volvió** a las seis y **cerró** las puertas.	*Rosa returned at six o'clock and closed the doors.*

♦ Spanish has no equivalent for the English word *did* used as an auxiliary verb in questions and negative sentences.

Yo no lo terminé.	*I did not finish it.*
¿Tú lo terminaste?	*Did you finish it?*

♦ The preterit tense is used to refer to actions or states that the speaker views as completed in the past.

Como el avión **salió** con dos horas de retraso, **llegamos** muy tarde.	*Since the plane left two hours behind schedule, we arrived very late.*

PRÁCTICA

A. What verb forms are missing in the following conversations?

1. —¿Tú _____ por teléfono con tus suegros ayer?
   —Sí, _____ con ellos. Los _____ por la mañana. _____ hasta las once. (hablar / llamar / charlar)
2. —¿A qué hora _____ ustedes?
   —Yo _____ a las cuatro y Mario _____ a las seis. (volver / volver / volver)
3. —¿ _____ tú las tarjetas que yo te _____ ?
   —No, no las _____ . (recibir / mandar / recibir)
4. —¿A qué hora _____ Ud., señorita?
   — _____ a las nueve y _____ a trabajar a las nueve y media. (llegar / llegar / comenzar)
5. —¿ _____ Uds. las puertas?
   —Sí, _____ las puertas y _____ las ventanas. (cerrar / cerrar / abrir)

B. The following people did something unusual yesterday. Say what they did using the preterit tense.

MODELO: Yo siempre como camarones...
Yo siempre como camarones, pero ayer **comí** *langosta.*

1. Ellos siempre trabajan por la tarde...
2. Tú siempre vuelves a las cinco...
3. Ana siempre me espera...
4. Yo siempre le escribo en español...
5. Nosotros siempre estudiamos por la mañana...
6. Yo siempre pago...
7. Ella siempre sale con Jorge...
8. Yo siempre empiezo a trabajar a las siete...

C. What did you and your friends do yesterday?

1. ¿Qué comieron Uds. ayer?
2. ¿Qué bebieron?
3. ¿Ud. estudió español ayer?
4. ¿A qué hora salió Ud. de su casa?
5. ¿A qué hora llegó Ud. a la universidad?
6. ¿Su papá trabajó ayer?
7. ¿Dónde almorzó su mamá?
8. ¿A qué hora volvió Ud. a su casa?

▶ **5. Direct and indirect object pronouns used together**
(Pronombres de complemento directo e indirecto usados juntos)

◆ When an indirect object pronoun and a direct object pronoun are used together, the indirect object pronoun always comes first.

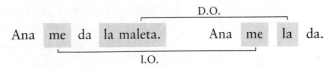

D.O.

Ana me da la maleta.   Ana me la da.

I.O.

◆ With an infinitive, the pronouns can either be placed before the conjugated verb or be attached to the infinitive.

I.O. D.O.

Ana me la va a dar.

Ana   va a dármela.[1]

---

[1] Note the use of the written accent, which follows the rules for accentuation. See Appendix A.

♦ With the present progressive, the pronouns can either be placed before the conjugated verb or be attached to the gerund.

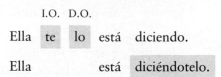

I.O.   D.O.

Ella   te   lo   está   diciendo.

Ella   está   diciéndotelo.

♦ If both pronouns begin with **l**, the indirect object pronoun (**le** or **les**) is changed to **se**.

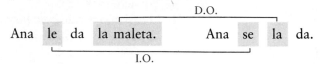

D.O.

Ana   le   da   la maleta.   Ana   se   la   da.

I.O.

For clarification, it is sometimes necessary to add **a él, a ella, a Ud., a Uds., a ellos,** or **a ellas.**

—¿A quién le da la maleta Ana?
—Se **la** da **a él.**

PRÁCTICA

A. You have a friend who is always willing to help others. Explain how, using the information provided.

MODELO: *Yo necesito una maleta.*   (comprar)
             Mi amigo **me** *la compra.*

1. *Yo necesito dos tarjetas postales.*   (comprar)
2. *Tú necesitas los discos.*   (traer)
3. *Nosotros queremos helado.*   (servir)
4. *Elsa necesita un bolso de mano.*   (prestar)
5. *Mis hermanos necesitan dinero.*   (dar)
6. *Mi prima necesita las maletas.*   (traer)
7. *Ud. necesita las cintas.*   (enviar)
8. *Yo quiero el periódico.*   (dar)

B. Whenever people ask Oscar to do something, he says he can't do it. Tell us how Oscar would respond to each request.

MODELO: —Oscar, ¿puedes traer*me el tocadiscos?*
            —*No, no puedo traértelo.*

1. —Oscar, ¿vas a mandar*me el dinero?*
2. —Oscar, ¿puedes dar*le los discos* a Julio?
3. —Oscar, ¿puedes comprar*le el periódico* a mamá?

4. —Oscar, ¿puedes prestar*me tus libros?*
5. —Oscar, ¿vas a traer*nos el helado?*
6. —Oscar, ¿puedes dar*le las maletas* a Luis?

C. Now repeat Exercise B, following the model below.

MODELO: —Oscar, ¿puedes traer*me el tocadiscos?*
—No, no **te lo puedo traer.**

D. Tell a classmate what you do for people and what people do for you.

1. Cuando tú necesitas dinero, ¿se lo pides a tu papá?
2. Cuando tú les pides dinero a tus padres, ¿te lo dan?
3. Si yo necesito tu libro de español, ¿me lo prestas?
4. Si ustedes no entienden algo, ¿se lo preguntan a su profesor(a)?
5. Si tú y yo somos amigos y yo necesito tu coche, ¿tú me lo prestas?
6. Necesito tu pluma. ¿Puedes prestármela?

E. Be an interpreter. What are these people saying?

1. Are you going to give me the tickets?
   Yes, I'm going to give them to you tonight, Miss Peña.
2. When did you send him the postcards?
   I sent them to him yesterday.
3. And the suitcase? Can you lend it to me?
   Yes, Anita, I am going to lend it to you.
4. Did your grandmother send you the cake, Mr. Vega?
   Yes, she sent it to us yesterday.

¡A ver cuánto aprendió!

A. ¡Conversemos!

Reread the dialogue in this lesson and be ready to discuss the following.

1. ¿Cuánto tiempo hace que Teresa y Silvia hablan por teléfono?
2. ¿Qué le está contando Teresa a su amiga?
3. ¿A Teresa le gustó más Machu Picchu o Lima?
4. ¿Silvia recibió una tarjeta postal de Teresa? ¿Por qué?
5. ¿Qué le prestó Silvia a Teresa para su viaje?
6. ¿Por qué pagó Teresa exceso de equipaje?
7. Teresa llevó la maleta de Silvia. ¿Llevó también la suya?
8. ¿Cuánto le costó a Teresa el pasaje?
9. ¿Por qué llegó el avión tarde a Lima?
10. ¿Qué pasó en la agencia de viajes?
11. Las vacaciones de Teresa son mejores que las vacaciones de Silvia. ¿Por qué?
12. ¿Cómo van a viajar Teresa y Silvia la próxima vez? ¿Por qué?

B. ¡Repase el vocabulario!

Complete the following with words from the lesson vocabulary.

1. No me gusta viajar en la _____ de fumar.
2. No es la puerta de entrada; es la puerta de _____ .
3. Le voy a _____ a Teresa las maletas que me prestó.
4. ¿Quiere un _____ de ventanilla o de pasillo?
5. Caracas es la _____ de Venezuela.
6. Teresa me está contando _____ su viaje a Machu Picchu.
7. Como Ana y yo viajamos _____ , conversamos durante _____ el viaje.
8. —¿Qué _____ el vuelo?
   —Un _____ largo.
9. Los viajeros llegaron tarde; llegaron con dos horas de _____ .
10. —¿Le vas a prestar mil dólares para ir a Las Vegas?
    ¡¿Estás _____ ?!
11. Yo les deseé un _____ viaje a los turistas.
12. Compré un pasaje de ida y _____ .
13. Le voy a enviar una _____ postal.
14. —¿Tienes seis maletas? ¡Vas a pagar exceso de _____ !
15. —¿Le vas a devolver el dinero que te prestó?
    —¡ _____ !

C. Situaciones

What would you say in the following situations? What might the other person say?

1. You are at a travel agency. Tell the travel agent you need to buy a first class, round-trip ticket to Mexico City. Ask the agent if you need a passport; then ask if there are any flights leaving on Saturday mornings.
2. You are at the airport. Tell the airline representative that you have two suitcases, and ask him or her if you can take your carry-on bag on the plane.
3. Wish someone a nice trip.
4. A friend has borrowed your suitcase. Ask him or her when he or she plans to return it to you, and tell him or her that you are going on a trip. Arrange to see your friend tomorrow at noon.

Para escribir

Complete the following dialogue.

En la agencia de viajes, el señor Vega compra un pasaje para Caracas.

SR. VEGA — _____

AGENTE —Un pasaje de ida y vuelta a Caracas cuesta cuarenta mil pesos.

SR. VEGA — _____

AGENTE —Turista.

SR. VEGA — _____

AGENTE —Necesita sólo el pasaporte.

SR. VEGA — _____

AGENTE —No, mañana no hay vuelos para Caracas. Hay vuelos los martes y los jueves.

SR. VEGA — _____

AGENTE —¿Para el martes? Está bien.

SR. VEGA — _____

AGENTE —El avión sale al mediodía.

SR. VEGA — _____

AGENTE —Puede llevar dos maletas y un bolso de mano. Buen viaje, señor Vega.

Lima-Sheraton Hotel

CASILLA POSTAL No. 588
PASEO DE LA REPUBLICA 170 — LIMA - PERU

En la vida real

Entrevista

Choose a partner and interview each other, using the **tú** form.

Pregúntele a su compañero(-a)...

1. ...adónde le gusta ir cuando tiene vacaciones.
2. ...si le gusta más viajar en avión o en tren.
3. ...si viaja en primera clase o en clase turista.
4. ...si cuando viaja les manda tarjetas postales a sus amigos.
5. ...si lleva mucho equipaje cuando viaja.
6. ...si conoció a alguien interesante en sus vacaciones. (¿A quién?)
7. ...si sus vacaciones son magníficas o aburridas.
8. ...adónde va a ir de vacaciones la próxima vez.

En una agencia de viajes

You and a classmate will play the roles of a travel agent and a traveler. Discuss the following.

1. ticket prices according to destination and different kinds of transportation
2. prices for first class or tourist class, one-way or round-trip
3. flight schedules
4. seat reservations
5. how much luggage can be taken

Selección de una aerolínea

Do the following activities based on the information contained in the advertisement for Eastern Airlines.

1. Un amigo suyo quiere viajar a Buenos Aires. ¿Qué ventajas *(advantages)* tiene si viaja con Eastern, teniendo en cuenta *(keeping in mind)* lo siguiente?

    - No habla inglés.
    - Quiere reservar el hotel y alquilar un coche en Buenos Aires.
    - Quiere ver una película *(movie)* en el avión, pero no entiende inglés.
    - Le gusta estar cómodo.
    - Le gusta comer bien.

2. Él necesita la siguiente información. ¿Puede Ud. dársela?

    - Cómo es el sistema de reservaciones de Eastern.
    - A cuántos países vuela Eastern.
    - Si puede volar a Puerto Rico por Eastern.

- A qué número de teléfono tiene que llamar para hacer reservaciones.
- Por qué llaman a Eastern «las alas *(wings)* de América».

Para todo un continente, toda una línea aérea.

Más de 130 ciudades en 24 países de América.

Eastern posee **el sistema computarizado de reservaciones más avanzado (SYSTEMONE®) y la flota aérea más grande y moderna** a través de América.

Con una sola llamada a Eastern usted puede hacer cuantas reservaciones de vuelos, hoteles y alquiler de autos desee. En un instante. Del Canadá a la Argentina. O a través del Caribe. Y luego volar a más destinos fascinantes a través de América que con ninguna otra línea aérea. Disfrutando de películas en inglés o español en la comodidad de nuestros **aviones L-1011 Whisperliner® de cabina ancha.** O escuchando música estereofónica. Y deleitándose con los menús exquisitos y vinos selectos de nuestro exclusivo servicio **El InterAmericano** en todos nuestros vuelos a través de Centro y Sudamérica. Sin costo alguno en Clase Económica. Sin límite al lujo en **Primera Clase.**

Consulte a su Agente de Viajes o llame al **873-3000** de Eastern Airlines en **Miami.** Para reservaciones en español, llame al **873-3780.**

EASTERN
Las alas de América

©1985 Eastern Air Lines, Inc.

UNA ACTIVIDAD ESPECIAL

The class is to be divided into several groups, each of which is to select an ideal vacation spot. Once this is done, all destinations will be listed on the board. You will then write a postcard to a member of another group describing your experiences during vacation. After each class member has received a card from a member of another group, cards may be read and discussed in groups.

Dos chicas españolas lavan los platos mientras conversan.

OBJECTIVES

Pronunciation   The Spanish **l, r, rr,** and **z**

Structure   Reflexive constructions • Some uses of the definitive article • Preterit of **ser, ir,** and **dar** • Preterit of **e:i** and **o:u** stem-changing verbs

Communication   You will learn vocabulary related to household chores and the beauty parlor.

Un día muy ocupado

Ana María e[1] Isabel se levantaron muy temprano hoy para limpiar el apartamento. Ana María está un poco cansada porque anoche no durmió muy bien. Isabel tiene turno en la peluquería por la tarde para cortarse el pelo.

Por la noche las dos están invitadas a la fiesta de cumpleaños de su amiga Eva.

ANA MARÍA —Ya barrí la cocina, le pasé la aspiradora a la alfombra y limpié el baño.

ISABEL —Yo cociné, planché mi vestido rojo y fui a la tienda a comprar el regalo para Eva.

ANA MARÍA —¡Ah!, ahora que me acuerdo, ¿tu hermano me consiguió las entradas para el concierto?

ISABEL —No, no le diste el dinero. Él te lo pidió anoche y tú te olvidaste de dárselo.

ANA MARÍA —¡Ah!, sí. ¡Qué tonta soy!... Oye, no sé qué ponerme para ir a la fiesta.

ISABEL —¿Por qué no te pones el vestido azul?

ANA MARÍA —Porque me lo probé ayer y no me queda bien.

ISABEL —¡Caramba! Ya es tarde. Tengo que bañarme y vestirme. Tengo turno en la peluquería a las tres.

ANA MARÍA —Yo voy a bañar al perro y más tarde me voy a lavar la cabeza. ¿Tenemos champú?

ISABEL —Sí, yo fui a la farmacia ayer y lo compré. Está en el botiquín.

En la peluquería, Isabel lee una revista mientras espera.

ISABEL —Quiero corte, lavado y peinado.

PELUQUERA —Tiene el pelo muy lacio. ¿No quiere una permanente?

ISABEL —No, no me gustan los rizos. ¡Ay, tengo el pelo muy largo!

PELUQUERA —Ahora está de moda el pelo corto. (*Le corta el pelo y, cuando termina, Isabel se mira en el espejo.*)

ISABEL —¡Muy bien! Ahora quiero pedir turno para mi amiga para la semana próxima.

PELUQUERA —¿El miércoles a las nueve y media? Generalmente hay menos gente por la mañana.

ISABEL —Está bien. Mi amiga se llama Ana María Rocha.

---

[1]Note that before a word beginning with i or hi, the equivalent of *and* is e.

A VERY BUSY DAY

Today Ana María and Isabel got up very early to clean the apartment. Ana María is a little tired because she didn't sleep very well last night. Isabel has an appointment to get a haircut at the beauty parlor in the afternoon.

In the evening, they're both invited to their friend Eva's birthday party.

A. I already swept the kitchen, vacuumed the rug, and cleaned the bathroom.

I. I did the cooking, ironed my red dress, and went to the store to buy the present for Eva.

A. Oh, now that I remember, did your brother get me the tickets for the concert?

I. No, you didn't give him the money. He asked you for it last night, but you forgot to give it to him.

A. Oh, yes. What a fool I am! . . . Listen, I don't know what to wear to go to the party.

I. Why don't you wear your blue dress?

A. Because I tried it on yesterday and it doesn't fit right.

I. Gee! It's late. I have to take a bath and get dressed. I have an appointment at the hairdresser's at three.

A. I'm going to bathe the dog, and afterwards I'm going to wash my hair. Do we have shampoo?

I. Yes, I went to the drugstore yesterday and bought it. It's in the medicine cabinet.

At the beauty parlor, Isabel reads a magazine while she waits.

Vocabulario

COGNADOS

el **apartamento**	apartment	**generalmente**	generally
el **concierto**	concert	**invitado(-a)**	invited
el **champú**	shampoo	la **permanente**	permanent
la **farmacia**	pharmacy, drugstore		

NOMBRES

la **alfombra** carpet, rug
la **aspiradora** vacuum cleaner
el **botiquín** medicine cabinet
la **cocina** kitchen
el **corte** cut, haircut
la **entrada** ticket (i.e., to a show)
el **espejo** mirror
la **gente**[1] people
el **lavado** shampoo, wash
el **peinado** hairdo, style
el **pelo** hair
la **peluquería**, el **salón de belleza** salon, beauty parlor
el (la) **peluquero(-a)** hairdresser, beautician
el **perro** dog
el **regalo** present, gift
la **revista** magazine
el **rizo** curl
la **semana** week
la **tienda** store
el (la) **tonto(-a)** fool
el **turno**, la **cita** appointment
el **vestido** dress

VERBOS

acordarse (o:ue)[2] to remember
bañar(se) to bathe (oneself)
barrer to sweep
cocinar to cook
cortar(se) to cut
esperar to wait (for)
levantarse to get up
limpiar(se) to clean (oneself)
llamarse to be called
olvidarse (de) to forget
planchar to iron
ponerse to put on
probarse (o:ue) to try on
quedar to fit
terminar to finish
vestirse (e:i) to get dressed

ADJETIVOS

lacio straight (hair)

OTRAS PALABRAS Y EXPRESIONES

anoche last night
ayer yesterday
cortarse el pelo to get a haircut
de moda in style
lavarse la cabeza to wash (one's) hair
pasar la aspiradora to vacuum
pedir turno, cita to make an appointment
temprano early

---

[1] **Gente** is used in the singular in Spanish. [2] **Acordarse** is always used with a reflexive pronoun.

I. I want my hair cut, washed, and styled.

B. Your hair is very straight. Would you like a permanent?

I. No, I don't like curls. Oh, my hair is very long!

B. Short hair is in style now. *(She cuts her hair and, when she finishes, Isabel looks at herself in the mirror.)*

I. Very nice! Now I would like to make an appointment for my friend for next week.

B. Wednesday at nine-thirty? Generally there are fewer people in the morning.

I. Fine. My friend's name is Ana María Rocha.

Vocabulario adicional

la **barbería**   barbershop
Tengo cita en la **barbería.**

el **barbero**   barber
El **barbero** me cortó el pelo.

ensuciar(se)   to get (oneself) dirty
Tú tienes que limpiar la cocina porque tú la **ensuciaste.**

la **escoba**   broom
No puedo barrer porque no tengo **escoba.**

la **máquina de afeitar**   razor
Me afeito con una **máquina de afeitar.**

pasado(-a)   last
Me corté el pelo la semana **pasada.**

peinar(se)   to comb somebody's (one's) hair
La peluquera me **peina** muy bien.

el **peine**   comb
Quiero peinarme. ¿Dónde está el **peine?**

regalar   to give (as a gift)
Marina me **regaló** un vestido rosado.

el **rizador**   curling iron
Si quieres rizos, tienes que usar el **rizador.**

el **secador**   hair dryer
¿Tienes el **secador?**

¿Lo sabía Ud.... ?

■ El nombre María es muy popular en los países de habla hispana. Generalmente se usa con otro nombre: María Isabel, María del Pilar, Ana María y otros. Es un nombre de mujer, pero también lo usan muchos hombres como segundo nombre: José María, Luis María, etc.

■ En los países de habla hispana, las peluquerías modernas usadas tanto por hombres como por mujeres no son tan comunes como en los Estados Unidos. La mayoría de los hombres van a las barberías *(barbershops)* y las mujeres van a los salones de belleza.

Pronunciación

▶ *A.* The Spanish **l**

The Spanish **l** is pronounced like the *l* in the English word *lean*. The tip of the tongue must touch the palate. Listen to your teacher and repeat the following words.

hola	Ángel	al rato
español	Julia	Aníbal
postal	él	telegrama

▶ *B.* The Spanish **r**

The Spanish **r** sounds something like the *dd* in the English word *ladder*. Listen to your teacher and repeat the folowing words.

periódico	ahora	tarde
caminar	Carlos	parado
certificado	giro	extranjero

▶ *C.* The Spanish **rr**   *(spelled **r** at the beginning of words and **rr** between vowels)*

The Spanish **rr** is a strong trill. Listen to your teacher and pronounce the following words.

correo	Rosa	Reyes
rato	arriba	Roberto
retirar	Raúl	reservación

▶ *D.* The Spanish **z**

In Latin America the Spanish **z** is pronounced like the *ss* in the English word *pressing*. In Spain it is pronounced like the *th* in the English word *think*. Avoid using the buzzing sound of the English *z* in the words *zoo* and *zebra*. Listen to your teacher and repeat the following words.

pizarra	cruz	Pérez
Zulema	zoológico	tiza
lápiz	zorro	azul

Estructuras gramaticales

▶ *1.* Reflexive constructions   *(Construcciones reflexivas)*

A. Reflexive pronouns

Subjects		Reflexive Pronouns
yo	me	*myself, to (for) myself*
tú	te	*yourself, to (for) yourself* (**tú** form)
nosotros	nos	*ourselves, to (for) ourselves*
vosotros	os	*yourselves, to (for) yourselves* (**vosotros** form)
Ud.		*yourself, to (for) yourself*
Uds.		*yourselves, to (for) yourselves*
él		*himself, to (for) himself*
ella	se	*herself, to (for) herself*
		itself, to (for) itself
ellos, ellas		*themselves, to (for) themselves*

- Reflexive pronouns are used whenever the direct or indirect object is the same as the subject of the sentence.

- Note that except for **se,** the reflexive pronouns have the same forms as the direct and indirect object pronouns.

- The third-person singular and plural **se** is invariable.

- Reflexive pronouns are positioned in the sentence in the same manner as object pronouns. They are placed in front of a conjugated verb: **Yo *me* levanto;** or they may be attached to an infinitive or to a present participle: **Yo voy a levantar*me*. Yo estoy levantándo*me*.**

B. Reflexive verbs

- Many verbs can be made reflexive in Spanish, that is, can be made to act upon the subject, by the use of a reflexive pronoun.

Julia baña al perro.

Julia se baña.

Elsa acuesta a su hijo a las siete.

Elsa se acuesta a las diez.

lavarse *(to wash oneself, to wash up)*	
Yo **me lavo**	*I wash (myself)*
Tú **te lavas**	*You wash (yourself)* (**tú** form)
Ud. **se lava**	*You wash (yourself)* (**Ud.** form)
Él **se lava**	*He washes (himself)*
Ella **se lava**	*She washes (herself)*
Nosotros **nos lavamos**	*We wash (ourselves)*
Vosotros **os laváis**	*You wash (yourselves)* (**vosotros** form)
Uds. **se lavan**	*You wash (yourselves)* (**Uds.** form)
Ellos **se lavan**	*They (m.) wash (themselves)*
Ellas **se lavan**	*They (f.) wash (themselves)*

♦ In addition to the verbs included in the dialogue, the following verbs are commonly used in reflexive constructions:

afeitarse *to shave*
acostarse (o:ue) *to go to bed*
despertarse (e:ie) *to wake up*
desvestirse (e:i) *to get undressed*
preocuparse (por) *to worry (about)*
sentarse (e:ie) *to sit down*

—¿A qué hora **se acuestan** Uds.?   *What time do you go to bed?*

—Yo **me acuesto** a las diez y Ana **se acuesta** a las doce.   *I go to bed at ten and Ana goes to bed at twelve.*

♦ Note that the Spanish reflexives are seldom translated using the reflexive pronouns in English: **Yo me acuesto** = *I go to bed*. Note also that the following verbs have different meanings when they are used with reflexive pronouns:

acostar (o:ue)	*to put to bed*	**acostarse**	*to go to bed*
dormir (o:ue)	*to sleep*	**dormirse**	*to fall asleep*
ir	*to go*	**irse**	*to go away, leave*
levantar	*to raise, lift*	**levantarse**	*to get up*
llamar	*to call*	**llamarse**	*to be called*
poner	*to put, place*	**ponerse**	*to put on*
probar (o:ue)	*to try; to taste*	**probarse**	*to try on*
quitar	*to take away*	**quitarse**	*to take off*

PRÁCTICA

A. Talk about what you and your relatives normally do by adding the missing verbs.

1. Mi tía siempre _____ (despertarse) tarde.
2. Yo _____ (levantarme) muy temprano.
3. Mi padre _____ (afeitarse) en el baño.
4. Nosotros _____ (bañarnos) por la mañana.
5. Mi hermana _____ (lavarse) la cabeza todos los días.
6. Mis primos _____ (vestirse) en diez minutos.
7. Yo _____ (desvestirme) y _____ (acostarme).
8. Mi mamá _____ (preocuparse) mucho cuando yo llego tarde.

B. Interview a classmate, asking him or her the following questions.

1. ¿A qué hora te levantaste hoy?
2. ¿A qué hora te acostaste anoche?
3. ¿Puedes bañarte y vestirte en diez minutos?
4. ¿Te lavas la cabeza cuando te bañas?
5. ¿Te miras en el espejo para peinarte?
6. ¿Te acordaste de traer el libro de español?
7. ¿Cómo se llama tu mejor amigo(-a)?
8. ¿Se preocupan tus padres por ti?

C. Say what these people are doing.

1. María _____ bien.

2. Los estudiantes _____ en la clase.

3. Juan le _____ el dinero al niño.

4. Pepito _____ el suéter.

5. Yo _____ la _____ en la clase.

6. Yo _____ a las seis.

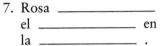

7. Rosa _____
   el _____ en
   la _____ .

8. Rosa _____
   el _____ azul.

9. Sergio _____ a
   Eva.

10. El muchacho _____
    Sergio _____ .

D. Be an interpreter. What are these people saying?

1. Did you try on the black dress?
   Yes, I tried it on, but I didn't like it.
2. What are you doing, Anita?
   I'm putting on the yellow sweater.
3. Where is the comb? I want to comb my hair.
   It's in the bathroom. I always put it there.

SUMMARY OF PERSONAL PRONOUNS

Subject	Direct object	Indirect object	Reflexive	Object of prepositions
yo	me	me	me	mí
tú	te	te	te	ti
usted *(f.)*	la			usted
usted *(m.)*	lo	le	se	usted
él	lo			él
ella	la			ella
nosotros(-as)	nos	nos	nos	nosotros(-as)
vosotros(-as)	os	os	os	vosotros(-as)
ustedes *(f.)*	las			ustedes
ustedes *(m.)*	los	les	se	ustedes
ellos	los			ellos
ellas	las			ellas

► *2.* **Some uses of the definite article** *(Algunos usos del artículo definido)*

The definite article has the following uses in Spanish.

♦ The possessive adjective is often replaced by the definite article in Spanish. An indirect object pronoun or a reflexive pronoun (if the subject performs the action upon himself or herself) usually indicates who the possessor is. Note the use of the definite article in Spanish in the following specific situations indicating possession.

◇ With parts of the body

Voy a cortar**le el pelo.**   *I'm going to cut his hair.*
Me lavé **las manos.**   *I washed my hands.*

◇ With articles of clothing and personal belongings

¿Te quitaste **el vestido?**   *Did you take off your dress?*
Ellos se quitaron **el suéter.**   *They took off their sweaters.*

ATENCIÓN

The number of the subject and verb generally does not affect the number of the thing possessed. Spanish uses the singular to indicate that each person has only one of any particular object.

Ellas se quitaron **el vestido.**	*They took off their dresses.*
(Each one has one dress.)	
but: Ellas se quitaron **los zapatos.**	*They took off their shoes.*
(Each one has two shoes.)	

♦ The definite article is used with nouns used in a general sense and with abstract nouns:

Me gusta **el té,** pero prefiero **el café.**	*I like tea, but I prefer coffee.*
Las madres siempre se preocupan por sus hijos.	*Mothers always worry about their children.*
La educación es muy importante.	*Education is very important.*

♦ The definite article is used with the nouns **cárcel** *(jail)*, **iglesia** *(church)*, and **escuela** when they are preceded by a preposition:

—¿Vas a **la iglesia** los viernes?	*Do you go to church on Fridays?*
—No, voy a **la escuela.**	*No, I go to school.*

♦ Remember that the definite article is also used with days of the week, when indicating titles in indirect address, and when telling time:

El señor Vega viene **el sábado** a **las tres** de la tarde.	*Mr. Vega is coming on Saturday at three o'clock in the afternoon.*

PRÁCTICA

A. Interview a classmate, asking him or her the following questions.

1. ¿Qué te gusta más, el pavo relleno o el arroz con pollo?
2. ¿Qué les gusta más a tus padres, el café o el té?
3. ¿Te gustan los muchachos rubios o los muchachos morenos (las chicas rubias o las chicas morenas)?
4. ¿Te gustan los idiomas extranjeros?
5. ¿Te gusta más el francés o el español?
6. ¿Quién te corta el pelo?
7. ¿Con qué champú te lavas la cabeza?
8. ¿Te quitas los zapatos cuando llegas a tu casa?
9. ¿Vas a la iglesia los domingos?
10. ¿Qué es más importante para ti, el amor o el dinero?

B. Be an interpreter. What are these people saying?

1. What are the girls doing?
   They are putting on their dresses.
2. Did you get your hands dirty, Paquito?
   Yes, but I washed them.
3. Women are more intelligent than men.
   Women always say that.
4. Is he in school?
   No, he is in jail.
5. I don't want to go to college.
   But education is very important!

▶ *3.* Preterit of **ser, ir,** and **dar**   *(Pretérito de los verbos* **ser, ir** y **dar***)*

♦ The preterits of ser, ir, and dar are irregular.

ser *to be*	ir *to go*	dar *to give*
fui	fui	di
fuiste	fuiste	diste
fue	fue	dio
fuimos	fuimos	dimos
fuisteis	fuisteis	disteis
fueron	fueron	dieron

♦ Note that **ser** and **ir** have identical forms in the preterit.

—Ayer **fue** el cumpleaños de
Lucía, ¿no?
—Sí, Ana y yo **fuimos** a su
casa y le **dimos** el regalo.

Yesterday was Lucía's birth-
day, right?
Yes, Ana and I went to her
house and gave her the pres-
ent.

PRÁCTICA

A. Which preterit verb forms are missing in the following
conversations?

1. —¿Adónde _____ tú ayer?
   — _____ a la barbería. El barbero
   me _____ un champú muy bueno.
2. —¿ _____ Uds. a casa de tía Eva ayer?
   —Sí, _____ y le _____ el regalo que tú
   le mandaste.

3. —¿Uds. _____ alumnos del Dr. Paz?
   —Carlos _____ su estudiante, pero Raquel y
   yo _____ alumnos de la Dra. Guerra.
4. —¿A quién le _____ la máquina de afeitar?
   —Se la _____ a Jorge.
5. —¿Adónde _____ ustedes anoche?
   — _____ al concierto. Los padres de Dora
   nos _____ las entradas.

B. Using the cues provided, answer the following questions.

1. ¿Quién fue su profesor? (el Sr. Soto)
2. ¿Le dio a Ud. una «A»? (no, una «B»)
3. ¿Fueron Uds. estudiantes de esta universidad el año
   pasado? (no)
4. ¿Fue Ud. a una fiesta anoche? (sí)
5. ¿Sus padres fueron tambień? (no)
6. ¿Quień dio la fiesta? (Maricarmen)
7. ¿Le dio Ud. un regalo a Maricarmen? (sí)
8. ¿Alguien fue a limpiar la casa después de la fiesta? (no)

▶ *4.* Preterit of **e:i** and **o:u** stem-changing verbs
 *(Pretérito de los verbos que cambian en la raíz: **e:i** y*
 o:u)

♦ Stem-changing verbs of the -**ir** conjugation change **e** to **i** and **o** to **u**
 in the third-person singular and plural of the preterit.

sentir *to feel*		**dormir** *to sleep*	
sentí	sentimos	dormí	dormimos
sentiste	sentisteis	dormiste	dormisteis
sintió	sintieron	durmió	durmieron

♦ Other verbs that follow the same pattern:

pedir	seguir
mentir	conseguir
servir	morir
repetir *(to repeat)*	

Ella dice que no **durmió**
anoche.

*She says she didn't sleep last
night.*

PRÁCTICA

A. Read the following story and supply the missing verbs from the list above.

Anoche Andrés no _____ muy bien porque se acostó muy tarde y se _____ muy mal toda la noche. Su mamá le _____ una taza de té esta mañana, pero él le _____ Pepto Bismol; ella _____ dándole té. Él _____ , «Quiero Pepto Bismol». Su mamá fue a la farmacia, pero no _____ la medicina y Andrés _____ .

Pero todo fue un sueño *(dream)*. Andrés se despertó a las siete y fue a trabajar.

B. Now do the same exercise as above, but add another character: **Anoche Andrés y su hermano Pablo...**

¡A ver cuánto aprendió!

A. ¡Conversemos!

Reread the dialogues in this lesson and be ready to discuss the following.

1. ¿Por qué se levantaron temprano Ana María e Isabel?
2. ¿Cómo durmió Ana María anoche?
3. ¿Las chicas van a estar aburridas esta noche? ¿Por qué no?
4. ¿Quién le pasó la aspiradora a la alfombra?
5. ¿Qué planchó Isabel?
6. ¿Para qué cree Ud. que lo planchó?
7. ¿Quién celebra su cumpleaños esta noche?
8. ¿Por qué dice Ana María que es una tonta?
9. ¿Por qué no se pone Ana María el vestido azul?
10. ¿Qué tiene que hacer Isabel antes de ir a la peluquería?
11. ¿Qué compró Ana María en la farmacia ayer?
12. ¿Por qué no quiere Isabel una permanente?
13. ¿Qué dice Isabel cuando se mira en el espejo?
14. ¿Por qué es mejor ir a la peluquería por la mañana?
15. ¿Cuál es el apellido de Ana María?

B. ¡Repase el vocabulario!

Say whether the following statements are logical or not. If they're not logical, give a statement that is.

1. El perro limpió el apartamento.
2. No puedo afeitarme porque no tengo escoba.
3. Elvira lee una revista en la peluquería.

4. Tengo el pelo muy lacio. Necesito un rizador.
5. Generalmente pongo los mariscos en el botiquín.
6. Tengo que ir a la tienda porque necesito corte, lavado y peinado.
7. No estoy haciendo nada. Estoy muy ocupado.
8. Ahora podemos comer porque yo ya cociné. Preparé cordero y arroz.
9. No quiero una permanente porque no me gustan los rizos.
10. Una semana tiene diez días.
11. Me voy. El peluquero no terminó de cortarme el pelo.
12. Nunca me olvido de nada. Siempre me acuerdo de todo.
13. El peluquero me cortó el pelo.
14. Necesito el secador para planchar mi vestido.
15. Generalmente hay menos gente en la peluquería por la mañana.

C. Situaciones

What would you say in the following situations? What might the other person say?

1. You are at home. Ask your younger sister (brother) if she or he bathed and combed her or his hair. Also ask if she or he cleaned her or his room, and tell her or him to sweep the kitchen.
2. Someone asks about your schedule. Tell him or her what time you generally go to bed and get up. Also say how long it takes you to bathe and get dressed.
3. You are at the beauty parlor (barbershop). Tell the hairdresser what you want done. Then make an appointment for next month.

En la vida real

ENTREVISTA
Choose a partner, then interview each other using the **tú** form.

Pregúntele a su compañero(-a) de clase...

1. ...si va a pedir turno en la peluquería y para cuándo.
2. ...si se lava la cabeza todos los días.
3. ...si cree que está de moda el pelo corto o el pelo largo.
4. ...si está invitado(-a) a alguna fiesta el sábado.
5. ...si tiene algo que ponerse para ir a una fiesta.
6. ...qué le va a regálar a su mejor amigo(-a) para su cumpleaños.
7. ...si barre la cocina o le pasa la aspiradora.
8. ...si sabe cocinar.

UNA VISITA IMPORTANTE
You and a classmate play the role of two roommates who are expecting an important visitor. Discuss what you have to do in order to get the house and yourselves ready for your guest.

¡VAMOS A LA PELUQUERÍA!
Carefully read the following ads for two hair salons, and then answer the questions that follow.

PELUQUERÍA MIRTA

Especiales de esta semana

Permanentes de	$35 a $50
Tinte	$15
Arreglo de uñas	$7
Corte	$8
Corte, lavado y peinado	$20

Abierto de martes a sábado
Martes a viernes de 9 a 5
Sábados de 8 a 6
Avenida Paz #28   Teléfono **287–3574**
Si presenta este anuncio Ud. recibe un **10%** de descuento.

SALÓN DE BELLEZA LA ÉPOCA

- Expertos peluqueros y barberos
- Especialidad en permanentes,
- Tenemos los mejores equipos y los precios más bajos para hombres y mujeres en toda Caracas.

Abierto de martes a domingo de 9 a 5
Para pedir su turno llame al teléfono 23–08–26
Calle Bolívar No. 439
Martes precios especiales para mayores de 50 años.

1. En la peluquería Mirta, ¿cuál es el precio mínimo de un permanente?
2. Si quiere cortarse el pelo el domingo, ¿a qué peluquería puede ir?
3. Mario desea afeitarse y cortarse el pelo. ¿Puede ir a la peluquería Mirta? ¿Por qué?
4. ¿Adónde puede ir? ¿Por qué?
5. ¿Por qué es importante tener el anuncio de la peluquería Mirta?
6. ¿Cuánto hay que pagar en Mirta para arreglarse las uñas y cortarse el pelo?
7. Mi abuela tiene 58 años. ¿Por qué debe ir a la peluquería La Época y qué día debe ir?
8. ¿A qué teléfono debe llamar para pedir turno?
9. ¿Cuál es la especialidad del salón de belleza La Época?
10. ¿Cuánto cuesta un tinte en la peluquería Mirta?

UNA ACTIVIDAD ESPECIAL

The class will be divided into two teams. The teacher will give each member a subject to draw on the board. The other members of the team try to guess what is being drawn. If they guess within one minute they get a point.

Y ahora, *¡vamos a leer!*

Todos los días...

Yo siempre me levanto temprano porque tengo que estar en la universidad a las ocho de la mañana. Me despierto a las seis y media y, después de bañarme, afeitarme y vestirme, desayuno. Me siento en la cocina y estudio, y salgo para la universidad a las siete y media. No llego tarde porque mi profesor de matemáticas es muy estricto.

Tengo clases toda la mañana, y por la tarde voy a la biblioteca a estudiar. A veces° me duermo leyendo algunos de mis libros.

At times

Vuelvo a casa a las cinco. Me desvisto, me quito los zapatos y duermo un rato. Cocino algo para la cena, estudio o hago mi tarea y luego miro las noticias.° Me acuesto a las once y media.

news

Los fines de semana, mis amigos y yo generalmente vamos a la playa o a la montaña.

¡A ver cuánto recuerda!

1. ¿Por qué me levanto siempre temprano?
2. ¿A qué hora me despierto?
3. ¿Qué hago después de bañarme, afeitarme y vestirme?
4. ¿Qué hago en la cocina?
5. ¿A qué hora salgo para la universidad?
6. ¿Por qué no llego tarde?
7. ¿Cuándo tengo clases?
8. ¿Qué hago por la tarde?
9. ¿Qué hago a veces en la biblioteca?
10. ¿A qué hora vuelvo a casa?
11. ¿Qué hago cuando llego a casa?
12. ¿Qué hago después de dormir un rato?
13. ¿A qué hora me acuesto?
14. ¿Adónde voy generalmente los fines de semana?

Una chica española maquillándose para salir con sus amigos.

Para escribir

Now write the answers to the questions above in paragraph form, add punctuation, and you will have a composition. Start this way: «**Ud.**...»

Costa Rica

América Central

PANORAMA HISPÁNICO 5

El Salvador

Guatemala

Honduras

Nicaragua

Panamá

- El canal de Panamá es actualmente la única vía de comunicación que conecta los dos grandes océanos. Ahorra 16.000 kilómetros de travesía para los barcos que antes tenían que doblar por el Cabo de Hornos.

- Costa Rica es el país centroamericano con el ingreso per cápita más alto, unos 3.200 dólares anuales. Frecuentemente llamada «la Suiza de Centroamérica», tiene además uno de los sistemas educativos más avanzados de Latinoamérica.

- En Guatemala tuvo su origen el gran imperio de los mayas. Las ruinas de Tikal, situadas en medio de la selva, representan el centro ritual y arqueológico del llamado período «clásico». En su apogeo, vivían en la ciudad unas 80.000 personas que ocupaban más de 3.000 edificaciones.

- A pesar de ser el país más pequeño de Centroamérica, El Salvador es la nación más densamente poblada. Más de cinco millones de habitantes viven en un área aproximadamente del tamaño del estado de Massachusetts. Nicaragua, en comparación, es cinco veces más grande que El Salvador, pero tiene una población de sólo unos tres millones de habitantes.

◄ Nicaragua se siente orgullosa de su poeta nacional, Rubén Darío, creador y líder del Modernismo, un movimiento literario que surgió a fines del siglo XIX y principios del XX. Las obras más importantes de Darío son: *Azul, Prosas profanas* y *Cantos de vida y esperanza*. En la foto aparece una de las muchas estatuas del gran poeta en el centro de Managua, la capital del país. ¿Qué otros poetas hispanoamericanos puede nombrar Ud.?

▲ La agricultura es la base económica de Guatemala. El producto principal es el café, de fama internacional por su alta calidad. Aquí vemos un secadero de café *(coffee drier)* a orillas del lago Atitlán, que se encuentra a 1.562 metros de altura sobre el nivel del mar en el cráter de un volcán inactivo. ¿Qué otros países latinoamericanos cultivan café?

◄ Estudiantes en la Universidad Nacional Autónoma de Honduras se dirigen a sus clases. Localizada en Tegucigalpa, la capital de Honduras, es el centro educativo más importante del país. ¿Cuál es la universidad más importante en el estado donde Ud. vive?

En la ciudad de Antigua, Guatemala, esta mujer indígena teje uno de los tapetes tradicionales de la región. Utilizando técnicas de tejido traídas por los españoles y diseños y colores típicamente indígenas, los indios han establecido una industria floreciente de telas y tapetes. Otros ejemplos de artesanía de la región son las joyas y los artículos de cerámica. ¿Qué tipos de artesanías se producen en la región donde Ud. vive?

▲ Tikal, situada en un bosque tropical al noroeste de Guatemala, es la ciudad más grande y más antigua de la civilización maya. Aquí se ve el Templo del Gran Jaguar, el edificio más alto y más importante de Tikal. ¿En qué otros países de Hispanoamérica encontramos ciudades mayas como Tikal?

▶ El cultivo del banano es una de las principales fuentes de ingreso de los países centroamericanos. El banano se cultiva en Panamá, Costa Rica, El Salvador, Honduras, Nicaragua y Guatemala. En la foto, un agricultor verifica el tamaño de los bananos en una hacienda de El Salvador. ¿De dónde son los bananos que Ud. compra en el supermercado?

▶ Oscar Arias, presidente de Costa Rica, aparece en la foto con su esposa, Margarita Penón. Arias recibió el Premio Nóbel de la Paz en 1987 por sus esfuerzos en favor de la paz en Centroamérica. En una región famosa por sus revoluciones, guerras y dictaduras, Costa Rica es un país democrático con elecciones libres, sin ejército y con un alto nivel cultural. ¿Sabe Ud. cuál es la capital de Costa Rica?

▲ La construcción del Canal de Panamá por parte del gobierno de los Estados Unidos duró siete años y fue terminada en el año 1914. El Canal mide 82,4 kilómetros y tiene tres esclusas a cada lado del istmo que cruza. ¿Qué otro canal muy famoso conoce Ud.?

Punta del Este, en Uruguay, es uno de los mejores centros turísticos del mundo.

OBJECTIVES

Pronunciation	La entonación
Structure	Irregular preterits • Uses of **por** • Uses of **para** • The imperfect
Communication	You will learn vocabulary related to leisure activities.

Planes de vacaciones

Marisa y Nora, dos chicas chilenas que viven en Buenos Aires, están sentadas en un café de la Avenida de Mayo. Están planeando sus vacaciones de verano, pero no pueden ponerse de acuerdo porque a Nora le gustan las actividades al aire libre y Marisa las odia.

MARISA —Traje unos folletos turísticos sobre excursiones a Punta del Este para mostrártelos.

NORA —Yo estuve allí el año pasado. Me gustó mucho la playa, pero había demasiada gente.

MARISA —Cuando yo era niña mi familia y yo siempre íbamos de vacaciones a Montevideo o a Río de Janeiro.

NORA —Nosotros íbamos al campo o a las montañas. Acampábamos, montábamos a caballo, pescábamos truchas en un lago...

MARISA —¡Qué horrible! Para mí, dormir en una tienda de campaña en un saco de dormir es como un castigo.

NORA —¿Pues sabes lo que yo hice ayer? Compré una caña de pescar para ir de pesca contigo.

MARISA —Tengo una idea. Podemos ir al Hotel del Lago y tú puedes pescar mientras yo nado en la piscina.

NORA —¿Por qué no alquilamos una cabaña en las montañas por unos días? Te vas a divertir...

MARISA —El año pasado me quedé en una cabaña con mi familia y me aburrí horriblemente.

NORA —*(Bromeando)* Porque yo no estaba allí para enseñarte a pescar.

MARISA —¡Por suerte! Oye, en serio, tenemos que ir a la playa porque mi traje de baño me costó un ojo de la cara.

NORA —Yo también quería comprarme uno, pero no pude ir a la tienda.

MARISA —Voy contigo a comprarlo si salimos para Punta del Este el sábado.

NORA —Está bien, pero en julio vamos a Bariloche a esquiar.

MARISA —¡Perfecto! Voy a casa para empezar a hacer las maletas.

LECCIÓN

9

...

VACATION PLANS

Marisa and Nora, two Chilean girls who are living in Buenos Aires, are sitting at a café on Avenida de Mayo. They are planning their summer vacation, but they can't agree (come to an agreement) because Nora likes outdoor activities and Marisa hates them.

M. I brought some tourist brochures about excursions to Punta del Este to show (them to) you.

N. I was there last year. I liked the beach very much, but there were too many people.

M. When I was a child, my family and I always used to go on vacation to Montevideo or to Rio de Janeiro.

N. We used to go to the country or to the mountains. We used to camp, ride horses, fish for trout in a lake . . .

M. How horrible! I think sleeping in a tent in a sleeping bag is like a punishment.

N. Well, do you know what I did yesterday? I bought a fishing rod to go fishing with you.

M. I have an idea. We can go to the Hotel del Lago and you can fish while I swim in the pool.

N. Why don't we rent a cabin in the mountains for a few days? You're going to have fun . . .

M. Last year I stayed in a cabin with my family and I got terribly bored.

N. *(Kidding)* Because I wasn't there to show you how to fish.

M. Luckily! Listen, seriously, we have to go to the beach because my

Vocabulario

COGNADOS

chileno(-a)   Chilean
la **excursión**   excursion
horriblemente   horribly

la **montaña**   mountain
perfecto(-a)   perfect
los **planes**   plans

NOMBRES

el **caballo**   horse
la **cabaña**   cabin
el **campo**   country
la **caña de pescar**   fishing rod
el **castigo**   punishment
el **folleto turístico**   tourist brochure
el **lago**   lake
el (la) **niño(-a)**   child
la **piscina**, la **alberca**
   (Mex.)   swimming pool
la **playa**   beach
el **saco** (la **bolsa**) de
   dormir   sleeping bag
la **tienda de campaña**   tent
el **traje de baño**   bathing suit
la **trucha**   trout

VERBOS

aburrirse   to be bored
acampar   to camp, to go camping
alquilar   to rent
bromear   to kid, to joke
divertirse (e:ie)   to have a good time
enseñar   to show, to teach
esquiar   to ski
montar   to mount, to ride

nadar   to swim
odiar   to hate
pescar   to fish, to catch (a fish)
planear   to plan
quedarse   to stay, remain

ADJETIVOS

sentado(-a)   sitting, seated

OTRAS PALABRAS Y EXPRESIONES

al aire libre   outdoors
demasiado(-a)   too many
en serio   seriously
está bien   fine, all right
hacer las maletas   to pack
ir a casa   to go home
ir de pesca   to go fishing
ir de vacaciones   to go on vacation
me costó un ojo de la cara   it cost me an arm and a leg
ponerse de acuerdo   to agree
por suerte   luckily
por supuesto   of course
pues   well
¡Qué horrible!   How horrible!
sobre   about
solamente   only

Vocabulario adicional

la **autopista**   freeway, highway
En California hay muchas **autopistas**.

cazar   to hunt
No quiero pescar; prefiero **cazar**.

bathing suit cost me an arm and a leg.
N. I wanted to buy myself one also, but I couldn't go to the store.
M. I'll go with you to buy it if we leave for Punta del Este on Saturday.
N. Fine . . . but in July we're going to Bariloche to ski.
M. Perfect! I'm going home to start packing my bags.

el **desierto**   desert
El Sahara es un **desierto.**

el **mar**   sea
Nosotros nadamos en el **mar.**

montar en bicicleta   to ride a bicycle
Ana no sabe **montar en bicicleta.**

la **nieve**   snow
Hay **nieve** en la montaña.

el **océano**   ocean
El **océano** Pacífico es muy grande.

el **país**   country, nation
España es un **país** magnífico.

el **río**   river
El **río** Amazonas está en el Brasil.

el (la) **salvavidas**   lifeguard
Es una buena idea tener **salvavidas** en las playas.

¿Lo sabía Ud.... ?

- Mar del Plata (Argentina), Viña del Mar (Chile) y Punta del Este (Uruguay) están entre las playas más hermosas e importantes de América del Sur. Estas ciudades son centros turísticos internacionales.
- Mucha gente va a Chile y al sur de Argentina (Bariloche) para esquiar durante junio, julio y agosto, que son los meses del invierno en el hemisferio sur *(southern).*

Vista de Mar del Plata, uno de los centros turísticos más importantes de Argentina.

Pronunciación

▶ La entonación

Intonation refers to the variations in the pitch of your voice when you are talking. Intonation patterns in Spanish are different from those in English. Note the following regarding Spanish intonation.

1. For normal statements, the pitch generally rises on the first stressed syllable.

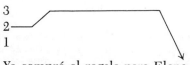

Yo compré el regalo para Elena.

2. For questions eliciting information, the pitch is highest on the stressed syllable of the interrogative pronoun.

¿Cómo está tu mamá?

3. For questions that can be answered with **sí** or **no,** the pitch is generally highest on the last stressed syllable.

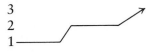

¿Fuiste al mercado ayer?

4. In exclamations, the pitch is highest on the first stressed syllable.

¡Qué bonita es esa alfombra!

Listen to your teacher and repeat the following sentences, imitating closely your teacher's intonation.

1. Marta no trabajó anoche.
2. ¿Dónde vive tu hermano?
3. ¿Le diste el dinero a Ramona?
4. ¡Qué delgado es ese muchacho!

Estructuras gramaticales

▶ *1.* Irregular preterits *(Pretéritos irregulares)*

◆ The following Spanish verbs are irregular in the preterit.

tener:	tuve, tuviste, tuvo, tuvimos, tuvisteis, tuvieron
estar:	estuve, estuviste, estuvo, estuvimos, estuvisteis, estuvieron
poder:	pude, pudiste, pudo, pudimos, pudisteis, pudieron
poner:	puse, pusiste, puso, pusimos, pusisteis, pusieron
saber:	supe, supiste, supo, supimos, supisteis, supieron
hacer:	hice, hiciste, hizo,[1] hicimos, hicisteis, hicieron
venir:	vine, viniste, vino, vinimos, vinisteis, vinieron
querer:	quise, quisiste, quiso, quisimos, quisisteis, quisieron
decir:	dije, dijiste, dijo, dijimos, dijisteis, dijeron[2]
traer:	traje, trajiste, trajo, trajimos, trajisteis, trajeron[2]
conducir:	conduje, condujiste, condujo, condujimos, condujisteis, condujeron[2]
traducir:	traduje, tradujiste, tradujo, tradujimos, tradujisteis, tradujeron[2]

—¿Por qué no **viniste** anoche?   *Why didn't you come last night?*

—No **pude**; **tuve** que trabajar.   *I wasn't able to; I had to work.*

ATENCIÓN

The preterit of **hay** (impersonal form of **haber**) is **hubo** *(there was, there were)*.

Anoche **hubo** una fiesta.   *Last night there was a party.*

PRÁCTICA

A. You and your friend are very efficient. When another friend asks whether you're going to do something, you say you already did it.

MODELO: ¿No vas a traer el saco de dormir?
     Ya lo traje.

1. ¿No vas a poner la caña de pescar en el coche?
2. ¿No vas a hacer la reservación?

---

[1] Note that in the third-person singular form, **c** changes to **z** in order to maintain the soft sound.
[2] Note that in the third-person plural ending of these verbs, the **i** is omitted.

3. ¿No vas a decirle que nos vamos?
4. ¿No van a traer los folletos?
5. ¿No van a poner los trajes de baño en la maleta?
6. ¿No vas a hacer las maletas?

B. Elsa and David are arguing. Supply the missing verbs that we can't hear.

ELSA   —¿Dónde _____ (estar) (tú) anoche?
          ¡ _____ (venir) muy tarde!
DAVID   —¡Te lo _____ (decir)! _____
          (Estar) en casa de mamá. _____ (Tener) que
          hablar con papá. No te llamé porque no
          _____ (poder).
ELSA   —¿No _____ (poder) o no _____
          (querer)?
DAVID   —Bueno. ¿Dónde _____ (poner) tú las cartas
          que yo _____ (traducir) ayer en la oficina?
ELSA   —¡Tú no _____ (traer) ninguna carta!
DAVID   —No... los empleados las _____ (traer) cuando
          _____ (venir) ayer.
ELSA   —Ellos no me _____ (decir) nada. ¡Son unos
          idiotas!

C. This is what always happens. Explain what happened yesterday by completing each sentence in an original manner.

MODELO: Siempre vengo temprano pero ayer...
         Siempre vengo temprano pero ayer vine tarde.

1. Siempre traen los cheques por la mañana pero ayer...
2. Siempre pongo el champú en el botiquín pero anoche...
3. Siempre hace la comida por la tarde pero ayer...
4. Siempre conduces bien pero anoche...
5. Siempre dicen algo pero ayer...
6. Siempre quiere ir al cine pero anoche...

D. Answer the following personal questions about yourself and your friends.

1. ¿Hubo una fiesta en su casa ayer?
2. ¿Dónde estuvieron Uds. anoche?
3. ¿Pudo venir Ud. temprano a la universidad ayer?
4. ¿Vino a la universidad la semana pasada?
5. ¿Qué hicieron sus amigos ayer?
6. ¿Condujo su coche ayer?

7. ¿Qué tuvo que hacer ayer?
8. ¿Uds. tuvieron que pasarle la aspiradora a la alfombra anoche?

▶ *2.* Uses of **por**　　*(Usos de **por**)*

The preposition **por** is used to indicate:

♦ motion *through, around, along, by,* or approximate location

Luis entró **por** la ventana.	*Luis came in through the window.*
Yo fui **por** la playa.	*I went along the beach.*
Enrique va **por** la calle Juárez.	*Enrique is going down Juárez Street.*
Gustavo pasó **por** la cabaña.	*Gustavo went by the cabin.*

♦ cause or motive of an action *(because of, on account of, on behalf of)*

Llegamos tarde **por** el tráfico.	*We were late because of the traffic.*
Lo hago **por** ellos.	*I do it on their behalf.*

♦ agency, means, manner, unit of measure *(by, for, per)*

Siempre viajamos **por** tren.	*We always travel by train.*
Le envié cien dólares **por** correo.	*I sent him a hundred dollars by mail.*
Van a 100 kilómetros **por** hora.	*They're going 100 kilometers per hour.*

♦ *in exchange for*

Te doy cien dólares **por** ese caballo.	*I'll give you a hundred dollars for that horse.*

♦ period of time during which an action takes place *(during, in, for)*

Lo veo mañana **por** la mañana.	*I'll see him tomorrow morning.*
Va a estar aquí **por** dos meses.	*He's going to be here for two months.*

♦ *in search of, for*

Mario fue **por** el doctor.	*Mario went in search of the doctor.*
Voy a venir **por** ti a las siete.	*I'll come by for you at seven.*

PRÁCTICA

A. Interview a classmate, asking him or her the following questions.

1. ¿Tienes una clase por la mañana?
2. Vas a llevar a tu amigo a la playa. ¿A qué hora vas por él?
3. ¿Cuánto pagaste por tu traje de baño?
4. ¿Prefieres viajar por tren o por avión?
5. ¿Pasaste por mi casa anoche?
6. Cuando tú pierdes la llave de tu casa, ¿entras por la ventana?
7. ¿Tú les escribes a tus padres o prefieres llamarlos por teléfono?
8. ¿Tus padres hacen mucho por ti?

B. Be an interpreter. What are these people saying?

1. How much did you pay for the tent, sir?
   I paid three hundred dollars. It cost me an arm and a leg.
2. Did you go through the desert?
   Yes, we went through the Sahara desert.
3. When we went on vacation last year we went by train.
   I prefer to travel by plane.
4. We were in Mexico for one week.
   How much did you pay for the excursion?
   A thousand dollars.

▶ *3.* Uses of **para**   *(Usos de **para**)*

The preposition **para** is used to indicate:

♦ destination in space

Quiero un pasaje **para** Lima.	*I want a ticket for Lima.*
¿A qué hora hay vuelos **para** La Paz?	*What time are there flights to La Paz?*

♦ direction in time, often meaning *by* or *for* a specific date in the future

Quiero un pasaje **para** el sábado.	*I want a ticket for Saturday.*
Debo estar allí **para** el mes de noviembre.	*I must be there by the month of November.*

♦ direction toward a recipient

Compré una escoba **para** la cocina.	*I bought a broom for the kitchen.*
Compramos los regalos **para** Fernando.	*We bought the gifts for Fernando.*

♦ *in order to*

Necesito mil dólares **para** pagar el viaje.

I need a thousand dollars in order to pay for the trip.

Vamos al teatro **para** celebrar nuestro aniversario de bodas.

We are going to the theater to celebrate our wedding anniversary.

♦ comparison *(by the standard of, considering)*

El niño es muy alto **para** su edad.

The child is very tall for his age.

Para norteamericano, habla muy bien el español.

For a North American he speaks Spanish very well.

♦ objective or goal

Nora y yo estudiamos **para** ingenieros.

Nora and I are studying to be engineers.

Mi novio estudia **para** médico.

My boyfriend is studying to be a doctor.

PRÁCTICA

A. Imagine that you and your best friend are planning a trip to Mexico. Answer the following questions.

1. ¿Cuánto dinero necesitan Uds. para pagar el viaje?
2. ¿Van a pedirles dinero a sus padres para el viaje?
3. ¿Para qué día quieren los pasajes?
4. ¿A qué hora sale el avión para México?
5. ¿Van a traer regalos para su familia?
6. Para norteamericanos, ¿hablan Uds. bien el español?
7. ¿Van Uds. a México para practicar el español?
8. John estudia para profesor de español y quiere visitar México. ¿Puede ir con Uds.?

B. Be an interpreter. What are these people saying?

1. This dress is for Lupita? It's very long . . .
   Well, she is very tall for her age.
2. I want a ticket to (for) Santiago for Tuesday.
   In order to leave on Tuesday you have to make a reservation today.
3. Is Adela studying at the university?
   Yes, she is studying to be a doctor.

C. Robert and I are telling you about plans for our trip to Paraguay. Complete the statements using **por** or **para**.

Robert y yo salimos ___*para*___ Asunción la semana próxima. Vamos a viajar ___*por*___ avión. Tenemos pasajes ___*para*___ el sábado ___*por*___ la mañana. Tuvimos que pagar tres mil dólares ___*para por*___ los billetes, pero como pensamos pasar ___*por*___ Caracas y ___*para por*___ Lima, donde vamos a estar ___*por*___ unos días, no es muy caro. Mañana ___*por*___ la tarde vamos a «Nordstrom» ___*para*___ comprar algunos regalos ___*para*___ nuestros amigos paraguayos. Desde Lima, vamos a llamar ___*por*___ teléfono a nuestros amigos en Asunción, y ellos van a ir al aeropuerto ___*por*___ nosotros. Robert me dice que, ___*para*___ americana, hablo muy bien el español y yo le digo que me van a tomar ___*por*___ paraguaya. ¡Pensamos divertirnos mucho!

▶ *4.* **The imperfect** *(El imperfecto de indicativo)*

As you have already learned, there are two simple past tenses in the Spanish indicative: the preterit, which you studied in **Lecciones 7, 8,** and **9,** and the imperfect.

A. Regular Forms

♦ To form the regular imperfect, add the following endings to the verb stem.

-ar verbs		-er and -ir verbs			
hablar		**comer**		**vivir**	
habl-	**aba**	com-	**ía**	viv-	**ía**
habl-	**abas**	com-	**ías**	viv-	**ías**
habl-	**aba**	com-	**ía**	viv-	**ía**
habl-	**ábamos**	com-	**íamos**	viv-	**íamos**
habl-	**abais**	com-	**íais**	viv-	**íais**
habl-	**aban**	com-	**ían**	viv-	**ían**

♦ Note that the endings of the **-er** and **-ir** verbs are the same. Note also that there is a written accent on the final **í** of the endings of the **-er** and **-ir** verbs.

♦ The Spanish imperfect tense is equivalent to three English forms.

Yo **vivía** en Lima. $\begin{cases} \textit{I used to live in Lima.} \\ \textit{I was living in Lima.} \\ \textit{I lived in Lima.} \end{cases}$

♦ The Spanish imperfect is used to refer to habitual or repeated actions in the past, with no reference to when they began or ended.

—¿Tu **asistías** a la universidad cuando **vivías** en Cuba?	*Did you attend the university when you were living in Cuba?*
—No, **trabajaba** cuando **vivía** en Cuba.	*No, I worked when I was living in Cuba.*

♦ The imperfect is also used to refer to actions, events, or states that the speaker views as *in the process of* happening in the past, again with no reference to when they began or ended.

Veníamos para casa cuando vimos a Raúl.	*We were coming home when we saw Raúl.*

B. Irregular Forms

♦ The only irregular verbs in the imperfect are as follows.

ser	ver	ir
era	veía	iba
eras	veías	ibas
era	veía	iba
éramos	veíamos	íbamos
erais	veíais	ibais
eran	veían	iban

—¿Siempre **ibas** a casa de tus abuelos cuando **eras** niño?	*Did you always used to go to your grandparents' house when you were a child?*
—Sí, los **veía** todos los sábados.	*Yes, I used to see them every Saturday.*

PRÁCTICA

A. Ten years ago María wrote this composition about her and her family. Rewrite her composition, using past tenses.

Mi familia y yo vivimos en Barcelona. Mi padre trabaja para la compañía Seat y mi madre enseña en la universidad. Es una profesora excelente. Mis hermanos y yo asistimos a la escuela. Generalmente pasamos las vacaciones en la playa de Sitges, en el mar Mediterráneo. Allí, nadamos, pescamos y tomamos el sol. Como a mi padre le gusta ir a la montaña para esquiar, en invierno vamos a los Pirineos. Mis abuelos viven en Sevilla y no los vemos mucho, pero siempre les escribimos.

B. Interview a classmate, asking him or her the following questions.

1. ¿Dónde vivías tú cuando eras niño(-a)?
2. ¿A qué escuela asistías?
3. ¿Odiabas estudiar o te gustaba?
4. ¿Eras buen estudiante?
5. ¿A dónde iban tú y tu familia de vacaciones?
6. ¿Qué les gustaba hacer?
7. ¿Preferías pasar las vacaciones en el campo o en la ciudad?
8. ¿Te divertías mucho o te aburrías?
9. ¿Veías mucho a tus abuelos?
10. ¿Vivías cerca o lejos de tus abuelos?

C. Use your imagination to complete these sentences in an original manner.

1. Yo iba al lago y tú...
2. Ernesto trabajaba de salvavidas y ellos...
3. Nosotros íbamos a la peluquería los sábados y ellos...
4. Ellos nunca se ponían de acuerdo, pero nosotros...
5. Yo no sabía montar en bicicleta, pero tú...
6. Tú nadabas en el río y él...
7. Ella siempre veía a sus abuelos, pero yo...
8. Yo era profesora y Ud....

¡A ver cuánto aprendió!

A. ¡Conversemos!

Reread the dialogue in this lesson and be ready to discuss the following.

1. ¿Quiénes están sentadas en un café de la Avenida de Mayo?
2. ¿Por qué no pueden ponerse de acuerdo las chicas?
3. ¿Para qué trajo Marisa los folletos turísticos?
4. ¿Cree Ud. que Punta del Este es un lugar popular? ¿Por qué?
5. ¿A qué países iban de vacaciones Marisa y su familia?
6. ¿Qué hacía Nora en sus vacaciones?
7. ¿Qué es un castigo para Marisa? ¿Nora piensa lo mismo?
8. ¿Qué idea tiene Marisa?
9. ¿Se divirtió Marisa en sus vacaciones el año pasado?
10. ¿Es caro el traje de baño de Marisa? ¿Cómo lo sabe Ud.?
11. ¿Qué van a hacer las chicas en Bariloche?
12. ¿Se pusieron de acuerdo las chicas? ¿Cómo lo sabe Ud.?

B. ¡Repase el vocabulario!

Indicate the correct choice, then read the sentence aloud.

1. Rosa nada en (el desierto, el mar, la nieve).
2. Ya hice (la propina, la playa, las maletas).
3. Los muchachos montaron (en el pasaje, a caballo, en el país).
4. Es de Santiago; es (argentino, uruguayo, chileno).
5. Está bien. No vamos a comprar la cabaña. Vamos a (barrerla, alquilarla, bañarla).
6. Supongo que no sabes nadar. Pues voy a (enseñarte, afeitarte, vestirte).
7. Por suerte los chicos se (aburrieron, murieron, divirtieron) mucho.
8. No quiero manejar en (la piscina, la autopista, la cabaña).
9. No te lo digo en serio. Estoy (planeando, bromeando, acampando).
10. El Misisipí es un (lago, río, mar).
11. ¡Perfecto! Todos podemos dormir en (la tienda de campaña, la trucha, el museo).
12. Mis vacaciones fueron magníficas. (Me aburrí horriblemente., No hice nada interesante., Me divertí muchísimo.)
13. Pagué cien dólares por ese espejo. (Fui de pesca., Pedí turno., Me costó un ojo de la cara.)
14. Fuimos de pesca y por supuesto llevamos la (máquina de afeitar, caña de pescar, autopista) nueva.
15. Hay demasiada gente en (el desierto, el océano, las ciudades grandes).

C. Situaciones

What would you say in the following situations? What might the other person say?

1. Someone asks you about your vacation. Say that you learned how to swim and ride a horse, and that you caught a trout.
2. Someone invites you to go camping. Say that you need a tent and a sleeping bag. Ask if you're going to need anything else.
3. You are trying to convince a friend to go camping. Tell him or her how much fun it can be.

Para escribir

Tomás and Víctor are very good friends, but their tastes differ. Tomás likes the outdoors while Víctor prefers city life. Using your imagination, write an account of how each of them spent his vacation last summer.

En la vida real

ENTREVISTA

Choose a partner, then interview each other, using the **tú** form.

Pregúntele a su compañero(-a) de clase...

1. ...si acampó este fin de semana.
2. ...si le gusta ir a las montañas.
3. ...si prefiere montar a caballo o en bicicleta.
4. ...si quiere ir a cazar con Ud. la próxima vez.
5. ...si quiere ir de pesca al lago.
6. ...si pescó alguna vez una trucha enorme.
7. ...si vive cerca del océano Pacífico o del océano Atlántico.
8. ...si es una buena idea tener un salvavidas en la playa.
9. ...si bromea mucho con el profesor (la profesora).
10. ...si le costó un ojo de la cara el libro de español.

PLANES PARA LAS VACACIONES

You and a classmate are going on a vacation. Make plans for the trip, including activities and things you might need to take with you.

Other words and phrases you might want to include:

la **mochila**   *backpack*
los **esquis**   *skis*
el **rifle**   *rifle*
hospedarse   *to stay* (i.e., at a hotel)
escalar   *to climb*

¡DE VIAJE!

Ángela y Elena fueron de vacaciones a Ixtapa y Alberto y Julio fueron a Playa Blanca en la costa del Pacífico de México. Los cuatro viajaron con el Club Mediterráneo.

Mire el siguiente anuncio del periódico y conteste las siguientes preguntas:

1. ¿Cómo son las excursiones en los viajes Bojorquez?
2. ¿Para qué tipo de viajeros son?
3. Las chicas viajaron con el plan 1 a Ixtapa. ¿Qué día salieron y cuántas noches estuvieron en Ixtapa?
4. ¿Cuánto pagaron?
5. Las chicas usaron la tarjeta American Express para pagar el viaje. ¿Qué beneficios recibieron?
6. Los muchachos viajaron con el plan 2 y estuvieron en Playa Blanca por cinco noches. ¿Cuánto les costó el viaje?

UNA ACTIVIDAD ESPECIAL

Imagine that your class is planning a special field trip. One group of students would like to do outdoor activities such as camping, fishing, swimming, etc. Another group would prefer a visit to a large city where one can stay in hotels, visit museums, see films, etc. After preparing for a discussion, both groups get together and try to convince the other of their views.

Take this test. When you finish, check your answers in the answer key provided for this section in Appendix E. Then use a red pen to correct any mistakes you may have made. Ready?

LECCIÓN 7

A. Construction with *gustar*

Write the following sentences in Spanish.

1. I don't like that travel agency.
2. He likes the aisle seat.
3. Do you like this handbag?
4. We don't like to travel by plane.
5. Do they like their hotel?

B. Possessive pronouns

Give the Spanish equivalent of the pronouns in parentheses.

1. El pasaje de Nora está en la mesa. _____ está en mi cuarto. *(Mine)*
2. Mis tarjetas están aquí. ¿Dónde están _____ , señor Vega? *(yours)*
3. Ellos van a enviar sus cartas hoy. ¿Cuándo vamos a enviar _____ ? *(ours)*
4. No tengo maletas. ¿Puedes prestarme _____ , Anita? *(yours)*
5. Aquí están los libros de Jorge. ¿Dónde están _____ ? *(ours)*
6. Enrique necesita tu cuaderno, Eva. _____ está en la universidad. *(His)*

C. Time expressions with *hacer*

Form sentences with the elements provided, using the expression **hace... que** to report how long an event has been going on. Follow the model.

MODELO: una hora / nosotros / trabajar
   Hace una hora que nosotros trabajamos.

1. dos días / yo / no dormir
2. un mes / tú / no llamarme
3. media hora / nosotros / estar sentados
4. un año / ellos / vivir / España
5. doce horas / mi hija / no comer

D. Preterit of regular verbs

Instead of talking about things that *are going to happen,* let's talk about things that *have already happened* by changing the following sentences to the preterit.

1. Mañana Luisa y yo vamos a comprar los billetes.   (Ayer)
2. La semana próxima yo voy a viajar.   (La semana pasada)
3. Ella va a esperarme en el aeropuerto.   (Ayer)
4. ¿No van a pagar Uds. la cuenta?   (Anoche)
5. Ellos van a abrir las ventanas.   (Al mediodía)
6. Nosotros vamos a comer en la cafetería.   (El lunes)
7. ¿Vas a empezar a estudiar?   (Esta mañana)
8. Yo voy a prestarle las maletas.   (Ayer)

E. Direct and indirect object pronouns used together

Answer the following questions, substituting direct object pronouns for the italicized words and using the cues provided.

1. ¿Cuándo *le* van a mandar *el pasaje* a Jorge?   (mañana)
2. ¿Quién *te* va a comprar *las tarjetas postales*?   (Elsa)
3. ¿Quién *les* va a traducir *las cartas* a Uds.?   (Luis)
4. ¿Cuándo *me* vas a traer *el pasaje*?   (esta tarde)
5. ¿Quién *le* va a dar *la pluma* a Ud.?   (la profesora)

F. Just words . . .

Complete the following sentences, using appropriate words or phrases from the vocabulary list in **Lección 7.**

1. Voy a la agencia de _____ para comprar el pasaje.
2. ¿Uds. van a volar a México mañana? ¡ _____ !
3. No puedo comprar un pasaje de primera clase. Quiero un pasaje de _____ .
4. Voy a Buenos Aires, pero no vuelvo. Quiero un pasaje de _____ .
5. ¡Son las cuatro! El avión tiene tres horas de _____ .
6. Mañana te voy a _____ el bolso de mano que me prestaste.
7. La _____ vez tenemos que viajar juntas.
8. Aquí está la entrada y ahí está la _____ .
9. No tengo valijas, sólo un bolso de _____ .
10. Tus vacaciones son siempre magníficas. Las mías son muy _____ .
11. Llevé cinco maletas y pagué _____ de equipaje.
12. Puedo ir de California a Arizona en avión, en coche, en tren o en ómnibus, pero no en _____ .

LECCIÓN <u>8</u>

A. Reflexive constructions

Rewrite each sentence according to the new cue. Follow the model.

MODELO: Yo *me despierto* a las nueve.   (levantarse)
   Yo me levanto a las nueve.

1. *La gente* se viste muy bien.   (Tú)
2. Ellos *se bañan* todos los días.   (afeitarse)
3. *Nosotros* nos acostamos a las once.   (Ellos)
4. ¿*Tú* no te preocupas por tus hijos?   (Ud.)
5. Yo *me pruebo* el vestido.   (ponerse)
6. *Nosotros* nos sentamos aquí.   (Juan)
7. *Ella* se lava la cabeza todos los días.   (Tú)
8. Yo no *me peiné*.   (cortarse el pelo)
9. *Ellos* no se acordaron de eso.   (Yo)
10. Yo me fui.   (Uds.)
11. ¿Cómo se llama *ella*?   (tú)
12. *Los niños* no se despertaron todavía.   (Daniel)

B. Some uses of the definite article

Form sentences with the elements given, adding the necessary connectors. Use verbs in the present tense. Follow the model.

MODELO: yo / ponerse / vestido
   Yo me pongo el vestido.

1. ¿ / tú / quitarse / zapatos / ?
2. el barbero / cortarme / el pelo
3. la peluquera / lavarme / cabeza
4. Uds. / no lavarse / manos
5. nosotros / preferir / té
6. madres / preocuparse / por / sus hijos
7. libertad / ser / lo más importante

C. Preterit of *ser, ir,* and *dar*

Change the following sentences according to the new subjects.

1. *Yo* fui a la cocina y comí hamburguesas.   (Nosotros)
2. *Ud.* no fue mi profesor el año pasado.   (Él)
3. ¿Le dio *Ud.* la revista, *señora*?   (tú, querido)
4. Alguien rompió el espejo. ¿Fuiste *tú, Anita*?   (Ud., señorita)
5. *Ella* no le dio el champú al peluquero.   (Nosotros)
6. *Ellos* fueron a la peluquería.   (Yo)
7. *Nosotros* no le dimos el rizador.   (Yo)

8. ¿Fueron *ellos* a la farmacia anoche?   (tú)
9. *Carlos y yo* fuimos a la barbería la semana pasada.   (Ellos)
10. ¿Fueron *Uds.* mis estudiantes el año pasado?   (Raúl y Eva)
11. *Nosotros* te dimos la alfombra.   (Yo)
12. *Ella* nos dio una escoba.   (Ellos)

D. Preterit of *e:i* and *o:u* stem-changing verbs

Complete the following sentences, using the preterit tense of the verbs in the list, as needed.

mentir	pedir	dormir	repetir
seguir	morir	conseguir	servir

1. ¿ _____ nosotros anoche en el hotel?
2. Los chicos _____ a sus padres.
3. Nosotros _____ sándwiches de jamón y queso.
4. Ella me _____ . No tiene veinte años; tiene diez y siete.
5. ¿No _____ Ud. el dinero para ir de vacaciones?
6. ¿Qué le _____ los niños a Santa Claus?
7. El hombre _____ en un accidente.
8. Ella me _____ la pregunta.

E. Just words . . .

Complete the following sentences, using the appropriate words and phrases learned in **Lección 8**.

1. Necesito la _____ para barrer la cocina.
2. Voy a pedir turno en la peluquería para corte, _____ y _____ .
3. Prefiero el pelo largo porque el pelo corto no está de _____ .
4. ¿Por qué no le pasas la _____ a la alfombra?
5. Siempre como en restaurantes porque no me gusta _____ .
6. Tengo que comprar _____ para lavarme la cabeza.
7. No tiene rizos; tiene el pelo muy _____ .
8. ¡Qué _____ soy! No le di el dinero para comprar la entrada.
9. No puedo peinarme porque no tengo _____ .
10. Voy a afeitarme. ¿Dónde está la _____ de _____ ?
11. No puedo hacer eso porque tengo mucho trabajo; estoy muy _____ .
12. Es el cumpleaños de Jorge. Tengo que comprarle un _____ .

LECCIÓN 9

A. Irregular preterits

Give the Spanish equivalent of the verbs in parentheses.

1. Ellos _____ que planear la excursión. *(had)*
2. ¿Dónde _____ Uds. anoche? *(were)*
3. Yo lo _____ al italiano. *(translated)*
4. Yo no _____ ir a esquiar. *(was able)*
5. ¿Dónde _____ tú el traje de baño? *(put)*
6. Anoche _____ una fiesta de Navidad. *(there was)*
7. Él no _____ . *(packed)*
8. Mi abuelo no _____ ayer. *(came)*
9. Ellos _____ nada. *(didn't say)*
10. Ella me _____ un saco de dormir. *(brought)*

B. Uses of *por* and *para*

Complete the following sentences with **por** or **para,** as needed.

Ayer fui a la agencia de viajes __para__ comprar un pasaje __para__ Madrid. Pagué setecientos dólares __por__ el pasaje, pero _____ un viaje así no es mucho. Quería el pasaje __para__ el sábado, pero no pude conseguirlo. El avión sale el domingo __por__ la mañana. __por__ la tarde fui otra vez al centro _____ comprar un regalo __para__ mi hermano, porque mañana es su aniversario de bodas. Llamé a mi padre __por__ teléfono __para__ decirle que no podía ir __para pu'__ él hasta las siete. Caminé __por__ el centro y pasé __por__ la casa de Julia, que estudia __para__ médica. Julia me deseó buen viaje.

C. Imperfect tense

Complete the following sentences with the imperfect tense of the verbs in the list.

montar	acampar	servir	divertirse	asistir
pescar	vivir	trabajar	gustar	

1. Nosotros nunca _____ porque no nos _____ el campo.
2. Yo siempre _____ a caballo y _____ truchas en mis vacaciones.
3. Ellos siempre _____ mucho en las fiestas.

4. Cuando nosotros _____ en Chile, yo
   _____ a la universidad.
5. Nosotros no _____ en el hospital.
6. ¿Tú siempre _____ vino con la cena?

D. Just words . . .

Match the questions in column A with the appropriate responses in column B.

A	B

A

1. ¿Van a comprar la cabaña?
2. ¿Te aburriste?
3. ¿No quieres ir de pesca?
4. ¿El Amazonas es un lago?
5. ¿Qué es el Pacífico?
6. ¿De qué color es la nieve?
7. ¿No van a la playa ellos?
8. ¿Compraste la caña de pescar?
9. ¿Vas a nadar?
10. ¿Qué pescaste?
11. ¿Quién te enseñó a nadar?
12. ¿Montaron en bicicleta?
13. ¿Sabes nadar?
14. ¿Fueron todos?
15. ¿Qué te dijo él?
16. ¿Se divirtieron mucho?

B

a. No, es un río.
b. Blanca.
c. Sí, en la piscina.
d. No, no les gusta el mar.
e. Mi novia.
f. No, a caballo.
g. No, solamente mis padres y yo.
h. No, me divertí mucho.
i. No, Carlos me va a enseñar.
j. Un océano.
k. Lo mismo que tú.
l. No, la vamos a alquilar.
m. Una trucha.
n. Sí, y me costó un ojo de la cara.
o. No, prefiero cazar.
p. Sí, fue una fiesta magnífica.

Hoy en día en España, muchas mujeres son profesionales. Aquí una médica le toma la presión a una de sus pacientes.

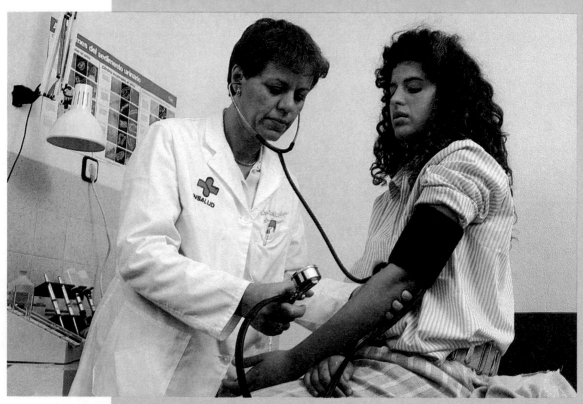

OBJECTIVES

Structure
The preterit contrasted with the imperfect • Verbs which change meaning in the preterit • **Hace** meaning *Ago* • Formation of adverbs

Communication
You will learn vocabulary related to medical emergencies and visits to the doctor's office.

En el hospital

Eran las dos de la tarde y llovía a cántaros. Gustavo iba en su motocicleta por la calle cuando un coche lo atropelló. Lo trajeron al hospital en una ambulancia, y ahora está en la sala de emergencia hablando con una enfermera.

ENFERMERA —¿Qué le pasó?

GUSTAVO —Tuve un accidente. Me atropelló un coche.

ENFERMERA —¿Cómo es que no lo vio venir?[1]

GUSTAVO —No sabía que era una calle de dos vías. Lo supe cuando me atropelló el coche.

ENFERMERA —¿Cómo se siente ahora?

GUSTAVO —Me duele mucho la pierna. Creo que me la rompí.

ENFERMERA —El doctor dijo que necesitaba una radiografía. Voy a llevarlo a la sala de rayos X.

GUSTAVO —También me corté el brazo. Me sangraba mucho.

ENFERMERA —Voy a desinfectarle y vendarle la herida. ¿Cuándo fue la última vez que le pusieron una inyección antitetánica?

GUSTAVO —Me pusieron una hace dos meses.

En otra sección del hospital, una señora está en el consultorio del médico.

DOCTOR —¿Hace mucho que tiene esos dolores de cabeza y esos mareos?

SEÑORA —Me empezaron hace dos semanas. Pero cuando era chica tomaba aspirina frecuentemente porque siempre me dolía la cabeza.

DOCTOR —¿La operaron alguna vez?

SEÑORA —Sí, me operaron de apendicitis cuando tenía veinte años.

DOCTOR —¿Es Ud. alérgica a alguna medicina?

SEÑORA —Sí, soy alérgica a la penicilina.

DOCTOR —¿Qué enfermedades tuvo cuando era niña?

SEÑORA —Varicela, sarampión... creo que las tuve todas porque siempre estaba enferma.

DOCTOR —¿Está Ud. embarazada?

SEÑORA —No, doctor.

DOCTOR —Bueno. Vamos a hacerle unos análisis.

SEÑORA —Y para los mareos, doctor, ¿va a recetarme alguna medicina?

DOCTOR —Sí, voy a recetarle unas pastillas. Debe tomarlas tres veces al día. Aquí tiene la receta.

---

[1]Note the use of the infinitive after the verb ver: **No lo vio venir.** = *You didn't see it coming.*

AT THE HOSPITAL

It was two o'clock in the afternoon, and it was raining cats and dogs. Gustavo was riding his motorcycle down the street when he was hit by a car. They brought him to the hospital in an ambulance, and he is now in the emergency room talking with a nurse.

N. What happened to you?
G. I had an accident. I was hit by a car.
N. How come you didn't see it coming?
G. I didn't know it was a two-way street. I found out when the car hit me.
N. How do you feel now?
G. My leg hurts a lot. I think I broke it.
N. The doctor said you needed an X-ray. I'm going to take you to the X-ray room.
G. I also cut my arm. It was bleeding a lot.
N. I'm going to disinfect and bandage the wound. When was the last time you had (they gave you) a tetanus shot?
G. I had (they gave me) one two months ago.

In a different section of the hospital, a woman is in the doctor's office.

D. Have you had those headaches and (those) dizzy spells for a long time?
W. They started two weeks ago. But when I was a child, I used to take aspirin frequently because I always had headaches.
D. Were you ever operated on?
W. I was operated on (they operated on me) for appendicitis when I was twenty years old.

Vocabulario

COGNADOS

el **accidente**   accident
   alérgico(-a)   allergic
la **ambulancia**   ambulance
la **apendicitis**   appendicitis
la **aspirina**   aspirin
   frecuentemente   frequently
la **emergencia**   emergency

la **inyección**   injection, shot
la **motocicleta**   motorcycle
la **medicina**   medicine
la **penicilina**   penicillin
la **sección**   section
el **tétano**   tetanus

NOMBRES

el **análisis**[1]   test, analysis
el **brazo**   arm
el **consultorio**   doctor's office
la **cabeza**   head
el **dolor**   pain
la **enfermedad**   disease, sickness
la **enfermera**   nurse
la **herida**   wound
el **mareo**   dizziness, dizzy spell
el **médico(-a)**   doctor
la **pastilla**   pill
la **pierna**   leg
la **radiografía**   X-ray
la **receta**   prescription
la **sala de emergencia**   emergency
   room
la **sala de rayos X**   X-ray room
el **sarampión**   measles
la **varicela**   chickenpox

VERBOS

atropellar   to run over, hit someone (i.e., with a car)
cruzar   to cross
desinfectar   to disinfect
doler[2]   (o:ue)   to hurt, ache

operar   to operate
recetar   to prescribe
romper(se), quebrar(se) (e:ie)   to break
sangrar   to bleed
sentir(se) (e:ie)   to feel
vendar   to bandage

ADJETIVOS

embarazada   pregnant
enfermo(-a)   sick
roto(-a), quebrado(-a)   broken

OTRAS PALABRAS Y EXPRESIONES

alguna vez   ever
calle de dos vías, calle de doble vía   two-way street
dolor de cabeza   headache
inyección antitetánica   tetanus shot
llover a cántaros   to rain cats and dogs
poner una inyección   to give an injection, a shot
la **última vez**   the last time

---

[1]Note that the article shows the number—singular: *el* **análisis**; plural: *los* **análisis**.   [2]The construction used with the verb **doler** is the same as the one used with **gustar**: Me duele la cabeza.

D. Are you allergic to any medicine?

W. Yes, I'm allergic to penicillin.

D. What diseases did you have when you were a child?

W. Chickenpox, measles . . . I think I had them all because I was always sick.

D. Are you pregnant?

W. No, doctor.

D. Good. We're going to run some tests (on you).

W. And for the dizzy spells, doctor, are you going to prescribe any medicine for me?

D. Yes, I'm going to prescribe some pills. You should take them three times a day. Here's the prescription.

Vocabulario adicional

1. el **pelo,** el **cabello**   hair
2. el **ojo**   eye
3. la **nariz**   nose
4. los **dientes**   teeth
5. la **lengua**   tongue
6. la **boca**   mouth
7. la **oreja**   ear
8. el **oído**   inner ear
9. la **cabeza**   head
10. la **cara**   face
11. el **pecho**   chest
12. el **estómago**   stomach
13. la **mano**   hand
14. la **rodilla**   knee
15. el **tobillo**   ankle
16. el **dedo del pie**   toe
17. el **pie**   foot
18. el **cuello**   neck
19. la **espalda**   back
20. el **dedo**   finger

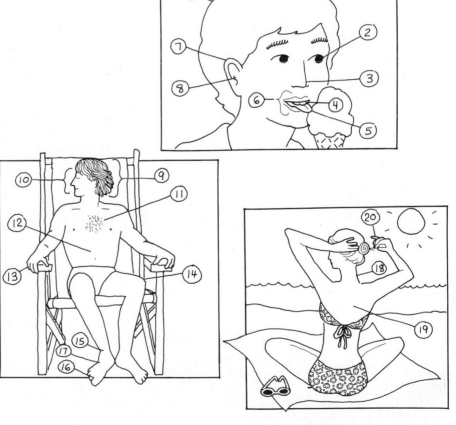

la **gripe**   flu
el **resfriado, resfrío**   cold

la **fiebre**   fever
la **tos**   cough

¿Lo sabía Ud.... ?

■ En la mayoría de los países de habla hispana, los hospitales son gratis *(free)* y subvencionados *(subsidized)* por el gobierno. Hay clínicas privadas para la gente de mejor posición económica que no quiere ir a un hospital del estado.

■ Especialmente en las grandes ciudades hispanas, la medicina está muy adelantada *(advanced)*, pero en muchos pueblos *(towns)* remotos no hay médicos ni hospitales. En ese caso, hay «curanderos» que pueden recomendar hierbas o tes o usar la magia *(magic)* para sus «curas». Muchas mujeres tienen su bebé con la ayuda de una partera *(midwife)*.

■ En España y en algunos países latinoamericanos, las farmacias venden principalmente medicinas. En algunos de estos países es posible comprar medicinas como penicilina sin tener prescripción médica.

Comprando medicina en una farmacia de Humacoa, Puerto Rico.

Estructuras gramaticales

▶ *1.* The preterit contrasted with the imperfect   *(El pretérito contrastado con el imperfecto)*

◆ The difference between the preterit and the imperfect can be visualized this way:

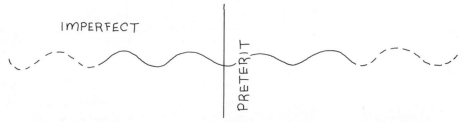

The continuous, moving line of the imperfect represents an action or event as it was taking place in the past. There is no reference to when the action began or ended. The vertical line represents the speaker's view of an event as a completed unit in the past: the preterit records such an action.

In many instances, the choice between the preterit and the imperfect depends on how the speaker views the action or event. The following table summarizes some of the most important uses of both tenses.

Preterit	*Imperfect*
1. Reports past actions that the speaker views as finished and completed. Gustavo **tuvo** un accidente anoche. Me **pusieron** una inyección ayer.	1. Describes past actions in the process of happening, with no reference to their beginning or end. **Iba** a la biblioteca cuando lo vi.
2. Sums up a condition or state viewed as a whole. Me **dolió** la pierna toda la noche.	2. Refers to repeated or habitual actions or events: *used to . . .* Cuando **era** niña, tomaba[1] aspirina todos los días.
	3. Describes a physical, mental, or emotional state or condition in the past. Me **dolía** mucho la cabeza.
	4. Expresses time in the past. **Eran** las dos de la tarde cuando lo trajeron al hospital.
	5. Is used in indirect discourse. El doctor dijo que **necesitaba** una radiografía.
	6. Is used when indicating age in the past. Cuando **tenía** veinte años, vivía en Chile.
	7. To describe in the past or to set the stage. **Hacía** frío y **llovía.**

---

[1]Note that this use of the imperfect also corresponds to the English *would* used to describe a repeated action in the past: *When I was a child, I used to take aspirin every day. = When I was a child, I would take aspirin every day.*

—¿Qué te **pasó?**   *What happened to you?*
—**Estaba** en la esquina cuando   *I was on the corner when a*
me **atropelló** un coche.   *car ran me over.*
—¿Qué te **dijo** el doctor?   *What did the doctor tell you?*
—**Me dijo** que **necesitaba** una   *He told me I needed an X-ray.*
radiografía.

PRÁCTICA

A. Write the Spanish equivalent of the following sentences, paying special attention to the use of the preterit or the imperfect in each situation.

Preterit

1. I *went* to the library with Peter last night. *(Narrates an action as a completed whole.)*
2. I *had* dizzy spells yesterday. *(Sums up a condition or state viewed as a whole.)*

Imperfect

1. I *was going* to the library when I saw Mary. *(Describes an action in progress.)*
2. I always *used to have* dizzy spells. *(Describes what used to happen.)*
3. I *was* cold. They *were* very happy here. *(A physical, mental, or emotional state or condition in the past.)*
4. He said he *wanted* a prescription. *(Indirect discourse.)*
5. It *was* six o'clock in the morning. *(Time in the past.)*
6. My niece *was* five years old. *(Age in the past.)*
7. My boyfriend *was* tall and handsome. *(Description in the past.)*

B. This interview takes place in Buenos Aires. Play the role of the reporter, interviewing a famous star. (You will want to know where she was born. The verb you need is **nacer.**)

— _____

—Yo nací en Sevilla, y no le digo cuándo.

— _____

—No, no vivíamos en Sevilla. Cuando yo tenía diez años nos fuimos a vivir a Madrid.

— _____

—¿Cuándo era niña? Era fea y un poco gorda.

— _____

—Sí, tenía un perro que se llamaba Chispita.

— _____

—Cuando era niña me gustaba la vida al aire libre. Me gustaba nadar y montar a caballo.

— _____

—Estudié en la Escuela de Arte Dramático.

— _____

—Empecé a trabajar en televisión en 1980.

— _____

—Primero trabajé con el famoso actor Pedro Lagar.

— _____

—Siempre hice comedias; nunca hice dramas.

— _____

—Vine a Buenos Aires en el año 1985.

— _____

—Sí, el año pasado fui a París y trabajé en un club nocturno.

— _____

—Estuve allí por tres meses.

— _____

—No, no pienso volver a España por ahora.

C. Read these two stories aloud, supplying the missing verbs (preterit or imperfect).

1. _____ (ser) la una y media de la tarde cuando Marta _____ (llegar) al hospital. La cabeza le _____ (doler) mucho y _____ (tener) una pierna rota. El médico _____ (venir) en seguida y le _____ (poner) una inyección. Marta le _____ (decir) al médico que le _____ (doler) mucho la cabeza y que _____ (tener) mareos. El doctor le dijo que _____ (necesitar) una radiografía. La enfermera la _____ (llevar) a la sala de rayos X.

2. Cuando nosotros _____ (ser) niños, _____ (vivir) en Acapulco. Todos los días _____ (ir) a la playa y _____ (nadar). Un día, cuando _____ (volver) de la playa, mi hermana _____ (cortarse) un pie y papá _____ (tener) que llevarla al hospital. El médico le _____ (desinfectar) y _____ (vendar) la herida, le _____ (recetar) penicilina y _____ (decir) que no _____ (deber) caminar por cinco días. Mi hermana _____ (estar) muy triste todo el día.

D. Write the following paragraph in Spanish, paying special attention to the proper uses of the preterit and the imperfect tenses.

It was nine o'clock in the morning. John was going to the university when a car ran him over. An ambulance came and took him to the hospital. His (the) leg was bleeding, and he was dizzy. Since the doctor said John needed an X-ray, the nurse took him to the X-ray room. When they went back to the doctor's office, the nurse gave John a tetanus shot.

▶ *2.* Verbs which change meaning in the preterit
(Verbos que cambian de significado en el pretérito)

♦ Some Spanish verbs change meaning when used in the preterit. Contrast the usage of the following verbs in the preterit and imperfect.

conocer:	conocí (preterit)	*I met*
	conocía (imperfect)	*I knew (was acquainted with)*

Anoche **conocí** a una enfermera muy simpática. *(met her for the first time)*
Yo no **conocía** la ciudad. *(I wasn't acquainted with the city.)*

saber:	supe (preterit)	*I found out, I learned*
	sabía (imperfect)	*I knew*

Yo no **sabía** que la calle era de dos vías. *(I wasn't aware of it.)*
Lo **supe** cuando me atropelló el coche. *(I found out or heard about it.)*

no querer: no quise (preterit) *I refused*
    no quería (imperfect) *I didn't want to (but . . .)*

Raúl **no quiso** comer. *(didn't want to and refused)*
Rita **no quería** ir pero después decidió ir. *(didn't want to at the time)*

—¿Tú **conocías** al cuñado de Carmen?	*Did you know Carmen's brother-in-law?*
—No, lo **conocí** anoche.	*No, I met him last night.*
—¿**Sabías** que teníamos un examen?	*Did you know that we had an exam?*
—No, lo **supe** esta mañana.	*No, I found (it) out this morning.*
—¿Y Roberto? ¿No vino?	*And Roberto? Didn't he come?*
—No, **no quiso** venir.	*No, he refused to come.*

PRÁCTICA

A. Interview a classmate, asking him or her the following questions.

1. ¿Conocías tú al profesor (a la profesora) antes de empezar esta clase?
2. ¿Cuándo lo (la) conociste?
3. ¿Sabías tú la nacionalidad de tu profesor(a)?
4. ¿Cuándo lo supiste?
5. Yo no quería venir a clase hoy. ¿Y tú?
6. Tú no viniste a mi fiesta anoche. ¿No pudiste o no quisiste?

B. The following is an excerpt from a soap opera (**telenovela**). Act it out with a partner. Provide the missing verbs.

ADRIÁN —¿Tú _____ que Rosaura estaba embarazada?

SARA —No, lo _____ anoche.

ADRIÁN —¡Qué horrible! Dicen que su esposo es un tonto. Los padres de ella no _____ ir a la boda. Ese día se fueron a Europa.

SARA —Pero, ¿dónde _____ Rosaura a Lorenzo?

ADRIÁN —En una fiesta. Rosaura no _____ ir, pero Olga la llevó.

SARA —¿Olga _____ a Lorenzo?

ADRIÁN —Sí, Olga es la ex-esposa de Lorenzo.

(Continuará...)

▶ *3.* **Hace...** meaning *ago*   (**Hace...** *como equivalente de ago)*

♦ In sentences using the preterit and in some cases the imperfect, **hace** + *period of time* is the equivalent of the English *ago.*
   The "formula" is as follows:

> **Hace** + *period of time* + **que**
> **Hace** + dos años   + **que** la conocí.

—¿Cuánto tiempo hace que   *How long ago did you meet*
conociste a tu novia?   *your girlfriend?*
—**Hace tres años que** la   *I met her three years ago.*
conocí.

PRÁCTICA

A. Tell us how long ago you did the following.

1. ir al médico
2. ir al dentista
3. tomar alguna medicina
4. tener dolor de cabeza
5. estar enfermo
6. empezar a estudiar español
7. ver a tus padres
8. ir de vacaciones
9. llamar a tu mejor amigo
10. levantarte

B. Be an interpreter. What are these people saying?

1. How long ago did they give you a tetanus shot?
   They gave me a tetanus shot four years ago.
2. Is he in the emergency room?
   Yes, they brought him to the hospital an hour ago.
3. How long ago did the pain start?
   It started two days ago.

▶ *4.* Formation of adverbs   (*La formación de los adverbios)*

♦ Most Spanish adverbs are formed by adding **-mente** (the equivalent of English *ly*) to the adjective.

especial *special*   especial**mente** *especially*
reciente *recent*   reciente**mente** *recently*

♦ Adjectives ending in **-o** change the **-o** to **-a** before adding **-mente.**

lento *slow*   lent**amente** *slowly*
rápido *rapid*   rápid**amente** *rapidly*

♦ If two or more adverbs are used together, both change the -o to -a, but only the last adverb takes the -mente ending.

Habló clara y **lentamente.** *He spoke clearly and slowly.*

♦ If the adjective has an accent, the adverb retains it.

difícil **difícilmente**

PRÁCTICA

A. Change the following adjectives to adverbs.

1. fácil *(easy)*
2. feliz *(happy)*
3. claro *(clear)*
4. raro *(rare)*
5. necesario *(necessary)*

6. frecuente *(frequent)*
7. triste *(sad)*
8. trágico *(tragic)*
9. alegre *(merry)*
10. desgraciado *(unfortunate)*

B. Complete the following sentences with the appropriate adverbs.

1. Ellos hablaron _____ y _____ .
2. Mis padres vienen a verme _____ .
3. Jaime llegó _____ .
4. El muchacho me habló _____ .
5. Tengo _____ diez dólares.
6. Los muchachos bailan _____ .
7. _____ no tengo dinero.
8. Compré ese champú _____ para ti.

¡A ver cuánto aprendió!

A. ¡Conversemos!

Reread the dialogues in this lesson and be ready to discuss the following.

1. ¿Qué estaba haciendo Gustavo cuando lo atropelló un coche?
2. ¿En qué lo llevaron al hospital?
3. ¿Sabía Gustavo que la calle era de dos vías?
4. ¿Qué dijo el doctor que necesitaba Gustavo?
5. ¿Tiene Gustavo el brazo roto?
6. ¿Por qué tomaba la señora aspirinas?
7. ¿A qué es alérgica la señora?

8. ¿De qué operaron a la señora cuando tenía veinte años?
9. ¿Está embarazada la señora?
10. ¿Le va a recetar el doctor alguna medicina a la señora? ¿Para qué?

B. Imagine you are talking with a friend, who asks you the following questions.

1. ¿Te hicieron radiografías del pecho?
2. ¿Adónde te llevaron para hacerte las radiografías?
3. ¿Eres alérgico(-a) a alguna medicina?
4. ¿Te operaron de apendicitis alguna vez?
5. ¿Qué haces cuando te duele la cabeza?
6. ¿Te sangra la nariz frecuentemente?
7. ¿Hay alguna persona diabética en tu familia?
8. ¿Cómo te sientes hoy?
9. ¿Te duelen los oídos?
10. Me corté un dedo del pie. ¿Puedes vendármelo?

C. ¡Repase el vocabulario!

¿Es lógico o no?

1. En serio. Los muchachos vinieron a esquiar en una ambulancia.
2. Cuando tengo dolor de estómago voy al médico.
3. Si necesito una radiografía voy al aeropuerto.
4. Me vendaron la herida porque me sangraba mucho.
5. Me operaron de apendicitis porque me dolía la nariz.
6. Algunas personas son alérgicas a la penicilina.
7. Las orejas sirven para planchar.
8. Le hicieron análisis para ver si era divorciado.
9. La lengua está en la boca.
10. La rodilla es parte de la cara.
11. Tenemos treinta dedos.
12. Necesitamos la nariz para caminar.
13. Para hacerle una radiografía, debemos ir a la sala de rayos X.
14. Roberto está embarazado.
15. Está enferma. Debe ir al consultorio del médico.
16. Cada vez que tengo dolor de cabeza tomo dos aspirinas.
17. Lo atropelló una bolsa de dormir en el mar.
18. Tuvo un accidente en la autopista.
19. Fuimos de pesca a la sala de emergencia y nos divertimos mucho.
20. Llovía a cántaros, pero por suerte pudimos dormir en la cabaña. No tuvimos que dormir afuera.

D. Name all the parts of the body numbered below.

E. Situaciones

What would you say in the following situations? What would the other person say?

1. A friend wants you to go to the store with her. Tell her you can't go for the following reasons: you've just taken two aspirins because you have a headache, your little brother cut his hand and you have to disinfect the wound, and it's raining cats and dogs and you don't like to go out when it rains.
2. You have had an accident and are at the emergency room, talking to a doctor. You tell him or her that your back hurts.
3. You are answering questions about your medical past during a visit to the doctor. Say that your headaches started three days ago, and that you are allergic to penicillin.

Para escribir

Adela is Doctor Vera's patient. We can hear the beginning of the conversation, but not the rest. Imagine what the patient is complaining about and what the doctor advises. Be sure to consult the **Vocabulario adicional** section.

DOCTOR   —¿Cómo se siente, señora?
ADELA   —Muy mal, doctor.
DOCTOR   —¿Qué problemas tiene, señora?
ADELA   — _____ ...

En la vida real

ENTREVISTA

Choose a partner, then interview each other, using the **tú** from.

Pregúntele a su compañero(-a) de clase...

1. ...si le hicieron radiografías del pecho alguna vez.
2. ...adónde lo (la) llevaron para hacerle las radiografías.
3. ...si es alérgico(-a) a alguna medicina.
4. ...si lo (la) operaron de apendicitis alguna vez.
5. ...qué hace cuando le duele la cabeza.
6. ...si le sangra la nariz frecuentemente.
7. ...cómo se siente hoy.
8. ...si le duelen los oídos.

CONVERSACIÓN

Have a conversation with a classmate, comparing your childhood experiences, including your date and place of birth. Ask each other what you used to do with your friends and family, how long ago you started school, and so on.

Some words and phrases you might want to include:

la **niñez** *childhood*
el, la **adolescente** *teenager*
la **escuela** { **primaria** *elementary school*
{ **secundaria** *junior high and high school*
casarse (**con**) *to get married*
divorciarse *to get divorced*

BUENOS CONSEJOS[1]

¿Qué consejos de la lista que sigue les daría Ud. *(would you give)* a estas personas?

Buenos consejos para conservar la salud[2]

Debe

- comer más vegetales y frutas
- dormir lo suficiente
- visitar al médico periódicamente
- hacer ejercicio
- consumir menos calorías
- aprender a relajarse
- evitar *(avoid)* la tensión *(stress)*
- pensar positivamente
- tener una dieta balanceada
- controlar su peso *(weight)*

No debe

- fumar *(smoke)*
- consumir mucho alcohol
- consumir mucha sal o azúcar *(sugar)*
- usar drogas
- comer mucha grasa
- trabajar en exceso

---

1. El señor Vega toma diez cervezas todos los días.
2. La señorita Díaz está siempre sentada *(sitting)*, mirando televisión.
3. Elsa come muchos dulces *(sweets)*.
4. El Dr. Álvarez trabaja catorce horas cada día.
5. La señora Carreras duerme sólo cuatro horas cada noche.
6. Estela se preocupa constantemente por todo.
7. Adela siempre come papas fritas, hamburguesas, mantequilla, pollo frito, etc.
8. Hace cinco años que Carlos no va a ver a su médico.
9. La dieta de Eduardo es de 5.000 calorías al día.
10. Raúl pesa *(weighs)* 300 libras *(pounds)*.
11. Raquel solamente come carne y pastas.
12. A Jorge le gustan mucho los cigarrillos.

---

[1] *Advice*   [2] *health*

UNA ACTIVIDAD ESPECIAL

With a classmate in the role of a patient, act out a doctor's visit in which you play the role of doctor. You may exchange roles after completing the situation. You may need to use the following words: **la fiebre** *(fever)*, **la infección** *(infection)*, **la gripe** *(flu)*, **tener tos** *(to have a cough)*, **el dolor de garganta** *(sore throat)*, and **el catarro, el resfrío** *(cold)*.

Y ahora, *¡vamos a leer!*

Del diario de Ana María

Miércoles, 14 de julio de 1990

Querido diario:

Ayer, martes trece,[1] fue un día de mala suerte. Me levanté a las ocho y llegué tarde a mi clase de química, que empieza a las ocho y diez. Cuando fui a mi clase de sicología, que es mi especialización, el profesor me dijo que tenía que estudiar más porque mi nota del último examen no era muy buena.

Por la tarde fui a la biblioteca para devolver unos libros y me caí en la escalera. Como me dolía mucho la pierna y tenía una herida en el brazo, Estela me llevó al hospital. Creíamos que yo tenía la pierna rota, pero me hicieron unas radiografías y el doctor me dijo que no había ningún problema. Me pusieron una inyección contra el tétano, me vendaron la herida y Estela me trajo a casa. Eran las ocho de la noche cuando llegamos, y llovía a cántaros.

Invité a Estela a cenar conmigo, pero cuando abrí el refrigerador, vi que no había nada para comer. Tomamos chocolate caliente, estudiamos un rato y miramos televisión. Estela se fue a las diez y yo me acosté porque estaba muy cansada.

A las diez y cuarto me llamó una compañera de clase para decirme que hoy teníamos un examen en la clase de matemáticas. ¡Yo no lo sabía!

Me levanté y empecé a estudiar pero, como me dolía muchísimo la cabeza y no entendía nada, me acosté pero no dormí bien. ¡El martes trece es realmente un día de mala suerte! El próximo martes trece no pienso salir de mi casa.

¡A ver cuánto recuerda!

1. ¿Qué fecha es hoy?
2. ¿Tuvo Ana María un buen día ayer?

---

[1] In Spanish-speaking countries, Tuesday, rather than Friday, the thirteenth is considered an unlucky day.

3. ¿Por qué llegó tarde a su clase de química?
4. ¿Qué le dijo el profesor de sicología?
5. ¿Cuál es la especialización de Ana María?
6. ¿Para qué fue Ana María a la biblioteca y qué le pasó allí?
7. ¿Por qué la llevó Estela al hospital?
8. ¿Qué le dijo el doctor después de ver las radiografías?
9. ¿Le pusieron una inyección a Ana María?
10. ¿Qué hora era cuando llegaron a la casa de Ana María y qué tiempo hacía?
11. ¿Qué pasó cuando Ana María abrió el refrigerador?
12. ¿Qué hicieron Ana María y Estela?
13. ¿Qué le dijo a Ana María su compañera de clase?
14. ¿Por qué se acostó Ana María?
15. ¿Qué dice Ana María del martes trece?
16. ¿Qué no piensa hacer Ana María el próximo martes trece?

Estudiante en una clase de literatura en una escuela secundaria de Barcelona, España.

Cuba

PANORAMA HISPÁNICO 6

El Caribe

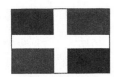

Rep. Dominicana

Puerto Rico

- El Viejo San Juan es la parte antigua de San Juan, la capital de Puerto Rico. Es uno de los barrios coloniales mejor conservados de las Américas y fue fundado en 1521. El barrio está casi totalmente rodeado de murallas de piedra construidas por los españoles.

- Puerto Rico es una de las áreas más densamente pobladas del mundo. Con una extensión de solamente 9.104 kilómetros cuadrados tiene una población de unos cuatro millones de habitantes.

- La isla en la que se encuentra la República Dominicana fue descubierta en 1492 durante el primer viaje de Colón al Nuevo Mundo. Colón le dio a la isla el nombre de La Española. La parte oriental de la isla está ocupada por la República de Haití, donde se habla francés.

- Santo Domingo, la más antigua de las ciudades de América, fue fundada en 1496 por Bartolomé Colón, hermano del descubridor. En la catedral de Santa María la Menor se dice que están enterrados los restos de Cristóbal Colón.

- La Habana, capital de Cuba, con sus dos millones de habitantes es la ciudad más grande del Caribe. Es también uno de los lugares donde mejor se conserva la arquitectura colonial española. Antes de la revolución de Castro, era uno de los mayores centros de atracción turística del Caribe.

Aunque *(although)* Puerto Rico forma parte de los Estados Unidos, conserva su cultura y sus tradiciones. Su lengua es el español, sus costumbres son las típicas de los países latinos y su música es la del Caribe, una mezcla de ritmos hispanos y africanos. Aquí vemos una fiesta de salsa en la Universidad de Puerto Rico, donde hay más de 35.000 estudiantes. ¿Qué otros tipos de música latina conoce Ud.?

La sección antigua de La Habana, capital de Cuba, se distingue por los numerosos edificios coloniales que aún conserva. «La Habana Vieja», como la llaman los habaneros, se caracteriza por sus calles estrechas, sus casas de tipo colonial y sus monumentos históricos. En la foto se ve la Plaza de la Fraternidad, parque moderno construido en la antigua Plaza de Marte, de la época colonial. ¿Cuál es el parque más importante de su ciudad?

La fortaleza del Morro está situada a la entrada de la bahía de San Juan, en Puerto Rico. Fue construida por los españoles en el siglo XVI para defender la isla de los ataques de los piratas. Hoy el Morro está considerado monumento nacional y constituye una importante atracción turística. ¿Qué monumentos históricos importantes se encuentran en el estado donde Ud. vive?

► El béisbol es el deporte más popular en Puerto Rico y de sus equipos locales han salido algunos de los mejores jugadores de las Grandes Ligas de los Estados Unidos. En otros países del Caribe y Centroamérica, como Cuba, la República Dominicana, Nicaragua y Panamá, el béisbol es también un deporte popular. ¿Puede Ud. nombrar algunos jugadores de béisbol hispanos de las Grandes Ligas?

▲ La Catedral de Santa María la Menor en Santo Domingo, capital de la República Dominicana, fue la primera catedral fundada en América. En 1514 Diego Colón, hijo de Cristóbal Colón, inició su construcción, que fue terminada en 1540. Santo Domingo fue la primera isla colonizada por los españoles en América. Hoy en esta isla coexisten dos países: la República Dominicana y Haití. ¿Sabe Ud. qué idioma se habla en Haití?

▲ Vista parcial de la Playa de las Croabas en Puerto Rico. La isla tiene numerosas playas de arena blanca y fina como ésta. Miles de turistas norteamericanos visitan estas playas todos los años en la temporada de invierno. ¿Puede mencionar Ud. algunas playas famosas cerca de donde Ud. vive?

► La Universidad de la Habana, la más antigua de la isla de Cuba, fue establecida en 1728. La universidad tiene dos sedes: la antigua está en el centro de la ciudad, y la moderna se encuentra en las afueras de la ciudad. La universidad fue autónoma hasta poco después de la llegada de Fidel Castro al poder. ¿Sabe Ud. cuál es la universidad más antigua de los Estados Unidos?

▼ El clima tropical del Caribe ofrece condiciones ideales para el cultivo de una gran variedad de frutas: el mango, la papaya, el banano y la guayaba, entre muchas otras. En la foto, un puesto de frutas en el Viejo San Juan muestra esta gran variedad. Indique cuáles son las distintas frutas que aparecen en la foto.

Banco en la ciudad de Bogotá, capital de Colombia.

OBJECTIVES

Structure   The relative pronouns **que** and **quien** • The subjunctive • The subjunctive with verbs of volition • The subjunctive with verbs of emotion

Communication   You will learn vocabulary related to daily occurrences and running errands.

Un martes trece

En una casa de la calle Ponce en San Juan, Puerto Rico, vive la familia Vargas. Sergio está muy cansado hoy y quiere quedarse en la cama hasta tarde. Su mamá quiere que haga varias diligencias, de modo que el pobre muchacho tiene que levantarse en cuanto suena el despertador a las siete de la mañana.

A las nueve, llega a la tintorería.

SERGIO —*(Piensa)* Ojalá que estén listos mis pantalones...*(Al empleado)* Vengo a recoger mis pantalones. Aquí está el comprobante.

EMPLEADO —Un momento, por favor. *(Al rato vuelve.)* Sus pantalones son rosados, ¿verdad?

SERGIO —¡Eran blancos cuando los traje... !

A las diez, Sergio está en el departamento de fotografía de la tienda La Francia.

SERGIO —La semana pasada traje un rollo de película en colores. Espero que esté listo.

EMPLEADO —A ver... ¿Sergio Vargas... ? Sí, las fotos salieron muy bien.

SERGIO —¿Y cuánto cobran por revelar un rollo de película?

EMPLEADO —Cinco dólares, señor.

SERGIO —Muy bien. *(Mira las fotografías.)* ¿Pero quién es esta señora? ¡Estas fotos no son mías!

A las once, Sergio estaciona su motocicleta frente al banco.

SERGIO —Quiero depositar este cheque, que está a nombre de mi madre. ¿Es necesario que lo firme ella?

EMPLEADO —Si lo va a depositar en la cuenta corriente de ella, no.

SERGIO —Muy bien, eso es lo que quiero hacer. También quiero sacar doscientos dólares de mi cuenta de ahorros.

EMPLEADO —Llene esta tarjeta, por favor.

SERGIO —Necesito que me dé el saldo de mi cuenta de ahorros.

EMPLEADO —Sólo tiene veinte dólares. Lo siento, señor Vargas, pero no tiene suficiente dinero.

Cuando Sergio sale del banco, no encuentra su motocicleta.

SERGIO —*(Grita)* ¡Oh, no! ¡Alguien me robó la motocicleta!

SEÑORA —El muchacho que se llevó su motocicleta dijo que usted era su hermano...

SERGIO —¡Yo soy hijo único!

ONE TUESDAY THE THIRTEENTH

In a house on Ponce Street in San Juan, Puerto Rico, lives the Vargas family. Sergio is very tired today and wants to sleep late. His mother wants him to run several errands, so the poor boy has to get up as soon as the alarm goes off at seven in the morning.

At nine, he arrives at the dry cleaner's.

S. *(Thinking)* I hope my pants are ready . . . *(To the clerk)* I'm here to pick up my pants. Here's the claim check.

E. One moment, please. *(He comes back a while later.)* Your pants are pink, right?

S. They were white when I brought them in . . . !

At ten, Sergio is in the photo section of the La Francia department store.

S. Last week I brought in a roll of color film. I hope it's ready.

E. Let's see . . . Sergio Vargas . . . ? Yes, the pictures came out very well.

S. And how much do you charge to develop a roll of film?

E. Five dollars, sir.

S. Very well. *(Looking at the photographs.)* But who is this lady? These pictures aren't mine!

At eleven, Sergio parks his motorcycle in front of the bank.

S. I want to deposit this check, which is in my mother's name. Is it necessary for her to sign it?

C. If you're going to deposit it in her checking account, no.

SEÑORA —*(Piensa)* Es una lástima que no sean hermanos... Se parecen mucho...

SERGIO —*(Piensa, mientras camina hacia la estación de policía)* ¡El próximo martes trece no salgo de casa!

Vocabulario

COGNADOS

el **banco**   bank
el **cheque**   check

el **departamento**   department, section
suficiente   enough, sufficient

NOMBRES

la **cama**   bed
el **comprobante**   claim check
la **cuenta**   account
la **cuenta corriente**   checking account
la **cuenta de ahorros**   savings account
el **despertador**   alarm clock
la **diligencia**   errand
la **estación de policía**   police station
el **pantalón**, los **pantalones**   pants, trousers
el **rollo de película**   roll of film
el **saldo**   balance
la **tintorería**   dry cleaner's

VERBOS

caminar   to walk
cobrar   to charge
depositar   to deposit
esperar   to hope
estacionar, aparcar, parquear   to park
gritar   to scream
llevarse   to take (away)
parecerse   to look like

recoger   to pick up
revelar   to develop (film)
robar   to steal
sacar   to take out, to withdraw
salir   to go out, to leave

ADJETIVOS

pobre   poor
varios(-as)   several

OTRAS PALABRAS Y EXPRESIONES

a ver...   let's see
al rato   a while later
de modo que, de manera que   so
es (una) lástima   it's a pity
en cuanto   as soon as
frente a   in front of
hacer diligencias   to run errands
hacia   toward
hijo(-a) único(-a)   only child
ojalá   I hope, God grant
quedarse en la cama hasta tarde   to sleep late
suena el despertador   the alarm goes off
¿verdad?   right?

s. Very well, that's what I want to do. I also want to withdraw two hundred dollars from my savings account.
c. Fill out this card, please.
s. I need you to give me the balance of my savings account.
c. You only have twenty dollars. I'm sorry, Mr. Vargas, but you don't have enough money.

When Sergio leaves the bank, he doesn't find his motorcycle.

s. *(Screaming)* Oh no! Somebody stole my motorcycle!
L. The young man who took (away) your motorcycle said he was your brother . . .
s. I'm an only child!
L. *(Thinking)* It's a pity that they're not brothers . . . They look a lot like each other . . .
s. *(Thinking, as he's walking to the police station)* Next Tuesday the thirteenth I'm not leaving the house!

Vocabulario adicional

a plazos on installments
Compré el coche **a plazos.**

ahorrar to save
Tienes que **ahorrar** más dinero.

al contado in cash
No voy a comprarlo a plazos; voy a comprarlo **al contado.**

en efectivo in cash
No pagué **en efectivo;** pagué con un cheque.

fechar to date (a check, a letter, etc.)
Tiene que firmar y **fechar** los documentos.

la firma signature
Necesito la **firma** de su padre en este cheque.

gratis free (of charge)
No cuesta nada; es **gratis.**

la libreta de ahorros savings passbook
¿Trajiste tu **libreta de ahorros?**

pedir prestado(-a) to borrow
Voy a **pedirle prestado** el libro de inglés.

pedir un préstamo to apply for a loan
Voy al banco para **pedir un préstamo** de cinco mil dólares.

el talonario de cheques checkbook
No puedo darte un cheque porque no tengo mi **talonario de cheques.**

¿Lo sabía Ud.... ?

■ Puerto Rico es una de las Antillas Mayores. Es un Estado Libre Asociado a los Estados Unidos, y sus lenguas oficiales son el español y el inglés. Su capital es San Juan.

Los indios llamaban a la isla de Puerto Rico «Borinquen», y hoy en día muchos de sus habitantes todavía usan ese nombre: en vez de *(instead of)* decir que son «puertorriqueños» dicen que son «boricuas» o «borinqueños».

■ Cada nación latinoamericana tiene un banco central encargado de *(in charge of)* emitir el dinero y de controlar la actividad de los bancos comerciales.

En la actualidad, América Latina está atravesando *(going through)* una gran crisis económica. Esto hace que los bancos centrales tengan que emitir grandes sumas *(quantities)* de dinero para financiar los déficits de sus gobiernos, y así la inflación resulta incontrolable.

Puerta de San Juan, en el Viejo San Juan, parte antigua de la capital de Puerto Rico.

Estructuras gramaticales

▶ *1.* The relative pronouns **que** and **quien** *(Los pronombres relativos* **que** *y* **quien***)*

Relative pronouns are used to combine two sentences that have a common element, usually a noun or a pronoun.

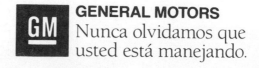

A. The relative pronoun *que*

¿Dónde está <u>la calculadora?</u>   Trajiste <u>la calculadora.</u> →

└──────────── common element ────────────┘

¿Dónde está la calculadora **que** trajiste?
                         R.P.

¿Cómo se llama <u>la chica?</u>   <u>La chica</u> vino esta mañana. →

└──────────── common element ────────────┘

¿Cómo se llama la chica **que** vino esta mañana?
                    R.P.

♦ Note that the relative pronoun **que** not only helps combine the two sentences above but also replaces the nouns **la calculadora** and **la chica** which are repeated in the second sentences.

♦ The relative pronoun **que** is invariable and is used for both persons and things. It is the Spanish equivalent of *that, which,* and *who.* Unlike its English equivalent, the Spanish **que** is never omitted.

Los libros **que** te di.   *The books (that) I gave you.*

B. The relative pronoun *quien*

—¿La muchacha **con quien**   *Is the girl with whom you*
hablabas es americana?   *were talking an American?*
—No, es extranjera.   *No, she's a foreigner.*

—¿Quiénes son esos señores?   *Who are those gentlemen?*
—Son los señores **de quienes**   *They are the gentlemen about*
te habló José.   *whom José spoke to you.*

♦ The relative pronoun **quien** is only used with persons.

♦ Note that the plural of **quien** is **quienes**. **Quien** does not change for gender.

♦ **Quien** is generally used after prepositions, i.e., **con quien, de quienes**.

♦ **Quien** is the Spanish equivalent of *whom* and *that*.

PRÁCTICA

A. Combine the following sentences, using **que, quien,** or **quienes.**

MODELO: Necesitan *la foto.* Yo traje *la foto.*
Necesitan la foto que yo traje.

1. ¿Quién es el profesor? / El profesor enseña literatura cubana.
2. ¿Quiénes son los estudiantes? / Tú hablaste con los estudiantes.
3. Preguntan cuál es la clase. / Nosotros queremos tomar la clase.
4. ¿Cómo se llama el empleado? / Me hablaste del empleado.
5. ¿Cuál es la señora? / La señora está embarazada.

B. Be an interpreter. What are these people saying?

1. Who was the girl who called you, Paquito?
   My sister. She broke her leg.
2. Where are the rolls of film that I bought?
   They're in your room, with the brochures of Mexico.
3. This is the girl about whom I spoke to you, Dr. Peña.
   Is she the person who had an accident?
   Yes, she's in the emergency room.

▶ *2.* The subjunctive   *(El subjuntivo)*

A. Use of the subjunctive

♦ The indicative is used to express factual, definite events. By contrast, the subjunctive is used to reflect the speaker's feelings or attitudes toward events, or when the speaker views events as uncertain, unreal, or hypothetical.

♦ Except for its use in main clauses to express commands, the Spanish subjunctive is most often used in subordinate or dependent clauses.

♦ The subjunctive is also used in English, although not as often as in Spanish. For example:

*I suggest that he **arrive** tomorrow.*

The expression that requires the use of the subjunctive is in the main clause, *I suggest*. The subjunctive appears in the subordinate clause, *that he **arrive** tomorrow*. The subjunctive is used because the action of arriving is not real; it is only what is *suggested* that he do.

B. Forms of the present subjunctive of regular verbs

♦ To form the present subjunctive, add the following endings to the stem of the first-person singular of the present indicative.

-ar verbs	-er verbs	-ir verbs
habl **-e**	com **-a**	viv **-a**
habl **-es**	com **-as**	viv **-as**
habl **-e**	com **-a**	viv **-a**
habl **-emos**	com **-amos**	viv **-amos**
habl **-éis**	com **-áis**	viv **-áis**
habl **-en**	com **-an**	viv **-an**

♦ Note that the endings for **-er** and **-ir** verbs are the same.

♦ The following table shows how to form the first-person singular of the present subjunctive. The stem is the same for all persons.

Verb	First-person singular present indicative	Subjunctive stem	First-person singular present subjunctive
tratar	trato	trat-	trate
aprender	aprendo	aprend-	aprenda
escribir	escribo	escrib-	escriba
decir	digo	dig-	diga
hacer	hago	hag-	haga
traer	traigo	traig-	traiga
venir	vengo	veng-	venga

PRÁCTICA

Give the present subjunctive of the following verbs.

1. *yo:* solicitar, recibir, traer, decir, recetar, comer, ver
2. *tú:* escribir, operar, decidir, regresar, venir, barrer
3. *él:* retirar, hacer, mandar, salir, anotar, atropellar
4. *nosotros:* cocinar, depositar, leer, poner, llegar[1]
5. *ellos:* caminar, deber, bajar, conocer, vender, sangrar

---

[1] Remember that in verbs with orthographic changes, **g** changes to **gu**, **c** changes to **qu**, and **c** changes to **z** before **e** and **i**. See **Lección 7** for rules on verbs with orthographic changes.

C. Subjunctive forms of stem-changing verbs

♦ Stem-changing verbs which end in **-ar** and **-er** maintain the basic pattern of the present indicative.

recomendar *to recommend*		**recordar** *to remember*	
recomiende	recomendemos	recuerde	recordemos
recomiendes	recomendéis	recuerdes	recordéis
recomiende	recomienden	recuerde	recuerden

entender *to understand*		**devolver** *to return (something)*	
entienda	entendamos	devuelva	devolvamos
entiendas	entendáis	devuelvas	devolváis
entienda	entiendan	devuelva	devuelvan

♦ In stem-changing verbs that end in **-ir,** the unstressed **e** changes to **i** and the unstressed **o** changes to **u** in the first- and second-persons plural.

mentir *to lie*		**dormir** *to sleep*	
mienta	mintamos	duerma	durmamos
mientas	mintáis	duermas	durmáis
mienta	mientan	duerma	duerman

D. Verbs that are irregular in the subjunctive

♦ The following verbs are formed irregularly in the subjunctive.

dar	estar	saber	ser	ir
dé	esté	sepa	sea	vaya
des	estés	sepas	seas	vayas
dé	esté	sepa	sea	vaya
demos	estemos	sepamos	seamos	vayamos
deis	estéis	sepáis	seáis	vayáis
den	estén	sepan	sean	vayan

ATENCIÓN

The subjunctive of **hay** (impersonal form of **haber**) is **haya.**

PRÁCTICA

Give the present subjunctive of the following verbs.

1. *yo:* dormir, mentir, recomendar, dar, haber, pensar, ir
2. *tú:* volver, estar, ser, preferir, recordar, morir, ver, pedir
3. *él:* cerrar, saber, perder, probar, dar, servir, seguir
4. *nosotros:* sentir, ir, dar, dormir, perder, cerrar, saber, ser
5. *ellos:* estar, ser, recordar, saber, haber, encontrar, repetir

E. Uses of the subjunctive

There are four main concepts that call for the use of the subjunctive in Spanish:

♦ Volition: demands, wishes, advice, persuasion, and other impositions of will

Ella **quiere** que yo **solicite** el trabajo.	*She wants me to apply for the job.*
Te **aconsejo** que no **vayas** a ese banco.	*I advise you not to go to that bank.*
Les **ruego** que no se **vayan.**	*I beg you not to leave.*

♦ Emotion: pity, joy, fear, surprise, hope, and so on

Espero que **lleguen** temprano.	*I hope they arrive early.*
Siento que no **puedas** venir a clase.	*I'm sorry you can't come to class.*
Me **sorprende** que no **vayas** a la fiesta.	*I'm surprised you're not going to the party.*

♦ Doubt, disbelief, denial, uncertainty, and negated facts

Dudo que **paguen** la cuenta.	*I doubt they'll pay the bill.*
No creo que ella **sea** una idiota.	*I don't think she's an idiot.*
No es verdad que Antonio sea médico.	*It isn't true that Anthony is a doctor.*

♦ Unreality, indefiniteness, and nonexistence

¿Hay alguien que **esté** libre hoy?	*Is there anyone who's free today?*
No hay nadie que **tenga** los documentos en regla.	*There's nobody that has his or her documents in order.*

▶ *3.* The subjunctive with verbs of volition *(El subjuntivo con verbos que indican voluntad o deseo)*

♦ All impositions of will, as well as indirect or implied commands, require the subjunctive in subordinate clauses. The subject in the main clause must be different from the subject in the subordinate clause. If there is no change of subject, the infinitive is used.

♦ Note the sentence structure for this use of the subjunctive in Spanish.

Él **quiere** que yo **estudie.**

He wants *me to study.*
main clause subordinate clause

—¿Quiere que le **dé** el número de mi cuenta?   *Do you want me to give you my account number?*

—Sí, y dígale a su esposa que **firme** la solicitud.   *Yes, and tell your wife to sign the application.*

♦ Some verbs of volition are:

querer *to want*	**sugerir** (e:ie) *to suggest*
mandar *to order*	**necesitar** *to need*
aconsejar *to advise*	**rogar** (o:ue) *to beg, plead*
pedir (e:i) *to ask for, request*	**recomendar** (e:ie) *to recommend*

PRÁCTICA

A. A friend of yours, María, always wants people to do the opposite of what they want or don't want to do. Say what she wants or doesn't want these people to do.

MODELO: Yo no quiero lavarme la cabeza ahora.
     María quiere que yo me lave la cabeza ahora.

1. Nosotros necesitamos comprar una motocicleta.
2. Yo no quiero probarme el vestido.
3. Tú quieres abrir una cuenta corriente.
4. Ellos no quieren ir al banco.
5. Esteban quiere dar una fiesta.
6. Mi hermano quiere ser barbero.
7. Anita y yo no queremos venir mañana.
8. Ud. no necesita ir al campo en bicicleta.
9. Alicia no quiere pagar la cuenta.
10. Nosotros queremos hacer la comida.

B. We will tell you our problems. Tell us what you suggest, recommend, or advise.

MODELO: Mañana tengo un examen. ¿Qué me aconseja que haga?
Le aconsejo que estudie mucho.

1. Yo no puedo lavar mis pantalones en casa. ¿Adónde me sugiere que los lleve?
2. Un Cadillac es muy caro para mí. ¿Qué coche me recomienda que compre?
3. A mi hermano le regalaron mil dólares. ¿Qué le sugiere que haga con el dinero?
4. Mi prima no tiene suficiente dinero para ir al teatro. ¿Le aconseja que se lo pida prestado a su papá o a su novio?
5. Alguien nos robó las maletas. ¿Adónde nos aconseja que vayamos?
6. Me duele la cabeza. ¿Qué me recomienda que tome?
7. Mi tía está enferma. ¿Qué le aconseja que haga?
8. Los chicos ensuciaron la alfombra. ¿Qué les sugiere que hagan?
9. A mi hermana no le gusta cocinar. ¿Qué le sugiere que haga?
10. Mañana es el cumpleaños de mi padre. ¿Qué me sugiere que le regale?

C. Be an interpreter. What are these people saying.

1. Where can I park?
   I suggest that you park in front of the bank.
2. Do I need to fill out this card?
   Yes, and I need you to sign it and date it.
3. I always sleep late, and now I have a job . . .
   Well . . . I advise you to buy an alarm clock.
4. My mother wants me to run errands tomorrow.
   Then I suggest that you get up early, Lupita.

Sí, deseo que me envíen información hoy mismo sobre los cursos en el Centro Koubek.

Manuela Rojas
Nombre
555 N. Beach Street
Dirección
Miami, Florida 33135
Ciudad / Estado / Código Postal

Envíe a: Koubek Memorial Center
School of Continuing Studies
University of Miami
2705 S.W. 3rd Street
Miami, Florida 33135
(305) 649-6000

DA8

► *4.* The subjunctive with verbs of emotion   *(El subjuntivo con verbos de emoción)*

♦ In Spanish, the subjunctive is always used in subordinate clauses
when the verb in the main clause expresses any kind of emotion,
such as fear, joy, pity, hope, pleasure, surprise, anger, regret, sor-
row, likes and dislikes, and so forth. Some of the verbs that call
for the subjunctive are **temer, alegrarse (de)** *(to be glad),* **sentir**
(to be sorry, regret), and **esperar;** also expressions like **ojalá** *(I
hope)* **es una lástima** *(it's a pity).*

—**Siento** que Julia no **venga**   *I'm sorry that Julia is not
hoy.*   *coming today.*
—**Espero** que **pueda** venir   *I hope she can come tomor-
mañana.   row.*

♦ If there is no change of subject, the infinitive is used instead of the
subjunctive.

Me alegro de no necesitar nada más. ⎫ *I'm glad I don't need
                                     ⎬ anything else.*
(**Yo** me alegro—**yo** no necesito.) ⎭

PRÁCTICA

A. You and Carmen are good friends. Tell us whether you are
glad (**Me alegro de que...**) or sorry (**Siento que...**) about what
is happening to Carmen and her family.

MODELO: Estoy enferma.
        Siento que estés enferma.

1. Yo quiero salir y tengo que quedarme en casa.
2. Mi hermano y yo no podemos ponernos de acuerdo.
3. Mi mamá estaba enferma pero ahora está mejor.
4. Mi hijo es muy inteligente.
5. Mi hija sabe cocinar muy bien.
6. No hay ningún cuarto libre.
7. Mis padres van a Buenos Aires.
8. Mis estudiantes me dan muchos problemas.

B. Be an interpreter. What are these people saying?

1. I'm going to go to bed.
   I hope the bed is comfortable.
2. I'm afraid she doesn't have much money in her checking account.
   I hope she has money in her savings account.

3. I'm glad you are here, ladies.
   We're glad to be here.
4. I'm afraid your pants aren't ready, sir.
   I hope they're ready tomorrow.
5. It's a pity that your brother isn't here.
   I hope (God grant) he comes back tomorrow.

C. Complete the following by expressing how you feel.

1. Yo me alegro mucho de...
2. Yo me alegro mucho de que mis amigos...
3. Yo temo no...
4. Yo temo que mi papá no...
5. Yo siento...
6. Yo siento que el profesor...
7. Yo espero...
8. Yo espero que mis padres...
9. Ojalá que...
10. Es una lástima que...

Abiertos Hoy
HASTA LAS 4:00 p.m

Esperamos que vengan a
nuestro supermercado

52 Años de Servicio

¡A ver cuánto aprendió!

A. ¡Conversemos!

Reread the dialogue in this lesson and be prepared to discuss the following.

1. ¿Cree usted que a Sergio le gusta dormir? ¿Cómo lo sabe?
2. ¿Qué pasa en cuanto suena el despertador?
3. ¿Por qué no puede quedarse en la cama hoy?
4. ¿Dónde estaban los pantalones de Sergio?
5. ¿De qué color eran los pantalones de Sergio originalmente? ¿Y ahora?
6. ¿A qué departamento de la tienda La Francia va Sergio?
7. Las fotos que él quiere revelar, ¿son en colores o en blanco y negro?
8. ¿Puede sacar Sergio doscientos dólares de su cuenta de ahorros? ¿Por qué no?
9. ¿Cuál es el saldo de su cuenta de ahorros?
10. ¿Por qué grita Sergio «¡Oh, no!»?
11. ¿Sergio tiene hermanos? ¿Cómo lo sabe?
12. ¿Qué piensa Sergio mientras camina a la estación de policía?

B. ¡Repase el vocabulario!

What words are missing?

1. Quiero que vayas a la _____ y me compres unos pantalones.
2. ¿Cuánto _____ Uds. por _____ un rollo de película en colores?
3. Voy a _____ mil dólares de mi cuenta de ahorros y los voy a _____ en mi cuenta corriente.
4. Necesita el _____ para retirar los pantalones.
5. ¡_____ Julio! ¡Los muchachos se llevaron su motocicleta y nunca se la devolvieron!
6. A ver... No puedo verte esta semana, de _____ que tienes que venir la semana _____ .
7. Llegó Antonio y al _____ llegó Luis.
8. Anita caminó _____ mí y me dio un beso.
9. ¿Lo vas a comprar al _____ o a plazos?
10. Tengo mi _____ de cheques, pero no quiero pagar con cheque; quiero pagar en _____ .
11. Si quieres asistir a la universidad, tienes que empezar a _____ tu dinero.

12. Tienes tu libreta de _____ contigo, ¿verdad? ¿O la dejaste en casa?
13. ¿Tengo que pagar o es _____ ?
14. No me desperté porque no sonó el _____ .
15. ¿Vas a salir o te vas a _____ en casa?

C. Situaciones

What would you say in the following situations? What might the other person say?

1. You are at the dry cleaner's and you want to pick up your pants. You are upset because they are not ready. You ask when they are going to be ready.
2. You are at the photo section of a large department store. Find out how much they charge to develop black and white and color film. Ask about the rolls of film you brought in last week for developing.
3. You are at the bank. You want to withdraw money from your savings account and deposit it in your checking account. Find out what you have to do.

Para escribir

Make a list of things you need to do the coming week.

¡Cosas muy importantes!

1.
2.
3.
4.
5.

Otras cosas que tengo que hacer

1.
2.
3.
4.
5.
6.
7.
8.
9.
10.

En la vida real

ENTREVISTA

Choose a partner, then interview each other using the **tú** form.

Pregúntele a su compañero(-a) de clase...

1. ...en qué calle y en qué ciudad vive.
2. ...si le gusta levantarse temprano o quedarse en la cama hasta tarde.
3. ...si hizo alguna diligencia ayer.
4. ...si lava su ropa o la lleva a la tintorería.
5. ...si prefiere que le tomen fotografías en colores o en blanco y negro.
6. ...si la última vez que tomó fotos, las fotos salieron bien.
7. ...si prefiere que le regalen un coche o una motocicleta.
8. ...si tiene hermanos o es hijo(-a) único(-a).
9. ...si se parece más a su mamá o a su papá.
10. ...si está ahorrando dinero para comprar algo especial. (¿Qué?)

CONVERSACIÓN

Have a conversation with a classmate about the errands you have had to run lately, including those that did not go as planned.

Some words and expressions you may want to include:

mala suerte   *bad luck*
todo me fue mal   *everything went wrong (for me)*
todo el día   *all day long*
el taller de mecánica   *mechanic's shop*

TALLERES VICTORIA
MOTORS & CIA. LTDA.
EDGARDO GONZALEZ
LUIS GAMA

VOLKSWAGEN

TRABAJOS GARANTIZADOS
Calle 67 N° 27-40
TELEFONOS:
240 3257 - 250 5993
Almacén de Repuestos
231 4021

Cosas por hacer

With a classmate, look at the list of errands that must be done tomorrow. Then take turns saying what you want each other to do, and give different reasons why you can't do it.

Modelo: Yo quiero que tú compres la medicina para Ernesto.
Yo no puedo comprarla porque tengo que estudiar.

	Cosas que debemos hacer.
	1. *Llevar los pantalones a la tintorería.*
	2. *Llevar a revelar el rollo de película.*
	3. *Depositar el cheque en el banco.*
	4. *Llevar la motocicleta al taller de mecánica.*
	5. *Comprar las bebidas para la fiesta.*
	6. *Llevar los discos a casa de Ana.*
	7. *Alquilar un video.*
	8. *Comprar los billetes para la excursión.*
	9. *Recoger las entradas para el concierto.*
	10. *Comprar la medicina para Ernesto.*
	11. *Pedirle prestada la grabadora a Rosita.*
	12. *Ir a la oficina de turismo para pedir la lista de hoteles.*
	13. *Comprar el regalo para Eva.*
	14. *Devolverle las maletas a Luis.*
	15. *Ir al aeropuerto a esperar (to meet) a Teresa.*

¿Qué dice tu horóscopo...?

CAPRICORNIO

(21 de diciembre–20 de enero)
Tú eres, como siempre, ¡superpráctico! Debes recordar, sin embargo *(however)*, que a veces es bueno ser impulsivo. Si recibes una invitación interesante... ¿por qué no aceptarla?

ACUARIO

(21 de enero–19 de febrero)
Si quieres progresar en tus estudios o en tu profesión, no debes dejar para mañana lo que puedes hacer hoy. Alguien muy importante te está observando.

PISCIS

(20 de febrero–20 de marzo)
Más que nunca, Cupido va a ser parte de tu vida *(life)* este año. Probablemente va a querer que estés preparado(-a) para cualquier cosa *(anything)*, incluso una boda.

ARIES

(21 de marzo–20 de abril)
¡Siempre empiezas proyectos con mucho entusiasmo pero casi nunca los terminas! Tienes que hacer lo posible por aprender a ser perseverante. Este año va a ser muy importante para ti.

TAURO

(21 de abril–20 de mayo)
Buena oportunidad para mejorar *(improve)* las finanzas. Un nuevo empleo... una beca *(scholarship)*... Pero tienes que hacer tu parte y aceptar nuevas responsabilidades.

GÉMINIS

(21 de mayo–20 de junio)
¡Tienes que salir de la rutina! ¿Por qué no tomas una clase o das una fiesta? Hay muchas personas que quieren ser tus amigos... pero tú no les das la oportunidad.

CÁNCER

(21 de junio–20 de julio)
Muy pronto vas a tener que tomar una decisión muy importante. Debes pensar en todas las posibilidades antes de decidir lo que vas a hacer. Hay alguien que está esperando ansiosamente *(anxiously)* tu decisión.

LEO

(21 de julio–20 de agosto)
Pronto vas a recibir noticias *(news)* de alguien que hace mucho que no ves. También debes tratar de llamar o escribirles a aquellas personas que son parte de tu pasado.

VIRGO

(21 de agosto–20 de septiembre)
Como siempre, estás trabajando demasiado. No debes sentirte culpable *(guilty)* si decides tomarte unas vacaciones o simplemente ir al cine o al teatro con tus amigos. Esta semana vas a tener muchas oportunidades de divertirte y debes aprovecharlas *(take advantage of them)*.

LIBRA

(21 de septiembre–20 de octubre)
Tú eres generalmente una persona muy equilibrada, pero últimamente *(lately)* le estás dando más importancia a tu trabajo y a tus proyectos que a tu familia. Tienes que pasar más tiempo con tu familia.

ESCORPIÓN

(21 de octubre–20 de noviembre)
Éstos son los momentos indicados para tomar decisiones importantes. Es muy posible que hagas un viaje muy largo, probablemente al extranjero *(abroad)*.

SAGITARIO

(21 de noviembre–20 de diciembre)
Hay una persona que está secretamente enamorada de *(in love with)* ti. Muy pronto vas a saber quién es. Debes aceptar las invitaciones de tus amigos porque vas a conocer a esa persona en una fiesta o en un picnic.

Now play a zodiac expert and see what is in store for your classmates and your teacher, according to the horoscope you just read. Talk to each one and discuss your fortune and theirs. Also check other people's horoscopes—your parents', your husband's or wife's, your boyfriend's or girlfriend's, and so on.

Una actividad especial

Get ready to complain and to receive complaints about different establishments. You will be divided into two groups owning different establishments. Group A owns a restaurant, a hotel, and a travel agency. Group B owns a bank, a beauty salon, and a maid service. Before the two groups express their complaints to each other about bad service, members of each group should get together to discuss the types of concerns and problems that they'll present.

Una mujer extranjera le pregunta a unos policías cómo llegar a la oficina de correos en Barcelona, España.

OBJECTIVES

Structure   The **Ud.** and **Uds.** commands • Position of object pronouns with direct commands • The subjunctive to express doubt, disbelief, and denial • Constructions with **se**

Communication   You will learn vocabulary related to asking for information at the post office.

Pidiendo información

Julia, una chica de Honduras, llegó a Madrid hace una semana. Con sus amigos españoles visitó el Parque del Retiro, el Palacio Real, Segovia, Ávila y la antigua ciudad de Toledo. En cada lugar compró un montón de tarjetas postales para enviárselas a sus padres y a sus amigos. Hoy decidió ir al correo para enviar las postales y recoger un paquete.

JULIA —*(Piensa)* Dudo que el correo esté abierto a esta hora. Creo que se abre a las nueve. *(A un señor que está parado en la esquina)* Dígame, señor, ¿dónde queda la oficina de correos?

SR. GÓMEZ —Está a cinco manzanas de aquí, en la Plaza de la Cibeles.

JULIA —Es que... soy extranjera y no conozco las calles. ¿Puede decirme cómo llegar ahí?

SR. GÓMEZ —¡Ah!, siga derecho por esta calle hasta llegar a la Plaza de Colón.

JULIA —¿Cuántas cuadras?

SR. GÓMEZ —Dos. Después doble a la derecha, en la calle Alcalá.

JULIA —¿La oficina de correos está en esa calle?

SR. GÓMEZ —Sí, ahí mismo. Es un edificio antiguo y está frente a la estación del metro.

A las nueve de la mañana, Julia llega a la oficina de correos.

JULIA —Perdón. Quiero recoger un paquete. Mi nombre es Julia Reyes.

EMPLEADO —¿Tiene un documento de identidad?

JULIA —Mi pasaporte... pero lo dejé en el hotel.

EMPLEADO —No creo que se lo den sin identificación.

JULIA —Bueno, vuelvo esta tarde. ¿Dónde puedo comprar sellos?

EMPLEADO —Vaya a la ventanilla número dos, a la izquierda.

En la ventanilla número dos, Julia le pide al empleado los sellos que necesita.

JULIA —Quiero enviar estas tarjetas postales por vía aérea y una carta certificada a Honduras.

EMPLEADO —Son dos mil quinientas pesetas[1], señorita.

JULIA —¿Adónde tengo que ir para enviar un telegrama?

EMPLEADO —Suba al segundo piso. La oficina de telégrafos está arriba.

---

[1] Spanish currency.

*Julia, a girl from Honduras,
arrived in Madrid a week
ago. With her Spanish friends
she visited the Parque del
Retiro, the Palacio Real, Segovia, Ávila, and the old city
of Toledo. At each place, she
bought a lot of postcards to
send to her parents and
friends. Today she decided to
go to the post office to send
the postcards and to claim a
package.*

J. *(Thinking)* I doubt
that the post office
is open at this time.
I think it opens at
nine. *(To a gentle-
man who is standing
on the corner)* Tell
me, sir, where is the
post office located?

MR. G. It's five blocks from
here, at the Plaza de
la Cibeles.

J. The fact is . . . I'm a
foreigner, and I
don't know the
streets. Can you tell
me how to get
there?

MR. G. Oh! Continue
straight ahead on
this street until you
get to the Plaza de
Colón.

J. How many blocks?

MR. G. Two. Then turn right
on Alcalá Street.

J. Is the post office on
that street?

MR. G. Yes, right there. It's
an old building, and
it's across from the
subway station.

*At nine o'clock in the morn-
ing Julia arrives at the post
office.*

J. Excuse me. I want to
claim a package. My
name is Julia Reyes.

Después de enviar el telegrama, Julia sale de la oficina de correos y camina
hacia la Gran Vía, donde la espera su amiga Pilar.

JULIA   —*(A Pilar)* Creía que no ibas a estar aquí.

PILAR   —Oye, guapa, no es verdad que los españoles siempre
lleguemos tarde como creéis vosotros. A veces somos
puntuales.

Vocabulario

COGNADOS

el **palacio** palace	**puntual** punctual
el **parque** park	

NOMBRES

el **camino**   road

el **documento de identidad**
   (identificación)   I.D.

el **edificio**   building

la **esquina**   (street) corner

la **estación del metro**   subway
   station

la **manzana**[1] *(Spain)*, la **cuadra**
   (Sp. Am.)   block (distance)

el **metro**   subway

la **oficina de correos**, el **correo**
   post office

la **oficina de telégrafos**   telegraph
   office

el **paquete**   package, parcel

el **sello**, la **estampilla**, el **timbre**
   (Mex.)   stamp

la **ventanilla**   window

VERBOS

doblar   to turn, bend

dudar   to doubt

quedar   to be located

subir   to go up, climb

ADJETIVOS

abierto(-a)   open

antiguo(-a), **viejo(-a)**[2]   old

certificado(-a)   registered, certified

extranjero(-a)   foreign

parado(-a)   standing

OTRAS PALABRAS Y
EXPRESIONES

ahí mismo   right there

arriba   upstairs

cada   each

derecho   straight (ahead)

después   then, afterwards

dígame   tell me

es que...   the fact is . . .

está a... de aquí   it is . . . from
   here

frente a   across from

por vía aérea   by airmail

sin   without

un montón de   a whole bunch of

---

[1] In Spanish America, **manzana** is used to refer to a block of buildings, not to the distance between
streets.   [2] When referring to people, use **viejo**, not **antiguo**.

E. Do you have some I.D.?
J. My passport . . . but I left it at the hotel.
E. I don't think they'll give it to you without identification.
J. Fine, I'll come back this afternoon. Where can I buy stamps?
E. Go to window number two, to the left.

At window number two, Julia asks the employee for the stamps she needs.

J. I want to send these postcards by air mail and a certified letter to Honduras.
E. It's two thousand five hundred pesetas, miss.
J. Where must I go to send a telegram?
E. Go up to the second floor. The telegraph office is upstairs.

After sending the telegram, Julia leaves the post office and walks toward the Gran Vía, where her friend Pilar is waiting for her.

J. *(To Pilar)* I thought you weren't going to be here.
P. Listen girl, it's not true that we Spaniards always arrive late like you think. Sometimes we are punctual.

Vocabulario adicional

abajo downstairs
No está arriba; está **abajo.**

bajar to descend, go down
Ud. debe **bajar** en seguida.

el buzón mailbox
¿Hay un **buzón** en el hotel?

el casillero mailbox (in an office)
La secretaria puso las cartas en mi **casillero.**

el correo mail
¿A qué hora llega el **correo?**

la estación station
El tren llega a la **estación** a las tres.

el giro postal money order
Deseo enviar un **giro postal** a Chile.

el semáforo traffic light
Caminé hasta llegar al **semáforo.**

¿Lo sabía Ud.... ?

Situada en la parte central de la Península Ibérica, Madrid es la capital de España. Su población de más de seis millones de habitantes y su importancia cultural y económica la hacen la principal ciudad española.

En los monumentos pueden apreciarse diferentes estilos: medieval, árabe, renacentista, barroco y otros. Entre los jardines, el más famoso es el Parque del Retiro.

Madrid tiene muchísimos museos de pintura, arquitectura, ciencias y otros, pero el más conocido de todos es el Museo del Prado.

Una de las calles principales de la ciudad es la Gran Vía, donde hay muchas tiendas elegantes y cafés al aire libre.

- El correo de Madrid, o el Palacio de Comunicaciones, es un edificio monumental. Está frente a la hermosa fuente *(fountain)* de La Cibeles, que, para muchos, es el símbolo de Madrid.

- El Palacio Real, situado frente a la Plaza de Oriente, fue la antigua residencia de los reyes de España. Está considerado uno de los mejores edificios de su tipo en Europa.

- El metro de Madrid es un sistema de transporte muy eficiente y barato. Es el medio *(means)* de transportación que usa la mayoría de los madrileños. También hay un metro en Barcelona.

- Segovia es un punto de atracción turístico. Entre sus muchos lugares de interés están el Alcázar, un castillo fortaleza *(fortress castle)*, y el famoso acueducto romano.

- Ávila es famosa por sus murallas *(walls)*, construidas en el siglo *(century)* XI. Las murallas tienen ochenta y ocho torres y nueve puertas *(gates)* y están en perfecto estado de conservación.

En Ávila nacieron *(were born)* los grandes poetas místicos San Juan de la Cruz y Santa Teresa de Jesús.

Estatua del Rey Alfonso XII en el estanque del Parque del Buen Retiro, en Madrid, España.

Estructuras gramaticales

▶ *1.* The **Ud.** and **Uds.** commands   *(Formas del imperativo para **Ud.** y **Uds.**)*

The command forms for **Ud.** and **Uds.**[1] are identical to the corresponding present subjunctive forms.

A. Regular forms

ENDINGS OF THE FORMAL COMMANDS

		Ud.	Uds.
-ar verbs	cantar	cant **-e**	cant **-en**
-er verbs	beber	beb **-a**	beb **-an**
-ir verbs	vivir	viv **-a**	viv **-an**

—¿Sigo derecho?	*Do I keep going straight ahead?*
—No, no **siga** derecho. **Doble** a la izquierda.	*No, don't keep going straight ahead. Turn left.*

ATENCIÓN

To give a negative **Ud./Uds.** command, just place **no** in front of the verb: No, **no siga** derecho.

B. Irregular forms

	dar	estar	ser	ir
Ud.	dé	esté	sea	vaya
Uds.	den	estén	sean	vayan

—¿Adónde tengo que ir?	*Where do I have to go?*
—**Vaya** a la ventanilla número dos.	*Go to window number two.*

---

[1] The commands for **tú** will be studied in **Lección 14.**

PRÁCTICA

What commands would these people give?

1. *El profesor a los estudiantes:*
   venir a clase temprano
   abrir el libro
   ir a la pizarra
   hacer los ejercicios
   cerrar el libro
   hablar solamente español
   no hablar inglés en la clase

2. *La directora a la secretaria:*
   estar en la oficina a las siete
   traer las cartas
   traducir los documentos
   llevar las cartas al correo
   comprar estampillas
   llamar por teléfono al señor Paz
   conseguir la dirección del Banco de Ponce
   no volver hasta las tres

► *2.* Position of object pronouns with direct commands *(Posición de los pronombres usados como complementos en el imperativo)*

♦ In all direct *affirmative* commands, the object pronouns are placed *after* the verb and attached to it, thus forming only one word.[1]

Ud. *form*		Uds. *form*	
Hága**lo.**	*Do it.*	Cómpren**lo.**	*Buy it.*
Dí**gales.**	*Tell them.*	Dígan**le.**	*Tell him.*
Tráiga**nosla.**	*Bring it to us.*	Tráigan**selo.**	*Bring it to him.*
Quéde**se.**	*Stay.*	Quéden**se.**	*Stay.*

♦ In all *negative* commands, the pronouns are placed *in front of the verb.*

Ud. *form*		Uds. *form*	
No **lo** haga.	*Don't do it.*	No **los** traigan.	*Don't bring them.*
No **le** hable.	*Don't speak to her.*	No **les** hablen.	*Don't speak to them.*
No **se lo** dé.	*Don't give it to him.*	No **se los** den.	*Don't give them to him.*

♦ Remember that when an indirect and a direct object pronoun are used together in the same sentence, the indirect object always precedes the direct object.

PRÁCTICA

A. You think that all these commands being given are wrong. Tell these people to do just the opposite of what they have been told to do.

MODELO: Siéntense aquí.
               No se sienten aquí.

1. No se levanten temprano.
2. Báñense con agua fría.
3. No se vistan aquí.
4. Sírvanme el desayuno temprano.
5. Tráigame las cartas, pero no las lea.
6. Dígale a Graciela que tenemos una fiesta, pero no se lo diga a Javier.

---

[1] Note the use of the written accent, which follows the rules for accentuation, as explained in Appendix A.

7. Dele las bebidas a Carlos; no se las dé a Ernesto.
8. Pídale la revista a Pastor; no me la pida a mí.

B. You are having dinner at a fancy restaurant. Tell the waiter what you want or don't want him to do.

MODELO: ¿Le traigo el menú?
Sí, tráigamelo, por favor.
No, no me lo traiga, por favor.

1. ¿Le traigo la lista de vinos?
2. ¿Le sirvo la ensalada primero?
3. ¿Le pongo pimienta a la ensalada?
4. ¿Abro la botella de vino ahora?
5. ¿Le traigo una tortilla a la española?
6. ¿Le sirvo el café ahora?
7. ¿Le traigo la cuenta ahora?
8. ¿Le llamo un taxi?

▶ *3.* **The subjunctive to express doubt, disbelief, and denial** *(Uso del subjuntivo para expresar duda, incredulidad y negación)*

◆ In Spanish, the subjunctive is always used in the subordinate clause when the main clause expresses doubt, uncertainty, disbelief, or denial.

◆ When the verb of the main clause expresses uncertainty or doubt, the verb in the subordinate clause is in the subjunctive.

Dudo que el correo **esté** abierto.	*I doubt that the post office is open.*
No están seguros de que ella **sea** alérgica.	*They are not sure that she is allergic.*
Dudo que yo **pueda** ir.	*I doubt that I can go.*

◆ Note that with the verb **dudar,** the subject in the subordinate clause can be the same as or different from the subject in the main clause.

ATENCIÓN

When no doubt is expressed and the speaker is certain of the reality, the indicative is used.

No dudo que el correo **está** abierto.
I don't doubt that the post office is open.

Están seguros de que ella **es** alérgica.
They are sure that she is allergic.

◆ The verb **creer** *(to believe, to think)* is followed by the subjunctive when used in negative sentences in which it expresses disbelief. It is followed by the indicative in affirmative sentences in which it expresses belief or conviction.

No creo que ellos se lo **den.**
I don't think they'll give it to you.

No creo que **podamos** conseguir reservaciones.
I don't think we can get reservations.

but:

Creo que ellos se lo **dan.**
I think they'll give it to you.

Creo que **podemos** conseguir reservaciones.
I think we can get reservations.

◆ When the main clause denies what is said in the subordinate clause, the subjunctive is used.

Niego que él **sea** mi hijo.
I deny that he is my son.

No es verdad que él **tenga** los pasajes.
It's not true that he has the tickets.

No es cierto que ellas **vayan** a la montaña.
It's not true that they are going to the mountains.

ATENCIÓN

When the main clause does not deny, but rather confirms, what is said in the subordinate clause, the indicative is used.

No niego que él **es** mi hijo.
I don't deny that he is my son.

Es verdad que él **tiene** los pasajes.
It's true that he has the tickets.

Es cierto que ellas **van** a la montaña.
It's true that they are going to the mountains.

PRÁCTICA

A. **¿Es verdad? ¿Es cierto?** Say whether the following statements are true or not.

MODELO: Nosotros celebramos la independencia de Chile.
No es verdad que celebremos la independencia de Chile.

1. Texas es más grande que Maine.
2. En Alaska hace más calor que en Arizona.
3. Buenos Aires es la capital de Chile.
4. Mi abuelo es menor que yo.
5. En las peluquerías venden champú.
6. Las aspirinas son buenas para el dolor de cabeza.
7. El 25 de diciembre celebramos la independencia de los Estados Unidos.
8. La Coca-Cola es una bebida alcohólica.
9. Revelan rollos de fotografía en el correo.
10. Ponemos las cartas en el buzón.
11. Necesitamos un documento de identidad para comprar estampillas.
12. El presidente de los Estados Unidos puede ser extranjero.

B. You and a friend are spending the weekend in a very small town. Your friend asks you questions about things to do, places to see, and so on. Answer, expressing belief or disbelief, doubt or certainty.

1. Son las siete; ¿tú crees que el correo esté abierto?
2. Vamos al centro. Quiero ir a una tienda elegante.
3. Tengo el pelo muy largo. Dicen que aquí hay peluquerías excelentes.
4. ¿Podemos alquilar un coche?
5. ¿Tú crees que hay habitaciones libres en el hotel?
6. ¿Tú crees que un cuarto cuesta más de cien dólares por noche?
7. ¿Tú crees que aceptan cheques de viajero en el hotel?
8. ¿Tú crees que hay un aeropuerto internacional aquí?
9. Quiero ir a cenar a un restaurante francés.
10. ¿Tú crees que vamos a volver aquí algún día?

► *4.* Constructions with **se**   *(Construcciones con **se**)*

♦ In Spanish the pronoun **se** + *the third-person singular or plural* form of the verb is used as an impersonal construction. This construction is equivalent to the English passive voice, in which the person doing the action is not specified. It is also equivalent to English sentences with the impersonal subjects *one, they, people,* and *you* (indefinite). This construction is widely used in Spanish.

Se habla español en Chile. { *Spanish is spoken in Chile.*
{ *They speak Spanish in Chile.*

—¿A qué hora **se abren** los bancos?   *What time do the banks open?*

—**Se abren** a las nueve de la mañana.   *They open at nine A.M.*

—¿Qué idioma **se habla** en Venezuela?   *What language is spoken in Venezuela?*

—**Se habla** español.   *Spanish is spoken.*

♦ This construction is often used in ads, instructions, or directions.

SE VENDE   SE PROHÍBE FUMAR   SE SALE POR LA DERECHA

(For sale)   *(No smoking)*   *(Exit to the right)*

PRÁCTICA

You are new in Quito, Ecuador, and you need to find out information about the country and the city. Ask pertinent questions, using constructions with **se**.

Ud. necesita saber...

1. el horario *(schedule)* de los bancos, del correo y de las tiendas
2. qué idiomas habla la gente
3. qué comen
4. si venden objetos de oro y de plata
5. dónde alquilan coches

¡A ver cuánto aprendió!

A. ¡Conversemos!

Reread the dialogues in this lesson and be ready to discuss the following.

1. ¿Cuánto tiempo hace que Julia está en Madrid?
2. ¿Qué lugares visitó con sus amigos españoles?
3. ¿A quién le pregunta dónde queda la oficina de correos?
4. ¿Qué debe hacer Julia en la calle Alcalá?
5. ¿Cómo es el edificio de correos y dónde está?
6. ¿Por qué no puede Julia recoger el paquete?
7. ¿En qué ventanilla puede comprar sellos?
8. ¿Cómo va a enviar las postales Julia?
9. ¿Hacia dónde camina Julia cuando sale de la oficina de correos?
10. ¿Qué dice Pilar de los españoles?

B. ¡Repase el vocabulario!

What words are missing?

1. Tengo que bajar porque la oficina de telégrafos no está _____ ; está abajo.
2. No estamos sentados; estamos _____ .
3. Hoy vamos a visitar el _____ del Retiro y el _____ Real.
4. La _____ del metro está en la calle Alcalá.
5. Mis padres me mandaron un _____ postal porque necesito dinero.
6. Recibí un _____ de tarjetas de Navidad el año pasado.
7. Le voy a decir a la secretaria que ponga las cartas certificadas en mi _____ .
8. Mandé el paquete por vía _____ .
9. Está ahí _____ , en la esquina.
10. Los colores del _____ son rojo, amarillo y verde.
11. Primero voy a estudiar y _____ voy a tratar de hacer el trabajo.
12. En _____ lugar que visitamos compramos tarjetas.
13. La oficina está arriba, pero dudo que ellos puedan _____ hasta el quinto piso.
14. Elsa pregunta dónde _____ la oficina de correos.
15. Para ir a la oficina de correos no debe seguir derecho. Debe _____ a la izquierda.

C. Situaciones

What would you say in the following situations? What might the other person say?

1. You are in Madrid. Ask someone where the telegraph office is located. Tell him or her that you are a foreigner and don't know the streets.
2. A foreigner asks you for directions to the post office in your town. Explain to him or her how to get there.
3. You are at the post office. Ask the clerk if there is a package for you.
4. Tell the post office clerk that you want to send some letters by airmail, and ask where you can buy stamps.
5. Ask the post office clerk how much it costs to send a registered letter to the United States.

Para escribir

You are in charge of writing the advice column for a newspaper in a Spanish-speaking country. Here are some problems that your readers are consulting you about. Using command forms, give them your advice in writing. Choose a name to sign your column.

1. Yo tengo 40 años y quiero vivir sola *(alone)* en un apartamento, pero mis padres no quieren que me vaya de la casa. ¿Qué me sugiere que haga?

Ansiosa de libertad

2. Pienso viajar a París este verano y tengo una amiga que quiere ir conmigo. Yo no quiero ofenderla, pero no deseo ir con ella porque es muy aburrida *(boring)* y siempre está cansada. ¿Qué puedo hacer?

Una viajera

3. Tengo un novio que es muy bueno, pero no es muy interesante. El sábado pasado fui a una fiesta y conocí a un hombre extraordinario y muy guapo que me invitó a salir. ¿Debo aceptar su invitación o no? ¿Qué me aconseja que haga?

Indecisa

4. Tenemos un vecino *(neighbor)* que tiene cinco hijos; los niños son terribles y todo lo rompen. Planeamos dar una fiesta muy elegante para celebrar el fin de año y queremos invitarlos pero ellos siempre llevan a sus hijos a todas partes *(everywhere)*. ¿Cómo les decimos que no traigan a sus hijos a la fiesta?

Entre la espada y la pared[1]

---

[1] *Between a rock and a hard place* (lit., *between the sword and the wall*).

En la vida real

ENTREVISTA

Choose a partner, then interview each other using the **tú** form.

Pregúntele a su compañero(-a) de clase...

1. ...si sabe dónde queda la oficina de correos.
2. ...si es verdad que el correo se abre a las siete de la mañana.
3. ...a cuántas cuadras de su casa queda el correo.
4. ...qué queda frente a su casa.
5. ...si prefiere los edificios antiguos o modernos.
6. ...si para ir a la cafetería debe seguir derecho o doblar a la izquierda o a la derecha.
7. ...si hay metro en la ciudad donde vive.
8. ...si sus padres son extranjeros.
9. ...si tiene pasaporte.
10. ...si cree que los norteamericanos son puntuales.

INSTRUCCIONES

With a classmate try to figure out how you would give directions to the following places.

Within the university:

¿Cómo voy de la clase de español...

1. a la biblioteca *(library)*?
2. al edificio de administración?
3. a la cafetería?
4. al baño?

Outside the university:

¿Cómo voy de la universidad...

1. al restaurante McDonald's?
2. a la oficina de correos?
3. a la estación de servicio *(service station)*?
4. a tu casa o apartamento?

En Granada

After spending a few weeks in Madrid, Julia decided to visit Granada. There she would like to visit many places, but doesn't know how to get to them. Using the map below, can you help her?

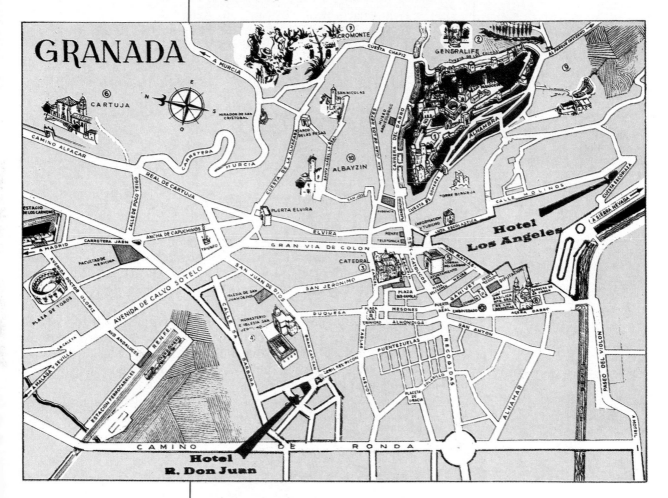

¿Cómo puede ir...

1. del hotel Don Juan a la Puerta Elvira?
2. de la Puerta Elvira a la Catedral?
3. del Albayzín al Sacramonte?
4. del Sacramonte a la Alhambra?
5. de la Alhambra al Generalife?
6. de la estación de trenes a la Plaza de Toros?

UNA ACTIVIDAD ESPECIAL

With two partners, go to the library to obtain additional information about one of the topics in the list below. Each group must select one item. Share the information you find with the rest of the class.

1. El Palacio Real
2. Toledo
3. El Greco
4. La Gran Vía
5. Segovia

6. Ávila
7. El Parque del Retiro
8. El Escorial
9. El Valle de los Caídos
10. Granada

Y ahora, *¡vamos a leer!*

La carta de Julia

8 de julio de 1990

Queridos padres:

Hace una semana que estoy aquí, y ya me siento un poco «española». ¡Madrid es una ciudad magnífica! Visité muchos lugares y compré un montón de tarjetas para enviárselas a ustedes y a todos mis amigos. Dudo que *somewhere* pueda escribirles a todos porque cada día voy a alguna parte° y no tengo mucho tiempo.

Ayer fui a Toledo y pasé todo el día allí. Es una ciudad antigua y muy interesante. Visité la casa de El Greco y vi algunos de sus cuadros, que son extraordinarios. También visité la Catedral, que me gustó mucho. Mañana quiero ir a El Escorial y al Valle de los Caídos, pero no creo que tenga suficiente tiempo para ver los dos lugares.

Say hi
Don't forget
Escríbanme y díganle a Rafael que me escriba también. Denle saludos° a Carmen. No se olviden° de mandarme la dirección de Ernesto.

Love
Cariños,°

Julia

¡A ver cuánto recuerda!

1. ¿Cuántos días hace que Julia está en Madrid?
2. ¿Cree Ud. que le gusta Madrid? ¿Cómo lo sabe Ud.?
3. ¿Para quiénes son las tarjetas que compró Julia?
4. ¿Ud. cree que Julia está aburrida *(bored)* en España?
5. ¿Quién es El Greco?
6. ¿Qué dice Julia de Toledo?
7. ¿Adónde piensa ir Julia mañana?
8. ¿Qué quiere Julia que hagan sus padres y Rafael?
9. ¿A quién le manda saludos Julia?
10. ¿De qué no quiere Julia que se olviden sus padres?

El puente Alcántara, sobre el río Tajo, en Toledo, España. Al fondo se observa el Alcazar.

Take this test. When you finish, check your answers in the answer key provided for this section in Appendix E. Then use a red pen to correct any mistakes you may have made. Ready?

LECCIÓN 10

A. Preterit vs. imperfect

Give the Spanish equivalent of the words in parentheses.

1. Mi hermano _____ un accidente ayer. Yo _____ una ambulancia. *(had / called)*
2. La semana pasada nosotros _____ al consultorio del doctor Mena. *(went)*
3. _____ las nueve de la noche cuando la enfermera me _____ a la sala de rayos X para tomarme una radiografía. *(It was / took)*
4. El médico me _____ si yo _____ embarazada. *(asked / was)*
5. Cuando ella _____ chica, siempre _____ mareos y dolores de cabeza. *(was / had)*
6. La doctora Nieto _____ que el niño _____ una inyección de penicilina. *(said / needed)*
7. Anoche _____ un accidente en la autopista. *(there was)*
8. Ayer nosotros _____ muy ocupados porque _____ mucha gente en nuestro restaurante. *(were / there were)*
9. Pedro y yo _____ a la sala de emergencia cuando _____ a Marcela. *(were going / we saw)*
10. La cabeza me _____ mucho. _____ dos aspirinas y _____ . *(hurt / I took / went to bed)*

B. Verbs which change meaning in the preterit

Write the following sentences in Spanish.

1. I refused to talk about my sickness.
2. We didn't know she was sick.
3. She found out I was sick.
4. I met your brother last night.
5. I didn't want to take the medicine, but I took it.
6. Paco, did you know Miss Rivera?

C. *Hace...* meaning *ago*

Write questions or statements using the elements provided and the expression **hace... que.** Follow the model.

MODELO: ¿ / cuánto tiempo / el doctor / recetarle / esa medicina / ?

¿Cuánto tiempo hace que el doctor le recetó esa medicina?

1. dos días / atropellarlo / un coche
2. tres meses / ellos / operarme / de apendicitis
3. una semana / morir / mi perro
4. ¿ / cuánto tiempo / Ud. / ver / al doctor / ?
5. ¿ / cuánto tiempo / ellos / hacerle / los análisis / ?

D. **Formation of adverbs**

Give the Spanish equivalent of the adverbs in parentheses.

1. Me gustan estas alfombras, _____ la alfombra verde. *(especially)*
2. Yo _____ paso la aspiradora. *(rarely)*
3. El profesor habló _____ . *(slowly and clearly)*
4. Tengo _____ diez dólares; no puedo comprar esa medicina. *(only)*
5. _____ ellos se van de vacaciones a California. *(Generally)*
6. No voy al teatro _____ porque no tengo dinero. *(frequently)*

E. **Just words . . .**

Choose the word or phrase in parentheses that best completes each of the following sentences.

1. Ella es alérgica a la (sección, penicilina, clase).
2. Comemos con (los oídos, los dientes, el pecho).
3. Hablamos con (la espalda, los dedos, la lengua).
4. Vemos con (los ojos, la boca, las orejas).
5. Caminamos con (las manos, el cuello, los pies).
6. Me desinfectaron (el dolor, la herida, la receta).
7. ¿Te (rompiste, atropellaste, pusiste) el brazo alguna vez?
8. Me sangraba mucho (la pierna, el pelo, el mareo).
9. Le vendé (el tobillo, el análisis, el corazón).
10. Era una calle de dos (narices, caras, vías).
11. ¿Cuándo fue la última vez que le (cortaron, quebraron, pusieron) una inyección contra el tétano?

12. ¿Por qué tomaste aspirinas? ¿Tenías (dolor de cabeza, apendicitis, tétano)?
13. ¿Tienes Alka Seltzer? Es para (el pecho, el estómago, los dedos de los pies).
14. Va a tener un niño. Está (cansada, enferma, embarazada).
15. ¿Qué le pasó a Raúl? Dicen que tiene el brazo (roto, alto, sentado).

LECCIÓN 11

A. The relatives pronouns *que* and *quien(es)*

Combine the following pairs of sentences, using **que, quien,** or **quienes,** as needed. Follow the model.

MODELO: Ayer hablé con el señor.
El señor quería tomar mi clase.
Ayer hablé con el señor que quería tomar mi clase.

1. Ésta es la señorita.
La señorita le va a dar los pantalones.
2. Éstos son los vestidos.
Los vestidos están de moda.
3. Ayer vi a las profesoras.
Ellos nos hablaron de las profesoras.
4. Ésta es la señora.
Yo le mostré las fotos a la señora.
5. Él compró una maleta.
La maleta es cara.

B. The subjunctive with verbs of volition

Give the Spanish equivalent of the words in parentheses.

1. Yo te sugiero que _____ al banco mañana. *(you go)*
2. Mis padres quieren _____ una cuenta de ahorros. *(to open)*
3. Elena quiere _____ un cheque. *(to cash)*
4. El empleado nos sugiere que _____ a plazos. *(we buy it)*
5. Dígales a ellos que _____ y _____ la solicitud. *(to date / to sign)*
6. Ella quiere que _____ al contado. *(I pay her)*
7. Deseo _____ con un billete de cien dólares. *(to pay him)*
8. Yo les recomiendo a Uds. que _____ el dinero en el banco. *(you deposit)*
9. Nosotros necesitamos _____ más. *(to save)*

10. Yo le sugiero que _____ su talonario de cheques. *(you bring)*
11. Mi esposo quiere que _____ sus pantalones a la tintorería. *(I take)*
12. Ella me sugiere que _____ aquí. *(I park)*
13. Ella quiere _____ por lo menos cincuenta dólares. *(to charge them)*
14. Ellos quieren que tú _____ todo el dinero en el banco. *(leave)*
15. ¿Qué cuenta quieren _____ Uds.? *(to open)*
16. Mis padres quieren que _____ temprano. *(I leave)*
17. Yo les sugiero que _____ cien dólares todos los meses. *(you save)*
18. Mi hermano quiere que su hijo _____ con nosotros por seis meses. *(live)*

C. The subjunctive with verbs of emotion

Write the Spanish equivalent of the following sentences.

1. I hope you have the claim check, Mr. Vega.
2. I'm sorry that they can't stay.
3. We're afraid that Juana will not come.
4. I'm glad you don't have to borrow money, dear.
5. I hope the photos are ready.

D. Just words . . .

Complete the following sentences with vocabulary learned in **Lección 11,** as appropriate.

1. No me desperté porque el _____ no sonó.
2. Si quiero pagar con cheques debo tener una cuenta _____ .
3. Necesito que pongan la fecha y la _____ en la solicitud.
4. No tengo mucho tiempo porque hoy tengo que hacer muchas _____ .
5. Tenía mil dólares en mi cuenta corriente. Escribí un cheque por doscientos. El _____ es de ochocientos dólares.
6. Quiero _____ este rollo de fotografías.
7. No voy a pagarlo al contado sino a _____ .
8. No es _____ ; cobran veinte dólares por persona.
9. Es una lástima que no se _____ a su padre.
10. Llamé a la policía porque me _____ el coche.
11. Voy a _____ mi coche aquí.
12. Estoy muy cansada. Voy a _____ en la cama hasta tarde.

LECCIÓN 12

A. The *Ud.* and *Uds.* commands

Complete the following sentences with the command form of the verbs in parentheses.

1. Señorita, _____ (mandar) las cartas por vía aérea y certificadas.
2. _____ (estar) aquí a las siete, señores.
3. _____ (ir) a la oficina de telégrafos ahora, señor.
4. Señora, _____ (caminar) dos cuadras y _____ (doblar) a la derecha.
5. No _____ (ser) impacientes, señoras.
6. _____ (caminar) Uds. hasta la esquina.
7. _____ (tratar) de comprar los sellos hoy, señor.
8. _____ (cerrar) las puertas, señoritas. Hace mucho frío.
9. No _____ (dar) su dirección, señoras.
10. No _____ (dejar) los paquetes aquí, señorita.

B. Position of object pronouns with direct commands

Give the Spanish equivalent of the words in parentheses.

1. Necesito las estampillas. _____ , señorita. *(Bring them to me)*
2. El señor quiere la cuenta. _____ , mozo. *(Give it to him)*
3. ¿Las cartas? _____ después, señoritas. *(Write them to him)*
4. La señora quiere leche fría. _____ , camarero. *(Take it to her)*
5. _____ que ellos son extranjeros, señor. *(Tell him)*
6. Necesito el periódico. _____ ahí mismo, señora. *(Leave it)*
7. Éste es el más caro pero _____ , señora. *(don't tell it to him)*
8. Yo no quiero los camarones. _____ , mozo. *(Don't bring them)*

C. The subjunctive to express doubt, disbelief, and denial

Rewrite the following sentences with the new beginnings.

1. Creo que el correo queda en la esquina.
   No creo que...
2. No es verdad que ella esté en la oficina de telégrafos.
   Es verdad que...
3. No dudo que tenemos que subir.
   Dudo que...

4. No niego que él maneja muy bien.
Niego que...
5. Estoy seguro de que Luis sabe dónde está el paquete.
No estoy seguro de que...
6. Es cierto que necesitamos un documento de identidad.
No es cierto que...

D. Constructions with *se*

Form questions with the elements given, adding the necessary connectors. Follow the model.

MODELO: a qué hora / abrir / las tiendas
¿A qué hora se abren las tiendas?

1. qué idioma / hablar / Chile
2. a qué hora / cerrar / los bancos
3. a qué hora / abrir / el correo
4. dónde / vender / estampillas
5. por dónde / subir / segundo piso

E. Just words . . .

Match the questions in column A with the appropriate responses in column B.

A	**B**
1. ¿Dónde queda la oficina?	a. No, está abajo.
2. ¿Vas a caminar?	b. Sí, hasta llegar al semáforo.
3. ¿Dónde puedo comprar estampillas?	c. Sí, necesito comprar estampillas.
4. ¿Qué le van a mandar?	d. Frente a la estación del metro.
5. ¿Vas a la oficina de correos?	e. No, tiene treinta años.
6. ¿Está arriba?	f. No, hacia la estación.
7. ¿Van a subir?	g. No, voy a tomar el metro.
8. ¿Es viejo?	h. No, el correo no llega hasta las diez.
9. ¿Sigo derecho?	i. Un telegrama.
10. ¿Está lejos?	j. No, un giro postal.
11. ¿Dónde están parados ellos?	k. No, vamos a bajar.
12. ¿Tienes la carta de Juan?	l. En Cuatro Caminos a dos cuadras.
13. ¿Va hacia el aeropuerto?	m. No, queda ahí mismo.
14. ¿Le van a mandar dinero?	n. Sí, todas las semanas.
15. ¿Les escribes a tus padres?	o. En la ventanilla número dos.
16. ¿Es un edificio moderno?	p. No, es muy antiguo.

Bolivia

PANORAMA HISPÁNICO

7

América del Sur (I)

Colombia

Ecuador

Perú

Venezuela

■ La cuenca *(basin)* del Amazonas, que comprende partes del Perú, Ecuador, Colombia, Brasil y Venezuela, es la más grande del mundo. El río Amazonas tiene más de 1.000 tributarios.

■ La Paz, capital de Bolivia, situada a más de diez mil pies de altura, es la sede de gobierno más alta del mundo. La ciudad se encuentra al pie del nevado Illimani, que alcanza una altura de más de veinte mil pies.

■ La ciudad de Cartagena, en el norte de Colombia, era uno de los puertos principales en la época de la colonia; desde allí los españoles enviaban las riquezas del Nuevo Mundo a Europa.

■ Las islas Galápagos, frente a las costas del Ecuador, se consideran una de las zonas ecológicas mejor conservadas. Las distintas especies de plantas y animales que allí se encuentran son exclusivas de las islas y no tienen similaridad con las especies del continente.

■ Caracas, capital de Venezuela, es el lugar de nacimiento de Simón Bolívar, el Libertador de América. Bolívar luchó por la independencia de Colombia, Venezuela, Ecuador, el Perú y Bolivia.

Brazalete de oro, usado en ritos funerarios preincaicos, que se encuentra en el Museo de Oro en Lima, Perú. En el museo existe una gran variedad de piezas precolombinas en oro, en plata y con piedras preciosas. Esta colección es una muestra incomparable del talento artístico y los conocimientos técnicos de las culturas indígenas que habitaban el continente antes de la llegada de Colón. ¿Ha visto Ud. piezas precolombinas en algún museo de los Estados Unidos?

La Avenida Doce de Octubre es una de las principales de Quito, la capital de Ecuador. Esta ciudad, situada al pie del volcán Pichincha, goza de un clima primaveral todo el año por estar a una altura de 9.250 pies sobre el nivel del mar. ¿Cómo se llaman las montañas que atraviesan el territorio del Ecuador?

En los llanos orientales de Colombia, la ganadería es la principal fuente de ingresos. Estos «llaneros» llevan una manada de caballos a los corrales de una hacienda en el departamento del Meta, situado al sureste de Colombia. ¿Qué región de los Estados Unidos es conocida por la importancia de la ganadería?

► El Salto Ángel *(Angel Falls)*, localizado en el Parque Nacional de Canaima en Venezuela, es el más alto del mundo, con una altura de 980 metros (unos 3.200 pies). Las cataratas se llaman Ángel en honor al piloto norteamericano Jimmy Ángel, quien fue el primero en aterrizar allí en 1937. ¿Qué cataratas de los Estados Unidos son famosas en todo el mundo?

▼ Todos los años se lleva a cabo en el Parque Central de Caracas, Venezuela un maratón internacional. El parque es en realidad una pequeña ciudad dentro de Caracas. Su construcción duró 16 años y contiene dos rascacielos *(skyscrapers)*, varios supermercados, una piscina olímpica, un centro para convenciones internacionales, numerosos museos y tiendas. ¿Ha participado Ud. en un maratón alguna vez?

► En la foto se aprecia una manada de alpacas en las montañas de Bolivia. La alpaca pentenece a la familia de las llamas, especie relacionada a los camellos y que habita la región de los Andes. La llama se usa primordialmente como animal de transporte mientras que la lana de la alpaca se utiliza para hacer alfombras y diferentes artículos de vestir. ¿En qué países de Suramérica podemos encontrar llamas y alpacas?

◀ Vista de una de las típicas calles coloniales de Cartagena de Indias en la costa norte de Colombia. Durante la Conquista y el período colonial, Cartagena fue el puerto principal desde donde los españoles exportaban las riquezas del Nuevo Mundo a Europa. La parte antigua de la ciudad estaba completamente amurallada para dar protección contra los ataques de piratas ingleses y franceses. ¿Por qué atacaban los piratas a los españoles?

▲ En el centro de Lima hay dos grandes plazas: la Plaza de Armas y la Plaza de San Martín, conectadas por la calle Jirón de la Unión. La Plaza de San Martín, que aparece en la foto, fue llamada así en honor a José de San Martín, considerado héroe nacional del Perú, por haber libertado este país, además de Argentina y Chile, del dominio español. ¿Conoce Ud. a otro famoso libertador sudamericano?

Una vista del hermoso parque Alameda en la Ciudad de México.

OBJECTIVES

Structure   The subjunctive to express indefiniteness and nonexistence • The subjunctive or indicative after certain conjunctions • ¿Qué? and ¿cuál? used with ser • Uses of sino and pero

Communication   You will learn vocabulary related to renting an apartment and to the various parts of a house.

Se alquila un apartamento

Irene y Lucía, dos chicas colombianas, están estudiando en la Universidad Nacional Autónoma de México. Ahora quieren mudarse porque necesitan un apartamento que esté más cerca de la universidad.

LUCÍA —¡Irene! En el periódico anuncian un apartamento que tiene dos dormitorios y está en un barrio elegante.

IRENE —¡A ver! *(Lee el anuncio.)*

Anuncios Clasificados

Se alquila: apartamento amueblado: dos recámaras, sala, comedor, cocina y cuarto de baño. Calefacción central. Barrio elegante. Llamar al teléfono 481-3520 de 1 a 5 de la tarde. Alquiler: $600.000.[1]

LUCÍA —Mañana, tan pronto como regresemos de la universidad, podemos llamar para ir a verlo.

IRENE —No sé... Nosotras necesitamos un apartamento que tenga garaje... Además, es muy caro para nosotras, Lucía.

LUCÍA —Bueno, mañana, cuando llamemos, podemos preguntar. A ver... ¿cuál es el número de teléfono?

Al día siguiente, en cuanto vuelven de la universidad, las chicas van a ver el apartamento.

LUCÍA —¡Me encantan los muebles y las cortinas!

IRENE —Con el sueldo que nosotras ganamos no vamos a poder pagar el alquiler.

LUCÍA —Entonces en vez de trabajar medio día podemos trabajar tiempo completo.

IRENE —¿Estás loca? No hay nadie que pueda trabajar tiempo completo y al mismo tiempo estudiar en la universidad.

LUCÍA —¡Eres tan pesimista, Irene!

IRENE —No soy pesimista, sino realista. Además, vamos a necesitar dinero para comprar mantas, sábanas, fundas y utensilios de cocina.

LUCÍA —*(No le hace caso y va a la cocina.)* La cocina tiene refrigerador y lavaplatos... y un fregadero grande.

IRENE —No podemos tomar una decisión hasta que veamos otros apartamentos.

---

[1]Based on a currency exchange rate of 2,300 Mexican pesos to one U.S. dollar.

APARTMENT FOR RENT

Irene and Lucía, two Colombian girls, are studying at the National University of Mexico. Now they want to move because they need an apartment which is closer to the university.

L. Irene! In the newspaper they are advertising an apartment which has two bedrooms and is in an elegant neighborhood.

I. Let's see! *(She reads the ad.)*

Classified Ads

For rent: furnished apartment: two bedrooms, living room, dining room, kitchen, and bathroom. Central heating. Elegant neighborhood. Phone 481-3520 between 1 and 5 P.M. Rent: $600,000.

L. Tomorrow, as soon as we return from the university, we can call to go see it.

I. I don't know . . . We need an apartment which has a garage . . . Besides, it's very expensive for us, Lucía.

L. Well, tomorrow, when we call, we can ask. Let's see . . . what's the phone number?

The following day, as soon as they return from the university, the girls go see the apartment.

L. I love the furniture and the curtains!

I. With the salary we are earning, we're not going to be able to pay the rent.

L. Then, instead of working part-time, we can work full-time.

LUCÍA —Pero, Irene, no vamos a encontrar ningún apartamento que sea tan bueno como éste.

IRENE —Tal vez, pero no podemos pagar el alquiler de este apartamento a menos que recibamos una herencia. ¡Vámonos!

LUCÍA —*(Enojada)* ¡Aguafiestas!

Vocabulario

COGNADOS

colombiano(-a) Colombian
la **decisión** decision
elegante elegant
el **garaje** garage
el (la) **pesimista** pessimist
el (la) **realista** realist
el **refrigerador** refrigerator
los **utensilios** utensils

NOMBRES

el (la) **aguafiestas** spoilsport
el **alquiler** rent
el **anuncio clasificado** classified ad
el **barrio** neighborhood
la **calefacción central** central heating
el **comedor** dining room
las **cortinas** curtains
el **dormitorio**, la **recámara** *(Mex.)* bedroom
el **fregadero** kitchen sink
la **funda** pillowcase
la **herencia** inheritance
el **lavaplatos** dishwasher
la **manta**, la **frazada**, la **cobija** blanket
los **muebles** furniture
la **sábana** sheet
la **sala** living room
el **sueldo**, el **salario** salary

VERBOS

anunciar to advertise
ganar to earn
mudarse to move (from one house or place to another)

ADJETIVOS

amueblado(-a) furnished
enojado(-a), **enfadado(-a)** angry

OTRAS PALABRAS Y EXPRESIONES

a menos que unless
al día siguiente the following day
al mismo tiempo at the same time
en vez de instead of
encantarle a uno to love *(same construction as **gustar**)*
hacer caso to pay attention
medio día half a day, part-time
se alquila for rent
tal vez maybe
tan so
tan pronto como as soon as
tiempo completo full-time
tomar una decisión to make a decision
¡Vámonos! Let's go!

I. Are you crazy? There's nobody who can work full-time and at the same time study at the university.

L. You are such a pessimist, Irene!

I. I'm not a pessimist, but a realist. Besides, we will need money to buy blankets, sheets, pillowcases, and kitchen utensils.

L. *(Doesn't pay attention to her and goes to the kitchen.)* The kitchen has (a) refrigerator and (a) dishwasher . . . and a big sink.

I. We can't make a decision until we see other apartments.

L. But, Irene, we're not going to find any apartment that's as good as this one.

I. Maybe, but we will not be able to pay the rent for this apartment unless we receive an inheritance. Let's go!

L. *(Angry)* What a spoilsport!

Vocabulario adicional

el **aire acondicionado**
    air-conditioning
La casa no tiene **aire acondicionado.**

la **almohada**   pillow
¿Estás cómoda? ¿Necesitas otra **almohada?**

la **cocina**   stove
Necesitamos una **cocina** nueva.

el **colchón**   mattress
El **colchón** no es muy cómodo.

la **cómoda**   chest of drawers
Necesito una **cómoda** más grande.

el **jardín**   garden
Mi cuarto tiene vista al **jardín.**

la **lámpara**   lamp
Compré dos **lámparas** para el dormitorio.

la **mesita de noche**   nightstand
El teléfono está en la **mesita de noche.**

El **salón de estar**   family room
El televisor está en el **salón de estar.**

el **sillón,** la **butaca**   armchair
Pongan el **sillón** en el salón de estar.

la **sobrecama**   bedspread
Ayer compré una **sobrecama** azul.

el **sofá**   couch, sofa
Pongan el **sofá** en la sala.

¿Lo sabía Ud.... ?

- En las grandes ciudades españolas y latino-americanas, la mayoría de la gente vive en apartamentos, que en España se llaman «pisos». Los apartamentos se alquilan o se compran. Muchos edificios tienen oficinas o tiendas en la planta baja y apartamentos en los otros pisos.
- La palabra «barrio» tiene una connotación negativa en muchos lugares de los Estados Unidos, pero en los países hispanos equivale simplemente al inglés «neighborhood».
- La Universidad Nacional Autónoma de México está situada en la parte sur de la ciudad de México. Está considerada como la principal institución de su tipo del país, y es una de las más grandes del mundo. Unos 400.000 estudiantes asisten a la UNAM.

Mural del pintor mexicano Alfaro Siqueiros en el edificio de la Administración de la Universidad de México.

Estructuras gramaticales

▶ *1.* **The subjunctive to express indefiniteness and nonexistence**   *(El subjuntivo para expresar lo indefinido y lo inexistente)*

◆ The subjunctive is always used when the subordinate clause refers to someone or something that is indefinite, unspecified, or nonexistent.

Necesitan un apartamento que **esté** cerca de la universidad.	*They need an apartment which is close to the university.*
En la oficina necesitan a alguien que **sepa** español.	*At the office they need someone who knows Spanish.*
Busco un empleado que **hable** inglés.	*I'm looking for an employee who speaks English.*
¡No hay nadie que **pueda** trabajar tiempo completo!	*There's nobody who can work full-time!*

◆ If the subordinate clause refers to existent, definite, or specific persons or things, the indicative is used instead of the subjunctive.

Viven en un apartamento que **está** cerca de la universidad.	*They live in an apartment which is near the university.*
En la oficina tienen a alguien que **sabe** español.	*At the office they have someone who knows Spanish.*
Busco al empleado que **habla** inglés.	*I'm looking for the employee who speaks English.*
Hay alguien que **puede** trabajar tiempo completo.	*There's someone who can work full-time.*

PRÁCTICA

A. You have just moved to Panama, where you will be staying for several years. Say what you need, want, or are looking for.

MODELO: una casa — tener piscina
Quiero una casa que tenga piscina.

1. una casa — tener tres dormitorios
2. una casa — estar cerca de la universidad
3. una casa — no costar un ojo de la cara
4. un coche — tener aire acondicionado
5. muebles — ser baratos
6. un empleo — pagar bien
7. alguien — ayudarme a mudarme
8. un restaurante — servir hamburguesas

B. Now play the role of a very helpful friend from Panama who gives positive answers to all the questions and statements in **Práctica A.**

C. A friend of yours is planning to move to the city or town where you presently live. Explain to him or her whether or not he or she can find the following.

1. ¿Hay alguna casa en un barrio elegante que sea barata?
2. ¿Hay alguna casa que tenga piscina?
3. ¿Hay algún apartamento que esté cerca del centro?
4. Yo necesito una secretaria. ¿Conoces a alguien que sepa hablar alemán y japonés?
5. A mí me gusta la comida argentina. ¿Hay algún restaurante que sirva comida argentina?
6. A mis padres les gusta la comida mexicana. ¿Hay algún restaurante que sirva comida mexicana?

D. Be an interpreter. What are these people saying?

1. I'm looking for a receptionist who can work full-time.
   I'm sorry. I only know students who can work part-time.
2. We want a hotel that has air-conditioning.
   There is a hotel which is near here and which has air-conditioning.
3. Is there anyone who can tell me the weather forecast for tomorrow?
   Yes, I know it. It's going to rain cats and dogs.

▶ *2.* The subjunctive or indicative after certain conjunctions   *(El subjuntivo o el indicativo después de ciertas conjunciones)*

A. Conjunctions followed by the subjunctive or indicative

♦ The subjunctive follows certain conjunctions when the main clause refers to a future action or is a command. Some of these conjunctions are **tan pronto como, en cuanto** (both meaning *as soon as*), **hasta que** *(until)*, and **cuando** *(when)*.

Mañana, **tan pronto como regresemos,** podemos llamar.	*Tomorrow, as soon as we return, we can call.*
No podemos tomar una decisión **hasta que** los **veamos.**	*We can't make a decision until we see them.*
En cuanto reciba mi primer sueldo, voy a comprar una cama.	*As soon as I receive my first paycheck (salary), I'm going to buy a bed.*
Cuando llamemos, podemos preguntar.	*When we call, we can ask.*

♦ If the action already happened or if there is no indication of a future action, the conjunction of time is followed by the indicative.

Ayer, **tan pronto como regresamos,** pudimos llamar.	*Yesterday, as soon as we returned, we were able to call.*
No tomamos una decisión **hasta que** los **vimos.**	*We didn't make a decision until we saw them.*
En cuanto recibí mi primer sueldo, compré una cama.	*As soon as I received my first paycheck (salary), I bought a bed.*
Siempre se lo preguntamos **cuando llamamos.**	*We always ask him (about it) when we call him.*

PRÁCTICA

Explain what kinds of things Alberto generally does, what he did yesterday, and what he intends to do tomorrow. Use the subjunctive or indicative as appropriate.

1. Todos los días / cuando llegar a casa / llamar a su mamá
   Mañana / cuando llegar a casa / va a llamar a su papá
2. Ayer / tan pronto como terminar el examen / ir al cine
   El próximo lunes / tan pronto como terminar el examen / va a ir a la biblioteca
3. Generalmente / esperar al profesor / hasta que llegar
   Ayer / esperar al profesor / hasta que llegar
4. Generalmente / en cuanto conseguir dinero / depositarlo en el banco
   La próxima semana / en cuanto conseguir dinero / depositarlo en el banco

B. Conjunctions followed by the subjunctive

◆ There are some conjunctions that by their very meaning imply uncertainty or condition and are, therefore, always followed by the subjunctive. Some of the conjunctions which are always followed by the subjunctive are:

con tal que *provided that*	**a menos que** *unless*
sin que *without*	**para que** *in order that*
en caso de que *in case*	**antes de que** *before*

Sale **sin que** lo **vean.**	He leaves without them seeing him.
Llámelo **antes de que salga.**	Call him before he leaves.
Voy a darle el dinero **en caso de que** lo **necesite.**	I'm going to give him the money in case he needs it.
Trabajo **para que** mis hijos **estudien.**	I work in order that my children may study.
Voy a visitarlo **a menos que** él **venga** a verme.	I'm going to visit him unless he comes to see me.
Lo voy a comprar **con tal que** no **sea** muy caro.	I'm going to buy it, provided that it's not very expensive.

PRÁCTICA

Víctor and Pablo are making plans for a friend's visit. Complete this conversation using **con tal que, sin que, en caso de que, a menos que, para que,** and **antes de que** and the verbs given.

VÍCTOR —Tenemos que limpiar el apartamento _____ (llegar) él.

PABLO —Yo voy a preparar unos sándwiches _____ (tener) hambre.

VÍCTOR —Sí, ¿y por qué no compras unos refrescos _____ (poder) tomar algo en cuanto llegue?

PABLO —Bueno, pero yo no puedo ir al mercado _____ tú me _____ (dar) el dinero.

VÍCTOR —Está bien. Yo te voy a dar el dinero _____ tú me lo _____ (devolver) mañana.

PABLO —Vale. Voy ahora mismo. Voy a salir _____ me _____ (ver) Paquito porque va a querer ir conmigo.

C. Aunque

♦ The conjunction **aunque** *(even if)* takes the subjunctive if the speaker wants to express uncertainty. If not, **aunque** takes the indicative and is equivalent to *although*.

Aunque la **busque,** no la va a encontrar.	*Even if he looks for her, he's not going to find her.*
Aunque la **buscó,** no la encontró.	*Although he looked for her, he didn't find her.*

PRÁCTICA

A. Complete the following statements, using the indicative or the subjunctive of the verb given as needed.

1. Aunque Rosalía _____ (trabajar) en una agencia de viajes, nunca viaja.
2. Aunque el pasaje de ida y vuelta _____ (ser) más barato, ella compró uno de ida.
3. No sé si está enfermo; pero aunque _____ (sentirse) mal no va a querer ir al médico.
4. Aunque _____ (hacer) buen tiempo el sábado, no vamos a ir a pescar porque no tenemos tiempo.

5. Aunque ellos _____ (ir) a California frecuentemente, nunca van a Disneylandia.

B. Be an interpreter. What are these people saying?

1. I love this lamp! As soon as I get money, I'm going to buy it.
Well, although it is pretty, I think it is expensive.
2. I'm going to give you five hundred dollars so you can pay the
rent.
Why don't you give me a little more in case Aurora wants to
sell us her chest of drawers?
3. A car ran over him?
Yes, and I waited until the ambulance came.

▶ 3. **¿Qué?** and **¿cuál?** used with **ser** *(Qué y cuál
usados con el verbo ser)*

A. *What* translates as **¿qué?** when it is used as the subject of
the verb and it asks for a definition.

—**¿Qué** es una sangría?   *What is a sangría?*
—Es una bebida que tiene   *It's a drink that has wine and*
vino y frutas.   *fruit.*

B. *What* translates as **¿cuál?** when it is used as the subject of
a verb and it asks for a choice. **Cuál** carries the idea of
selection from among several or many available objects,
ideas, and so on.

—**¿Cuál** es su número de telé-   *What is your phone number?*
fono?
—792–4856   *792–4856.*

PRÁCTICA

Write the questions you would ask to get the following information. Use
qué or **cuál,** as needed.

1. — _____
—Mi apellido es Velázquez.
— _____
—Calle Rosales, número 420.
— _____
—8–35–21–92.

2. —¿Quiere una sangría?

— _____

—Es una bebida que se hace con frutas y vino tinto. ¿Quiere comer una paella?

— _____

—Una paella es un plato español que se prepara con arroz, pollo y mariscos.

▶ *4.* Uses of **sino** and **pero**   *(Usos de **sino** y **pero**)*

A. Sino, meaning *but* in the sense of *rather* or *on the contrary,* can be used only after negative statements. The second part of the sentence must negate or contradict the first.

No es la ventanilla número siete **sino** la seis.	*It's not window number seven, but number six.*
No quiero una cuenta corriente **sino** una cuenta de ahorros.	*I don't want a checking account, but a savings account.*

B. Pero is used for *but* in all other cases.

La casa es pequeña **pero** cómoda.	*The house is small but comfortable.*
El cliente no leyó la solicitud **pero** la firmó.	*The customer did not read the application, but he signed it.*

PRÁCTICA

A. Complete the following, using **sino** or **pero,** as needed.

1. Trabaja, _____ no gana mucho dinero.
2. No vive en una casa _____ en un apartamento.
3. No es rubia _____ pelirroja.
4. No tengo sábanas, _____ tengo dos frazadas.
5. No es médico _____ enfermero.
6. No está en el salón de estar _____ en la sala.

B. Be an interpreter. What are these people saying?

1. Do you need sheets and pillowcases?
   We don't need pillowcases, but we (do) need pillows.
2. Is he angry?
   He's not angry, but tired.
3. Is Alberto her son?
   No, he's not her son, but her nephew.
4. Did you buy a bedspread?
   No, but I bought a mattress for David's room.

¡A ver cuánto aprendió!

A. ¡Conversemos!

Reread the dialogue in this lesson and be ready to discuss the following.

1. ¿Irene y Lucía están estudiando en su país?
2. ¿Por qué quieren mudarse?
3. Si las chicas alquilan el apartamento que anuncian en el periódico, ¿van a tener que comprar muebles?
4. Describa el apartamento del anuncio.
5. ¿Qué quiere hacer Lucía tan pronto como regresen mañana de la universidad?
6. ¿Cree Ud. que las chicas tienen automóvil? ¿Cómo lo sabe?
7. ¿Cuál es el número de teléfono al que las chicas tienen que llamar?
8. ¿Qué hacen al día siguiente en cuanto regresan de la universidad?
9. ¿Le gustan a Lucía los muebles y las cortinas del apartamento?
10. ¿Por qué le dice Irene a Lucía que está loca?
11. ¿Qué tiene la cocina del apartamento?
12. Según Irene, ¿qué van a necesitar para poder pagar el alquiler del apartamento?

B. ¡Repase el vocabulario!

Choose the best answer for each of the following questions.

1. ¿Es de Bogotá?
   a. Sí, es uruguayo.   b. Sí, es chileno.   c. Sí, es colombiano.
2. ¿Dónde vas a poner el sofá?
   a. En el comedor.   b. En la sala.   c. En el ascensor.
3. ¿Por qué estás enojado con tu hermano?
   a. Porque no me hace caso.   b. Porque es de estatura mediana.   c. Porque no tiene nada que ponerse.
4. ¿Para qué quieres la frazada?
   a. Para cruzar la calle.   b. Para ponerla en la cama.
   c. Para que me hagan una radiografía.
5. ¿Por qué no puedes alquilar ese apartamento?
   a. Porque no gano suficiente dinero.   b. Porque se alquila.
   c. Porque tengo que pagar exceso de equipaje.
6. ¿Para dónde son las cortinas?
   a. Para aquella butaca.   b. Para aquella ventana.
   c. Para aquel jardín.

7. ¿Por qué no te gusta Emilio?
   a. Porque es muy simpático.   b. Porque trabaja tiempo
   completo.   c. Porque es muy antipático.
8. ¿Qué vas a poner en la sala en vez del sofá?
   a. Un asiento de ventanilla.   b. Un asiento de pasillo.
   c. Una butaca.
9. ¿Es amueblado el apartamento?
   a. Sí, pero no tiene lavaplatos.   b. Sí, pero no tiene tienda
   de campaña.   c. Sí, pero no tiene consultorio.
10. ¿Qué necesitas para el dormitorio?
    a. Una caña de pescar.   b. Un rizador y un secador.
    c. Una mesita de noche.

C. Situaciones

What would you say in the following situations? What might the other
person say?

1. You are talking to a real estate agent. Tell him or her you
   want a house that is in a very exclusive (elegant) neighborhood, with at least five bedrooms, air-conditioning, and a
   three-car garage.
2. You are describing the house or apartment where you live to a
   friend.
3. You and your friend are going to share an apartment. Describe
   one you have just seen telling him or her why you should take
   the apartment.

Para escribir

Write a composition describing the house of your dreams (**sueños**).
Include the following information.

- location
- kind of neighborhood
- what type of rooms you want
- number of bedrooms and bathrooms
- backyard (patio)
- color scheme
- furniture you would have in each room
- conveniences
- what you will have to do to be able to afford such a house

En la vida real

ENTREVISTA

Choose a partner, then interview each other using the **tú** form.

Pregúntele a su compañero(-a) de clase...

1. ...si su casa tiene calefacción central y aire acondicionado.
2. ...qué muebles tiene en su dormitorio.
3. ...si se va a mudar cuando termine este semestre.
4. ...si prefiere una casa que tenga garaje para tres coches o una casa que tenga piscina.
5. ...si trabaja tiempo completo o medio día.
6. ...si prefiere alquilar un apartamento o comprar una casa.
7. ...qué va a hacer mañana en cuanto regrese a su casa.
8. ...si cree que va a recibir una herencia. (¿De quién?)
9. ...si es pesimista, optimista o realista.
10. ...si es un(a) aguafiestas.

INTERCAMBIO

You and a classmate are going to exchange houses or apartments. Describe your present living accommodations to each other and what you each can expect.

EN BUSCA DE APARTAMENTO

Some friends of yours are looking for an apartment. Help them by using the information provided in the ads below to answer their questions.

E—ALQUILERES

Veranee todo el año en Barcelona. Vista panoramica, por encima capa polución ciudad, 135 m. sobre el nivel del mar

APARTAMENTOS
(JUNTO AL PARQUE GUINARDO)

Calle Dr. Cadevall, 1-3 Barcelona (entrada por Avda. V.de Montserrat y calle Fco. Alegre)
Gran calidad, estar-comedor, 2 ó 3 dorm., cocina, baño, calef. ind., terraza, antena colectiva, y parabólica, 70 a 90 m². A partir de ptas. 7.000.000

*Información: MANSUR, S.A. De 5.30 a 8.30 h. tarde
Tel. 257-53-45. Con financiación de Caja Postal*

VIVA EN EL CENTRO
DE BLANES
A 5 minutos de la playa
APARTAMENTOS

Con Plazas de Parking, 1 y 2 hab. Salón - Comedor – Cocina equipada – Baño completo - Acabados
ALTO STANDING. Información: **FINCAS VERA.**
*C. Muralla, n.º 3. BLANES. Tels.: (972) 33-53-74
y (972) 33-70-47*

TORREDEMBARRA

Apartamentos 2 habitaciones, salón comedor, cocina, baño completo con instalación para lavadora. Situados en el centro del pueblo.
Avda. Catalunya. 11.
Precio: 4.000.000 pesetas
Vd. puede ser propietario con 1 millón de pesetas más 3 millones de hipoteca (a 15 años)
Vea apartamento de muestra y compruebe su calidad.

Información en la misma obra laborable de 10 a 14 h. y de 16.30 a 20 hs. Excepto lunes y martes

CONJUNTO RESIDENCIAL DE TIANA

Con participación en Club Social. Piscina, tenis, squash, y zona ajardinada de recreo.

ALTING
Tel. 321 32 36

Vivir todo el año a 8 Km. de Barcelona.
4 dormitorios (1 suite) • cocina office • salón con chimenea • 3 baños • 1 aseo • 1 estudio • 1 solarium y terraza • garaje 3 coches.
Acabados de calidad. 225 m² + jardín individual.

1. ¿Hay algún apartamento que esté cerca de la ciudad de Barcelona? ¿Cuál? ¿Cuántos dormitorios tiene? ¿Tiene piscina? ¿Cuál es el número de teléfono?
2. ¿Hay algún apartamento que quede cerca de la playa? ¿Cuál es la dirección? ¿Los apartamentos son grandes o pequeños? ¿Se puede estacionar coches allí?
3. ¿Hay algún apartamento que quede cerca de un parque? ¿Qué parque? ¿A qué hora se puede ver? ¿Cuánto cuesta el más barato?
4. ¿Hay algún apartamento donde se pueda poner una lavadora *(washer)*? ¿Cuánto tiempo hay para pagarlo? ¿Se puede ver cualquier *(any)* día de la semana? ¿Cuánto cuesta?

UNA ACTIVIDAD ESPECIAL

Imagine that you and several classmates own a real estate agency. Prepare ads for the following types of houses.

1. A very expensive house in an elegant neighborhood
2. A small house in a student neighborhood
3. Two different types of apartments for rent

Put all the ads up on the bulletin board in the classroom.

De compras en uno de los grandes almacenes de ropa de Madrid, España.

OBJECTIVES

Structure   The past participle • The present perfect • The past perfect (pluperfect) • The familiar commands (**tú** and **vosotros**)

Communication   You will learn vocabulary related to clothing and shopping.

De compras en El Corte Inglés

Anita y su esposo Hugo han abierto el armario y han dicho, casi al mismo tiempo, «¡No tengo nada que ponerme!» Han decidido, pues, ir de compras a El Corte Inglés.

Cuando llegan, la tienda no está abierta todavía, pero ya hay mucha gente porque hoy hay una gran rebaja. A las nueve entran en la tienda con muchas otras personas. Anita sube por la escalera mecánica hasta el segundo piso, donde está el departamento de ropa para señoras. Hugo se queda en el departamento de ropa para caballeros, que está en la planta baja.

En el departamento de ropa para señoras, Anita se encuentra con su amiga Tere.[1]

ANITA —Dime, Tere, ¿cuánto cuesta esa blusa anaranjada?

TERE —Mil ochocientas pesetas. ¿Qué talla usas?

ANITA —Uso talla treinta y ocho.[2] Voy a probármela.

TERE —Pruébate también esta falda. El probador está a la izquierda.

ANITA —Oye, hazme un favor. Tráeme una blusa talla treinta y seis.

TERE —Espera... Lo siento, no hay tallas más pequeñas.

Anita compró la blusa, pero no compró la falda porque le quedaba grande y era demasiado cara. Fue a la zapatería para comprar un par de zapatos rojos, porque Hugo le había regalado una bolsa roja.

ANITA —¿Tiene zapatos rojos?

DEPENDIENTE —Lo siento, señora, pero en rojo solamente tengo estas sandalias.

ANITA —Yo calzo el treinta y seis.[3] *(A Tere)* Hacen juego con mi bolsa.

El dependiente le prueba las sandalias.

ANITA —Me aprietan un poco, pero me las llevo.

DEPENDIENTE —¿Se las envuelvo o quiere llevárselas puestas?

ANITA —Envuélvamelas, por favor.

En el departamento de ropa para caballeros, Hugo ha comprado un traje, dos pantalones, tres camisas y una chaqueta. También ha cambiado un par de

---

[1] Nickname for Teresa. [2] Equivalent to an American size 10. [3] Equivalent to an American size 6.

SHOPPING AT EL
CORTE INGLÉS

*Anita and her husband Hugo
have opened the closet and
have said, almost at the same
time, "I have nothing to
wear!" They have decided,
therefore, to go shopping at
El Corte Inglés.*

*When they arrive, the
store is not yet open, but
there are already many people (there) because there is a
big sale today. At nine they
enter the store with many
other people. Anita takes the
escalator to the second floor,
where the women's depart-
ment is located. Hugo stays
in the men's department,
which is on the ground floor.*

*In the women's depart-
ment, Anita meets her friend
Tere.*

A. Tell me, Tere, how much
does that orange blouse
cost?

T. One thousand eight
hundred pesetas. What
size do you wear?

A. I wear size thirty-eight.
I'm going to try it on.

T. Also try on this skirt.
The fitting room is to
your left.

A. Listen, do me a favor.
Bring me a size thirty-six
blouse.

T. Wait . . . I'm sorry, there
are no smaller sizes.

*Anita bought the blouse, but
did not buy the skirt because
it was too big on her and was
too expensive. She went to
the shoe department to buy
a pair of red shoes, because
Hugo had given her a red
purse.*

A. Do you have any red
shoes?

C. I am sorry, Miss, but in
red I only have these
sandals.

botas que había comprado, porque le quedaban chicas. Hugo, Anita y Tere se
encuentran a la salida.

ANITA   —Hugo, llévanos a comer algo. ¡Estamos muertas de hambre!
HUGO   —¡Yo también! Esperadme aquí. Yo voy por el coche.

Vocabulario

COGNADOS

la **blusa**   blouse
el **par**   pair

las **sandalias**   sandals

NOMBRES

el **armario,** el **ropero**   closet
la **bolsa,** la **cartera**   handbag,
   purse
la **bota**   boot
la **camisa**   shirt
la **chaqueta**   jacket
el **departmento de (ropa para) caballeros**   men's department
el **departamento de (ropa para)
   señoras (damas)**   women's
   department
el (la) **dependiente(-a)**   store clerk
la **escalera mecánica**   escalator
la **falda**   skirt
la **planta baja**   ground floor
el **probador**   fitting room
la **rebaja,** la **liquidación**   sale
la **ropa**   clothes
la **talla,** la **medida**   size
el **traje**   suit
la **zapatería**   shoe department,
   shoe store
el **zapato**   shoe

VERBOS

calzar   to take (a certain size in
   shoes)
cambiar   to exchange, change
encontrarse (o:ue) (con)   to meet
envolver (o:ue)   to wrap
llevarse   to take (buy)
quedarse   to stay, remain
usar   to wear, use

ADJETIVOS

abierto(-a)   open

OTRAS PALABRAS Y
EXPRESIONES

casi   almost
comer algo[1]   to have something
   to eat
hacer juego   to match
ir de compras   to go shopping
llevar puesto(-a)   to wear, have on
me aprietan   they feel tight
muerto(-a) de hambre   starving
no tener nada que ponerse   not to
   have anything to wear
pues   therefore, for, then
quedarle grande (chico) a uno   to
   be too big (small) on someone
todavía   yet

---

[1] **tomar algo** = *to have something to drink.*

A. I wear a thirty-six. *(To Tere)* They match my purse.

The clerk tries the sandals on her.

A. They're a little tight on me, but I'll take them.

C. Shall I wrap them up, or do you want to wear them?

A. Wrap them up for me, please.

In the men's department, Hugo has bought a suit, two (pairs of) pants, three shirts, and a jacket. He has also exchanged a pair of boots he had bought, because they were too small for him. Hugo, Anita, and Tere meet at the exit.

A. Hugo, take us out to eat something. We're starving!

H. Me too! Wait for me here. I'm going to get the car.

Vocabulario adicional

la **billetera**, la **cartera**   wallet
Puse la **billetera** en la bolsa.

los **calcetines**   socks
Necesito un par de **calcetines**.

el **camisón**   nightgown
El **camisón** está en la cama.

la **corbata**   tie
Aníbal lleva puesta una **corbata** roja.

la **escalera**   stairs
Subió por la **escalera**.

el **guante**   glove
Tengo las manos frías. ¿Dónde están mis **guantes?**

las **pantimedias**   panty hose
Estas **pantimedias** son muy grandes.

el **pañuelo**   handkerchief, scarf
Compré un **pañuelo** blanco.

la **ropa interior**   underwear
¿Pusiste la **ropa interior** en la maleta?

la **talla mediana**   medium size
¿Usas **talla** grande, pequeña o **mediana?**

el **vestido de noche**   evening gown
Se puso el **vestido de noche** rojo para ir a la fiesta.

El Corte Inglés

Gran Vía, 25
Teléfono: **415111 - 416111**

¿Lo sabía Ud.... ?

- Lo que *(What)* en los Estados Unidos es el primer piso es la planta baja en los países hispanos. Entonces el primer piso en España, por ejemplo, corresponde al segundo piso en los Estados Unidos.
- En las ciudades hispanas hay excelentes tiendas donde se puede comprar ropa hecha *(ready-to-wear)*, pero hay personas que prefieren utilizar los servicios de un sastre *(tailor)* o de una modista *(dressmaker)*.
- Aunque ahora hay muchas tiendas por departamento, todavía existen en los países hispanos muchas tiendas pequeñas especializadas en un producto. Por ejemplo, se vende **perfume** en la **perfumería, joyas** *(jewelry)* en la **joyería** y **relojes** en la **relojería.**
- Actualmente *(Nowadays)* en España, los dependientes de las tiendas a menudo tutean *(use the **tú** form of address)* a los clientes.

Una elegante joyería en la Ciudad de México.

Estructuras gramaticales

▶ *1.* The past participle   *(El participio pasado)*

A. Forms of the past participle

PAST PARTICIPLE ENDINGS		
-ar verbs	**-er** verbs	**-ir** verbs
habl-**ado** *(spoken)*	com-**ido** *(eaten)*	decid-**ido** *(decided)*

♦ The following verbs have irregular past participles.

abrir	**abierto**	*opened*
cubrir	**cubierto**	*covered*
decir	**dicho**	*said*
hacer	**hecho**	*done*

escribir	**escrito**	*written*
morir	**muerto**	*died*
poner	**puesto**	*put*
ver	**visto**	*seen*
volver	**vuelto**	*returned* (somewhere)
romper	**roto**	*broken*
devolver	**devuelto**	*returned* (something)
envolver	**envuelto**	*wrapped*

*The past participle of the verb **ir** is **ido**.

PRÁCTICA

Supply the past participle of each of the following verbs.

1. tener	9. romper	17. abrir
2. traer	10. cubrir	18. escribir
3. cerrar	11. vendar	19. ver
4. decir	12. sentir	20. aceptar
5. quebrar	13. entrar	21. devolver
6. apretar	14. salir	22. leer
7. cortar	15. hacer	23. operar
8. volver	16. poner	24. recetar

B. Past participles used as adjectives

♦ In Spanish, most past participles may be used as adjectives. As such, they agree in number and gender with the nouns they modify.

La peluquería está **abierta** hoy.	*The beauty parlor is open today.*
El restaurante está **abierto** hoy.	*The restaurant is open today.*
Las peluquerías están **abiertas** hoy.	*The beauty parlors are open today.*
Le mandé dos cartas **escritas** en inglés.	*I sent him two letters written in English.*
No dejen los libros **abiertos**.	*Don't leave the books open.*

ATENCIÓN

Verbs ending in **-er** and **-ir** whose stem ends in a vowel require an accent mark on the **i** of the **-ido** ending.

leer	**leído**	*read*
oír	**oído**	*heard*
traer	**traído**	*brought*

PRÁCTICA

You are very efficient. When a friend asks whether you did something, you say it is already done.

> MODELO: ¿Ya pusiste la mesa?
> *Sí, ya está puesta.*

1. ¿Ya cerraste la puerta?
2. ¿Ya abriste las ventanas?
3. ¿Ya hiciste la gelatina?
4. ¿Ya envolviste el regalo?
5. ¿Ya escribiste las cartas?
6. ¿Ya pagaste la cuenta?
7. ¿Ya cubriste los muebles?
8. ¿Ya lavaste la blusa?

▶ 2. The present perfect *(El pretérito perfecto)*

- The present perfect tense is formed by using the present tense of the auxiliary verb **haber** with the past participle of the verb that expresses the action or state.

- This tense is equivalent to the use in English of the auxiliary verb *have + past participle*, as in *I have spoken*.

present of **haber**

he	hemos
has	habéis
ha	han

FORMATION OF THE PRESENT PERFECT TENSE

	hablar	**tener**	**venir**
yo	**he** hablado	**he** tenido	**he** venido
tú	**has** hablado	**has** tenido	**has** venido
Ud. ⎫ él ⎬ ella ⎭	**ha** hablado	**ha** tenido	**ha** venido
nosotros(-as)	**hemos** hablado	**hemos** tenido	**hemos** venido
vosotros(-as)	**habéis** hablado	**habéis** tenido	**habéis** venido
Uds. ⎫ ellos ⎬ ellas ⎭	**han** hablado	**han** tenido	**han** venido

present perfect

—¿Cuánto te **ha costado** esa blusa?

How much has that blouse cost you?

—Me **ha costado** dos mil pesetas.

It has cost me two thousand pesetas.

—¿**Has visto** a Teresa?

Have you seen Teresa?

—No, no la **he visto**.

No, I haven't seen her.

♦ Note that when the past participle is part of a perfect tense, it is invariable. The past participle only changes in form when used as an adjective.

♦ In the Spanish present perfect tense the auxiliary verb **haber** can never be separated from the past participle as it can in English.

Yo nunca **he estado** en Lima.　　*I have never been in Lima.*

♦ Remember that when using reflexive or object pronouns with compound tenses, these are placed immediately before the auxiliary verb.

Le ha dado mucho dinero a su hijo.

He has given a lot of money to his son.

María y José **se** han ido.

María and José have left.

PRÁCTICA

Ricardo has broken his leg and cut his arm in an accident. Using the cues given, tell what everybody has done for him.

MODELO: Su hermana / llevarlo al hospital
　　　　Su hermana lo ha llevado al hospital.

1. El doctor / hacerle una radiografía
2. La enfermera / ponerle una inyección
3. El médico / vendarle la herida
4. Elsa y Rosa / limpiar el apartamento
5. Nosotros / escribirles a sus padres
6. Yo / hacer la comida
7. Tú / hablar con el médico
8. Sus padres / mandarle una tarjeta

Una celebración que ha hecho historia

▶ 3. The past perfect (pluperfect) *(El pluscuamperfecto)*

♦ The past perfect tense is formed by using the imperfect tense of the auxiliary verb **haber** with the past participle of the verb that expresses the action or state.

♦ This tense is equivalent to the use in English of the auxiliary verb *had + past participle,* as in *I had spoken.* Generally, the past perfect tense expresses an action that has taken place before another action in the past.

imperfect of **haber**

había	habíamos
habías	habíais
había	habían

FORMATION OF THE PAST PERFECT TENSE

	estudiar	beber	ir
yo	**había** estudiado	**había** bebido	**había** ido
tú	**habías** estudiado	**habías** bebido	**habías** ido
Ud. él ella	**había** estudiado	**había** bebido	**había** ido
nosotros(-as)	**habíamos** estudiado	**habíamos** bebido	**habíamos** ido
vosotros(-as)	**habíais** estudiado	**habíais** bebido	**habíais** ido
Uds. ellos ellas	**habían** estudiado	**habían** bebido	**habían** ido

—¿No hablaste con Teresa?   *Didn't you speak with Teresa?*
—No, cuando yo llegué, ella   *No, when I arrived, she had*
ya **se había ido.**   *already left.*

PRÁCTICA

When Olga came back from her vacation she thought she had a lot to do, but her friends had already done everything. Express this, using the cues provided.

MODELO: Nosotros / lavar los platos
          Cuando Olga llegó nosotros ya habíamos lavado los platos.

1. Yo / barrer la cocina
2. Los chicos / pasarle la aspiradora a la alfombra
3. Roberto / hacer la comida

4. Elsa y yo / planchar la ropa
5. Tú / limpiar el refrigerador
6. Carmen y Elena / bañar al perro
7. Anita / poner la mesa
8. Raúl y Carlos / comprar la comida

▶ *4.* The familiar commands (**tú** and **vosotros**) *(Las formas imperativas de **tú** y de **vosotros**)*

In Spanish, the familiar affirmative commands (corresponding to the **tú** and **vosotros** forms) are the only commands that do not use the subjunctive.

A. *Tú* commands

◆ The affirmative command form for **tú** has exactly the same form as the third-person singular form of the present indicative.

Verb	*Present Indicative*	*Familiar Command* (tú)
hablar	él habla	**habla** (tú)
comer	él come	**come** (tú)
abrir	él abre	**abre** (tú)
cerrar	él cierra	**cierra** (tú)
volver	él vuelve	**vuelve** (tú)

¡Espera!	*Wait!*
Habla español.	*Speak Spanish.*
¡Come el biftec!	*Eat the steak!*
Abre el refrigerador.	*Open the refrigerator.*
Cierra la puerta.	*Close the door.*
Vuelve a la piscina.	*Go back to the swimming pool.*

◆ Spanish has eight irregular command forms of **tú**.

decir	**di**	*say, tell*	salir	**sal**	*go out*
hacer	**haz**	*do, make*	ser	**sé**	*be*
ir	**ve**	*go*	tener	**ten**	*have*
poner	**pon**	*put*	venir	**ven**	*come*

Di la verdad.	*Tell the truth.*
Haz tu trabajo.	*Do your work.*
Ve al sexto piso.	*Go to the sixth floor.*
Ponlo en la mesa.	*Put it on the table.*
¡Sal de mi dormitorio!	*Get out of my bedroom!*
Sé bueno.	*Be good.*
Ten paciencia.	*Have patience.*
Ven lo antes posible.	*Come as soon as possible.*

B. *Vosotros* commands

◆ The affirmative command form for **vosotros** is formed by changing the final **r** of the infinitive to **d.**

Infinitive	*Familiar Command* (vosotros)
hablar	hablad
comer	comed
escribir	escribid
ir	id
salir	salid

◆ When the affirmative command of **vosotros** is used with the reflexive pronoun **os,** the final **d** is dropped.

bañar	bañad	**bañaos**
poner	poned	**poneos**
vestir	vestid	**vestíos**[1]

Bañaos antes de cenar.	*Bathe before dinner.*
Poneos los zapatos.	*Put on your shoes.*
Vestíos aquí.	*Get dressed here.*

◆ Only one verb doesn't drop the final **d** when the pronoun **os** is added.

irse *(to go away)*   **¡Idos!** *(Go away!)*

C. Negative forms

◆ The negative commands of **tú** and **vosotros** use the corresponding forms of the present subjunctive.

hablar	no **hables** tú	no **habléis** vosotros
vender	no **vendas** tú	no **vendáis** vosotros
decir	no **digas** tú	no **digáis** vosotros
salir	no **salgas** tú	no **salgáis** vosotros

ATENCIÓN

The position of object and reflexive pronouns with familiar commands follows the same rules as those for the formal commands.

Pon**lo** aquí.	*Put it here.*
No **lo** pongas ahí.	*Don't put it there.*
Vénde**nosla.**	*Sell it to us.*
No nos **la** vendas.	*Don't sell it to us.*

---

[1]Note that -ir verbs take a written accent over the **i** when the reflexive pronoun **os** is added.

PRÁCTICA

A. Your younger brother or sister is staying by himself or herself. Tell him or her what to do and what not to do.

1. Levantarse temprano
2. Estudiar
3. Hacer la tarea
4. No hablar por teléfono con sus amigos
5. No dejar al perro adentro
6. Ir al mercado y comprar frutas
7. No salir a la calle después de volver del mercado
8. No abrirle la puerta a nadie
9. No olvidarse de cerrar las ventanas
10. Llamar por teléfono a Carlos y decirle que no venga hoy
11. Lavar el mantel y las servilletas
12. Tener la comida lista para las siete
13. Poner la mesa
14. No probarse la ropa de su mamá
15. No preocuparse si tú vienes tarde

B. Juana always has a hard time deciding what to do. Give her some suggestions, using the cues provided.

MODELO: No sé qué clase tomar. (francés)
Toma una clase de francés.

1. No sé adónde ir esta noche.   (cine)
2. No sé con quién salir.   (Mauricio)
3. No sé qué hacer mañana.   (ir de compras)
4. No sé qué comprar.   (un traje de baño)
5. No sé qué regalarle a papá.   (una camisa y una corbata)
6. No sé qué comprarle a mamá.   (una falda y unas pantimedias)
7. No sé qué hacer para comer.   (sopa y pollo)
8. No sé qué decirle a Jorge.   (que te lleve al baile)
9. No sé en qué banco poner mi dinero.   (en el Banco de Ponce)
10. No sé qué hacer con mi pelo.   (cortártelo)

C. Someone is telling your friends what to do and what not to do. You don't agree with him, so tell your friends just the opposite.

MODELO: No habléis español.
Hablad español.

1. Idos.
2. No vengáis mañana.
3. Haced algo.

4. No cerréis las ventanas.
5. No dejéis la puerta abierta.
6. Sentaos aquí.
7. No os lavéis la cabeza aquí.
8. No os pongáis la chaqueta.
9. Quitaos los zapatos.
10. Traed a los niños.

¡A ver cuánto aprendió!

A. ¡Conversemos!

Reread the dialogues in this lesson and be ready to discuss the following.

1. ¿Por qué han decidido ir de compras Anita y Hugo?
2. ¿Está cerrado El Corte Inglés cuando llegan Anita y Hugo?
3. ¿Cómo va Anita al segundo piso?
4. ¿Tiene Hugo que subir para ir al departamento de caballeros? ¿Por qué?
5. ¿Es Anita alta y muy gorda?
6. ¿Qué no compra Anita y por qué?
7. ¿Por qué quiere Anita comprar unos zapatos rojos?
8. ¿Tiene Anita los pies grandes?
9. ¿Le quedan bien las sandalias?
10. ¿Qué ha comprado Hugo? ¿Dónde?
11. ¿Por qué ha cambiado Hugo las botas que había comprado?
12. ¿Cómo van a casa Hugo y las chicas?

B. ¡Repase el vocabulario!

Choose the word or phrase that best completes each sentence, then read the sentences aloud.

1. Puede probarse (la lengua, la falda, el cuello) en el probador.
2. Mi bolsa (hace juego, está muerta de hambre, va de compras) con mis zapatos.
3. Yo calzo el número siete y estos zapatos son número diez. (Me aprietan mucho. Me quedan grandes. Me quedan bien.)
4. Necesito un par de (calcetines, mundos, otoños).
5. Pagué solamente treinta dólares por el vestido; hoy hubo una gran (alfombra, liquidación, sorpresa) en Sears.
6. Estos pantalones son muy caros, pero no los he devuelto todavía pues (me gustan mucho, no me gustan, no me quedan bien).
7. Hace frío. Póngase (la chaqueta, el camino, la cabeza).

8. ¿Quiere llevar las sandalias puestas o se las (desinfecto, envuelvo, peino)?
9. ¿Qué medida (vuela, usa, cruza)?
10. El traje tiene que hacer juego con (la corbata, la ropa interior, el camisón).
11. Voy a ponerle una inyección. Quítese los (calcetines, pantalones, rizos).
12. Puse el dinero en (la billetera, la máquina de afeitar, el secador).
13. No hay ropa en mi ropero. No tengo nada que (ponerme, bañarme, afeitarme).
14. ¿Usa Ud. talla grande, chica o (breve, lacia, mediana)?
15. Me sangra la nariz. ¿Tienes (pantimedias, un pañuelo, un vestido de noche)?
16. Pues yo me quedo en la (taza, trucha, planta baja).

C. Situaciones

What would you say in the following situations? What would the other person say?

1. You are shopping in a large department store. Tell the clerk you need a pair of gloves, a white shirt, and a blue tie. You also saw a brown suit in the window that you liked; ask the clerk how much it costs.
2. You are a clerk. Ask your customer if she wants the pink blouse. Ask her what size she wears, and tell her the fitting room is on the left.
3. A clerk at a shoe store wants to sell you a pair of boots. Tell him that they are too expensive and that they are too tight on you.
4. Tell your friend that you haven't eaten yet, that you are starving, and that you want to have something to eat.

Para escribir

Write a dialogue between yourself and a clerk at a department store. You should mention what size you wear, what colors you like, and whether or not something fits you; you should talk about different things you want to buy.

En la vida real

ENTREVISTA

Choose a partner, then interview each other using the **tú** form.

Pregúntele a su compañero(-a) de clase...

1. ...si va a ir de compras mañana.
2. ...qué talla de camisa (blusa) usa.
3. ...qué número calza.
4. ...si le aprietan los zapatos que lleva puestos.
5. ...si cuando compra un par de zapatos se los lleva puestos.
6. ...dónde ha comprado esa falda (chaqueta, camisa).
7. ...si su camisa (blusa) y sus pantalones siempre hacen juego.
8. ...cuál es la tienda que más le gusta.
9. ...si prefiere comprar cuando hay una liquidación y por qué.
10. ...si prefiere usar la escalera o la escalera mecánica.

VACACIONES

You and a classmate are going on vacation. You are going to Hawaii in August and she or he is going to Colorado in December. Help each other select the type of clothes you will need for the trip, according to the different activities you are planning.

Other words and phrases you may want to include are:

la **bufanda** *scarf*
el **abrigo** *coat*
de lana *made of wool*
de algodón *made of cotton*
el **suéter** *sweater*

¡DE COMPRAS!

Help a friend of yours who is shopping at El Corte Inglés in Madrid. Answer her questions, using the information provided in the ad.

1. ¿En qué mes son las rebajas?
2. Tengo una hija de nueve años. ¿Qué puedo comprarle?
3. Mi esposo necesita zapatos. ¿Qué tipo de zapatos venden y cuánto cuestan?
4. No tengo nada que ponerme. ¿Qué puedo comprar para mí?
5. Pensamos ir a la playa. ¿Qué puedo comprar para mí y para mis hijos?
6. Es el cumpleaños de mi padre. ¿Qué puedo regalarle? ¿Cuánto me va a costar?
7. ¿Para cuántas personas son los manteles?
8. ¿Cuánto cuesta el sillón?

UNA ACTIVIDAD ESPECIAL

A few students will play the role of live mannequins, and other students will describe the clothes and shoes the mannequins are wearing. The rest of the class will be customers and will ask the price and size of the clothes and shoes the mannequins are wearing.

Y ahora, *¡vamos a leer!*

La cinta de José Luis

A José Luis no le gusta escribir, y por eso todos los meses les manda a sus padres una cinta, contándoles cómo le va. Ésta es la que les mandó el mes pasado.

¡Hola! ¿Cómo están todos? Yo estoy bien, pero muy cansado porque Carlos y yo hemos estado trabajando mucho para limpiar y arreglar nuestro nuevo apartamento. Nos mudamos el sábado pasado y, como el apartamento sólo° estaba parcialmente amueblado, tuvimos que comprar una cómoda, un sofá y dos mesitas de noche. ¡Gracias por el cheque! En cuanto me gradúe° de la universidad y consiga un buen trabajo, les voy a devolver todo lo que les debo.° Bueno... ¡no creo que pueda devolvérselo todo!

only

I graduate
owe

Ayer fui de compras porque tenían una gran liquidación en mi tienda favorita. Ya compré casi todos los regalos de Navidad. A abuelo le compré unos pañuelos y a abuela un camisón. Para Anita compré una blusa rosada y para Jorge una corbata. No les digo lo que compré para ustedes porque quiero que sea una sorpresa.

Yo había pensado invitar a Carlos a pasar la Navidad con nosotros, pero ya lo invitaron unos tíos que viven en Rosario.[1]

still

¡Ah! Todavía° estoy buscando a alguien que me lleve en coche a Córdoba[1] en diciembre; si no encuentro a nadie, voy a tomar el tren.

Mamá, hazme un favor: dile a Silvia que me escriba o me llame por teléfono.

love

Bueno, denle cariños° a toda la familia. Los veo en diciembre. ¡Chau!

---

[1] Cities in Argentina.

¡A ver cuánto recuerda!

1. ¿Cuánto tiempo hace que José Luis y Carlos se mudaron al nuevo apartamento?
2. ¿Se mudaron durante un fin de semana?
3. ¿El apartamento tenía todos los muebles que los muchachos necesitaban? ¿Cómo lo sabe?
4. ¿José Luis ya terminó sus estudios en la universidad? ¿Cómo lo sabe?
5. ¿Por qué fue José Luis de compras a su tienda favorita?
6. ¿Los abuelos de José Luis viven todavía? ¿Cómo lo sabe?
7. ¿Quiénes cree Ud. que son Anita y Jorge?
8. ¿Carlos va a pasar la Navidad en Córdoba? ¿Por qué?
9. ¿Ya ha encontrado José Luis a alguien que lo lleve a Córdoba?
10. ¿Qué quiere José Luis que haga Silvia?

Argentina

PANORAMA HISPÁNICO 8

América del Sur (II)

Chile

Paraguay

Uruguay

■ En la región andina de Chile y Argentina se puede esquiar durante los meses de invierno (de junio a septiembre en el hemisferio sur). Los centros de esquí más famosos son Bariloche en Argentina y Portillo en Chile.

■ Buenos Aires, capital de Argentina, tiene una población de más de diez millones de habitantes y su área metropolitana es una de las más extensas del mundo. El sistema del metro, llamado «el subterráneo», es el más antiguo de Latinoamérica.

■ Uruguay es el país más pequeño de América del Sur. El 45% de la población del país está concentrado en Montevideo, la capital. Esta ciudad tiene muy cerca las famosas playas de Pocitos y Punta del Este.

■ La represa *(dam)* de Itaipú, entre el Brasil y Paraguay, es la represa hidroeléctrica más grande del mundo y fue construida por los gobiernos de Brasil y Paraguay.

■ Paraguay es conocido por sus joyas de oro y de plata, sus objetos de madera tallada *(carved)* y sus encajes *(laces)* de «ñandutí». Estos encajes están hechos a mano y para hacerlos se utilizan más de cien diseños diferentes.

◀ El centro de Santiago, capital de Chile, se distingue por el contraste de sus modernos rascacielos y sus construcciones coloniales. Entre estas últimas están la Casa Colorada, residencia del primer presidente de la República; el Palacio de la Moneda, palacio presidencial actual; y la catedral, construida en 1780. ¿Cómo se llama en español la residencia del presidente de los Estados Unidos?

▶ Entre los numerosos teatros que existen en Buenos Aires, el Teatro Colón es el más impresionante y el de mayor importancia artística. Fue en el Teatro Colón donde Arturo Toscanini dirigió por primera vez una orquesta. ¿En qué calle de Nueva York están los teatros más famosos?

▲ El gaucho argentino, inmortalizado en la literatura y en la música popular argentinas, es hoy día más una leyenda que un personaje real. Una de las costumbres de los gauchos que persiste es la del rodeo, como lo podemos apreciar en la foto. ¿En qué son similares los vaqueros norteamericanos y los gauchos argentinos?

▶ Vista del Obelisco y la Avenida Nueve de Julio, en Buenos Aires. La Avenida Nueve de Julio es considerada la más ancha del mundo y lleva este nombre para conmemorar la fecha de la independencia de Argentina. ¿Le gustaría a Ud. vivir en una gran ciudad como Buenos Aires?

► Vista panorámica del puerto de Asunción, la capital de Paraguay. En esta ciudad se mezclan armoniosamente la arquitectura colonial y la moderna. Aquí vemos la Plaza de los Héroes y, al fondo, el río Paraguay, que sirve como vía de comunicación con el Océano Atlántico. Nombre Ud. tres ciudades norteamericanas que también son puertos importantes.

◄ Vista de las cataratas de Iguazú, formadas por los ríos Iguazú y Paraná, entre los países de Argentina, Brasil y Paraguay. Se consideran las cataratas más anchas y caudalosas del mundo, y de ahí su nombre, que en el idioma guaraní significa «agua grande». ¿Son exclusivamente americanas las Cataratas del Niágara?

La argentina Gabriela Sabatini es hoy día una de las tenistas más famosas del mundo. A los quince años empezó a jugar como profesional, y a los dieciséis fue la jugadora más joven en clasificar para los semifinales de Wimbledon. En 1988, a los 17 años de edad, quedó clasificada como una de las cuatro mejores tenistas del mundo. ¿Cuál es su deporte favorito?

Viña del Mar es uno de los centros turísticos más populares de Suramérica y está situada al noreste de Valparaíso en Chile. En Viña del Mar encontramos numerosas playas, parques, hoteles y casinos. La ciudad es también un importante centro comercial e industrial. ¿Cómo sabemos al mirar esta foto que ésta es una playa muy popular?

Vista de una calle céntrica de Montevideo, la capital de Uruguay. Los habitantes de esta ciudad son, en su mayoría, de ascendencia europea y poseen uno de los más altos niveles de educación de Hispanoamérica. Montevideo es además un centro cultural de primer orden con numerosos museos, teatros, galerías y centros educativos. ¿De qué ascendencia es la mayoría de los habitantes de la ciudad donde Ud. vive?

En una gasolinera cerca de Cali, Colombia.

OBJECTIVES

Structure   The future • The future to express probability in the present • The conditional • The conditional to express probability in the past

Communication   You will learn vocabulary related to automobiles, including going to a service station and dealing with road emergencies.

Camino a San José

Gloria y Julio, una pareja de recién casados, están de vacaciones en Costa Rica.
Ahora están en la carretera, camino a San José.

GLORIA —Julio, ¡estás manejando muy rápido! La velocidad máxima
es de noventa kilómetros por hora. ¡Te van a poner una
multa!

JULIO —No te preocupes. ¿Dónde estaremos? ¿Tú tienes el mapa?

GLORIA —Está en el portaguantes, pero según ese letrero estamos a
cuarenta kilómetros de San José.

JULIO —¿Habrá una gasolinera cerca? El tanque está casi vacío.

GLORIA —Yo creo que tendrás que esperar hasta llegar a San José.
¡Ah, no! Allí hay una.

Julio para en la estación de servicio para comprar gasolina.

JULIO —(Al empleado) Llene el tanque, por favor. Además, ¿podría
revisar el aceite y ponerle agua al radiador?

EMPLEADO —Sí, señor.

JULIO —Ayer tuve un pinchazo y el mecánico me dijo que
necesitaba neumáticos nuevos...

EMPLEADO —Sí, yo los cambiaría... y también el acumulador.

GLORIA —¡Caramba! También te dijo que tendrías que arreglar los
frenos e instalar una bomba de agua nueva.

JULIO —Haremos todo eso en San José.

GLORIA —¿No dijiste que también cambiarías el filtro del aceite y que
comprarías limpiaparabrisas nuevos?

JULIO —Sí, pero ahora pienso que sería mejor comprar un coche
nuevo.

GLORIA —Ayer el motor estaba haciendo un ruido extraño. ¿Qué
sería?

JULIO —Sería el silenciador...

Cuando Julio trata de arrancar, el coche no funciona.

JULIO —¡Ay, no! Tendremos que llamar una grúa para remolcar el
coche hasta San José.

GLORIA —¿Cuánto costará un Chevrolet nuevo?

*Gloria and Julio, a couple of
newlyweds, are on vacation
in Costa Rica. Now they are
on the highway, on the way
to San Jose.*

G. Julio, you're driving very
fast! The speed limit is
ninety kilometers per
hour. They're going to
give you a ticket!

J. Don't worry. Where do
you suppose we are? Do
you have the map?

G. It's in the glove com-
partment, but according
to that sign we're forty
kilometers from San
Jose.

J. I wonder if there's a gas
station close by. The
tank is almost empty.

G. I think you'll have to
wait until we get to San
Jose. Oh, no! There's
one over there.

*Julio stops at the service sta-
tion to buy gasoline.*

J. *(To the attendant)* Fill
the tank, please. Also,
could you check the oil
and put water in the
radiator?

A. Yes, sir.

J. Yesterday I had a flat,
and the mechanic told
me that I needed new
tires . . .

A. Yes, I'd change them
. . . and also the battery.

G. Gee! He also said you'd
have to fix the brakes
and install a new water
pump.

J. We'll do all of that in
San Jose.

G. Didn't you also say that
you'd change the oil fil-
ter and buy new wind-
shield wipers?

J. Yes, but now I think it
would be better to buy a
new car.

Vocabulario

COGNADOS

el **filtro** filter
la **gasolina** gasoline
el **kilómetro** kilometer
el **mecánico** mechanic

el **motor** motor, engine
el **radiador** radiator
el **tanque** tank

NOMBRES

el **aceite** oil
el **acumulador**, la **batería**
   battery
el **agua** *(f.)*[1] water
la **bomba de agua** water pump
la **carretera** highway
el **freno** brake
la **gasolinera**, la **estación de
   servicio** service station
la **grúa** tow truck
el **letrero** sign
el **limpiaparabrisas** windshield
   wiper
el **neumático**, la **llanta**, la **goma**
   tire
la **pareja** couple
el **portaguantes**, la **guantera**
   glove compartment
los **recién casados** newlyweds
el **ruido** noise
el **silenciador** muffler
la **velocidad** speed

VERBOS

arrancar to start (a car)
arreglar to fix
funcionar to work, function
instalar to install
parar to stop
preocuparse to worry
remolcar to tow
revisar, chequear to check
tratar (de) to try

ADJETIVOS

extraño(-a) strange, funny
vacío(-a) empty

OTRAS PALABRAS Y
EXPRESIONES

camino a... on the way to . . .
poner (dar) una multa to give a
   ticket (fine)
rápido fast
tener un pinchazo to have a flat
velocidad máxima speed limit

Vocabulario adicional

el **carburador** carburetor
El mecánico revisó el **carburador.**

la **chapa** license plate
La **chapa** de mi coche es 24808.

descompuesto(-a) out of order
No pude usar el coche porque
   estaba **descompuesto.**

---

[1] The definite article **el** or the indefinite article **un** is used instead of **la** or **una** with feminine singular
nouns beginning with *stressed* **a** or **ha.**

G. Yesterday the motor was making a strange noise. What do you suppose it was?

J. It was probably the muffler . . .

When Julio tries to start (it), the car doesn't work.

J. Oh, no! We'll have to call a tow truck to tow the car to San Jose.

G. I wonder how much a new Chevrolet costs . . .

la **licencia** (el **carnet**) **de conducir** driver's license
Él me pidió la **licencia de conducir.**

lleno(-a) full
El tanque está **lleno.**

el **maletero,** la **cajuela** *(Mex.)* trunk
¿Pusiste **las maletas** en el maletero?

la **milla** mile
Hay 300 **millas** de aquí a Lima.

sucio(-a) dirty
Tu coche está muy **sucio.**

el **taller** repair shop
¿Hay un **taller** cerca de aquí?

¿Lo sabía Ud.... ?

■ En las grandes ciudades como Madrid, Caracas, la Ciudad de México y Buenos Aires, hay muchísimos automóviles y autobuses, lo cual *(which)* está causando graves problemas de contaminación del aire *(smog)*. Sin embargo, en muchas zonas rurales de los países hispanos, particularmente en Hispanoamérica, hay muy pocos automóviles, ya que no hay carreteras, o las que existen están en muy malas condiciones.

■ En la mayoría de los países hispanos, los automóviles y la gasolina son excesivamente caros. Por esta razón es muy popular la motocicleta, especialmente entre la gente joven.

■ En los países hispanos, se usa el sistema métrico decimal. Un kilómetro equivale a 0,6 millas; un galón equivale a 3,8 litros.

La Calle Mayor de Madrid, donde se ve un anuncio de la Feria del Libro, que se celebra todos los años.

Estructuras gramaticales

▶ *1.* The future   *(El futuro)*

♦ Most Spanish verbs are regular in the future. The infinitive serves as the stem of almost all Spanish verbs. The endings are the same for all three conjugations.

THE FUTURE TENSE

Infinitive		*Stems*	*Endings*	
trabajar	yo	trabajar-	é	trabajaré
aprender	tú	aprender-	ás	aprenderás
escribir	Ud.	escribir-	á	escribirá
hablar	él	hablar-	á	hablará
decidir	ella	decidir-	á	decidirá
dar	nosotros(-as)	dar-	emos	daremos
ir	vosotros(-as)	ir-	éis	iréis
caminar	Uds.	caminar-	án	caminarán
perder	ellos	perder-	án	perderán
recibir	ellas	recibir-	án	recibirán

ATENCIÓN

Note that all the endings, except the one for the **nosotros** form, have written accents.

—¿**Venderán** Uds. la compañía?	*Will you sell the company?*
—No sé; lo **decidiremos** mañana.	*I don't know; we will decide tomorrow.*

♦ The English equivalent of the Spanish future is *will* or *shall* + *a verb*. As you have already learned, Spanish also uses the construction **ir a** + *infinitive* or *the present tense with a time expression* to express future action, very much like the English present tense or the expression *going to*.

Vamos a ir al cine esta noche. *or:* **Iremos** al cine esta noche.	} *We're going (We'll go) to the movies tonight.*
Anita **toma** el examen mañana. *or:* Anita **tomará** el examen mañana.	} *Anita is taking (will take) the exam tomorrow.*

ATENCIÓN

The Spanish future is *not* used to express willingness, as is the English future. In Spanish this is expressed with the verb **querer.**

¿Quieres llamar a Tomás?   *Will you call Tomás?*

♦ A small number of verbs are irregular in the future. These verbs use a modified form of the infinitive as a stem but the endings are the same as the ones for regular verbs.

IRREGULAR FUTURE STEMS

Infinitive	Modified Form (Stem)	First-Person Singular
decir	dir-	**diré**
hacer	har-	**haré**
querer	querr-	**querré**
saber	sabr-	**sabré**
poder	podr-	**podré**
caber	cabr-	**cabré**
poner	pondr-	**pondré**
venir	vendr-	**vendré**
tener	tendr-	**tendré**
salir	saldr-	**saldré**
valer[1]	valdr-	**valdré**

—¿Qué les **dirás** a tus padres?   *What will you tell your parents?*

—Les **diré** que no **podremos** venir en enero y que **vendremos** en febrero.   *I will tell them that we won't be able to come in January and that we will come in February.*

ATENCIÓN

The future of **hay** is **habrá.**

¿Habrá una reunión?   *Will there be a party?*

---

[1] *To be worth.*

PRÁCTICA

A. After classes are over, these people will do many different things. Using the future tense and the words and expressions given, say what they will do.

1. Jorge / ir de vacaciones / México
2. Marta y yo / salir para Colombia / julio
3. Mis padres / venir / a visitarme / agosto
4. Ana / tener que / trabajar / verano
5. Yo / tomar / una clase / francés
6. Uds. / poner / alfombra nueva / casa
7. Tú / viajar / por Latinoamérica
8. Ud. / pasar / dos semanas / Sevilla

B. You will be traveling to Spain next year with two friends. Answer these questions about your trip.

1. ¿Adónde irán?
2. ¿Cuándo saldrán de viaje?
3. ¿Viajarán en barco o en avión?
4. ¿Cuánto tiempo estarán viajando?
5. ¿Podrán visitar muchas ciudades?
6. ¿Qué lugares visitarán?
7. ¿Les enviarán tarjetas postales a sus amigos?
8. ¿Cuánto dinero necesitarán para el viaje?
9. ¿Se lo pedirán a sus padres?
10. ¿Cuándo volverán?

C. You and your parents are traveling across the country by car. Say what everybody will do, according to the circumstances.

Antes del viaje:

1. El radiador no tiene agua. ¿Qué hará su padre?
2. Los frenos no están funcionando muy bien. ¿Qué hará Ud.?
3. El tanque del coche está casi vacío. ¿Qué hará su mamá?
4. El coche está muy sucio. ¿Qué harán Uds.?
5. Hace cinco meses que Uds. no cambian el aceite. ¿Qué harán sus padres?

Durante el viaje:

1. Uds. no saben cómo llegar a algún lugar. ¿Qué hará su mamá?
2. Ud. está manejando demasiado rápido. ¿Qué hará el policía?
3. Tienen un pinchazo. ¿Qué hará su papá?
4. El coche no arranca. ¿Qué harán Uds.?
5. El coche está descompuesto y el mecánico dice que nadie puede arreglarlo. ¿Qué harán sus padres?

▶ *2.* The future to express probability in the present
(*El futuro para expresar probabilidad en el presente*)

♦ The future is also used to indicate a conjecture or statement of probability concerning an action in the present. English uses expressions such as *I wonder, probably, can it be that, it must be,* and *do you suppose* where Spanish uses the future tense.

—No tengo reloj. ¿Qué hora **será**?	*I don't have a watch. I wonder what time it is.*
—No sé. **Serán** las tres...	*I don't know. It must be three o'clock.*
—Dónde **estará** Eva?	*Where do you suppose Eva is?*
—No sé... **Estará** en la universidad.	*I don't know . . . I suppose she's at the university.*

♦ **Deber** + *infinitive* is also used to express either obligation or probability.

Debe ser porque el silenciador no funciona bien.

Será porque el silenciador no funciona bien.

} *It must be because the muffler doesn't work well.*

PRÁCTICA

A. You and a classmate are at Mario's party and are wondering about many things. Take turns asking these questions and trying to guess what the answer may be. Use the future of probability.

1. Oye, ¿tú sabes lo que está celebrando Mario?
2. ¿Quién es la chica que está hablando con él?
3. Es muy joven... ¿Cuántos años crees que tiene?
4. ¿Qué está haciendo la mamá de Mario en la cocina?
5. Estela no está aquí todavía. ¿A qué hora va a venir?
6. Oye, esta carne está muy sabrosa. ¿Tú sabes qué es?
7. Mario me dijo que íbamos a bailar. ¿Cuándo empieza el baile?
8. Mario no tiene discos... ¿Quién los va a traer?
9. Mario no toma bebidas alcohólicas. ¿Qué crees que va a servir para tomar?
10. No tengo mi reloj. ¿Qué hora es?

B. Be an interpreter. What are these people saying? Use the future of probability.

1. How much do you suppose that car is worth?
   It must be worth twenty thousand dollars.
2. What do you suppose the speed limit is?
   It must be eighty kilometers an hour.
3. The car is making a strange noise. What do you suppose it is?
   The muffler must be broken.
4. Do you think we can park here?
   No! They're going to give us a ticket.
5. Where do you think the maps are?
   They must be in the trunk or in the glove compartment.

▶ *3.* The conditional *(El condicional)*

♦ The conditional tense in Spanish is equivalent to the conditional in English, expressed by *should* or *would* + *a verb*.[1] Like the future tense, the conditional uses the infinitive as the stem and has only one set of endings for all three conjugations.

THE CONDITIONAL TENSE

Infinitive		*Stem*	*Endings*	
trabajar	yo	trabajar-	ía	trabajaría
aprender	tú	aprender-	ías	aprenderías
escribir	Ud.	escribir-	ía	escribiría
ir	él	ir-	ía	iría
ser	ella	ser-	ía	sería
dar	nosotros(-as)	dar-	íamos	daríamos
hablar	vosotros(-as)	hablar-	íais	hablaríais
servir	Uds.	servir-	ían	servirían
estar	ellos	estar-	ían	estarían
preferir	ellas	preferir-	ían	preferirían

♦ All of the conditional endings have written accents.

| —Él dijo que **cambiaría** el filtro. | *He said that he would change the filter.* |
| —Sí, y también dijo que **revisaría** los frenos. | *Yes, and he also said that he would check the brakes.* |

---

[1] The conditional is never used in Spanish as an equivalent of *used to*.
Cuando era pequeño siempre **iba** a la playa. *When I was little I would always go to the beach.*

♦ The conditional is also used as the future of a past action. The future states what *will* happen; the conditional states what *would* happen.

Future	**Conditional**
(states what *will* happen)	(states what *would* happen)
Él **dice** que **estará** aquí mañana.	Él **dijo** que **estaría** aquí mañana.
He says that he will be here tomorrow.	*He said that he would be here tomorrow.*

♦ The same verbs that have irregular stems in the future tense are also irregular in the conditional. The endings are the same as those for regular verbs.

IRREGULAR CONDITIONAL STEMS[1]

Infinitive	*Modified Form (Stem)*	*First-Person Singular*
decir	dir–	**diría**
hacer	har–	**haría**
querer	querr–	**querría**
saber	sabr–	**sabría**
poder	podr–	**podría**
caber	cabr–	**cabría**
poner	pondr–	**pondría**
venir	vendr–	**vendría**
tener	tendr–	**tendría**
salir	saldr–	**saldría**
valer	valdr–	**valdría**

| —¿A qué hora te dijo que **vendría?** | *What time did he tell you he would come?* |
| —Dijo que **saldría** de casa a las dos. | *He said he would leave home at two.* |

El mejor regalo que usted les podría dar a sus hijos

Una tarjeta de biblioteca*

---

[1] The conditional of **hay** is **habría** (*there would be*).

PRÁCTICA

A. Nobody would do the things that Carlos does. Express this by telling us what you and these other people would do. Use the conditional tense.

MODELO: Carlos come en la cafetería. (yo)
          Yo no comería en la cafetería; comería en mi casa.

1. Carlos se levanta a las cinco.   (Uds.)
2. Carlos estudia por la mañana.   (Ana y Luis)
3. Carlos viene a la universidad en ómnibus.   (nosotros)
4. Carlos toma clases de alemán.   (yo)
5. Carlos se baña por la noche.   (Elsa)
6. Carlos se acuesta a las nueve de la noche.   (Ud.)
7. Carlos va a la montaña los fines de semana.   (ellos)
8. Carlos sale con Margarita.   (tú)

B. Choose a partner, and ask each other the following questions.

1. ¿Qué harías con mil dólares?
2. ¿Adónde irías de vacaciones?
3. ¿Preferirías un asiento de ventanilla o un asiento de pasillo?
4. ¿Preferirías un cuarto en la planta baja o en el séptimo piso?
5. ¿Manejarías sin tu licencia para conducir?
6. Vamos a tener una fiesta. ¿Qué podrías traer?
7. ¿Te gustaría tener la oportunidad de practicar el español todos los días?
8. ¿Dijiste que vendrías a la universidad el domingo?

C. Using the conditional, say what you would do in the following situations.

1. Su coche no arranca.
2. El tanque de su coche está vacío.
3. Ud. tuvo un pinchazo en la carretera.
4. Le duele la cabeza.
5. Ud. tiene el pelo largo y ahora está de moda el pelo corto.
6. Un amigo le pide diez dólares.
7. Ud. tiene un examen muy difícil mañana.
8. Está lloviendo a cántaros.
9. Ud. quiere ir a la playa y no tiene traje de baño.
10. Su amigo(-a) se ha roto un brazo.

► *4.* The conditional to express probability in the past
  (*El condicional para expresar probabilidad en el pasado*)

♦ The conditional tense is also used to express probability or conjecture in the past.

—¿Por qué no **vendría** Eva
   ayer?   *Why do you suppose Eva*
                                            didn't come yesterday?
—No sé... ; **estaría** enferma.   *I don't know . . . ; I suppose*
                                            she was sick.

PRÁCTICA

A. Andrés and Sergio came home very late last night. With a classmate, use your imagination to try to guess the answer to each of the following questions. Use the conditional to express probability in the past.

1. ¿Qué hora sería cuando llegaron?
2. ¿Dónde estarían?
3. ¿Quién sería el muchacho que vino con ellos?
4. ¿Dónde cenarían?
5. ¿Qué comerían?
6. No vinieron en el coche. ¿Dónde lo dejarían?
7. No me trajeron el disco que les pedí. ¿Por qué no lo comprarían?
8. Un policía llamó a Sergio esta mañana. ¿Qué le diría?

B. Be an interpreter. What are these people saying? Use the conditional to express probability in the past.

1. Why do you think the policeman gave him a ticket?
   He was probably driving too fast.
2. Why do you think they took him to the hospital?
   He probably had an accident.
3. Who do you suppose gave Paco the money to buy the water pump?
   I guess his father gave it to him.
4. What time do you think Carlos went to bed last night?
   I suppose he went to bed around twelve o'clock.

¡A ver cuánto aprendió!

A. ¡Conversemos!

Reread the dialogue in this lesson and be ready to discuss the following.

1. ¿Quiénes están en la carretera, camino a San José?
2. ¿Hace mucho tiempo que ellos están casados?
3. ¿Por qué dice Gloria que le van a poner una multa a Julio?
4. Según el letrero, ¿a cuántos kilómetros de San José están Gloria y Julio?
5. ¿Por qué necesitan ir a una gasolinera?
6. ¿Qué tiene que hacer el empleado de la gasolinera?
7. ¿Qué dijo el mecánico que necesitaban arreglar?
8. ¿Dónde arreglarán el coche?
9. Según Julio, ¿qué sería mejor?
10. ¿Por qué tendrán que llamar una grúa?

B. ¡Repase el vocabulario!

Circle the word or phrase that best completes each sentence, then read the sentences aloud.

1. Tuve un pinchazo. Tendré que cambiar el (platillo, neumático, helado).
2. Voy a llevar el coche al taller porque está (sabroso, sentado, descompuesto).
3. Tendré que lavar el coche porque está muy (preocupado, sucio, vacío).
4. Te van a poner una multa porque estás (manejando, declarando, pescando) muy rápido.
5. No pude parar porque los (frenos, pedidos, lavaplatos) no funcionaban.
6. Íbamos (autopista, carretera, camino) a Quito cuando tuvimos un accidente.
7. Vino (un edificio, una ambulancia, una grúa) para remolcar el coche.
8. Le puse (pimienta, agua, sal) al radiador.
9. Según (ese letrero, esa valija, esa lluvia), estamos a 100 kilómetros de la capital.
10. Pondré los mapas en el (diente, peine, portaguantes).

C. Situaciones

What would you say in the following situations? What would the other person say?

1. Ask your mechanic if he or she can check your car. Tell him or her you think the brakes are out of order.
2. Tell a tourist that he or she can buy gasoline at the service station located at the next corner, and that he or she has a flat tire.
3. You are a police officer, and you have stopped a motorist. Tell the motorist that his or her car doesn't have a license plate and that the lights aren't working. Ask to see his or her driver's license.
4. Tell someone to call a tow truck because your car won't start.

Para escribir

What if **Romeo** and **Julieta** were living now? Write an account of what their circumstances would be and what they would be doing. In our story, of course, they *don't* die! Start out with: **Romeo y Julieta vivirían en...**

En la vida real

ENTREVISTA

Choose a partner, then interview each other using the **tú** form.

Pregúntele a su compañero(-a) de clase...

1. ...si tendrá que ir a la gasolinera mañana.
2. ...si está lleno o vacío el tanque de su coche.
3. ...si tiene que ponerle agua al radiador de su coche.
4. ...cuándo piensa comprar neumáticos para su coche.
5. ...si le gustaría manejar un Mercedes Benz.
6. ...si tiene que cambiar el filtro de aceite de su coche.
7. ...cuál es la velocidad máxima en la autopista.
8. ...a qué velocidad maneja generalmente en la autopista.
9. ...cuál es el número de la chapa de su coche.
10. ...cuántas millas hay de su casa a la universidad.

PLANES DE VIAJE

You and a classmate are planning to drive to Mexico. Working together, make a list of everything you need to do before you leave. Make sure you include things you need to do to get the car ready and to prepare yourselves.

COMPRANDO COCHE

What questions would you ask before buying a car? Carefully read the following brochure and provide questions that would cover these topics:

- la condición del coche (dos preguntas)
- la garantía
- las reparaciones (dos preguntas)
- la inspección del estado
- el precio de reventa (resale)

Cuando vaya a comprar un automóvil, ¡pregunte!

Ciertas preguntas le ahorrarán dinero.
Determine primero qué automóvil necesita y cuánto dinero puede invertir.
Consulte por lo menos con tres comerciantes de automóviles antes de decidir a cuál le comprará.

Pregunte a cada comerciante:
— ¿Qué garantía tiene el automóvil?
— Si el automóvil se descompone, ¿quién va a componerlo?
— ¿El automóvil será aprobado en la inspección del Estado?
— ¿Qué precio de reventa tendrá el automóvil cuando Ud. quiera venderlo?
— ¿Está el automóvil en perfectas condiciones?
— ¿Le dejarán probar el automóvil antes de entregárselo?
— Si el automóvil necesita ser reparado, ¿quién pagará la reparación?
    Recuerde hacer estas preguntas y ahorrará mucho dinero.
    Asegúrese de que el vendedor no lo engañe. Muchos vendedores tratarán de engañarlo para hacer la venta.

¡PREGUNTE EL PRECIO!
Hágale saber al vendedor que Ud. ya conoce los precios de otros competidores.
    Recuerde que los vendedores a veces pueden cambiar el precio. No cierre el trato si el precio que le ofrecen no le parece correcto o justo.

RECUERDE, ES SU DINERO.

Take this test. When you finish, check your answers in the answer key provided for this section in Appendix E. Then use a red pen to correct any mistakes you may have made. Ready?

LECCIÓN 13

A. The subjunctive to express indefiniteness and nonexistence

Give the Spanish equivalent of the following sentences.

1. Is there anybody here who can speak Spanish?
2. We have a house that has five bedrooms.
3. I don't know anybody who is from Spain.
4. Do you want a house that has a swimming pool?
5. I need an armchair that is comfortable.
6. There is a girl who speaks French, but there is no one who speaks Russian.

B. The subjunctive or indicative after certain conjunctions

Give the Spanish equivalent of the verbs in parentheses.

1. Tan pronto como Marta _____ a casa, le voy a mostrar la cómoda nueva. *(arrives)*
2. Voy a esperarlos hasta que _devuelvan_ . *(they return)*
3. Cuando ellos _vayan_ a trabajar, siempre dejan las ventanas abiertas. *(go)*
4. Cuando lo _____ , dile que somos seis. *(see)*
5. Vamos antes de que _____ la lámpara que te gusta. *(they sell)*
6. Ella va a ir a la fiesta con tal que tú _____ con ella. *(go)*
7. No puedo sacar el sillón de la casa sin que ellos me _____ . *(see)*
8. En caso de que ella _____ otra almohada, aquí está la mía. *(needs)*
9. No puedo comprar las fundas a menos que tú me _____ el dinero. *(give)*
10. Voy a hacer todo lo posible para que él _____ el dinero. *(gets)*
11. Aunque _____ el rojo, no creo que sea un buen color para la recámara. *(I like)*
12. Vamos a ir a la playa el sábado aunque _____ . *(it rains)*

C. *Qué* and *cuál* used with *ser*

Supply the question that elicited the following responses, beginning with **qué** or **cuál,** as needed.

1. Mi número de teléfono es 862–4031.
2. El apellido de mi madre es Lovera.
3. Un pasaporte es un documento que necesitamos para viajar a un país extranjero.
4. Las lecciones que necesitamos son la once y la doce.
5. Su dirección es calle Universidad número treinta.
6. La sidra es una bebida hecha de manzanas.

D. Uses of *sino* and *pero*

Combine the following pairs of sentences into one, using **pero** or **sino** as needed. Follow the model.

MODELO: Ella es morena.
Ella no es rubia.
Ella no es rubia sino morena.

1. No voy a comprarlo a plazos.
   Voy a comprarlo al contado.
2. No quiere alquilar la casa.
   Quiere comprarla.
3. El coche vale solamente setecientos dólares.
   Nosotros no podemos comprarlo.
4. Carlos no dijo que tenía el dinero.
   Carlos dijo que tenía los cheques.
5. Ella no quiere que firmemos la solicitud.
   Ella quiere que la leamos.

Ahora, una máquina no trabaja junto a las otras, sino con las otras.

E. Just words . . .

Match the questions in column A with the appropriate responses in column B.

A	B
1. ¿Tienes frío?	a. Pienso viajar a México.
2. ¿Por qué es tan cara la casa?	b. No, tengo fregadero.
3. ¿Por qué necesitas un garaje tan grande?	c. Sí, la cama era muy cómoda.
4. ¿Cuánto va a costar el edificio?	d. Porque era más cómodo.
5. ¿Cuáles son tus planes para el verano?	e. La semana próxima.
6. ¿Es optimista?	f. Está en un barrio muy elegante.
7. ¿Dormiste bien?	g. Una cómoda y una butaca.
8. ¿Tienes lavaplatos?	h. No, tiempo completo.
9. ¿Cuándo se mudan?	i. No, muy pesimista.
10. ¿Tienen dinero?	j. Sí, pero no tenemos fundas.
11. ¿Por qué compraste este sofá en vez del otro?	k. ¡Tengo tres coches!
12. ¿Vas a trabajar medio día?	l. Póngalo en la sala.
13. ¿Qué muebles necesitas?	m. Sí, cierra la ventana, por favor.
14. ¿Dónde pongo el sofá?	n. Sí, recibieron una herencia.
15. ¿Tienen almohadas?	o. Cinco millones de dólares.

LECCIÓN 14

A. The past participle

Give the Spanish equivalent of the following past participles.

1. written
2. opened
3. seen
4. done
5. broken

6. gone
7. spoken
8. eaten
9. drunk
10. received

B. Past participles used as adjectives

Give the Spanish equivalent of the words in parentheses.

1. Los espejos están _____ . (broken)
2. ¿Están _____ las puertas de la tienda? (open)
3. El hombre estaba _____ . (dead)
4. El departamento de señoras está _____ . (closed)
5. Estas sandalias están _____ aquí. (made)

C. The present perfect

Complete the sentences with the present perfect tense of the verbs in the list, as needed.

decir	usar	comer
quedarse	hacer	envolver

1. ¿Tú nunca _____ esa falda?
2. Él me _____ los zapatos. No voy a llevarlos puestos.
3. Ellos me _____ que no tienen nada que hacer.
4. Nosotros _____ demasiado.
5. Yo me _____ en la planta baja.
6. ¿Uds. no _____ el trabajo todavía?

D. The past perfect

Complete the following sentences with the past perfect tense of the verbs in parentheses.

1. Cuando yo llegué, la liquidación ya _____ . (terminar)
2. Elsa dijo que ellos _____ (ir) al departamento de ropa para caballeros.
3. El dependiente me _____ (decir) que la cartera costaba cincuenta dólares.
4. Yo ya _____ (abrir) el probador.
5. Nosotros todavía no _____ (comprar) la camisa.
6. ¿Tú le _____ (preguntar) qué talla usaba?

E. The familiar command (*tú* form)

Give the Spanish equivalent of the words in parentheses.

1. _____ , Paco. ¿Pusiste los platos en el fregadero? *(Tell me)*
2. _____ el trabajo y luego _____ la cocina, Ana. *(Do / clean)*
3. _____ de mi recámara, Carlos. *(Get out)*
4. _____ con ella y _____ las cortinas para el cuarto, Pepe. *(Go / buy)*
5. ¿Los libros? _____ en la mesa, querida. *(Put them)*
6. _____ conmigo. *(Come)*
7. _____ buena y _____ las sábanas y la frazada, Anita. *(Be / bring me)*
8. _____ paciencia. _____ unos minutos más. *(Have / Wait for me)*

9. _____ la casa si no tiene aire acondicionado, Luis. *(Don't buy)*
10. ¿El té? _____ todavía, Petrona. *(Don't serve it)*
11. _____ , querido. *(Don't go away)*
12. _____ a las seis y _____ hasta las once. *(Get up / work)*

F. Just words . . .

Choose the appropriate answer to the following questions.

1. ¿Qué número calza Ud.?
   a. Talla mediana.
   b. El treinta y seis.
   c. No tengo pantimedias.
2. ¿Quiere las botas negras y la bolsa azul?
   a. No, no hacen juego.
   b. Casi al mismo tiempo.
   c. No, me gusta la ropa interior.
3. ¿Puedo probarme estos zapatos?
   a. Sí, pero antes tiene que ponerse calcetines.
   b. Sí, pero necesita esta corbata.
   c. Sí, pero necesita ponerse estos guantes.
4. ¿Va a llevar este par de zapatos?
   a. No, me quedan muy bien.
   b. No, están en la zapatería.
   c. No, me aprietan un poco.
5. ¿Dónde pusiste el traje?
   a. ¡En la billetera, por supuesto!
   b. ¡En el ropero, por supuesto!
   c. ¡En la escalera, por supuesto!
6. ¿Tiene frío, señora?
   a. Sí, tráigame el pañuelo.
   b. Sí, tráigame las sandalias.
   c. Sí, tráigame la chaqueta.
7. ¿Quieres comer algo?
   a. Sí, estoy muerta de hambre.
   b. Sí, me gusta este vestido.
   c. Sí, quiero esa camisa y esa blusa.
8. ¿Cómo subieron al tercer piso?
   a. Nos encontramos en la planta baja.
   b. Por la escalera mecánica.
   c. Compramos ropa.

LECCIÓN 15

A. The future

Give the Spanish equivalent of the words in parentheses.

1. El mecánico _____ que su coche está descompuesto, señora. *(will tell you)*
2. ¿Quién _____ el carburador y la batería? *(will bring)*
3. Yo _____ las maletas en el maletero. *(will put)*
4. Nosotros _____ un limpiaparabrisas nuevo. *(will buy)*
5. ¿Tú _____ esta noche? *(will speak to him)*
6. Yo _____ todo lo posible por los niños. *(will do)*
7. Ellos _____ hasta la gasolinera para comprar gasolina. *(will drive)*
8. El mecánico _____ el motor. *(will check)*
9. Papá _____ el coche al taller. *(will take)*
10. _____ más tarde, querido. *(I will see you)*

B. The future to express probability in the present

Rewrite the following sentences with the future of probability. Follow the model.

MODELO: ¿Quién *crees tú que es* esa chica?
　　　　¿Quién será esa chica?

1. Mi coche hace mucho ruido. *Debe ser* porque el silenciador no funciona.
2. ¿Cuántos años *crees tú que tiene* Gustavo?
3. ¿Dónde *crees tú que hay* una estación de servicio?
4. Ese coche *debe costar* unos diez mil dólares.
5. San Diego *debe estar* a unas cincuenta millas de Los Ángeles.

C. The conditional

Give the Spanish equivalent of the words in parentheses.

1. Él dijo que ellos _____ el aceite. *(would change)*
2. ¡Yo sabía que el tanque _____ vacío! *(would be)*
3. Yo te dije que el coche _____ con la lluvia. *(would get dirty)*
4. Yo les dije que Uds. _____ un filtro nuevo. *(would need)*
5. Nosotros le _____ agua al radiador. *(would put)*
6. ¿Qué le _____ tú? *(would tell)*

D. The conditional to express probability in the past

Rewrite the following sentences with the conditional to express probability in the past. Follow the model.

MODELO: ¿Quién *crees tú que era* esa mujer?
¿Quién *sería* esa mujer?

1. *Me pregunto qué hora era* cuando llegaron los muchachos.
2. ¿*Crees tú que era* el acumulador?
3. ¿Cuántos años *crees tú que tenía* el dependiente?
4. *Me pregunto* quién *instaló* la bomba de agua.
5. ¿Quién *crees tú que vino* con Lola?

E. Just words . . .

Choose the word or phrase in parentheses that best completes each of the following sentences.

1. Tendré que cambiar (la chapa, el freno, el filtro) del aceite.
2. ¡Caramba! Los frenos de mi coche no (funcionan, manejan, arreglan).
3. Tuve que parar porque tuve (un pinchazo, un letrero, un portaguantes) en la carretera.
4. La (carretera, velocidad, grúa) máxima es de noventa kilómetros por hora.
5. No necesito gasolina porque el tanque está (lleno, rápido, extraño).
6. Camino a Madrid, me dieron una multa porque (las llantas eran negras, el coche no arrancaba, iba muy rápido).
7. La (goma, bomba de agua, chapa) de mi carro es ANA 325.
8. Según ese letrero, no podemos (tener neumáticos, estacionar aquí, tener licencia para conducir).
9. Va a venir una grúa para (remolcar, instalar, funcionar) el coche.
10. No puedo ver el camino porque el coche no tiene (maletero, freno, luces).

Cine en Buenos Aires, Argentina. En Argentina, como en toda Latinoamérica, las películas norteamericanas son muy populares.

OBJECTIVES

Structure   First-person plural commands • The future perfect • The conditional perfect • Reciprocal reflexives

Communication   You will learn vocabulary related to shopping for groceries and typical weekend activities (attending movies, concerts, etc.).

Un fin de semana

Hoy es feriado. Oscar y Jorge, dos estudiantes cubanos que viven en Miami, deciden ir al supermercado para hacer las compras de la semana. Por la noche piensan salir con dos chicas: Elsa y Adela. Tienen una cita para ir al cine, pero primero van a cocinar una cena para ellas en su apartamento. El supermercado se abre a las nueve y los muchachos son los primeros en llegar.

OSCAR —Necesitamos mantequilla, leche, una docena de huevos, pan, azúcar...

JORGE —¿No vamos a comprar carne?

OSCAR —Sí, compremos carne, pescado y pollo. También dos latas de frijoles y una de salsa de tomate.

JORGE —De haber sabido que ibas a invitar a las chicas, habría limpiado el apartamento.

OSCAR —Tú siempre te preocupas demasiado. A ver... necesitamos manzanas, uvas, naranjas, melón y peras para la ensalada de frutas...

JORGE —¿Dónde están las verduras? Tenemos que comprar lechuga, tomates, papas, zanahorias y cebollas.

OSCAR —¡Caramba! Esto va a costar una fortuna. Tendremos que ponernos a dieta.

JORGE —Buena idea. Pongámonos a dieta.

La cena estuvo muy buena. Ahora Oscar, Elsa, Jorge y Adela están en el cine, haciendo cola para comprar las entradas.

OSCAR —Dicen que esta película es magnífica.

ADELA —Sí, ganó el premio como la mejor película en el Festival de Cannes.

ELSA —Es un drama, ¿verdad? De haberlo sabido, no habría venido. Prefiero las comedias.

JORGE —El próximo sábado podemos ir a ver una película musical.

OSCAR —No, no vayamos al cine otra vez. Vamos a un club a bailar.

ADELA —Tengo ganas de comer algo. ¿Por qué no vamos a la cafetería Versailles cuando termine la película?

JORGE —¿No habrán cerrado para esa hora? Ésta es la última función.

OSCAR —No, esa cafetería se cierra muy tarde.

La película termina a las doce. Los chicos van a la cafetería a comer algo y a charlar un rato. Como el día siguiente es sábado, Oscar y Adela deciden verse otra vez para ir a la playa. Elsa y Jorge se van a encontrar en la biblioteca para estudiar.

A Weekend

Today is a holiday. Oscar and Jorge, two Cuban students who live in Miami, decide to go to the supermarket to do the weekly shopping. This evening they're planning on going out with two girls: Elsa and Adela. They have a date to go to the movies, but first they are going to cook dinner for them at their apartment. The supermarket opens at nine, and the boys are the first to arrive.

o. We need butter, milk, a dozen eggs, bread, sugar . . .

j. Aren't we going to buy meat?

o. Yes, let's buy meat, fish, and chicken. Also two cans of beans and one (can) of tomato sauce.

j. Had I known that you were going to invite the girls, I would have cleaned the apartment.

o. You always worry too much. Let's see . . . we need apples, grapes, oranges, melon, and pears for the fruit salad . . .

j. Where are the vegetables? We have to buy lettuce, tomatoes, potatoes, carrots, and onions.

o. Gee! This is going to cost a fortune. We'll have to go on a diet.

j. Good idea! Let's go on a diet.

The dinner was very good. Now Oscar, Elsa, Jorge, and Adela are at the movie theater, standing in line to buy the tickets.

o. They say this movie is great.

a. Yes, it won the prize for best film at the Cannes Festival.

Vocabulario

COGNADOS

la **dieta**   diet
la **docena**   dozen
el **drama**   drama
la **fortuna**   fortune

el **melón**   melon
musical   musical
el **supermercado**   supermarket
el **tomate**   tomato

NOMBRES

el **azúcar**   sugar
la **biblioteca**   library
la **carne**   meat
la **cebolla**   onion
el **feriado**   holiday
la **función**   show
el **huevo,** el **blanquillo** *(Mex.)*   egg
la **lata,** el **bote** *(Mex.)*   can
la **lechuga**   lettuce
la **mantequilla**   butter
la **manzana**   apple
la **naranja**   orange
el **pan**   bread
la **película**   movie
la **pera**   pear
el **pescado**   fish
el **premio**   prize
la **salsa**   sauce

la **verdura**   vegetable
la **zanahoria**   carrot

VERBOS

ganar   to win

ADJETIVO

siguiente   following, next

OTRAS PALABRAS Y EXPRESIONES

de haber sabido   had I known
hacer cola   to stand in line
hacer compras   to shop, do the shopping
otra vez   again
ponerse a dieta   to go on a diet
tener ganas de   to feel like (doing something)

E. It's a drama, right? Had I known, I wouldn't have come. I prefer comedies.

J. Next Saturday we can go see a musical.

O. No, let's not go to the movies again. Let's go to a club to dance.

A. I feel like having something to eat. Why don't we go to the Versailles cafeteria when the movie ends?

J. Won't they have closed by that time? This is the last show.

O. No, that cafeteria closes very late.

The movie ends at twelve. The group goes to the cafeteria to have something to eat and to chat for a while. Since the following day is Saturday, Oscar and Adela decide to see each other again to go to the beach. Elsa and Jorge are going to meet at the library to study.

Vocabulario adicional

el **apio**   celery
Voy a comer mucho **apio** porque estoy a dieta.

el **durazno**, el **melocotón**   peach
No me gustan las manzanas; prefiero los **duraznos.**

las **fresas**   strawberries
Las **fresas** no tienen muchas calorías.

la **margarina**   margarine
No compré mantequilla; compré **margarina.**

el **papel higiénico**   toilet paper
¿Pusiste el **papel higiénico** en el baño?

el **parque de diversiones**   amusement park
Disneylandia es mi **parque de diversiones** favorito.

la **piña**   pineapple
Cuando fui a Hawaii comí mucha **piña.**

la **sandía**   watermelon
Compré **sandía** para la ensalada de frutas.

la **toronja**   grapefruit
¿Quieres jugo de naranja o jugo de **toronja?**

el **vinagre**   vinegar
Yo le pongo aceite y **vinagre** a la ensalada.

el **zoológico**   zoo
En ese **zoológico** hay muchos animales de África.

HOY
CINE METRO 2
(En Exclusivo)
3:00 6:00 9:00 PM (T)

ELEPHANT

Quien engañó a
ROGER RABBIT

¿Lo sabía Ud.... ?

■ Aunque hoy en día hay un gran número de supermercados en los países hispanos, muchas personas prefieren comprar en los mercados al aire libre o en las tiendas pequeñas que generalmente se especializan en uno o dos productos. Por ejemplo, se vende **carne** en la **carnicería, frutas** en la **frutería, verduras** en la **verdulería** y **pan** en la **panadería.**

■ En países de habla hispana como España, México, Argentina y Cuba, la producción de películas ha tenido gran importancia. Recientemente, directores como Carlos Saura, que dirigió **Carmen** y **Bodas de sangre** (*Blood Wedding*), así como María Luisa Bemberg, directora de **La historia oficial** (*The Official Story*), que ganó el Oscar como la mejor película extranjera en 1986, se han hecho conocer en Europa y los Estados Unidos.

En muchos países hispánicos se producen muy buenas películas, muchas de las cuales son de tipo socio-político. En 1983, una película española, **Volver a empezar** (*To Begin Again*), ganó el Oscar como la mejor película extranjera.

■ Las películas norteamericanas son muy populares en el mundo hispánico. Generalmente tienen subtítulos en español o están dobladas (*dubbed*). Muchos de los títulos en español son completamente diferentes a los del inglés. Por ejemplo, la película *Beverly Hills Cop* se llama **Un detective suelto en Hollywood;** *Out of Africa* se titula **África mía.**

Oferta de zumos (jugos) en el supermercado de la famosa tienda El Corte Inglés, en Madrid, España.

Estructuras gramaticales

▶ *1.* First-person plural commands *(El imperativo de la primera persona del plural)*

♦ The first-person plural of an affirmative command *(let's + verb)* may be expressed in two different ways:

◇ by using the first-person plural of the present subjunctive

Compremos carne y pescado.	*Let's buy meat and fish.*

◇ by using the expression **vamos a** + *infinitive*

Vamos a comprar carne y pescado.	*Let's buy meat and fish.*

♦ The verb **ir** does not use the subjunctive for the first-person plural affirmative command.

Vamos a la playa.	*Let's go to the beach.*

♦ For the negative command, the subjunctive is used.

No vayamos a la playa.	*Let's not go to the beach.*

♦ In all direct affirmative commands, the object pronouns are attached to the verb. An accent must be used to maintain the original stress.

Llamémos**lo**.	*Let's call him.*
Escribámos**les**.	*Let's write to them.*

♦ If the pronouns **nos** or **se** are attached to the verb, the final **-s** of the verb is dropped before adding the pronoun.

Sentémo**nos** aquí.	*Let's sit here.*
Vistámo**nos** ahora.	*Let's get dressed now.*
Démo**selo** a los niños.	*Let's give it to the children.*
Digámo**selo** a ella.	*Let's tell (it to) her.*

♦ In direct negative commands, the object pronouns are placed in front of the verb.

No **lo** planchemos.	*Let's not iron it.*
No **nos** vistamos ahora.	*Let's not get dressed now.*

PRÁCTICA

A. Imagine that you are going to a restaurant with a friend. He or she will ask for suggestions about what you should do. Tell him or her, using the first-person plural command.

Antes de ir:

1. ¿A qué restaurante vamos?
2. ¿Hacemos reservaciones?
3. ¿Llevamos el coche o tomamos un taxi?

En el restaurante:

1. ¿Dónde nos sentamos?
2. ¿Qué pedimos para comer?
3. ¿Qué tomamos?
4. ¿Qué comemos de postre?
5. ¿Pedimos algo más?
6. ¿Cuánto le dejamos de propina al mozo?
7. ¿Adónde vamos ahora?
8. ¿Invitamos a alguien?

B. Be an interpreter. What are these people saying?

1. Let's do the shopping today.
   Yes, let's go to the supermarket.
2. Let's buy (some) butter.
   No, let's not buy it. I want to go on a diet.
3. Where do you want to sit?
   Let's sit near the window.
4. Let's go to bed early tonight.
   Why?
   Because we have to get up at six o'clock.

▶ *2.* The future perfect *(El futuro perfecto)*

♦ The future perfect in Spanish corresponds closely in formation and meaning to the same tense in English. The Spanish future perfect is formed with the future tense of the auxiliary verb **haber** + *the past participle* of the main verb.

THE FUTURE PERFECT

yo	habré terminado	*I will have finished*
tú	habrás vuelto	*you will have returned*
él (ella)	habrá comido	*he (she) will have eaten*
nosotros(-as)	habremos escrito	*we will have written*
vosotros(-as)	habréis dicho	*you (fam.) will have said*
ellos (ellas)	habrán salido	*they will have left*

♦ Like its English equivalent, the future perfect is used to indicate an action that will have taken place by a certain time in the future.

—¿Tus padres estarán aquí para el dos de junio?

Will your parents be here by June second?

—Sí, para esa fecha ya **habrán vuelto** de Madrid.

Yes, by that date they will have returned from Madrid.

PRÁCTICA

Provide the future perfect of the missing verbs in the following dialogues. Choose from this list:

limpiar	salir	volver
acostarse	cenar	terminar

1. TERESA —Esta noche a las once voy a llamar a Quique.

   SILVIA —¿Estás loca? Para esa hora él ya _____ . Llámalo mañana a las siete.

   TERESA —Para esa hora ya _____ de su casa.

2. JORGE —¿Uds. _____ de México para el cuatro de julio?

   SR. VERA —No, no _____ todavía. Vamos a estar allí hasta agosto.

3. PABLO —Tú y yo podemos salir para España el 12 de diciembre porque ya estaremos de vacaciones.

   ANDRÉS —Bueno, tú _____ las clases para entonces, pero yo no las _____ todavía.

4. ANA —No podemos traer a mis amigos esta noche porque la casa está muy sucia.

   NORA —No te preocupes. Para cuando Uds. vengan, las chicas ya la _____ .

5. PACO —¿Quieres cenar con nosotros hoy?

   RAFA —Gracias, pero para cuando yo vuelva, ustedes ya _____ .

▶ *3.* The conditional perfect   *(El condicional perfecto)*

◆ The conditional perfect is formed with the conditional of the auxiliary verb **haber** + *the past participle* of the main verb.

THE CONDITIONAL PERFECT

yo	habría vuelto	*I would have returned*
tú	habrías comido	*you would have eaten*
él (ella)	habría salido	*he (she) would have left*
nosotros(-as)	habríamos estudiado	*we would have studied*
vosotros(-as)	habríais hecho	*you (fam.) would have done*
ellos (ellas)	habrían muerto	*they would have died*

◆ Like the English conditional perfect, the Spanish conditional perfect is used to indicate an action that would have taken place but didn't.

—Compramos piña.   *We bought pineapple.*
—Yo **habría comprado** sandía.   *I would have bought water-*
                                    melon.

PRÁCTICA

A. Last summer, my family, a friend, and I took a trip to New York. Based on what I tell you about our trip, tell me what you and each member of your family would have done differently, if anything.

MODELO: Mi padre llevó tres maletas.
         *Mi padre **habría llevado** una maleta.*

1. Nosotros fuimos a Nueva York.
2. Viajamos en tren.
3. Yo me senté en la sección de no fumar.
4. Mi mamá preparó sándwiches para el viaje.
5. Mi amigo y yo bebimos refrescos en el café del tren.
6. En Nueva York, mi amigo se quedó en casa de su abuelo.
7. Nosotros nos quedamos en un hotel.
8. Mis padres fueron a ver una comedia musical.
9. Yo fui a bailar.
10. Nosotros visitamos el Museo de Arte Moderno.
11. Mi amigo visitó la Estatua de la Libertad.
12. Estuvimos en Nueva York por dos semanas.

B. Be an interpreter. What are these people saying?

1. I invited my uncle to spend the weekend with us.
   Had I known that you were going to invite him, I would have bought more vegetables and fish.

2. I won the prize!
   Had I gone, I would have won it.
3. They went to an amusement park last Saturday.
   I would have gone to the zoo.
4. What fruits would you have bought, Tito?
   I would have bought watermelon, strawberries, and pineapple.
5. She said she felt like having something to eat.
   I would have taken her to a good restaurant.

▶ *4.* Reciprocal reflexives *(Pronombres reflexivos en función recíproca)*

♦ As you have already learned in **Lección 8,** the reflexive pronouns are used whenever the subject does the action to itself. The reflexive pronouns may also be used in the plural form (**nos, os, se**) to express a mutual or reciprocal relationship. The reflexive then translates as the expressions *(to) each other* or *(to) one another.*

Nos queremos mucho. | *We love **each other** very much.*

Los amigos **se** escriben. | *The friends write **to each other**.*

Ustedes **se** ven. | *You see **each other**.*

PRÁCTICA

Be an interpreter. What are these people saying?

1. Do you and your mother write to each other often, Miss Vega?
   No, we call each other on the phone.
2. Are they going to meet at the theater?
   No, at the zoo.
3. Tell Carlos that we need vinegar and sauce.
   I'm sorry, but Carlos and I don't talk to each other.
4. When are you going to see each other again?
   Never. We don't love each other.

¡A ver cuánto aprendió!

A. ¡Conversemos!

Reread the dialogues in this lesson and be ready to discuss the following.

1. ¿Adónde van Jorge y Oscar para hacer las compras de la semana?

2. ¿Qué piensan hacer por la noche?
3. ¿A qué hora se abre el supermercado?
4. Según Oscar, ¿qué necesitan comprar?
5. ¿Cuántas latas de frijoles compran los muchachos?
6. De haber sabido que Oscar iba a invitar a las chicas, ¿qué habría hecho Jorge?
7. ¿Qué frutas necesitan para la ensalada?
8. ¿Por qué dice Oscar que tendrán que ponerse a dieta?
9. ¿Para qué tienen que hacer cola los muchachos?
10. ¿Qué premio ganó la película que van a ver?
11. ¿Adónde van a ir después de ver la película?
12. ¿Qué tiene ganas de hacer Adela?
13. ¿Se cierra temprano la cafetería Versailles?
14. ¿Dónde se van a encontrar Elsa y Jorge?

B. ¡Repase el vocabulario!

Choose the appropriate response to each of the following questions.

1. ¿Vas a hacer ravioles?
   a. Sí, necesito una lata de frijoles.
   b. Sí, necesito dos latas de salsa de tomate.
   c. Sí, necesito las naranjas.
2. ¡Caramba! La comida está muy cara, ¿verdad?
   a. Sí, es muy barata.
   b. Sí, ahora cuesta menos.
   c. Sí, cuesta una fortuna.
3. ¿Hay mucha gente que quiere comprar entradas?
   a. Sí, tenemos que hacer cola.
   b. Sí, tenemos que llamar una grúa.
   c. Sí, tenemos que ir a la estación de servicio.
4. A ver... ¿qué verduras necesitamos?
   a. Agua y aceite.
   b. Pescado y pollo.
   c. Lechuga y zanahorias.
5. ¿Cuándo estuvieron listas las radiografías?
   a. Mañana.
   b. Al día siguiente.
   c. La semana próxima.
6. ¿Dónde queda el supermercado?
   a. Frente a la gasolinera.
   b. En la barbería.
   c. En el río.
7. ¿No tienes una cita con Juan Carlos?
   a. Sí, pero no puedo ir porque él es famoso.
   b. Sí, pero no puedo ir porque me duele la espalda.
   c. Sí, pero no puedo ir porque no tengo visa.

8. ¿Qué vas a usar para hacer el jugo?
   a. Huevos.
   b. Toronjas.
   c. Sellos.
9. ¿Bailamos?
   a. No, tengo que ponerme a dieta.
   b. No, me duelen los pies.
   c. No, no tengo el menú.
10. Dicen que esa película es fantástica.
    a. Sí, ganó el primer premio.
    b. Sí, ganó la licencia para conducir.
    c. Sí, a mí tampoco me gustó.
11. Mi hermano quiere ver los elefantes.
    a. Llévalo al parque de diversiones.
    b. Llévalo al zoológico.
    c. Llévalo a la biblioteca.
12. ¿Tienes ganas de tomar algo?
    a. Sí, pescado.
    b. Sí, carne.
    c. Sí, una copa de vino blanco.

C. Situaciones

What would you say in the following situations? What would the other person say?

1. Tell a friend what you feel like having to eat and drink in a restaurant.
2. Tell a group of friends you are going to meet them at the amusement park.
3. Tell your roommate what ingredients are needed to make a good fruit salad.
4. Your friends dropped in to see you. Tell them that, had you known they were coming, you would have cleaned your apartment.
5. Invite a friend to go see a movie with you this weekend. Tell him or her what movie you'd like to see and at what time.

Para escribir

1. Write a grocery shopping list.
2. Write a dialogue between you and a friend, making plans for the weekend.

En la vida real

ENTREVISTA

Choose a partner, then interview each other using the **tú** form.

Pregúntele a su compañero(-a) de clase...

1. ...si aceptaría una cita con una persona a quien no conoce.
2. ...si prefiere ver una comedia musical o un drama.
3. ...si salió con una chica (un chico) y no se divirtió y si saldría con ella (él) otra vez.
4. ...qué hace cuando es feriado.
5. ...si se preocupa cuando alguien viene a comer a su casa, y por qué o por qué no.
6. ...cuántas docenas de huevos compra para una semana.
7. ...qué frutas y qué verduras le gustan.
8. ...si prefiere comer carne, pescado o pollo.
9. ...si sabe a qué hora se cierra el mercado.
10. ...si sabe a qué hora se abre la biblioteca de la universidad.

DISCUSIÓN

With a classmate, discuss a movie or a T.V. program you have both seen recently and try to summarize the plot. Say whether you liked it or not and give reasons why.

Some words and phrases you might want to include:

actor *actor*
actriz *actress*

(la) película
- de acción
- de ciencia ficción
- cómica
- dramática
- de guerra
- de horror
- de misterio
- policiaca

Telecaribe

12:00 Cocinando.	5:00 Tal para cual.	8:00 Misión secreta.
12:30 Estelares del vallenato.	5:30 Los Ropers.	9:00 Agente secreto.
1:30 Telerevista Sucesos.	6:00 Emociones.	10:00 Risas y lentejuelas.
2:00 Sábados espectaculares.	6:30 Oro puro.	10:30 Telecaribe.
3:00 Fútbol alemán.	7:00 Tv Noticias.	11:00 Buenas noches.
4:00 Telecaribe especial.	7:30 Serie Satel Tv.	

De la cocina a la mesa

With a classmate read the following recipes for enchiladas and flan. Imagine that you will prepare these at home tonight. One of you should make a list of utensils or any special items you will need in order to cook these dishes. The other person should make a list of the food items and quantities you will need.

ENCHILADAS

Ingredientes:

    1 docena de tortillas de maíz
    1 lata de salsa de enchilada
    ¼ taza de aceite
    1 libra de queso rallado
    1 cebolla grande, rallada

Preparación:

Caliente la salsa en una sartén. En otra sartén caliente las tortillas en el aceite, sin freírlas. Sáquelas del aceite y mójelas en la salsa. Póngalas en un plato, y cúbralas con queso y cebolla. Enrolle las tortillas como tubos y cúbralas con el resto del queso. Póngalas en el horno a 325 grados por cinco minutos.

FLAN

Ingredientes:

Para el flan:
    2 tazas de leche evaporada
    4 huevos
    8 cucharadas de azúcar
    1 cucharadita de vainilla

Para el caramelo:
    3 cucharadas de azúcar

Preparación:

En el molde donde va a hacer el flan, ponga a derretir al fuego tres cucharadas de azúcar. Después de unos minutos el azúcar va a tener un color dorado. Mueva el molde para cubrirlo todo con el caramelo y déjelo enfriar.

Bata los huevos. Añada el azúcar, la leche y la vainilla y revuélvalo bien. Póngalo todo en el molde y cocínelo a Baño María en el horno a 350 grados por una hora. (Para saber si ya está cocinado, introduzca un cuchillo en el flan y si sale limpio, ya está listo.)

Sáquelo del horno y déjelo enfriar. Póngalo en el refrigerador. Antes de servirlo, voltee el molde en un plato.

Y ahora, *¡vamos a leer!*

Antonio hace planes

Antonio, un muchacho mexicano que vive en Los Ángeles y asiste a la Universidad de California, está pensando en todo lo que tendrá que hacer el próximo fin de semana. Trata de organizar su tiempo porque el sábado por la noche tiene una cita con María Isabel, una compañera de la universidad. Esto es lo que Antonio piensa:

¡Caramba! ¿Qué hora será? No sé si tendré tiempo para llevar el coche al taller. ¿Estará allí el mecánico? Los frenos no funcionan bien y un día de estos no voy a poder parar... Creo que el coche necesita neumáticos nuevos... ¿Cuánto costarán? No sé si tendré suficiente dinero, porque tengo que hacer las compras de la semana. El refrigerador está vacío. Necesito carne, pescado, leche, mantequilla, huevos, verduras... Mamá me dirá otra vez que no como suficientes verduras y que tendré que ponerme a dieta... Tengo ganas de comer pizza... ¿Qué le gustará a María Isabel... ? Tendré que preparar una cena magnífica cuando venga... Langosta, filete... ¿No será más barato llevarla a un restaurante? Tendré que limpiar el apartamento, lavar el coche y recoger mi chaqueta azul de la tintorería... ¡A María Isabel le encanta esa chaqueta! ¿Y dónde estaría anoche cuando la llamé? ¿Saldría con Ernesto? Voy a llamarla otra vez. Supongo que para las once ya habrá vuelto a su casa... ¡Caramba! ¿Qué hora será... ?

¡A ver cuánto recuerda!

1. ¿Antonio es extranjero?
2. ¿Cree Ud. que Antonio va a estar muy ocupado el próximo fin de semana? ¿Por qué?
3. ¿Antonio tiene reloj? ¿Cómo lo sabe Ud.?
4. ¿Qué problemas tiene el coche de Antonio?
5. ¿Cree Ud. que Antonio tiene mucho dinero? ¿Por qué?
6. ¿Qué necesita comprar Antonio?
7. ¿Cree Ud. que la mamá de Antonio se preocupa por él? ¿Por qué?
8. ¿Quién va a cocinar cuando venga María Isabel?
9. ¿Qué más tendrá que hacer para la visita de María Isabel?
10. ¿Antonio habló con María Isabel anoche? ¿Por qué no?
11. ¿Para qué hora habrá vuelto María Isabel a su casa?
12. ¿Cree Ud. que a Antonio le gusta María Isabel?

Estados Unidos

Las minorías hispanas en los Estados Unidos

PANORAMA HISPÁNICO 9

■ Muchas de las estrellas *(stars)* de cine y de televisión en los Estados Unidos son de ascendencia hispana: Raquel Welch, Ricardo Montalbán, Martín Sheen, Emilio Estévez, Edward J. Olmos, María Conchita Alonso y Linda Ronstadt, entre muchos otros.

■ En la ciudad de Nueva York hay más de dos millones de hispano hablantes, la mayoría de los cuales son puertorriqueños. Otros grupos hispanos concentrados en Nueva York son los dominicanos, los centroamericanos y los cubanos.

■ La minoría hispana más numerosa en los Estados Unidos es la de origen mexicano, que se concentra principalmente en los estados de Texas, Colorado, Nuevo México, Arizona y California.

■ Más de medio millón de cubanos viven en Miami, donde ejercen una gran influencia tanto cultural como económica. En La Pequeña Habana, el centro comercial de los cubanos en Miami, casi todos los establecimientos son de propiedad cubana y el español es el idioma dominante.

■ Los hispanos adquieren cada día mayor importancia en el campo de la política en los Estados Unidos. Hoy día muchos son elegidos para ocupar posiciones políticas importantes. Los alcaldes de Miami, Xavier Suárez, y de Denver, Federico Peña, son de origen hispano. En el primer gabinete del Presidente Bush, dos hispanos, Lauro Cabazos y Manuel Luján, han sido nombrados Secretarios de Educación y del Interior respectivamente.

◀ La calle Olvera con sus aceras adoquinadas *(tiled)*, sus piñatas, sus mariachis y sus puestos de artesanía mexicana es realmente un trozo del viejo México en el corazón de Los Ángeles. Aquí encontramos el edificio Ávila, construido de adobe y considerado el más antiguo de los edificios existentes en Los Ángeles. Describa Ud. lo que se ve en esta foto.

▼ En América Latina tiene mucha importancia para las muchachas la celebración de los quince años. En México la fiesta recibe el nombre de «quinceañera»; en otros países se refieren a ella como la celebración de «los quince». La mayor parte de las familias latinas en los Estados Unidos sigue la tradición con un baile y una comida especial. ¿Qué cumpleaños es muy importante para una chica en los Estados Unidos?

▶ Los hispanos constituyen el grupo minoritario más populoso de la ciudad de Nueva York. Aquí se ve un festival hispano en la calle 14 de Manhattan, en el centro de Nueva York. ¿Hay festivales hispanos en la ciudad donde Ud. vive?

Aquí aparece la locutora hispana, Ana Martínez, en los estudios de televisión del canal KVUE, en Austin Texas. Cada vez hay más locutores hispanos, no sólo en los canales hispanos, sino también en los de habla inglesa. ¿Hay un canal de televisión hispano en la ciudad donde Ud. vive?

▲ La cantante cubana Gloria Estefan y el grupo *Miami Sound Machine* alcanzaron fama en los Estados Unidos en 1986. Entre sus mayores éxitos están «*1-2-3*» y «*The rhythm is gonna get you*». ¿Cuál es su grupo musical favorito?

◄ Edward James Olmos ganó fama al representar el papel de Martín Castillo en la popular serie de televisión «*Miami Vice*». Nacido de padres mexicanos en Los Ángeles, Olmos es uno de los artistas hispanos más conocidos en los Estados Unidos. Su reciente actuación en la película, «*Stand and Deliver*», le valió numerosos elogios. ¿Cuál es su actor favorito?

▶ Basta una vuelta por la ciudad de San Antonio, Texas, para convencerse de que la cultura mexicana es la predominante. En la foto, una familia está comiendo en el restaurante mexicano «Mi Tierra». ¿Cuál es su restaurante mexicano favorito?

◀ Xavier Suárez, actual alcalde de Miami, sirve como ejemplo del poder político de los cubanos en Miami. Suárez, un abogado graduado de la Universidad de Harvard, nació en Cuba en 1949, y vino a los Estados Unidos cuando sus padres se exiliaron después de la revolución de Castro. ¿Cómo se llama el alcalde (la alcaldesa) de su ciudad?

Estudiantes universitarios en Madrid, España.

OBJECTIVES

Structure   The present perfect subjunctive • The imperfect subjunctive • Uses of the imperfect subjunctive • The pluperfect subjunctive

Communication   You will learn vocabulary related to college activities and careers.

Dos estudiantes conversan

Alina y Daniel son dos jóvenes latinoamericanos que están estudiando en la Universidad de California en Los Ángeles. Alina es cubana y Daniel es argentino. Los dos están tomando una clase de administración de empresas.

ALINA —Es una lástima que no te hayas matriculado en la clase de sociología de la doctora Parker. Siempre tenemos unas discusiones muy interesantes.

DANIEL —Mi consejero me sugirió que la tomara, pero yo quería tomar una clase de física o de química a esa hora.

ALINA —¡Ah, sí... ! A ti te gustan las ciencias... Pero dime, ¿cuál es tu especialización?

DANIEL —Todavía no lo sé. Mi padre quería que fuera abogado, como él, pero yo asistí a la Facultad de Derecho en Buenos Aires y no me gustó.

ALINA —Yo tampoco seguí los consejos de mi papá. A él le gustaría que yo estudiara ingeniería, pero yo decidí estudiar periodismo.

DANIEL —¿Qué otras asignaturas estás tomando? ¿Estás tomando algunos requisitos?

ALINA —¡Qué va! Este semestre solamente estoy tomando materias que me gustan... ¡incluyendo una clase de danza aeróbica!

DANIEL —(Bromeando) Claro, eso es muy importante para una periodista.

ALINA —Pues chico,[1] es necesario hacer ejercicio, y habría sido una buena idea que tú también la hubieras tomado.

DANIEL —Es verdad. Che,[2] Alina, hay un partido de fútbol esta noche en el estadio universitario. ¿Quieres ir conmigo?

ALINA —No, lo siento pero esta noche tengo que ir a la biblioteca para hacer la tarea de literatura y estudiar para el examen de sicología que, según la profesora, será muy difícil.

DANIEL —¡No es necesario preocuparse tanto por las notas!

ALINA —Es que yo tengo una beca y necesito mantener un buen promedio.

---

[1] An informal expression used in Cuba and other hispanic countries to address someone. [2] Used in Argentina as an equivalent of "Listen" or "Hey" when addressing someone informally.

Two Students Chat

Alina and Daniel are two young Latin Americans who are studying at the University of California in Los Angeles. Alina is Cuban and Daniel is Argentinian. They're both taking a class in business administration.

A. It's a pity that you haven't registered for Dr. Parker's sociology class. We always have very interesting discussions.

D. My advisor suggested that I take it, but I wanted to take a physics or a chemistry class at that time.

A. Oh yes . . . ! You like sciences . . . But tell me, what is your major?

D. I don't know that yet. My father wanted me to be a lawyer, like him, but I attended law school in Buenos Aires and I didn't like it.

A. I didn't follow my Dad's advice, either. He would like me to study engineering, but I decided to study journalism.

D. What other classes are you taking? Are you taking any requirements?

A. No way! This semester I'm only taking classes that I like . . . including an aerobic dance class!

D. *(Jokingly)* Of course, that's very important for a journalist.

A. Well, my friend, it's necessary to exercise, and it would have been a good idea if you had also taken it.

D. That's true. Hey, Alina, there's a soccer game tonight at the university stadium. Would you like to go with me?

DANIEL —¡Ah! Yo quería que fueras al partido conmigo pero ahora que me acuerdo, tengo un examen parcial en mi clase de matemáticas.

ALINA —Supongo que tendré que prestarte mi calculadora, como siempre.

DANIEL —Gracias, flaca.[1] Me voy, porque David quería que lo ayudara con su tarea de biología y ya es tarde. ¡Chau!

ALINA —Adiós, Daniel. Buena suerte en el examen.

Vocabulario

COGNADOS

argentino(-a) Argentinian
la **biología** biology
la **calculadora** calculator
la **ciencia** science
la **discusión** discussion
el **estadio** stadium
el **examen** exam
importante important

la **ingeniería** engineering
latinoamericano(-a) Latin American
la **literatura** literature
las **matemáticas** mathematics
el **semestre** semester
la **(p)sicología** psychology
la **sociología** sociology

NOMBRES

el (la) **abogado(-a)** lawyer
la **administración de empresas** business administration
la **asignatura,** la **materia** subject
la **beca** scholarship
el (la) **consejero(-a)** counselor, advisor
el **consejo** advice
la **danza aeróbica** aerobic dance
la **especialización** major (field of study)
el **examen parcial** midterm exam

la **facultad de derecho** law school
la **física** physics
el **fútbol** soccer
el **joven** (los **jóvenes**) young person(s)
la **nota** grade
el **partido** game
el **periodismo** journalism
el (la) **periodista** journalist
el **promedio** grade point average
la **química** chemistry
el **requisito** requirement
la **tarea** assignment, homework

---

[1] **Flaca** literally means *"skinny,"* but is also used affectionately in many Hispanic countries to address close friends regardless of the person's physical characteristics. Comparable expressions in English are "kid," "pal," and "buddy."

A. No, I'm sorry, but tonight I have to go to the library to do the assignment for literature and to study for the sociology exam, which, according to the professor, will be very difficult.

D. It's not necessary to worry so much about grades!

A. The fact is that I have a scholarship, and need to maintain a good average.

D. Ah! I wanted you to go to the game with me, but now that I remember, I have a midterm exam in my math class.

A. I suppose I'll have to lend you my calculator, as usual.

D. Thanks, kid. I'm leaving because David wanted me to help him with his biology assignment, and it's late. Bye!

A. Good-bye, Daniel. Good luck on the test.

VERBOS

ayudar   to help
incluir[1]   to include
mantener   to maintain *(conj. like* **tener***)*
matricularse   to register
suponer   to suppose *(conj. like* **poner***)*

OTRAS PALABRAS Y EXPRESIONES

como   like
como siempre   as usual

es necesario   it's necessary
hacer ejercicio   to exercise
no gustarle nada a uno   not to like it at all
¡qué va!   no way!
tanto   so much
todavía no   not yet

Vocabulario adicional

aprobar (o:ue)   to pass (an exam), to approve
Aprobé el examen de química ayer.

la contabilidad   accounting
La clase de **contabilidad** no es fácil.

el diccionario   dictionary
¿Qué quiere decir «*better*»? Necesito un **diccionario**.

entregar   to turn in, deliver
Le **entregué** la tarea al profesor.

la escuela primaria   grade school
Ella asiste a la **escuela primaria**.

la escuela secundaria   high school
Tenía muy buenas notas en la **escuela secundaria**.

el horario   schedule
Este semestre tengo un **horario** muy bueno.

la matrícula   registration, tuition
No tengo dinero para pagar la **matrícula**.

la palabra   word
Voy a buscar esta **palabra** en el diccionario.

sacar   to get (a grade in school)
Sacó una «A» en sicología.

el trimestre   quarter
Este **trimestre** tengo una clase de matemáticas.

---

[1] Present Tense: **incluyo, incluyes, incluye, incluimos, incluís, incluyen.**

¿Lo sabía Ud.... ?

- En la mayoría de las universidades hispanas no existe el concepto de ''major'' usado en los Estados Unidos. Los estudiantes españoles y latinoamericanos toman muy pocas clases optativas *(electives)*, ya que la mayoría comienza a especializarse a partir de su primer año en la universidad.

- En España y en Latinoamérica, las universidades se dividen en «facultades» *(colleges)*, donde los estudiantes toman clases directamente relacionadas con su especialización (por ejemplo, la Facultad de Medicina, la Facultad de Ingeniería, la Facultad de Arquitectura, etc.). Por lo general, los planes de estudios son rígidos y no hay cursos electivos. Tampoco hay requisitos generales, pues éstos se toman en la escuela secundaria o en los institutos.

- El fútbol *(soccer)* es el deporte *(sport)* más popular en España y Latinoamérica (excepto en la región del Caribe, donde el deporte favorito es el béisbol). Otro deporte popular en España, México y Cuba es el *jai alai*, o pelota vasca.

- En lugar de letras, el sistema de calificaciones *(grading system)* en las universidades hispanas es numérico. Por lo general, se califica asignando notas de 1 a 5 en Hispanoamérica y de 1 a 10 en España. Una nota de 3 o 6 es normalmente la nota mínima para aprobar una clase o examen.

El fútbol es uno de los deportes favoritos en los países de habla hispana. Aquí vemos un partido de fútbol en Buenos Aires, Argentina.

Estructuras gramaticales

▶ *1.* The present perfect subjunctive *(El presente perfecto del subjuntivo)*

◆ The present perfect subjunctive is formed by combining the present subjunctive of the auxiliary verb **haber** with the past participle of the main verb.

PRESENT PERFECT SUBJUNCTIVE

Present Subjunctive of haber	+	Past Participle of the Main Verb
yo	haya	cambiado
tú	hayas	temido
él (ella)	haya	sufrido
nosotros(-as)	hayamos	hecho
vosotros(-as)	hayáis	puesto
ellos (ellas)	hayan	visto

◆ The present perfect subjunctive is used in sentences in which the main clause calls for the use of the subjunctive in the subordinate clause. It is used to describe events which have ended prior to the time indicated in the main clause.

—Me alegro de que **hayas venido.**   *I'm glad you have come.*

—Es una lástima que papá no **haya podido** venir conmigo.   *It is a pity that Dad has not been able to come with me.*

UNIVERSIDAD AUTONOMA DEL CARIBE

FACULTAD DE ADMINISTRACION HOTELERA Y DE TURISMO

INFORMAN:

Que están abiertas las Inscripciones para su JORNADA NOCTURNA Período Enero - Junio de 1989

PRÁCTICA

A. Imagine that you overhear these conversations in the student cafeteria. With a classmate, act out the following mini-dialogues, providing the missing verbs. Use the present perfect subjunctive of the verbs given.

conseguir	ser	traer
poder	ir	volver
decir	venir	dar

1. —Es una lástima que (ellos) no te _____ la beca.
   —Sí. Ojalá que mis padres _____ el dinero para pagar la matrícula.
2. —Espero que Irma _____ su calculadora, porque hoy tengo un examen de matemáticas.
   —No creo que ella _____ hoy, porque ayer no se sentía bien.
3. —Es una lástima que tú no _____ a la clase de química hoy.
   —Dudo que _____ muy interesante.
4. —Uds. siempre dicen que la biología y la sociología son muy fáciles.
   —No es verdad que nosotros _____ eso.
5. —Me alegro mucho de que ustedes _____ hablar con su consejero.
   —Yo también, porque nos ayudó mucho.
6. —Mis padres están muy contentos de que yo _____ de España.
   —Sí, ellos te extrañaban mucho.

B. Express your own feelings and those of others according to the given cues. Use the present perfect subjunctive in your answers.

1. Yo espero que el profesor...
2. Ojalá que mis padres...
3. Es una lástima que mis compañeros de clase...
4. Mis padres no creen que yo...
5. No es verdad que mi amigo...
6. Me alegro mucho de que Ud....

► *2.* The imperfect subjunctive *(El imperfecto de sub-juntivo)*

♦ Spanish has two forms for the imperfect subjunctive: the **-ra** form and the **-se** form. Both forms may be used interchangeably in almost every case, but the **-ra** ending is more commonly used.

To form the imperfect subjunctive of all regular and irregular verbs, the **-ron** ending of the third-person plural preterit is dropped and the following endings are added to the stem.

IMPERFECT SUBJUNCTIVE ENDINGS

-ra *form*		-se *form*	
-ra	-ramos	-se	-semos
-ras	-rais	-ses	-seis
-ra	-ran	-se	-sen

Verb	Third-Person Plural Preterit	Stem	First-Person Singular Imperfect Subjunctive	
			(-ra form)	(-se form)
hablar	hablaron	habla-	**hablara**	**hablase**
aprender	aprendieron	aprendie-	**aprendiera**	**aprendiese**
vivir	vivieron	vivie-	**viviera**	**viviese**
dejar	dejaron	deja-	**dejara**	**dejase**
ir	fueron	fue-	**fuera**	**fuese**
saber	supieron	supie-	**supiera**	**supiese**
decir	dijeron	dije-	**dijera**	**dijese**
poner	pusieron	pusie-	**pusiera**	**pusiese**
pedir	pidieron	pidie-	**pidiera**	**pidiese**
estar	estuvieron	estuvie-	**estuviera**	**estuviese**

ATENCIÓN

Make sure you have mastered the forms of the preterit tense. If you need to review them, you will find them in **Lecciones 7, 8,** and **9.**

PRÁCTICA

Supply the imperfect subjunctive of the following verbs.

1. *yo:* aprobar, volver, pedir, decir, mantener
2. *tú:* matricularse, ser, dormir, querer, dar
3. *él:* ir, estar, poner, conducir, servir
4. *nosotros:* saber, poder, regresar, conseguir, hacer
5. *ellos:* tener, pescar, comenzar, seguir, mentir

▶ *3.* **Uses of the imperfect subjunctive** *(Usos del imperfecto de subjuntivo)*

◆ The imperfect subjunctive is used in a subordinate clause when the verb of the main clause is in the past and calls for the subjunctive.

—¿Qué te dijo el médico?	*What did the doctor tell you?*
—Me dijo que **hiciera** ejercicio.	*He told me to exercise.*
—Yo esperaba que el profesor me **diera** una buena nota.	*I was hoping that the teacher would give me a good grade.*
—Bueno... te dio una «B».	*Well . . . he gave you a "B."*

◆ When the verb of the main clause is in the present, but the subordinate clause refers to the past, the imperfect subjunctive is used.

—**Es** una lástima que no **fueras** al partido ayer.	*It's a pity that you didn't go to the game yesterday.*
—No me sentía bien.	*I wasn't feeling well.*

PRÁCTICA

A. When Adriana went away to college, her parents gave her many suggestions about what she should and shouldn't do once she got there. Change all the verbs on both lists to the imperfect subjunctive in order to express her parents' wishes.

Los padres de Adriana querían que ella...

1. *escribirles* todas las semanas
2. *llamarlos* por teléfono los domingos
3. *tomar* varios requisitos el primer semestre
4. *mantener* un buen promedio
5. *abrir* una cuenta corriente en el banco
6. *hacer* ejercicios todos los días
7. *levantarse* temprano
8. *aprobar* todos los exámenes

Los padres de Adriana no querían que ella...

1. *vivir* lejos de la universidad
2. *ir* a muchas fiestas
3. *comer* hamburguesas todos los días
4. *pedirles* dinero extra todos los meses
5. *conducir* muy rápido
6. *olvidarse* de escribirles a sus abuelos
7. *acostarse* muy tarde

B. Combine the items in columns A, B, and C to form sentences using the imperfect subjunctive. Several combinations are possible. Compare your sentences with those of a classmate.

A	B	C
Los estudiantes esperaban	Elsa	venir a verlo
Mi papá quería	tú	poder hacerlo
El consejero le dijo a	Juan	vender el coche viejo
Luis se alegró de	yo	tomar física
Siento	usted	no conseguir la beca
El mecánico quería	una secretaria	ser abogado
Fue una lástima	nosotros	estar enfermo ayer
Buscábamos	el profesor	romperse el tobillo
No había	sus amigos	tener tiempo
Mamá dudaba	Uds.	saber francés
Yo no creía	ellos	darles buenas notas
Ellos temían	nadie	comer tanto

▶ *4.* The pluperfect subjunctive *(El pluscuamperfecto de subjuntivo)*

♦ The pluperfect subjunctive is formed by combining the imperfect subjunctive of the auxiliary verb **haber** with the past participle of the main verb. It is used in much the same way as the past perfect is used in English, but in sentences in which the main clause calls for the subjunctive.

THE PLUPERFECT SUBJUNCTIVE

	Imperfect Subjunctive of haber	+	*Past Participle of the Main Verb*
yo	hubiera		hablado
tú	hubieras		comido
él (ella)	hubiera		vivido
nosotros(-as)	hubiéramos		visto
vosotros(-as)	hubierais		hecho
ellos (ellas)	hubieran		vuelto

—¿No había nadie que   *Wasn't there anybody who*
  hubiera visto esa película?   *had seen that movie?*
—Sí, Eva la había visto ya.   *Yes, Eva had already seen it.*

PRÁCTICA

A. Say what your mother had expected you to do by the time she got home yesterday.

MODELO: Aída / *planchar* la ropa
         *Mamá esperaba que Aída **hubiera planchado** la ropa.*

Mamá esperaba que...

1. yo / hacer la comida
2. Quique / lavar el coche
3. nosotros / llevar a Raulito a la escuela
4. tú / escribirle a tío Carlos
5. ustedes / devolver los libros a la biblioteca
6. Eva y Luis / traer el postre
7. Irma / poner la mesa
8. Eva y yo / pasarle la aspiradora a la alfombra

B. Say that the following things which occurred last week are not true.

MODELO: Carlos / *venir* muy tarde
         *No era verdad que Carlos **hubiera venido** tarde.*

No era verdad que...

1. Pepe / sacar una «F» en literatura
2. mis amigos / darme malos consejos
3. nosotros / perder el partido de fútbol
4. yo / llegar tarde a casa
5. tú / solicitar ese empleo
6. ustedes / dejar todas las puertas abiertas
7. la niña / decir una mala palabra
8. tú y yo / no hacer la tarea

ESCUELAS

¡A ver cuánto aprendió!

A. ¡Conversemos!

Reread the dialogue in this lesson and be ready to discuss the following.

1. ¿De dónde son Alina y Daniel?
2. ¿Qué clase están tomando juntos?
3. ¿Cree Ud. que la doctora Parker es una buena profesora? ¿Por qué?
4. Daniel no tomó la clase que su consejero le sugirió que tomara. ¿Por qué?
5. ¿Cuál es la profesión del padre de Daniel?
6. ¿Cree Ud. que a Alina le gustan las ciencias?
7. ¿Cuál de los dos jóvenes podría trabajar para el *New York Times*? ¿Por qué?
8. ¿Cómo sabemos que Daniel no está tomando una clase de danza aeróbica?
9. ¿Por qué no puede ir Alina al partido de fútbol?
10. ¿Cuál de los dos jóvenes está preocupado por mantener un buen promedio? ¿Por qué?
11. ¿De qué se había olvidado Daniel?
12. ¿Daniel tiene una calculadora? ¿Cómo lo sabe?
13. ¿Cree Ud. que la clase de biología es difícil para David? ¿Cómo lo sabe Ud.?
14. ¿Qué le desea Alina a Daniel?

B. ¡Repase el vocabulario!

Complete the following sentences using words and phrases from this lesson. Read the sentences aloud.

1. Los jóvenes son _____ ; son de Buenos Aires.
2. Estoy tomando una clase de administración de _____ .
3. La química es la _____ que menos me gusta.
4. Quiere ser abogado. Estudia en la Facultad de _____ .
5. ¿Tienes un examen parcial? ¡Buena _____ !
6. En nuestra clase de sicología, tenemos unas _____ muy interesantes.
7. No me _____ nada este horario porque tengo que venir muy temprano.
8. —¿Vas a la fiesta?
   —¡Qué _____ ! Tengo que estudiar.

9. Hoy es viernes y yo _____ no he entregado la tarea.
10. Es _____ , pero no es de La Habana.
11. Escribe para la revista *Time*. Es _____ .
12. Para ser ingeniero tienes que estudiar en la Facultad de
_____ .
13. _____ siempre, mi hijo me pidió dinero.
14. ¿Cuál es tu _____ ? ¿Matemáticas o contabilidad?
15. Son _____ . Pedro es de Chile y Ana de México.

C. Situaciones

What would you say in the following situations? What might the other person say?

1. A freshman asks you what classes are required. Tell him or her what some of the requirements are.
2. Tell someone which classes you like, which you don't like, and explain why.
3. One of your friends wants to lose weight. Give him or her some good advice.
4. Your friend wants you to go to a football game. Tell him or her you can't go, and explain why.

Para escribir

Write a composition about your college activities. Include the following.

- your major
- classes you are taking this semester
- classes you took last semester
- classes you like and classes you don't like
- some extracurricular activities

ENTREVISTA

Choose a partner, then interview each other using the **tú** form.

Pregúntele a su compañero(-a) de clase...

1. ...si conoce a algún estudiante latinoamericano. (¿De qué país?)
2. ...cuál es la materia que más le gusta.
3. ...dónde vivía cuando asistía a la escuela primaria (secundaria).
4. ...si ha tomado todos los requisitos generales.
5. ...qué querían sus padres que estudiara.
6. ...si le gustaría tomar una clase de danza aeróbica.
7. ...cuándo tiene exámenes parciales (finales).
8. ...qué clases piensa tomar el próximo trimestre (semestre).
9. ...si puede prestarle un diccionario de español.
10. ...qué nota espera sacar en esta clase.

HORARIO DE CLASES

With a classmate, use the course listing below to plan your schedules for next semester (quarter). You should include your work schedule, time spent exercising, studying, and other activities. In your discussion you should also give reasons why you are taking the classes you choose.

LISTA DE MATERIAS

Administración de empresas	Ciencias Políticas	Historia
Alemán	Contabilidad	Humanidades
Álgebra	Drama	Inglés
Antropología	Educación Física	Literatura
Arte	Electrónica	Matemáticas
Astronomía	Español	Música
Biología	Estadística	Química
Cálculo	Física	Relaciones Públicas
Cibernética *(Computer Science)*	Francés	Ruso
Ciencias Económicas	Geología	Sociología
	Geometría	Telecomunicaciones

AHORA UD. ES PROFESOR(-A)

Choose one of the ads shown below and imagine that you are an instructor for one of the schools. Study the ad carefully, noting all of the features that are described. Then try to convince a classmate why he or she should take a course there. You should allow your classmate an opportunity to ask questions after you have spoken.

UNA ACTIVIDAD ESPECIAL

Work with several classmates to conduct a survey about one of your professors. As a group, try to arrive at a consensus about each question in the questionnaire below. After you have completed all the questions, briefly discuss the results among yourselves and other members of the class.

	Malo	*Regular*	*Bueno*	*Muy bueno*
	1	2 3	4 5	6 7
1. ¿Está siempre bien preparado el profesor?	1	2 3	4 5	6 7
2. ¿Es entusiasta?	1	2 3	4 5	6 7
3. ¿Presenta la materia de una manera eficiente?	1	2 3	4 5	6 7
4. ¿Muestra interés por los estudiantes?	1	2 3	4 5	6 7
5. ¿Trata a los estudiantes con respeto?	1	2 3	4 5	6 7
6. ¿Estimula a los estudiantes a participar en la clase?	1	2 3	4 5	6 7
7. ¿Permite preguntas y discusión en clase?	1	2 3	4 5	6 7
8. ¿Está usted aprendiendo y progresando en esta clase?	1	2 3	4 5	6 7
9. ¿Cómo evalúa usted este curso en su totalidad?	1	2 3	4 5	6 7
10. ¿Cuál es su opinión general sobre el profesor?	1	2 3	4 5	6 7

La estación de trenes de Chamartín, en Madrid, España.

OBJECTIVES

Structure   *If* clauses • Sequence of tenses with the subjunctive • Summary of the uses of the subjunctive • Letter writing

Communication   You will learn vocabulary related to traveling by train and renting a car. You will also learn how to write personal and business letters in Spanish.

10

De viaje a Sevilla

Alicia y Rosa han decidido viajar por el sur de España. Ahora están en el despacho de billetes en la estación de trenes de Barcelona. En la ventanilla número dos:

ALICIA —Por favor, señor, ¿me podría decir cuándo hay trenes para Sevilla?

EMPLEADO —Hay dos trenes diarios: uno por la mañana y otro por la noche. El tren de la noche es el expreso.[1]

ALICIA —*(A Rosa)* Si quieres, sacamos pasajes para el expreso.

ROSA —Bueno, pero entonces es mejor que reservemos literas.

ALICIA —*(Al empleado)* ¿Tiene coche-cama el tren?

EMPLEADO —Sí, señorita. Tiene coche-cama y coche-comedor.

ROSA —Queremos dos literas, una alta y una baja.

EMPLEADO —Dudo que haya literas bajas. En verano viaja mucha gente.

ALICIA —¡Caramba! Si lo hubiéramos sabido, habríamos hecho la reserva antes.

EMPLEADO —¿Quieren billetes sólo de ida o de ida y vuelta? El pasaje de ida y vuelta tiene una tarifa especial. Damos el veinte por ciento de descuento.

ROSA —¿Por cuánto tiempo es válido el billete de ida y vuelta?

EMPLEADO —Por seis meses, señorita.

ROSA —Bueno, deme dos pasajes de ida y vuelta para el sábado. ¿Puede darme un itinerario?

EMPLEADO —Sí, un momento. Aquí tiene los billetes y el cambio.

ALICIA —*(A Rosa)* Espero que no tengamos que trasbordar.

El día del viaje, Alicia y Rosa llegan a la estación y van al andén número cuatro, de donde sale el tren. Después de un largo viaje, llegan a Sevilla y deciden alquilar un coche.

ROSA —*(Al empleado de la agencia)* Queremos alquilar un coche compacto de dos puertas. ¿Cobran Uds. por kilómetro?

EMPLEADO —Depende. Si lo alquila por día, sí; si lo alquila por semana, no.

ROSA —Necesitamos el coche por una semana. Queremos uno de cambios mecánicos.

EMPLEADO —Dudo que tengamos coches de cambios mecánicos. Ahora sólo tenemos automáticos.

---

[1] In some Spanish-speaking countries, **rápido** is used for **expreso.**

TRAVELING TO SEVILLE

Alicia and Rosa have decided to travel through southern Spain. They are now at the ticket office of the train station in Barcelona. At window number 2:

A. Please sir, could you tell me when are there trains to Seville?

E. There are two daily trains: one in the morning and the other in the evening. The evening train is the express.

A. *(To Rosa)* If you want, we can buy tickets for the express train.

R. Fine, but then it's better that we reserve berths.

A. *(To the clerk)* Does the train have a sleeper?

E. Yes, Miss. It has a sleeper and a dining car.

R. We would like two berths, an upper (berth) and a lower (berth).

E. I doubt that there are lower berths. During the summer many people travel.

A. Gee! If we had known we would have made the reservation before.

E. Do you want only one-way or round-trip tickets? The round-trip ticket has a special rate. We give a 20 percent discount.

R. For how long is the round-trip ticket valid?

E. For six months, Miss.

R. Fine, give me two round-trip tickets for Saturday. Can you give me a timetable?

E. Yes, one moment. Here are the tickets and the change.

A. *(To Rosa)* I hope that we don't have to transfer.

On the day of the trip, Alicia and Rosa arrive at the station,

ROSA —Es una lástima que no tengan coches mecánicos. Gastan menos gasolina.

ALICIA —*(Al empleado)* Queremos sacar seguro. Siempre es mejor estar asegurado.

EMPLEADO —Muy bien. Llene esta planilla.

ROSA —Nosotras somos ciudadanas chilenas. ¿Necesitamos un permiso especial para manejar en España?

EMPLEADO —No, no es necesario.

ROSA —*(A Alicia)* Vamos a comer algo. Estoy muerta de hambre.

ALICIA —¿Otra vez? ¡Hablas como si no hubieras desayunado!

ROSA —Bueno, entonces esperaré hasta que sirvan el almuerzo en el hotel.

Después de unos días en Sevilla, Rosa les manda a sus padres una tarjeta postal.

Sevilla 5/7/90

Queridos padres:

Sevilla es una ciudad encantadora. Ojalá estuvieran Uds. con nosotras. Si pudiera, me quedaría a vivir aquí. Mañana salimos para el norte donde visitaremos Galicia y Asturias. Los extraño mucho.
Un abrazo,

Rosa

Sr. Javier Villas

C/ San Martín 489

Santiago

Chile

Vocabulario

COGNADOS

automático(-a) automatic
compacto(-a) compact
especial special

Sevilla Seville
válido(-a) valid

NOMBRES

el **abrazo** hug, embrace
el **andén** platform
el **billete**, el **boleto**, el **pasaje** ticket

el **cambio**, el **vuelto** change
el (la) **ciudadano(-a)** citizen
el **coche**, el **vagón** car, coach
el **coche-cama** sleeping car, sleeper (Pullman)

and go to platform number four, from which the train leaves. After a long trip, they arrive in Seville and decide to rent a car.

R. *(To the agency employee)* We would like to rent a two-door, compact car. Do you charge per kilometer?

E. It depends. If you rent it by the day, we do; if you rent it by the week, we don't.

R. We need the car for a week. We would like one with a standard shift.

E. I doubt that we have cars with standard shift. Now we only have automatics.

R. It's a pity that they don't have standard shift cars. They use less gasoline.

A. *(To the employee)* We would like to take out insurance. It's always better to be insured.

E. Very well. Fill out this form.

R. We are Chilean citizens. Do we need a special permit to drive in Spain?

E. No, it's not necessary.

R. *(To Alicia)* Let's go have something to eat. I'm starving.

A. Again? You talk as if you hadn't had any breakfast!

R. Well, then I'll wait until they serve lunch in the hotel.

After a few days in Seville, Rosa sends her parents a postcard.

Seville 5/7/90
Dear parents:
Seville is a charming city. I wish you were here with us. If I could, I would stay here to live. Tomorrow we leave for the North where we will visit Galicia and Asturias. I miss you a great deal.
A hug, *Rosa*

el **coche-comedor**   dining car
el **descuento**   discount
el **despacho de billetes**   ticket office
el **itinerario**, el **horario**   schedule, timetable
la **litera**   berth
la **litera alta**   upper berth
la **litera baja**   lower berth
el **norte**   north, the North
el **permiso**   permit
la **planilla**   form
el **rápido**, el **expreso**   express (train)
el **seguro**   insurance
el **sur**   south, the South
la **tarifa**   rate

VERBOS

depender (**de**)   to depend (on)
desayunar   to have breakfast

gastar   to use; to spend
reservar   to reserve
trasbordar   to transfer

ADJETIVOS

asegurado(-a)   insured
diario(-a)   daily
encantador(a)   charming

OTRAS PALABRAS Y EXPRESIONES

de cambios mecánicos   (with) a standard shift
de dos puertas   two-door
por ciento   percent
¿Por cuánto tiempo es válido...?   For how long is it valid . . . ?
sacar pasajes   to buy (get) tickets

Vocabulario adicional

a tiempo   on time
El tren no va a llegar **a tiempo**; tiene dos horas de atraso.

bajarse   to get off
Si quieres **bajarte** del tren, tenemos veinte minutos.

el **este**   east, the East
Boston está en el **este** de los Estados Unidos.

la **frontera**   border
¿Cuándo llegamos a la **frontera** de México?

hacer escala   to make a stopover
Voy a Buenos Aires pero quiero **hacer escala** en Lima.

llegadas y salidas   arrivals and departures
Pregunte la hora de **llegada y salida** del tren.

el **oeste**   west, the West
Phoenix está al **oeste** de Dallas.

la **sala de equipajes**   baggage room
Sus maletas están en la **sala de equipajes**, señora.

subirse   to get on
Ellos **se subieron** al avión en Las Vegas, no en Los Ángeles.

¿Lo sabía Ud.... ?

■ Sevilla es una de las cinco provincias que forman parte de Andalucía, la región situada en el sur de España. Sevilla fue la capital de la España Mora *(Moorish)*, y hoy es un centro de atracción turística. Entre los lugares de interés están la Catedral, que es uno de los templos más grandes del mundo cristiano; la Giralda, que es la torre *(tower)* de una antigua mezquita *(mosque)* del siglo *(century)* XII y la Torre del Oro.

　　Sevilla es famosa también por sus hermosos patios, sus plazas y sus casas pintadas de blanco con balcones llenos de flores. Por eso dicen los españoles: «Quien no ha visto Sevilla no ha visto maravilla».

■ España tiene hoy día un excelente sistema de transportación. Tiene aeropuertos grandes y muy modernos y una aerolínea, Iberia, que vuela a todas las ciudades españolas y comunica a España con el extranjero. Tiene también un servicio muy bueno de autobuses y trenes. El Talgo y el Ter están entre los trenes más cómodos y rápidos de Europa.

La famosa Torre del Oro a orillas del río Guadalquivir, en Sevilla, España.

Estructuras gramaticales

▶ *1. If* clauses　　*(Cláusulas que comienzan con **si**)*

◆ In Spanish, as in English, the imperfect subjunctive is used in *if* clauses when a contrary-to-fact statement is made.

—Si **tuviera** dinero, sacaría los pasajes hoy.   *If I had money, I would get the tickets today.*
—Usa tu tarjeta de crédito.   *Use your credit card.*

◆ Note that the imperfect subjunctive is used in the *if* clause and the conditional is used in the main clause. When a statement expresses a contrary-to-fact situation in the past, the pluperfect subjunctive is used in the *if* clause and the verb in the main clause is in the conditional perfect.

—No pude dormir bien en el tren.	*I couldn't sleep well on the train.*
—Si **hubieras reservado** una litera, **habrías dormido** bien.	*If you had reserved a berth, you would have slept well.*

◆ The imperfect subjunctive is also used in *if* clauses that express an unlikely fact, or simply the Spanish equivalent of the English *if . . . were to . . .*

—Si Raúl me **invitara** a salir con él, aceptaría.	*If Raul were to ask me to go out with him, I would accept.*
—No creo que te invite...	*I don't think he'll ask you . . .*

◆ The imperfect subjunctive is also used after the expression **como si** *(as if)*.

—Pepe se compró otro coche.	*Pepe bought himself another car.*
—Ese hombre gasta dinero como si **fuera** millonario.	*That man spends money as if he were a millionaire.*

◆ In no other situation is the imperfect subjunctive used after *if,* not even when *if* means *whether.*

—¿Me vas a comprar los zapatos?	*Are you going to buy me the shoes?*
—Si **tengo** dinero, te los compro.	*If I have money, I'll buy them for you.*

ATENCIÓN

Note that the present subjunctive is *never* used in an *if* clause.

PRÁCTICA

A. At the train station in Madrid, you overhear these dialogues. Provide the missing verbs using the present indicative, the imperfect subjunctive, or the pluperfect subjunctive.

1. —Si tú _____ (sacar) pasajes para el expreso, habríamos llegado a tiempo a Sevilla.
   —Si tú _____ (querer), podemos comer algo mientras esperamos el otro tren.

2. —Si el tren _____ (parar) en Ávila, podríamos
   quedarnos allí por un día.
   —Sería mejor si _____ (poder) quedarnos por dos
   o tres días.

3. —Si yo _____ (tener) dinero, le compraría un regalo a Teresa.
   —Yo puedo prestártelo. Puedes ir a comprarlo si la tienda
   _____ (estar) abierta.

4. —¿Por qué no alquilaron Uds. un coche?
   —Habríamos alquilado uno si ellos _____ (tener)
   coches automáticos de dos puertas.

5. —¿Viste el vestido de Susana? ¡Le costó un ojo de la cara!
   —Esa mujer gasta dinero como si _____ (ser)
   millonaria.
   —Si yo _____ (ser) ella lo gastaría en viajar, no en
   ropa.

6. —Si nosotros _____ (pedir) un itinerario,
   habríamos sabido las horas de salidas y llegadas del tren.
   —Si tú _____ (llamar) por teléfono a la estación,
   no habríamos tenido que esperar tanto.

7. —Si Uds. _____ (ver) a Marta, denle un abrazo.
   —Si tú _____ (quedarse) en Madrid, podrías
   dárselo tú.

8. —Si Juan _____ (saber) francés, le daría el empleo.
   —Si él _____ (necesitar) un empleo, yo puedo darle
   trabajo.

B. Be an interpreter. What are these people saying?

1. If we had reserved a room, we wouldn't have any problems
   now.
   If my aunt is home, we can go to her house.

2. If you buy a car with a standard shift, you will spend less
   money on gasoline.
   I don't like them.

3. If it weren't so cold in Ohio, I would live there.
   If you were to move to Ohio, I would never visit you in the
   winter.

4. He always talks as if he knew it all!
   If he comes to see us, let's not open the door.

▶ *2.* Sequence of tenses with the subjunctive   *(La se-cuencia de los tiempos con el subjuntivo)*

♦ In multiple clause sentences, the tense of the verb used in the subordinate clause depends on the tense used in the main clause.

Main clause– Indicative	Subordinate clause– Subjunctive
present future present perfect	present subjunctive present perfect subjunctive
command	present subjunctive

♦ If the verb of the main clause is in the present, future, or present perfect, the verb of the subordinate clause must be in the present subjunctive or present perfect subjunctive. If the verb of the main clause is a command, the present subjunctive is used in the subordinate clause.

Yo le **digo** que **venga**.	*I tell her to come.*
Yo le **diré** que **venga**.	*I will tell her to come.*
Yo le **he dicho** que **venga**.	*I have told her to come.*
Me alegro de que **haya venido**.	*I'm glad she has come.*
Dile que **venga**.	*Tell her to come.*

Main clause– Indicative	Subordinate clause– Subjunctive
preterit imperfect conditional	imperfect subjunctive pluperfect subjunctive

♦ If the verb of the main clause is in the preterit, imperfect, or conditional, the verb of the subordinate clause must be in the imperfect subjunctive or the pluperfect subjunctive.

Le **dije** que **viniera**.	*I told her to come.*
Le **decía** que **viniera**.	*I was telling her to come.*
Le **diría** que **viniera**.	*I would tell her to come.*
Me alegré de que Rosa **hubiera venido**.	*I was glad that Rosa had come.*

Main clause– Indicative	Subordinate clause– Subjunctive
present	imperfect subjunctive

♦ The imperfect subjunctive is used in a subordinate clause when the verb in the main clause is in the present indicative, if the action referred to describes a past action.

Me alegro de que **vinieran** anoche.	*I'm glad that they came last night.*
Es lástima que tú no **arreglaras** el fregadero ayer.	*It's a pity that you didn't fix the sink yesterday.*

PRÁCTICA

A. What expectations do these people have or have they had of you? Complete the statements.

1. Cuando yo era chico(-a), mi mamá siempre quería que yo...
2. Mi papá siempre me dice que...
3. Mis amigos me han pedido que...
4. Mi profesor querrá que yo...
5. Ayer un amigo me sugirió que...
6. A mi hermana le gustaría que yo...
7. Papá dice que es una lástima que ayer yo...
8. Mis padres me habrían dado más dinero si yo...

B. Be an interpreter. What are these people saying?

1. What do you want me to tell her?
   Tell her to give you the change.
2. I'm glad they have come to see me.
   Yes, but it's a pity they didn't bring their son.
3. We were sorry that they had moved to the South.
   We (were) too, because we used to visit them every week.

▶ 3. Summary of the uses of the subjunctive
(Resumen de los usos del subjuntivo)

EL SUBJUNTIVO: RESUMEN GENERAL

♦ Use the subjunctive . . .

a. After verbs of volition (when there is change of subject):

Yo quiero que él **salga.**

b. After verbs of emotion (when there is change of subject):

Me alegro de que tú **estés** aquí.

c. After impersonal expressions (when there is a subject):

Es necesario que él **estudie.**

♦ Use the subjunctive . . .

a. To refer to something indefinite or non-existent:

Busco una casa que **sea** cómoda.
No hay nadie que lo **sepa.**

b. If the action is to occur at some indefinite time in the future as a condition of another action:

Cenarán cuando él **llegue.**

c. To express doubt and denial:

Dudo que **pueda** venir.
Niego que él **esté** aquí.

d. In an *if*-clause, to refer to something contrary-to-fact or to something impossible or very improbable:

Si **pudiera,** iría.
Si el presidente me **invitara** a la Casa Blanca, yo aceptaría.

♦ Use the infinitive . . .

a. After verbs of volition (when there is no change of subject):

Yo quiero **salir.**

b. After verbs of emotion (when there is no change of subject):

Me alegro de **estar** aquí.

c. After impersonal expressions (when speaking in general):

Es necesario **estudiar.**

♦ Use the indicative . . .

a. To refer to something specific:

Tengo una casa que **es** cómoda.
Hay alguien que lo **sabe.**

b. If the action has been completed or is habitual:

Cenaron cuando él **llegó.**
Siempre cenan cuando él **llega.**

c. When there is no doubt or denial:

No dudo que **puede** venir.
No niego que él **está** aquí.

d. In an *if*-clause, when not referring to anything that is contrary-to-fact, impossible, or very improbable:

Si **puedo,** iré.
Si Juan me **invita** a su casa, aceptaré.

PRÁCTICA

Read the following, and choose the correct forms.

1. Es necesario que Uds. (sacar, saquen) seguro.
2. Mamá quería que ellos le (dar, dieran) un descuento.
3. Dudo que ella (quiera, quiere) vivir en el oeste.
4. Hay muchas personas que (tienen, tengan) que bajarse en esa estación.
5. Espero que el tren (tiene, tenga) coche-cama y coche-comedor.
6. Aunque mañana (llueva, llueve), iremos a la playa.
7. Aquí no hay nadie que (es, sea) ciudadano argentino.
8. Estoy segura de que el tren (salga, sale) del andén número cuatro.
9. Yo no quiero (trasborde, trasbordar).
10. Cuando (viene, venga) Roberto, pregúntale por cuánto tiempo es válido el boleto.
11. No es verdad que ellos (viven, vivan) en la frontera.
12. Si tú (estás, estés) asegurado, no tienes que pagar la cuenta.
13. Busco una secretaria que (hable, habla) alemán.
14. Es necesario (estudie, estudiar) mucho para sacar una «A».
15. Si yo (tuve, tuviera) dinero, compraría un coche compacto.

► *4.* Letter writing

Richard Smith
809 Fairview St.
Columbus, Ohio 67212
U.S.A

19 de mayo de 1990

Señor Director
Programa para Estudiantes Extranjeros
Instituto Caro y Cuervo
Apartado Postal 6411
Bogotá, Colombia

Distinguido señor:

I am writing to you / with the purpose of / following matter
At present

Me dirijo a Ud.° con el fin de° solicitar su amable cooperación respecto al siguiente asunto.° Actualmente° estudio lengua y literatura españolas en la Universidad de California en Santa Bárbara, pero tengo interés en poder estudiar, por lo menos durante un semestre, en una universidad hispanoamericana.

I would be very grateful (to you) / as soon as possible

Mucho le agradecería° si pudiera Ud. enviarme a la mayor brevedad posible° la descripción del nuevo programa de estudios para estudiantes extranjeros que ha establecido su Instituto. Le pido, además, que me mande informes sobre el procedimiento° de

procedure

admisión (ingreso) y sobre cualquier otro detalle que Ud. considere pertinente al caso.

Awaiting your reply,

En espera de sus noticias,° se despide cordialmente,[1]

Richard Smith

---

[1] Lit., *Richard Smith cordially says good-bye*. Spanish business letters are generally more formal than English ones.

- Date line
  Caracas, 5 de febrero de 1990

- Address

  ◇ *to a person:*
  Sr. Ernesto Montoya
  Avenida 19 de Mayo 756
  La Habana, Cuba

  ◇ *a business letter to a company:*
  Sres. Juárez Menéndez y Cía.,[1] S.A.[2]
  Apdo. Postal[3] 148
  Santiago, Chile

- Salutations

  ◇ *business letters:*
  Muy señor(a) mío(-a): (from one person to another)
  Muy señores(-as) míos(-as): (from one person to more than one person)
  Distinguido(-a) señor (señora, señorita):

  ◇ *familiar:*
  Querido Luis, (to a close friend or relative)
  Estimado Raúl, (informal)
  Queridísimo(-a), *(Dearest,)*

- Conclusions

  ◇ *social and business letters:*
  Sinceramente, *(Sincerely,)*
  Atentamente, (lit., *"Politely,"*)

  ◇ *to family and friends:*
  Abrazos de,
  Con todo cariño, *(Love,)*
  Besos, *(Kisses,)*
  Afectuosamente, *(Affectionately,)*
  Cariñosos saludos de, *(Affectionate greetings from,)*

---

[1] **Cía.** = **Compañía**   [2] **S.A.** = **Sociedad Anónima** (equivalent to the English *Inc.* or *Incorporated*)
[3] **Apartado Postal:** *Post Office Box*

PRÁCTICA

Write a letter to the personnel director of a company or an institution, applying for a position in your field. Provide all pertinent information about yourself. You may include the following.

- education
- work experience
- foreign language(s) you speak
- whether you are applying for a part-time or a full-time job
- salary requirements
- any other information you think may help you obtain the job

¡A ver cuánto aprendió!

A. ¡Conversemos!

Reread the dialogues in this lesson and be ready to talk about the following.

1. ¿Qué están haciendo Alicia y Rosa en el despacho de billetes?
2. ¿Dónde van a dormir las chicas?
3. ¿Qué descuento dan en los billetes de ida y vuelta?
4. ¿Por cuánto tiempo es válido el billete de ida y vuelta?
5. ¿Qué quiere Rosa que le dé el empleado?
6. ¿Qué tipo de coche quieren alquilar?
7. ¿Cobran por kilómetro?
8. Rosa dice que es una lástima que no tengan coches de cambios mecánicos. ¿Por qué?
9. ¿Es verdad que las chicas necesitan un permiso especial para manejar en España?
10. ¿Qué quiere hacer Rosa?

B. ¡Repase el vocabulario!

Choose the correct response to each of the following questions or statements.

1. —Perdón, ¿tienen Uds. tarifas especiales?
   —Sí, (si las pide prestadas / a veces ganamos más interés / le damos el 20 por ciento de descuento / acaban de poner otro vagón).
2. —Vamos a comprar los boletos.
   —Espero que (no estén sentados en el andén / no tengan esa enfermedad / no tengamos que hacer cola / me sirvan la especialidad de la casa).

3. —¿En qué puedo servirle?

—Señor, (aquí servimos langosta y lechón / quiero llevarlo puesto / quiero alquilar un coche automático, de dos puertas / aquí sirven platos muy sabrosos).

4. —¿Qué hay de nuevo?

—Pues... (mañana me voy para el sur de España / están abajo / creo que sí / allí están las llegadas y salidas de los aviones).

5. —Yo no quiero dormir en el asiento del tren.

—Pues entonces (vamos a la liquidación / montemos a caballo / compremos cañas de pescar / reservemos literas).

6. —Tengo mucho dolor de cabeza.

—Tendrás que (pasar la frontera / tomar aspirinas / comprar el jamón / lavar los platos).

7. —El tren no va a llegar a tiempo.

—Ojalá que no (tenga seguro / tenga mucho atraso / venga en octubre / traiga el equipaje).

8. —Este tren no llega hasta mañana.

—Siento que (no tengas tarjetas de crédito / no podamos cazar / no podamos ir en el rápido / no haya nieve).

9. —¿Pagaste la cuenta?

—Sí, pero no me dieron (la talla / la niebla / los rizos ni los rizadores / el vuelto).

10. —Si no viajamos hoy podemos viajar mañana.

—Es difícil que (haga viento mañana / haya trenes diarios para Lima / el silenciador haga ruido / sea una calle de dos vías).

11. —¿Conviene tomar el expreso?

—Sí, porque (es riquísimo / no es ciudadano / tiene una cuenta de ahorros / es mucho más rápido).

12. —¿Lleva el tren coche-cama?

—Sí, y también (probadores / paraguas muy elegantes / coche-comedor / libretas de ahorro).

13. —¿Tengo que trasbordar?

—Sí, (si calza el número diez / en la próxima estación / si le aprietan los zapatos / si grita).

14. —¿Quiere un coche de cambios mecánicos?

—No, uno (lleno / vacío / automático / sin llantas).

15. —¿Por qué no manejas mi coche?

—No puedo. No tengo (cuello / luz / hambre / licencia para conducir).

C. Situaciones

What would you say in the following situations? What might the other person say?

1. You are at a train station in Madrid. Ask the clerk when there are trains for Barcelona. Also ask him if the train has a sleeper and a dining car. Tell him you want a lower berth.
2. You are buying tickets to travel by train. Ask the clerk if they give a special rate or a discount when you buy a round-trip ticket. Also ask her for how long the ticket is valid and if you have to transfer. Finally, ask her to give you a timetable.
3. You are traveling with a friend. Tell him or her that you will probably have to wait because the train is two hours behind schedule. Suggest that you both go have something to eat.
4. You are at the car rental agency. Tell the clerk you want to rent a car. Tell him you want a four-door compact model. Also tell him that you hope they have automatics, because you don't like standard shifts.

Para escribir

1. Write a composition describing a memorable trip you took. Include the following information.

   - means of transportation
   - place(s) you visited
   - things and people you saw
   - places of interest
   - where you stayed
   - things that happened
   - duration of the trip
   - whether or not you're planning to take the same trip again

2. Now that you know how to write letters in Spanish, write a letter to a friend who has moved away, giving him or her the latest news about you and your family. You may include the following.

   - news about school and work
   - any projects in which you are involved
   - plans for your vacation
   - parties you have attended and traveling you have done
   - news about your family
   - any health problem you may have had
   - any specific question(s) you may wish to ask your friend about what's happening in his or her life

En la vida real

ENTREVISTA

Choose a partner, then interview each other using the **tú** form.

Pregúntele a su compañero(-a) de clase...

1. ...si vive en el norte, sur, este u oeste de los Estados Unidos.
2. ...si es ciudadano(-a) de los Estados Unidos.
3. ...si tiene asegurado su coche.
4. ...si las clases de español son diarias.
5. ...si tiene un coche grande o un modelo compacto.
6. ...si su coche es automático o de cambios mecánicos.
7. ...si es necesario viajar en coche-cama cuando se viaja de Nueva York a Boston.
8. ...si los pasajes de ida y vuelta tienen tarifas especiales.
9. ...si es posible que los pasajes para Puerto Rico sean gratis.
10. ...si está muerto(-a) de hambre.

UN VIAJE EN TREN

With a classmate, discuss travel plans for going somewhere by train. Decide where you are going, what accommodations you would like and can afford, and how long you will be traveling. When you reach your destination, you will be renting a car. Discuss what kind of car you want and why.

¡Pᴀsᴀᴊᴇʀᴏs, ᴀʟ ᴛʀᴇɴ!

Carefully read the following brochure about services provided by RENFE, the Spanish Rail Company which provides train service throughout Spain. Then answer the questions that follow.

Tᴀʀᴊᴇᴛᴀ Rᴇɴғᴇ

Cᴏɴ KILOMETROS DE VENTAJAS

Sea cual sea la clase y la frecuencia con que usted viaja, la Tarjeta Renfe le ofrece interesantes ventajas.

Todos los titulares de la tarjeta disfrutan de servicios extraordinarios: seguro de viaje por 25 millones de pesetas, recepción de la revista "Cliente Renfe", participación en promociones, sorteos de viajes en trenes turísticos, descuentos en las tiendas de las estaciones, parking gratuito y, además, cuanto más viaje, más ventajas obtendrá. Para usted, directamente, cheques de viaje.

Para su empresa u organización, importantes descuentos en las compras de billetes.

Vɪᴀᴊᴇ A NUESTRA CUENTA

Viaje sólo con su Tarjeta Renfe.

Cargue en ella sus billetes de tren y disfrute de otros muchos servicios de Renfe (parking, utilización salas "Rail Club", "Hotel de día"). Todo ello sin dinero. Sólo con su Tarjeta Renfe.

Eɴ COMODOS PLAZOS

Disfrute de su viaje con toda comodidad, y, si no le conviene pagar en el momento, hágalo más tarde.

La Tarjeta Renfe le da la posibilidad de aplazar hasta tres meses los pagos de su tarjeta. Sin apenas recargo. Ahora puede viajar cuando quiera. Y con su Tarjeta Renfe, pagar después.

Cᴏɴ LA MEJOR RESERVA

Cualquier hora es válida para decidir viajar, y cualquier hora es buena para reservar sus billetes con la tarjeta en puntos de venta Renfe y en Agencias de Viaje.

Utilice también la reserva telefónica de plazas, cargando el importe de sus billetes a su Tarjeta Renfe.

Decida usted el viaje. Su Tarjeta Renfe le ayudará a viajar.

1. ¿Qué tipo de tarjeta es la Tarjeta RENFE?
2. ¿De cuánto es el seguro de viaje que ofrece?
3. ¿Qué sorteos *(drawings)* ofrecen?
4. ¿Dónde ofrecen descuentos?
5. ¿Qué revistas reciben las personas que tienen la tarjeta?
6. ¿Qué ventajas *(advantages)* ofrece para el estacionamiento de coches?
7. ¿Qué tiempo dan para pagar los billetes de tren?
8. Si no pudiera ir a la estación para comprar los billetes, ¿qué podría hacer con la tarjeta RENFE?
9. ¿Le gustaría tener una Tarjeta RENFE? ¿Por qué?

UNA ACTIVIDAD ESPECIAL
A College Bowl

Turn to Appendix D, where you will find questions that will check your knowledge of the information presented in the **¿Lo sabía Ud....?** sections and the **Panorama hispánico** photo essays. Your instructor will be the host of the College Bowl and will ask the questions. May the best team win!

Y ahora, *¡vamos a leer!*

La carta de Graciela

Desde Sevilla, Graciela le escribe una carta a Irma, una compañera de la universidad.

15 de agosto de 1990

Querida Irma:

Te estoy escribiendo desde Sevilla, una ciudad maravillosa que está en el sur de España. Vinimos en tren, y fue una experiencia muy interesante. El viaje fue largo, pero como teníamos litera, pudimos dormir bien.

Es una lástima que tú no hayas podido venir con nosotras. Alquilamos un coche compacto cuando llegamos a Sevilla. Es automático, pero no gasta mucha gasolina. Yo creía que íbamos a necesitar un permiso especial para manejar aquí, pero no fue necesario. Mañana salimos para Galicia, donde vamos a pasar unos días. No fuimos a Marruecos porque Gloria no quiso ir. Si tú hubieras venido, habríamos ido las dos.

Espero que ya te hayas matriculado. ¿Vas a tomar la clase de química conmigo? ¡A ti te gustan las ciencias! Mi consejero me dijo que la tomara, pero yo no creo que sea fácil para mí... ¿Qué has decidido? ¿Vas a cambiar tu especialización o no? ¿Qué asignaturas vas a tomar? Yo quiero terminar con todos los requisitos el semestre próximo. Además, voy a tomar danza aeróbica porque necesito hacer ejercicio. La comida española es excelente y Gloria y yo estamos comiendo mucho.

Bueno, pensamos estar de vuelta en Tejas para septiembre.

Cariños,

Graciela

¡A ver cuánto recuerda!

1. ¿Le gusta Sevilla a Graciela?
2. ¿El viaje en tren fue cómodo?
3. ¿Graciela siente que Irma no haya venido con ellas a España?
4. ¿Qué clase de coche alquilaron las chicas en Sevilla?
5. ¿Adónde le habría gustado ir a Graciela?
6. ¿Por qué no fue?
7. ¿Por qué va a tomar química Graciela?
8. ¿Qué quiere saber Graciela de Irma?
9. ¿Por qué va a tomar danza aeróbica Graciela?
10. ¿Por qué cree Ud. que Graciela y Gloria tienen que estar de vuelta para septiembre?

La famosa Plaza de España en el Parque de María Luisa, en Sevilla, España.

Take this test. When you finish, check your answers in the answer key provided for this section in Appendix E. Then use a red pen to correct any mistakes you may have made. Ready?

LECCIÓN 16

A. First-person plural commands

Change the following sentences according to the model.

MODELO: Yo creo que sería una buena idea estudiar con Roberto.
Estudiemos con Roberto.

1. Yo creo que sería una buena idea llamar a Juan.
2. Yo creo que sería una buena idea alquilar un coche de dos puertas.
3. Yo creo que sería una buena idea no decirle que no tenemos ganas de salir con él.
4. Yo creo que sería una buena idea preguntarle a María si va a ir a la biblioteca hoy.
5. Yo creo que sería una buena idea vestirnos ahora para llegar a tiempo.
6. Yo creo que sería una buena idea decirles que el coche no estaba asegurado.

B. The future perfect

Give the Spanish equivalent of the words in parentheses.

1. Para mañana _____ las entradas. *(I will have bought)*
2. Para entonces, la función ya _____ . *(will have finished)*
3. Para las diez, ellos ya _____ el supermercado. *(will have closed)*
4. Para las doce, nosotros ya _____ del concierto, ¿verdad? *(will have returned)*
5. ¿Tú _____ con ellos en el parque de diversiones para las once? *(will have met)*

C. The conditional perfect

Complete the following sentences with the conditional perfect of the verbs in the list.

preocuparse   comprar   volver   aceptar   hacer

1. De haberlo sabido, yo no _____ esas latas de durazno.
2. Nosotros no _____ cola otra vez.

3. Él no _____ por eso.
4. ¿Tú _____ una cita con Rubén?
5. Ellos _____ al día siguiente.

D. Reciprocal reflexives

Write sentences with the elements given. Follow the model.

MODELO: hace / un año / nosotros / no hablarse
Hace un año que nosotros no nos hablamos.

1. hace / tres meses / ellos / escribirse
2. hace / mucho tiempo / Uds. / conocerse
3. hace / un mes / ellas / no verse
4. hace / quince días / Julio y Marisa / no llamarse por teléfono
5. hace / mucho tiempo / tú y yo / quererse

E. Just words . . .

Match the questions in column A with the appropriate responses in column B.

A	**B**
1. ¿Está muy gorda?	a. Lechuga, cebolla, papas, tomates y apio.
2. ¿Quieres ver un drama?	
3. ¿Cuántos huevos quieres?	b. No, solamente como verduras.
4. ¿Qué frutas usas para la ensalada?	c. En el baño.
5. ¿Trabajas el lunes?	d. Sí, ganó el primer premio.
6. ¿Qué necesitas para la ensalada?	e. No, es barato.
7. ¿No quieres azúcar?	f. Pescado.
8. ¿Es buena esa película?	g. Yo no como frutas.
9. ¿Dónde está el papel higiénico?	h. No, prefiero una comedia musical.
10. ¿Qué quieres desayunar?	i. No, solamente aceite.
11. ¿Alquilaste el apartamento?	j. Zanahorias.
12. ¿Qué se vende allí?	k. No, es feriado.
13. Cuesta una fortuna, ¿verdad?	l. Para hacer ravioles.
14. ¿No quieres carne?	m. No, nunca le pongo nada al café.
15. ¿Qué come Bugs Bunny?	n. No, se puso a dieta.
16. ¿Prefieres toronja o sandía?	o. Pan y mantequilla.
17. ¿Tú le pones vinagre a la ensalada?	p. Naranjas, peras, piña, manzanas, fresas y melón.
18. ¿Cuánto es?	q. No, es demasiado caro.
19. ¿Para qué necesitas la salsa de tomate?	r. Dos docenas.
20. ¿Qué vas a hacer hoy?	s. Voy a hacer unas compras.
	t. A ver... veinte dólares.

LECCIÓN 17

A. The present perfect subjunctive

Combine the following pairs of sentences, using the verbs in the main clauses in the present indicative and the verbs in the subordinate clauses in the present perfect subjunctive. Follow the model.

MODELO: Yo (alegrarme).
          Tú (venir).
          Yo me alegro de que tú hayas venido.

1. Nosotros (sentir) mucho.
   Uds. no (tomar) el examen parcial.
2. Yo (dudar).
   Ella (asistir) a la Facultad de Derecho.
3. (Ser) una lástima.
   Tú no (mantener) un buen promedio este semestre.
4. Ellos (alegrarse).
   Nosotros (tomar) la clase de danza aeróbica.
5. Yo (sentir) mucho.
   Esa periodista (morir).
6. (Ser) difícil.
   Pedro (entregar) la tarea a tiempo, como siempre.

B. Uses of the imperfect subjunctive

Give the Spanish equivalent of the words in parentheses.

1. Yo quería que tú _____ en la clase de física. *(register)*
2. Yo sentí mucho que él _____ conseguir la beca. *(wasn't able to)*
3. Fue una lástima que Ud. no _____ todos los días. *(exercise)*
4. Mi hermano me pidió que lo _____ . *(help)*
5. Es una lástima que ellos _____ a la discusión. *(didn't come)*
6. Nuestros padres querían que _____ periodistas. *(we were)*
7. Ella me pidió que yo _____ la calculadora. *(lend her)*
8. Yo me alegré mucho de que Uds. _____ . *(knew him)*

C. The pluperfect subjunctive

Give the Spanish equivalent of the words in parentheses.

1. Yo dudaba que María _____ la comida. *(had brought)*
2. Ellos temían que nosotros _____ . *(had left)*
3. Él se alegró mucho de que Ud. le _____ la tarea. *(had returned)*
4. Él esperaba que yo _____ que Ud. tenía una «C». *(had told you)*
5. Yo sentí muchísimo que tú _____ al partido. *(hadn't come)*

D. Just words . . .

Complete the following sentences with the appropriate words or phrases from the vocabulary in **Lección 17.**

1. Me gusta mucho la física. Ésa es mi _____ en la universidad.
2. Como _____ , jugamos al fútbol ayer.
3. Mi _____ me dijo que tomara algunos requisitos.
4. Es de La Habana. Es _____ .
5. Leímos *Don Quijote* en nuestra clase de _____ española.
6. El trimestre pasado tomé varios _____ generales, y ya los tengo todos.
7. ¿Tienen un examen mañana? ¡Buena _____ !
8. No puedo tomar clases si no tengo dinero para pagar la _____ .
9. Esa modelo está muy _____ . Está a dieta.
10. Fuimos juntos a la escuela _____ y a la escuela _____ .
11. Este trimestre quiero _____ una «A» en matemáticas, en sociología y en contabilidad.
12. ¿De dónde es la palabra «che»? ¿Es _____ ?
13. ¿Vamos juntos al _____ de fútbol hoy?
14. Necesito hacer _____ . Voy a tomar una clase de danza _____ .
15. Te voy a dar mi _____ de clases, para ver si puedes tomar la clase de periodismo conmigo.
16. Mi _____ en la clase de administración de negocios es «B».
17. Nunca tomo química, porque no me gusta esa _____ .
18. Para ser _____ hay que asistir a la Facultad de Derecho.

LECCIÓN 18

A. *If* clauses

Give the Spanish equivalent of the words in parentheses.

1. Si ellos _____ literas, habría sido mejor. *(had reserved)*
2. Si tú _____ a Juan, habríamos ido al cine. *(had called)*
3. Si yo _____ un buen descuento, iría de vacaciones. *(were to get)*
4. Si _____ tiempo, compraré los pasajes. *(I have)*
5. Gasta dinero _____ millonaria. *(as if she were)*
6. Si Uds. _____ un coche, yo puedo prestarles el mío. *(need)*
7. ¿Qué le dirías tú al profesor si él _____ a clase? *(didn't come)*
8. Salimos mañana si Alejandro _____ de Sevilla. *(comes back)*

B. Summary of the uses of the subjunctive

Give the Spanish equivalent of the words in parentheses.

1. El empleado quiere que _____ los billetes ahora. *(we reserve)*
2. El señor Peña sugiere que _____ un descuento, señora Mena. *(you give her)*
3. ¿ _____ el itinerario, querido? *(Do you want to see)*
4. Espero que _____ un buen viaje. *(she has)*
5. Me alegro mucho de _____ , señorita Alvarado. *(see you)*
6. Necesitamos una secretaria que _____ eficiente y _____ por lo menos dos idiomas. *(is / speaks)*
7. Aquí no hay nadie que _____ nada de química. *(knows)*
8. Tenemos dos secretarias que _____ alemanas. *(are)*
9. Hay muchas personas que _____ vivir en un apartamento. *(prefer)*
10. Voy a esperar hasta que Ud. _____ empezar a trabajar. *(are able to)*
11. Cuando _____ mis padres, les daré el regalo. *(arrive)*
12. Siempre la esperamos hasta que ella _____ . *(arrives)*

13. La semana pasada, cuando ellos _____ a Buenos Aires, hablé con ellos por unos minutos. *(came)*
14. Anoche no cenamos hasta que todos _____ allí. *(were)*
15. Dudo que él _____ comprar un coche de dos puertas. *(wants)*
16. Es probable que él _____ el seguro para el coche hoy. *(gets)*
17. Estoy segura de que él _____ a sus amigos. *(will want to see)*
18. No es verdad que ellos _____ tiempo para trasbordar. *(don't have)*
19. No niego que nosotros _____ . *(are in a hurry)*
20. Aunque mañana _____ , iremos a tu casa. *(it rains)*

C. Just words . . .

Match the questions in column A with the appropriate responses in column B.

A	**B**
1. ¿Es automático?	a. No, en abril tienen una tarifa especial.
2. ¿Son Uds. norteamericanos?	b. No, prefiero la litera alta.
3. ¿De dónde sale el tren?	c. Depende del professor.
4. ¿Llega a tiempo?	d. No, en el sur.
5. ¿Cenamos en el tren?	e. No, somos ciudadanos chilenos.
6. ¿Quieres dormir aquí?	f. Sí, porque gasta menos gasolina.
7. ¿Qué tren vas a tomar?	g. No, sólo dos veces por semana.
8. ¿Viven en el norte?	h. Del andén número cinco.
9. ¿Es muy caro el pasaje?	i. No, no le gusta el este.
10. ¿No te dio el vuelto?	j. No, tiene tres horas de retraso.
11. ¿Cuándo tenemos exámenes?	k. Sí, dos dólares.
12. ¿Prefieres un coche mecánico?	l. No, de cambio.
13. ¿Hay trenes diarios?	m. El rápido.
14. ¿Dónde está El Paso?	n. No, no tiene coche-comedor.
15. ¿Va a vivir en Nueva York?	o. En la frontera con México.

APPENDIXES
APPENDIX A
Spanish Sounds
VOWELS

There are five distinct vowels in Spanish: **a, e, i, o,** and **u.** Each vowel has only one basic, constant sound. The pronunciation of each vowel is constant, clear, and brief. The length of the sound is practically the same whether it is produced in a stressed or unstressed syllable.[1]

While producing the sounds of the English stressed vowels that most closely resemble the Spanish ones, the speaker changes the position of the tongue, lips, and lower jaw, so that the vowel actually starts as one sound and then *glides* into another. In Spanish, however, the tongue, lips, and jaw keep a constant position during the production of the sound.

English: banana   **Spanish:** banana

The stress falls on the same vowel and syllable in both Spanish and English, but the English stressed *a* is longer than the Spanish stressed **a.**

English: banana   **Spanish:** banana

Note also that the English stressed *a* has a sound different from the other *a*'s in the word, while the Spanish **a** sound remains constant.

a   in Spanish sounds similar to the English *a* in the word *father.*

alta	casa	palma	Ana
cama	Panamá	alma	apagar

e   is pronounced like the English *e* in the word *eight.*

mes	entre	este	deje
ese	encender	teme	prender

i   has a sound similar to the English *ee* in the word *see.*

fin	ir	sí	sin	dividir	Trini	difícil

o   is similar to the English *o* in the word *no,* but without the glide.

toco	como	poco	roto
corto	corro	solo	loco

u   is pronounced like the English *oo* sound in the word *shoot,* or the *ue* sound in the word *Sue.*

su	Lulú	Úrsula	cultura
un	luna	sucursal	Uruguay

---

[1] In a stressed syllable, the prominence of the vowel is indicated by its loudness.

441

Diphthongs and Triphthongs

When unstressed **i** or **u** falls next to another vowel in a syllable, it unites with that vowel to form what is called a *diphthong*. Both vowels are pronounced as one syllable. Their sounds do not change; they are only pronounced more rapidly and with a glide. For example:

traiga	Lidia	treinta	siete	oigo	adiós
Aurora	**agua**	**bueno**	**antiguo**	**ciudad**	**Luis**

A triphthong is the union of three vowels: a stressed vowel between two unstressed ones (**i** or **u**) in the same syllable. For example: Paraguay, estudiéis.

NOTE: Stressed **i** and **u** do not form diphthongs with other vowels, except in the combinations **iu** and **ui**. For example: rí-o, sa-bí-ais.

In syllabication, diphthongs and triphthongs are considered a single vowel; their components cannot be separated.

CONSONANTS

p   Spanish **p** is pronounced in a manner similar to the English *p* sound, but without the puff of air that follows after the English sound is produced.

pesca	pude	puedo	parte	papá
postre	piña	puente	Paco	

k   The Spanish **k** sound, represented by the letters **k**, **c** before **a, o, u** or a consonant, and **qu**, is similar to the English *k* sound, but without the puff of air.

casa	comer	cuna	clima	acción	que
quinto	queso	aunque	kiosko	kilómetro	

t   Spanish **t** is produced by touching the back of the upper front teeth with the tip of the tongue. It has no puff of air as in the English *t*.

todo	antes	corto	Guatemala	diente
resto	tonto	roto	tanque	

d   The Spanish consonant **d** has two different sounds depending on its position. At the beginning of an utterance and after **n** or **l**, the tip of the tongue presses the back of the upper front teeth.

día	doma	dice	dolor	dar
anda	Aldo	caldo	el deseo	un domicilio

In all other positions the sound of **d** is similar to the *th* sound in the English word *they*, but softer.

medida	todo	nada	nadie	medio
puedo	moda	queda	nudo	

g   The Spanish consonant **g** is similar to the English *g* sound in the word *guy* except before **e** or **i**.

goma	glotón	gallo	gloria	lago	alga
gorrión	garra	guerra	angustia	algo	Dagoberto

j   The Spanish sound **j** (or **g** before **e** and **i**) is similar to a strongly exaggerated English *h* sound.

gemir	juez	jarro	gitano	agente
juego	giro	bajo	gente	

b, v   There is no difference in sound between Spanish **b** and **v**. Both letters are pronounced alike. At the beginning of an utterance or after **m** or **n**, **b** and **v** have a sound identical to the English *b* sound in the word *boy*.

vivir	beber	vamos	barco	enviar
hambre	batea	bueno	vestido	

When pronounced between vowels, the Spanish **b** and **v** sound is produced by bringing the lips together but not closing them, so that some air may pass through.

sábado	autobús	yo voy	su barco

y, ll   In most countries, Spanish **ll** and **y** have a sound similar to the English sound in the word *yes*.

el llavero	trayecto	su yunta	milla
oye	el yeso	mayo	yema
un yelmo	trayectoria	llama	bella

NOTE: When it stands alone or is at the end of a word, Spanish **y** is pronounced like the vowel **i**.

rey	hoy	y	doy	buey
muy	voy	estoy	soy	

r   The sound of Spanish **r** is similar to the English *dd* sound in the word *ladder*.

crema	aroma	cara	arena	aro
harina	toro	oro	eres	portero

rr   Spanish **rr** and also **r** in an initial position and after **n**, **l**, or **s** are pronounced with a very strong trill. This trill is produced by bringing the tip of the tongue near the alveolar ridge and letting it vibrate freely while the air passes through the mouth.

rama	carro	Israel	cierra	roto
perro	alrededor	rizo	corre	Enrique

s   Spanish **s** is represented in most of the Spanish world by the letters **s**, **z**, and **c** before **e** or **i**. The sound is very similar to the English sibilant *s* in the word *sink*.

sale	sitio	presidente	signo
salsa	seda	suma	vaso
sobrino	ciudad	cima	canción
zapato	zarza	cerveza	centro

h   The letter **h** is silent in Spanish.

hoy	hora	hilo	ahora
humor	huevo	horror	almohada

ch   Spanish **ch** is pronounced like the English *ch* in the word *chief*.

hecho	chico	coche	Chile
mucho	muchacho	salchicha	

f   Spanish **f** is identical in sound to the English *f*.

difícil	feo	fuego	forma
fácil	fecha	foto	fueron

l   Spanish **l** is similar to the English *l* in the word *let*.

dolor	lata	ángel	lago	sueldo
los	pelo	lana	general	fácil

m   Spanish **m** is pronounced like the English *m* in the word *mother*.

mano	moda	mucho	muy
mismo	tampoco	multa	cómoda

n   In most cases, Spanish **n** has a sound similar to the English *n*.

nada	nunca	ninguno	norte
entra	tiene	sienta	

The sound of Spanish **n** is often affected by the sounds that occur around it. When it appears before **b, v,** or **p,** it is pronounced like an **m.**

tan bueno	toman vino	sin poder
un pobre	comen peras	siguen bebiendo

ñ   Spanish **ñ** is similar to the English *ny* sound in the word *canyon*.

señor	otoño	ñoño	uña
leña	dueño	niños	años

x   Spanish **x** has two pronunciations depending on its position. Between vowels the sound is similar to English *ks*.

examen	exacto	boxeo	éxito
oxidar	oxígeno	existencia	

When it occurs before a consonant, Spanish **x** sounds like *s*.

expresión	explicar	extraer	excusa
expreso	exquisito	extremo	

NOTE: When **x** appears in **México** or in other words of Mexican origin, it is pronounced like the Spanish letter **j.**

RHYTHM

Rhythm is the variation of sound intensity that we usually associate with music. Spanish and English each regulate these variations in speech differently, because they have different patterns of syllable length. In Spanish the length of the stressed and unstressed syllables remains almost the same, while in English stressed syllables are considerably longer than unstressed ones. Pronounce the following Spanish words, enunciating each syllable clearly.

es-tu-dian-te	bue-no	Úr-su-la
com-po-si-ción	di-fí-cil	ki-ló-me-tro
po-li-cí-a	Pa-ra-guay	

Because the length of the Spanish syllables remains constant, the greater the number of syllables in a given word or phrase, the longer the phrase will be.

LINKING

In spoken Spanish, the different words in a phrase or a sentence are not pronounced as isolated elements but are combined together. This is called *linking*.

Pepe come pan.	Pe-pe-co-me-pan
Tomás toma leche.	To-más-to-ma-le-che
Luis tiene la llave.	Luis-tie-ne-la-lla-ve
La mano de Roberto.	La-ma-no-de-Ro-ber-to

1. The final consonant of a word is pronounced together with the initial vowel of the following word.

Carlos anda	Car-lo-san-da
un ángel	u-nán-gel
el otoño	e-lo-to-ño
unos estudios interesantes	u-no-ses-tu-dio-sin-te-re-san-tes

2. A diphthong is formed between the final vowel of a word and the initial vowel of the following word. A triphthong is formed when there is a combination of three vowels (see rules for the formation of diphthongs and triphthongs on page 442).

su hermana	suher-ma-na
tu escopeta	tues-co-pe-ta
Roberto y Luis	Ro-ber-toy-Luis
negocio importante	ne-go-cioim-por-tan-te
lluvia y nieve	llu-viay-nie-ve
ardua empresa	ar-duaem-pre-sa

3. When the final vowel of a word and the initial vowel of the following word are identical, they are pronounced slightly longer than one vowel.

A-nal-can-za	Ana alcanza	tie-ne-so	tiene eso
lol-vi-do	lo olvido	Ada-tien-de	Ada atiende

The same rule applies when two identical vowels appear within a word.

cr*e*s   crees
Te-rán   Teherán
cor-di-na-ción   coordinación

4. When the final consonant of a word and the initial consonant of the following word are the same, they are pronounced as one consonant with slightly longer than normal duration.

e-*la*-do   el lado   tie-ne-*s*ed   tienes sed
Car-lo-*sal*-ta   Carlos salta

INTONATION

Intonation is the rise and fall of pitch in the delivery of a phrase or a sentence. In general, Spanish pitch tends to change less than English, giving the impression that the language is less emphatic.

As a rule, the intonation for normal statements in Spanish starts in a low tone, raises to a higher one on the first stressed syllable, maintains that tone until the last stressed syllable, and then goes back to the initial low tone, with still another drop at the very end.

Tu amigo viene mañana.   José come pan.
Ada está en casa.   Carlos toma café.

SYLLABLE FORMATION IN SPANISH

General rules for dividing words into syllables:

Vowels

1. A vowel or a vowel combination can constitute a syllable.

a-lum-no   a-bue-la   Eu-ro-pa

2. Diphthongs and triphthongs are considered single vowels and cannot be divided.

bai-le   puen-te   Dia-na   es-tu-diáis   an-ti-guo

3. Two strong vowels (**a, e, o**) do not form a diphthong and are separated into two syllables.

em-ple-ar   vol-te-ar   lo-a

4. A written accent on a weak vowel (**i** or **u**) breaks the diphthong, thus the vowels are separated into two syllables.

trí-o   dú-o   Ma-rí-a

Consonants

1. A single consonant forms a syllable with the vowel that follows it.

   po-der   ma-no   mi-nu-to

   NOTE: **ch, ll,** and **rr** are considered single consonants: **a-ma-ri-llo, co-che, pe-rro.**

2. When two consonants appear between two vowels, they are separated into two syllables.

   al-fa-be-to   cam-pe-ón   me-ter-se   mo-les-tia

   EXCEPTION: When a consonant cluster composed of **b, c, d, f, g, p,** or **t** with **l** or **r** appears between two vowels, the cluster joins the following vowel: **so-bre, o-tros, ca-ble, te-lé-gra-fo.**

3. When three consonants appear between two vowels, only the last one goes with the following vowel.

   ins-pec-tor   trans-por-te   trans-for-mar

   EXCEPTION: When there is a cluster of three consonants in the combinations described in rule 2, the first consonant joins the preceding vowel and the cluster joins the following vowel: **es-cri-bir, ex-tran-je-ro, im-plo-rar, es-tre-cho.**

ACCENTUATION

In Spanish, all words are stressed according to specific rules. Words that do not follow the rules must have a written accent to indicate the change of stress. The basic rules for accentuation are as follows.

1. Words ending in a vowel, **n,** or **s** are stressed on the next-to-the-last syllable.

   hi-jo   **ca**-lle   **me**-sa   fa-**mo**-sos
   flo-**re**-cen   **pla**-ya   **ve**-ces

2. Words ending in a consonant, except **n** or **s,** are stressed on the last syllable.

   ma-**yor**   a-**mor**   tro-pi-**cal**   na-**riz**   re-**loj**   co-rre-**dor**

3. All words that do not follow these rules must have the written accent.

   ca-**fé**   **lá**-piz   **mú**-si-ca   sa-**lón**
   án-gel   **lí**-qui-do   fran-**cés**   **Víc**-tor
   sim-**pá**-ti-co   rin-**cón**   a-**zú**-car   de-**mó**-cra-ta
   sa-**lió**   **dé**-bil   e-**xá**-me-nes

4. Pronouns and adverbs of interrogation and exclamation have a written accent to distinguish them from relative pronouns.

   ¿**Qué** comes?   *What are you eating?*
   La pera que él no comió.   *The pear that he did not eat.*

¿**Quién** está ahí?   *Who is there?*
El hombre a quien tú llamaste.   *The man whom you called.*

¿**Dónde** está?   *Where is he?*
En el lugar donde trabaja.   *At the place where he works.*

5. Words that have the same spelling but different meanings take a written accent to differentiate one from the other.

el	*the*	él	*he, him*	te	*you*	té	*tea*
mi	*my*	mí	*me*	si	*if*	sí	*yes*
tu	*your*	tú	*you*	mas	*but*	más	*more*

APPENDIX B *Verbs*

REGULAR VERBS

Model **-ar, -er, -ir,** verbs

INFINITIVE

amar *(to love)*   comer *(to eat)*   vivir *(to live)*

PRESENT PARTICIPLE

amando *(loving)*   comiendo *(eating)*   viviendo *(living)*

PAST PARTICIPLE

amado *(loved)*   comido *(eaten)*   vivido *(lived)*

SIMPLE TENSES

Indicative Mood

PRESENT

(I love)		*(I eat)*		*(I live)*	
amo	amamos	como	comemos	vivo	vivimos
amas	amáis	comes	coméis	vives	vivís
ama	aman	come	comen	vive	viven

IMPERFECT

(I used to love)		*(I used to eat)*		*(I used to live)*	
amaba	amábamos	comía	comíamos	vivía	vivíamos
amabas	amabais	comías	comíais	vivías	vivíais
amaba	amaban	comía	comían	vivía	vivían

PRETERIT

(I loved)		*(I ate)*		*(I lived)*	
amé	amamos	comí	comimos	viví	vivimos
amaste	amasteis	comiste	comisteis	viviste	vivisteis
amó	amaron	comió	comieron	vivió	vivieron

FUTURE

(I will love)		*(I will eat)*		*(I will live)*	
amaré	amaremos	comeré	comeremos	viviré	viviremos
amarás	amaréis	comerás	comeréis	vivirás	viviréis
amará	amarán	comerá	comerán	vivirá	vivirán

CONDITIONAL

(I would love)		*(I would eat)*		*(I would live)*	
amaría	amaríamos	comería	comeríamos	viviría	viviríamos
amarías	amaríais	comerías	comeríais	vivirías	viviríais
amaría	amarían	comería	comerían	viviría	vivirían

Subjunctive Mood

PRESENT

([that] I [may] love)		*([that] I [may] eat)*		*([that] I [may] live)*	
ame	amemos	coma	comamos	viva	vivamos
ames	améis	comas	comáis	vivas	viváis
ame	amen	coma	coman	viva	vivan

IMPERFECT (two forms: **ara, ase**)

([that] I [might] love)	*([that] I [might] eat)*	*([that] I [might] live)*
amara(-ase)	comiera(-iese)	viviera(-iese)
amaras(-ases)	comieras(-ieses)	vivieras(-ieses)
amara(-ase)	comiera(-iese)	viviera(-iese)
amáramos(-ásemos)	comiéramos(-iésemos)	viviéramos(-iésemos)
amarais(-aseis)	comierais(-ieseis)	vivierais(-ieseis)
amaran(-asen)	comieran(-iesen)	vivieran(-iesen)

IMPERATIVE MOOD

(love)	*(eat)*	*(live)*
ama (tú)	come (tú)	vive (tú)
ame (Ud.)	coma (Ud.)	viva (Ud.)
amemos (nosotros)	comamos (nosotros)	vivamos (nosotros)
amad (vosotros)	comed (vosotros)	vivid (vosotros)
amen (Uds.)	coman (Uds.)	vivan (Uds.)

COMPOUND TENSES

PERFECT INFINITIVE

haber amado	haber comido	haber vivido

PERFECT PARTICIPLE

habiendo amado	habiendo comido	habiendo vivido

Indicative Mood

PRESENT PERFECT

(I have loved)		*(I have eaten)*		*(I have lived)*	
he amado	hemos amado	he comido	hemos comido	he vivido	hemos vivido
has amado	habéis amado	has comido	habéis comido	has vivido	habéis vivido
ha amado	han amado	ha comido	han comido	ha vivido	han vivido

PLUPERFECT

(I had loved)	*(I had eaten)*	*(I had lived)*
había amado	había comido	había vivido
habías amado	habías comido	habías vivido
había amado	había comido	había vivido
habíamos amado	habíamos comido	habíamos vivido
habíais amado	habíais comido	habíais vivido
habían amado	habían comido	habían vivido

FUTURE PERFECT

(I will have loved)	*(I will have eaten)*	*(I will have lived)*
habré amado	habré comido	habré vivido
habrás amado	habrás comido	habrás vivido
habrá amado	habrá comido	habrá vivido
habremos amado	habremos comido	habremos vivido
habréis amado	habréis comido	habréis vivido
habrán amado	habrán comido	habrán vivido

CONDITIONAL PERFECT

(I would have loved)	*(I would have eaten)*	*(I would have lived)*
habría amado	habría comido	habría vivido
habrías amado	habrías comido	habrías vivido
habría amado	habría comido	habría vivido
habríamos amado	habríamos comido	habríamos vivido
habríais amado	habríais comido	habríais vivido
habrían amado	habrían comido	habrían vivido

Subjunctive Mood

PRESENT PERFECT

([that] I [may] have loved)	*([that] I [may] have eaten)*	*([that] I [may] have lived)*
haya amado	haya comido	haya vivido
hayas amado	hayas comido	hayas vivido
haya amado	haya comido	haya vivido
hayamos amado	hayamos comido	hayamos vivido
hayáis amado	hayáis comido	hayáis vivido
hayan amado	hayan comido	hayan vivido

PLUPERFECT (two forms: -ra, -se)

([that] I [might] have loved)	*([that] I [might] have eaten)*	*([that] I [might] have lived)*
hubiera(-iese) amado	hubiera(-iese) comido	hubiera(-iese) vivido
hubieras(-ieses) amado	hubieras(-ieses) comido	hubieras(-ieses) vivido
hubiera(-iese) amado	hubiera(-iese) comido	hubiera(-iese) vivido

hubiéramos(-iésemos) amado	hubiéramos(-iésemos) comido	hubiéramos(-iésemos) vivido
hubierais(-ieseis) amado	hubierais(-ieseis) comido	hubierais(-ieseis) vivido
hubieran(-iesen) amado	hubieran(-iesen) comido	hubieran(-iesen) vivido

STEM-CHANGING VERBS

The -ar and -er stem-changing verbs

Stem-changing verbs are those that have a spelling change in the root of the verb. Stem-changing verbs that end in -ar and -er change the stressed vowel e to ie, and the stressed o to ue. These changes occur in all persons, except the first- and second-persons plural, of the present indicative, present subjunctive, and imperative.

INFINITIVE	Indicative	Imperative	Subjunctive
cerrar *(to close)*	cierro cierras cierra	—— cierra cierre	cierre cierres cierre
	cerramos cerráis cierran	cerremos cerrad cierren	cerremos cerréis cierren
perder *(to lose)*	pierdo pierdes pierde	—— pierde pierda	pierda pierdas pierda
	perdemos perdéis pierden	perdamos perded pierdan	perdamos perdáis pierdan
contar *(to count;* *to tell)*	cuento cuentas cuenta	—— cuenta cuente	cuente cuentes cuente
	contamos contáis cuentan	contemos contad cuenten	contemos contéis cuenten
volver *(to return)*	vuelvo vuelves vuelve	—— vuelve vuelva	vuelva vuelvas vuelva
	volvemos volvéis vuelven	volvamos volved vuelvan	volvamos volváis vuelvan

Verbs that follow the same pattern are:

acordarse	*to remember*	entender	*to understand*
acostar(se)	*to go to bed*	llover	*to rain*

almorzar	to have lunch	mover	to move
atravesar	to go through	mostrar	to show
cocer	to cook	negar	to deny
colgar	to hang	nevar	to snow
comenzar	to begin	pensar	to think; to plan
confesar	to confess	probar	to prove; to taste
costar	to cost	recordar	to remember
demostrar	to demonstrate, show	rogar	to beg
		sentar(se)	to sit down
despertar(se)	to wake up	soler	to be in the habit of
empezar	to begin	soñar	to dream
encender	to light; to turn on	tender	to stretch; to unfold
encontrar	to find	torcer	to twist

The -ir stem-changing verbs

There are two types of stem-changing verbs that end in -ir: one type changes stressed e to ie in some tenses and to i in others, and stressed o to ue or u; the second type changes stressed e to i only in all the irregular tenses.

Type I: -ir: e > ie / o > ue or u

These changes occur as follows.

Present Indicative: all persons except the first- and second-persons plural change e to ie and o to ue. *Preterit:* third person, singular and plural, changes e to i and o to u. *Present Subjunctive:* all persons change e to ie and o to ue, except the first- and second-persons plural, which change e to i and o to u. *Imperfect Subjunctive:* all persons change e to i and o to u. *Imperative:* all persons except the first- and second-persons plural change e to ie and o to ue; first-person plural changes e to i and o to u. *Present Participle:* changes e to i and o to u.

INFINITIVE	Indicative		Imperative	Subjunctive	
sentir **(to feel)**	PRESENT	PRETERIT		PRESENT	IMPERFECT
	siento	sentí		sienta	sintiera(-iese)
PRESENT	sientes	sentiste	siente	sientas	sintieras
PARTICIPLE	siente	sintió	sienta	sienta	sintiera
sintiendo	sentimos	sentimos	sintamos	sintamos	sintiéramos
	sentís	sentisteis	sentid	sintáis	sintierais
	sienten	sintieron	sientan	sientan	sintieran
dormir **(to sleep)**	duermo	dormí		duerma	durmiera(-iese)
	duermes	dormiste	duerme	duermas	durmieras
PRESENT	duerme	durmió	duerma	duerma	durmiera
PARTICIPLE					
durmiendo	dormimos	dormimos	durmamos	durmamos	durmiéramos
	dormís	dormisteis	dormid	durmáis	durmierais
	duermen	durmieron	duerman	duerman	durmieran

Other verbs that follow the same pattern are:

advertir	*to warn*	herir	*to wound, hurt*
arrepentirse	*to repent*	mentir	*to lie*
consentir	*to consent; to pamper*	morir	*to die*
convertir(se)	*to turn into*	preferir	*to prefer*
discernir	*to discern*	referir	*to refer*
divertir(se)	*to amuse oneself*	sugerir	*to suggest*

Type II: -ir: e > i

The verbs in the second category are irregular in the same tenses as those of the first type. The only difference is that they have only one change: e > i in all irregular persons.

INFINITIVE	Indicative		Imperative	Subjunctive	
pedir *(to ask for, request)*	PRESENT	PRETERIT		PRESENT	IMPERFECT
	pido	pedí		pida	pidiera(-iese)
PRESENT PARTICIPLE	pides	pediste	pide	pidas	pidieras
	pide	pidió	pida	pida	pidiera
pidiendo	pedimos	pedimos	pidamos	pidamos	pidiéramos
	pedís	pedisteis	pedid	pidáis	pidierais
	piden	pidieron	pidan	pidan	pidieran

Verbs that follow this pattern:

concebir	*to conceive*	reír(se)	*to laugh*
competir	*to compete*	repetir	*to repeat*
despedir(se)	*to say good-bye*	reñir	*to fight*
elegir	*to choose*	seguir	*to follow*
impedir	*to prevent*	servir	*to serve*
perseguir	*to pursue*	vestir(se)	*to dress*

ORTHOGRAPHIC-CHANGING VERBS

Some verbs undergo a change in the spelling of the stem in some tenses in order to maintain the sound of the final consonant. The most common ones are those with the consonants **g** and **c**. Remember that **g** and **c** in front of **e** or **i** have a soft sound, and in front of **a, o,** or **u** have a hard sound. In order to keep the soft sound in front of **a, o,** or **u, g** and **c** change to **j** and **z,** respectively. In order to keep the hard sound of **g** or **c** in front of **e** and **i, u** is added to the **g** (**gu**) and the **c** changes to **qu.** The most important verbs that are regular in all the tenses but change in spelling are the following.

1. Verbs ending in **-gar** change **g** to **gu** before **e** in the first person of the preterit and in all persons of the present subjunctive.

pagar *to pay*
Preterit: pagué, pagaste, pagó, etc.
Pres. Subj.: pague, pagues, pague, paguemos, paguéis, paguen
Verbs that follow the same pattern: **colgar, llegar, navegar, negar, regar, rogar, jugar.**

2. Verbs ending in **-ger** or **-gir** change **g** to **j** before **o** and **a** in the first person of the present indicative and in all the persons of the present subjunctive.

    proteger *to protect*
    Pres. Ind.: protejo, proteges, protege, etc.
    Pres. Subj.: proteja, protejas, proteja, protejamos, protejáis, protejan
    Verbs that follow the same pattern: **coger, dirigir, elegir, escoger, exigir, recoger, corregir.**

3. Verbs ending in **-guar** change **gu** to **gü** before **e** in the first persons of the preterit and in all persons of the present subjunctive.

    averiguar *to find out*
    Preterit: averigüé, averiguaste, averiguó, etc.
    Pres. Subj.: averigüe, averigües, averigüe, averigüemos, averigüéis, averigüen
    The verb **apaciguar** follows the same pattern.

4. Verbs ending in **-guir** change **gu** to **g** before **o** and **a** in the first person of the present indicative and in all persons of the present subjunctive.

    conseguir *to get*
    Pres. Ind.: consigo, consigues, consigue, etc.
    Pres. Subj.: consiga, consigas, consiga, consigamos, consigáis, consigan
    Verbs that follow the same pattern: **distinguir, perseguir, proseguir, seguir.**

5. Verbs ending in **-car** change **c** to **qu** before **e** in the first person of the preterit and in all persons of the present subjunctive.

    tocar *to touch; to play (a musical instrument)*
    Preterit: toqué, tocaste, tocó, etc.
    Pres. Subj.: toque, toques, toque, toquemos, toquéis, toquen
    Verbs that follow the same pattern: **atacar, buscar, comunicar, explicar, indicar, sacar, pescar.**

6. Verbs ending in **-cer** or **-cir** preceded by a consonant change **c** to **z** before **o** and **a** in the first person of the present indicative and in all persons of the present subjunctive.

    torcer *to twist*
    Pres. Ind.: tuerzo, tuerces, tuerce, etc.
    Pres. Subj.: tuerza, tuerzas, torzamos, torzáis, tuerzan
    Verbs that follow the same pattern: **convencer, esparcir, vencer.**

7. Verbs ending in **-cer** or **-cir** preceded by a vowel change **c** to **zc** before **o** and **a** in the first person of the present indicative and in all persons of the present subjunctive.

    conocer *to know, be acquainted with*
    Pres. Ind.: conozco, conoces, conoce, etc.
    Pres. Subj.: conozca, conozcas, conozca, conozcamos, conozcáis, conozcan
    Verbs that follow the same pattern: **agradecer, aparecer, carecer, establecer, entristecer** *(to sadden)*, **lucir, nacer, obedecer, ofrecer, padecer, parecer, pertenecer, relucir, reconocer.**

8. Verbs ending in **-zar** change **z** to **c** before **e** in the first person of the preterit and in all persons of the present subjunctive.

rezar *to pray*
Preterit: recé, rezaste, rezó, etc.
Pres. Subj.: rece, reces, rece, recemos, recéis, recen
Verbs that follow the same pattern: **alcanzar, almorzar, comenzar, cruzar, empezar, forzar, gozar, abrazar.**

9. Verbs ending in **-eer** change the unstressed **i** to **y** between vowels in the third-person singular and plural of the preterit, in all persons of the imperfect subjunctive, and in the present participle.

creer *to believe*
Pres. Part.: creyendo
Preterit: creí, creíste, creyó, creímos, creísteis, creyeron
Imp. Subj.: creyera(-ese), creyeras, creyera, creyéramos, creyerais, creyeran
Past Part.: creído
Verbs that follow the same pattern: **leer, poseer.**

10. Verbs ending in **-uir** change the unstressed **i** to **y** between vowels (except **-quir**, which has the silent **u**) in the following tenses and persons.

huir *to escape flee*
Pres. Part.: huyendo
Pres. Ind.: huyo, huyes, huye, huimos, huís, huyen
Preterit: huí, huiste, huyó, huimos, huisteis, huyeron
Imperative: huye, huya, huyamos, huid, huyan
Pres. Subj.: huya, huyas, huya, huyamos, huyáis, huyan
Imp. Subj.: huyera(-ese), huyeras, huyera, huyéramos, huyerais, huyeran
Verbs that follow the same pattern: **atribuir, concluir, constituir, construir, contribuir, destituir, destruir, disminuir, distribuir, excluir, incluir, influir, instruir, restituir, sustituir.**

11. Verbs ending in **-eír** lose the **e** in the third-person singular and plural of the preterit, in all persons of the imperfect subjunctive, and in the present participle.

reír *to laugh*
Pres. Ind.: río, ríes, ríe, reímos, reís, ríen
Preterit: reí, reíste, rió, reímos, reísteis, rieron
Pres. Subj.: ría, rías, ría, riamos, riáis, rían
Imp. Subj.: riera(-ese), rieras, riera, riéramos, rierais, rieran
Pres. Part.: riendo
Verbs that follow the same pattern: **sonreír, freír.**

12. Verbs ending in **-iar** add a written accent to the **i,** except in the first- and second-persons plural of the present indicative and subjunctive.

fiar(se) *to trust*
Pres. Ind.: (me) fío, (te) fías, (se) fía, (nos) fiamos, (os) fiais, (se) fían
Pres. Subj.: (me) fíe, (te) fíes, (se) fíe, (nos) fiemos, (os) fiéis, (se) fíen
Verbs that follow the same pattern: **enviar, ampliar, criar, desviar, enfriar, guiar, telegrafiar, vaciar, variar.**

13. Verbs ending in **-uar** (except **-guar**) add a written accent to the **u,** except in the first- and second-persons plural of the present indicative and subjunctive.

actuar *to act*
Pres. Ind.: actúo, actúas, actúa, actuamos, actuáis, actúan
Pres. Subj.: actúe, actúes, actúe, actuemos, actuéis, actúen
Verbs that follow the same pattern: **continuar, acentuar, efectuar, exceptuar, graduar, habituar, insinuar, situar.**

14. Verbs ending in -**ñir** lose the **i** of the diphthongs **ie** and **ió** in the third-person singular and plural of the preterit and all persons of the imperfect subjunctive. They also change the **e** of the stem to **i** in the same persons and in the present indicative and present subjunctive.

teñir *to dye*
Pres. Ind.: tiño, tiñes, tiñe, teñimos, teñís, tiñen
Preterit: teñí, teñiste, tiñó, teñimos, teñisteis, tiñeron
Pres. Subj.: tiña, tiñas, tiña, tiñamos, tiñáis, tiñan
Imp. Subj.: tiñera(-ese), tiñeras, tiñera, tiñéramos, tiñerais, tiñeran
Verbs that follow the same pattern: **ceñir, constreñir, desteñir, estreñir, reñir.**

SOME COMMON IRREGULAR VERBS

Only those tenses with irregular forms are given below.

adquirir *to acquire*
Pres. Ind.: adquiero, adquieres, adquiere, adquirimos, adquirís, adquieren
Pres. Subj.: adquiera, adquieras, adquiera, adquiramos, adquiráis, adquieran
Imperative: adquiere, adquiera, adquiramos, adquirid, adquieran

andar *to walk*
Preterit: anduve, anduviste, anduvo, anduvimos, anduvisteis, anduvieron
Imp. Subj.: anduviera (anduviese), anduvieras, anduviera, anduviéramos, anduvierais, anduvieran

avergonzarse *to be ashamed, to be embarrassed*
Pres. Ind.: me avergüenzo, te avergüenzas, se avergüenza, nos avergonzamos, os avergonzáis, se avergüenzan
Pres. Subj.: me avergüence, te avergüences, se avergüence, nos avergoncemos, os avergoncéis, se avergüencen
Imperative: avergüénzate, avergüéncese, avergoncémonos, avergonzaos, avergüénzense

caber *to fit, to have enough room*
Pres. Ind.: quepo, cabes, cabe, cabemos, cabéis, caben
Preterit: cupe, cupiste, cupo, cupimos, cupisteis, cupieron
Future: cabré, cabrás, cabrá, cabremos, cabréis, cabrán
Conditional: cabría, cabrías, cabría, cabríamos, cabríais, cabrían
Imperative: cabe, quepa, quepamos, cabed, quepan
Pres. Subj.: quepa, quepas, quepa, quepamos, quepáis, quepan
Imp. Subj.: cupiera (cupiese), cupieras, cupiera, cupiéramos, cupierais, cupieran

caer *to fall*
Pres. Ind.: caigo, caes, cae, caemos, caéis, caen
Preterit: caí, caíste, cayó, caímos, caísteis, cayeron
Imperative: cae, caiga, caigamos, caed, caigan
Pres. Subj.: caiga, caigas, caiga, caigamos, caigáis, caigan

Imp. Subj.: cayera (cayese), cayeras, cayera, cayéramos, cayerais, cayeran
Past Part.: caído

conducir *to guide, to drive*
Pres. Ind.: conduzco, conduces, conduce, conducimos, conducís, conducen
Preterit: conduje, condujiste, condujo, condujimos, condujisteis, condujeron
Imperative: conduce, conduzca, conduzcamos, conducid, conduzcan
Pres. Subj.: conduzca, conduzcas, conduzca, conduzcamos, conduzcáis, conduzcan
Imp. Subj.: condujera (condujese), condujeras, condujera, condujéramos,
condujerais, condujeran
(All verbs ending in **-ducir** follow this pattern)

convenir *to agree (see* **venir**)

dar *to give*
Pres. Ind.: doy, das, da damos, dais, dan
Preterit: di, diste, dio, dimos, disteis, dieron
Imperative: da, dé, demos, dad, den
Pres. Subj.: dé, des, dé, demos, deis, den
Imp. Subj.: diera (diese), dieras, diera, diéramos, dierais, dieran

decir *to say, tell*
Pres. Ind.: digo, dices, dice, decimos, decís, dicen
Preterit: dije, dijiste, dijo, dijimos, dijisteis, dijeron
Future: diré, dirás, dirá, diremos, diréis, dirán
Conditional: diría, dirías, diría, diríamos, diríais, dirían
Imperative: di, diga, digamos, decid, digan
Pres. Subj.: diga, digas, diga, digamos, digáis, digan
Imp. Subj.: dijera (dijese), dijeras, dijera, dijéramos, dijerais, dijeran
Pres. Part.: diciendo
Past Part.: dicho

detener *to stop; to hold; to arrest (see* **tener**)

entretener *to entertain, amuse (see* **tener**)

errar *to err; to miss*
Pres. Ind.: yerro, yerras, yerra, erramos, erráis, yerran
Imperative: yerra, yerre, erremos, errad, yerren
Pres. Subj.: yerre, yerres, yerre, erremos, erréis, yerren

estar *to be*
Pres. Ind.: estoy, estás, está, estamos, estáis, están
Preterit: estuve, estuviste, estuvo, estuvimos, estuvisteis, estuvieron
Imperative: está, esté, estemos, estad, estén
Pres. Subj.: esté, estés, esté, estemos, estéis, estén
Imp. Subj.: estuviera (estuviese), estuvieras, estuviera, estuviéramos, estuvierais,
estuvieran

haber *to have*
Pres. Ind.: he, has, ha, hemos, habéis, han
Preterit: hube, hubiste, hubo, hubimos, hubisteis, hubieron
Future: habré, habrás, habrá, habremos, habréis, habrán
Conditional: habría, habrías, habría, habríamos, habríais, habrían
Pres. Subj.: haya, hayas, haya, hayamos, hayáis, hayan
Imp. Subj.: hubiera (hubiese), hubieras, hubiera, hubiéramos, hubierais, hubieran

hacer *to do, make*

Pres. Ind.: hago, haces, hace, hacemos, hacéis, hacen
Preterit: hice, hiciste, hizo, hicimos, hicisteis, hicieron
Future: haré, harás, hará, haremos, haréis, harán
Conditional: haría, harías, haría, haríamos, haríais, harían
Imperative: haz, haga, hagamos, haced, hagan
Pres. Subj.: haga, hagas, haga, hagamos, hagáis, hagan
Imp. Subj.: hiciera (hiciese), hicieras, hiciera, hiciéramos, hicierais, hicieran
Past Part.: hecho

imponer *to impose; to deposite (see* **poner***)*

ir *to go*

Pres. Ind.: voy, vas, va, vamos, vais, van
Imp. Ind.: iba, ibas, iba, íbamos, ibais, iban
Preterit: fui, fuiste, fue, fuimos, fuisteis, fueron
Imperative: ve, vaya, vayamos, id, vayan
Pres. Subj.: vaya, vayas, vaya, vayamos, vayáis, vayan
Imp. Subj.: fuera (fuese), fueras, fuera, fuéramos, fuerais, fueran

jugar *to play*

Pres. Ind.: juego, juegas, juega, jugamos, jugáis, juegan
Imperative: juega, juegue, juguemos, jugad, jueguen
Pres. Subj.: juegue, juegues, juegue, juguemos, juguéis, jueguen

obtener *to obtain (see* **tener***)*

oír *to hear*

Pres. Ind.: oigo, oyes, oye, oímos, oís, oyen
Preterit: oí, oíste, oyó, oímos, oísteis, oyeron
Imperative: oye, oiga, oigamos, oíd, oigan
Pres. Subj.: oiga, oigas, oiga, oigamos, oigáis, oigan
Imp. Subj.: oyera (oyese), oyeras, oyera, oyéramos, oyerais, oyeran
Pres. Part.: oyendo
Past Part.: oído

oler *to smell*

Pres. Ind.: huelo, hueles, huele, olemos, oléis, huelen
Imperative: huele, huela, olamos, oled, huelan
Pres. Subj.: huela, huelas, huela, olamos, oláis, huelan

poder *to be able to*

Preterit: pude, pudiste, pudo, pudimos, pudisteis, pudieron
Future: podré, podrás, podrá, podremos, podréis, podrán
Conditional: podría, podrías, podría, podríamos, podríais, podrían
Imperative: puede, pueda, podamos, poded, puedan
Imp. Subj.: pudiera (pudiese), pudieras, pudiera, pudiéramos, pudierais, pudieran
Pres. Subj.: pudiendo

poner *to place, put*

Pres. Ind.: pongo, pones, pone, ponemos, ponéis, ponen
Preterit: puse, pusiste, puso, pusimos, pusisteis, pusieron
Future: pondré, pondrás, pondrá, pondremos, pondréis, pondrán
Conditional: pondría, pondrías, pondría, pondríamos, pondríais, pondrían
Imperative: pon, ponga, pongamos, poned, pongan

Pres. Subj.: ponga, pongas, ponga, pongamos, pongáis, pongan
Imp. Subj.: pusiera (pusiese), pusieras, pusiera, pusiéramos, pusierais, pusieran
Past Part.: puesto

querer *to want, wish; to like, love*
Preterit: quise, quisiste, quiso, quisimos, quisisteis, quisieron
Future: querré, querrás, querrá, querremos, querréis, querrán
Conditional: querría, querrías, querría, querríamos, querríais, querrían
Imp. Subj.: quisiera (quisiese), quisieras, quisiera, quisiéramos, quisierais, quisieran

resolver *to decide on*
Past Part.: resuelto

saber *to know*
Pres. Ind.: sé, sabes, sabe, sabemos, sabéis, saben
Preterit: supe, supiste, supo, supimos, supisteis, supieron
Future: sabré, sabrás, sabrá, sabremos, sabréis, sabrán
Conditional: sabría, sabrías, sabría, sabríamos, sabríais, sabrían
Imperative: sabe, sepa, sepamos, sabed, sepan
Pres. Subj.: sepa, sepas, sepa, sepamos, sepáis, sepan
Imp. Subj.: supiera (supiese), supieras, supiera, supiéramos, supierais, supieran

salir *to leave; to go out*
Pres. Ind.: salgo, sales, sale, salimos, salís, salen
Future: saldré, saldrás, saldrá, saldremos, saldréis, saldrán
Conditional: saldría, saldrías, saldría, saldríamos, saldríais, saldrían
Imperative: sal, salga, salgamos, salid, salgan
Pres. Subj.: salga, salgas, salga, salgamos, salgáis, salgan

ser *to be*
Pres. Ind.: soy, eres, es, somos, sois, son
Imp. Ind.: era, eras, era, éramos, erais, eran
Preterit: fui, fuiste, fue, fuimos, fuisteis, fueron
Imperative: sé, sea, seamos, sed, sean
Pres. Subj.: sea, seas, sea, seamos, seáis, sean
Imp. Subj.: fuera (fuese), fueras, fuera, fuéramos, fuerais, fueran

suponer *to assume (see* **poner***)*

tener *to have*
Pres. Ind.: tengo, tienes, tiene, tenemos, tenéis, tienen
Preterit: tuve, tuviste, tuvo, tuvimos, tuvisteis, tuvieron
Future: tendré, tendrás, tendrá, tendremos, tendréis, tendrán
Conditional: tendría, tendrías, tendría, tendríamos, tendríais, tendrían
Imperative: ten, tenga, tengamos, tened, tengan
Pres. Subj.: tenga, tengas, tenga, tengamos, tengáis, tengan
Imp. Subj.: tuviera (tuviese), tuvieras, tuviera, tuviéramos, tuvierais, tuvieran

traducir *to translate (see* **conducir***)*

traer *to bring*
Pres. Ind.: traigo, traes, trae, traemos, traéis, traen
Preterit: traje, trajiste, trajo, trajimos, trajisteis, trajeron
Imperative: trae, traiga, traigamos, traed, traigan
Pres. Subj.: traiga, traigas, traiga, traigamos, traigáis, traigan
Imp. Subj.: trajera (trajese), trajeras, trajera, trajéramos, trajerais, trajeran

Pres. Part.: trayendo
Past Part.: traído

valer *to be worth*

Pres. Ind.: valgo, vales, vale, valemos, valéis, valen
Future: valdré, valdrás, valdrá, valdremos, valdréis, valdrán
Conditional: valdría, valdrías, valdría, valdríamos, valdríais, valdrían
Imperative: vale, valga, valgamos, valed, valgan
Pres. Subj.: valga, valgas, valga, valgamos, valgáis, valgan

venir *to come*

Pres. Ind.: vengo, vienes, viene, venimos, venís, vienen
Preterit: vine, viniste, vino, vinimos, vinisteis, vinieron
Future: vendré, vendrás, vendrá, vendremos, vendréis, vendrán
Conditional: vendría, vendrías, vendría, vendríamos, vendríais, vendrían
Imperative: ven, venga, vengamos, venid, vengan
Pres. Subj.: venga, vengas, venga, vengamos, vengáis, vengan
Imp. Subj.: viniera (viniese), vinieras, viniera, viniéramos, vinierais, vinieran
Pres. Part.: viniendo

ver *to see*

Pres. Ind.: veo, ves, ve, vemos, veis, ven
Imp. Ind.: veía, veías, veía, veíamos, veíais, veían
Preterit: vi, viste, vio, vimos, visteis, vieron
Imperative: ve, vea, veamos, ved, vean
Pres. Subj.: vea, veas, vea, veamos, veáis, vean
Imp. Subj.: viera (viese), vieras, viera, viéramos, vierais, vieran
Past Part.: visto

volver *to return*
Past Part.: vuelto

APPENDIX C Glossary of Grammatical Terms

adjective: A word that is used to describe a noun: *tall* girl, *difficult* lesson.

adverb: A word that modifies a verb, an adjective, or another adverb. It answers the questions "How?", "When?", "Where?": She walked *slowly.* She'll be here *tomorrow.* She is *here.*

agreement: A term applied to changes in form that nouns cause in the words that surround them. In Spanish, verb forms agree with their subjects in person and number (**yo** habl**o**, **él** habl**a**, etc.). Spanish adjectives agree in gender and number with the noun they describe. Thus, a feminine plural noun requires a feminine plural ending in the adjective that describes it (cas**as** amarill**as**) and a masculine singular noun requires a masculine singular ending in the adjective (libro negr**o**).

auxiliary verb: A verb that helps in the conjugation of another verb: I *have* finished. He *was* called. She *will* go. He *would* eat.

command form: The form of the verb used to give an order or a direction: *Go! Come* back! *Turn* to the right!

conjugation: The process by which the forms of the verb are presented in their different moods and tenses: I *am*, you *are*, he *is*, she *was*, we *were*, etc.

contraction: The combination of two or more words into one: *isn't, don't, can't.*

definite article: A word used before a noun indicating a definite person or thing: *the* woman, *the* money.

demonstrative: A word that refers to a definite person or object: *this, that, these, those.*

diphthong: A combination of two vowels forming one syllable. In Spanish, a diphthong is composed of one *strong* vowel (**a, e, o**) and one *weak* vowel (**u, i**) or two weak vowels: **ei, au, ui.**

exclamation: A word used to express emotion: *How* strong! *What* beauty!

gender: A distinction of nouns, pronouns, and adjectives, based on whether they are masculine or feminine.

indefinite article: A word used before a noun that refers to an indefinite person or object: *a* child, *an* apple.

infinitive: The form of the verb generally preceded in English by the word *to* and showing no subject or number: *to do, to bring.*

interrogative: A word used in asking a question: *Who?, What?, Where?.*

main clause: A group of words that includes a subject and a verb and by itself has complete meaning: *They saw me. I go now.*

noun: A word that names a person, place, or thing: *Ann, London, pencil,* etc.

number: Number refers to singular and plural: *chair, chairs.*

object: Generally a noun or a pronoun that is the receiver of the verb's action. A direct object answers the question *"What?"* or *"Whom?"*: We know *her.* Take *it.* An indirect object answers the question *"To whom?"* or *"To what?"*: Give *John* the money. Nouns and pronouns can also be objects of prepositions: The letter is *from Rick.* I'm thinking *about you.*

past participle: Past forms of a verb: *gone, worked, written,* etc.

person: The form of the pronoun and of

the verb that shows the person referred to: *I* (first-person singular), *you* (second-person singular), *she* (third-person singular), etc.

possessive: A word that denotes ownership or possession: This is *our* house. The book isn't *mine*.

preposition: A word that introduces a noun or pronoun and indicates its function in the sentence: They were *with* us. She is *from* Nevada.

pronoun: A word that is used to replace a noun: *she, them, us,* etc. A **subject pronoun** refers to the person or thing spoken of: *They* work. An **object pronoun** receives the action of the verb: They arrested *us* (direct object pronoun). She spoke to *him* (indirect object pronoun). A pronoun can also be the object of a preposition: The children stayed with *us*.

reflexive pronoun: A pronoun that refers back to the subject: *myself,* *yourself, himself, herself, itself, ourselves,* etc.

subject: The person, place, or thing spoken of: *Robert* works. *Our car* is new.

subordinate clause: A clause that has no complete meaning by itself but depends on a main clause: They knew *that I was here*.

tense: The group of forms in a verb that show the time in which the action of the verb takes place: *I go* (present indicative), *I'm going* (present progressive), *I went* (past), *I was going* (past progressive), *I will go* (future), *I would go* (conditional), *I have gone* (present perfect), *I had gone* (past perfect), *that I may go* (present subjunctive), etc.

verb: A word that expresses an action or a state: We *sleep*. They baby *is* sick.

APPENDIX D Questions for the "College Bowl"

The following questions will be answered by students participating in the "College Bowl," which is described in the **Actividad especial** at the end of Lección 18. The instructor should first divide the class into equal teams, then ask questions of each student, assigning points for correct answers.

The questions are based on the cultural information provided in the **¿Lo sabía Ud.... ?** and the **Panorama hispánico** sections of the text.

1. ¿Dónde dicen «oigo» cuando contestan el teléfono?
2. ¿Qué idioma hablan en Brasil?
3. ¿Qué otro nombre se le da al idioma español?
4. ¿Cuál es el sobrenombre de una persona que se llama Antonia?
5. ¿Cuál es el nombre de una persona a la que llaman Pepe (Quique)?
6. Generalmente, ¿cuántos apellidos usan las personas en los países de habla hispana?
7. Si una persona se llama José Pérez Rivas, ¿cuál es el apellido de su padre? ¿Cuál es el de su madre?
8. ¿Qué hay que tener en cuenta al alfabetizar los nombres de personas en español?
9. ¿Qué celebran muchos hispanos además de su cumpleaños?
10. ¿Cuál es la edad mínima para comprar bebidas alcohólicas en algunos países de habla hispana?
11. ¿Cuál es uno de los museos de pintura más importantes de España?
12. Cite algunos pintores famosos de España.
13. ¿Qué diferencia hay entre la manera de escribir la fecha en los Estados Unidos y en los países de habla hispana?
14. ¿Qué fecha es 3–10–92 en los países de habla hispana?
15. ¿Cuál es la capital del Perú?
16. ¿Cómo se llama la moneda del Perú? ¿de España?
17. ¿A qué altura está situada la ciudad de Cuzco?
18. ¿Cuál fue la capital del antiguo Imperio Inca?
19. ¿En qué cordillera está situada Machu Picchu?
20. ¿Qué países abarcaba (*encompassed*) el Imperio Inca?
21. El nombre de María, ¿es exclusivamente femenino?
22. ¿Qué diferencia hay entre las estaciones en el hemisferio norte y en el hemisferio sur?
23. Cuando en los Estados Unidos es verano, ¿qué estación es en Argentina?
24. ¿Cuáles son las playas más conocidas de Argentina, Chile y Uruguay?
25. ¿Cuáles son los idiomas oficiales de Puerto Rico?
26. ¿Qué nombre le dieron los indios a la isla de Puerto Rico?
27. ¿A qué grupo de islas pertenece Puerto Rico?
28. ¿Es Puerto Rico una república independiente?
29. ¿Cuál es la capital de España?
30. ¿Cuál es la población de Madrid?
31. Mencione dos estilos arquitectónicos que pueden apreciarse en los edificios de Madrid.

32. ¿Cuál es el parque más famoso de Madrid?
33. ¿Cuál es, para muchos españoles, el símbolo de Madrid?
34. ¿En qué ciudades de España hay metro?
35. ¿Por qué es famosa la ciudad de Ávila?
36. ¿Qué famosos escritores nacieron en Ávila?
37. ¿Por qué muchos jóvenes hispanos prefieren usar motocicleta?
38. ¿Qué sistema de medidas se utiliza en los países de habla hispana?
39. ¿A qué equivale un kilómetro?
40. ¿Cómo se llaman las tiendas donde se vende carne? ¿frutas? ¿pan?
41. ¿A qué equivale un galón?
42. ¿Qué película española ganó el *Oscar* en 1983?
43. ¿Cuál es el título en inglés de la película *Un detective suelto en Hollywood*?
44. ¿A qué facultad debe asistir una persona que quiere ser médico?
45. ¿Qué otro nombre tiene el jai-alai?
46. ¿Cuál fue la capital de la España mora?
47. ¿Cuál fue la primera universidad fundada en España?
48. ¿Cuál es el puerto comercial más activo de España?
49. ¿En qué ciudad española está el templo de La Sagrada Familia?
50. ¿Quiénes construyeron la Alhambra?
51. ¿Quién creó el personaje de Don Quijote?
52. ¿De qué época data la celebración del Corpus Christi?
53. ¿En qué mes se celebra el Corpus Christi en España?
54. ¿Cuál es la paella más famosa de España?
55. ¿Cuál es el baile típico del Sur de España?
56. ¿Quién es Joan Miró?
57. ¿Dónde está la pirámide del Mago?
58. ¿En qué ciudad está el Castillo de Chapultepec?
59. De los monumentos que hay en el Paseo de la Reforma, ¿cuál es el más importante para los mexicanos?
60. ¿Qué es lo más famoso de la artesanía de Oaxaca?
61. ¿Qué famoso presidente y patriota mexicano nació en Oaxaca?
62. ¿Quién es un famoso muralista mexicano?
63. ¿Dónde está el Museo de Antropología en México?
64. ¿Qué se celebra el primero y el dos de noviembre en México?
65. ¿Qué canal une el Océano Pacífico con el Océano Atlántico?
66. ¿Cuál es la base principal de la economía de Guatemala?
67. ¿Cuál es uno de los productos principales de Guatemala?
68. ¿Cuál es la capital de Honduras?
69. ¿En qué país están las playas de Luquillo, Isla Verde y Las Croabas?
70. ¿Dónde se cree que están enterrados los restos de Cristóbal Colón?
71. ¿Cuál es el deporte más popular en Puerto Rico?
72. ¿Cuál es la universidad más antigua de Cuba?
73. ¿En qué país están las cataratas del Ángel?
74. ¿Cuál es el río más grande de América del Sur?
75. ¿En qué país está la ciudad de Cartagena?
76. ¿Cuál es la capital de Ecuador?
77. ¿A qué distancia de la línea del Ecuador está Quito?
78. ¿En que país está el lago navegable más alto del mundo?
79. ¿Qué animal se usa principalmente para transportar carga en los Andes?

80. ¿Qué río nace en los llanos de Colombia?
81. ¿Cuál es uno de los barrios más elegantes de Buenos Aires?
82. ¿Cuál es la capital de Paraguay?
83. ¿Qué cataratas encontramos en la frontera entre Argentina, Brasil y Paraguay?
84. Además del español, ¿qué otro idioma se habla en el Paraguay?
85. ¿Cuál es la capital de Uruguay?
86. ¿Cuál es el teatro más famoso de Buenos Aires?
87. ¿En qué cuidad de California está la calle Olvera?
88. ¿En qué estado vive la mayor parte de los cubanos radicados en los Estados Unidos?
89. ¿Quiénes dominaron España por más de 700 años?
90. ¿Cuál es la capital de Cataluña?
91. ¿Cómo se llama el rey de España?
92. ¿Qué se celebra el siete de julio en Pamplona?
93. ¿Cuál es la ciudad que tiene más habitantes en todo el mundo?
94. ¿A qué país se le llama *la Suiza de Centro América*?
95. ¿En qué país tuvo su origen el gran imperio de los Mayas?
96. ¿Cuál es el país más pequeño de Centro América?
97. ¿Qué nombre le dio Colón a la isla de Santo Domingo?
98. ¿Cuál es la capital de Cuba?
99. ¿Qué país tiene como capital una ciudad llamada Santiago?
100. ¿Qué islas están consideradas como uno de los centros ecológicos mejor conservados?

APPENDIX E *Answer Key to the Self-Tests*

SELF-TEST PASOS 1–3

A. Cardinal numbers 0–30

nueve / cinco / trece / dos / cero / diez / veintisiete (veinte y siete) / once / catorce / dieciocho (diez y ocho) / treinta / doce / quince

B. Gender of nouns

1. la / una 2. el / un 3. el / un 4. la / una 5. el / un 6. el / un 7. la / una 8. el / un 9. el / un 10. la / una

C. Plural forms

1. los señores y las señoritas 2. unos relojes 3. las doctoras y los profesores 4. unos lápices 5. las conversaciones 6. unas mujeres 7. las ventanas 8. las plumas y los cuadernos

D. Colors

1. amarillo 2. rojo 3. azul 4. rojo, blanco y azul 5. verde 6. negro 7. marrón (café) 8. anaranjado

E. Telling time

1. Es la una y media. 2. Son las tres menos cuarto. 3. Son las cuatro y diez. 4. Son las doce. 5. Son las dos y cuarto.

F. Just words . . .

1. g 2. j 3. h 4. a 5. d 6. f 7. i 8. b 9. l 10. o 11. n 12. m 13. e 14. k 15. c

SELF-TEST LECCIONES 1–3

Lección 1

A. Subject pronouns and present indicative of regular -ar verbs

1. Nosotras hablamos inglés y español. 2. Uds. trabajan en el hospital. 3. Ellas llaman más tarde. 4. Ellos estudian ruso y chino. 5. Nosotros necesitamos dinero. 6. Nosotros deseamos hablar con Eva.

B. Gender, Part II

1. la 2. las 3. la 4. los 5. la 6. el 7. la 8. las 9. el 10. el 11. las 12. los

C. Negative and interrogative sentences

1. —¿Hablas (Habla Ud.) francés? / —No, no hablo francés. 2. —¿Necesita él la lección l? / —No, él no necesita la lección l. 3. —¿Llaman ellos más tarde? / —No, (ellos) no llaman más tarde. 4. —¿Trabajas (Trabaja Ud.) en la universidad? / —No, no trabajo en la universidad.

D. Cardinal numbers 31–1,000

1. el año mil cuatrocientos noventa y dos 2. el año mil setecientos setenta y seis 3. el año mil ochocientos sesenta y cinco 4. el año mil novecientos noventa 5. Calle Paz, número dos mil quinientos cincuenta y dos 6. Calle Bolívar, número cinco mil ciento veintitrés

E. Present indicative of ser

1. Yo soy de México, pero ellos son de California. 2. ¿Eres (tú) de Chile? Nosotros somos de Chile también. 3. El Sr. Vera es profesor. 4. ¿Son ustedes de Venezuela?

F. Just words . . .

1. i 2. d 3. l 4. a 5. c 6. k 7. b 8. g 9. j 10. f 11. e 12. h

Lección 2

A. Possession with **de**

1. ¿Cuál es el número de teléfono de Nora?
2. ¿Es difícil la clase de la doctora Peña?
3. ¿Cuál es la dirección de los hijos de Ernesto?

B. Agreement of adjectives, articles, and nouns

1. La chica es alta. 2. La doctora es española. 3. Las señoras son inglesas. 4. La profesora es mexicana. 5. Las hijas de ella no son felices.

C. Possessive adjectives

1. Sí, es su esposa. 2. Sí, nuestro profesor es divorciado. 3. Sí, sus hijos beben café. 4. Sí, nuestros hijos solicitan el trabajo. 5. Sí, sus estudiantes deben llenar otra solicitud.

D. Present indicative of regular **-er** and **-ir** verbs

1. como 2. vive 3. leen / escriben / aprenden 4. Beben 5. crees 6. lee 7. escribimos 8. recibe 9. como 10. decide / debe

E. Present indicative of the irregular verbs **tener** and **venir**

1. tienen 2. viene 3. tenemos 4. viene 5. tengo / vienen 6. vengo

F. Uses of **tener que** + *infinitive*

1. Tengo que llenar la solicitud. 2. Tenemos que escribir el anuncio. 3. Ellos tienen que trabajar. 4. Mi esposo tiene que venir a las once.

G. Just words . . . (Part I)

1. conocimiento 2. rubio 3. solicitud 4. difícil 5. café / comen / jamón 6. lee / periódico 7. libre 8. lejos

H. Just words . . . (Part II)

1. Nombre 2. Dirección 3. Edad 4. Lugar de nacimiento 5. Estado civil 6. Ocupación 7. Lugar donde estudia

Lección 3

A. Expressions with **tener**

1. Mis compañeros de clase tienen prisa. 2. Yo no tengo hambre, pero tengo mucha sed. 3. ¿Tienes (Tiene Ud.) calor? ¡Yo tengo frío! 4. Mis amigos tienen sueño. 5. Nosotros no tenemos miedo. 6. Ud. tiene razón, señorita Peña. Mary tiene treinta años.

B. The personal **a**

1. Yo llevo a mis hermanos a la fiesta de Navidad. 2. Nosotros llevamos la cerveza a la cafetería. 3. Ellos invitan a Julio y a su novia. 4. Nosotros tenemos cuatro hijos.

C. Contractions

1. Venimos del club. 2. Voy al baile de fin de año. 3. Llama al hermano de su compañero. 4. Invitan a las chicas. 5. Vengo de la terraza. 6. Llevamos a las muchachas uruguayas. 7. Viene del hospital. 8. Es de la ciudad de México.

D. Present indicative of the irregular verbs **ir, dar,** and **estar**

1. voy 2. damos 3. está 4. está 5. van 6. dan 7. estoy 8. van 9. estás 10. doy

E. **Ir a** + *infinitive*

1. Yo no voy a hablar con mi hermana. 2. Mis hijos van a estudiar en España. 3. Mi amiga va a leer el anuncio. 4. Ustedes van a bailar en la fiesta. 5. Tú no vas a vivir cerca de la universidad. 6. Nosotros vamos a brindar con sidra.

F. Present indicative of **e:ie** stem-changing verbs

1. quiere / piensa 2. entendemos 3. pierde 4. Cierras 5. empiezan / comienzan 6. empezamos / comenzamos 7. pienso / quiero 8. preferimos

G. Just words . . .

1. Invitamos 2. comemos 3. sidra 4. magnífica 5. nuevo 6. coctel 7. brindamos 8. discos

SELF-TEST LESSONS 4–6

Lección 4

A. Comparison of adjectives and adverbs

1. Alfredo es el estudiante más inteligente de la clase. 2. La Lección 12 es menos interesante que la lección 7. 3. Mi novia es más bonita que tu novia. 4. Roberto es el más guapo de la familia. 5. El profesor tiene menos de veinte estudiantes. 6. Ana es tan alta como Roberto.

B. Irregular comparison of adjectives and adverbs

1. más grande 2. mejor 3. mejor / peor 4. mayor 5. más / menos 6. más pequeño

C. Ordinal numbers

1. tercer 2. quinto 3. cuarto 4. décimo 5. octavo 6. primer

D. Present indicative of **o:ue** stem-changing verbs

1. cuesta 2. pueden 3. Recuerda 4. cuento 5. almorzamos 6. vuelves

E. Weather expressions

1. Llueve 2. Hace mucho frío. 3. calor 4. nieva 5. hace mucho sol 6. niebla

F. Just words . . .

1. nieto 2. bajo 3. delgado 4. las pinturas 5. cartas 6. mirar 7. extrañas 8. ¡Qué lástima! 9. manejan su auto 10. fotos 11. pronóstico 12. mediana

Lección 5

A. Present indicative of **e:i** stem-changing verbs

1. En el restaurante México sirven la cena a las nueve. 2. Ella pide una habitación con vista a la calle. 3. Nosotros seguimos al botones a la habitación. 4. ¿Consiguen Uds. reservaciones en diciembre? 5. Yo digo que él debe firmar el registro ahora.

B. Pronouns as objects of prepositions

1. mí 2. ti 3. ellos 4. nosotros 5. conmigo 6. contigo

C. Affirmative and negative expressions

1. Ellos van a querer algo. 2. Hay alguien en el baño. 3. Tengo unos objetos de oro y plata. 4. Ellos siempre pasan por la aduana. 5. Yo también ceno a las nueve. 6. Siempre tiene las listas de los hoteles. 7. Puedes ir o a la derecha o a la izquierda. 8. Ellos siempre quieren algo también.

D. Present progressive

1. está diciendo 2. estoy hablando 3. estamos leyendo 4. estás comiendo 5. está durmiendo 6. están pidiendo

E. Direct object pronouns

1. comprarlo 2. te llamo 3. la sirven 4. declararla 5. me lleva 6. las necesito 7. los aceptan 8. llevarlo 9. las tengo 10. llamarla

F. Just words . . .

1. c 2. a 3. b 4. c 5. b 6. a 7. b
8. a 9. a 10. b 11. c 12. c

Lección 6

A. Demonstrative adjectives and pronouns

1. estos cuchillos y aquéllos 2. ese mantel y éste 3. estas oficinas y aquéllas 4. este teatro y aquél 5. este mozo y aquél 6. estas servilletas y aquéllas

B. Summary of the uses of **ser** and **estar**

1. Ella es la mamá de María 2. El club nocturno está en la calle Siete. 3. ¡Hmmm! Este lechón asado está muy sabroso. 4. Roberto es de España, pero ahora está en los Estados Unidos. 5. La sopa está fría. 6. El reloj es de oro. 7. Hoy es martes y mañana es miércoles. 8. El mozo está sirviendo la comida. 9. La fiesta es en casa de Julia. 10. El teatro es muy grande.

C. Irregular first person

1. conduzco 2. sé 3. quepo 4. salgo 5. traduzco 6. veo 7. hago 8. pongo 9. conozco 10. traigo

D. **Saber** vs. **conocer; pedir** vs. **preguntar**

1. Voy a preguntar cuándo es su aniversario de bodas. 2. Yo sé que ellos quieren ir a ese restaurante. 3. Yo no conozco a su suegra, Sra. Peña. 4. Él va a pedir el menú. 5. Yo no sé hablar ruso.

E. Indirect object pronouns

1. Ella les trae la torta helada. 2. Yo te voy a preparar (voy a prepararte) / un puré de papas. 3. Él le trae el flan y el helado. 4. Ana me va a comprar (va a comprarme) las tazas. 5. El camarero nos trae una botella de vino tinto. 6. Les traen el filete y la langosta.

F. Just words . . .

1. s 2. i 3. a 4. m 5. q 6. t 7. o 8. d 9. g 10. h 11. c 12. f 13. b 14. r 15. e 16. k 17. n 18. j 19. l 20. p

SELF-TEST LECCIONES 7–9

Lección 7

A. Construction with **gustar**

1. No me gusta esa agencia de viajes. 2. A él le gusta el asiento de pasillo. 3. ¿Le (Te) gusta este bolso de mano? 4. No nos gusta viajar por avión. 5. Les gusta (a ellos) su hotel?

B. Possessive pronouns

1. El mío 2. las suyas 3. las nuestras 4. las tuyas 5. los nuestros 6. El suyo

C. Time expressions with **hacer**

1. Hace dos días que yo no duermo. 2. Hace un mes que tú no me llamas. 3. Hace media hora que nosotros estamos sentados. 4. Hace un año que ellos viven en España. 5. Hace doce horas que mi hija no come.

D. Preterit of regular verbs

1. Ayer Luisa y yo compramos los billetes. 2. La semana pasada yo viajé. 3. Ayer ella me esperó en el aeropuerto. 4. ¿No pagaron Uds. la cuenta anoche? 5. Ellos abrieron las ventanas al mediodía. 6. El lunes nosotros comimos en la cafetería. 7. ¿Empezaste a estudiar esta mañana? 8. Ayer yo le presté las maletas.

E. Direct and indirect object pronouns used together

1. Se lo van a mandar (Van a mandárselo) mañana. 2. Elsa me las va a comprar (va a comprármelas). 3. Luis nos las va a traducir

(va a traducírnoslas). 4. Se (Te) lo voy a traer (voy a traértelo)(traérselo) esta tarde. 5. La profesora me la va a dar (va a dármela).

F. Just words . . .

1. viajes 2. Buen viaje 3. turista 4. ida 5. retraso 6. devolver 7. próxima 8. salida 9. mano 10. aburridas 11. exceso 12. barco

Lección 8

A. Reflexive constructions

1. Tú te vistes muy bien. 2. Ellos se afeitan todos los días. 3. Ellos se acuestan a las once. 4. ¿Ud. no se preocupa por sus hijos? 5. Yo me pongo el vestido. 6. Juan se sienta aquí. 7. Tú te lavas la cabeza todos los días. 8. Yo no me corté el pelo. 9. Yo no me acuerdo de eso. 10. Uds. se fueron. 11. ¿Cómo te llamas (tú)? 12. Daniel no se despertó todavía.

B. Some uses of the definite article

1. ¿Tú te quitas los zapatos? 2. El barbero me corta el pelo. 3. La peluquera me lava la cabeza. 4. Uds. no se lavan las manos. 5. Nosotros preferimos el té. 6. Las madres se preocupan por sus hijos. 7. La libertad es lo más importante.

C. Preterit of ser, ir, and dar

1. Nosotros fuimos a la cocina y comimos hamburguesas. 2. Él no fue mi profesor el año pasado. 3. ¿Tú le diste la revista, querido? 4. Alguien rompió el espejo. ¿Fue Ud., señorita? 5. Nosotros no le dimos el champú al peluquero. 6. Yo fui a la peluquería. 7. Yo no le di el rizador. 8. ¿Fuiste tú a la farmacia anoche? 9. Ellos fueron a la barbería la semana pasada. 10. ¿Fueron Raúl y Eva mis estudiantes el año pasado?

11. Yo te di la alfombra. 12. Ellos nos dieron una escoba.

D. Preterit of e:i and o:u stem-changing verbs

1. ¿Dormimos nosotros anoche en el hotel? 2. Los chicos siguieron a sus padres. 3. Nosotros servimos / pedimos sándwiches de jamón y queso. 4. Ella me mintió. No tiene veinte años; tiene diez y siete. 5. ¿No consiguió Ud. el dinero para ir de vacaciones? 6. ¿Qué le pidieron los niños a Santa Claus? 7. El hombre murió en un accidente. 8. Ella me repitió la pregunta.

E. Just words . . .

1. escoba 2. lavado / peinado 3. moda 4. aspiradora 5. cocinar 6. champú 7. lacio 8. tonto 9. peine 10. máquina / afeitar 11. ocupado 12. regalo

Lección 9

A. Irregular preterits

1. tuvieron 2. estuvieron 3. traduje 4. pude 5. pusiste 6. hubo 7. hizo las maletas 8. vino 9. no dijeron 10. trajo

B. Por v. para

para / para / por / para / para / por / Por / para / para / por / para / por / por / por / para

C. Imperfect tense

1. acampábamos / gustaba 2. montaba / pescaba 3. se divertían 4. vivíamos / asistía 5. trabajábamos 6. servías

D. Just words . . .

1. l 2. h 3. o 4. a 5. j 6. b 7. d 8. n 9. c 10. m 11. e 12. f 13. i 14. g 15. k 16. p

SELF-TEST LECCIONES 10–12

Lección 10

A. Preterit vs. imperfect

1. tuvo / llamé 2. fuimos 3. Eran / llevó 4. preguntó / estaba 5. era / tenía 6. dijo / necesitaba 7. hubo 8. estuvimos / había 9. íbamos / vimos 10. dolía / Tomé / me acosté

B. Verbs which change meaning in the preterit

1. No quise hablar de mi enfermedad. 2. No sabíamos que ella estaba enferma. 3. Ella supo que yo estaba enfermo(-a). 4. Conocí a tu (su) hermano anoche. 5. No quería tomar la medicina, pero la tomé. 6. Paco, ¿conocías a la Srta. Rivera?

C. **Hace...** meaning *ago*

1. Hace dos días que lo atropelló un coche. 2. Hace tres meses que ellos me operaron de apendicitis. 3. Hace una semana que murió mi perro. 4. ¿Cuánto tiempo hace que Ud. vio al doctor? 5. ¿Cuánto tiempo hace que ellos le hicieron los análisis?

D. Formation of adverbs

1. especialmente 2. raramente 3. lenta y claramente 4. solamente 5. Generalmente 6. frecuentemente

E. Just words . . .

1. penicilina 2. los dientes 3. la lengua 4. los ojos 5. los pies 6. la herida 7. rompiste 8. la pierna 9. el tobillo 10. vías 11. pusieron 12. dolor de cabeza 13. el estómago 14. embarazada 15. roto

Lección 11

A. The relative pronouns **que** and **quien(es)**

1. Ésta es la señorita que le va a dar los pantalones. 2. Éstos son los vestidos que están de moda. 3. Ayer vi a las profesoras de quienes ellos nos hablaron. 4. Esta es la señora a quien yo le mostré las fotos. 5. Él compró una maleta que es cara.

B. The subjunctive with verbs of volition

1. vayas 2. abrir 3. cobrar 4. lo compremos 5. fechen / firmen 6. yo le pague 7. pagarle 8. depositen 9. ahorrar 10. Ud. traiga 11. yo lleve 12. yo aparque / yo estacione 13. cobrarles 14. dejes 15. abrir 16. yo salga 17. Uds. ahorren 18. viva

C. The subjunctive with verbs of emotion

1. Espero que Ud. tenga el comprobante, Sr. Vega. 2. Siento que no puedan quedarse. 3. Tememos que Juana no venga. 4. Me alegro de que no tengas que pedir un préstamo, querido(-a). 5. Espero que estén listas las fotos.

D. Just words . . .

1. despertador 2. corriente 3. firma 4. diligencias 5. saldo 6. revelar 7. plazos 8. gratis 9. parezcan 10. robaron 11. estacionar / aparcar / parquear 12. quedarme

Lección 12

A. The **Ud.** and **Uds.** commands

1. mande 2. Estén 3. Vaya 4. camine / doble 5. sean 6. Caminen 7. Trate 8. Cierren 9. den 10. deje

B. Position of object pronouns with direct commands

1. Tráigamelas 2. Désela 3. Escríbanselas 4. Llévesela 5. Dígale 6. Déjelo 7. no se lo diga 8. No me los traiga

C. The subjunctive to express doubt, disbelief, and denial

1. No creo que el correo quede en la esquina. 2. Es verdad que ella está en la oficina de telégrafos. 3. Dudo que tengamos que subir. 4. Niego que él maneje muy bien. 5. No estoy seguro de que Luis sepa dónde está el paquete. 6. No es cierto que necesitemos un documento de identidad.

D. Constructions with se

1. ¿Qué idioma se habla en Chile? 2. ¿A qué hora se cierran los bancos? 3. ¿A qué hora se abre el correo? 4. ¿Dónde se venden estampillas? 5. ¿Por dónde se sube al segundo piso?

E. Just words . . .

1. l 2. g 3. o 4. i 5. c 6. a 7. k 8. e 9. b 10. m 11. d 12. h 13. f 14. j 15. n 16. p

SELF-TEST LECCIONES 13–15

Lección 13

A. The subjunctive to express indefiniteness and nonexistence

1. ¿Hay alguien aquí que sepa hablar español? 2. Tenemos una casa que tiene cinco dormitorios. 3. No conozco a nadie que sea de España. 4. ¿Quiere / quieres una casa que tenga piscina? 5. Necesito un sillón que sea cómodo. 6. Hay una chica que habla francés, pero no hay nadie que hable ruso.

B. The subjunctive or indicative after certain conjunctions

1. llegue 2. vuelvan 3. van 4. veas 5. ellos vendan 6. vayas 7. vean 8. necesite 9. des 10. consiga 11. me gusta 12. llueva

C. Qué and cuál used with ser

1. ¿Cuál es su (tu) número de teléfono? 2. ¿Cuál es el apellido de su (tu) madre? 3. ¿Qué es un pasaporte? 4. ¿Cuáles son las lecciones que Uds. necesitan? 5. ¿Cuál es su dirección? 6. ¿Qué es la sidra?

D. Uses of sino and pero

1. No voy a comprarlo a plazos sino al contado. 2. No quiere alquilar la casa sino comprarla. 3. El coche vale solamente setecientos dólares pero no podemos comprarlo. 4. Carlos no dijo que tenía el dinero sino que tenía los cheques. 5. Ella no quiere que firmemos la solicitud sino que la leamos.

E. Just words . . .

1. m 2. f 3. k 4. o 5. a 6. i 7. c 8. b 9. e 10. n 11. d 12. h 13. g 14. l 15. j

Lección 14

A. The past participle

1. escrito 2. abierto 3. visto 4. hecho 5. roto 6. ido 7. hablado 8. comido 9. bebido 10. recibido

B. Past participles used as adjectives

1. rotos 2. abiertas 3. muerto 4. cerrado 5. hechas

C. The present perfect

1. has usado 2. ha envuelto 3. han dicho 4. hemos comido 5. he quedado 6. han hecho

D. The past perfect

1. había terminado 2. habían ido 3. había dicho 4. había abierto 5. habíamos comprado 6. habías preguntado

E. The familiar command (tú form)

1. Dime 2. Haz / limpia 3. Sal 4. Ve / compra 5. Ponlos 6. Ven 7. Sé / tráeme 8. Ten / Espérame 9. No compres 10. No lo sirvas 11. No te vayas 12. Levántate / trabaja

F. Just words . . .

1. b 2. a 3. a 4. c 5. b 6. c 7. a 8. b

Lección 15

A. The future

1. le dirá 2. traerá 3. pondré 4. compraremos 5. le hablarás 6. haré 7. conducirán / manejarán 8. revisará 9. llevará 10. Te veré

B. The future to express probability in the present

1. Mi coche hace mucho ruido. Será porque el silenciador no funciona. 2. ¿Cuántos años tendrá Gustavo? 3. ¿Dónde habrá una estación de servicio? 4. Ese coche costará unos diez mil dólares. 5. San Diego estará a unas cincuenta millas de Los Ángeles.

C. The conditional

1. cambiarían 2. estaría 3. se ensuciaría 4. necesitarían 5. pondríamos 6. dirías

D. The conditional to express probability in the past

1. ¿Qué hora sería cuando llegaron los muchachos? 2. ¿Sería el acumulador? 3. ¿Cuántos años tendría el dependiente? 4. ¿Quién instalaría la bomba de agua? 5. ¿Quién vendría con Lola?

E. Just words . . .

1. el filtro 2. funcionan 3. un pinchazo 4. velocidad 5. lleno 6. iba muy rápido 7. chapa 8. estacionar aquí 9. remolcar 10. luces

SELF-TEST LECCIONES 16–18

Lección 16

A. First-person plural commands

1. Llamemos a Juan. 2. Alquilemos un coche de dos puertas. 3. No le digamos que no tenemos ganas de salir con él. 4. Preguntémosle a María si va a ir a la biblioteca hoy. 5. Vistámonos ahora para llegar a tiempo. 6. Digámosles que el coche no estaba asegurado.

B. The future perfect

1. habré comprado 2. habrá terminado 3. habrán cerrado 4. habremos vuelto 5. te habrás encontrado

C. The conditional perfect

1. habría comprado 2. habríamos hecho 3. se habría preocupado 4. habrías aceptado 5. habrían vuelto

D. Reciprocal reflexives

1. Hace tres meses que ellos se escriben. 2. Hace mucho tiempo que Uds. se conocen. 3. Hace un mes que ellas no se ven. 4. Hace quince días que Julio y Marisa no se llaman por teléfono. 5. Hace mucho tiempo que tú y yo nos queremos.

E. Just words . . .

1. n 2. h 3. r 4. p 5. k 6. a 7. m 8. d 9. c 10. o 11. q 12. f 13. e 14. b 15. j 16. g 17. i 18. t 19. l 20. s

Lección 17

A. The present perfect subjunctive

1. Nosotros sentimos mucho que Uds. no hayan tomado el examen parcial. 2. Yo

dudo que ella haya asistido a la Facultad de Derecho. 3. Es una lástima que tú no hayas mantenido un buen promedio este semestre. 4. Ellos se alegran de que nosotros hayamos tomado la clase de danza aeróbica. 5. Yo siento mucho que esa periodista haya muerto. 6. Es difícil que Pedro haya entregado la tarea a tiempo.

B. Uses of the imperfect subjunctive

1. te matricularas 2. no pudiera 3. hiciera ejercicio 4. ayudara 5. no vinieran 6. fuéramos 7. le prestara 8. lo conocieran

C. The pluperfect subjunctive

1. hubiera traído 2. hubiéramos salido 3. hubiera devuelto 4. le hubiera dicho 5. no hubieras venido

D. Just words . . .

1. especialización 2. siempre 3. consejero 4. cubano(-a) 5. literatura 6. requisitos 7. suerte 8. matrícula 9. flaca 10. primaria / secundaria 11. sacar 12. argentina 13. partido 14. ejercicio / aeróbica 15. horario 16. nota 17. asignatura 18. abogado

Lección 18

A. *If* clauses

1. hubieran reservado 2. hubieras llamado 3. consiguiera 4. tengo 5. como si fuera 6. necesitan 7. no viniera 8. vuelve

B. Summary of the uses of the subjunctive

1. reservemos 2. le dé 3. Quieres ver 4. ella tenga 5. verla 6. sea / hable 7. sepa 8. son 9. prefieren 10. pueda 11. lleguen 12. llega 13. vinieron 14. estuvieron 15. quiera 16. consiga 17. querrá ver 18. no tengan 19. tenemos prisa 20. llueva

C. Just words . . .

1. l 2. e 3. h 4. j 5. n 6. b 7. m 8. d 9. a 10. k 11. c 12. f 13. g 14. o 15. i

VOCABULARY

The Spanish–English vocabulary contains all active and passive words that appear in the student text. It includes words and expressions used in the photo captions, **Panorama hispánico** and **¿Lo sabía Ud.?** sections, readings, and authentic documents that are part of activities and exercises, and grammar examples. Active words and expressions are identified with a number that indicates the lesson in which they were first introduced.

The English–Spanish Vocabulary contains only those words and expressions that are considered active. This includes words that appear in the lesson vocabulary lists, grammar examples, and end-of-lesson readings.

The following abbreviations are used in the vocabularies:

adj.	adjective	*lang.*	language	*p.p.*	past participle
adv.	adverb	*m.*	masculine noun	*sing.*	singular
aux.	auxiliary	*Mex.*	Mexico	*Sp.*	Spain
f.	feminine noun	*pl.*	plural	*Sp. Am.*	Spanish America
fam.	familiar	*prep.*	preposition		
form.	formal	*pron.*	pronoun		

Spanish–English

A

a at, 1; to, 1
   _____ **menudo** often
   _____ **pesar de** in spite of
   _____ **plazos** in installments, 11
   _____ **tiempo** on time, 18
   _____ **través de** throughout
   _____ **veces** sometimes, 8
   _____ **ver** let's see, 11
abajo downstairs, 12
abierto(-a) *(p.p. of abrir and adj.)* open, 12
abogado(-a) *(m., f.)* lawyer, 17
abrazo *(m.)* hug, embrace, 18
abrigo *(m.)* coat, 4
abril April, 4
abrir open, 2
abuela *(f.)* grandmother, 4
abuelo *(m.)* grandfather, 4
aburrido(-a) bored, 7; boring, 7
aburrirse be bored, 9
acabado *(m.)* decoration
acabar de have just, 5
acampar camp, 9
accidente *(m.)* accident, 10
aceite *(m.)* oil, 15
aceituna *(f.)* olive
aceptar accept, 5
acero *(m.)* steel

aconsejar advise, 11
acordarse (de) (o:ue) remember, 8
acostar (o:ue) put to bed, 8
   _____se go to bed, 8
actividad *(f.)* activity
actuación *(f.)* act
actualmente at the present time, nowadays
acumulador *(m.)* battery, 15
adelantado(-a) advanced
adelante come in, P2
además besides, 3
adiós good-bye, P1
administración de empresas *(f.)* business administration, 17
adónde where (to), 3
adoquinar tile
aduana *(f.)* customs, 5
aeropuerto *(m.)* airport, 5
afectuosamente affectionately, 18
afeitar(se) shave, 8
afueras *(f. pl.)* outskirts
agencia de viajes *(f.)* travel agency, 7
agente *(m., f.)* agent
agosto August, 4
agrícola agricultural
agua *(f.)* water, 15
   _____ **mineral** mineral water, 6
aguafiestas *(m., f.)* spoilsport, 13

águila *(f.)* eagle
ahí mismo right there, 12
ahora now, 3
ahorrar save, 11
ahorros *(m. pl.)* savings, 11
aire acondicionado *(m.)* air conditioning, 13
al *(m. sing.) (contraction)* to the, 1
   _____ **aire libre** outdoors, 9
   _____ **contado** in cash, 11
   _____ **mismo tiempo** at the same time, 13
   _____ **rato** a while later, 11
   _____ **teléfono** on the phone, 1
ala *(f.)* wing
alberca *(f.) (Mex.)* swimming pool, 9
albóndiga *(f.)* meatball, 6
alcalde *(m.)* mayor
alcaldesa *(f.)* mayor
alcanzar achieve
alegrarse (de) be glad, 11
alegre cheerful, merry, 10
alegremente cheerfully, 10
alemán *(m.)* German *(lang.),* 1
alérgico(-a) allergic, 10
alfabetizar alphabetize
alfombra *(f.)* carpet, rug, 8
algo something, anything, 5
algodón *(m.)* cotton

alguien someone, somebody, 5
algún, alguna any, some, 5
alguna parte somewhere, 12
alguna vez ever, 10
alguno(-a) any, some, 5
algunos(-as) some, 4
almohada *(f.)* pillow, 13
almorzar (o:ue) have lunch, 4
almuerzo *(m.)* lunch, 5
alojamiento *(m.)* lodging
alquilar rent, 9
    se alquila for rent, 13
alquiler *(m.)* rent, 13; rental
alto(-a) tall, high, 2
altura *(f.)* height
allí there, 2
amante *(m., f.)* lover
amarillo(-a) yellow, P3
ambiente *(m.)* atmosphere
ambos(-as) both
ambulancia *(f.)* ambulance, 10
amigo(-a) *(m., f.)* friend, 2
amistad *(f.)* friendship
amor *(m.)* love, 6
amueblado(-a) furnished, 13
amurallado(-a) walled in
análisis *(m.)* analysis, test, 10
anaranjado(-a) orange, P3
ancho(-a) wide
andén *(m.)* platform, 18
aniversario *(m.)* anniversary, 6
    _____ de bodas *(m.)* wedding anniversary, 6
anoche last night, 8
anotar write down, 6
antes (de) before, 5
    _____ de que before, 13
anticipado(-a) advance
antiguo(-a) former, old, 12
antipático(-a) unpleasant, 2
antiquísimo(-a) ancient, very old
anunciar announce, 13
anuncio *(m.)* advertisement, ad, 2
    _____ clasificado classified ad, 13
año *(m.)* year, 2
    tener... _____s to be . . . years old, 3
aparcar park, 11
apartado postal *(m.)* post office box, 18
apartamento *(m.)* apartment, 8
apellido *(m.)* surname, 2
apendicitis *(f.)* appendicitis, 10
apio *(m.)* celery, 16
apreciar appreciate
aprender learn, 2

apretar (e:ie) be too tight, squeeze, 14
aprobar (o:ue) pass, 17
aprovechar take advantage of
aquel(los), aquella(s) *(adj.)* that, those *(distant),* 6
aquél(los), aquélla(s) *(pron.)* that one, those *(distant),* 6
aquello *(neuter pron.)* that, 6
aquí here, 3
arena *(f.)* sand
argentino(-a) Argentinian, 17
armario *(m.)* closet, 14
arrancar start *(car),* 15
arreglar fix, 15; arrange, 14
arriba upstairs, 12
arroz *(m.)* rice, 6
    _____ con leche *(m.)* rice pudding, 6
    _____ con pollo *(m.)* chicken with rice, 6
artesanía *(f.)* crafts
artículo *(m.)* article
    _____s deportivos sporting goods
asado(-a) roasted, 6
ascendencia *(f.)* origin
ascensor *(m.)* elevator, 5
asegurado(-a) insured, 18
asegurarse make sure
así como as well as
asiento *(m.)* seat, 7
    _____ de pasillo *(m.)* aisle seat, 7
    _____ de ventanilla *(m.)* window seat, 7
    tome _____ have a seat, P2
asignatura *(f.)* subject, 17
asistir (a) attend, 4
aspiradora *(f.)* vacuum cleaner, 8
aspirina *(f.)* aspirin, 10
asunto *(m.)* matter
atentamente politely, 18
aterrizar land *(plane),* 18
atraso *(m.)* delay, 7
    tener... de _____ be . . . behind schedule, 7
atravesar (e:ie) go through
atropellar run over, 10
aunque although, 13
autobús *(m.)* bus, 4
automático(-a) automatic, 18
automóvil *(m.)* car, 4
autopista *(f.)* freeway, highway, 9
avenida *(f.)* avenue, 2
avión *(m.)* plane, 7
¡ay! oh!, 4
ayer yesterday, 8

ayuda *(f.)* assistance, help, aid
ayudar help, assist, 17
azúcar *(m.)* sugar, 16
azul blue, P3

B

bahía *(f.)* bay
bailar dance, 3
baile *(m.)* dance, 3
bajar(se) go down, 12; get off, 18
bajo *(prep.)* under
bajo(-a) *(adj.)* short, 2
banco *(m.)* bank, 11
bañar(se) bathe, 8
baño *(m.)* bathroom, 5
barato(-a) cheap, inexpensive, 5
barbería *(f.)* barber shop, 8
barbero(-a) *(m., f.)* barber, 8
barco *(m.)* boat, ship, 7
barrer sweep, 8
barrio *(m.)* neighborhood, 13
barro *(m.)* clay
básquetbol *(m.)* basketball
bastar be enough, suffice
batería *(f.)* battery, 15
    _____ de cocina *(f.)* cookware
beber drink, 2
bebida *(f.)* drink, beverage, 3
beca *(f.)* scholarship, 17
béisbol *(m.)* baseball
belleza *(f.)* beauty, 8
    salón de _____ *(m.)* beauty salon, 8
bello(-a) beautiful
    Bellas Artes Fine Arts
beso *(m.)* kiss, 6
biblioteca *(f.)* library, 16
bicicleta *(f.)* bicycle, 9
    montar en _____ ride a bicycle, 9
bien well, fine, Pl; okay, 7
    no muy _____ not very well, Pl
billete *(m.)* ticket, 7
billetera *(f.)* wallet, 14
biología *(f.)* biology, 17
bistec *(m.)* steak, 6
blanco(-a) white, P3
blanquillo *(m.) (Mex.)* egg, 16
blusa *(f.)* blouse, 14
boca *(f.)* mouth, 10
bocadillo *(m.)(Sp.)* sandwich, 2
boda *(f.)* wedding
boleta *(m.)* ticket, 18
bolsa *(f.)* purse, 14
bolso de mano *(m.)* handbag, 7
bomba de agua *(f.)* water pump, 15

bonito(-a) pretty, 2
borrador *(m.)* eraser, P3
bosque *(m.)* woods
bota *(f.)* boot, 14
bote *(m.) (Mex.)* can, 16
botella *(f.)* bottle, 6
botica *(f.)* drugstore
botiquín *(m.)* medicine cabinet, 8
botones *(m.)* bellhop, 5
brazo *(m.)* arm, 10
brindar toast, 3
bromear joke, kid, 9
bueno(-a) good, 3; hello *(phone)*, 1;
　okay, 7; well, 2
　buena suerte good luck, 2
　buenas noches good evening, good
　　night, P1
　buenas tardes good afternoon, P1
　buenos días good morning, P1
　buen provecho enjoy your meal
　buen viaje have a nice trip, 7
bufanda *(f.)* scarf
buscar look for, search for, 7
butaca *(f.)* armchair, 13
buzón *(m.)* mailbox, 12

C

caballo *(m.)* horse, 9
　montar a _____ ride a horse, 9
cabaña *(f.)* cabin, 9
cabello *(m.)* hair, 10
caber fit, 6
cabeza *(f.)* head, 10
cada each, 12
caer(se) fall
café *(m.)* coffee, 2; cafe, 4
　_____ **al aire libre** *(m.)* sidewalk
　　cafe
cafetería *(f.)* cafeteria, 2
cajuela *(f.) (Mex.)* trunk *(car)*, 15
calcetín *(m.)* sock, 14
calculadora *(f.)* calculator, 17
calefacción central *(f.)* central heating,
　13
calidad *(f.)* quality
cálido(-a) hot, warm
caliente hot, 6
calificaciones *(f. pl.)* grades, 18
calor *(m.)* heat, 3
　hacer _____ be hot *(weather)*, 4
　tener _____ be hot, 3
calzar take . . . size *(in shoes)*, 14
calle *(f.)* street, P2

_____ **de dos vías (de doble vía)**
　two-way street, 10
cama *(f.)* bed, 11
cámara fotográfica *(f.)* camera, 5
camarero(-a) *(m., f.)* waiter, waitress, 6
camarones *(m. pl.)* shrimp, 6
cambiar change, exchange, 14
cambio *(m.)* change, 18
　¿a cómo está el _____ **de moneda?**
　　what is the exchange rate?, 5
　de _____**s mecánicos** standard
　　shift, 18
camello *(m.)* camel
caminar walk, 11
camino *(m.)* road, 12
　_____ **a** on the way to, 15
camión de pasajeros *(m.) (Mex.)* bus, 4
camisa *(f.)* shirt, 14
camiseta *(f.)* tee-shirt
camisón *(m.)* nightgown, 14
campestre rustic
campo *(m.)* country, 9
cancelar cancel, 5
canción *(f.)* song
cansado(-a) tired, 3
cantante *(m., f.)* singer
caña de pescar *(f.)* fishing rod, 9
capa *(f.)* layer
capaz capable
capital *(f.)* capital, 7
cara *(f.)* face, 10
¡caramba! gee!, P1
carburador *(m.)* carburetor, 15
Caribe *(m.)* Caribbean
cariños *(m. pl.)* love *(letter closing)*, 12
cariñoso(-a) affectionate, 18
carne *(f.)* meat, 6
carnet de conducir *(m.)* driver's license,
　15
carnicería *(f.)* meat market
caro(-a) expensive, 5
carretera *(f.)* highway, 15
carro *(m.)* car, 4
carta *(f.)* letter, 4
cartera *(f.)* purse, 14
casa *(f.)* house, home, 3
casado(-a) married, 2
casarse (con) get married (to)
casete *(m.)* cassette, tape, 3
casi almost, 14
casillero *(m.)* mailbox, 12
castaño brown *(hair, eyes)*, 4
castellano *(m.)* Spanish *(lang.)*
castigo *(m.)* punishment, 9

castillo *(m.)* castle
catarata *(f.)* waterfall
catorce fourteen, P2
caudaloso(-a) voluminous
Cayo Largo *(m.)* Key Largo
cazar hunt, 9
cebolla *(f.)* onion, 16
celebrar celebrate, 3
cementerio *(m.)* cemetery
cena *(f.)* dinner, supper, 5
cenar have dinner, 5
centro *(m.)* downtown, 5
cerca *(adv.)* near, 2
　_____ **de** *(prep.)* close to, near, 2
cereal *(m.)* cereal
cero zero, P1
cerrar *(e:ie)* close, 3
certificado(-a) certified, registered, 12
cerveza *(f.)* beer, 3
cesta *(f.)* basket
cibernética *(f.)* computer science
cielo *(m.)* sky
cien, ciento one hundred, 1
ciencia *(f.)* science, 17
cierto true, 12
cinco five, P1
cincuenta fifty, 1
cine *(m.)* movie theater, 6; movies, 6
cinta *(f.)* cassette, tape, 3
cita *(f.)* appointment, 8; date, 16
ciudad *(f.)* city, 1
ciudadano(-a) citizen, 18
claramente clearly, 10
claro(-a) light, P3
clase *(f.)* class, 1
　_____ **turista** *(f.)* tourist class, 7
　de primera _____ first-class, 7
clasificado(-a) classified, 13
clasificarse qualify
club *(m.)* club, 3
cobija *(f.)* blanket, 13
cobrar charge, 11
cocina *(f.)* kitchen, 8; stove, 13; cuisine
cocinar cook, 8
coctel *(m.)* cocktail, 3
coche *(m.) (Sp.)* car, 4; coach, 18
　_____**-cama** *(m.)* sleeper car, 18
　_____**-comedor** *(m.)* dining car, 18
colchón *(m.)* mattress, 13
colombiano(-a) Colombian, 13
color *(m.)* color, P3
colorado(-a) red
comedor *(m.)* dining room, 13
comenzar *(e:ie)* begin, 3

comer eat, 2

    _____ **algo** have something to eat, 14

comida *(f.)* meal, food, 6

como since, 7; like, 17

    _____ **siempre** as usual, 17

cómo how, P2; what, P1

    ¿a _____ **está el cambio de moneda?** what is the exchange rate?, 5

    ¿ _____ **es... ?** what is . . . like?, 4

    ¿ _____ **se dice... ?** how do you say . . . ?, P2

    ¿ _____ **se llama usted?** what is your name? *(form.)*, P1

    ¿ _____ **te llamas?** what is your name? *(fam.)*, P2

cómoda *(f.)* chest of drawers, 13

comodidad *(f.)* comfort

cómodo(-a) comfortable, 4

compacto(-a) compact, 18

compañero(-a) classmate, 3

compañía *(f.)* company, 2

componer fix *(car)*

comprar buy, 5

comprobante *(m.)* claim check, 11

comprobar (o:ue) check

computadora *(f.)* computer, 2

con with, 1

    _____ **tal que** provided that, 13

concierto *(m.)* concert, 8

conducir conduct, 6; drive *(Sp.)*, 6

confirmar confirm, 5

conjunto *(m.)* development *(housing)*

conmigo with me, 5

conocer know, be acquainted with, 6; meet, 7

conocimiento *(m.)* knowledge, 2

conseguir (e:i) get, obtain, 5

consejero(-a) *(m., f.)* advisor, counselor, 17

consejo *(m.)* advice, 17

consultorio *(m.)* doctor's office, 10

contabilidad *(f.)* accounting, 17

contar (o:ue) tell, 7; count, 4

contento(-a) happy, glad, 3

contestar answer

contigo *(fam. sing.)* with you, 5

contra against

conversación *(f.)* conversation, 1

conversar talk, converse, 2

copa *(f.)* goblet, 6; glass of wine

corazón *(m.)* heart

corbata *(f.)* tie, 14

cordero *(m.)* lamb, 6

cordillera *(f.)* mountain range

coro *(m.)* choir

correro *(m.)* mail, post office, 12

correspondencia *(f.)*: **tener** _____ correspond

corrida de toros *(f.)* bullfight

cortar(se) cut (oneself), 8

    cortarse el pelo get a haircut, 8

corte *(m.)* haircut, hairstyle, 8

cortina *(f.)* curtain, 13

corto(-a) short, 7

costa *(f.)* coast

costar (o:ue) cost, 4

    _____ **un ojo de la cara** cost an arm and a leg, 9

costillas *(f. pl.)* ribs

costumbre *(f.)* custom, habit

creado(-a) created

creer believe, think, 2

crema *(f.)* cream, 6

cruz *(f.)* cross

cruzar cross, 10

cuaderno *(m.)* notebook, P3

cuadra *(f.) (Sp. Am.)* block, 12

cuadro *(m.)* picture, painting, 4

cuál(es) which, what, P2

cualquier(a) any, anybody

cuando when

    de vez en _____ from time to time

cuándo when, 3

cuánto(-a) how much, 3

    ¿ _____ **cuesta... ?** how much does . . . cost?, 1

cuántos(-as) how many, 3

cuarenta forty, 1

cuarto *(m.)* room, 5

    _____ **de baño** bathroom, 5

    y _____ quarter past, P2

cuarto(-a) fourth, 4

cuatro four, P1

cuatrocientos four hundred, 1

cubano(-a) Cuban, 6

cubierto(-a) *(p. p. of* **cubrir** *and adj.)* covered, 14

cubrir cover, 14

cuchara *(f.)* spoon, 6

cucharita *(f.)* teaspoon, 6

cuchillo *(m.)* knife, 6

cuello *(m.)* neck, 10

cuenta *(f.)* account, 11; bill, 6

    _____ **corriente** *(f.)* checking account, 11

    _____ **de ahorros** *(f.)* savings account, 11

culpable guilty

cumpleaños *(m.)* birthday, 3

cuñada *(f.)* sister-in-law, 4

cuñado *(m.)* brother-in-law, 4

curandero *(m.)* medicine man

CH

champán *(m.)* champagne, 3

champú *(m.)* shampoo, 8

chapa *(f.)* license plate, 15

chaqueta *(f.)* jacket, 14

charlar talk, chat, 2

chau bye, P2

cheque *(m.)* check, 11

    _____ **de viajero** *(m.)* traveler's check, 5

chequear check, 15

chica *(f.)* girl, 2

chico *(m.)* boy, 2

chileno(-a) Chilean, 9

chimenea *(f.)* fireplace

chino *(m.)* Chinese *(lang.)*, 1

chocolate *(m.)* chocolate, 6

    _____ **caliente** *(m.)* hot chocolate, 6

D

danza aeróbica *(f.)* aerobic dance, aerobics, 17

dar give, 3

    _____ **saludos a...** say hi to . . . , 12

    _____ **una multa** fine, 15

de of, 1; from, 1; about, 7

    _____ **haber sabido** if I had known, 16

    _____ **la mañana (noche, tarde)** in the morning (evening, afternoon), 1

    _____ **manera que** so, 11

    _____ **moda** in style, 8

    _____ **modo que** so, 11

    _____ **nada** you're welcome, P2

    _____ **postre** for dessert, 6

    _____ **quién(es)** whose, 3

    _____ **vacaciones** on vacation, 9

    _____ **vez en cuando** from time to time

deber must, ought to, 2; owe, 14

    _____**se a** be due to

decidir decide, 2

décimo(-a) tenth, 4

decir (e:i) say, tell, 5
    ¿cómo se dice... ? how do you say . . . ? , P2
    se dice... you say . . . , P2
    ¿qué quiere _____... ? what does . . . mean?, P2
    quiere _____... it means . . . , P2
decisión (f.) decision, 13
declarar declare, 5
dedo (m.) finger, 10
    _____ del pie (m.) toe, 10
dejar leave, 6
del (m. sing.) (contraction) of the, 1; from the, 1
deleitarse (en) delight (in)
deletrear spell
delgado(-a) thin, slender, 2
demasiado too, too much, 9
departamento (m.) department, section, 11
    _____ de (ropa para) caballeros (m.) men's department, 14
    _____ de (ropa para) señoras women's department, 14
depender (de) depend (on), 18
dependiente(-a) (m., f.) store clerk, 14
deporte (m.) sport
deportivo(-a) sports-related
    artículos _____s (m. pl.) sporting goods
depositar deposit, 11
derecho (m.) law, 17; (adv.) straight ahead, 12
derecho(-a) (adj.) right, 5
    a la derecha on (to) the right, 5
desarrollarse develop
desayunar have breakfast, 18
desayuno (m.) breakfast, 5
descomponerse break down
descompuesto(-a) out of order, 15
descuento (m.) discount, 18
desde from
desear want, wish, 1
desgraciadamente unfortunately, 10
desgraciado(-a) unfortunate, 10
desierto (m.) desert, 9
desinfectar disinfect, 10
despacho de boletos (m.) ticket office, 18
despertador (m.) alarm clock, 11
despertar(se) (e:ie) wake up, 8
después afterwards, 12
    _____ de after, 6
destacar stand out
desvestir(se) (e:i) undress, 8

devolver (o:ue) return, 7
devuelto(-a) (p. p. of devolver and adj.) returned, 14
día (m.) day, P1
    al _____ siguiente the next day, 13
diario (m.) newspaper, 2
diario(-a) daily, 18
dibujo (m.) design
diccionario (m.) dictionary, 17
diciembre December, 4
dictado (m.) dictation, P3
dictadura (f.) dictatorship
dicho(-a) (p. p. of decir and adj.) said, told, 14
diecinueve nineteen, P2
dieciocho eighteen, P2
dieciséis sixteen, P2
diecisiete seventeen, P2
diente (m.) tooth, 10
dieta (f.) diet, 16
diez ten, P1
difícil difficult, 2
¡diga!, ¡dígame! hello! (phone), 1
diligencia (f.) errand, 11
    hacer _____s run errands, 11
dinero (m.) money, 1
dirección (f.) address, P2
dirigir direct, conduct
    _____se a head for
disco (m.) record, 3
discoteca (f.) discotheque
discusión (f.) discussion, 17
diseñar design
diseño (m.) design
disfrutar enjoy
distinguido(-a) distinguished, 18
divertirse (e:ie) have a good time, 9
divorciado(-a) divorced, 2
doblar turn, bend, 12; dub
doble double, 5
doce twelve, P2
docena (f.) dozen, 16
doctor(a) (m., f.) doctor, P1
documento (m.) document, 11
    _____ de identidad (identificación) identification, I.D., 12
dólar (m.) dollar, 5
doler (o:ue) ache, hurt, 10
dolor (m.) pain, 10
    _____ de cabeza (m.) headache, 10
domicilio (m.) address, P2
domingo (m.) Sunday, P2
dónde where, 3
dormir (o:ue) sleep, 4
    _____se fall asleep, 8

dormitorio (m.) bedroom, 13
dos two, P1
doscientos two hundred, 1
drama (m.) drama, play, 16
dudar doubt, 11
dulce (m.) sweet, candy
durante during, 7
durar last
durazno (m.) peach, 16

E

económico(-a) financial, economic, 1
echar de menos miss, 4
edad (f.) age, 2
    Edad Media Middle Ages
edificio (m.) building, 12
efectivo (m.) cash, 11
    en _____ in cash, 11
ejemplo (m.) example
ejercicio (m.) exercise, P3
    hacer _____ exercise, 17
ejército (m.) army
el the (m. sing.), P3
él he, 1; him, 5
elegante elegant, 13
elevador (m.) elevator, 5
ella she, 1; her, 5
ellas (f. pl.) they, 1; them, 5
ellos (m. pl.) they, 1; them, 5
embajada (f.) embassy, 5
embarazada pregnant, 10
emergencia (f.) emergency, 10
empanada (f.) meat pie
emparedado (m.) (Sp.) sandwich, 2
emperador (m.) emperor
empezar (e:ie) begin, start, 3
empleado(-a) (m., f.) clerk, 5
empleo (m.) job, 2
en in, P2; at, P2; on, 1
    _____ cuanto as soon as, 11
    _____ efectivo in cash, 11
    _____ regla in order, 5
    _____ seguida right away, 5
    _____ serio seriously, 9
    _____ vez de instead of, 13
enamorado(-a) in love
encantado(-a) a pleasure (to meet you), 1
encantador(a) charming, 18
encantar: me encanta... I love . . . , 13
encargado(-a) in charge
encima de above, on top of
encontrar (o:ue) find, 4
    _____se (con) meet, 14
enero January, 4

enfadado(-a) angry, 13
enfermedad *(f.)* disease, sickness, 10
enfermero(-a) *(m., f.)* nurse, 10
enfermo(-a) sick, 10
engañar deceive
enojado(-a) angry, 13
ensalada *(f.)* salad, 3.
enseñanza *(f.)* teaching
enseñar show, teach, 9
ensuciar(se) get dirty, 8
entender (e:ie) understand, 3
entonces then, in that case, 1
entrada *(f.)* entrance, 7; ticket, 8
entre between, among
_____ la espada y la pared
 between a rock and a hard place
entregar deliver, turn in, 17
entremeses *(m. pl.)* hors d'oeuvres, 3
entretener(se) *(like tener)* entertain (one-self)
entrevista *(f.)* interview
enviar send, 2
envolver (o:ue) wrap, 14
envuelto(-a) *(p. p. of envolver and adj.)* wrapped, 14
equilibrado(-a) balanced
equipaje *(m.)* luggage, 7
equipo *(m.)* team
escala *(f.)* stopover, 18
 hacer _____ make a stopover, 18
escalar climb
escalera *(f.)* stairs, 14
_____ mecánica *(f.)* escalator, 14
escenario *(m.)* setting, stage
esclusa *(f.)* lock *(canal)*
escoba *(f.)* broom, 8
escribir write, 2
escrito(-a) *(p.p. of escribir and adj.)* written, 14
escritor(a) *(m., f.)* writer
escritorio *(m.)* desk, P3
escuela *(f.)* school, 4
_____ primaria *(f.)* elementary school, 17
_____ secundaria *(f.)* high school, 17
escultura *(f.)* sculpture
ese(-os), esa(s) *(adj.)* that, those *(nearby)*, 6
ése(-os), ésa(s) *(pron.)* that one, those, 6
esfuerzo *(m.)* effort
esmerado(-a) esteemed
eso *(neuter pron.)* that, 6
espalda *(f.)* back, 10
España Spain, 4

español *(m.)* Spanish *(lang.)*, P2
especial special, 10
especialidad *(f.)* specialty, 6
especialización *(f.)* major, specialization, 17
especialmente especially, 10
especie *(f.)* kind, sort, species
espectáculo *(m.)* show, spectacle
espejo *(m.)* mirror, 8
esperar wait (for), 8; hope, 11
esposa *(f.)* wife, 2
esposo *(m.)* husband, 2
es que... the fact is . . . , 12
esquí *(m.)* ski
esquiar ski, 9
esquina *(f.)* street corner, 12
estación *(f.)* station, 12
_____ del metro *(f.)* subway station, 12
_____ de ómnibus *(f.)* bus station
_____ de policía *(f.)* police station, 11
_____ de servicio *(f.)* service station, 15
estacionar park, 11
estadio *(m.)* stadium, 17
estado *(m.)* state
_____ civil *(m.)* marital status, 2
Estados Unidos *(m. pl.)* United States, 2
estampado(-a) printed
estampilla *(f.)* stamp, 12
estancia *(f.)* lodging; room rate
estanque *(m.)* pond
estar be, 3
_____ a... de aquí be . . . from here, 12
 ¿cómo está usted? how are you?, P1
estatura *(f.)* height, 4
este *(m.)* east, 18
este(-os), esta(s) *(adj.)* this, 4; these, 6
éste(-os), ésta(s) *(pron.)* this one; these, 6
estilo *(m.)* style
estimado(-a) dear, 18
esto *(neuter pron.)* this, 6
estómago *(m.)* stomach, 10
estrecho(-a) narrow
estudiante *(m., f.)* student, P3
estudiar study, 1
evitar avoid
examen *(m.)* examination, exam, test, P3
_____ parcial midterm exam, 17
excelente excellent, 6
exceso *(m.)* excess, 7

_____ de equipaje *(m.)* excess baggage, 7
excursión *(f.)* excursion, 9
exigente demanding
éxito *(m.)* success, hit
experiencia *(f.)* experience, 18
expreso *(m.)* express *(train)*, 18
extranjero(-a) foreign, 12
 al extranjero abroad
extrañar miss, 4
extraño(-a) strange, funny, 15

F

fácil easy, 2
fácilmente easily, 10
facultad *(f.)* college, 17
falda *(f.)* skirt, 14
fama *(f.)* fame, reputation
familia *(f.)* family, 4
famoso(-a) famous, 4
farmacia *(f.)* pharmacy, 8
favorito(-a) favorite, 6
febrero February, 4
fecha *(f.)* date, 4
fechar date, 11
feliz happy, 2
felizmente happily, 10
femenino(-a) feminine, 2
feo(-a) ugly, homely, 4
feriado *(m.)* holiday, 16
festivo *(m.)* holiday
festón *(m.)* fringe
fiebre *(f.)* fever, 10
fiesta *(f.)* party, 3
filete *(m.)* tenderloin steak, 6
filtro *(m.)* filter, 15
fin *(m.)* end
_____ de año *(m.)* New Year's Eve, 3
_____ de semana *(m.)* weekend, 4
firma *(f.)* signature, 11
firmar sign, 5
física *(f.)* physics, 17
flan *(m.)* custard, 6
floreciente flourishing
florería *(f.)* flower shop
flota *(f.)* fleet
folleto *(m.)* brochure, 9
fondo *(m.)* background
fortaleza *(f.)* fort
fortuna *(f.)* fortune, 16
foto *(f.)* photograph, 4
fotografía *(f.)* photograph, 4
francés *(m.)* French *(lang.)*, 1
frazada *(f.)* blanket, 13

frecuentemente   frequently, 10
fregadero *(m.)*   sink, 13
freno *(m.)*   brake, 15
frente a   opposite, across from, 11
fresa *(f.)*   strawberry, 16
frijol *(m.)*   bean, 6
frío *(m.)*   cold, 3
    hacer _____   be cold *(weather)*, 4
    tener _____   be cold, 3
frito(-a)   fried, 6
frontera *(f.)*   border, 18
fruta *(f.)*   fruit, 6
frutería *(f.)*   fruit store
fuente *(f.)*   fountain, source
fuera de   outside
fumar   smoke
función *(f.)*   show, 16
funcionar   work, function, 15
funda *(f.)*   pillowcase, 13
fundar   found
fútbol *(m.)*   soccer, 17
    _____ **americano**   football

G

ganadería *(f.)*   cattle raising
ganar   earn, 13; win, 16
garaje *(m.)*   garage, 13
gasolina *(f.)*   gasoline, 15
gasolinera *(f.)*   service station, 15
gastar   spend *(money)*, 18; use, 18
gelatina *(f.)*   gelatin, 6
generalmente   generally, 8
gente *(f.)*   people, 8
gira *(f.)*   tour
giro postal *(m.)*   money order, 12
gobierno *(m.)*   government
goma *(f.)*   tire, 15
gordo(-a)   fat, 2
gozar (de)   enjoy
grabadora *(f.)*   tape recorder, 5
gracias   thank you, P1
    muchas _____   thank you very much, P2
graduarse   graduate, 14
gran, grande   big, large, 4
grasa *(f.)*   grease
gratis   free *(of charge)*, 11
gripe *(f.)*   flu, 10
gris   gray, P3
gritar   scream, shout, 11
grúa *(f.)*   tow truck, 15
guante *(m.)*   glove, 14
guantera *(f.)*   glove compartment, 15
guapo(-a)   handsome, 2
güero(-a) *(Mex.)*   blonde, 2
guerra *(f.)*   war

guía telefónica *(f.)*   telephone book
gustar   appeal to, 7
    me gusta(n)...   I like . . . , 7
    no gustarle nada a uno   not to like at all, 17
gusto *(m.)*   pleasure, P2
    el _____ **es mío**   the pleasure is mine, P2

H

haber *(aux.)*   have, 15
habitación *(f.)*   room, 5
habitante   inhabitant
habla *(f.)*   speech
    de _____ **hispana**   Spanish-speaking
hablar   speak, talk, 1
hacer   do, make, 6
    buen tiempo   be good weather, 4
    _____ **calor**   be hot, 4
    _____ **caso**   pay attention, 13
    _____ **cola**   stand in line, 16
    _____ **diligencias**   run errands, 11
    _____ **ejercicio**   exercise, 17
    _____ **escala**   stop over, 18
    _____ **frío**   be cold, 4
    _____ **juego**   match, 14
    _____ **las compras**   do the shopping, 16
    _____ **las maletas**   pack, 9
    _____ **mal tiempo**   be bad weather, 4
    _____ **sol**   be sunny, 4
    _____ **viento**   be windy, 4
    _____ **hace...**   . . . ago, 10
hacia   toward, 11
hacienda *(f.)*   farm
hambre *(f.)*   hunger, 3
    tener _____   be hungry, 3
hamburguesa *(f.)*   hamburger, 6
haragán, haragana   lazy
hasta   until, 5
    _____ **la vista**   until I see you again, P2
    _____ **luego**   see you later, P1
    _____ **mañana**   see you tomorrow, P1
hay   there is, there are, P3
hecho(-a) *(p. p. of* **hacer** *and adj.)*   done, made, 14
helado *(m.)*   ice cream, 6
helado(-a)   iced, 6
    torta helada *(f.)*   ice cream cake, 6
herencia *(f.)*   inheritance, 13
herida *(f.)*   wound, 10
hermana *(f.)*   sister, 3

hermano *(m.)*   brother, 3
hermoso(-a)   beautiful
hierba *(f.)*   herb
hija *(f.)*   daughter, 3
hijo *(m.)*   son, 3
    _____ **único**   only child, 11
hijos *(m. pl.)*   children, 2
hipoteca *(f.)*   mortgage
hola   hello, hi, P1
hombre *(m.)*   man, P3
hora *(f.)*   time, P2; hour, 7
    ¿a qué _____ **... ?**   at what time . . . ?, 1
    ¿qué _____ **es?**   what time is it?, P2
horario *(m.)*   schedule, 17
horriblemente   horribly, 9
hospedarse   stay *(at a hotel)*
hospital *(m.)*   hospital, 1
hotel *(m.)*   hotel, 5
hoy   today, P1
    _____ **en día**   today, nowadays
huevo *(m.)*   egg, 6

I

ida *(f.):* **de** _____   one-way *(ticket)*, 7
    de _____ **y vuelta**   round-trip, 7
idea *(f.)*   idea, 3
idioma *(m.)*   language, 1
iglesia *(f.)*   church
imperio *(m.)*   empire
impermeable *(m.)*   raincoat, 4
importante   important, 17
incluir   include, 17
incómodo(-a)   uncomfortable, 4
indígena *(invariable adj.)*   native
información *(f.)*   information, 5
ingeniería *(f.)*   engineering, 17
Inglaterra   England
inglés *(m.)*   English *(lang.)*, 1
ingreso *(m.)*   revenue
inigualable   unequalled
inspector(a) *(m., f.)*   inspector, 5
instalar   install, 15
instituto *(m.)*   high school
inteligente   intelligent, 2
interés *(m.)*   interest, 5
interesante   interesting, 4
invertir (e:ie)   invest
invierno *(m.)*   winter, 4
invitado(-a) *(m., f.)*   guest, 8
invitar   invite, 3
inyección *(f.)*   injection, shot, 10
    _____ **antitetánica**   tetanus shot, 10
    poner una _____   give a shot, 10

ir go, 3; **irse** go away, 8
    a casa go home, 9
        _____ **de compras** go shopping, 14
        _____ **de pesca** go fishing, 9
        _____ **se de vacaciones** go on vacation, 9
italiano *(m.)* Italian *(lang.)*, 1
italiano(-a) Italian, 1
itinerario *(m.)* schedule, timetable, 18
izquierdo(-a) left, 5
    a la izquierda on (to) the left, 5

J

jabón *(m.)* soap, 5
jamón *(m.)* ham, 6
japonés *(m.)* Japanese *(lang.)*, 1
jardín *(m.)* garden, 13
jefe(-a) *(m., f.)* chief, head
joven *(m., f.)* young person, 17
joya *(f.)* jewel
joyería *(f.)* jewelry store
juego *(m.):* **hacer** _____ match, 14
jueves *(m.)* Thursday, P2
jugador(a) *(m., f.)* player
jugo *(m.)* juice, 6
julio July, 4
junio June, 4
junto a next to
juntos(-as) together, 7

K

kilómetro *(m.)* kilometer, 15

L

la *(f. sing.)* the, P3; *(pron.)* her, it, 5
laborales *(m. pl.)* workdays
lacio(-a) straight, 8
lago *(m.)* lake, 9
lámpara *(f.)* lamp, 13
lana *(f.)* wool
langosta *(f.)* lobster, 6
lápiz *(m.)* pencil, P3
largo(-a) long, 7
    a lo _____ along the length of
las *(f. pl.)* the, P3; *(pron.)* them, 5
lástima *(f.)* pity, shame, 11
    ¡qué _____! what a pity!, 4
lata *(f.)* can, 16
latinoamericano(-a) Latin American, 17
lavado *(m.)* shampoo, 8
lavadora *(f.)* washing machine
lavaplatos *(m.)* dishwasher, 13
lavar(se) wash (oneself), 16
    _____ **la cabeza** to wash one's hair, 8

le (to) her, him, you, 6
lección *(f.)* lesson, P3
leche *(f.)* milk, 6
lechón *(m.)* piglet, 6
lechuga *(f.)* lettuce, 16
leer read, 2
lejos *(adv.)* far, 2
    _____ **de** *(prep.)* far from, 2
lengua *(f.)* tongue, 10
lentamente slowly, 10
lento(-a) slow, 10
león *(m.)* lion
les (to) them, (to) you, 6
letrero *(m.)* sign, 15
levantar lift, raise, 8
levantarse get up, 8
leyenda *(f.)* legend
libertad *(f.)* liberty, 1
libra *(f.)* pound
libre vacant, free, 2
libreta de ahorros *(f.)* savings passbook, 11
libro *(m.)* book, P3
licencia de conducir *(f.)* driver's license, 2
liga *(f.)* league
    Grandes Ligas major leagues
ligeramente slightly
limitar con border
limpiaparabrisas *(m.)* windshield wiper, 15
limpiar(se) clean (oneself), 8
limpio(-a) clean
lindo(-a) pretty, 2
liquidación *(f.)* sale, 14
liso(-a) solid-color
lista *(f.)* list, 5
    _____ **de espera** *(f.)* waiting list, 5
listo(-a) ready, 6
litera *(f.)* berth, 18
    _____ **alta** upper berth, 18
    _____ **baja** lower berth, 18
literatura *(f.)* literature, 17
lo him, it, you, 5
localidad *(f.)* location, seat
localizado(-a) located
loco(-a) crazy, 7
locutor(a) *(m., f.)* announcer
los *(m. pl.)* the, P3; *(pron.)* them, you, 5
luego later, then, 5
lugar *(m.)* place, 2
    tener _____ take place
lujo *(m.)* luxury
    de _____ deluxe
lujoso(-a) luxurious

lunes *(m.)* Monday, P2
luz *(f.)* light, P3

LL

llamar call, 1
llamarse be called, 8
    ¿cómo se llama usted? what is your name? *(form.)*, P1
    ¿cómo te llamas? what is your name? *(fam.)*, P2
    me llamo... my name is . . . , P1
llanero *(m.)* plainsman
llanta *(f.)* tire, 15
llanura *(f.)* plain
llave *(f.)* key, 5
llegada *(f.)* arrival, 18
llegar arrive, 5
llenar fill, 2
lleno(-a) full, 15
llevar take, 3
    _____ **a cabo** carry out
    _____ **puesto(-a)** wear, 14
llevarse take away, 11; buy, 14
llover *(o:ue)* rain, 4
    _____ **a cántaros** rain cats and dogs, 10
lloviznar drizzle, 4
lluvia *(f.)* rain, 4

M

madre *(f.)* mother, 4
magia *(f.)* magic
magnífico(-a) magnificent, 3
mago(-a) magician, wizard
maíz *(m.)* corn
mal bad, badly, 4
malabarismo *(m.)* juggling
maleta *(f.)* suitcase, 5
    hacer las _____**s** pack, 9
maletero *(m.)* trunk, 15
malo(-a) bad, 3
mamá Mom, 4
manada *(f.)* herd
mandar send, 2; order, 11
manejar drive, 4
manera *(f.)* way
    de _____ **que** so, 11
mano *(f.)* hand, P3
manta *(f.)* blanket, 13
mantel *(m.)* tablecloth, 6
mantelería *(f.)* table linens
mantener maintain, 17
mantequilla *(f.)* butter, 16
manzana *(f.)* apple, 16; *(Sp.)* block, 12

mañana (f.) morning, 1; (adv.) tomorrow, 1
    de la _____ in the morning, 1
    hasta _____ see you tomorrow, P1
    por la _____ in the morning, 1
mapa (m.) map, P3
maquillarse apply makeup
máquina de afeitar (f.) razor, 8
mar (m.) sea, 9
maravilla (f.) marvel
maravilloso(-a) marvelous, 18
marca (f.) brand
marea (f.) tide
mareo (m.) dizziness, dizzy spell, 10
margarina (f.) margarine, 16
mariscos (m. pl.) seafood, 6
marrón brown, P3
Marruecos (m.) Morocco, 18
Marte (m.) Mars
martes (m.) Tuesday, P2
marzo March, 4
más more, 4
    el (la) _____ the most, 4
    _____ **o menos** so-so, more or less, 1
    _____ **tarde** later, 1
máscara (f.) mask
masculino male, 2
matemáticas (f. pl.) math, 17
materia (f.) subject matter, 17
matrícula (f.) registration, 17; tuition, 17
matricularse register, 17
mayo May, 4
mayor older, 4
    el (la) _____ the oldest, 4
mayoría (f.) majority
me me, 5; (to) me, 6; (to) myself, 8
mecánico (m.) mechanic, 15
mediano(-a) medium, 4
medianoche (f.) midnight, 3
    a la _____ at midnight, 3
medicina (f.) medicine, 4
médico(-a) (m., f.) doctor, 10
medida (f.) size, 14
medio(-a) half, 6
    _____ **día** half a day, part-time, 13
mediodía (m.) noon, 3
    al _____ at noon, 3
medios (m. pl.) means
medir (e:i) measure
mejor better, 4
    el (la) _____ the best, 4
mejorar improve
melocotón (m.) peach, 16

melón (m.) melon, 16
menaje (m.) household
menor younger, 4
    el (la) _____ youngest, 4
menos less, 4
    a _____ **que** unless, 13
    el (la) _____ the least, 4
mentir (e:ie) lie, 8
menú (m.) menu, 6
mercado (m.) market
mermelada (f.) jam
mes (m.) month, 2
mesero(-a) (Mex.) waiter, waitress, 6
mesita de noche (f.) nightstand, 13
metro (m.) subway, 12
mezcla (f.) mix
mezquita (f.) mosque
mi (adj.) my, 2
mí (pron.) me, 5
miedo (m.) fear, 3
    tener _____ be afraid, 3
mientras while, 2
miércoles (m.) Wednesday, P2
mil one thousand, 1
milla (f.) mile, 15
minoritario(-a) (adj.) minority
mío(s), mía(s) (pron.) mine, 7
mirar look at, watch, 2
mochila (f.) backpack
moda (f.) fashion
    de _____ in style, 8
moderno(-a) modern, 5
módico(-a) modest
modista (f.) dressmaker
modo (m.) way
    de _____ **que** so, 11
molino de viento (m.) windmill
momento (m.) moment, 1
moneda (f.) currency
montaña (f.) mountain, 9
montar mount, ride, 9
    _____ **a caballo** ride a horse, 9
    _____ **en bicicleta** ride a bicycle, 9
montón (m.) a lot, 12
morado(-a) purple, P3
moreno(-a) dark-haired, 2
morir (o:ue) die, 8
moro(-a) Moorish
mostrar (o:ue) show, 5
motocicleta (f.) motorcycle, 10
motor (m.) motor, 15
mozo (m.) waiter, 6
muchacha (f.) girl, young woman, 2
muchacho (m.) boy, young man, 2
mucho(-a) much, a lot (of), 3

muchas gracias thank you very much, P2
muchos(-as) many, 3
mudarse move (from one house to another), 13
muebles (m. pl.) furniture, 13
muerto(-a) (p. p. of morir and adj.) dead, 14
    _____ **de hambre** starving, 14
muestra (f.) sample
mujer (f.) woman, P3
multa (f.) fine, 15
    poner una _____ fine, 15
mundo (m.) world, 4
muralla (f.) wall
museo (m.) museum, 4
musical musical, 16
muy very, P1

N

nacer be born
nacimiento (m.) birth, 2
nacionalidad (f.) nationality, 2
nada nothing, 1
    de _____ you're welcome, P2
    _____ **más** nothing else, 5
nadar swim, 9
nadie nobody, no one, 5
naranja (f.) orange, 16
nariz (f.) nose, 10
Navidad (f.) Christmas, 3
necesariamente necessarily, 10
necesario(-a) necessary, 10
necesitar need, 1
negar (e:ie) deny, 12
negro(-a) black, P3
neumático (m.) tire, 15
nevar (e:ie) snow, 4
ni nor, 5
    _____ **... ni...** neither . . . nor . . . , 5
niebla (f.) fog, 4
nieta (f.) granddaughter, 4
nieto (m.) grandson, 4
nieve (f.) snow, 9
ningún, ninguna no, none, not any, 5
ninguno(-a) no, none, not any, 5
niñez (f.) childhood
niño(-a) (m., f.) child, 9
nivel (m.) level
no no, not, P1
noche (f.) evening, night, 1
    de la _____ in the evening, 1
    esta _____ tonight, 1
    por la _____ in the evening, 1

nombre *(m.)* name, 2
noreste *(m.)* northeast
noroeste *(m.)* northwest
norte *(m.)* north, 18
norteamericano(-a) North American, 2
nos us, 5; (to) us, 6; (to) ourselves, 8
nosotros(-as) we, 1; us, 5
nota *(f.)* grade, 17
noticias *(f. pl.)* news, 8
novecientos nine hundred, 1
novedades *(f. pl.)* novelties
noveno(-a) ninth, 4
noventa ninety, 1
novia *(f.)* girlfriend, fiancée, 3
noviembre November, 4
novio *(m.)* boyfriend, fiancé, 3
nublado cloudy
nudos *(m. pl.)* knots
nuera *(f.)* daughter-in-law, 4
nuestro(s), nuestra(s) *(adj.)* our, 2;
  (pron.) ours, 7
nueve nine, P1
nuevo(-a) new, 3
número *(m.)* number, P3
  _____ **de teléfono** *(m.)* phone
  number, P3
nunca never, 4

O

o or, 1
  _____ **...o...** either . . . or . . . , 5
objeto *(m.)* object, 5
obra *(f.)* work
  _____ **de teatro** *(f.)* play, 6
  _____ **maestra** *(f.)* masterpiece
océano *(m.)* ocean, 9
ochenta eighty, 1
ocho eight, P1
ochocientos eight hundred, 1
octavo(-a) eighth, 4
octubre October, 4
ocupación *(f.)* occupation, 2
ocupado(-a) busy, occupied, 3
odiar hate, 9
oeste *(m.)* west, 18
oferta *(f.)* special offer
oficina *(f.)* office, 5
  _____ **de correos** *(f.)* post office,
  12
  _____ **de telégrafos** *(f.)* telegraph
  office, 12
  _____ **de turismo** *(f.)* tourist office, 5
ofrecer offer
oído *(m.)* ear *(internal)*, 10

oír hear, 14
  ¡oigo! hello! *(phone) (Cuba)*, 1
ojalá God grant, I hope, 11
ojo *(m.)* eye, 10
  un _____ **de la cara** an arm and a
  leg, 9
ola *(f.)* wave
olvidar(se) (de) to forget (about), 8
ómnibus *(m.)* bus, 4
once eleven, P2
operar operate, 10
oportunidad *(f.)* opportunity, 4
optativo(-a) elective
orden *(f.)* order, 6
  a sus órdenes at your service
oreja *(f.)* ear, 10
organizar organize, 16
orilla *(f.)* bank *(river)*; shore
oro *(m.)* gold, 5
orquesta *(f.)* orchestra, 3
os you *(fam. pl.)*, 5; (to) you, 6; (to)
  yourselves, 8
oscuro(-a) dark, P3
otoño *(m.)* autumn, fall, 4
otro(-a) another, other, 4
  otra vez again, 16
¡oye! listen!, 1

P

padre *(m.)* father, 4
padres *(m. pl.)* parents, 4
paella *(f.) (Sp.)* chicken and seafood
  with rice
pagar pay, 6
página *(f.)* page, P3
país *(m.)* country, 9
palabra *(f.)* word, 17
palacio *(m.)* palace, 12
pan *(m.)* bread, 16
panqueque *(m.)* pancake
pantalón *(m.)* pants, 11
  pantalones *(m. pl.)* pants, 11
pantimedias *(f. pl.)* pantyhose, 14
pañuelo *(m.)* handkerchief, 14
papa *(f.)* potato, 6
  _____ **s fritas** *(f. pl.)* French fries, 6
papá Dad, 4
papel higiénico *(m.)* toilet tissue, 16
paquete *(m.)* package, 12
par *(m.)* pair, 14
para to, 2; for, 5; by, 9; in order to, 2
  _____ **que** in order that, 13
parado(-a) standing, 12
parar stop, 15
parecerse (a) look like, 11

pared *(f.)* wall, P3
pareja *(f.)* couple, 15
parque *(m.)* park, 12
  _____ **de diversiones** *(m.)* amusement park, 16
parquear park, 11
parrillada *(f.) (Arg.)* grilled beef and
  sausage
parte *(f.):* **a todas** _____ **s** everywhere
  a alguna _____ somewhere
partido *(m.)* game, 17
pasado(-a) last, 8
pasaje *(m.)* ticket, 7
pasaporte *(m.)* passport, 5
pasar spend *(time)*, 5
  _____ **la aspiradora** vacuum, 8
  _____ **por** go by, pass through, 5
  pase come in, P2
paseo *(m.)* median, walkway
pasillo *(m.)* aisle, 7
pastilla *(f.)* pill, 10
patinaje *(m.)* skating
pavo *(m.)* turkey, 6
paz *(f.)* peace
pecho *(m.)* chest, 10
pedido *(m.)* order, 6
pedir (e:i) ask for, 6; request, 5; order, 6
  _____ **prestado** borrow, 11
  _____ **turno** make an appointment, 8
  _____ **un préstamo** apply for a
  loan, 11
peinado *(m.)* hairstyle, hairdo, 8
peinarse comb one's hair, 8
peine *(m.)* comb, 8
película *(f.)* movie, film, 16
pelirrojo(-a) red-headed, 2
pelo *(m.)* hair, 8
peluquería *(f.)* beauty parlor, 8
peluquero(-a) hairdresser, 8
penicilina *(f.)* penicillin, 10
pensar (e:ie) think, 3; plan, 3
pensión *(f.)* boarding house, 4
peor worse, 4
  el (la) _____ the worst, 4
pequeño(-a) small, little, 4
pera *(f.)* pear, 16
perder (e:ie) lose, 3
perdón *(m.)* excuse me, P1
perezoso(-a) lazy
perfectamente perfectly, 4
perfecto(-a) perfect, 9
perfume *(m.)* perfume
perfumería *(f.)* perfume shop
periódico *(m.)* newspaper, 2

periodismo *(m.)* journalism, 17
periodista *(m., f.)* journalist, 17
permanente *(f.)* permanent, 8
permiso *(m.)* permit, 8
　　con ——— excuse me, P2
pero but, 2
perro(-a) *(m., f.)* dog, 8
　　——— **caliente** *(m.)* hot dog
personaje *(m.)* character
pesar weigh
pesca *(f.)* fishing, 9
　　ir de ——— go fishing, 9
pescado *(m.)* fish, 6
pescar fish, catch a fish, 9
pesimista *(m., f.)* pessimist, 13
peso *(m.)* weight
pesquero(-a) fishing
picado(-a) choppy
pico *(m.)* bill *(bird)*
pie *(m.)* foot, 10
piedra *(f.)* stone
piel *(f.)* leather
pierna *(f.)* leg, 10
pimienta *(f.)* pepper, 6
pinchazo *(m.)* flat tire, 15
pintor *(m.)* painter
pintura *(f.)* painting
piña *(f.)* pineapple, 16
piscina *(f.)* swimming pool, 9
piso *(m.)* floor, P3; *(Sp.)* apartment
pizarra *(f.)* blackboard, P3
plan *(m.)* plan, 9
planchar iron
planear plan, 9
planilla *(f.)* form, 18
planta baja *(f.)* ground floor, 14
plata *(f.)* silver, 5
platillo *(m.)* saucer, 6
plato *(m.)* dish, plate, 6
playa *(f.)* beach, 9
playero *(m.)* beach coverup
plaza *(f.)* square
　　Plaza Mayor main square
plazo *(m.)* term, 11
　　a plazos in installments, 11
pluma *(f.)* pen, P3
pobre poor, 11
poco(-a) little *(quantity)*, 4
pocos(-as) few, 5
poder *(o:ue)* be able to, 4
poder *(m.)* power
policiaco(-a) detective
pollo *(m.)* chicken, 3
poner put, place, 6
　　——— **una inyección** give an injection, 10

——— **una multa** fine, 15
——— **una obra de teatro** put on a play, 6
ponerse put on, 8
　　——— **a dieta** go on a diet, 16
　　——— **de acuerdo** agree, 9
por around, 9; along, 9; by, 9; for, 5; per, 5; through, 9
　　——— **aquí** around here, 5; this way, 6
　　——— **ciento** percent, 18
　　——— **encima** above
　　——— **eso** that's why, 4
　　——— **favor** please, P1
　　——— **por la mañana (noche, tarde)** in the morning (evening, afternoon), 1
　　¿——— **qué?** why?, 1
　　——— **suerte** luckily, 9
　　——— **supuesto** of course, 9
　　——— **teléfono** on the phone, 7
porque because, 3
portaguantes *(m. sing.)* glove compartment, 15
portugués *(m.)* Portuguese *(lang.)*, 1
poseer have, own, possess
postre *(m.)* dessert, 6
　　de ——— for dessert, 6
practicar practice, 4
preferir *(e:ie)* prefer, 3
preguntar ask *(a question)*, 6
premio *(m.)* prize, 16
prensa *(f.)* press
preocuparse (por) worry (about), 8
preparar(se) prepare (oneself), 6
presente present, here, P3
presión *(f.)* blood pressure
préstamo *(m.)* loan, 11
prestar lend, 7
primavera *(f.)* spring, 4
primero(-a) first, 4
　　de primera clase first-class, 7
primo(-a) *(m., f.)* cousin, 3
prisa *(f.):* **tener** ——— be in a hurry, 3
privado(-a) private, 5
probador *(m.)* fitting room, 14
probar *(o:ue)* try, 8; taste, 8
probarse try on, 8
problema *(m.)* problem, 1
procedente de coming from
profesor(a) *(m., f.)* professor, teacher, P1
programa *(m.)* program
promedio *(m.)* average, 17
pronóstico del tiempo *(m.)* weather forecast, 4

pronto soon
propietario(-a) *(m., f.)* owner
propina *(f.)* tip, 6
proseguir *(e:i)* continue
próximo(-a) next, 7
psicología *(f.)* psychology, 17
pueblo *(m.)* town
puente *(m.)* bridge
puerta *(f.)* door, P2; gate, 7
　　——— **de entrada** *(f.)* point of entry
　　——— **de salida** *(f.)* airline departure gate, 7
puerto marítimo *(m.)* seaport
pues for, 14; then, 7; therefore, 4; well, 9
puesto *(m.)* stand
puesto(-a) *(p. p. of* **poner** *and adj.)* set, placed, 14
puntual punctual, 12
puré de papas *(m.)* mashed potatoes, 6

Q

que *(rel. pron.)* that, 3; who, 11; which, 5; whom, 11; *(conj.)* than, 4
¿qué? what, P1
　　¡qué... ! how . . . !, 9
　　¿——— **hora es?** what time is it?, P2
　　¿——— **lástima!** what a pity!, 4
　　¿——— **quiere decir... ?** what does . . . mean?, P2
　　¿——— **tal... ?** how's it going?, P1; how was . . . ?, 7
　　¡——— **va!** no way!, 17
quebrado(-a) broken, 10
quedar be located, 12
　　——— **le grande (chico) a uno** be too big (small) on someone, 14
quedarse remain, stay, 9
　　——— **en la cama hasta tarde** sleep late, 11
querer *(e:ie)* want, wish, 3; love, 3
　　no quise I refused, 10
querido(-a) dear, 18
queridísimo(-a) dearest, 18
queso *(m.)* cheese, 2
quien(es) whom, 11
quién(es) who, 1
　　¿de ———? whose?, 3
química *(f.)* chemistry, 17
quince fifteen, P2
quinientos five hundred, 1
quinto(-a) fifth, 4
quitar take away, 8
quitarse take off, 8

R

radiador *(m.)* radiator, 18
radicarse gather
radiografía *(f.)* X-ray, 10
rallar grate
Ramblas *(f.)* boulevards
rápidamente rapidly, 10
rápido *(m.)* express *(train)*, 18
rápido(-a) rapid, fast, 10
raramente rarely, 10
raro(-a) strange, rare, 10
rascacielos *(m.)* skyscraper
rato *(m.)* while, 11
   al _____ a while later, 11
razón *(f.)*: **tener** _____ be right, 3
   a _____ **de** at a rate of
real royal
realista *(m., f.)* realist, 13
rebaja *(f.)* sale, 14
recámara *(f.)* *(Mex.)* bedroom, 13
recepcionista *(m., f.)* receptionist, 2
receta *(f.)* prescription, 10
recetar prescribe, 10
recibir receive, 2
recién casados *(m. pl.)* newlyweds, 15
reciente recent, 10
recientemente recently, 10
recoger pick up, 11
recomendar (e:ie) recommend, 6
recordar (o:ue) remember, 4
recorrer travel all over *(a place)*
red *(f.)* net
refresco *(m.)* soft drink, soda, 3
refrigerador *(m.)* refrigerator, 13
regalar give *(a gift)*, 8
regalo *(m.)* gift, 8
registro *(m.)* register, 5
regresar return, 1
relajarse relax
reloj *(m.)* clock, P3
relojería *(f.)* watch store
relleno(-a) stuffed, 6
remar row
remolcar tow, 15
renacentista Renaissance
repetir (e:i) repeat, 8
representación *(f.)* show
requisito *(m.)* requirement, 17
reserva *(f.)* reservation, 5
reservación *(f.)* reservation, 5
reservar reserve, 18
resfriado *(m.)* cold, 10
resfrío *(m.)* cold, 10
respaldo *(m.)* back *(chair)*
restaurante *(m.)* restaurant, 4

retraso *(m.)* delay, 7
   tener... de _____ be ... behind schedule, 7
revelar develop *(film)*, 11
reventa *(f.)* resale
revisar check, 15
revista *(f.)* magazine, 8
rey *(m.)* king
rezar pray
río *(m.)* river, 9
riqueza *(f.)* riches, wealth
ritmo *(m.)* rhythm
rizador *(m.)* curling iron, 8
rizo *(m.)* curl, 8
robar steal, 11
rodeado(-a) **(de)** surrounded (by)
rodilla *(f.)* knee, 10
rogar (o:ue) beg, 11
rojo(-a) red, P3
rollo de película *(m.)* roll of film, 11
romper(se) break, 10
ropa *(f.)* clothes, 14
   _____ **interior** *(f.)* underwear, 14
ropero *(m.)* closet, 14
rosado(-a) pink, P3
roto(-a) *(p. p. of* **romper** *and adj.)* broken, 10
rubio(-a) blond, 2
ruido *(m.)* noise, 15
ruinas *(f. pl.)* ruins, 5
ruso *(m.)* Russian *(lang.)*, 1

S

sábado *(m.)* Saturday, P2
sábana *(f.)* sheet, 13
saber know, 6; find out, 10
saborear taste
sabroso(-a) tasty, 6
sacar take out, withdraw, 11; get *(a grade)*, 17
   _____ **pasaje** buy a ticket, 18
saco de dormir *(m.)* sleeping bag, 9
Sagrada Familia *(f.)* Holy Family
sal *(f.)* salt, 6
sala *(f.)* living room, 13
   _____ **de clase** classroom, P3
   _____ **de emergencia** emergency room, 10
   _____ **de equipajes** baggage room, 10
   _____ **de espera** waiting room, 10
   _____ **de rayos X (equis)** X-ray room, 10
salario *(m.)* salary, 13
saldo *(m.)* balance, 11
salida *(f.)* exit, 7; departure, 18

salir leave, go out, 6
salmón *(m.)* salmon, 6
salón *(m.)* room
   _____ **de belleza** *(m.)* beauty parlor, 8
   _____ **de estar** *(m.)* family room, 13
salsa *(f.)* sauce, 16
¡salud! cheers!
saludo *(m.)* greeting, 18
   _____**s a...** say hello to . . . , P2
salvavidas *(m., f.)* lifeguard, 9
sandalia *(f.)* sandal, 14
sandía *(f.)* watermelon, 16
sándwich *(m.)* sandwich, 2
sangrar bleed, 10
santo *(m.)* saint
sarampión *(m.)* measles, 10
sarape *(m.)* poncho
sastre *(m.)* tailor
se (to) himself, (to) herself, (to) yourself, (to) yourselves, (to) themselves, 8
secadero *(m.)* dryer *(coffee)*
secador *(m.)* hair dryer, 8
sección *(f.)* section, 7
   _____ **de (no) fumar** (non-) smoking section, 7
secretario(-a) *(m., f.)* secretary, P3
sed *(f.)* thirst, 3
   tener _____ be thirsty, 3
sede *(f.)* headquarters
seguir (e:i) follow, 5; continue, 5
según according to, 4
segundo(-a) second, 4
seguro(-a) sure, 12
   estar _____ be sure, 12
seguro *(m.)* insurance, 18
   _____ **social** *(m.)* social security, 2
seis six, P1
seiscientos six hundred, 1
sello *(m.)* stamp, 12
semáforo *(m.)* traffic light, 12
semana *(f.)* week, 8
semanal weekly
semestre *(m.)* semester, 17
sencillo(-a) single, 5; simple, 5
sentado(-a) seated, sitting, 9
sentar(se) (e:ie) sit (down), 8
sentimental romantic, sentimental, 1
sentir(se) (e:ie) feel, 8; be sorry, regret, 11
   lo siento I'm sorry, P1
señor *(abr.* **Sr.***)* Mister, sir, gentleman, P1
   muy _____**es míos** Dear Sirs, 18
señora *(abr.* **Sra.***)* Mrs., Madam, Ma'am, lady, P1

muy _____s **mías** Dear Ladies, 18
señorita *(abr.* **Srta.***)* Miss, young lady, P1
septiembre September, 4
séptimo(-a) seventh, 4
ser be, 1
servicio de habitación *(m.)* room service, 5
servilleta *(f.)* napkin, 6
servir (e:i) serve, 5
sesenta sixty, 1
setecientos seven hundred, 1
setenta seventy, 1
sexo *(m.)* sex, 2
sexto(-a) sixth, 4
si if, 4
sí yes, 1
sicología *(f.)* psychology, 17
sidra *(f.)* cider, 3
siempre always, 3
siete seven, P1
siglo *(m.)* century
siguiente following, 13
silenciador *(m.)* muffler, 15
silla *(f.)* chair, P3
sillón *(m.)* armchair, 13
simpático(-a) nice, charming, 2
sin without, 12
_____ **embargo** however
_____ **que** without, 13
sinceramente sincerely, 18
sino but, 13
_____ **que** but rather
sitio *(m.)* place
sobre about, 9; over
sobrecama *(f.)* bedspread, 13
sobremesa *(f.)* after-dinner conversation
sobrenombre *(m.)* nickname
sobresalir be outstanding
sobrina *(f.)* niece, 4
sobrino *(m.)* nephew, 4
sobrio(-a) somber
Sociedad Anónima *(f.)* Incorporated
sociología *(f.)* sociology, 17
sofá *(m.)* couch, 13
sol *(m.)* sun, 4
hacer _____ be sunny, 4
solamente only, 9
soleado(-a) sunny
solicitar apply for, 2
solicitud *(f.)* application, 2
sólo only, 7
solo(-a) alone
soltero(-a) single, 2
sombrilla *(f.)* parasol, 4

sonar (o:ue) ring, go off *(alarm)*, 11
sopa *(f.)* soup, 6
sorprender surprise, 11
sorpresa *(f.)* surprise, 6
sorteo *(m.)* drawing *(lottery)*
su his, her, its, your *(form.)*, their, 2
subir climb, go up, 12
subirse get on, 18
subvencionado(-a) subsidized
sucio(-a) dirty, 15
suegra *(f.)* mother-in-law, 4
suegro *(m.)* father-in-law, 4
sueldo *(m.)* salary, 13
sueño: tener _____ be sleepy, 3
suerte *(f.)* luck, P2
suéter *(m.)* sweater, 4
suficiente enough, sufficient, 11
sugerir (e:ie) suggest, 11
supermercado *(m.)* supermarket, 16
suponer *(conj. like* **poner***)* suppose, 17
sur *(m.)* south, 18
suroeste *(m.)* southwest
suyo(s), suya(s) *(pron.)* his, hers, theirs, yours, 7

T

talonario de cheques *(m.)* checkbook, 11
talla *(f.)* size, 14
taller *(m.)* repair shop, 15
_____ **de mecánica** *(m.)* automobile repair shop, 15
también also, too, 1
tan as, so, 4
_____ **... como...** as . . . as . . . , 4
tanque *(m.)* tank, 15
tanto(-a) as much, 4
_____ **como** as much as, 4
tantos(-as) as many, 4
_____ **como** as many as, 4
tapa *(f.) (Sp.)* hors d'oeuvre
tapete *(m.)* tapestry
tarde *(f.)* afternoon, 1; *(adv.)* late, 7
de la _____ in the afternoon, 1
por la _____ in the afternoon, 1
tarea *(f.)* homework, 17
tarifa *(f.)* rate, 18
tarjeta *(f.)* card, 7
_____ **de crédito** *(f.)* credit card, 5
_____ **de turista** *(f.)* tourist card, 5
_____ **postal** *(f.)* postcard, 7
taxi *(m.)* taxi, 5
taza *(f.)* cup, 6

te *(pron.)* you *(fam.)*, 5; (to) you, 6; (to) yourself, 8
té *(m.)* tea, 6
teatro *(m.)* theater, 6
tejer weave
tejido *(m.)* weaving
teléfono *(m.)* telephone, 2
al _____ on the phone, 1
por _____ on the phone, 7
telegrama *(m.)* telegram
televisión *(f.)* television, 1
temer fear, be afraid, 11
temporada *(f.)* season
temprano early, 8
tenedor *(m.)* fork, 6
tener have, 2
_____ **... años (de edad)** be . . . years old, 3
_____ **calor** be hot, 3
_____ **frío** be cold, 3
_____ **ganas** feel like, 16
_____ **hambre** be hungry, 3
_____ **lugar** take place
_____ **miedo** be afraid, 3
_____ **prisa** be in a hurry, 3
_____ **que** have to, 2
_____ **razón** be right, 3
_____ **sed** be thirsty, 3
_____ **sueño** be sleepy, 3
_____ **... de atraso** be . . . late, behind, 7
tenista *(m., f.)* tennis player
tercero(-a) third, 4
terminar finish, 8
terraza *(f.)* terrace, 3
tétano *(m.)* tetanus, 10
ti you *(fam. sing.)*, 5
tía *(f.)* aunt, 4
tiempo *(m.)* time, 2; weather, 4
de _____ **completo** full-time, 13
tienda *(f.)* store, 8
_____ **de campaña** *(f.)* tent, 9
timbre *(m.) (Mex.)* stamp, 12
tinto red *(wine)*, 6
tintorería *(f.)* dry cleaner, 11
tío *(m.)* uncle, 4
tiza *(f.)* chalk, P3
toalla *(f.)* towel, 5
tobillo *(m.)* ankle, 10
tocadiscos *(m.)* record player, 3
tocino *(m.)* bacon
todavía yet, still 14
_____ **no** not yet, 17
todo(-a) all, 2; *(pron.)* everything, 5
todos(-as) everybody, 3

tomar take, 5; drink, 2

    ——— **una decisión** make a decision, 13

    tome asiento have a seat, P2

tomate *(m.)* tomato, 16

tonto(-a) *(m., f.)* fool, 8

toronja *(f.)* grapefruit, 16

torre *(f.)* tower

torta *(f.)* cake, 6

    torta helada *(f.)* ice cream cake, 6

tortilla *(f.)* omelette, 6

    ——— **de maíz** *(f.)* Mexican corn tortilla, 6

tos *(f.)* cough, 10

trabajar work, 1

trabajo *(m.)* job, 2

traducir translate, 6

traer bring, 3

traje *(m.)* suit

    ——— **de baño** *(m.)* bathing suit, 9

tramo *(m.)* set

trasbordar transfer, 18

tratar (de) try (to), 15

trato *(m.)* deal

trece thirteen, P2

treinta thirty, P2

tren *(m.)* train, 7

tres three, P1

trescientos three hundred, 1

trimestre *(m.)* quarter, 17

triste sad, 10

tristemente sadly, 10

trozo *(m.)* piece

trucha *(f.)* trout, 6

tu your *(fam. sing.)*, 2

tú you *(fam. sing.)*, P1

turbonadas *(f. pl.)* gusts

turista *(m., f.)* tourist, 7

    clase ——— *(f.)* tourist class, 7

turno *(m.)* appointment, 8

    pedir ——— to make an appointment, 8

tuyo(s), tuya(s) *(pron.)* yours *(fam. sing.)*, 7

U

últimamente lately

último(-a) last, 10

un(a) a, an, one, P3

un rato a short while

un poco (de) a little (of)

único(-a) only, unique, 11

    lo ——— the only thing

unido(-a) united

uniforme uniform

unir unite

universidad *(f.)* university, 1

uno *(m.)* one, 1

uruguayo(-a) Uruguayan, 3

usar wear, use, 14

usted (Ud.) you *(form.)*, 1

ustedes (Uds.) you *(pl.)*, 1

uva *(f.)* grape, 3

V

vacaciones *(f. pl.)* vacation, 9

    irse de ——— go on vacation

vacío(-a) empty, 15

valer be worth, 15

válido(-a) valid, 18

valija *(f.)* suitcase, 5

¡vamos!, ¡vámonos! come on!, let's go!, 4

vaquero *(m.)* cowboy

varicela *(f.)* chickenpox, 10

varios(-as) several, various, 11

vasija *(f.)* pot

vaso *(m.)* glass, 6

vecino(-a) *(m., f.)* neighbor

veinte twenty, P2

veinticinco twenty-five, P2

veinticuatro twenty-four, P2

veintidós twenty-two, P2

veintinueve twenty-nine, P2

veintiocho twenty-eight, P2

veintiséis twenty-six, P2

veintisiete twenty-seven, P2

veintitrés twenty-three, P2

veintiuno twenty-one, P2

vela *(f.)* candle

velocidad *(f.)* speed, 15

    ——— **máxima** *(f.)* speed limit, 15

vendar bandage, 10

vendedor(a) *(m., f.)* salesperson

vender sell, 2

venir come, 2

venta *(f.)* sale

ventaja *(f.)* advantage

ventana *(f.)* window, P3

ventanilla *(f.)* window *(of a vehicle)*, 12

ver see, 4

    a ——— let's see, 11

veranear spend the summer

verano *(m.)* summer, 4

¿verdad? right?, 11

verdulería *(f.)* greengrocer's

vermut *(m.)* vermouth, 6

vestido *(m.)* dress, 8

    ——— **de noche** *(m.)* evening gown, 14

vestir (e:i) dress, 8

vestirse (e:i) get dressed, 8

vez *(f.)* time, 7

    de ——— **en cuando** from time to time

vía *(f.)* street, way

    ——— **aérea** air mail, 12

    la Gran ——— Main Street

viajar travel, 4

viaje *(m.)* trip, 7

viajero(-a) *(m., f.)* traveler, 7

vida *(f.)* life

viejo(-a) old, 12

viento *(m.)* wind, 4

    hacer ——— be windy, 4

viernes *(m.)* Friday, P2

vinagre *(m.)* vinegar, 16

vino *(m.)* wine, 3

    ——— **blanco** white wine, 6

    ——— **tinto** red wine, 6

visitar visit, 5

vista *(f.)* view

    con ——— **a** overlooking, 5

visto(-a) *(p. p. of* **ver** *and adj.)* seen, 14

vitrificado glazed porcelain

viuda *(f.)* widow, 2

viudo *(m.)* widower, 2

vivir live, 2

volar (o:ue) fly, 4

volver (o:ue) return, 4

vosotros(-as) you *(fam. pl.)*, 1; *(pron.)* you, 5

vuelo *(m.)* flight, 7

vuelta *(f.)* tour

vuelto *(m.)* change, 18

vuelto(-a) *(p. p. of* **volver** *and adj.)* returned, 14

vuestro(-a) your *(fam. pl.)*, 2

vuestro(-a) *(pron.)* yours *(fam. pl.)*, 7

Y

y and, 1

ya already, 6

yerno *(m.)* son-in-law, 4

yo I, 1

Z

zanahoria *(f.)* carrot, 16

zapatería *(f.)* shoe department, shoe store, 14

zapato *(m.)* shoe, 14

zona postal *(f.)* zip code, 2

zoológico *(m.)* zoo, 16

English–Spanish

A

a, an un(a), P3
about de, 7; sobre, 9
accept aceptar, 5
accident accidente *(m.)*, 10
according to según, 4
account cuenta *(f.)*, 11
    checking _____ cuenta corriente *(f.)*, 11
    savings _____ cuenta de ahorros *(f.)*, 11
accounting contabilidad *(f.)*, 17
ache doler (o:ue), 10
across from frente a, 11
ad anuncio *(m.)*, 2
    classified _____ anuncio clasificado *(m.)*, 2
address dirección *(f.)*, P2; domicilio *(m.)*, P2
advance anticipado(-a), 12
advertisement anuncio *(m.)*, 2
advice consejo *(m.)*, 17
advise aconsejar, 11
advisor consejero(-a) *(m., f.)*, 17
affectionate cariñoso(-a), 18
affectionately afectuosamente, 18
afraid: to be _____ tener miedo, 3
after después (de), 6
afternoon tarde *(f.)*, 1
    good _____ buenas tardes, P1
    in the _____ de la tarde, 1; por la tarde, 1
afterwards después, 12
again otra vez, 16
age edad *(f.)*, 2
ago: . . . ago hace... , 10
agree ponerse de acuerdo, 9
air aire *(m.)*
    conditioning aire acondicionado *(m.)*, 13
airmail (por) vía aérea, 9
airport aeropuerto *(m.)*, 5
alarm clock despertador *(m.)*, 11
all todo(-a), 2; todos(-as), 3
    right bien, P2; bueno, 7
allergic alérgico(-a), 10
almost casi, 14
along por, 9
already ya, 6
also también, 1
although aunque, 13
always siempre, 3
ambulance ambulancia *(f.)*, 10

amusement park parque de diversiones *(m.)*, 16
analysis análisis *(m.)*, 10
and y, 1
angry enfadado(-a), 13; enojado(-a), 13
ankle tobillo *(m.)*, 10
anniversary aniversario *(m.)*, 6
    wedding _____ aniversario de bodas *(m.)*, 6
announce anunciar, 13
another otro(-a), 4
any algún(a), 5; alguno(-a), 5
    not _____ ningún(a), 5
anyone alguien, 5
anything algo, 5
    _____ **else?** ¿algo más?, 5
apartment apartamento *(m.)*, 8; piso *(m.) (Sp.)*, 8
appeal (to) gustar, 7
appendicitis apendicitis *(f.)*, 10
apple manzana *(f.)*, 16
application solicitud *(f.)*, 2
apply (for) solicitar, 2
    _____ **for a loan** pedir un préstamo, 11
appointment cita *(f.)*, 8; turno *(m.)*, 8
    to make an _____ pedir turno, 8
April abril, 4
Argentinian argentino(-a), 17
arm brazo *(m.)*, 10
    an _____ **and a leg** un ojo de la cara, 9
armchair butaca *(f.)*, 13; sillón *(m.)*, 13
around por, 9
    _____ **here** por aquí, 5
arrange arreglar, 14
as como, 7
    _____ **. . .** _____ tan... como, 4
    _____ **many** tantos(-as), 4
    _____ **many . . .** _____ tantos(-as)... como, 4
    _____ **much** _____ tanto como, 4
    _____ **soon** _____ en cuanto, 11
    _____ **usual** como siempre, 17
ask preguntar, 6
    _____ **(for)** pedir (e:i), 6
aspirin aspirina *(f.)*, 10
assist ayudar, 17
at a, 1; en, P2
    _____ **the** al *(m. sing.) (contraction)*, 1; a la *(f. sing.)*
    _____ **the left** a la izquierda, 5
    _____ **what time?** ¿a qué hora?, 1

attend asistir (a), 4
August agosto, 4
aunt tía *(f.)*, 4
automatic automático(-a), 18
autumn otoño *(m.)*, 4
avenue avenida *(f.)*, 2
average promedio *(m.)*, 17

B

back espalda *(f.)*, 10
bad malo(-a), 3
badly mal, 4
baggage room sala de equipajes *(f.)*, 18
balance *(bank)* saldo *(m.)*, 11
bandage vendar, 10
bank banco *(m.)*, 11
barber barbero(-a) *(m., f.)*, 8
    _____ **shop** barbería *(f.)*, 8
bathe bañar(se), 8
bathing suit traje de baño *(m.)*, 9
bathroom baño *(m.)*, 5; cuarto de baño *(m.)*, 5
battery acumulador *(m.)*, 5; batería *(f.)*, 15
be estar, 3; ser, 1
    _____ **able to** poder (o:ue), 4
    _____ **acquainted with** conocer, 6
    _____ **afraid** temer, 11; tener miedo (de), 3
    _____ **bad** *(weather)* hacer mal tiempo, 4
    _____ **. . . behind schedule** tener... de retraso, 7
    _____ **cold** *(weather)* hacer frío, 4; tener frío, 3
    _____ **. . . from here** estar a... de aquí, 12
    _____ **glad** alegrarse (de), 11
    _____ **good** *(weather)* hacer buen tiempo, 4
    _____ **hot** *(weather)* hacer calor, 4; tener calor, 3
    _____ **hungry** tener hambre, 3
    _____ **in a hurry** tener prisa, 3
    _____ **located** quedar, 12
    _____ **named** llamarse, P2
    _____ **right** tener razón, 3
    _____ **sleepy** tener sueño, 3
    _____ **sorry** sentir (e:ie), 11
    _____ **sunny** hacer sol, 4
    _____ **sure** estar seguro(-a), 12
    _____ **thirsty** tener sed, 3

_____ **too big** (**small**) quedar grande (chico), 14

_____ **too tight** apretar (e:ie), 14

_____ **windy** hacer viento, 4

_____ **worth** valer, 15

_____ **. . . years old** tener... años, 3

beach playa *(f.)*, 9

bean frijol *(m.)*, 6

beauty parlor peluquería *(f.)*, 8; salón de belleza *(m.)*, 8

bed cama *(f.)*, 11

bedroom dormitorio *(m.)*; recámara *(f.)* *(Mex.)*, 13

bedspread sobrecama *(f.)*, 13

beer cerveza *(f.)*, 3

before antes (de), 5; antes de que, 13

beg rogar (o:ue), 11

begin comenzar (e:ie), 3; empezar (e:ie), 3

believe creer, 2

bellhop botones *(m.)*, 12

bend doblar, 12

berth litera *(f.)*, 18

lower _____ litera alta, 18

upper _____ litera baja, 18

besides además, 3

best el (la) mejor, 4

better mejor, 4

beverage bebida *(f.)*, 3

bicycle bicicleta *(f.)*, 9

big grande, 4

be too _____ quedar grande, 14

bill cuenta *(f.)*, 6

biology biología *(f.)*, 17

birth nacimiento *(m.)*, 2

birthday cumpleaños *(m.)*, 3

black negro(-a), P3

blackboard pizarra *(f.)*, P3

blanket cobija *(f.)*, 13; frazada *(f.)*, 13; manta *(f.)*, 13

bleed sangrar, 10

block cuadra *(f.)*, 12; manzana *(f.)* *(Sp.)*, 12

blonde güero(-a) *(Mex.)*, 2; rubio(-a), 2

blouse blusa *(f.)*, 14

blue azul, P3

boarding house pensión *(f.)*, 4

boat barco *(m.)*, 7

book libro *(f.)*, P3

boot bota *(f.)*, 14

border frontera *(f.)*, 18

bore aburrir, 9

bored aburrido(-a), 7

get _____ aburrirse, 9

boring aburrido(-a) 7

borrow pedir prestado, 11

bottle botella *(f.)*, 6

boy chico *(m.)*, 2; muchacho *(m.)*, 2

boyfriend novio *(m.)*, 3

brake freno *(m.)*, 15

bread pan *(m.)*, 16

break romper(se), 10

_____ **down** descomponerse, 15

breakfast desayuno *(m.)*, 5

have _____ desayunar, 18

bring traer, 3

brochure folleto *(m.)*, 9

broken quebrado(-a), 10; roto(-a), 10

broom escoba *(f.)*, 8

brother hermano *(m.)*, 3

brother-in-law cuñado *(m.)*, 4

brown *(hair, eyes)* castaño, 4; marrón, P3

building edificio *(m.)*, 12

bus autobús *(m.)*, 4; camión *(m.)* *(Mex.)*, 4; ómnibus, 4

business administration administración de empresas *(f.)*, 17

busy ocupado(-a), 3

but pero, 3; sino, 13

butter mantequilla *(f.)*, 16

buy comprar, 5; llevarse, 14

by para, 9; por, 9

go _____ pasar (por), 5

bye chau, P2

C

cabin cabaña *(f.)*, 9

cafe café *(m.)*, 4

cafeteria cafetería *(f.)*, 2

cake torta *(f.)*, 6

ice cream _____ torta helada *(f.)*, 6

calculator calculadora *(f.)*, 17

call llamar, 1

camera cámara fotográfica *(f.)*, 5

camp acampar, 9

can bote *(m.)* *(Mex.)*, 16; lata *(f.)*, 16

cancel cancelar, 5

capital capital *(f.)*, 7

car automóvil *(m.)*, 4; carro *(m.)*, 4; coche *(m.)*, 4

dining _____ coche-comedor *(m.)*, 18

sleeping _____ coche-cama *(m.)*, 18

carburetor carburador *(m.)*, 15

card tarjeta *(f.)*, 8

credit _____ tarjeta de crédito *(f.)*, 5

tourist _____ tarjeta de turista *(f.)*, 5

carpet alfombra *(f.)*, 8

carrot zanahoria *(f.)*, 16

cash efectivo *(m.)*, 11

in _____ al contado, 11; en efectivo, 11

cassette casete *(m.)*, 3; cinta *(f.)*, 3

catch *(a fish)* pescar, 9

celebrate celebrar, 3

celery apio *(m.)*, 16

central heating calefacción central *(f.)*, 13

certified certificado(-a), 12

chair silla *(f.)*, P3

chalk tiza *(f.)*, P3

champagne champán *(m.)*, 3

change cambio *(m.)*, 18; vuelto *(m.)*, 18; cambiar, 14

charge cobrar, 11

charming encantador(a), 18; simpático(-a), 2

cheap barato(-a), 5

check cheque *(m.)*, 11; chequear, 15; revisar, 15

traveler's _____ cheque de viajero *(m.)*, 5

checkbook talonario de cheques *(m.)*, 11

checking account cuenta corriente *(f.)*, 11

cheerful alegre, 10

cheerfully alegremente, 10

cheese queso *(m.)*, 2

chemistry química *(f.)*, 17

chest pecho *(m.)*, 10

_____ **of drawers** cómoda *(f.)*, 13

chicken pollo *(m.)*, 3

_____ **with rice** arroz con pollo *(m.)*, 6

chickenpox varicela *(f.)*, 10

child hijo(-a), 3; niño(-a), 9

only _____ hijo(-a) único(-a), 11

children hijos *(m. pl.)*, 2

Chilean chileno(-a), 9

Chinese *(lang.)* chino *(m.)*, 1

chocolate chocolate *(m.)*, 6

hot _____ chocolate caliente *(m.)*, 6

Christmas Navidad *(f.)*, 3

cider sidra *(f.)*, 3

citizen ciudadano(-a) *(m., f.)*, 18

city ciudad *(f.)*, 1

claim check comprobante *(m.)*, 11
class clase *(f.)*, 1
    first _____ (de) primera clase, 7
    tourist _____ clase turista *(f.)*, 7
classified ad anuncio clasificado *(m.)*, 2
classmate compañero(-a) de clase *(m., f.)*, 3
clean (oneself) limpiar(se), 8
clear claro(-a), P3
clearly claramente, 10
clerk empleado(-a), 5
climb subir, 12
close cerrar (e:ie)
    _____ **to** *(prep.)* cerca de, 2
closet amario *(m.)*, 14; ropero *(m.)*, 14
clothes ropa *(f.)*, 14
club club *(m.)*, 3
coach coche *(m.)*, 18
coat abrigo *(m.)*, 4
cocktail coctel *(m.)*, 3
coffee café *(m.)*, 2
cold frío *(m.)*, 3; resfriado *(m.)*, 10; resfrío *(m.)*, 10
    be _____ *(weather)* hacer frío, 4; tener frío, 3
college facultad *(f.)*, 17
color color *(m.)*, P3
comb peine *(m.)*, 8
    _____ **(one's hair)** peinar(se), 8
come venir, 2
    _____ **in!** ¡adelante!, P2; ¡pase!, P2
    _____ **on!** ¡vamos!, 4; ¡vámonos!, 13
comfortable cómodo(-a), 4
compact compacto(-a), 18
company compañía *(f.)*, 2
computer computador(a), 2
concert concierto *(m.)*, 8
conduct conducir, 6
confirm confirmar, 5
conversation conversación *(f.)*, 1
converse conversar, 2
cook cocinar, 8
corn maíz *(m.)*, 6
corner *(street)* esquina *(f.)*, 12
cost costar (o:ue), 4
    _____ **an arm and a leg** costar un ojo de la cara, 9
couch sofá *(m.)*, 13
cough tos *(f.)*, 10
counselor consejero(-a) *(m., f.)*, 17
country campo *(m.)*, 9; país *(m.)*, 9
couple pareja *(f.)*, 15
cousin primo(-a) *(m., f.)*, 13
cover cubrir, 14 *(past part. cubierto)*

crazy loco(-a), 7
cream crema *(f.)*, 6
cross cruzar, 10
Cuban cubano(-a), 6
cup taza *(f.)*, 6
curl rizo *(m.)*, 8
curling iron rizador *(m.)*, 8
curtain cortina *(f.)*, 13
custard flan *(m.)*, 6
customs aduana *(f.)*, 5
cut (oneself) cortar(se), 8

D

Dad papá *(m.)*, 4
daily diario(-a), 18
dance baile *(m.)*, 3; bailar, 3
dark oscuro(-a), P3
    _____-**haired** moreno(-a), 2
date cita *(f.)*, 16; fecha *(f.)*, 4; fechar, 11
daughter hija *(f.)*, 3
    _____-**in-law** nuera *(f.)*, 4
day día *(m.)*, P1
    the next _____ al día siguiente, 13
dead muerto(-a), 14
dear estimado(-a), 18; querido(-a), 18
    _____ **Madam** muy señora mía, 18
    _____ **Sir** muy señor mío, 18
dearest queridísimo(-a), 18
December diciembre, 4
decide decidir, 2
decision decisión *(f.)*, 13
    to make a _____ tomar una decisión, 13
declare declarar, 5
delay retraso *(m.)*, 7
deliver entregar, 17
deny negar (e:ie), 12
department departamento *(m.)*, 11
    men's _____ departamento (de ropa) para caballeros, 14
    women's _____ departamento (de ropa) para señoras, 14
departure salida *(f.)*, 18
    _____ **gate** puerta de salida *(f.)*, 7
depend (on) depender (de), 18
deposit depositar, 11
descend bajar, 12
desert desierto *(m.)*, 9
desk escritorio *(m.)*, P3
dessert postre *(m.)*, 6
    for _____ de postre, 6
develop *(film)* revelar, 11
dictation dictado *(m.)*, P3
dictionary diccionario *(m.)*, 17
die morir (o:ue), 8

diet dieta *(m.)*, 16
    to go on a _____ ponerse a dieta, 16
difficult difícil, 2
dining car coche-comedor *(m.)*, 18
dining room comedor *(m.)*, 13
dinner cena *(f.)*, 5
    to have _____ cenar, 5
dirty sucio(-a), 15
    to get (something) _____ ensuciar, 8
    to get _____ ensuciarse, 8
discount descuento *(m.)*, 18
discussion discusión *(f.)*, 17
disease enfermedad *(f.)*, 10
dish plato *(m.)*, 6
dishwasher lavaplatos *(m.)*, 13
disinfect desinfectar, 10
distinguished distinguido(-a), 18
divorced divorciado(-a), 2
dizziness mareo *(m.)*, 10
do hacer, 6
    _____ **the shopping** hacer las compras, 16
doctor doctor(a) *(m., f.)*, P1; médico(-a) *(m., f.)*, 10
    _____**'s office** consultorio *(m.)*, 10
document documento *(m.)*, 11
dog perro(-a), 8
dollar dólar *(m.)*, 5
door puerta *(f.)*, P2
double doble, 5
doubt dudar, 11
downstairs abajo, 12
downtown centro *(m.)*, 5
dozen docena *(f.)*, 16
drama drama *(f.)*, 16
dress vestido *(m.)*, 8; vestir(se) (e:i), 8
drink bebida *(f.)*, 3; beber, 2; tomar, 2
drive conducir, 6; manejar, 4
driver's license carnet de conducir *(m.)*, 15; licencia de conducir *(f.)*, 2
drizzle lloviznar, 4
dry cleaner tintorería *(f.)*, 11
during durante, 7

E

each cada, 12
ear *(inner)*, oído *(m.)*, 10; *(external)* oreja *(f.)*, 10
early temprano, 8
earn ganar, 13
easily fácilmente, 10
east este *(m.)*, 18
easy fácil, 2

eat comer, 2
    have something to _____ comer algo, 14
economic económico(-a), 1
egg blanquillo *(m.) (Mex.),* 16; huevo *(m.),* 6
eight ocho, P1
    _____ hundred ochocientos, 1
eighteen dieciocho, P2
eighth octavo(-a), 4
eighty ochenta, 1
elegant elegante, 13
elevator ascensor *(m.),* 5; elevador *(m.),* 5
eleven once, P2
embassy embajada *(f.),* 5
embrace abrazo *(m.),* 18
emergency emergencia *(f.),* 10
    _____ room sala de emergencia *(f.),* 10
empty vacío(-a), 15
engineering ingeniería *(f.),* 17
English *(lang.)* inglés *(m.),* 1
enough suficiente, 11
entrance entrada *(f.),* 7
eraser borrador *(m.),* P3
errand diligencia *(f.),* 11
    to run _____s hacer diligencias, 11
escalator escalera mecánica *(f.),* 14
especially especialmente, 10
evening noche *(f.),* 1
    _____ gown vestido de noche *(m.),* 14
in the _____ de la noche, 1; por la noche, 1
ever alguna vez, 10
everybody todos(-as), 3
everything todo, 5
exam examen *(m.),* P3
    midterm _____ examen parcial *(m.),* 17
excellent excelente, 6
excess exceso *(m.),* 7
    _____ baggage exceso de equipaje *(m.),* 7
exchange cambio *(m.),* 18; cambiar, 14
    _____ rate cambio de moneda *(m.),* 5
excursion excursión *(f.),* 14
excuse me perdón, P1; con permiso, P2
exercise ejercicio *(m.),* P3; hacer ejercicio, 17
exit salida *(f.),* 7
expensive caro(-a), 5
experience experiencia *(f.),* 18

express *(train)* expreso *(m.),* 18; rápido *(m.),* 18
eye ojo *(m.),* 10

F

face cara *(f.),* 10
fact: the _____ is . . . es que... , 12
fall otoño *(m.),* 4
fall asleep dormirse (o:ue), 8
family familia *(f.),* 4
family room salón de estar *(m.),* 13
famous famoso(-a), 4
far (from) lejos (de), 2
fast rápido(-a), 10
fat gordo(-a), 2
father padre *(m.),* 4
father-in-law suegro *(m.),* 4
favorite favorito(-a), 6
fear miedo *(m.);* temer, 11
February febrero, 4
feel sentir (e:ie), 8
    _____ like tener ganas de, 16
feminine femenino(-a), 2
fever fiebre *(f.),* 10
few pocos(-as), 5
fiancé novio *(m.),* 3
fiancée novia *(f.),* 3
fifteen quince, P2
fifth quinto(-a), 4
fifty cincuenta, 1
fill llenar, 2
film película *(f.),* 16
filter filtro *(m.),* 15
find encontrar (o:ue), 4
    _____ out saber, 10
fine multa *(f.),* 15; poner (dar) una multa, 15; *(adv.)* bien, P1
finger dedo *(m.),* 10
finish terminar, 8
first primero(-a), 4
    _____-class de primera clase, 7
fish pescado *(m.),* 6; pescar, 9
fishing pesca *(f.),* 16
    go _____ ir de pesca, 9
fishing rod caña de pescar *(f.),* 9
fit caber, 6
fitting room probador *(m.),* 14
five cinco, P1
    _____ hundred quinientos, 1
fix arreglar, 15
flat tire pinchazo *(m.),* 7
flight vuelo *(m.),* 7
floor piso *(m.),* P3
fly volar (o:ue), 4
fog niebla *(f.),* 4

follow seguir (e:i), 5
following siguiente, 13
food comida *(f.),* 6
fool tonto(-a), 8
foot pie *(m.),* 10
for para, 5; por, 5
    _____ rent se alquila, 13
forecast *(weather)* pronóstico del tiempo *(m.),* 4
foreign extranjero(-a), 12
forget olvidar, 8
    _____ about olvidarse de, 8
fork tenedor *(m.),* 6
form planilla *(f.),* 18
fortune fortuna *(f.),* 16
forty cuarenta, 1
four cuatro, P1
    _____ hundred cuatrocientos, 1
fourteen catorce, P2
fourth cuarto(-a), 4
free gratis, 11; libre, 2
freeway autopista *(f.),* 9
French *(lang.)* francés *(m.),* 1
    _____ fries papas fritas *(f. pl.),* 6
frequently frecuentemente, 10
Friday viernes *(m.),* P2
fried frito(-a), 6
friend amigo(-a), *(m., f.),* 2
from de, 1
    to be . . . _____ here estar a... de aquí, 12
fruit fruta *(f.),* 6
full lleno(-a), 15
    _____-time de tiempo completo, 13
function funcionar, 15
funny extraño(-a), 15
furnished amueblado(-a), 13
furniture muebles *(m. pl.),* 13

G

game partido *(m.),* 17
garage garaje *(m.),* 13
garden jardín *(m.),* 13
gasoline gasolina *(f.),* 15
gate puerta *(f.),* 7
    departure _____ puerta de salida *(f.),* 7
gee! ¡caramba!, P1
gelatin gelatina *(f.),* 6
generally generalmente, 8
gentleman caballero *(m.),* 14; señor *(m.),* P1
German *(lang.)* alemán *(m.),* 1
get conseguir (e:i), 5; *(grade)* sacar, 17

_____ **a haircut** cortarse el pelo, 8
_____ **dirty** ensuciar(se), 8
_____ **off** bajarse, 18
_____ **on** subirse, 18
_____ **undressed** desvestirse (e:i), 8
_____ **up** levantarse, 8
gift regalo *(m.)*, 8
girl chica *(f.)*, 2; muchacha *(f.)*, 2
girlfriend novia *(f.)*, 3
give dar, 3; *(gift)* regalar, 8
_____ **an injection** poner una inyección, 10
glad contento(-a), 3
be _____ alegrarse, 11
glass vaso *(m.)*, 6
glove guante *(m.)*, 4
_____ **compartment** guantera *(f.)*, 15; portaguantes *(m.)*, 15
go ir, 3
_____ **away** irse, 8
_____ **by** pasar por, 5
_____ **down** bajar, 12
_____ **fishing** ir de pesca, 9
_____ **home** ir a casa, 9
_____ **off** *(alarm)* sonar (o:ue), 11
_____ **on a diet** ponerse a dieta, 16
_____ **on vacation** irse de vacaciones, 9
_____ **out** salir, 6
_____ **shopping** ir de compras, 14
_____ **to bed** acostarse (o:ue), 8
_____ **up** subir, 12
let's go! ¡vámonos!, 13; ¡vamos!, 4
goblet copa *(f.)*, 6
gold oro *(m.)*, 5
good bueno(-a), 3
_____ **afternoon** buenas tardes, P1
_____ **evening** buenas noches, P1
_____ **luck!** ¡buena suerte!, 2
_____ **morning** buenos días, P1
_____ **night** buenas noches, P1
good-bye adiós, P1
grade calificación *(f.)*, 18; nota *(f.)*, 17
graduate graduar(se), 14
granddaughter nieta *(f.)*, 4
grandfather abuelo *(m.)*, 4
grandmother abuela *(f.)*, 4
grandson nieto *(m.)*, 4
grape uva *(f.)*, 3
grapefruit toronja *(f.)*, 16
gray gris, P3
green verde, P3
greeting saludo *(f.)*, 18
ground floor planta baja *(f.)*, 14

H

hair cabello *(m.)*, 9; pelo *(m.)*, 8
comb one's _____ peinarse, 8
wash one's _____ lavarse la cabeza, 8
haircut corte *(m.)*, 8
get a _____ cortarse el pelo, 8
hairdo peinado *(m.)*, 8
hairdresser peluquero(-a) *(m., f.)*, 8
hair dryer secador *(m.)*, 8
hairstyle peinado *(m.)*, 8
half medio(-a), 6
ham jamón *(m.)*, 6
hamburger hamburguesa *(f.)*, 6
hand mano *(f.)*, P3
handbag bolso de mano *(m.)*, 7
handkerchief pañuelo *(m.)*, 14
handsome guapo(-a), 2
happen pasar, 7
happily felizmente, 10
happy contento(-a), 3; feliz, 2
hate odiar, 9
have haber *(aux.)*, 15; tener, 2
_____ **a good time** divertirse (e:ie), 9
_____ **a nice trip** buen viaje, 7
_____ **a seat** tome asiento, P2
_____ **dinner** cenar, 5
_____ **just . . .** acabar de... , 5
_____ **lunch** almorzar (o:ue), 4
_____ **something to eat** comer algo, 14
_____ **to** tener que, 2
he él, 1
head cabeza *(f.)*, 10
headache dolor de cabeza *(m.)*, 10
hear oír, 14
heat calor *(m.)*, 3
central _____ calefacción central *(f.)*, 13
height estatura *(f.)*, 4
hello *(on the phone)* bueno, 1; buenos días, 1; *(on the phone)* dígame, 1; *(on the phone)* oigo, 1
say _____ to . . . saludos a... , P2
help ayudar, 17
her ella, 5; la, 5; le, 6; su, 2
here aquí, 3; presente, P3
hers suyo(-a)(s), 7
herself se, 8
hi hola, P1
say _____ to . . . (dar) saludos a... , 12
high alto(-a), 2
high school escuela secundaria *(f.)*, 17

highway autopista *(f.)*, 9; carretera *(f.)*, 15
him él, 5; le, 6; lo, 5
himself se, 8
his su, 2; suyo(-a)(s), 7
holiday feriado *(m.)*, 16
home casa *(f.)*, 3
go _____ ir a casa, 9
homely feo(-a), 4
homework tarea *(f.)*, 17
hope esperar, 11
I _____ . . . ojalá... , 11
horribly horriblemente, 9
hors d'oeuvres entremeses *(m. pl.)*, 3
horse caballo *(m.)*, 9
hot caliente, 6
be _____ *(weather)* hacer calor, 4; tener calor, 3
_____ **chocolate** chocolate caliente *(m.)*, 6
hotel hotel *(m.)*, 5
hour hora *(f.)*, 7
house casa *(f.)*, 3
how cómo, P2
_____ . . . ! ¡qué... !, 9
_____ **are you?** ¿cómo está Ud.?, P1
_____ **do you say . . . ?** ¿cómo se dice... ? , P2
_____ **many** cuántos(-as), 3
_____ **much** cuánto(-a), 3
_____ **'s it going?** ¿qué tal?, P1
hug abrazo *(m.)*, 18
hundred cien, 1
hungry: be _____ tener hambre, 3
hunt cazar, 9
hurry: be in a _____ tener prisa, 3
hurt doler (o:ue), 10
husband esposo *(m.)*, 2

I

I yo, 1
ice cream helado *(m.)*, 6
_____ **cake** torta helada *(f.)*, 6
iced helado(-a), 6
idea idea *(f.)*, 3
identification documento de identidad *(m.)*, 12
if si
important importante, 17
in en, P2
_____ **cash** al contado, 11; en efectivo, 11
_____ **order** en regla, 5
_____ **order that** para que, 13

_____ **order to** para, 2
_____ **that case** entonces, 1
_____ **the afternoon** de la tarde, 1; por la tarde, 1
_____ **the evening** de la noche, 1; por la noche, 1
_____ **the morning** de la mañana, 1; por la mañana, 1
include incluir, 17
incorporated Sociedad Anónima *(f.)*, 18
inexpensive barato(-a), 5
information información *(f.)*, 5
inheritance herencia *(f.)*, 13
injection inyección *(f.)*, 10
give an _____ poner una inyección, 10
inspector inspector(a) *(m., f.)*, 5
install instalar, 15
installments plazos *(m. pl.)*, 11
in _____ a plazos, 11
instead of en vez de, 13
insurance seguro *(m.)*, 18
insured asegurado(-a), 18
interest interés *(m.)*, 5
interesting interesante, 4
invite invitar, 3
invited invitado(-a), 8
it la, 5; lo, 5
its su, 2
Italian *(lang.)* italiano *(m.)*, 1; italiano(-a), 1

J

jacket chaqueta *(f.)*, 14
January enero, 4
Japanese *(lang.)* japonés *(m.)*, 1
job empleo *(m.)*, 2; trabajo *(m.)*, 2
joke bromear, 9
journalism periodismo *(m.)*, 17
journalist periodista *(m., f.)*, 17
juice jugo *(m.)*, 6
July julio, 4
June junio, 4

K

key llave *(f.)*, 5
kid bromear, 9
kilometer kilómetro *(m.)*, 15
kiss beso *(m.)*, 6
kitchen cocina *(f.)*, 8
knee rodilla *(f.)*, 10
knife cuchillo *(m.)*, 6
know conocer, 6; saber, 6

if I had known de haber sabido, 16
knowledge conocimiento *(m.)*, 2

L

lady señora *(f.)*, P1
young _____ señorita *(f.)*, P1
lake lago *(m.)*, 9
lamb cordero *(m.)*, 6
lamp lámpara *(f.)*, 13
language idioma *(m.)*, 1
large grande, 4
last último(-a), 10
_____ **night** anoche, 8
late tarde, 7
later luego, 5; más tarde, 1
a while _____ al rato, 11
see you _____ hasta luego, P1
Latin American latinoamericano(-a), 17
law derecho *(m.)*, 17
lawyer abogado(-a) *(m., f.)*, 17
learn aprender, 2
least el (la) menos, 4
leave dejar, 6; salir, 6
left izquierdo(-a), 5
on the _____ a la izquierda, 5
leg pierna *(f.)*, 10
lend prestar, 7
less menos, 4
more or _____ más o menos, 1
lesson lección *(f.)*, P3
letter carta *(f.)*, 4
lettuce lechuga *(f.)*, 16
liberty libertad *(f.)*, 1
library biblioteca *(f.)*, 16
license carnet de conducir *(m.)*, 5; licencia de conducir *(f.)*,
_____ **plate** chapa *(f.)*, 15
lie mentir (e:ie), 8
lifeguard salvavidas *(m., f.)*, 9
lift levantar, 8
light luz *(f.)*, P3, claro(-a), P3
traffic _____ semáforo *(m.)*, 12
like como, 17
feel _____ tener ganas de, 16
I _____ . . . me gusta(n)... , 7
not to _____ **at all** no gustarle nada a uno, 17
what is . . . _____? ¿cómo es... ? , 4
line cola *(f.)*, 16
to stand in _____ hacer cola, 16
list lista *(f.)*, 5
waiting _____ lista de espera *(f.)*, 5

listen! ¡oye!, 1
literature literatura *(f.)*, 17
little pequeño(-a), 4; poco(-a), 4
live vivir, 2
loan préstamo *(m.)*, 11
apply for a _____ pedir un préstamo, 11
lobster langosta *(f.)*, 6
located: be _____ quedar, 12
long largo(-a), 7
look mirar, 2
_____ **for** buscar, 7
_____ **like** parecerse (a), 11
lot (of) un montón *(m.)*, 12; mucho(-a), 3
love amor *(m.)*, 6; cariños *(m. pl.)*, 12; querer (e:ie), 3
I _____ . . . me encanta(n)... , 13
lower berth litera baja *(f.)*, 18
luck suerte *(f.)*, 2
good _____! ¡buena suerte!, 2
luckily por suerte, 9
luggage equipaje *(m.)*, 7
lunch almuerzo *(m.)*, 5
have _____ almorzar (o:ue), 4

M

Ma'am, Madam señora *(f.)*, P1
made hecho(-a), 14
magazine revista *(f.)*, 8
magnificent magnífico(-a), 3
mail correo *(m.)*, 12
mailbox buzón *(m.)*, 12; casillero *(m.)*, 12
maintain mantener, 17
major especialización *(f.)*, 17
make hacer, 6
_____ **an appointment** pedir turno (e:i), 8
_____ **a phone call** llamar por teléfono, 1
_____ **a stopover** hacer escala, 18
man hombre *(m.)*, P3
many muchos(-as), 3
as _____ tantos(-as), 4
how _____ cuántos(-as), 3
map mapa *(m.)*, P3
March marzo, 4
margarine margarina *(f.)*, 16
marital status estado civil *(m.)*, 2
married casado(-a), 2
marvelous maravilloso(-a), 18
mashed potatoes puré de papas *(m.)*, 6
match hacer juego, 14
mattress colchón *(m.)*, 13

May mayo, 4
me me, 5, 6; mí, 5
meal comida *(f.)*, 6
mean: what does . . . _____? ¿qué quiere decir... ? , 2
    it _____s . . . quiere decir... , 2
measles sarampión *(m.)*, 10
meat carne *(f.)*, 6
meatball albóndiga *(f.)*, 6
mechanic mecánico *(m.)*, 15
medicine medicina *(f.)*, 4
    _____ cabinet botiquín *(m.)*, 8
medium mediano(-a), 4
meet conocer, 7; encontrarse (o:ue) (con), 14
melon melón *(m.)*, 16
menu menú *(m.)*, 6
merry alegre, 10
midnight medianoche *(f.)*, 3
    at _____ a la medianoche, 3
midterm exam examen parcial *(m.)*, 17
mile milla *(f.)*, 15
milk leche *(f.)*, 6
mine mío(-a)(s), 7
mineral water agua mineral *(f.)*, 6
mirror espejo *(m.)*, 8
miss echar de menos, 4; extrañar, 4
Miss señorita *(f.)*, P1
Mister señor *(m.)*, P1
modern moderno(-a), 5
Mom mamá *(f.)*, 4
moment momento *(m.)*, 1
Monday lunes *(m.)*, P2
money dinero *(m.)*, 1
    _____ order giro postal *(m.)*, 12
month mes *(m.)*, 2
more más, 4
    _____ or less más o menos, 1
morning mañana *(f.)*, 1
    good _____ buenos días, P1
    in the _____ de la mañana, 1; por la mañana, 1
Morocco Marruecos *(m.)*, 18
most el (la) más, 4
mother madre *(f.)*, 4
mother-in-law suegra *(f.)*, 4
motor motor *(m.)*, 15
motorcycle motocicleta *(f.)*, 10
mountain montaña *(f.)*, 9
move mudarse, 13
movie película *(f.)*, 16
movies cine *(m.)*, 6
movie theater cine *(m.)*, 6
Mrs. señora *(f.)*, P1
much mucho(-a), 3

as _____ tanto(-a), 4
how _____ cuánto(-a), 3
how _____ does it cost? ¿cuánto cuesta?, 1
too _____ demasiado, 9
muffler silenciador *(m.)*, 15
museum museo *(m.)*, 4
musical musical, 16
must deber, 2
my mi(s), 2
myself me, 8

N

name nombre *(m.)*, 2
    my _____ is . . . me llamo... , P1
    What is your _____? ¿Cómo se llama Ud.? *(form.)*, P1; ¿Cómo te llamas? *(fam.)*, P2
napkin servilleta *(f.)*, 6
nationality nacionalidad *(f.)*, 2
near *(adv.)* cerca, 2; *(prep.)* cerca de, 2
necessarily necesariamente, 10
necessary necesario(-a), 10
neck cuello *(m.)*, 10
need necesitar, 1
nephew sobrino *(m.)*, 4
never nunca, 4
new nuevo(-a), 3
    New Year's Eve fin de año *(m.)*, 3
newlyweds recién casados *(m. pl.)*, 15
news noticias *(f. pl.)*, 8
newspaper diario *(m.)*, 2
next próximo(-a), 7
    the _____ day al día siguiente, 13
nice simpático(-a), 2
niece sobrina *(f.)*, 4
night noche *(f.)*, 1
    at _____ de la noche, 1; por la noche, 1
    good _____ buenas noches, P1
nightgown camisón *(m.)*, 14
nightstand mesita de noche *(f.)*, 13
nine nueve, P1
    _____ hundred novecientos, 1
nineteen diecinueve, P2
ninety noventa, 1
ninth noveno(-a), 4
no no, P1; ningún(a), 5
    _____ one nadie, 5
    _____ way! ¡qué va!, 17
nobody nadie, 5
none ningún(a), 5; ninguno(-a), 5
noon mediodía *(m.)*, 3
    at _____ al mediodía, 3
nor ni, 5

neither . . . _____ . . . ni... ni... , 5
north norte *(m.)*, 18
North American norteamericano(-a), 2
nose nariz *(f.)*, 10
not no, 1
notebook cuaderno *(m.)*, P3
nothing nada, 1
    _____ else nada más, 5
November noviembre, 4
now ahora, 3
number número *(m.)*, P3
nurse enfermero(-a) *(m., f.)*, 10

O

object objeto *(m.)*, 5
obtain conseguir (e:i), 5
occupation ocupación *(f.)*, 2
occupied ocupado(-a), 3
ocean océano *(m.)*, 9
October octubre, 4
of de, 1; del, 1
    _____ course! ¡cómo no!, 4
office oficina *(f.)*, 5
    doctor's _____ consultorio *(m.)*, 10
    post _____ oficina de correos *(f.)*, 12
    telegraph _____ oficina de telégrafos *(f.)*, 12
    ticket _____ despacho de boletos *(m.)*, 18
    tourist _____ oficina de turismo *(f.)*, 5
oh! ¡ay!, 4
oil aceite *(m.)*, 15
okay bien, 7; bueno, 7; ¡vale!, 4
old antiguo(-a), 12; viejo(-a), 12
    to be . . . years _____ tener... años, 3
older mayor, 4
oldest el (la) mayor, 4
omelette tortilla *(f.)*, 6
on en, 1
    _____ the phone al teléfono, 1; por teléfono, 7
    _____ the way to camino a, 5
    _____ time a tiempo, 18
    _____ vacation de vacaciones, 9
one uno, 1
    _____ hundred cien, 1; ciento, 1
    _____-way de ida, 7
onion cebolla *(f.)*, 16
only solamente, 9; sólo, 7; único(-a), 11
    _____ child hijo(-a) único(-a), 12
open abrir, 2; abierto(-a), 12

operate operar, 10
opportunity oportunidad *(f.)*, 4
opposite frente a, 11
or o, 1
orange naranja *(f.)*, 16; anaranjado(-a), P3
orchestra orquesta *(f.)*, 3
order orden *(f.)*, 6; pedido *(m.)*, 6; pedir (e:i), 6
    in _____ en regla, 5
    in _____ that para que, 13
    in _____ to para, 2
organize organizar, 16
other otro(-a), 4
ought deber, 2
our nuestro(-a)(s), 2
ours nuestro(-a)(s), 7
out of order descompuesto(-a), 15
overlooking con vista a, 5
owe deber, 14

P

pack hacer las maletas, 9
package paquete *(m.)*, 12
page página *(f.)*, P3
pain dolor *(m.)*, 10
painting cuadro *(m.)*, 4
pair par *(m.)*, 14
palace palacio *(m.)*, 12
pants pantalón *(m.)*, 11; pantalones *(m. pl.)*, 11
pantyhose pantimedias *(f. pl.)*, 14
parasol sombrilla *(f.)*, 4
parents padres *(m. pl.)*, 4
park parque *(m.)*, 12; aparcar, 11; estacionar, 11; parquear, 11
    amusement _____ parque de diversiones *(m.)*, 16
party fiesta *(f.)*, 3
pass aprobar (o:ue), 17
    _____ through pasar por, 5
pay pagar, 6
    _____ attention hacer caso, 13
peach durazno *(m.)*, 16; melocotón *(m.)*, 16
pear pera *(f.)*, 16
pen pluma *(f.)*, P3
pencil lápiz *(m.)*, P3
penicillin penicilina *(f.)*, 10
people gente *(f.)*, 8
pepper pimienta *(f.)*, 6
percent por ciento, 18
perfect perfecto(-a), 9
perfectly perfectamente, 4
permanent permanente *(f.)*, 8

permit permiso *(m.)*, 18
pessimist pesimista *(m., f.)*, 13
pharmacy farmacia *(f.)*, 8
phone teléfono *(m.)*, P3
    _____ number número de teléfono *(m.)*, P3
    on the _____ al teléfono, 1; por teléfono, 7
photograph fotografía *(f.)*, 4; foto *(f.)*, 4
physics física *(f.)*, 17
pick up recoger, 11
picture cuadro *(m.)*, 4
piglet lechón *(m.)*, 6
pill pastilla *(f.)*, 10
pillow almohada *(f.)*, 13
pillowcase funda *(f.)*, 13
pineapple piña *(f.)*, 16
pink rosado(-a), P3
pity lástima *(f.)*, 11
    what a _____! ¡qué lástima!, 4
place poner, 6
placed puesto(-a), 14
plan plan *(m.)*, 9; pensar (e:ie), 3; planear, 9
plane avión *(m.)*, 7
plate plato *(m.)*, 6
platform andén *(m.)*, 18
play obra de teatro *(f.)*, 6
please por favor, P1
pleasure gusto *(m.)*, P2
    a _____ (to meet you) encantado(-a), 1
    the _____ is mine el gusto es mío, P2
police station estación de policía *(f.)*, 11
politely atentamente, 18
pool piscina *(f.)*, 9
Portuguese *(lang.)* portugués *(m.)*, 1
post office correo *(m.)*, 12; oficina de correo *(f.)*, 12
    _____ box apartado postal *(m.)*, 18
postcard tarjeta postal *(f.)*, 7
potato papa *(f.)*, 6
    mashed _____ puré de papas *(f.)*, 6
practice practicar, 4
prefer preferir (e:ie), 3
pregnant embarazada, 10
prepare preparar(se), 6
prescribe recetar, 10
prescription receta *(f.)*, 10
present presente, P3
pretty bonito(-a), 2; lindo(-a), 2
private privado(-a), 5

prize premio *(m.)*, 16
problem problema *(m.)*, 1
professor profesor(a) *(m., f.)*, 1
provided that con tal que, 13
psychology psicología *(f.)*, 17; sicología *(f.)*, 17
punctual puntual, 12
punishment castigo *(m.)*, 9
purple morado(-a), P3
purse bolsa *(f.)*, 14; cartera *(f.)*, 14
put poner, 6
    _____ on ponerse, 8
    _____ on a play poner una obra de teatro, 6
    _____ to bed acostar (o:ue), 8

Q

quarter trimestre *(m.)*, 17
    _____ past ...y cuarto, 4

R

radiator radiador *(m.)*, 18
rain lluvia *(f.)*, 4; llover (o:ue), 4
    _____ cats and dogs llover a cántaros, 10
raincoat impermeable *(m.)*, 4
raise levantar, 8
rapid rápido(-a), 10
rapidly rápidamente, 10
rare raro(-a), 10
rarely raramente, 10
rate tarifa *(f.)*, 18
razor máquina de afeitar *(f.)*, 8
read leer, 2
ready listo(-a), 6
receive recibir, 2
recent reciente, 10
recently recientemente, 10
receptionist recepcionista *(m., f.)*, 2
recommend recomendar (e:ie), 6
record disco *(m.)*, 3
    _____ player tocadiscos *(m.)*, 3
red rojo(-a), P3; *(wine)* tinto, 6
red-headed pelirrojo(-a), 2
refrigerator refrigerador *(m.)*, 13
refuse no querer (e:ie) *(preterit)*
register registro *(m.)*, 5; matricularse, 17
registered certificado(-a), 12
registration matrícula *(f.)*, 17
regret sentir (e:ie), 11
remain quedarse, 9
remember recordar (o:ue), 4
rent alquiler *(m.)*, 13; alquilar, 9
repair shop taller *(m.)*, 15

automobile _____ _____ taller de mecánica, 15

repeat repetir (e:i), 8

request pedir (e:i), 5

requirement requisito (m.), 17

reservation reservación (f.), 5

reserve reservar, 18

restaurant restaurante (m.), 4

return devolver (o:ue), 7; regresar, 1; volver (o:ue), 4

returned devuelto(-a), 14; vuelto(-a), 14

rice arroz (m.), 6

_____ **pudding** arroz con leche (m.), 6

ride *(a bicycle)* montar en bicicleta, 9; *(a horse)* montar a caballo, 9

right derecho(-a), 5

_____? ¿verdad?, 11

_____ **away** en seguida, 5

_____ **there** ahí mismo, 12

be _____ tener razón, 3

to (on, at) the _____ a la derecha, 5

ring sonar (o:ue), 11

river río (m.), 9

road camino (m.), 12

roasted asado(-a), 6

roll of film rollo de película (m.), 11

romantic sentimental, 1

room cuarto (m.), 5

round-trip de ida y vuelta, 7

run errands hacer diligencias, 11

run over atropellar, 10

Russian *(lang.)* ruso (m.), 1

S

sad triste, 10

sadly tristemente, 10

said dicho(-a), 14

salad ensalada (f.), 3

salary salario (m.), 13; sueldo (m.), 13

sale liquidación (f.), 14; rebaja (f.), 14

salmon salmón (m.), 6

salt sal (f.), 6

sandal sandalia (f.), 14

sandwich bocadillo (m.) (Sp.), 2; emparedado (m.) (Sp.), 2; sándwich (m.), 2

Saturday sábado (m.), P2

sauce salsa (f.), 16

saucer platillo (m.), 6

save ahorrar, 11

savings ahorros (m. pl.), 11

_____ **account** cuenta de ahorros (f.), 11

_____ **passbook** libreta de ahorros (f.), 11

say decir (e:i), 5

_____ **hi to** dar saludos a, 12; saludos a, 18

how do you _____ ... ? ¿cómo se dice... ? , P2

you _____ ... se dice... , P2

schedule horario (m.), 17; itinerario (m.), 18

be ... **behind** _____ tener... de atraso, 7

scholarship beca (f.), 17

school escuela (f.), 4

elementary _____ escuela primaria, 17

high _____ escuela secundaria, 17

science ciencia (f.), 17

scream gritar, 11

sea mar (m.), 9

seafood mariscos (m. pl.), 6

search for buscar, 7

seat asiento (m.), 7

aisle _____ asiento de pasillo, 7

window _____ asiento de ventanilla, 7

seated sentado(-a), 9

second segundo(-a), 4

secretary secretario(-a), (m., f.), P3

section sección (f.), 7

(non-)smoking _____ sección de (no) fumar, 7

see ver, 4

let's _____ ... a ver... , 11

_____ **you later** hasta luego, P1

_____ **you tomorrow** hasta mañana, P1

until I _____ **you again** hasta la vista, P2

seen visto(-a), 14

sell vender, 2

semester semestre (m.), 17

send enviar, 2; mandar, 2

sentimental sentimental, 1

September septiembre, 4

seriously en serio, 9

serve servir (e:i), 5

seven siete, P1

_____ **hundred** setecientos, 1

seventeen diecisiete, P2

seventh séptimo(-a), 4

seventy setenta, 1

several varios(-as), 11

sex sexo (m.), 2

shame lástima (f.), 11

what a _____! ¡qué lástima!, 11

shampoo champú (m.), 8; lavado (m.), 8

shave (oneself) afeitar(se), 8

she ella, 1

sheet sábana (f.), 13

ship barco (m.), 7

shirt camisa (f.), 14

shoe zapato (m.), 14

_____ **department** zapatería (f.), 14

_____ **store** zapatería (f.), 14

shopping: do the _____ hacer las compras, 16

go _____ ir de compras, 14

short bajo(-a), 2; corto(-a), 7

shot inyección (f.), 10

tetanus _____ inyección antitetánica, 10

give a _____ poner una inyección, 10

shout gritar, 11

show enseñar, 9; mostrar (o:ue), 5

shrimp camarones (m. pl.), 6

sick enfermo(-a), 10

sickness enfermedad (f.), 10

sign letrero (m.), 15; firmar, 5

signature firma (f.), 11

silver plata (f.), 5

simple sencillo(-a), 5

since como, 7

sincerely sinceramente, 18

single sencillo(-a), 5; soltero(-a), 2; único(-a), 11

sink fregadero (m.), 13

sir señor, P1

Dear Sir(s) muy señor(es) mío(s), 18

sister hermana (f.), 4

sister-in-law cuñada (f.), 4

sit sentarse (e:ie), 8

six seis, P1

_____ **hundred** seiscientos, 1

sixteen dieciséis, P1

sixth sexto(-a), 4

sixty sesenta, 1

size medida (f.), 14; talla (f.), 14

take _____ ... *(in shoes)* calzar... , 14

ski esquiar, 9

skirt falda (f.), 14

sleep dormir (o:ue), 4

sleeper-car coche-cama (m.), 18

sleepy: be _____ tener sueño, 3

slender delgado(-a), 2

slow lento(-a), 10

slowly lentamente, 10

small pequeño(-a), 4

be too _____ **(on someone)** quedar(le) chico(-a) (a uno), 14

snow   nieve *(f.)*, 4; nevar (e:ie), 4

so   tan, 4; de manera que, 11; de modo que, 11

soap   jabón *(m.)*, 5

soccer   fútbol *(m.)*, 17

sociology   sociología *(f.)*, 17

sock   calcetín *(m.)*, 14

soda   refresco *(m.)*, 3

soft drink   refresco *(m.)*, 3

some   algún(a), 5; alguno(-a), 5

somebody   alguien, 5

someone   alguien, 5

something   algo, 5

sometimes   a veces, 8

somewhere   alguna parte *(f.)*, 12

son   hijo *(m.)*, 4

son-in-law   yerno *(m.)*, 4

soon: as _____ as   en cuanto, 11

so-so   más o menos, 1

sorry: be _____   sentir (e:ie), 11
   I'm _____   lo siento, P1

soup   sopa *(f.)*, 6

south   sur *(m.)*, 18

Spain   España *(f.)*, 4

Spanish   *(lang.)* español *(m.)*, P2

speak   hablar, 1

special   especial, 10

specialization   especialización *(f.)*, 17

specialty   especialidad *(f.)*, 6

speed   velocidad *(f.)*, 15
   _____ limit   velocidad máxima, 15

spend   *(money)* gastar, 18; *(time)* pasar, 5

spoilsport   aguafiestas *(m., f.)*, 13

spoon   cuchara *(f.)*, 6

spring   primavera *(f.)*, 4

stadium   estadio *(m.)*, 17

stairs   escalera *(f.)*, 14

stamp   estampilla *(f.)*, 12; sello *(m.)*, 12; timbre *(m.)* *(Mex.)*, 12

stand in line   hacer cola, 16

standard shift   de cambios mecánicos, 18

standing   parado(-a), 12

start   arrancar *(car)*, 15; empezar (e:ie), 3

starving   muerto(-a) de hambre, 14

state   estado *(m.)*, 2

station   estación *(f.)*, 12
   police _____   estación de policía *(f.)*, 11
   service _____   estación de servicio *(f.)*, 15; gasolinera *(f.)*, 15
   subway _____   estación del metro *(f.)*, 12

stay   quedarse, 9

steak   bistec *(m.)*, 6

steal   robar, 11

still   todavía, 14

stomach   estómago *(m.)*, 10

stop   parar, 15

stopover   escala *(f.)*, 18
   to make a _____   hacer escala, 18

store   tienda *(f.)*, 8

store clerk   dependiente(-a) *(m., f.)*, 14

stove   cocina *(f.)*, 13

straight ahead   derecho, 12

strange   extraño(-a), 15; raro(-a), 10

strawberry   fresa *(f.)*, 16

street   calle *(f.)*, P2
   _____ corner   esquina *(f.)*, 12

student   estudiante *(m., f.)*, P3

study   estudiar, 1

stuffed   relleno(-a), 6

style   moda *(f.)*, 8
   in _____   de moda, 8

subject   asignatura *(f.)*, 17

subway   metro *(m.)*, 12
   _____ station   estación del metro *(f.)*, 12

sufficient   suficiente, 11

sugar   azúcar *(m.)*, 16

suggest   sugerir (e:ie), 11

suit   traje *(m.)*, 14

suitcase   maleta *(f.)*, 5; valija *(f.)*, 5

summer   verano *(m.)*, 4

sun   sol *(m.)*, 4

Sunday   domingo *(m.)*, P2

sunny: be _____   hacer sol, 4

supermarket   supermercado *(m.)*, 16

supper   cena *(f.)*, 5

suppose   suponer, 17

sure   seguro(-a), 12
   be _____   estar seguro(-a), 12

surname   apellido *(m.)*, 2

surprise   sorpresa *(f.)*, 6; sorprender, 11

sweater   suéter *(m.)*, 4

sweep   barrer, 8

swimming poll   alberca *(f.)* *(Mex.)*, 9; piscina *(f.)*, 9

T

tablecloth   mantel *(m.)*, 6

take   llevar, 3; llevarse, 14; tomar, 15
   _____ away   quitar, 8
   _____ out   sacar, 11
   _____ size . . .   *(in shoes)* calzar... , 14

talk   conversar, 2; charlar, 2; hablar, 1

tall   alto(-a), 2

tank   tanque *(m.)*, 15

tape   casete *(m.)*, 3; cinta *(f.)*, 3

tape recorder   grabadora *(f.)*, 3

taste   probar (o:ue), 8

tasty   sabroso(-a), 6

taxi   taxi *(m.)*, 5

tea   té *(m.)*, 6

teach   enseñar, 9

teacher   profesor(a) *(m., f.)*, P1

teaspoon   cucharita *(f.)*, 6

telegraph office   oficina de telégrafos *(f.)*, 12

telephone   teléfono *(m.)*, 2
   on the _____   al teléfono, 1; por teléfono, 7

television   televisión *(f.)*, 1

tell   contar (o:ue), 7; decir (e:i), 5

ten   diez, P1

tenderloin   *(steak)* filete *(m.)*, 6

tent   tienda *(f.)*, 9

tenth   décimo(-a), 4

terrace   terraza *(f.)*, 3

test   *(medical)* análisis *(m.)*, 10; examen *(m.)*, P3

tetanus   tétano *(m.)*, 10
   _____ shot   inyección antitetánica *(f.)*, 10

than   que, 4

thank you   gracias, P1
   _____ very much   muchas gracias, P2

that   *(adj.)* aquel(la), 6; *(adj.)* ese, 6; *(adj.)* esa, 6; *(neuter pron.)* aquello, 6; *(neuter pron.)* eso, 6; *(rel. pron.)* que, 5
   _____ one   aquél(la), 6; ése, 6; ésa, 6

the   el, P3; la, P3; las, P3; los, P3

theater   cine *(m.)*, 6; teatro *(m.)*, 6

their   su(s), 2

theirs   suyo(-a)(s), 7

them   ellas, 5; ellos, 5; las, 5; les, 6; los, 5

themselves   se, 8

then   entonces, 1; luego, 5; pues, 7

there   allí, 2
   _____ is (are)   hay, P3

therefore   pues, 4

these   *(adj.)* estos(-as), 6; *(pron.)* éstos(-as), 6

they   ellos, 1; ellas, 1

thin   delgado(-a), 2

think   creer, 2; pensar (e:ie), 3

third   tercero(-a), 4

thirsty: be _____   tener sed, 3

thirteen   trece, P2

thirty   treinta, P2

this   *(adj.)* este, 6; *(adj.)* esta, 6; *(neuter pron.)* esto, 6
   _____ one   *(pron.)* éste(-a), 6
   _____ way   por aquí, 6

_____ **time is it?** ¿qué hora es?, P2
when cuándo, 3
where adónde, 3; dónde, 3
which cuál(es), P2; *(rel. pron.)* que, 5
while rato *(m.)*, 11; *(conj.)* mientras, 2
    a _____ **later** al rato, 11
white blanco(-a), P3
who *(rel. pron.)* que, 5; quién, 1
whom quiénes, 11
whose de quién(es), 3
why? ¿por qué?, 1
    that's _____ por eso, 4
widow viuda *(f.)*, 2
widower viudo *(m.)*, 2
wife esposa *(f.)*, 2
win ganar, 16
window ventana *(f.)*, P3; *(vehicle)* ventanilla *(f.)*, 12
    _____ **seat** asiento de ventanilla *(m.)*, 12
windshield wiper limpiaparabrisas *(m.)*, 15
windy: be _____ hacer viento, 4
wine vino *(m.)*, 3
    red _____ vino tinto, 6
    white _____ vino blanco, 6
winter invierno *(m.)*, 4
wish desear, 1; querer (e:ie), 3

with con, 1
    _____ **me** conmigo, 5
    _____ **you** *(fam. sing.)* contigo, 5
withdraw sacar, 11
without sin, 12
woman mujer *(f.)*, P3
    _____**'s department** departamento de señoras *(m.)*, 14
word palabra *(f.)*, 17
work trabajo *(m.)*, 2; funcionar, 15; trabajar, 1
world mundo *(m.)*, 4
worry (about) preocuparse (de), 18
worse peor, 4
worst el (la) peor, 4
worth: be _____ valer, 15
wound herida *(f.)*, 10
wrap envolver (o:ue), 14
wrapped envuelto(-a), 14
write escribir, 2
    _____ **down** anotar, 6
written escrito(-a), 14

X

X-ray radiografía *(f.)*, 10
    _____ **room** sala de rayos X *(f.)*, 10

Y

year año *(m.)*, 2
    be . . . _____**s old** tener... años, 3
    New Year's Eve fin de año *(m.)*, 3
yellow amarillo(-a), P3
yes sí, 1
yesterday ayer, 8
yet todavía, 14
    not _____ no todavía, 17
you *(subj.)* tú, usted, P1; ustedes, vosotros(-as), 1; *(d.o. pron.)* la(s), lo(s), os, te, 5; *(i.o. pron.)* le(s), os, te, 6; *(obj. of prep.)* ti, usted(es), vosotros(-as), 5
    _____**'re welcome** de nada, P2
    with _____ contigo *(fam.)*, con usted, 5
younger menor, 4
youngest el (la) menor, 4
your su, tu vuestro(-a), 2
yours suyo(-a)(s), tuyo(-a)(s), vuestro(-a)(s), 7
yourself se, te, 8
yourselves os, se, 8

Z

zero cero, P1
zip code zona postal *(f.)*, 2
zoo zoológico *(m.)*, 16

INDEX

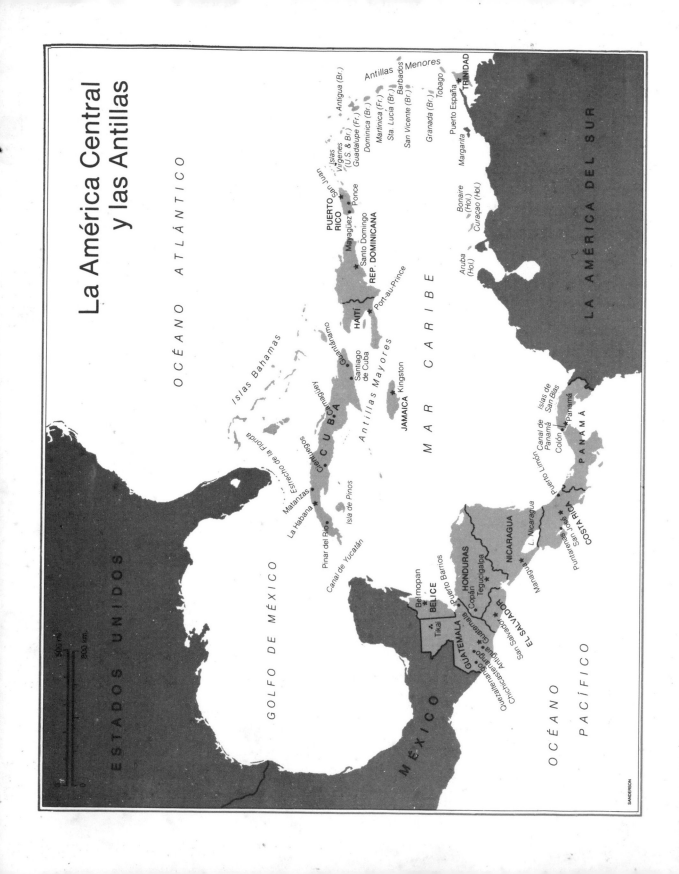

La América Central
y las Antillas

OCÉANO ATLÁNTICO

ESTADOS UNIDOS

GOLFO DE MÉXICO

MÉXICO

Islas Bahamas

Estrecho de la Florida

Pinar del Río
La Habana
Matanzas
Cienfuegos
Isla de Pinos
CUBA
Camagüey
Santiago de Cuba
Guantánamo

Canal de Yucatán

Antillas Mayores

JAMAICA
Kingston

MAR CARIBE

HAITÍ
Port-au-Prince
REP. DOMINICANA
Santo Domingo
PUERTO RICO
Mayagüez
Ponce
San Juan

Islas Vírgenes (U.S. & Br.)
Guadalupe (Fr.)
Antigua (Br.)
Dominica (Br.)
Martinica (Fr.)
Sta. Lucía (Br.)
San Vicente (Br.)
Barbados
Granada (Br.)
Tobago
TRINIDAD
Puerto España
Margarita

Antillas Menores

Bonaire (Hol.)
Curaçao (Hol.)
Aruba (Hol.)

LA AMÉRICA DEL SUR

Islas de San Blas
Panamá
Colón
PANAMÁ
Canal de Panamá
Puerto Limón
COSTA RICA
San José
Puntarenas
L. Nicaragua
NICARAGUA
Managua
HONDURAS
Tegucigalpa
Copán
Puerto Barrios
Belmopan
BELICE
Tikal
GUATEMALA
Guatemala
Quetzaltenango
Chichicastenango
Antigua
San Salvador
EL SALVADOR

OCÉANO PACÍFICO

500 mi
800 km.

SANDERSON